The Psychology of Language

SAGE was founded in 1965 by Sara Miller McCune to support the dissemination of usable knowledge by publishing innovative and high-quality research and teaching content. Today, we publish more than 750 journals, including those of more than 300 learned societies, more than 800 new books per year, and a growing range of library products including archives, data, case studies, reports, conference highlights, and video. SAGE remains majority-owned by our founder, and after Sara's lifetime will become owned by a charitable trust that secures our continued independence.

Los Angeles | London | Washington DC | New Delhi | Singapore | Boston

The Psychology of Language

An Integrated Approach

David Ludden

Georgia Gwinnett College

Los Angeles | London | New Delhi
Singapore | Washington DC | Boston

Los Angeles | London | New Delhi
Singapore | Washington DC | Boston

FOR INFORMATION:

SAGE Publications, Inc.

2455 Teller Road

Thousand Oaks, California 91320

E-mail: order@sagepub.com

SAGE Publications Ltd.

1 Oliver's Yard

55 City Road

London EC1Y 1SP

United Kingdom

SAGE Publications India Pvt. Ltd.

B 1/I 1 Mohan Cooperative Industrial Area

Mathura Road, New Delhi 110 044

India

SAGE Publications Asia-Pacific Pte. Ltd.

3 Church Street

#10-04 Samsung Hub

Singapore 049483

Printed in the United States of America

Cataloging-in-publication data available for this title from the Library of Congress.

ISBN 978-1-4522-8880-2

This book is printed on acid-free paper.

SFI Certified Sourcing
www.sfiprogram.org
SFI-00453

Acquisitions Editor: Reid Hester

Digital Content Editor: Lucy Berbeo

Production Editor: Laura Barrett

Copy Editor: Lynn Weber

Typesetter: C&M Digitals (P) Ltd.

Proofreader: Kris Bergstad

Indexer: Will Ragsdale

Cover Designer: Gail Buschman

Marketing Manager: Shari Countryman

15 16 17 18 19 10 9 8 7 6 5 4 3 2 1

Brief Table of Contents

Detailed Table of Contents

Preface

I got to psychology rather late in my career. From an early age, I'd had a driving curiosity about language. In school, English was always my favorite subject, and I took four years of French in high school. My interest in languages led me to a bachelor's degree in French and German, followed naturally by a master's degree in linguistics. During my Asia years, I picked up Japanese and two dialects of Chinese. In the meanwhile, I dabbled in a number of languages, working through beginning texts in Spanish, Russian, Latin, and Ancient Greek. Well into my thirties, I thought of myself as a linguist, a scholar of languages.

That all changed during my second year working on a PhD in linguistics at the University of Iowa. Just out of curiosity, I signed up for a Psychology of Language course offered way across campus. It was Gregg Oden who showed me the light (or turned me to the dark side, depending on whose version of the story you choose to believe). After taking Gregg's class, I finally knew what I wanted to be when I grew up—a psycholinguist!

The following year, I transferred to the psychology department at Iowa, where I benefited from the mentorship of many outstanding scholars. In particular, I'd like to thank my advisor Prahlad Gupta for putting up with my impertinence and bullheadedness on many an occasion while managing to teach me far more about the science of psycholinguistics than I had realized at the time. Thanks also to my other mentors at Iowa who guided me down a path that I have never regretted taking. These include Steve Luck, Shaun Vecera, Larissa Samuelson, and also Rochelle Newman, who is now at the University of Maryland.

My first job out of graduate school was at a small liberal arts college where I was half of the psychology department. As a result, I taught most of the psychology curriculum at one time or another, and it was this experience with a wide range of courses that turned me into a generalist. However, as I taught classes like Social Psychology or History and Issues, in which I knew only marginally more about the subject matter than my students, I was repeatedly impressed by the importance of language in every area of psychology, even though it was rarely acknowledged by the scholars of those fields.

Like the air we breathe, language is often taken for granted. Yet language is every bit as vital for our human existence as oxygen. We cannot live without air, and we cannot live a fully human life without language. Philosophers may debate whether it's worse to lose the faculty of sight or the faculty of hearing, but blind people and deaf people still manage to lead happy and productive lives. The same simply cannot be said for those who've lost the faculty of language. These unfortunates are relegated to the sidelines of humanity, unable to take part in the most basic of human institutions—family, friendship, and community. Indeed, it's language above all else that defines us as a species.

This broad view of the role of language in human psychology is what I've attempted to portray in this book. I didn't want to just write another psycholinguistics textbook, as there are plenty of fine options available for the instructor who wants to take a traditional cognitive approach to the study of language processes. Instead, I wanted to write a book about the psychology of language that integrated all the major approaches of the field—including social, cognitive, evolutionary, biological, cultural, and developmental—into the discussion. This was my goal, although you the reader will be the one to judge how well I've succeeded at the task.

I wish to thank my colleague Morris Grubbs and my wife, Yawen, for convincing me, over a lunch of Thai curry, that I really could—and should—write this book. Likewise, I owe an immense debt of gratitude to my editor Reid Hester, who all along has had more faith in this project than I could ever muster. Without Reid imposing "impossible" deadlines—that I always somehow managed to meet—this completed textbook would still be lingering in the conceptual stage. The rest of the SAGE team has been wonderful as well. Thanks to Eve Oettinger, my initial contact at SAGE who passed my idea for a textbook on to Reid; to Sarita Sarak, who helped me put together my proposal; and to Nathan Davidson, for his insightful comments on the manuscript reviews. Special thanks go to Lucy Berbeo for her diligence, persistence, and incredible detective skills. Lucy has taught me a lot about the nitty-gritty aspects of putting together a book.

On the homefront, I'd like to thank my children Jennifer and Jason, who as recent grads were able to give me a college-student perspective on portions of the text. I'd also like to thank my parents, Carol and David, for asking "So how's the book coming along?" every time we talked. Their confidence in my ability sustained me through hard times. Finally, I need to thank my wife Yawen again for all the emotional and material support she provided me during the two years it took to complete this project. Without her constant encouragement, I never could have written this book.

Publisher's Acknowledgments

SAGE gratefully acknowledges the contributions of the following reviewers:

Tamiko Azuma, Arizona State University
Natalie Kacinik, CUNY Brooklyn College
Anna B. Cieślicka, Texas A&M International University
Neal J. Pearlmutter, Northeastern University
Lydia Volaitis, Massachusetts Institute of Technology, Program in Writing and
    Humanistic Studies
Laura Sabourin, University of Ottawa
Ann R. Eisenberg, The University of Texas at San Antonio
Shannon N. Whitten, University of Central Florida
Stephani Foraker, SUNY Buffalo State
Daniel S. McConnell, University of Central Florida
Susan Baillet, University of Portland
Wind Cowles, University of Florida
Dirk-Bart den Ouden, University of South Carolina
Gretchen Sunderman, Florida State University
Jan Berkhout, Psychology Department, University of South Dakota
Usha Lakshmanan, Southern Illinois University Carbondale
Kathleen M. Eberhard, University of Notre Dame
Daniel S. McConnell, University of Central Florida
Annie J. Olmstead, SUNY New Paltz
Patrick Rebuschat, Lancaster University, Department of Linguistics and English
    Language
Daniel S. Koo, Gallaudet University

About the Author

David Ludden is a professor of psychology at Georgia Gwinnett College near Atlanta. He considers himself a generalist, and he has taught a wide variety of psychology courses, including cognitive, physiological, evolutionary, social, and cross-cultural psychology as well as research methods and the psychology of language. Showing a penchant for languages from an early age, he majored in French and German as an undergraduate at Ohio University, where he returned, after a brief stint in Japan, to complete a master's degree in linguistics. Following a second, much longer stint in East Asia, he earned a PhD in cognitive psychology from the University of Iowa. His research extends far beyond his traditional psycholinguistics training to include a consideration the evolutionary, biological, developmental, and social factors that make all human languages so incredibly similar.

CHAPTER 1

Animal Communication and Human Language

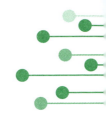

Kanzi watched one of the keepers play the game with his mother. They did this most afternoons, and she often got cross with him during these sessions. But if he sat quietly on her shoulders, he could watch them. The keeper pointed at some colorful squiggles on a plastic sheet, and then Kanzi's mother was supposed to do the same. But she wasn't very good at the game, and she'd just made another mistake. Kanzi squealed and shook his finger, but they both ignored him.

It seemed to Kanzi that the keepers used the plastic sheet to communicate with. Sometimes he even thought he knew what they were trying to say and how his mother was supposed to respond. But she just didn't get it. The keepers also made noises to communicate with each other, but neither Kanzi nor his mother understood that.

One day during a session, another keeper came into the room. The two keepers squawked at each other, and then they led Kanzi's mother out of the room, leaving him behind. Kanzi climbed onto the table and started pointing at the squiggles on the plastic sheet. The patterns were easy, and he had no idea why his mother found them so difficult.

When one of the keepers returned, he traced out a pattern with his finger. She looked, and he did it again. The keeper traced a different pattern, and Kanzi gave the response. They did this several more times, and then the keeper scooped little Kanzi into her arms and laughed. Now laughter Kanzi understood—even bonobos do that.

From then on, Sue Savage-Rumbaugh and her colleagues focused their attention on Kanzi instead of his mother (Savage-Rumbaugh & Lewin, 1994; Savage-Rumbaugh, Shanker, & Taylor, 1998). In retrospect, it was obvious. Human adults have difficulty learning a language, so why should they have expected more from an adult bonobo? Little Kanzi, however, picked up the symbol language quickly and could use it to communicate with his keepers. Later, he even learned to understand their speech, even though he couldn't speak himself.

Not all scientists agree that Kanzi has learned language. He may use words, they contend, but he doesn't understand syntax—the rules for combining words into sentences. And syntax, according to the traditional view, is what separates human languages from animal communication systems. Kanzi's understanding of syntax may be weak, others argue, but his ability to express novel ideas far exceeds anything that animals can do in the wild. Perhaps, then, Kanzi and other linguistically trained apes can tell us something about how our ancestors transitioned from a limited set of animal calls to the infinitely expressive communication system we call human language.

SECTION 1.1: ANIMAL COMMUNICATION SYSTEMS

- Animals use various communication systems to aid survival and reproductive needs; these usually center around foraging for food, avoiding predators, recognizing friends, and finding a mate.
- Honeybees perform a waggle dance to communicate with hive mates about the location of resources.
- Vervet monkeys vocalize to warn group members about three kinds of predators: leopards, eagles, and snakes; alarm calls lead to appropriate evasive action.
- Many social species use vocalizations to maintain social structure and to establish a dominance hierarchy; in this way, members understand their relationships with other members of the group.
- Animals use many means to attract mates; these include vocalizations, bright colors, and flashing lights.
- Animal communication systems:(1) have a limited range of meanings, (2) consist of holophrases that refer to an entire situation, (3) cannot combine elements to create novel ideas, and (4) can only refer to the current situation.

If you want to find a mate, you've got to advertise. This is certainly true in our digital age, but it's equally true in the animal kingdom. It's five o'clock in the morning, and there's a cardinal singing outside my bedroom window. Birdsong is the Facebook of the avian world.

That cardinal is simply playing the game of life, the whole point of which is to get your genes into the next generation. But before you can do that, you need to know four things: who you can eat, who wants to eat you, who is part of your group, and who you can mate with. An **ethologist**, that is, *a scientist who studies animal behavior*, often refers to these as the four Fs—food, foe, friend, and finding a mate.

Animals communicate with each other about the four Fs through a variety of means. We can define **communication** as *any behavior on the part of one organism intended to* *influence the emotions, thoughts, or behaviors of another organism.* Communication is often vocal, but it can also take the form of facial expressions, body postures, movements, odors—even flashing lights if you're a firefly. Most of this communication is directed at a **conspecific**, that is, *a member of the same species*, but interspecies communication happens as well, and so does interspecies eavesdropping (Lea et al., 2008; Magrath, Pitcher, & Gardner, 2009).

Food

The sun is streaming through my bedroom window, so I get up and dress for my morning run. I dash out the door and down the street. Along the side of the road is a patch of clover, and I see a honeybee flitting from blossom to blossom. She's a scout, foraging for nectar. But there are too many flowers in this patch for just one bee to harvest, so she lifts up and flies away. She's heading back to the nest to tell her hive mates what she's found, and she'll do this by means of a dance.

Austrian ethologist Karl von Frisch (1967) first deciphered the honeybee waggle dance in the mid-twentieth century. Scientists had long been aware of the bee dance, and they had also long suspected that bees somehow communicated about the location of resources, but it was von Frisch who finally put the two together.

When our honeybee returns to her nest, hundreds of hive mates will gather around her, and she'll perform a figure-eight dance. She'll start with a waggle-run, followed by a turn to the right to circle back to her starting point. Then she'll do the waggle-run again, this time circling back on the left. She may do this a hundred times or more as hive mates fly off to gather the nectar she has just told them about.

Through a series of experiments in which he systematically changed the location of a nectar source after a scouting bee had found it, von Frisch learned that the waggle dance gave hive mates two pieces of information: direction and distance. This dance is performed on the vertical surface of the honeycombs, and if the scout waggles straight upward, she is telling the others to fly in the direction of the sun. If she dances to the left or right of the vertical axis, she is telling them the angle from the sun in which they need to fly. She also tells her hive mates how far to fly, as the length of the waggle is correlated with the distance from the hive.

Thus, honeybees can communicate about two things, direction and distance to fly. Yet she can't tell them what they'll find when they get there. She could have been scouting for nectar, but bees need water too, and she could have been scouting for that. And if the hive is in the market for a new home, she might be bringing news about some prime real estate. But that much she simply can't tell, as animal communication systems are always quite limited in their range of expression.

Honeybees aren't the only animals to communicate about food sources. Some primate species vocalize when they find a new food source, and these food calls will evoke

Figure 1.1   Honeybee Waggle Dance

Honeybees perform a dance to tell hive mates about the location of sources of nectar or water. They communicate two pieces of information: the direction relative to the sun and the distance. The hive mates know where to fly, but they don't know what they'll find when they get there.

1 s = 1 km

α

foraging behaviors among other members of their group (Kitzmann & Caine, 2009). In the case of honeybees, the evolutionary advantage of food communication is clear. In a honeybee colony, just the queen bee reproduces, and her daughters can only get their genes into the next generation if the queen survives and mates. But birds and mammals are generally in competition with other members of their group for food (and mates), so the purpose of food calls is less clear. Perhaps they're helping family members, who share their genes. But some ethologists suspect that food calls are less about communicating a food source than they are vocalizations of unrestrained excitement at finding a tasty treat (Clay, Smith, & Blumstein, 2012).

Foe

My morning run takes me across the campus lawn, graced with hundred-year-old oaks and pines. A squirrel scampers about, gathering food. She sees me approach and rears up on her hind legs. And then she chatters, drops the acorn in her paws, and scampers up a tree. Her chattering is what is known as an **alarm call**. Many social species use such *a vocalization to warn other members of the group about approaching predators*. But American red squirrels are solitary creatures, and ethologists are still not sure why they make alarm calls (Digweed & Rendall, 2009, 2010). They might be warning relatives in nearby trees, or they may be directing the call at the predator, as if to say, "I see you."

Better understood is the system of alarm calls used by vervet monkeys in Africa (Seyfarth, Cheney, & Marler, 1980a, 1980b). Vervets are a social species living in groups of up to seventy individuals, and they spend their days foraging for food. Vervets have three enemies: leopards, which want to eat them; eagles, which can carry off their young; and snakes, whose venomous bite can kill them. Avoiding each of these foes requires a different strategy, and vervets have a different call for each predator. When a vervet sees a leopard and makes the "leopard" call, all the other members of the group scamper up the nearest tree. When the "eagle" call is made, they scamper under the nearest bush or overhanging rock. And when the "snake" call is made, they look down and watch carefully where they tread.

Seyfarth, Cheney, and Marler (1980a, 1980b) deciphered this system first by careful observation and then by experimentation. They recorded what they suspected were "leopard," "eagle," and "snake" calls, and then they played them back through speakers hidden in trees. Sure enough, the vervets reacted as expected based on the type of call

Figure 1.2 Vervet Monkeys

Vervet monkeys use alarm calls to warn other members of their group about predators.

Source: © AiStockphoto.com / Laitho.

that was played. So it appears that vervets have a "language" consisting of three words. And like human languages, this communicative behavior is partially innate and partially learned. For example, young vervets at first will use the "leopard" call for just about any four-legged mammal (just as a young human will call just about any four-legged mammal "doggie"), but mother vervets will punish mistakes, and the young ones quickly learn.

The call system of Diana monkeys, close relatives of the vervets, has been systematically studied as well (Zuberbühler, Cheney, and Seyfarth, 1999). Diana monkeys make two different alarm calls, one for leopards and one for eagles, their two main predators. The researchers used a prime-probe task to evaluate the meaningfulness of these alarm calls. In the baseline condition, they played a recording of an eagle vocalization (the prime) and measured the number of alarm calls per minute for the next six minutes. After six minutes, they played the eagle vocalization again (the probe), but this time the vocalization elicited no new alarm calls. In the test condition, they played a recording of an eagle alarm call, and the monkeys responded with more eagle calls. But six minutes later, when the researchers played an eagle vocalization, the monkeys did not respond. In the control condition, the researchers played a leopard alarm call, which elicited more leopard alarm calls. Six minutes later, the researchers played an eagle vocalization, which this time elicited eagle vocalizations. They also repeated the three conditions, swapping eagle and leopard alarms and vocalizations. In this way, the researchers were able to determine that the alarm calls referred to specific predators and not to danger in general.

Compared with human languages, monkey talk is extremely limited. To start with, they only have two or three words. And moreover, monkey words can't be used in as wide a range of contexts as human words. To a vervet or Diana monkey, the "leopard" call means "leopard here and now," and never, "I saw a leopard yesterday down by the river." Nor could a monkey use the "eagle" call to say, "If you see an eagle, keep a close eye on the kiddies." Monkey alarm calls, like animal communication systems in general—and specifically unlike human language—are stuck in the here and now.

Friend

My morning run next takes me out a country lane, past a herd of cattle grazing in a field. One cow moos, and then another. Cattle express a variety of emotional states through vocalizations, but one reason they vocalize is to maintain social structure within the herd. Like other social species, cattle herds are structured according to a **dominance hierarchy**, *a social system in which each member of a group knows who ranks above and who ranks below.* Vocalizations are one way these relationships are acknowledged (Hall et al., 1988; Watts & Stookey, 2000). Furthermore, cows and calves use vocalizations as part of the attachment process, and calves separated from their mothers just two weeks after birth can still recognize their mother's voice three weeks later (Barfield, Tang-Martinez, and Trainer, 1994).

Vocalizations are an important aspect of mother-infant bonding in a wide variety of species. For example, rat pups that have fallen out of the nest will emit high-pitched

Figure 1.3 Eagle and Leopard Alarm of the Diana Monkey

Zuberbühler, Cheney, and Seyfarth (1999) tested the meaningfulness of alarm calls in Diana monkeys using a prime-probe task. In the baseline condition, monkeys were primed with an eagle vocalization, and alarm calls per minute were counted for the next six minutes. This was followed by an eagle vocalization probe, which elicited no more alarm calls. In the test condition, the monkeys were primed with an eagle alarm call and probed with an eagle vocalization, yielding results similar to the baseline condition. In the control condition, the monkeys were primed with a leopard alarm call and probed with an eagle vocalization. This time, the probe elicited additional alarm calls. In this way, the researchers were able to determine that the alarm calls referred to specific predators and not to danger in general.

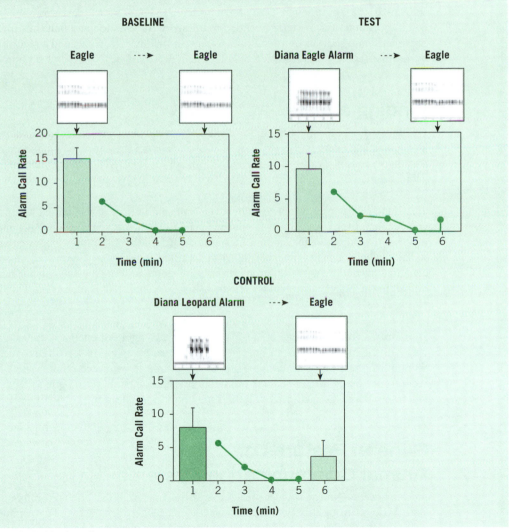

Source: Zuberbühler (2005).

whines (Brunelli, Shair, & Hofer 1994). These ultrasonic calls are above the range of human hearing, and presumably that of most predators as well; but rat moms can hear them, and when they do, they search for their lost little ones and bring them back to the nest. Human infants likewise make high-pitched whines that bring their mothers running for them. And, like cow and calf, human mom and baby will often exchange vocalizations that clearly have positive emotional value for both.

The social role of vocalizations in our closest cousins, the chimpanzees and bonobos, is not well studied (Zuberbühler, 2005). However, **social grooming** has been widely studied in these species, and it is clear that in the primate world, friendships are built through *the practice of picking fleas and dirt from the fur of conspecifics* (Fedurek & Dunbar, 2009). Although it may seem a stretch to count social grooming as communication, it is behavior intended to influence the emotion and behavior of other organisms, and so it fits our definition. We'll visit the practice of social grooming again in our discussion of the evolution of language in Section 1.3.

Finding a Mate

I've finished my morning run, and as I walk across my front yard, I see the cardinal that was singing earlier. He's still at it. You eat, you avoid predators, you make friends, and then you find a mate—that's how the game of life is played. And through the entire game, animals are communicating with each other.

You only have to open your ears to hear the hustle and bustle of the animal world competing for the opportunity to put their genes into the next generation. And under no circumstances is animal communication rowdier, flashier, or more elaborate than when it's about sex. The peacock unfurls his feathers for every peahen he fancies. On a warm summer night, the bullfrog croaks in his pond, and the firefly lights up his tail, all in the hopes of attracting a female (Akre & Ryan, 2010; Stanger-Hall, Lloyd, & Hillis, 2007).

Humans play the same game of life. We eat our meals, fight our enemies, spend time with our friends, find someone special to settle down with, and raise a family. And to accomplish these tasks, we use language to communicate with each other. Many of us seem to be talking through all our waking hours, and when there's no one around, we talk to ourselves—sometimes out loud, sometimes in our head.

General Features of Animal Communication Systems

Although we use human language to achieve all the same goals that animal communication systems do, there are also some fundamental differences between the two. First, animal communication systems always have a very limited range of expression. Bees can communicate about the direction and distance to a resource, but they can't tell what that resource is. Vervets can warn other members of their group about an approaching predator—if it's a leopard, eagle, or snake. But they can't talk about anything else.

Second, an utterance in an animal communication system is always a **holophrase**, in other words, *a single vocalization or gesture that refers to the entire situation and not to the specific objects and events in that situation*. That is, the vervet "leopard" call really means something like, "Look out, there's a leopard coming this way!" and the "snake" call something like, "Yikes, I just saw a snake in the grass!"

Human toddlers start their language development with holophrases as well. "Ball!" can mean "Give me the ball!" or "Look, there's a ball!" And "No!" means something like, "I don't want that!" Even human adults, under emotional duress, often resort to holophrases. The reaction of most humans to a snake in the grass is not much different from that of a vervet monkey: "Snake! Ahh!"

Third, animal communication systems generally lack the ability to combine symbols together to express novel ideas. It is still a matter for further research what a vervet would say if it encountered both a leopard and a snake at the same time, but we just don't see vervets combining symbols to express novel ideas. The honeybee dance does complicate this issue somewhat. Each honeybee dance will be different, because each time the distance and direction will different. Still, honeybees have no ability to express any sort of meaning beyond that. It's this ability to combine symbols to express novel ideas that gives human language its expressive power, and how this is accomplished is the topic of Section 1.2.

Finally, we can point out one last hallmark of animal communication systems, namely that they are always about the here and now. A vervet "eagle" call is about an eagle flying overhead at this very moment, and not about an eagle the vervet saw last week. When a cow says "moo," she's saying, "Here I am, right now," and not, "See you down by the water trough in half an hour." Again, honeybee dance complicates the picture, since she's telling her hive mates about a resource she found some distance away some time ago. But still, she's talking about a distance a bee can quickly fly, and presumably the resource is still there now.

Much of human language is also communication about the present time and place: "What's up?" "Not much." "Hey, watch out for that truck!" But human language also allows us to escape the confines of the here and now to talk about the past, to think about the future, to wonder what's happening on the other side of the planet, and to imagine times and places that never existed.

In Sum

Five million years ago, our ancestors split with those of the chimps and bonobos (Bradley, 2008). Sometime after that, language evolved. Modern humans started making their mark on this world within the last hundred thousand years, probably at about the same time that human language became fully formed. This powerful new tool for communicating—as well as thinking—allowed humans to transcend the limits of animal life, to bend nature to our will. And then in the blink of an eye, in evolutionary terms, language transported us from the Stone Age to the Space Age.

Review Questions

1. Ethologists say there are four basic categories animals must understand to survive and reproduce. What are they? Give an example of an animal communication system relevant to each of these categories.

2. Describe the honeybee communication system. Explain how von Frisch deciphered it.

3. Describe the vervet monkey communication system. Explain how Seyfarth and colleagues deciphered it.

4. What are the four characteristics of animal communication systems that make them different from human language?

Thought Questions

1. Chimpanzees live in complex social groups in which they build friendships, forge political alliances (in which they jostle for position within the dominance hierarchy), and engage in cooperative hunting and warfare. How are they capable of accomplishing all this without language?

2. Imagine you were suddenly transported to a remote village where no one spoke English and you didn't speak their language. How would you communicate your needs to these people? Likewise, imagine you have joined a cloistered community and taken a vow of silence. How will you be able to cooperate with the other members if you can't talk with them?

3. The scenarios in the previous question involve the loss of language as a communication tool. But we also use language for thinking. Brain damage can lead to aphasia, or a total loss of language abilities. Presumably, these patients cannot use language to think with, either. (They can still use other means for thinking, though.) What would life be like if you could see and hear, but you could not use language even for thinking? How is such a condition different from ordinary existence for a chimpanzee?

Google It! Honeybee Waggle Dance

There are plenty of videos and articles on the Internet about animal communication systems. Try googling **bee dance** or **waggle dance, vervet monkey alarm call** (or just **alarm call**), and **mating call.**

SECTION 1.2: HUMAN LANGUAGE

- Laughter is a social vocalization we share with chimpanzees; we use it together with conversation to enhance social interactions.

- Language bears three important features as a communication system: (1) it is governed by rules, (2) it consists of structured components, and (3) it makes use of arbitrary symbols. Certain animal communication systems share some, but not all, of these features.

- Language is conveyed in three different modes: (1) in a vocal mode, which we call spoken language or speech; (2) in a manual mode, which we call signed language; and (3) a visual mode, which we call writing. By far, the vocal mode is most common.

- Duality of patterning gives language its expressive power; it is a process that takes units at a lower level and combines them according to rules into new units at a higher level. By repeating this process many times, a multilayered structure of great complexity can be built out of a small set of simple elements.

- The building blocks of language are phonemes, which are meaningless speech sounds. Phonemes combine to form morphemes, which are the basic units of meaning. Morphemes combine to form words, words combine to form phrases, phrases combine to form sentences, and sentences combine to form discourse.

- While animal communication systems are always about the here and now, human languages allow us to talk about events happening in other times and places; this is known as displacement.

In humans, language hasn't simply replaced the vocalizations of our primate cousins. Rather, we use language on top of the communication system we inherited from our prelinguistic predecessors. We laugh with joy, cry with despair, shriek with terror, shout with anger. And when we are overcome with emotion, our language faculty shuts down altogether, leaving us with nothing but our animal vocalizations and facial expressions. Because their body forms are somewhat different from ours, chimpanzees do not share all of the same vocalizations and facial expressions we have, and they even have some we don't. But there is one emotional expression widely found in the primate world that is uncannily similar in humans and chimps, and that is laughter (Davila-Ross et al., 2011; Palagi & Mancini, 2011; Vettin & Todt, 2005).

Laugh, and the World Laughs With You

Laughter isn't just the fare of comedy clubs and late-night TV; it's an integral part of our social communication. We laugh so frequently and so automatically that we're often but vaguely aware we've done so and have no idea why. In fact, our very intuitions about why we laugh are completely wrong. Most of the time when we laugh, we do so not because someone said something funny, but simply because they said something, and we'd like them to say more (Mehu & Dunbar, 2008). We laugh to say, "I like you." In other words, it is a kind of social vocalization, not unlike the mooing of cows in a herd.

Laughter evolved from the labored breathing of rough-and-tumble play, but it's come to mean playful intent in both chimpanzees and humans (Provine, 2004). We punctuate our conversations with laughter, and by so doing, we encourage our conversation partners to stay in the chit-chat game. Chimpanzees likewise use short bursts of laughter during social interactions, and they'll mimic the laugh patterns of those they are engaging with, presumably to promote social cohesion (Davila-Ross et al., 2011). In short, both species use laughter as a tool for building friendships.

In humans, there is a clear gender difference in laugh production (Provine, 2004). By far, women do most of the laughing, and men do most of the laugh-getting. It seems that laughter is part of the mate attraction process in humans. Human females laugh in the presence of males they find attractive, and the more a woman laughs during an encounter with the opposite sex, the greater is her reported interest in that man. Whether female chimpanzees use laughter to signal sexual interest is still an open topic for research.

Laughter and language bear an interesting relationship. Each involves the same vocal apparatus, and so you can't do both at the same time, even though they are almost always used in the same context. Rather, in conversational interactions we alternate between talking and laughing, using laughter as a sort of punctuation between phrases and sentences (Provine, 2004). Even listeners usually wait until the end of the speaker's sentence to laugh.

While it isn't likely that language evolved out of laughter, differences between the way humans and chimpanzees laugh suggest something about what was needed for language to evolve. When chimpanzees laugh, they typically produce one long "ha" per breath. But humans have much greater control over their breathing, which they need for producing speech, and they typically produce a series of short bursts—"ha-ha-ha"—with each breath.

Speech! Speech!

In our modern world, human language can take several forms. For the most part, we use language in its spoken form, or speech. Speech is the form of human language that, at least on the surface, most resembles the vocalized communication systems of our primate cousins. But communities of the deaf use human languages in a manual mode, which we call signed languages. Primates in laboratory settings have been taught to use simplified signed languages, but they don't use them in the wild. Over the last few thousand years, we've devised ways to represent language in a visual mode, and we call this writing. It's important to note that signed languages are not just manual versions of spoken languages, but rather they are full-fledged languages in their own right. Furthermore, writing is not just a visual representation of speech, but rather it has taken on its own forms and conventions to fit the medium.

Nevertheless, speech is the primary form of human language. For millennia, speech was the only form of language, and even in today's world of near-universal literacy, we listen and speak far more than we read or write. Likewise, the users of signed languages are but a small fraction of a society that is dominated by spoken language users.

For this reason, in this textbook we'll emphasize the **primacy of speech**, that is, *the observation that virtually all language use is in the spoken mode* (Hockett, 1960). We'll do this in spite of the fact that much of the psycholinguistic research we will look at has studied language in its visual mode. It's much easier to present stimuli to research participants in a visual mode rather than in an auditory mode, and so most of the classical studies in psycholinguistics involved written language, with researchers working under the assumption that their findings would extrapolate to speech as well.

Rules, Structure, and Arbitrary Symbols

Laughter is a typical example of animal communication. It's holistic in expression, emotional by nature, and referential to the current situation. Language is also a form of communication, but it's quite different from anything seen elsewhere in the animal kingdom.

Defining language is difficult, but we've been avoiding it for too long, so let's take a stab at it. First, language is a communication system governed by rules. But even this definition doesn't completely get at the uniqueness of human language. Even animal communication systems have rules. You can't just make the "leopard" call whenever you feel like it, as every young vervet soon learns.

Second, language is a communication system consisting of structured components. Again, this doesn't uniquely specify human language. Even the honeybee waggle dance consists of components that are organized in a structure, in that the returning scout must structure her dance so that the length of the waggle correlates with the distance to the source, and the direction of the waggle correlates with the direction to fly.

Third, many language researchers claim that a key feature of language is the **arbitrary symbol**. That is, a word is *a symbol that bears no resemblance to what it refers to*. This observation is generally true of human languages. The word we use in English to refer to that furry, four-legged creature we keep as a pet is *dog*, but in Chinese it's *gǒu*, and in Japanese it's *inu*. And yet we also have onomatopoeia, which are words that sound like what they refer to, such as the *moo* of cows or the *woof-woof* of dogs. But even onomatopoeia differs from language to language. In Chinese, for example, cows go *móu* and dogs go *wàng-wàng*.

Each component of the honeybee waggle dance, on the other hand, is an **iconic symbol**, meaning it's *a symbol that bears a clear resemblance to what it refers to*. The longer the dance, the longer the distance. Likewise, the greater the angle from the vertical, the greater the angle from the sun. Yet vervet alarm calls, as far as we know, are arbitrary. At least, there's nothing obvious, to human observers, in the relationship between the call and the predator it's referring to.

Table 1.1 A Rose by Any Other Name . . .

"What's in a name? that which we call a rose by any other name would smell as sweet." So wrote William Shakespeare in *Romeo and Juliet*. Below is the name for ROSE in ten different languages. Notice that the word is similar across the various European languages because of borrowing. Outside of Europe, the name varies considerably. (The source for some of these items is from the Bab.la Online Dictionary, available at http://en.bab.la.)

Chinese	méigui
Czech	růže
Finnish	ruusu
Hindi	gulaab
Hungarian	rózsa
Indonesian	bunga mawar
Japanese	bara
Spanish	rosa
Swahili	waridi
Turkish	gül

We want to make the case that human language is somehow unique. And yet it shares each of its three of its major features—rules, structure, and arbitrary symbols—with other animal communication systems. What makes human language unique is the combination of these three features into a complex system that linguists call **duality of patterning** (Hockett, 1960). This is *a structuring process that takes units at a lower level and combines them according to rules into new units at a higher level*. Furthermore, by repeating this process to build layer upon layer like a pyramid, languages can take a handful of simple elements (whether speech sounds, hand gestures, or squiggles on a page) and turn them into structures of exquisite complexity. Duality of patterning gives language users the ability to express virtually anything and likewise to think virtually anything. It's exactly this power of language that has lifted us out of the animal world in a few tens of thousands of years.

Pyramid Scheme

Standard American English (SAE) is just one of the many thousands of languages that's been spoken over the eons of human existence, and as far as languages go, it's pretty ordinary. At its most basic level, SAE is composed of about forty **phonemes**, which are

Figure 1.4 Duality of Patterning

Meaningless phonemes, which are the smallest units of speech sound, combine according to the rules of phonology to form morphemes, which are the smallest units of meaning. Morphemes then combine according to the rules of morphology to form words.

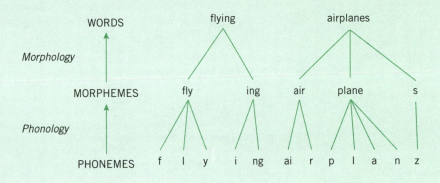

meaningless speech sounds that serve as the fundamental building blocks of language. For example, the name of the language, English, is composed of six phonemes, namely *i-ng-g-l-i-sh*. The letters we use to write English attempt to represent the phonemes of the language, but we borrowed the alphabet from the Romans, and it's not a good fit. So don't be thrown off by double-letter combinations like *sh* that represent a single phoneme.

Stand-alone phonemes are meaningless. We would never say "ng" in English—it just doesn't mean anything. We do under certain circumstances say "sh," and it does have a definite meaning, but it's more like one of those animal communication signals we still use—it's holistic, emotional, and referential to the current situation. Anyway, "sh" has no meaning when it occurs as a phoneme in "English" or any other word. As we said, SAE has an inventory of about forty phonemes, which is fairly typical for a human language.

According to the principle of duality of patterning, units at a lower level are combined by rules into units at a higher level. *The set of rules for combining phonemes into larger units* is called **phonology**. We learn these rules implicitly as youngsters. Any native speaker of English can tell you that *glunt, obligrate,* and *thessily* are possible words in the language, even though they don't happen to be actual words. On the other hand, sequences such as *zwckl, brznsk,* and *uioeaaio* are not even possible words in the language. But the rules of phonology do differ somewhat from language to language. For example, speakers of Japanese are baffled that English speakers hear *street* as a single syllable, which to them sounds like the five-syllable sequence *su-to-re-e-to,* based on the rules of Japanese phonology. On the other hand, the Japanese word for "moon," which is *tski,* is hard to pronounce as a single syllable for native speakers of English.

The rules of phonology take the lower level units, the phonemes, and combine them into units at the next higher level. These units are called **morphemes**, and they represent *the basic units of meaning in a language*. Some morphemes can stand alone as words, and these are called free morphemes. Other morphemes cannot stand alone but rather must be combined with other morphemes to form words, and these are called bound morphemes. Bound morphemes are the prefixes and suffixes we attach to words.

In some languages, like English and Chinese, many words consist of a single free morpheme. Consider the following example English sentence and its Chinese equivalent.

English: I want to go, but I have no money.

Chinese: *Wǒ yào qù, dàn wǒ méi yǒu qián.*

             'I want go, but I not have money.'

In both cases, each word consists of a single morpheme. That is to say, there is no way to divide any of the words into parts that are also meaningful.

Still, both English and Chinese make use of bound morphemes, in the form of suffixes and prefixes. Sometimes bound morphemes are there strictly for the grammar and add little or no meaning. One example is the -*s* suffix on verbs, as in the sentence:

Malcolm want-s to come to the party, and I want to also.

Due to the quirky history of English, this relic from an ancient form of the language is still hanging around vexing native speakers, who are often perplexed about when it's needed and when it's not.

English has other bound morphemes that serve a more reasonable grammatical function. All verbs can take the -*ing* suffix indicating that the action is ongoing, and all regular verbs can take the -*ed* suffix indicating that the action happened in the past, as in the sentence:

We were play-ing Guitar Hero when Kyle bump-ed his head.

All English nouns can take the -'*s* suffix indicating possession, and all regular English nouns can take the -*s* suffix indicating plural. And when a noun is both possessive and plural, the suffix is -*s*', as in the sentence:

Miriam-'s boy-s' bicycle-s are blocking the driveway.

Notice that while the three suffixes are distinguished in writing by the strategic use of an apostrophe, in speech all three sound exactly the same, and that's why English writers are so confused in their use.

The set of rules for combining morphemes together to form words is called **morphology**. English and Chinese morphology are relatively simple, but it can be quite complex in some languages. One such language is Japanese, at least in the case of verbs, which consist of a verb root that can almost never stand alone, followed by one or more suffixes indicating various grammatical distinctions. My favorite is *ik-ase-rare-na-katta*, which means "I was not caused to go."

The important thing to notice in this discussion of morphemes, morphology, and words is that we once again see duality of patterning. Just as phonemes combine according to the rules of phonology to form morphemes, morphemes combine according to the rules of morphology to form words. It's this repeating pattern of units at a lower level combining according to rules to form units at a higher level—in other words, duality of patterning—that gives human language such power of expression.

Sentences and Discourse

Human language is built in a hierarchical structure, layer upon layer, with this same duality of patterning linking adjacent levels. In the simple view, words combine according to rules to form sentences, but in fact there is an intermediate step. Words first group themselves into phrases, and these phrases then group themselves into sentences. *The set of rules for ordering words and phrases into sentences* is called **syntax**. If we want to be more precise about the rules ordering words first into phrases and then into sentences, we mention phrase structure rules.

When we consider phrase structure rules from a cognitive psychology perspective, it's clear why we need two stages to go from words to sentences. It has to do with working memory constraints. If we think of **working memory** as *a kind of short-term memory that holds whatever we are currently thinking about,* and if we keep in mind that working memory has a very limited capacity—generally considered to be around seven items—we can see that many sentences exceed this capacity in terms of number of words. But we can only talk about what we're currently thinking about; likewise, we can only understand what someone is saying if we can hold it in working memory long enough to process it. So if we went straight from words to sentences, we'd have to keep our sentences short.

Classical cognitive psychology teaches us that we can increase working memory capacity through a process known as **chunking**, which is *a process that groups meaningless items into larger meaningful units in order to increase working memory capacity*. (This should sound suspiciously like duality of patterning.) For example, if I tell you (and I'll be lying) that my office phone number is 207-834-0880, chances are you won't be able to remember it. But if you are a student on my campus, you'll know that 207 is the local area code and that 834 is the campus prefix. You can chunk these, leaving enough room in working memory to hold the four random digits of my office extension. And so it is when we go from words to sentences.

If the idea of phrase structure is still unclear to you, let's consider for a moment the following totally random sentence:

The man in the Santa Claus suit used to be my history professor.

Imagine you're going to pause somewhere in this sentence, perhaps to laugh. You'll probably do it this way:

The man in the Santa Claus suit [hah, hah] used to be my history professor.

This is the most natural way to break this sentence because what comes before the laugh is a single unit, namely the subject of the sentence. It's what the sentence is about. The string of words following the laugh is also a single unit, namely the predicate. The predicate makes some kind of comment about the subject. Generally speaking, that's what we do when we talk—we point something out, and then we make a comment about it.

It's possible to insert laughter at other places in the sentence. For example, you could also laugh here:

The man [hee, hee] in the Santa Claus suit [hah, hah] used to be my history professor.

We can do this because the subject phrase of this sentence is complex, consisting of the noun phrase *the man* and the prepositional phrase *in the Santa Claus suit*. Furthermore, if you're feeling especially giggly, you could even laugh here:

The man [hee, hee] in the Santa Claus suit [hah, hah] used to be [ho, ho] my history professor.

The predicate phrase is also complex, consisting of the verb phrase *used to be* and the object noun phrase *my history professor*.

Linguists like to illustrate the hierarchical structure of sentences by means of tree diagrams. Each branch in a tree diagram represents an instance of duality of patterning, units at a lower level combining to form a unit at the next higher level.

Traditionally, linguists have viewed the sentence as the basic unit of language. In fact, most of the linguistic research of the last half of the twentieth century focused on teasing out the structure of sentences, following the lead of noted linguist Noam Chomsky. However, people just don't go around uttering random sentences. Instead, they utter sentences within larger linguistic structures, such as conversations and narratives. These are examples of **discourse**, which is *a language structure consisting of a sequence of sentences that are ordered according to rules*. Conversations have rules for taking turns and changing topics. And narratives, or stories, have rules for how events need to be ordered. We implicitly learn the rules of discourse as we grow up, and we are all aware of violations of these rules, even though we can rarely articulate them. Any careful analysis of a conversation or a story will reveal duality of patterning once again as the structuring agent.

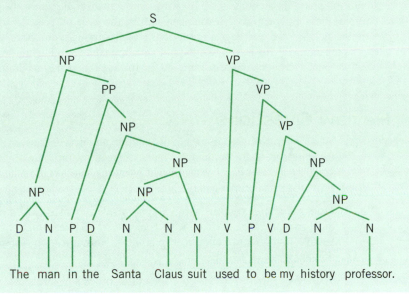

Figure 1.5   Sentence Tree

Tree diagram for the sentence: "The man in the Santa Claus suit used to be my history professor." Note the various instances of recursion in the structure, especially the nesting of noun phrases within noun phrases and verb phrases within verb phrases. Abbreviations: D = determiner, N = noun, P = preposition, V = verb, NP = noun phrase, VP = verb phrase, PP = prepositional phrase, and S = sentence. (We will discuss recursion in Section 1.3.)

Long, Long Ago, in a Galaxy Far, Far Away . . .

Before we end this section, we need to briefly discuss one other feature of human language that distinguishes it from animal communication systems. We have already seen that animal communication is about the here and now. Human communication, even with language, is also to a great extent about the here and now. However, embedded within the complex hierarchical structure of language are devices that allow us to escape the confines of the eternal present. Because we have so many words, we can use some of them to indicate that we are talking about past events or future events or even hypothetical events, and furthermore those events could have happened at some other place than where speaker and the listener currently are, perhaps down by the river, or on the other side of the boulder, or even in some place that we only imagined.

The ability to refer to things and events beyond the here and now is called **displacement**. We have already seen in the case of the honeybee waggle dance that some animal communication systems also exhibit limited displacement. Nevertheless, the complexity of human language allows for displacement on a far grander scale than is capable in any other communication system. Furthermore, it is this power of displacement in human language that allows us to think in terms of hypothetical situations, to consider alternative worlds—and what we would need to do to make them reality.

In Sum

It is the hierarchical structure of human language that lends it such expressive power. The ability to combine meaningless sounds into meaningful words allows for a vocabulary of unlimited size, and the ability to combine words into sentences allows for the expression of complex ideas. Although we often use language for the same purposes as animal communication systems, language also supports complex thought processes, and it also allows us to efficiently convey information from one human to another and from one generation to next. In sum, language is the single attribute that makes us uniquely human.

Review Questions

1. What is the evolutionary origin of laughter, and how is it used in chimpanzees and humans? What is the relationship between laughter and language? What insight into the evolution of language is provided by a comparison of chimpanzee and human laughter?

2. Rules, structure, arbitrary symbols, and displacement are all features of human language. Explain what is meant by each feature. For each feature, also give an example of an animal communication system that exhibits that feature.

3. What is duality of patterning? Explain this process in terms of phonemes, morphemes, and phonology. What happens next?

4. Explain the organization of words into phrases and sentences in terms of working memory constraints.

5. What is discourse? What are the two main types of spoken discourse? How are they similar? How are they different?

Thought Questions

1. Why is laughter contagious? Laughter evolved from the labored breathing of rough-and-tumble play, but what is the relationship between play and language?

2. Linguists and psychologists maintain that signed languages have all the features of spoken languages, and in fact both signed and spoken languages are processed in the same regions of the brain. But what would be the phonemes and morphemes of a signed language?

3. Besides modality, what are some differences between spoken and written languages? What circumstances in the way the two are used can account for these differences?

4. Duality of patterning is not just a phenomenon of human languages. In fact, it is a structuring principle that is also found in the physical and biological worlds as well as in the structure of human societies. Can you think of some concrete examples?

Google It! Chimpanzee Laughter

There are plenty of video clips about **chimpanzee laughter** on YouTube. You can also find out something in common between the way chimpanzees and human babies laugh.

SECTION 1.3 EVOLUTION OF LANGUAGE

- Humans and chimpanzees share a common ancestor; *Homo erectus* was an ancestor of both the Neanderthals and modern humans.

- Recursion, or the process of extending a pattern by placing it inside itself, is an important feature of human language in particular and human thought in general.

- The question of whether human language evolved gradually or rapidly is known as the continuity debate; both continuity and discontinuity theories have been proposed.

- Evidence for discontinuity theories includes (1) the specific language impairment of the KE family, (2) the FOXP2 gene, and (3) the disparity between animal communication and human language.

- Evidence for continuity theories includes (1) the fact that these theories are consistent with the principles of natural selection, and (2) the existence of pidgins, which suggests the possibility that pre-humans spoke a protolanguage halfway between animal calls and full language.

- Social theories of language evolution emphasize (1) the special nature of mother–infant interactions, (2) the relationship between music and speech, or (3) the role of conversation in building and maintaining social relationships.

A great king of India once invited six blind monks to his palace to examine an elephant. The first blind monk placed his hands against the side of the elephant and declared, "This is a wall." The second grabbed the elephant's ear and said, "This is a fan." The third had the elephant's tail and called it a snake. The fourth held the elephant's trunk and said it was a tree limb. The fifth said the smooth, pointed tusk was a sword. And the last one, wrapping his arms around one of its legs, said he'd found a pillar. The six blind monks commenced fighting among themselves until the king ordered them to stop. "You are all right," said the king. "And you are all wrong."

This story is an apt parable for the endeavor of science. We believe there's something called reality out there, but each of us has only the faintest glimpse of it. We must remember to always be humble and not to assume that we know all there is to know, as did the blind monks in the parable. Instead, we need to keep in mind that what we know is only our current best guess as to the true nature of the world. And furthermore, we have to always remember that other people have different insights from our own. Neither our view nor theirs is totally correct, but rather the truth lies somewhere in between. As scientists, we need to collect as much evidence as we can, fill in the blanks with reasonable assumptions, and keep an open mind to the fact that, as new evidence comes to light, our understanding of the world will change. It is with this open, humble frame of mind that we recount the natural history of our species and the role in it played by our most wonderful invention, language.

Out of Africa

Our home is in Africa. Our chimpanzee cousins still live there, as do many of our human siblings. But others of us spread out through the world until we covered every continent except snow-capped Antarctica. The story goes back five million years, but first we need to understand something about **speciation**, or *the processes involved in the evolution of new species*.

A common metaphor for evolution is a ladder. According to this view, we humans are higher up the evolutionary ladder than are the chimpanzees. But this view is inappropriate. Instead, a better metaphor for evolution is a tree. The tree of life is three billion years old, with branches upon branches upon branches, and the leaves on the tips of those branches are the species currently in existence.

Species do not evolve from one form to another as they ascend the ladder of evolution. Rather, populations that were once a single species split in two, and as these two groups go their separate ways, they each adapt to their new environments and thus evolve into different species. One way to determine whether two populations are one or two species is to see if they can interbreed. Humans from the various continents of the world can (and frequently do) interbreed, so we can say all humans belong to one species. On the other hand, dogs and cats cannot interbreed, and so they are clearly separate species.

Humans did not evolve from chimpanzees. Rather, humans and chimpanzees have a common ancestor about five million years ago (Bradley, 2008). After the split, various pre-human species arose and then disappeared, as species have been doing since life began on this planet. Sometimes several species of pre-humans existed at the same time, perhaps even competing for the same territory and resources. This is not surprising. After all, there are two species of chimpanzee—the common chimp and the bonobo—living not far apart from each other back on the African homestead. Indeed, there's something very suspicious about the fact that there's only one living human species today, especially given that other human species once shared this planet with our ancestors.

The first important human ancestor for our story is *Homo erectus*, which arose in Africa about 1.8 million years ago (Disotell, 2012). *H. erectus* was the first human-like creature to walk truly upright. The members of this species lived in hunter-gatherer societies, used fire and stone tools, and probably had a communication system more complex than the vocalizations of our chimp cousins but still not nearly as complex as the full language of modern humans (Bickerton, 1990). They were similar in height to modern humans, though stockier, and they had a cranial capacity much larger than modern chimpanzees but still somewhat smaller than that of modern humans. Dressed in modern clothes, a member of *H. erectus* riding the New York subway might not catch anyone's attention.

By all accounts, *H. erectus* was a successful species. Its members were fruitful and multiplied, and some of them migrated from the African home base, eventually occupying large swaths of Europe and Asia, reaching all the way to China and Southeast Asia. But then, around 200,000 years ago, the fossil record on *H. erectus* fizzles out (Ben-Dor et al., 2011; Disotell, 2012). Still, a million and a half years is a pretty good run for a species. Incidentally, 200,000 years ago is about the time *Homo sapiens*—us!—begins to appear in the fossil record. Before we look at our own history, though, let's briefly consider our sibling species, the Neanderthals.

There are no fossil remains of *Homo neanderthalensis* in Africa, only in Europe and Asia. From this we can only guess that the Neanderthals branched off from those members of *H. erectus* that had already left Africa. The earliest Neanderthal fossils date to 400,000 years ago (Hublin, 2009). They were somewhat larger and stronger than modern humans, and their brains were slightly larger as well. They too used fire and tools, and they lived in hunter-gatherer societies. There really is no reason to think that they did not have a communication system at least approaching the sophistication of our modern language (Wynn & Coolidge, 2012).

Our branch of the family, *Homo sapiens*, has its origins in Africa around 200,000 years ago, and by 50,000 years ago we see clear signs of stone-age culture. Like our *erectus* forebears a million and a half years before us, we too were fruitful and multiplied, and we began the second wave of human migration out of Africa. Our *erectus* ancestors had already died out, but we met our Neanderthal cousins in Europe 40,000 years ago. For 10,000 years, two species of humans lived side by side, but then the Neanderthals died out—under rather suspicious circumstances.

Some scientists think we killed them (Banks et al., 2008). Perhaps it was outright warfare between the two species of humans, or perhaps it was a competition for resources. But for some reason, the Neanderthals—with their bigger brains and stronger bodies—were no match for us. As a psycholinguist, I prefer to think that perhaps we had more fully developed language than they did, and that's what gave us the edge. But then I'm just a blind monk holding a part of an elephant.

Other scientists believe we made love, not war, with the Neanderthals (Smith, Janković, & Karavanić, 2005). According to this theory, when our ancestors, coming out of

Africa, met with the Neanderthals in Europe, we recognized members of the same species, and we interbred with them. In fact, there is some evidence of Neanderthal ancestry in the DNA of people of European descent. If this theory is true, there really are Neanderthals riding the New York subway!

Hopeful Monster

Timmy and Tommy are having a counting contest. "One," says Timmy. "Two," says Tommy. "Three," Timmy replies. "Four," Tommy responds. Timmy pauses. He can't think of a higher number, and neither can Tommy. Of course, counting contests are pointless. As any grade school pupil can tell you, no matter how high you count, there's always a higher number. Mathematicians put it this way: for any n, there is $n + 1$. This property of numbers is known as recursion.

Put simply, **recursion** is *the process of extending a pattern by placing it inside itself*. When we count, we know that the next number is one more than the last number, or as mathematicians put it, $n_1 = n_0 + 1$. Recursive patterns occur widely in nature, from the

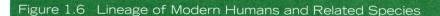

Figure 1.6 Lineage of Modern Humans and Related Species

Approximate family tree for the hominid lineage. Species marked with an asterisk are considered extinct. Note that the dates are approximate. Estimated dates for the branching of gorilla and chimpanzee from the common ancestor vary by several million years; the dates given in this figure are based on Bradley (2008).

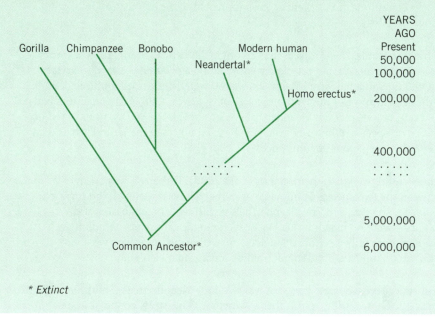

* Extinct

structure of DNA to the number of petals on a daisy. Likewise, recursion is a feature of many of our day-to-day behaviors, for example, when we wash, rinse, and repeat.

Recursion is a characteristic of human languages as well. Just as there is no such thing as a highest number, there is no such thing as a longest sentence. Children pick up on the recursive nature of language even before they enter grade school, and they play language games in which they challenge each other to extend sentences indefinitely. *I saw the dog . . . that chased the cat . . . that caught the rat. . . .* And so on. In this game, you extend the sentence by tacking on an additional relative clause at the end. However, unlike a counting contest, this game is a memory challenge. The sentence never has to end, but eventually your memory for repeating it will fail, and then you're out of the game.

According to linguist Noam Chomsky (2011), recursion is the key to understanding how human languages evolved from more primitive communication systems. Chomsky leads a school of linguistics that emphasizes the **centrality of syntax**. This is *the view that the ability to organize words into phrases and sentences according to recursive rules is the distinguishing feature of language*. If this is the case, then what evolved first

Figure 1.7 Recursion in Russian Dolls

A set of Russian dolls, known as *matryoska*, provides a concrete example of recursion. Each doll resembles the others, but one fits inside another, those inside a third, and so on. Likewise in language, we can nest sentences inside each other. This is a unique aspect of human language as a communication system.

Source: © iStockphoto.com / BomBeR_irk.

was not language but rather an understanding of recursion. Once the ability to think recursively was hardwired into our brains, Chomsky argues, language in its full form naturally emerged.

Many animal species, including human babies, have a simple number sense (Xu, Spelke, & Goddard, 2005). That is, they can distinguish sets of two items from sets of three items or sets of four items. But they usually do not show an understanding of relationships among numbers, such as that three is greater than two but less than four. Nor do they understand counting as a recursive pattern.

Generally speaking, evolution proceeds incrementally. For example, a complex eye evolves, through countless steps, from a patch of light-sensitive skin (Land & Nilsson, 2002). At every step in the process, this "partial eye" provided a survival and reproductive advantage to those who had it, and so it was passed on to future generations. But Chomsky argues that language did not evolve this way. Instead, he proposes that a single mutation transformed the pre-human brain into a recursive thinking machine and that this mutation spread quickly through the population in one or a few generations (Hauser, Chomsky, & Fitch, 2002). In other words, our species was quickly transformed from one that communicated with grunts and gestures to one that spoke in complete sentences.

Chomsky's ideas on language were influential for much of the last half of the twentieth century. Still, his theory of language evolution is not without its detractors. Evolutionary biologists in particular question *the idea that a single mutation could lead to a rapid transition from one form to another*, calling it a **hopeful monster hypothesis** (Theißen, 2006). In general, *the question of whether human language evolved gradually or rapidly* is known as the **continuity debate**.

A Language Gene?

Chomsky's argument is philosophical, not empirical. That is to say, he presents his case based on logic and not on scientific evidence. He doesn't claim to know which gene has mutated, only that one must have. In the late twentieth century, though, it looked as though there might indeed be a language gene after all.

In 1990, linguist Myrna Gopnik (1990) reported on the so-called **KE family**, *an extended family living in London that exhibits a language disorder appearing to have a genetic cause*. Some members of the family exhibit an extreme form of **specific language impairment**, which is *a language processing and production disorder that cannot be attributed to other causes such as brain damage or hearing loss*. By tracking the occurrence of specific language impairment in members of the family through three generations, researchers were able to isolate the responsible gene, known as FOXP2. Family members with normal language abilities had the normal version of the FOXP2 gene, and those with specific language impairment had a defective version of the gene.

FOXP2 is *a gene found widely among vertebrates that plays a role in brain development as well as serving other functions*. In songbirds, for example, a mutation of the FOXP2 gene leads to disruptions in the ability to learn song (Bolhuis, Okanoya, & Scharff, 2010). Furthermore, newborn mice with a disrupted FOXP2 gene exhibit an alteration or absence of the ultrasonic vocalizations they use to call for their mother when they fall from the nest (Shu et al., 2005), leading these researchers to propose that FOXP2 plays a role in social communication across a wide variety of species.

In the end, FOXP2 is probably not the language gene Chomsky proposed. While it is true that chimpanzee FOXP2 is different from the human, it's also not the disrupted version found in the KE family (Konopka et al., 2009). Rather, it seems that a disruption of human FOXP2 leads to language impairments, just as a disruption of songbird FOXP2 leads to difficulties in learning birdsong (Bolhuis et al., 2010).

In fact, this discussion about the role of FOXP2 provides a good lesson in the proper way to think about genetics. Genes code for the production of proteins, which can have cascading effects both during embryonic development and the entire lifespan of the organism. FOXP2 influences not only the development of neural structures but also the cartilage and connective tissue of the face, all of which are important for spoken language but which serve other functions as well. In other words, there is no single "language gene," but instead our ability to speak is likely influenced by many genes that also subserve other functions besides language (Bolhuis et al., 2010).

Perhaps Chomsky has only described one part of the elephant. That is, while recursion is an important characteristic of human language, perhaps it's not the sole distinguishing feature. Instead, it's far more likely that human language evolved gradually from simple animal communication systems to its present complex form (Pinker & Bloom, 1990). Along the way, each addition to the communication toolkit of our early ancestors provided them with reproductive advantage, and thus the development of language was driven by the same forces of natural selection that we see at play throughout the natural world.

Continuity theories, which are *theories that propose a steady transition from animal communication systems to human language*, also have problems. First, there are no species alive today that display communicative skills between those of animals and humans. Indeed, this fact is taken as evidence for **discontinuity theories**, which are *theories that propose a sudden transition from animal communication systems to human language*.

Second, there is no way to tell for sure, just by looking at the fossils and artifacts of ancestral humans, what sort of communication system they had. Perhaps members of *Homo erectus* already had full language a million years ago, and they sat by the campfire at night telling each other stories. Or maybe the reason their culture stalled at campfires and rock tools was precisely because they had no effective means of communicating and thus transmitting culture. On the other hand, there is evidence from living human populations to suggest that human language does indeed come in incremental forms.

Long Time No See

When British traders arrived in southern China in the eighteenth century, no one on board spoke Chinese, and no one on land spoke English. Yet each had what the other wanted—the British offering silver and gold, and the Chinese offering tea and porcelain—so they had to find a way to communicate. They did this by developing a **pidgin**, which is a *simple language consisting of a few hundred words and a very basic grammar*, and it was just good enough to get the business done (Bolton, 2002). (In fact, it's believed that the word "pidgin" comes from the Chinese pronunciation of the English word "business.") Although this pidgin is no longer in use, several of its expressions, such as *long time no see* and *no can do*, have made their way into the English language.

Throughout history, whenever two human populations speaking different languages have come into extended contact with each other, the speakers of those two languages have developed a pidgin for the purpose of basic communication. It's important to note that pidgins are not languages by design, but rather they emerge naturally through the repeated interactions of humans who do not speak each other's language.

Although every pidgin is unique, they share some common features (Holm, 2000). They all have a limited vocabulary and a simple phonology, so the words are easy to pronounce and distinguish from one another. Pidgin syntax typically allows for simple subject-verb-object sentences but doesn't provide for the recursion necessary to build the complex sentences typical of full-fledged human languages. Thus, the expressive power of pidgins stands somewhere between the holophrases of animal language and the complex expressions of human language.

This observation has led linguist Derek Bickerton (1990, 2009) to propose that *Homo erectus* probably spoke a sort of pidgin. Since this was the only language they had, he calls it protolanguage to distinguish it from the general meaning of the term pidgin, which refers to a supplemental communication system used by people who already speak a full language. In other words, **protolanguage** is *a hypothetical pidgin-like language spoken by ancestral humans*. Pidgins can be an effective means of communication, and so if *Homo erectus* did have protolanguage, it would certainly have given the species an edge over other pre-human populations. And *Home erectus* was a very successful species, spreading across three continents during its tenure on this planet.

At first glance, the protolanguage hypothesis appears to propose a two-step program from animal communication to human language. As such, it's still a discontinuity theory with all the weaknesses of Chomsky's proposal. Yet two observations from living species suggests the transition from animal communication to protolanguage, and then from protolanguage to full language, may not be as abrupt as first imagined.

First, attempts to teach language to chimpanzees have shown that they are capable of learning pidgin-like communication systems, even though they have not developed these spontaneously in the wild. Thus, our ancestors may have been poised to acquire at least some aspects of language, and maybe all it took was a little nudge, perhaps some small reorganization of the brain, for them to develop protolanguage spontaneously.

Second, when children grow up in an environment where all the adults around them speak a pidgin, they develop a **creole**, which is *a full-fledged language based on a pidgin*. Thus, the transition from pidgin to creole only takes one generation, but of course this is with children who already have an innate understanding of recursion, as well as all the biological machinery necessary for language.

The "living fossils" of pidgins and creoles will be the topic of Section 1.4, but for now let's review a few other current theories on language evolution.

Hush, Little Baby, Don't You Cry

Kids say the darndest things, and so do mothers. Moms coo to their babies, and the babies coo back. It doesn't matter what mom actually says—after all, the kid doesn't understand any of it. Rather, it's how she says it that counts. **Motherese**, or *the type of language caregivers use to interact with their infants*, is quite different from ordinary speech. (Since it's not just mothers but caregivers in general who use this type of language, motherese is also known as caregiver speech or infant-directed speech.) The range of pitch is greater, the rhythms are more regular, and there's plenty of repetition. In other words, motherese has a number of features in common with music.

Several theorists have looked at the connections between motherese and music and the evolution of language. For example, anthropologist Dean Falk (2009) has proposed that language evolved out of the vocalizations of mothers soothing their young. The **mother tongue hypothesis** is *a model of language evolution proposing that maternal vocalizations took on meaning over the course of many generations, developing into a way for family members to communicate*. After even more generations had passed, these mother tongues spread through communities until everyone in the group spoke the same language.

Archaeologist Steven Mithen (2005) proposes that it wasn't motherese per se but rather singing that became the origin of speech. There is clearly a relationship between language and music, but the exact nature of that relationship is unclear, and scholars debate at length about which came first (Ross, 2009). Mithen claims that pre-human mothers made humming sounds to soothe their babies. Over evolutionary time, these wordless songs were segmented into meaningful units that became the words of language. Likewise, the habit of singing to babies was extended to other situations, such as religious ceremonies and to coordinate group behaviors. This idea, called the **singing Neanderthal hypothesis**, is *a model of language evolution proposing that both music and language derive from the same source, the humming of pre-human social interactions*. It's important to note here that Mithen uses the term Neanderthal loosely, using it to refer to early humans in general and not just the species *Homo neanderthalensis*.

Also considering the social aspects of language is evolutionary psychologist Robin Dunbar (1998). Our chimpanzee cousins live in relatively complex societies, and they build and maintain social relationships through mutual grooming. Although grooming serves a hygienic purpose, cleaning the fur and skin of insects and debris, it also solidifies friendships. Humans also engage in social grooming—doing each other's hair, primping each other's clothes. But according to Dunbar, we've found an easier and more effective way of building and maintaining relationships—idle chit-chat. Thus, the **social grooming hypothesis** is *a model of language evolution proposing that gossip for humans serves the same purpose of social network building as does grooming for chimpanzees.*

These three hypotheses focus on the social aspects of language use and don't really get at the specifics of how language evolved. But they do challenge us to think about what language really is. Traditional approaches, such as the one taken by Chomsky, view language as a system for transmitting thoughts from one person to another. Certainly, language does have that function, as for example when your professor lectures in class. Although you would prefer your teachers to speak in an engaging manner, what's most important is content. Yet two friends will chit-chat for hours, and when they part ways the only thing engraved in their memories is that they had a great time, even though they can't remember the details of what they talked about. In other words, it's not the content that's important but rather the communication of feelings, that is, the building of mutual trust and affection. Chit-chat with friends is a lot like motherese—it's not so much what you say but how you say it that counts.

Figure 1.8   Photo of Baboons Engaged in Social Grooming

Baboons, like many primate species, live in groups and groom each other as a way of developing social relationships. Some scientists think social grooming may be an evolutionary precursor of language.

Source: © iStockphoto.com / mrtom-uk.

In Sum

There are a number of theories of language evolution, all of which have some support. Discontinuity theories focus on the disparity between animal communication and human language, proposing a sudden evolutionary shift to explain this observation. Continuity theories are more in line with the principles of natural selection, but they have a difficult time explaining the gulf between animal and human communicative abilities in the present. Social theories of language evolution emphasize the role of language in building and maintaining relationships, but they do not explain why such a complex system as language is necessary for achieving this goal.

Review Questions

1. Describe the evolutionary history of humans. What is our relationship with chimpanzees? What is our relationship with Neanderthals?

2. Explain Chomsky's hopeful monster hypothesis. What is the evidence for and against it?

3. Explain the continuity debate. What is the evidence for and against the continuity and discontinuity hypotheses?

4. Explain how research on the KE family led to the discovery of the FOXP2 gene. Why is it not likely to be a "language gene" after all?

5. What is a pidgin, and under what circumstances does one develop? What is a creole, and under what circumstances does one develop? What is Bickerton's concept of protolanguage, and how does it relate to pidgins?

6. Describe each of the three social theories of language evolution presented in this section: (1) the mother tongue hypothesis; (2) the singing Neanderthal hypothesis; and (3) the social grooming hypothesis.

Thought Questions

1. A friend of yours asks: "If humans evolved from monkeys, why haven't chimpanzees evolved into humans?" How do you respond?

2. In the previous section, we considered Hockett's view that duality of patterning is the key distinguishing characteristic of human language. In this section, we considered Chomsky's view that centrality of syntax is the key feature. Consider carefully what these two concepts mean. Are they fundamentally different? Are they the same thing?

3. Chomsky argues that the essential thought process necessary for human language is an understanding of recursion. But since it is characteristic of

human thought, not language per se, we should see recursion occurring elsewhere in human behavior. Can you think of some examples?

4. As you go through this course, try to become more aware of your language use. In particular, pay attention to when you are using language to communicate information and when you are using it to communicate feelings.

Google It! Pidgins

There is plenty of information (as well as misinformation) about human origins on the web. If you are interested in learning more about **human origins**, google it! Also, if you're mathematically inclined, you can google **recursion**. You'll find it has all sorts of uses in computer science, and it crops up repeatedly in nature. You can also google **pidgin** to see some specific examples. See if you can understand them. (But be careful, some so-called pidgins, such as Hawaiian Pidgin and Tok Pisin, are actually creoles. Still, can you make any sense out of them?)

SECTION 1.4: LIVING FOSSILS

- Pidgins are simplified languages, but they are very useful for communication when no common language is available. They also suggest that an intermediate step between animal communication systems and full-fledged human languages is evolutionarily viable; the one-generation transition from pidgin to creole lends some support to discontinuity theories.

- All pidgins have certain characteristics in common: (1) they have simple phonology, (2) they generally lack morphology, (3) they have limited vocabularies, (4) they have little or no syntax, and (5) they are effortful to produce and comprehend.

- Early attempts to teach speech to primates failed because they lack the vocal tract structures required to produce the full range of speech sounds.

- Later attempts to teach signed or visual-symbol language to primates have shown that they can acquire a small vocabulary and can actively produce two- and three-word utterances, but the complexities of full language seem beyond their grasp.

- Language development suggests a trajectory for language evolution; the shift from short utterances to full sentences shows that the change is continuous, consistent with continuity theories, but rapid, consistent with discontinuity theories.

- Brain damage can lead to a loss of language abilities; these patients often are only capable of pidgin-like utterances that are short, ungrammatical, and effortful to produce.

Continuity theories of language evolution are consistent with Darwin's (1859) theory of natural selection, which has been very successful in explaining the origin of species. An important line of evidence for evolutionary biologists is the fossil record, which has preserved the forms of plants and animals that went extinct long ago. On the other hand, the debate about language evolution based on fossil evidence from early humans, such as *Homo erectus* and the Neanderthals, has generated more heat than light. Some researchers maintain the fossil record suggests that spoken language was not anatomically possible before modern humans (Holden, 1999; Lieberman, Crelin, & Klatt, 1972; Lieberman & McCarthy, 2007). However, other researchers do find evidence in the fossil record for language ability in pre-modern humans (Boë et al., 2004; Hayden, 2012; Krause et al.,2007; Wolpoff et al., 2004). Little of the fossil record was known at the time Darwin developed his theory of natural selection. Instead, he looked for clues about evolutionary history in existing forms. In this section, we will consider some of the "living fossils" that provide a glimpse into how language could have evolved.

Half an Eye

Those who oppose evolution on religious grounds often challenge the theory with the question: "What good is half an eye?" Darwin himself recognized this as a potential problem for his theory, which maintains that every feature of a species evolved slowly across many generations and that, in every step in the process, these halfway features were beneficial to those who bore them. The half-an-eye question is interesting not in its logic but rather in that fact that it has been smugly repeated so many times in spite of the unassailable evidence that the eye did in fact evolve from a patch of light-sensitive skin—and not just once but dozens of times (Lamb, Collin, & Pugh, 2007).

At bottom, the half-an-eye question is not really about the evolution of visual systems; instead, it's a question about the status of humans in comparison with all the other animals that occupy this planet. We want to believe we are special, different. We use the words "human" and "animal" as if they referred to two separate categories. Yet at a biological level there is nothing to distinguish us from other animals. We share at least 98% of our genes with our cousins, the chimpanzees, and we're not much farther genetically from gorillas and orangutans either (Bradley, 2008).

Scientists who understand this still use the human/animal distinction. But when they say human, they mean an animal of the genus *Homo*, and when they say animal they mean any animal outside the genus *Homo*. This usage is less precise though more elegant than the politically correct but linguistically clunky "human animal" and "nonhuman animal." In this book, we'll go with elegance over precision, but now you know what I mean by "human" and "animal."

Still, all of us have lurking inside us the implicit bias that we humans are qualitatively different from (and hence superior to) all other animals. It's this implicit bias that's at the heart of the continuity debate, which centers on the question of whether human language could have evolved through a series of gradual steps, or whether there's something unique about human language that could have only occurred through a sudden and considerable reorganization of the human brain.

In part, this debate also hinges on how you define language. If you think of language as a communication system for transmitting thoughts from one person to another, you will be pushed toward the discontinuity side of the debate. This is because any meaningful definition of "thought" would have to include some concept of recursion or combinatory power. On the other hand, if you think of language as a communication system for building and maintaining social relationships, then it will seem obvious how human language could have evolved gradually out of animal communication. Viewing language as an all-or-nothing phenomenon, the discontinuity theorist asks, "What good is half a language?" But the continuity theorist merely retorts, "Far better than no language at all." As any traveler to a foreign country knows, even a few words of the local language, combined with a friendly expression and the appropriate gestures, can get you pretty far.

If implicit human arrogance drives the discontinuity theories of language evolution, a different implicit bias haunts the continuity side of the debate, and that is **anthropomorphism**. In other words, we have *the tendency to assign human-like qualities to animals, natural phenomena, and even abstract concepts*. Anyone who has ever spent some time with nonhuman primates knows it's hard not to think, "They're so much like us!" But we need to ask ourselves to what extent they really are just like us and to what extent we're merely projecting our own thoughts and intentions on them, just as we beg our car to start on a cold winter's morning, as if it had a will of its own.

In weighing the evidence on both sides of the debate, we need to steer between arrogance and anthropomorphism, to weigh the facts with all the objectivity we can muster. Regardless of which side of the debate we favor, there is one fact that is inescapable—in the natural realm, continuity rules, and hopeful monsters are rare (Theißen, 2006).

Me Tarzan, You Jane

Whenever people who don't share a common language meet, they'll find a way to communicate. We've already seen this when British traders landed in China in the eighteenth century, and it's a process that has repeated itself countless times throughout history. Hawaiian pidgin is one such example. In the nineteenth century, English-speaking plantation owners imported workers from Japan, Korea, the Philippines, and other countries. With no common language among all these different groups, a pidgin emerged based on the dominant language of the plantation owners. Thus, Hawaiian pidgin consisted mainly of English words with a smattering of items from other languages (McWhorter, 1999). Likewise, a number of pidgins arose in the eighteenth century in the West Indies and southern United States due to the slave trade.

Regardless of where they have arisen, all pidgins bear certain characteristics in common (Holm, 2000). First, pidgins have simple phonology. Consonant clusters are reduced or broken apart, only common vowel sounds are used, and tones are avoided altogether.

Difficult sounds, such as the *th* sound in *them* and *there*, are replaced with sounds that are easier to produce, such as *dem* and *dere*. Oftentimes words are reduced from their original form, as in the case of the word *pidgin*, a reduced form of the word *business*. This simplification of phonology makes the words easy to pronounce and to distinguish from one another.

Second, pidgins generally lack morphology. In English we distinguish singular from plural nouns (*hand* and *hands*, *foot* and *feet*) and present from past verbs (*chase* and *chased*, *run* and *ran*). We also distinguish subject from object pronouns (*I* and *me*, *they* and *them*). But pidgins do not generally make such distinctions, using the same word form in all cases, such as *one man, two man* or *go today, go yesterday*).

Third, pidgins have quite limited vocabularies, usually just a few hundred words. Mostly, these are **content words**, such as concrete nouns, action verbs, and common adjectives, which are *words that carry the bulk of meaning in language*. There are few, if any, **function words**, such as *the* and *a*, *is* and *of*, which are *words that express grammatical relationships but carry little meaning*.

Fourth, pidgins have little or no syntax. Words can be combined to form simple sequences, but word order is generally free and probably based, at least in part, on the syntax of the speaker's native language. Pidgin speakers rely heavily on context to convey grammatical functions, and this context is generally sufficient as long as the sentences are short and the conversation is about everyday events. But the lack of word-order rules as well as function words precludes complex sentences.

Fifth, pidgins require effort to produce and to comprehend. It's important to keep in mind that nobody speaks a pidgin as a native language. If you've ever studied a foreign language, you know how challenging it is to come up with both the right vocabulary and the right grammar when speaking. The simplified structure of pidgins reduces the cognitive load on both the speaker and the listener, who can each focus on meaning without having to attend to proper form. It also makes pidgins much easier to learn than full-fledged languages.

The existence of pidgins demonstrates that humans can make use of communication systems that are more complex than animal calls or gestures but still much less complex than full human languages. In other words, pidgins provide an answer to the half-a-language question. In Section 1.3 we saw how linguist Derek Bickerton (1990, 2009) proposed that the full language capacity of modern humans evolved not out of the primate vocalizations but rather out of something that he called protolanguage, the pidgin-like communication system supposedly used by early humans.

Psychologists Steven Pinker and Paul Bloom also see pidgins as support for the continuity hypothesis. They point out that pidgin-like structures occur not only in the realm of intercultural communication but also in more mundane contexts such as the speech of toddlers and of people suffering from **aphasia**, which is *a language deficit due to brain damage* (Pinker & Bloom, 1990). Furthermore, attempts to teach some form of human language to non-human animals has shown that several species can learn simple pidgins, even though full language seems beyond their grasp (Bickerton, 2009). Thus, we can view pidgins as a sort of living fossil that can provide insight into what intermediate forms of language in early humans might have looked like.

Planet of the Apes

The great apes—chimpanzees, bonobos, gorillas, and orangutans—are our closest relatives, sharing up to 98% of their DNA with humans (Bradley, 2008). Thus, it's only logical to look first among these primate species for signs of latent linguistic ability.

The first known attempt to teach language to a nonhuman primate occurred in the 1930s (Kellogg & Kellogg, 1933). Psychologists Winthrop and Luella Kellogg brought the infant chimpanzee Gua into their home, raising her along with their own infant Donald as if they were brother and sister. At that time, the social sciences were dominated by **behaviorism**, *a school of psychology that emphasized the role of learning in shaping behavior.* So the Kelloggs' research question was whether a chimpanzee raised as a human would learn to behave like a human. The Kelloggs tested Gua and Donald

---

Figure 1.9 Photo of a Bonobo

The bonobo is one of the most closely related species to humans, along with the chimpanzee and the gorilla. We share about 98% of our genes with these species. Members of these species have been able to learn simple sign languages to communicate with their human caregivers.

Source: © iStockphoto.com / seeingimages.

each month on a number of cognitive tasks. The boy generally outperformed the chimp, even though Gua did learn a number of typically human behaviors. But the key difference was in language. By eighteen months, Donald was already producing words, but Gua, at a similar age, was not. The Kelloggs decided to end the experiment after nine months because Donald was imitating Gua's vocalizations.

Two decades later, another husband and wife team tried to teach language to a chimpanzee (Hayes, 1951; Hayes & Hayes, 1952, 1953; Hayes & Nissen, 1971). Keith and Cathy Hayes raised the infant chimpanzee Viki as if she were a human baby. The Hayes's even gave Viki speech therapy, but at the end of three years, she could only produce four words, "mama," "papa," "cup," and "up." Considering that the average human three-year-old has a vocabulary numbering in the thousands of words, Viki's meager performance seemed to indicate that chimpanzees were incapable of learning language. However, it is now known that Viki's limitations were at least as much physical as they were cognitive. The **vocal tract** is *the system of air passages, including the throat, mouth and nose, where speech is produced*. But the shape of the vocal tract in other primates is somewhat different from that in humans, and this difference prevents them from producing the full range of human speech sounds (Lieberman, 2012). Nonhuman primates also appear to have less fine motor control over the tongue, jaw, and lips, which is also essential for producing speech.

Primates do, however, have a degree of manual dexterity similar to humans, and so the next attempt to teach language to a chimpanzee made use of signed instead of spoken language. In 1967, Allen and Beatrix Gardner adopted the infant chimpanzee Washoe and raised her as a human infant, the only difference being that they used American Sign Language (ASL) instead of spoken English (Gardner & Gardner, 1969, 1975, 1984, 1998; Gardner, Gardner, & Van Cantfort, 1989). Scientists are creatures of habit, just like the rest of us, and at first the Gardners tried teaching Washoe by means of **operant conditioning**, which is *a method for reinforcing desired behavior through the use of systematic rewards and punishments*. However, they soon discovered that Washoe was able to pick up new signs by observing others use them, just as human children do, and the Gardners switched to natural conversation and interaction with Washoe instead. Washoe acquired a vocabulary of several hundred words, and she was able to combine signs to express novel concepts. For example, on seeing a swan, Washoe made the signs for "water" and "bird."

Shortly thereafter, Penny Patterson reported similar results with the female lowland gorilla Koko (Bonvillian & Patterson, 1993; Patterson, 1978). After thirty months of training, Koko had an active vocabulary of around a hundred words. According to Patterson, Koko not only used these words spontaneously, she also could combine signs to express novel meanings. For example, she is reported to have made the signs for "finger" and "bracelet" to refer to a ring.

Another workaround to the lack of vocal control in apes has been the use of **lexigrams**, which are *visual symbols that stand for words*. These lexigrams can be made out of plastic tokens, printed on a laminated sheet, or even placed on a keyboard and displayed on a computer monitor. A number of ape-language projects have used this approach. Early projects using lexigrams investigated the question of whether primates could learn elements of syntax. To this end, a simple grammar for ordering lexigrams was designed. The first success with this approach involved a chimpanzee named Sarah, who was able to respond appropriately to "if-then" and "more-less" statements (Premack & Premack, 1984). Another team of researchers also reported success with a chimpanzee named Lana, who, they claimed, could also construct novel, grammatically correct utterances with the lexigrams (Rumbaugh, 1977).

To date, the most successful attempt to teach language to an ape has involved the bonobo Kanzi (Gillespie-Lynch et al., 2011; Lyn et al., 2011; Savage-Rumbaugh, Shanker & Taylor, 1998). Bonobos are a separate species from common chimpanzees. They're also less aggressive and therefore easier to train. Originally, Savage-Rumbaugh and her colleagues were attempting to teach Kanzi's mother to communicate with lexigrams arranged on a laminated sheet, but she was often distracted by baby Kanzi and was disengaged by the monotonous operant-conditioning approach the researchers were using. When Kanzi spontaneously began using the lexigrams to communicate with the researchers, they turned their efforts to him instead. According to Savage-Rumbaugh and her colleagues, Kanzi also picked up some sign language by watching tapes of Koko the signing gorilla. More important, they also claim that Kanzi can understand spoken English, even though he can't speak. In a controlled listening comprehension task, nine-year-old Kanzi performed at 72% correct compared with the 66% performance of a two-and-a-half-year-old human child.

In short, these studies show that, under the right conditions, primates can acquire small vocabularies, and they can combine the words they know to form short, novel utterances. However, this is no easy feat for these primates to accomplish, and they take many years of training and interaction with humans to achieve a similar level of communication to that of a human toddler. In other words, they learn pidgin but not full-fledged human language.

The ape-language research program has ignited a heated debate in the literature, reminding us that scientists are primates too. On the one hand, researchers who view syntax as the key defining feature of language argue that so-called language-trained primates are not really using language. For example, Terrace and his colleagues carefully examined thousands of two- and three-sign utterances made by the language-trained chimpanzee Nim Chimsky and found little evidence of grammatical structure in novel utterances (Terrace et al., 1979). Rather, most of Nim's utterances either were repetitions of what his teacher had just signed or were memorized sequences, and they found little evidence of syntactic structure in novel utterances.

On the other hand, researchers such as Savage-Rumbaugh push the social interaction aspect of language (Givón & Rumbaugh, 2009). Furthermore, they emphasize the fact that human language development moves from nongrammatical pidgin-like utterances to grammatical sentences. As Trachsel (2010) points out, this is also the likely evolutionary trajectory of human language, as it's consistent with Darwinian evolution. Savage-Rumbaugh and her colleagues concede that language-trained apes don't exhibit complex syntax in their utterances, but they also insist that their utterances are nonetheless communicative, a point Terrace and colleagues also concede.

Baby Talk

Babies aren't born talking. Rather, they go through a very predictable sequence of language development. They spend most of their first year vocalizing, at first in ways that don't sound very language-like, but gradually their vocalizations take on aspects of the language spoken around them. As infants babble, they practice making the speech sounds they'll use later when they speak.

Around one year of age, they utter their first words, and for the next half year or so, their vocabulary is limited to a few dozen words (Ganger & Brent, 2004). During this time period, the child produces holophrases (Braine, 1974; Dore, 1975). Thus, "Kitty!" means something like, "Look, there's a kitty!" Likewise, "Milk!" means something like, "Give me the cup of milk." And "Ball!" means something like "Here's the ball!" These holophrases are much like the animal calls we learned about in Section 1.1, in that they refer to an event taking place at the current place and time, and they cannot be used to speak about events at other times or places.

At first, word learning appears slow and effortful, but halfway through the second year, there is a shift in the way the child approaches new words. This period is known as the **vocabulary spurt**, and it is *a time in which the child begins learning new words at a rapid pace, usually starting around eighteen months of age* (Goldfield & Reznick, 1990; Nazzi & Bertoncini, 2003). Around the same time, children begin making two-word combinations (McEachern & Haynes, 2004; Starr, 1975). These two-word utterances have all the hallmarks of pidgin sentences, in that they are strung together based on semantic relationships rather than syntactic structure. Over the next few years, vocabulary and syntax develop hand in hand, so that by age five or so the child has become a competent speaker of the language.

To the extent that the development of the individual mimics the evolution of the species, a child's first language acquisition may shed light on the stages of language evolution from pre-humans to the present day. Infants emit cries that elicit nurturing behavior in their mothers; rat pups behave similarly, producing ultrasonic vocalizations when they need their mother's attention (Stern, 1997). Around their first birthday, children begin producing one-word holophrases, similar to those of animal communication systems we've already looked at. By their second birthday, toddlers are producing pidgin-like utterances of two or three words. They also go through a vocabulary and syntax spurt as they transition to full language. Although this transition is continuous, it's also rapid, and so it's consistent with either continuity or discontinuity theories. In short, language development in individual humans suggests a plausible trajectory for language evolution in the human species.

At a Loss for Words

If you put your finger just in front of, and a little above, your left ear, you'll be pointing at a part of your brain known as Broca's area. In 1861, French surgeon Paul Broca reported the case of a patient with damage to this area (Lorch, 2011). Although the patient appeared to still be able to understand spoken language, he'd lost the ability to speak (except for the nonsense syllable *tan* and a few choice obscenities). **Broca's aphasia**, then, is *a type of aphasia characterized by disjointed or ungrammatical speech* (Sahraoui & Nespoulous, 2012). Patients with Broca's aphasia appear to be exerting great effort just to find words in memory and produce them, and their speech largely consists of content words with few function words and little regard for syntax (Rochon et al., 2000). In other words, the speech of Broca's aphasics has many of the properties of a pidgin.

Broca's area is right next to the motor cortex area of the brain that controls the movement of the speech articulators, such as the jaw, lips, and tongue. This arrangement seems reasonable, given that it's *an area of the brain that plays a role in speech production*. It's possible that Broca's area evolved from brain areas that were responsible for producing vocalizations in our pre-human ancestors; in fact, a similar area in primate brains is activated when calls are produced (Gil-da-Costa et al., 2006).

However, Broca's aphasia doesn't just disrupt spoken language; it similarly affects those who use signed language (Horwitz et al., 2003). This suggests that Broca's area isn't responsible specifically for speech production but rather more generally for language production, whether spoken or signed. On the one hand, this is an unexpected finding because native signers generally don't move their speech articulators when they sign (though many people learning ASL do vocalize the English equivalent while signing).

Figure 1.10 Broca's Area

Damage to Broca's area leads to difficulty in producing speech, although the patient can still understand speech.

Broca's area

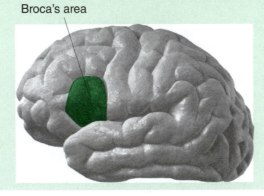

On the other hand, signed languages display the same hierarchical structure and complexity of syntax as spoken languages, so maybe there's more to Broca's area than just producing speech.

Furthermore, Broca's area isn't only involved in language production. Rather, activation in this area also underlies tool use, both in humans and in primates (Hopkins, 2010). Although the connection between language and tool use isn't immediately obvious, there's a relationship at a more abstract level. Both involve the precise sequences of fine motor movements. Specifically, we're referring to the jaw, tongue, and lips in the case of speech and the arms, hands, and fingers in the case of tool use. Language and tool use are also both activities that are organized in hierarchical structures (Greenfield, 1991). This suggests a connection between developing tool use in the primate line and the use of meaningful vocalizations that later developed into language (Higuchi et al., 2009).

Whatever the original purpose of Broca's area was, it's clear that we humans depend on it for fluently sequencing words into sentences. When this area is damaged, we can no longer arrange words according to the rules of grammar. That is to say, we can no longer build hierarchical structures for organizing our words, but instead we produce words like beads on a string, roughly related in meaning but not held in place by an overarching sentence structure. It's also commonly observed that Broca's aphasics will augment their communicative attempts with pointing and gestures and even drawing pictures (Cicone, 1979). People communicating by pidgin often resort to gestures and pictures as well to get their point across (Wilkinson, Beeke, & Maxim, 2010).

In Sum

The "living fossils" of language suggest a continuous evolution from holophrases to pidgins to full language. However, the single-generation transition from pidgin to creole and the rapid development of vocabulary and syntax in children can be interpreted as evidence for discontinuity theories. Primate language research also shows that chimpanzees and gorillas have some of the cognitive abilities necessary for language, but they require extensive human interaction to develop.

Review Questions

1. Describe the five common characteristics of pidgins. How do these features make pidgins simplified compared with full languages?

2. What methods have been used to teach language to primates? What are the results of primate language research?

3. Briefly describe the progression of language acquisition in children. What does this process suggest about the evolution of language?

4. What are the symptoms of Broca's aphasia? What does this suggest about the function of Broca's area? What is the role of Broca's area in primates?

Thought Questions

1. How is the half-an-eye question relevant to the debate on the evolution of language?

2. There are two major approaches to teaching language to primates. One involves creating a natural environment similar to that in which human children learn language, and the other involves rigorous behavioral methods such as operant conditioning. What are the advantages and disadvantages of each approach?

3. What evidence suggests that Broca's area may be involved in more than just speech production?

4. Greenfield (1991) proposes that language and tool use are related because both are organized in hierarchical structures. This suggests that there is also a duality of patterning in tool use, namely a set of meaningless actions that can be combined according to rules into meaningful sequences. Try coming up with a grammar for a simple tool use such as brushing your teeth; be very specific about all the component actions and the restrictions on how these can be sequenced. If you find this easy, try developing a grammar for driving a car.

Google It! Washoe, Koko, and Kanzi

You can find more information, including pictures and videos, about some of the language-trained primates you read about in this section, including **Washoe**, **Koko**, and **Kanzi**. Also, Pepperberg (2002) has reported on a language-trained African grey parrot named **Alex.** You can watch videos **of Alex the parrot** interacting with Pepperberg on YouTube. Are you convinced Alex understands what he's saying? You can also find videos on YouTube of patients who've suffered from **Broca's aphasia.** Imagine what it must be like to be one of these patients. How do they try to compensate for their language loss?

CONCLUSION

Many animal species use communication systems to attract mates, warn others about threats, and maintain group cohesion. Humans communicate for these reasons as well, but human languages are structurally far more complex, allowing humans a much wider range of expression. It's unclear how human language evolved, but a number of theories touch on some aspects of this process. Some insights into the origin of human language can be gleaned from "living fossils": pidgins and creoles, attempts to teach human language to chimps, human infant language development, and language loss due to brain damage.

Humans express emotions in ways similar to animal communication systems, using vocalizations, gestures, posture, and facial expressions. However, human language has a much wider range of expression by combining elements to create novel utterances. Language also lets us to escape the here and now to discuss events that took place at other times and places. These unique features are due to the hierarchical structure of language. Speech sounds combine to form words, words combine to form sentences, and sentences combine to form larger units such as conversation.

The question of whether human language evolved gradually or rapidly is known as the continuity debate. Discontinuity theories propose that human language arose rapidly, perhaps as the result of a single genetic mutation, and they emphasize the disparity between present-day animal communication and human language. Continuity theories assume a more gradual evolution of human language from animal communication, and they're more in line with standard evolutionary theory. However, they have difficulty explaining the lack of intermediate stages between animal communication and human language. Although language is the unique feature of humans that makes us different from all other animal species, we still need to keep in mind our humble origins and the fact that we left the wild not that long ago.

CROSS-CULTURAL PERSPECTIVE:
Hawaiian Pidgin

Whenever groups of people who don't speak the same language find themselves living and working together, they develop a pidgin to communicate with each other. A pidgin is a simple language with a small vocabulary and a simple grammar, but it's good enough for basic interactions. As global trade developed in the eighteenth and nineteenth centuries, pidgins cropped up in many locales around the world.

One place where a pidgin emerged was Hawaii. In the nineteenth century, English-speaking plantation owners brought in workers from East and Southeast Asia. Words were borrowed from English, Hawaiian, Japanese, and other languages (Sakoda & Siegel, 2003). The children of these workers then developed their parents' speech into a language they called "Pidgin." Despite its name, Hawaiian Pidgin is in fact a creole, and it's still widely spoken across the Hawaiian islands today.

Many Hawaiians grow up speaking Pidgin, which they see as an important part of their ethnic identity. Billboards and TV advertisements in Hawaii often incorporate Pidgin expressions to appeal to the local population. Hawaiian Pidgin even has a written form based loosely on English spelling conventions. See if you can recognize the following well-known psalm verses, as presented in the Hawaiian Pidgin Bible (*Da Hawai'i Pidgin Bible*, 2000).

> Da Boss Above, he take care me, jalike da sheep farma take care his sheeps.
> He goin give me everyting I need. He let me lie down wea da sweet an soft

grass stay. He lead me by da water wea I can rest. He give me new kine life. He lead me in da road dat stay right, cuz I his guy. (Psalm 23: 1–3)

It might make more sense to you if you read it out loud. (The only tricky word here is *wea*, which is pronounced *way-uh* and means "where.")

If you'd like to hear what Pidgin sounds like, you can listen to Kathy Collins's (2009) open letter congratulating Barack Obama as the first president from Hawaii. Google

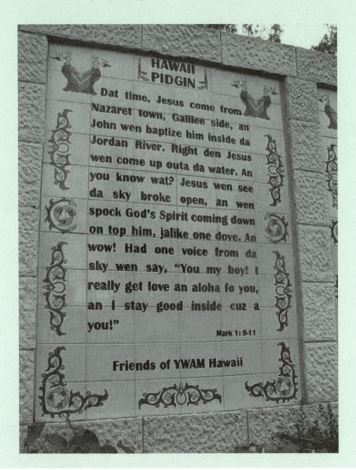

Maui Magazine and then search for "Dear Prezadent Obama." Both the text and the audio are available, so you can read along as you listen.

Because English provides most of its vocabulary, many people criticize Pidgin as nothing more than broken English. While Pidgin doesn't follow the forms of Standard American English, it nevertheless has a structure of its own. It's important to keep in mind that there's no such thing as a "pure" form of a language. Instead, languages are constantly changing to fit the needs of the speech communities that use them. Pidgin is a living language and an important component of the Hawaiian identity for many thousands of people.

KEY TERMS

Alarm call

Anthropomorphism

Aphasia

Arbitrary symbol

Behaviorism

Broca's aphasia

Broca's area

Centrality of syntax

Chunking

Communication

Conspecific

Content words

Continuity debate

Continuity theories

Creole

Discontinuity theories

Discourse

Displacement

Dominance hierarchy

Duality of patterning

Ethologist

FOXP2

Function words

Holophrase

Hopeful monster hypothesis

Iconic symbol

KE family

Lexigrams

Morphemes

Morphology

Mother tongue hypothesis

Motherese

Operant conditioning

Phonemes

Phonology

Pidgin

Primacy of speech

Protolanguage

Recursion

Singing Neanderthal hypothesis

Social grooming

Social grooming hypothesis

Speciation

Specific language impairment

Syntax

Vocabulary spurt

Vocal tract

Working memory

CHAPTER

2

The Science of Language

Something had gone terribly wrong. They'd been running experiments like these for months now, always with the same result. When they'd started this experiment—really no more than a simple tweak on the basic design—they were quite confident they knew what the data would look like.

They were using a new technique to monitor brain activity, and the equipment was state of the art. But the experiments were also tricky to perform. First you had to carefully glue dozens of electrodes in just the right locations on the scalp of a willing and patient research participant. Then you presented the stimuli—usually a series of words or pictures—to the participant while an electroencephalograph recorded his or her brain activity. After that, the data were fed into a powerful computer, which extracted isolated waveforms known as event-related potentials, or ERPs. There was plenty that could go wrong with an ERP experiment, but that would just lead to garbage output, not the clean data they were looking at.

The researchers had been studying an ERP component known as the P300. The brain produces a P300 every time it encounters an unexpected stimulus, such as an item that's out of order in a series. They'd found that they could also get a P300 to linguistic stimuli, such as when the last word of a sentence is presented in larger font, as in:

SHE PUT ON HER HIGH HEELED SHOES.

This time, they'd changed the meaning instead of the size of the final word, as in:

HE SPREAD THE WARM BREAD WITH SOCKS.

They were expecting a P300 this time as well, but that's not what they got. Instead, the waveform went in the opposite direction. It was totally unexpected.

This is the story of how young Marta Kutas, working as a postdoctoral student in the lab of noted neuroscientist Steven Hillyard, discovered the N400, one of the most important and influential findings in the history of psycholinguistics (van

Petten, Federmeier, & Holcomb, 2010). Their paper reporting on the N400 in the prestigious journal *Science* (Kutas & Hillyard, 1980) has been cited more than a thousand times, and the N400 is now a standard tool for studying how the brain processes language.

In this chapter, you'll learn about how psychologists use the scientific method to study the mental processes involved in language perception and production. You'll read about ERP research, the P300, and the N400 as well as many other many other tricks of the psycholinguistics trade. Also you'll see that sometimes the greatest discoveries are made when things go terribly wrong—and that's the true wonder of science!

SECTION 2.1: SCIENTIFIC METHOD

- A theory provides a conceptual framework for explaining a set of observations; it should make predictions about future observations that can be tested in experiments.

- A prediction that is derived from a theory is known as a hypothesis; the researcher then collects data to test the hypothesis.

- Hypotheses derived from a theory must have the possibility of being disconfirmed by data; this is known as the falsifiability criterion.

- Science has three successive goals: (1) naturalistic observations are used to describe phenomena, (2) correlational methods find patterns in the data that can be used to make predictions, and (3) experimental methods seek to explain phenomena by testing hypotheses derived from theories.

- Theories are often expressed as models, which attempt to explain underlying mechanisms, typically in the form of a graph, a set of mathematical equations, or a computer simulation.

- Constructs provide scientists with useful ways of thinking about the world, and operational definitions then define those constructs in terms of how they are to be measured; operational definitions must be both valid and reliable.

Two of the most important concepts in science are theory and hypothesis. But the way these terms are used in the common language is quite a bit different from the way scientists use them, which often leads to misunderstandings about the enterprise of science. In everyday language, the words *theory* and *hypothesis* are used more or less interchangeably to refer to a hunch or conjecture. A detective will gather clues and formulate a hypothesis about the identity of the murderer, and your highly opinionated uncle may have a theory about the global recession that involves a conspiracy between the Freemasons and the Michigan Militia. "Well, it's just a theory," he rebuts when you point out the inconsistencies in his argument.

Just a Theory

The "just a theory" comment aptly sums up the common view of what a theory is. This public misconception about what scientists mean by theory provides ammunition for those who wish to attack science on religious grounds, as for example when the Cobb County (Georgia) school district placed stickers on biology textbooks warning students that evolution is a theory, not a fact (Holden, 2006). Evolution is a theory, but not in the Cobb County sense.

Scientists use the term **theory** to refer to *a conceptual framework that explains a set of observations in such a way that it also makes predictions about future observations.* For example, in the 1950s noted psychologist George Miller thought he had detected a pattern in the data from a number of experiments testing people's ability to discriminate sensory inputs, attend to objects, and recall information. In his famous "Magic Number Seven" paper, Miller (1956) proposed that short-term memory capacity is limited to about seven meaningful chunks of information. This theory explains results from the **digit span task**, which is *a procedure that assesses short-term memory capacity by having research participants repeat lists of digits.* But the theory also predicts you'll get similar results if you use lists of words instead of lists of digits because words, like digits, are meaningful units, or chunks.

Theories can only be tested if they make predictions. *A prediction about future observations that is derived from a theory* is called a **hypothesis**. It's the hypotheses we formulate that allow us to test the theory. In other words, a hypothesis states what we expect to observe in a particular situation if the theory is correct. We then make that observation, and if the observation matches our expectation, we say that we have found support for the theory. In fact, further observations do support Miller's theory of short-term memory capacity, since you get similar results to the digit span task if you use lists of common words instead (Baddeley, Thomson, & Buchanan, 1975).

You Can't Prove It

You can never prove a theory true, but you can prove it false. When our observations of the real world don't match the hypotheses we derive from a theory, intellectual honesty dictates we must conclude that the theory is wrong. Thus, the true test of a theory isn't whether it leads to hypotheses that can be confirmed by observation. Rather, we follow *the principle that a theory must make predictions that have the potential to be disconfirmed by data.* This principle is known as the **falsifiability criterion**, and its importance in the scientific enterprise was first emphasized by philosopher Karl Popper (1959). Thus, a good theory will be very specific about expected outcomes (Stanovich, 2007), and the scientist proposing it must be willing to take the risk of being wrong (Ben-Ari, 2005).

Miller's (1956) theory of short-term memory capacity meets the falsifiability criterion. The theory predicts that people can recall about seven chunks of information—whether words or digits—immediately after hearing them. Immediate recall tasks of digits or common words lend support to this theory. In a strong version of this theory, you should be able to hold onto about seven chunks of information, regardless of their size. However, Alan Baddeley suspected that size did matter, conceptualizing short-term memory instead as a buffer limited by length of time. In a classic set of experiments, Baddeley et al. (1975) had research participants repeat lists of short words and lists of long words. On the short word task, participants were able to repeat about seven items on average. But on the long word task, their performance was much worse. Thus, the data support Baddeley's model and disconfirm Miller's.

Baddeley's model is also superior because it accounts for the data that originally supported Miller's model. Baddeley proposed a mechanism called the **phonological loop**, which is *a short-term memory buffer that can hold about two seconds of spoken language*. The average speaking rate is about three or four syllables per second, and most of the digit names consist of a single syllable (zero and seven are the exceptions). Hence, you can say about seven digits in two seconds, and Baddeley proposed that you say them to yourself as you hold them in memory until it's time to repeat them. If there are more than seven or so digits, the list takes longer than two seconds to say, and you overwhelm the phonological loop. Likewise, if most of the words in the list are multisyllabic, you will reach the end of the loop before the end of the list. Baddeley also referred to short-term memory as working memory instead to emphasize its active nature.

From Observation to Explanation

The scientific method is a cyclical process, but it always has its starting point in the real world. Scientists observe the real world, making observations and collecting facts, and then they formulate a theory to account for the data they've collected so far. *The logical process of going from specific examples to general statements* is known as **induction**. But recall that a theory must also make predictions about future observations, and *the logical process of going from general statements to specific examples* is called **deduction**. Scientists then go back to the real world to see if these predictions are accurate. A hypothesis that is confirmed by the data (observations) lends support to a theory, but still the theory needs to be tested multiple times to strengthen our confidence in it, so we do more hypothesis testing. If the hypothesis fails to support the theory, we revise the theory and generate new hypotheses. Either way, the cycle starts again.

It may surprise you to read that scientists go to the "real world" to collect data, since many scientists work in laboratories. To most people, a laboratory is the farthest thing from the real world. But for a scientist, the laboratory *is* the real world, stripped down to the bare bones to rid it of all its "blooming, buzzing confusion" (James, 1890/1981, p. 462). Still, scientists can test the real-world validity of their theory by doing *a study conducted under natural circumstances outside of the laboratory*, and this is called a **field study**. The tests that Zuberbühler et al. (1999) performed on Diana monkey alarm calls that we discussed in Chapter 1 are an excellent example of this.

Until now, we've been talking about the scientific method as if it were a single, unified approach, but in fact science has a number of methods at its disposal, depending on the

Figure 2.1 The Research Cycle

Scientists make observations to detect patterns, from which they propose a theory. They then generate hypotheses, which are predictions about future observations. These new observations, called experiments, test the hypotheses and provide evidence for or against the theory. The process from patterns to theory involves induction, while the process from theory to hypotheses involves deduction.

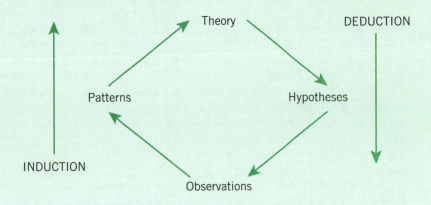

research question being asked and how much we already know about the phenomenon under study. At the beginning of a research program on a new topic, it's generally best just to watch carefully and take detailed notes. *The process of observing and describing a phenomenon* is known as **naturalistic observation**. As an example of naturalistic observation, consider the study of speech errors. Although researchers have speculated for years about why people make slips of the tongue, linguist Victoria Fromkin (1971) decided to approach the phenomenon in a more systematic fashion. She began by simply recording in a notebook examples of speech errors that she heard. Eventually, she amassed a database of several thousand items.

This database, by itself, doesn't tell us much about the nature of speech errors. However, by searching through this database, Fromkin found that speech errors followed predictable patterns. Now we know that even when we make mistakes in speaking we still follow rules! (You'll learn more about these patterns in Chapter 4.) When the data we collect come in the form of numbers, we can use **correlation**, which is *a mathematical technique that searches for relationships among variables in a set of data*. For example, college GPA and ACT scores are correlated, which means that admissions officers can roughly predict how well applicants will do in college based on their ACT scores.

Ultimately, scientists seek to understand the underlying factors that cause the phenomenon they're studying. Fromkin's initial work in collecting speech errors and detecting patterns in their production has led to a fruitful research program involving a number of language scientists. Researchers developed methods for inducing speech errors in the laboratory (Baars, Motley, & MacKay, 1975). This enabled scientists to use the **experimental method**, *a means for systematically testing hypotheses in controlled situations*, to investigate the factors leading to speech errors. For instance, Motley and Baars (1979) found that male college students were more likely to make speech errors of a sexual nature in the presence of a provocatively clad female researcher. Since explanation is the ultimate goal of science, the experimental method is considered the gold standard of science.

While a good theory needs to make specific predictions about future observations, a better theory also proposes an underlying mechanism to account for those observations (Ben-Ari, 2005). When scientists study complex phenomena (such as human psychology), they often build models to help them understand the processes behind the behavior they observe. A **model** is *a simplified version of the phenomenon under investigation, typically in the form of a graph or set of mathematical equations*. Because models are proposed mechanisms for how theories work, the two terms, *model* and *theory*, are often used interchangeably.

Oftentimes, models are implemented as computer programs, and the model is considered good if it mimics the behavior that's being studied. Humans are notoriously flawed at logic, and scientists can easily make unwarranted assumptions when working out models with pen and paper. But computers are, quite literally, logic machines, and so expressing the model in computer code forces the theorist think in a logical, step-by-step fashion. Thus, a good model lends plausibility to a theory, but only data from experiments can support or falsify a theory. We will learn about a number of models in the chapters that follow.

Constructs

Science is a process of systematic observation, and yet many of the topics we study as psychologists are abstract and not directly observable. Concepts such as memory, cognition, emotion—and even language—don't represent real objects in the real world. Rather, each of these is a **construct**, which is a *label given to a set of observations that seem to be related*. For example, there's no way to measure memory, because it's an abstract concept. Instead, we measure outward behaviors, such as digit span and list recall, and make inferences about something we call memory on the basis of those behaviors.

A construct provides scientists with a useful way of thinking about the world, but they don't worry about what the construct actually means. Rather, the construct is given an **operational definition**. That is, scientists make a *definition of a construct in terms of how the construct is measured*. Perhaps the most infamous example of an operational definition in psychology is by Edwin Boring, who defined intelligence as what is measured on an intelligence test (Boring, 1923). Although Boring's definition sounds circular, it's not. Instead of quibbling about the true nature of intelligence, Boring proposes we avoid that question altogether and focus instead on the data, in this case scores on IQ tests. Operational definitions let scientists dodge the philosophical "true nature of" type of questions and focus their energy instead on doing science.

Operational definitions are only as good at the measurements on which they are based. There are two criteria for evaluating an operational definition. The first criterion is **validity**, which refers to *the degree to which the measuring instrument actually measures what it is claimed to measure*. If I stand on my bathroom scale, I'll get a three-digit number, which I take to be my weight. Scales are specifically designed to measure weight, and so I believe my bathroom scale to be valid. My IQ is also a three-digit number, but I don't take the number on my bathroom scale to be a measure of my intelligence, since there's no evidence that weight is related to intelligence. (If it were, I'd be a genius!) The second criterion is **reliability**, which is *the degree to which the instrument gives consistent measurements for the same thing*. My bathroom scale is old, and depending on the temperature and humidity on a given day, my weight (as measured by the scale) can vary by ten pounds. I doubt my body weight really fluctuates by that much, so I consider my bathroom scale to have low reliability.

By testing and refining our theories, we gain a deeper understanding of the world, but the truth—as we understand it—is always tentative, not absolute. Scientists as individuals suffer the same frailties and vanities that all humans possess, yet science as a social enterprise is a self-correcting process. Thus, science is the most powerful tool we have for understanding the world, and ourselves.

In Sum

Science is a set of methods for systematically observing the world. These observations are guided by theories, which are tentative explanations for how things work. Hypotheses are expected observations based on the theory, and we can use them to test the theory by checking whether our hypotheses and observations match. We can never prove a theory correct, because there is always the possibility that new evidence will disconfirm the theory. Scientists use naturalistic observations to describe phenomena and search for patterns, and they use experimental methods to seek explanations for those phenomena. Models are attempts to explain the underlying processes that account for observed patterns. Models are often set up in the form of a computer simulation. Constructs are labels given to sets of observations that seem to be related. Operational definitions are used to define constructs in terms of how they are to be measured.

Review Questions

1. What is a theory? What is a hypothesis? What is a model?

2. Why can't you prove a theory true? How can you prove a theory false?

3. What are constructs? Why do they need to be operationally defined? What are validity and reliability?

Thought Questions

1. If someone tells you that evolution is just a theory and hasn't been proven as a fact, how would you respond?

2. Miller's "Magic Number Seven" is more accurately described as seven-plus or minus-two, in other words, the range between five and nine. Virtually anyone can repeat back a list of four digits or short words, and very few can reliably repeat back a list of ten or more. This limitation of short-term memory impacts the way we format large numbers. Think about the important numbers in your life, such as telephone, Social Security, and credit card numbers. How many digits are they? How would you read these numbers to another person so that he or she could write them down?

Google It! Digit Span

There are a number of **digit span** and **word list recall** demonstrations available online. Some are offered by companies claiming they can help boost your cognitive performance. Try out the demos, but don't give them your credit card number!

SECTION 2.2: EXPERIMENT DESIGN

- Hypotheses are derived from a theory by the logical process of deduction; an experiment is then designed to test the hypothesis.

- Experiments compare the performance of different groups; the experimental group is given a treatment to test the hypothesis, and the control group goes without the treatment in order to provide a baseline for comparison.

- An experiment can be viewed as a stimulus-response test. The independent variable is the type of stimulus, or treatment, each group is given; the dependent variable is a measure of the response each participant makes to the treatment.

- When each participant is assigned to only one condition, we say the experiment has a between-subjects design; when each participant is assigned to multiple conditions, we say the experiment has a within-subjects design.

- We express the hypothesis as a greater-than or less-than relationship between the groups, and if the data go in the predicted direction, we say they support the hypothesis.

- Because there are always alternative explanations for a set of results, no single experiment ever makes or breaks a theory.

Grandma loves to cook, and she's quite adventurous in the kitchen. She likes to "experiment" with recipes, changing ingredients and adding new items, just to see what will happen. The last time she baked her famous oatmeal cookies, she used dried cranberries instead of raisins and tossed in some butterscotch morsels just for the heck of it. "You never know how an experiment will turn out," Grandma says, and that's half the fun. Unlike Grandma, scientists never perform an experiment "just to see what will happen." In fact, they have a very clear expectation of what is going to happen in the experiment, and that expectation is called a hypothesis.

Elements of an Experiment

An **experiment** is *a tightly controlled situation that has been intentionally designed to test a hypothesis*. In its simplest form, an experiment involves a comparison between two groups. The hypothesis makes a prediction about a difference between these two groups in terms of their observable behavior. More complex experiments contain more groups, but still the hypothesis predicts how each group will perform compared with the other groups. We often refer to these groups as conditions because they each experience a different situation or treatment. The **experimental condition** refers to *the group that is given a treatment to test the hypothesis*, and the **control condition** refers to *the group that is treated differently from the experimental group to provide a baseline for comparison*. In the Baddeley et al. (1975) experiment, the presentation of the short-word list constituted the control condition. This is because its purpose was to demonstrate that the experimental technique would yield results similar to Miller's (1956) digit-span task. On the other hand, the presentation of the long-word list made up the experimental condition because it directly tested the hypothesis.

You can think of an experiment in terms of stimulus and response. Each group is given a different stimulus, or treatment, and then the response of each group is measured. *The various types of treatment given to the different groups in an experiment* are known collectively as the **independent variable**. In Baddeley et al.'s (1975) experiment, the independent variable was whether the participants were given a short-word list or a long-word list. *The measurement of the response each participant makes to the treatment in an experiment* is known as the **dependent variable**. The dependent variable that Buchanan and colleagues measured was the number of words recalled in each condition.

If an experiment compares the performance of different groups under different conditions, you would expect each of these groups to be composed of different participants, and this is often the case. *An experiment design that assigns each participant to only one condition* is called a **between-subjects design**. However, it's also possible, in some circumstances, to reuse participants through multiple conditions of the experiment. *An experiment design that assigns each participant to every condition* is said to be a **within-subjects design**.

Practical issues determine whether the experiment design should be between or within subjects. For example, Bransford and Johnson (1972) investigated the effect

Figure 2.2   List Recall of Short Words and Long Words

Lists of short words were recalled better than lists of long words, providing support for the phonological loop hypothesis.

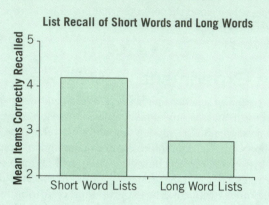

List Recall of Short Words and Long Words

Source: Baddeley, Thomson, and Buchanan (1975).

of context on story comprehension. All participants heard the same ambiguous story, but some saw a disambiguating picture first (the Context condition), while others listened to the story without the picture (the No Context condition). Obviously, once participants had taken part in the Context condition, they could no longer be in the No Context condition, because they were already familiar with the picture. And if they served in the No Context condition before the Context condition, they would already be familiar with the story. So in this case there really was no choice but to use a between-subjects design.

However, research participants are a valuable commodity, and so it makes sense to recycle them whenever possible. That's what Baddeley et al. (1975) did. Since there's no reason to believe that repeating a list of short words will have any effect on your later ability to repeat a list of long words (or vice versa), it made sense to use a within-subjects design. In fact, the participants not only took part in both conditions, they also underwent multiple trials in each condition. A **trial** is *a single application of the treatment in an experiment.* In this case, each participant repeated eight short-word lists and eight long-word lists, for sixteen trials total. In short, running participants in multiple conditions and multiple trials can be a very efficient way to gather data, and psychologists take this approach whenever possible.

The Experimentation Process

The experimentation process is an extension of the inductive-deductive method. First, we deduce a hypothesis from the theory. Second, we design and conduct an experiment to test the hypothesis. Third, we do an analysis of the data. And fourth, we make an interpretation of the results. In our interpretation we must not only consider how the data provide support for the hypothesis, and hence for the theory, we need to also evaluate any shortcomings in the experiment as well as other possible interpretations of the results. This leads to new hypotheses that need to be tested, and the wheel spins another turn.

In the first step, we formulate our hypothesis in terms of an expected difference in the dependent variable between the groups. Bransford and Johnson (1972) expected that people who are given context for an ambiguous story will comprehend that story better than other people who are given no context. When the hypothesis is formulated in such a precise fashion, it not only dictates the basic design of the experiment but also states the expected outcome.

In the second step, we design a procedure that's expected to produce the hypothesized difference between the groups. Bransford and Johnson (1972) developed the following ambiguous story, which they read to the participants in the No Context condition:

> If the balloons popped, the sound wouldn't be able to carry since everything would be too far away from the correct floor. A closed window would also prevent the sound from carrying, since most buildings tend to be well insulated. Since the whole operation depends on a steady flow of electricity, a break in the middle of the wire would also cause problems. Of course, the fellow could shout, but the human voice is not loud enough to carry that far. An additional problem is that a string could break on the instrument. Then there could be no accompaniment to the message. It is clear that the best situation would involve less distance. Then there would be fewer potential problems. With face to face contact, the least number of things could go wrong.

The researchers then asked these participants to rate how difficult the passage was to understand, and they were tested on how many items from the story they could recall. Participants in the Context condition followed the same procedure, but they first got to see a disambiguating picture.

In the third step, we analyze the data to determine whether they provide support for the hypothesis, which is stated in terms of a "greater than" or "less than" relationship between the group means. Bransford and Johnson (1972) predicted that the comprehension rating for the Context group would be greater than the comprehension rating for the No Context. As you can imagine, the participants in the Context condition rated the story easier to comprehend and they recalled more details from the story than did the No Context. In other words, the data support the hypothesis.

Figure 2.3   Disambiguating Picture

Participants in the Context condition viewed this picture first before listening to the ambiguous story.

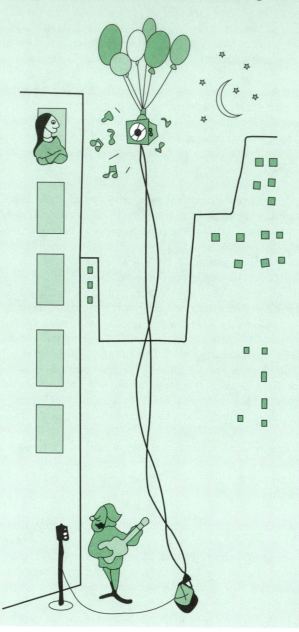

Source: Bransford and Johnson (1972).

Figure 2.4   The Role of Context in Story Comprehension

Participants who first viewed a disambiguating picture (the Context condition) rated an ambiguous story easier to comprehend than did those who listened to the story without viewing the picture (the No Context condition). Those in the Context condition also recalled more details from the story.

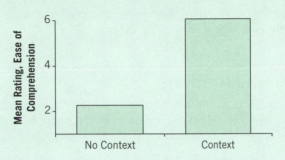

Source: Bransford and Johnson (1972).

In the fourth step, we interpret our results. Obtaining data that support the hypothesis is always cause for celebration, but we should consider any weaknesses in the current experiment that may have biased the results. We also need to consider alternative explanations for the pattern of data we obtained other than the explanation provided by the hypothesis. This kind of careful deliberation generally leads to the generation of new hypotheses that need to be tested, which means more experiments that need to be performed. In the case of Bransford and Johnson (1972), the key experiment was Experiment I, but they also performed three other experiments to test alternative hypotheses, and the results of these experiments provided further support for their initial hypothesis by testing and eliminating alternative explanations.

No single experiment ever makes or breaks a theory. Even when the data support the hypothesis, we need to consider alternative explanations for the results and test these with additional experiments. It's only when we get consistent results under a variety of related conditions that we gain confidence our theory is a reasonable explanation of the phenomenon we are studying. This is why we view the experimental process as a cycle, starting with a hypothesis tested in an experiment, the results of which then suggest new experiments that need to be performed.

In Sum

Scientists use the logical process of deduction to derive a hypothesis from a theory. They then set up an experiment to test the hypothesis. Experiments compare the performance of groups that are treated differently. The experimental group is given the treatment that tests the hypothesis, while the control group receives a different or no treatment to provide a baseline for comparison. The independent variable refers to the type or stimulus or treatment given to each group, and the dependent variable is a measure of how each group responds to the treatment. The hypothesis is expressed as a greater-than or less-than relationship between the groups, and when the data go in the predicted direction, we say they support the hypothesis. Since there are many different ways to explain a given set of data, no single experiment ever makes or breaks a theory.

Review Questions

1. What is the difference between induction and deduction? Why do we say that theories are derived by induction, but hypotheses are derived by deduction?

2. Explain the difference between an experimental group and a control group. Point out the experimental and control groups in Baddeley et al.'s (1975) Experiment I (Figure 2.2) and in Bransford and Johnson (1972)'s Experiment I (Figure 2.4).

3. Explain the difference between an independent variable and a dependent variable within the context of an experiment.

4. What is the difference between a between-subjects design and a within-subjects design?

Thought Questions

1. Can you think of alternative explanations for Bransford and Johnson's (1972) results? What experiments would you want to perform to test these alternative hypotheses?

2. Suppose you read in the news about a "revolutionary new experiment that completely changes the way scientists think about" some subject. Do you think this report is likely to be accurate? Explain why you should be skeptical about such claims.

Google It! Mythbusters

Mythbusters is a popular TV show on the Discovery Channel that uses the scientific method to test claims in the popular media (with a fair number of explosions mixed in for fun). You can find clips from the show online. Watch a few and see if you can tease out the experimental design in each. In particular, see if you can identify the independent and dependent variables and the experimental and control groups. Keep in mind that some *Mythbusters* episodes involve naturalistic observation or proof of concept, so you won't be able to tease out the experimental design in these. Still, observation and demonstration are important tools of the trade in science.

SECTION 2.3: BEHAVIORAL TECHNIQUES

- Two important behavioral measures in psycholinguistics are latency and accuracy. Latency, also known as reaction time, measures how quickly the participant responds; accuracy may be reported either as the percentage of correct or incorrect responses.

- The lexical decision task has participants distinguish between words and nonwords as quickly and as accurately as possible; the latency to words is generally shorter than to nonwords.

- Priming is an implicit memory process in which recall is enhanced due to previous exposure; associated words (such as *doctor* and *nurse*) prime each other; combined with the lexical decision task, priming can be used to test a wide range of hypotheses about language processing.

- Recall tasks can be divided into four types, depending on whether the time between presentation and recall is immediate or delayed and whether the order of recall is serial or free; the tendency for the first and last items in a list to be recalled best is known as primacy and recency effects.

- Implicit learning is a form of learning that takes place outside of conscious awareness; it is typically tested with a forced-choice task in which the participant needs to rely on intuition to select between options.

- Head-mounted eye-tracking devices can be used to record eye movements during reading tasks or for observing how people scan the environment for context cues to aid in discourse comprehension; the general finding is that the eyes do not move in a smooth fashion but rather in a series of saccades and fixations.

Psycholinguistics is *the scientific study of the cognitive processes involved in comprehending and producing language*. However, cognitive processes can't be observed directly. That is to say, they're constructs. Instead, psycholinguists make careful observations of outward behavior in order to make inferences about inward mental processes. Careful observation involves measurement, and two of the most basic measures of behavior are latency and accuracy.

Measured Response

Recall that we can think of a trial in an experiment as a stimulus-response test, and so the behavior we want to measure is the response that the participant makes to the stimulus that the experimenter presents. **Latency** is a measure of *the difference in time between the presentation of a stimulus and the initiation of a response by the participant*. Latency is also referred to as reaction time, and it's measured in milliseconds, abbreviated as ms or msec. (A millisecond is one one-thousandth of a second.)

Sometimes we're less interested in how quickly the participant responds but rather in whether the participant gives the correct response. This measure is known as **accuracy**, and it measures *the percentage of correct responses over a set of trials*. Sometimes accuracy is reported instead as **error rate**, which is *the percentage of incorrect responses over a set of trials*. Accuracy is an important behavioral measure in memory tasks, where we're testing the participant's ability to recall a set of previously learned items.

Accuracy is also frequently used as a secondary measure in addition to latency. There's often a trade-off between speed (latency) and accuracy, and participants are frequently encouraged to work both as quickly and as accurately as possible. Inspecting error rates allows researchers to determine whether a difference in latency between two conditions was a result of a speed-accuracy trade-off instead of being due to the manipulation of the independent variable. For example, if both latency and error rate increase in one condition compared with another, we infer that the stimuli in the first condition were more difficult to process than those in the second condition.

Bread and Butter

One commonly used procedure in the psycholinguistics laboratory is the **lexical decision task**. This is *an experimental procedure in which the participant sees a string of letters and responses as quickly as possible, indicating whether it is a word or not*. Word trials present strings such as TIME or STEM, while nonword trials present strings such as MOBE and SPEM. Notice that a **nonword** is a *pronounceable letter string that just happens to not be a word in English*. Nonwords are also sometimes called nonce words or pseudowords, and they're distinguished from nonsense strings such as ZYGWQ or PTVSS, which are unpronounceable and could not even be possible words in English. Generally speaking, participants respond faster to words (by pressing the "Yes" key) than they do to nonwords (by pressing the "No" key).

The lexical decision task can be used to test for priming effects. **Priming** is *an implicit memory process in which the recall of a particular item is enhanced due to previous exposure of similar items*. For example, reaction time in a lexical decision task for the item NURSE is faster when the preceding word is DOCTOR than when it's TORCH. Because DOCTOR and NURSE are frequently associated words, we find that DOCTOR primes NURSE. The first item in a priming pair is called the prime, and the second item in a priming pair is called the probe or the target.

Meyer and Schvaneveldt (1971) pioneered the use of the lexical decision task as a means of measuring priming effects. They showed participants pairs of words and asked them to indicate by key press whether both were English words. In the Associated condition, the word pairs were highly associated, such as BREAD-BUTTER. In the Unassociated condition, the word pairs were not related to each other, such as CAKE-STEM. In three other conditions, the pair consisted of one or two nonwords (Word-Nonword, Nonword-Word, and Nonword-Nonword).

Associated word pairs exhibited a shorter latency than unassociated word pairs, as predicted by the hypothesis (Meyer & Schvaneveldt, 1971). But you may be wondering about the purpose of the nonword conditions. The answer is simple— they gave the participant a reason to respond. If the experiment had consisted only of the Associated and Unassociated conditions, there would have been no decision to make, and participants would simply press a key as soon as something appeared on the screen. However, because half of the trials contained a nonword, and because the trials were presented in random order, the participant needed to remain vigilant and make a lexical decision each time. Thus, only half of the trials produced data to test the hypothesis, but all of the trials were needed in order to generate those data.

Building Blocks

Priming effects in the lexical decision task are robust and easily replicated, and so they form part of the foundation for further psycholinguistic research. In fact, quite complex hypotheses can be tested using the lexical decision task. Consider a sentence like the following:

> The gymnast loved the professor from the northwestern city who complained about the bad coffee.

In this sentence, the word *who* is a relative pronoun that links *the professor* with *complained about the bad coffee*. In other words, when we're listening to this sentence and hear the word *who*, we're reminded of *the professor*, and we understand that the professor (and not the gymnast) complained about the bad coffee. This ability to match up pronouns with the nouns they refer to is an essential part of language processing.

If pronouns activate memories of the nouns they refer to, then we should expect to see the same priming effect with the pronoun as we do with its referent. Researchers tested this hypothesis using a lexical decision task (Swinney et al., 1979). Participants listened to a series of sentences with relative pronouns like the example sentence above. At the same time, they had to perform a lexical decision task for words appearing on a computer screen. Unbeknownst to the participants, PROFESSOR was a prime, and the item on screen was a probe that was either semantically related to the prime, such as TEACHER, or else it was semantically unrelated, such as ADDRESS. Furthermore, in some trials the probe appeared just before the participants heard "who," and in other trials it

Figure 2.5   Priming in a Lexical Decision Task

Mean reaction time was faster in the Associated Pair (BREAD-BUTTER) condition than it was in the Unassociated Pair (CAKE-STEM) condition, suggesting that the first word of the associated pair primed the second word. Participants also made more errors in the Unassociated Pair condition.

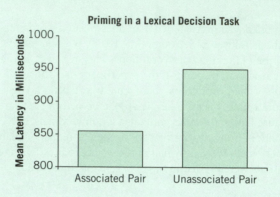

Priming in a Lexical Decision Task

Source: Meyer and Schvaneveldt (1971).

appeared just after they heard the pronoun. Consistent with the hypothesis, Swinney and colleagues found a priming effect after "who," presumably because the participants were now thinking of PROFESSOR. However, they found no priming effect before "who," presumably because the participants weren't thinking of PROFESSOR at that time.

This result establishes a procedure that can be used to tackle other questions, such as syntactic processing in patients suffering from aphasia. Depending on the region of the brain involved, different language functions may be disrupted. As we learned in Chapter 1, Broca's aphasia is characterized by disjointed or ungrammatical speech, although speech perception is still largely unimpaired. Another type of language loss is known as **Wernicke's aphasia**, which is *a condition characterized by fluent speech that is filled with vocabulary errors accompanied by difficulty in comprehending speech.* In other words, Broca's aphasia is viewed as mainly a deficit in language production, whereas Wernicke's aphasia is seen largely as a deficit in language perception.

There are differences between these two types of aphasia in terms of syntactic processing. Evidence suggests that Broca's aphasics make rough-and-ready interpretations of sentences based on semantic and contextual cues rather than processing them at a syntactic level. For example, Broca's aphasics have difficulty processing certain passive sentences, such as *The girl was kissed by the boy*, interpreting it instead as the non-equivalent active sentence *The girl kissed the boy*. In this task, Wernicke's aphasics perform similarly to normally functioning participants, suggesting that their ability to process syntax is still intact despite frequent grammatical errors in their speech. However, Broca's aphasics showed no priming effect, corroborating previous findings that Broca's aphasics had difficulty comprehending sentences that could only be understood through syntactic processing (Zurif et al., 1993).

These are just two examples of how complex experiments testing abstract hypotheses can be built out of simple, well-established building blocks. Latency is a useful behavioral measurement for exploring questions about the cognitive processes involved in comprehending and producing language, as they provide a rough measure of the time frame involved in these processes. In the early days of psycholinguistics, researchers had to depend on mechanical means for measuring latency; for example, Meyer and Schvaneveldt measured reaction time "by counting the cycles of a 1,000-Hz. oscillator" (1971, p. 228). Nowadays researchers program their experiments on computers, which can accurately control stimulus presentation and measure the speed of responses.

Total Recall

Psychologists distinguish two types of memory, short-term memory (STM) and long-term memory (LTM). It's important to keep in mind that these are constructs and not physically

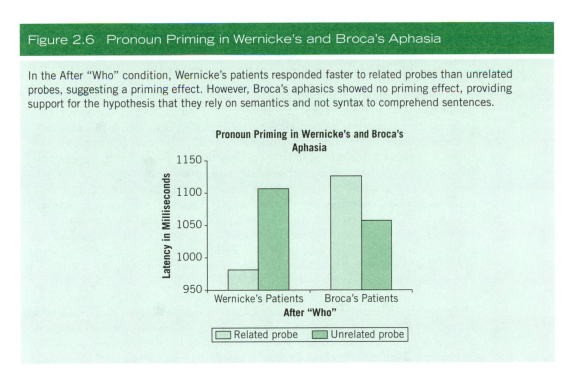

Figure 2.6   Pronoun Priming in Wernicke's and Broca's Aphasia

In the After "Who" condition, Wernicke's patients responded faster to related probes than unrelated probes, suggesting a priming effect. However, Broca's aphasics showed no priming effect, providing support for the hypothesis that they rely on semantics and not syntax to comprehend sentences.

Source: Zurif et al. (1993).

observable phenomena. We operationally define short-term memory as the number of items that can be immediately recalled and long-term memory as the number of items that can be recalled after a delay. Short-term memory is also called working memory.

The properties of short-term memory are studied using an **immediate recall task**, which is *a memory task in which participants hear or see a series of items and then repeat them without delay*. The digit span and word lists tasks that we've already looked at are examples of immediate recall tasks. You should remember that each of these was *a memory task in which participants are required to repeat the items in the correct order*, also known as a **serial recall task**. Serial recall predictably produces what are known as **primacy and recency effects**, referring to *the observation that the first and last items in a list are more accurately recalled than those in the middle*.

Immediate serial recall is a useful task for exploring the role of working memory in language processing. Consider for a moment what happens when you encounter a new word for the first time. (As a college student, you should experience this a lot.) Let's say your professor is lecturing and tosses out some technical term:

Professor: Blah blah blah antriskoldate blah blah . . .

Classmate whispers to you: What did he say?

You whisper back: I don't know. Ant-something-date.

Only remembering the beginning and the end of the new word is an instance of primacy and recency effects.

Gupta (2005) proposed that newly encountered multisyllable words are treated by the language processing system as lists of syllables. If this is the case, you would expect to see primacy and recency effects in the repetition of multisyllabic nonwords, as in the fictional conversation above. After all, a word you've never encountered before is the same as a nonword to you. This hypothesis was tested with sets of four-syllable nonwords that were decomposable into four one-syllable words. For example, *antriskoldate* breaks down into *ant, risk, old,* and *ate*. In the Nonword condition, the participants heard a nonword like *antriskoldate* and repeated it right away. In the Word List condition, they heard a list of words like *ant, risk, cold, ate,* which they repeated right away. When the researcher measured serial recall accuracy of the nonword repetition on a syllable-by-syllable basis, he found primacy and recency effects, just as he did in the Word List condition. Overall, though, nonword repetition was less accurate than word repetition.

The properties of long-term memory are explored by using a **delayed recall task**, which is *a memory task in which participants hear or see a series of items and then recall those items after a delay*. The delay can range from minutes and hours to even days and weeks. The Bransford and Johnson (1972) study that we looked at in Section 2.2 used a delayed recall task. Remember that participants heard an ambiguous story with or without the aid of a disambiguating picture. In addition to rating the comprehension difficulty of the story, the participants were also asked to recall as many events from the story as possible in any order. Such *a memory task in which participants are allowed to repeat the items in any order* is called a **free recall task**. In other words, Bransford and Johnson used a delayed free recall task, meaning that the participants heard a story (a series of events) and after a delay were asked to recall those events as they came to mind.

In short, recall tasks can be classified as immediate, tapping into short-term memory processes, or as delayed, tapping into long-term memory processes. Each of these types of recall tasks can be further distinguished as serial or free, depending on whether the response is required to be in the same order as the presentation.

Learning Without Knowing

Native speakers have good intuitions about which sentences in their language are grammatical and which are not, but they usually can't explain why. This is because

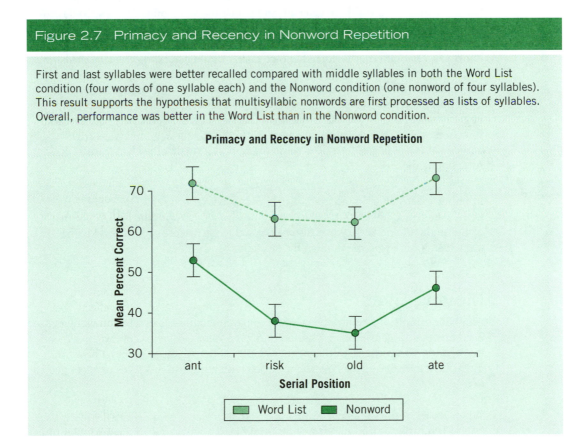

Figure 2.7 Primacy and Recency in Nonword Repetition

First and last syllables were better recalled compared with middle syllables in both the Word List condition (four words of one syllable each) and the Nonword condition (one nonword of four syllables). This result supports the hypothesis that multisyllabic nonwords are first processed as lists of syllables. Overall, performance was better in the Word List than in the Nonword condition.

Source: Gupta (2005).

language acquisition is largely based on **implicit learning,** which is *a form of learning that takes place outside of conscious awareness.* Hypotheses about implicit language learning are usually tested with two-part experiments that consist of a learning phase followed by a test phase. During the learning phase, participants see or hear a set of stimuli that have been organized according to certain rules. In the test phase that follows, the participants experience a new set of stimuli and indicate whether each item follows the rules that formed the set of stimuli in the learning phase.

A classic demonstration of implicit learning is Reber's (1967) artificial grammar learning task. First, Reber constructed a simple grammar in the form of a directed graph with arrows connecting nodes. Each arrow is labeled with a letter, and any path through the graph constitutes a grammatical string. Conversely, if a letter string can't be constructed by a path through the graph, it is not a grammatical string. For example, in Reber's grammar, TPTS is a grammatical string, but VPTS is not.

During the learning phrase, Reber asked his participants to study a list of letter strings for a subsequent memory test. At the beginning of the test phase, he informed them that the letter strings had been generated from an artificial grammar. He also told them that they were now going to see more letter strings, some generated by the grammar and some violating the grammar. For each item, they were to indicate yes or no. This is known as a **two-alternative forced-choice task,** meaning *an experimental task requiring the participant to decide between two options.* "I don't know" is not an option, and the participants must respond on every trial, forcing them to rely on implicit knowledge to complete the task. Reber's participants were able to distinguish grammatical from ungrammatical strings at a rate greater than chance, suggesting that they had learned something about the rules of the grammar. However, in follow-up interviews the participants were unable to express those rules, indicating that they had learned the rules implicitly.

In implicit learning tasks, accuracy is the key behavioral measure. However, participants are often encouraged to work quickly or to go with the first choice that comes to mind, and latency may also be tracked to get a sense of how quickly the participants were working through the test items.

Moving Eyes

Another example of a behavioral measure in psycholinguistics involves tracking eye movements during reading or while scanning the visual scene for context cues to aid in discourse comprehension (Rayner, 1978, 1998; Tanenhaus & Spivey-Knowlton, 1995). Eye movements are typically recorded with a head-mounted camera connected to a computer.

When we read, the subjective impression is that our eyes move smoothly along the line of print, but in fact our eyes jump from one content word to the next, skipping

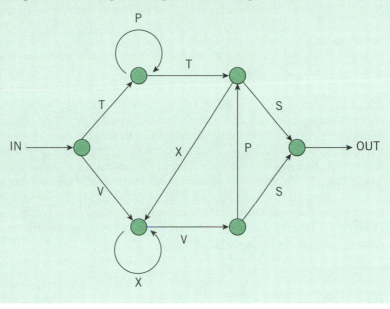

Figure 2.8 Artificial Grammar

Grammatical letter strings like TPTXVS follow a path through the graph, whereas ungrammatical letter strings like TTPVS do not. After studying a list of grammatical strings, participants were able to distinguish novel grammatical strings from ungrammatical strings.

Source: Reber (1967).

function words like "is" and "the" (which is why it's so hard to catch typos). *A quick movement of the eyes while reading* is known as a **saccade**, and *a momentary gaze of the eyes on a single location while reading* is known as a **fixation**. Most saccades move forward in the text, but sometimes we saccade backward, perhaps to reread a word we'd misread the first time. *A movement of the eyes back to a previously viewed location* is called a **regression**. These observations suggest that we read words as wholes and not as a series of letters.

You may have seen the following text, which circulated on the Internet in September 2003 (Davis, n.d.):

> Aoccdrnig to a rscheearch at Cmabrigde Uinervtisy, it deosn't mttaer in waht oredr the ltteers in a wrod are, the olny iprmoetnt tihng is taht the frist and lsat ltteer be at the rghit pclae. The rset can be a toatl mses and you can sitll raed it wouthit a porbelm. Tihs is bcuseae the huamn mnid deos not raed ervey lteter by istlef, but the wrod as a wlohe.

The story is a hoax, in that no researcher at Cambridge University had conducted such a study. Nevertheless, this hoax inspired Rayner and his colleagues to investigate the phenomenon (Rayner et al., 2006). Using a head-mounted eye-tracking device, the researchers recorded the eye movements of participants as they read sentences containing jumbled words. There were four conditions in the experiment, with all words of five letters or more being manipulated. In the Normal condition, the sentences contained no transposed letters. In the Beginning condition, the first two letters of each manipulated word were transposed (*could* became *oculd*). In the End condition, the last two letters of each of these words was transposed (*could* became *coudl*). And in the Internal condition, two letters in the middle of each manipulated word were transposed (*could* became *cuold*).

For each sentence, Rayner and colleagues counted the number of fixations, calculated the percentage of saccades that were regressions, and measured the length (in milliseconds) of each fixation. We already know from many years of reading research that each of these numbers is a good indicator of reading difficulty (Rayner, 1978, 1998). That is, when we have more difficulty in reading a text, we make more and longer fixations and more regressions. On the basis of these measurements, Rayner and his colleagues concluded that internal transpositions had less negative impact on reading than did transpositions at the beginning or ends of words, consistent with the claim on the Internet. However, the claim that internal transpositions do not impose a reading cost was not supported by the data.

In Sum

Although we can't observe cognitive processes directly, we can make inferences about them on the basis of outward behavior. Latency provides a rough measure of the time course of cognitive processes, and accuracy is a common measure for assessing learning. Priming paired with a lexical decision task provides a useful tool for exploring cognitive processing involved in language comprehension. Recall tasks probe the organization of various memory systems, with immediate recall testing short-term memory and delayed recall testing long-term memory. The tendency for first and last items to be best recalled is known as primacy and recency effects. Implicit learning, which largely takes place outside of conscious awareness, is often measured with forced-choice tasks that require the participant to rely on intuition. Head-mounted eye-tracking devices are a useful tool for studying reading and discourse comprehension.

Review Questions

1. Explain latency and accuracy. What are the other names these measures go by?

2. Describe the standard lexical decision and priming task. What is the purpose of having participants distinguish between words and nonwords?

As proposed by the Internet hoax story, words with internal transpositions were easier to read than words with either beginning or end transpositions. However, contrary to the story, words with internal transpositions were still harder to read than normally spelled words. The same pattern of results was obtained for three measures of reading difficulty: number of fixations (shown), percentage of regressions, and average fixation duration.

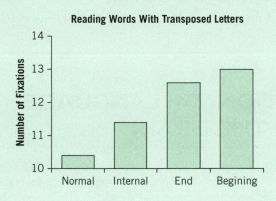

Source: Rayner et al. (2006).

3. Distinguish the four types of recall tasks described in this section. What are they used for?

4. Describe the standard format of an implicit learning task. Why does the test phase typically employ a forced-choice task?

5. What are the established findings from eye-tracking studies of reading?

Thought Questions

1. The field study of Diana monkey calls presented in Chapter 1 (Zuberbühler et al., 1999) was described by the researchers as a priming experiment. Why? (You may want to review the design of this experiment.) In what sense were the expected responses different from the standard priming task?

2. In addition to the recall tasks we examined in this section, there's another type known as cued recall. In a cued recall task, participants are trained on random word pairs and then tested on their ability to recall these pairs, with either the first or second word serving as the recall cue for the other word. (For example, if you learned the pair

APPLE-HOUSE, you might be cued with APPLE to respond HOUSE, or you might be cued with HOUSE to respond APPLE.) This type of paired associate learning is common in the real world. Can you think of some examples?

Google It! Eye Tracking

Search YouTube for videos of **head-mounted eye tracker** studies. Eye tracking is used in a wide variety of research fields.

SECTION 2.4: LANGUAGE AND THE BRAIN

- In most people, language functions are lateralized on the left side of the brain; two important regions are Broca's area, responsible for language production, and Wernicke's area, responsible for language comprehension.

- Subcortical structures such as the hippocampus, amygdala, and basal ganglia also play a role in language acquisition and language processing.

- Event-related potentials (ERP) are waveforms extracted from the EEG that can track the time course of cognitive processes at the millisecond level; particular ERP components are associated with particular cognitive processes.

- The N400 is an ERP response to a semantic anomaly and is probably the most commonly tracked ERP component in psycholinguistic research.

- Neuroimaging techniques measure brain activity by tracking blood flow. The two most commonly used techniques are PET and fMRI; for safety and practical reasons, fMRI is now far more commonly used than PET.

- ERP and fMRI results are frequently compared; ERP provides excellent temporal resolution, while fMRI provides good spatial resolution.

Inside your skull sits a three-pound blob of fat and protein. Although it has no moving parts, it controls all action within your body, and it directs your body as you navigate through the environment. Consuming one-fifth of all the energy your body produces, your brain is without doubt the most important body part you possess, the thing that defines who you are as a person.

What's Inside Your Head

The brain is structured like a mushroom, with a stem rising up in the middle and surrounded by a cap that largely envelops the stem. The **brainstem** is *the interior portion of the brain that is charged with regulating body functions and and keeping the body alive*, and *the walnut-sized structure behind the brainstem that is responsible for coordinating movement* is called the **cerebellum**. The tissue surrounding the brainstem is known as the forebrain, and it's divided into two hemispheres, left and right. The **corpus callosum** is *a band of fibers connecting the left and right hemispheres, allowing for communication between the two hemispheres of the brain*. The **cerebral cortex** is *the outer covering of the forebrain where most of the brain activity giving rise to conscious experience takes place*.

Each hemisphere is divided into four lobes. The **occipital lobe** is *the lobe at the back of the head that processes visual input from the eyes*. It contains line detectors of various orientations (horizontal, vertical, diagonal) that are important in detecting letters in written language. The **temporal lobe** is *the lobe at the side of the head that processes auditory input from the ears and is also responsible for object recognition*. Damage to this

Figure 2.10 Lobes and Functional Areas of the Cerebral Cortex

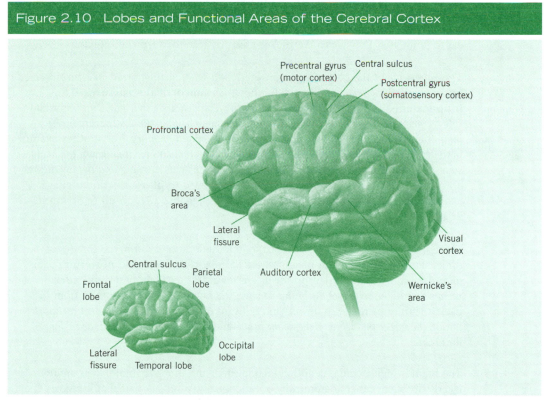

Source: Garrett, Figure 3.8, Lobes and Functional Areas on the Surface of the Hemispheres.

lobe can lead to an inability to name objects. The **parietal lobe** is *the lobe at the top of the head that monitors body position and navigation through the environment.* The results of some brain-imaging studies suggest that the parietal lobe may play a role in higher-level language processing, but the evidence is still inconclusive (Geranmayeh et al., 2012). Finally, the **frontal lobe** is *the lobe at the front of the head that generates motor movement and is also responsible for planning and decision making.* The region of the brain that programs muscle movement for speech articulation is located toward the back of the frontal lobe.

For the most part, the two hemispheres are symmetrical, with the left hemisphere controlling the right side of the body, and the right hemisphere controlling the left side of the body. However, some functions are lateralized. **Lateralization** refers to *the fact that some cognitive functions are processed in only one of the two hemispheres of the brain.* For the vast majority of people, language functions are lateralized on the left side of the brain.

Two areas of the cerebral cortex are especially important for language processing. The first language location is known as Broca's area, which, as we learned in Chapter 1, is a region in the left frontal lobe that is generally described as the language production area of the brain. Damage to Broca's area can lead to Broca's aphasia. The second language location is called **Wernicke's area**, which is *a region in the left temporal lobe that is generally described as the language comprehension area of the brain.* Touch behind your left ear to point at it. Damage to Wernicke's area may lead to Wernicke's aphasia.

The functions of the cortex are supported by *a set of distinct brain structures located below the cerebral cortex,* collectively known as **subcortical structures**. The **hippocampus** is *a subcortical structure of the temporal lobe that plays an important role in memory and learning.* The **amygdala** is also *a subcortical structure of the temporal lobe that plays a role in regulating emotion and memory.* Yet another example is the **basal ganglia**, which is *a set of subcortical structures located where the brain stem joins the cerebrum that are responsible for procedural learning and the execution of routine actions.* All of these structures are believed to play a role in language acquisition and processing (Bohrn, Altmann, & Jacobs, 2012; Duff & Schmidt, 2012; Enard, 2011).

Three pairs of direction words are used to indicate locations within the three-dimensional brain. **Anterior** means *toward the front of the brain,* and **posterior** means *toward the back of the brain.* **Superior** means *toward the top of the brain,* and **inferior** means *toward the bottom of the brain.* Because the brain is symmetrical from front to back, the third pair refer to inward and outward directions. That is, **lateral** means *toward the side (either left or right) of the brain,* and **medial** means *toward the midline of the brain.*

The brain is highly complex and interconnected, and in reality brain areas are not clearly divisible, either anatomically or functionally. While it's true that we have identified consistent functions for certain areas of the brain, as we learn more about

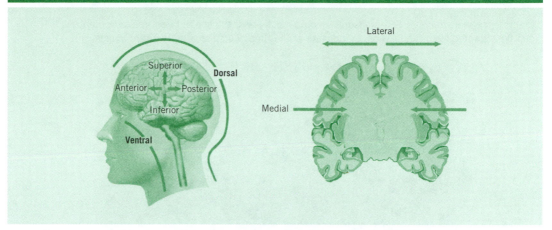

Figure 2.11   Terms Used to Indicate Directions in the Brain

Source: Garrett, Figure 3.9(a) Terms Used to Indicate Direction and Orientation in the Nervous System.

the brain, we find other areas also getting involved in those tasks. Furthermore, the same area of the brain will generally take part in a variety of cognitive functions. Nevertheless, the functional description of the brain presented here provides a reasonable basis for understanding research on language and the brain.

"Listening" to the Brain

The brain works by shunting around electrical impulses, working in much the same way as the computers and other electronic devices we have grown so accustomed to. The electrical activity in the brain spreads to the scalp, where it can measured. By tracking this electrical activity at the scalp, we can "listen in" to what is going on inside the brain.

Electroencephalography (EEG) is *a technique that uses electrodes attached to various locations on the scalp to record voltage fluctuations originating in the brain.* EEG is commonly used in clinical settings as a tool for diagnosing epilepsy, coma, and brain trauma. It's also extensively used in research on sleep and other forms of altered consciousness. EEG provides continuous real-time information about the activity of the brain. However, the electrical activity at the scalp that EEG records is a summation of all the electrical activity going on within the brain, and for this reason it's not possible to pinpoint the location in the brain where any particular action is taking place.

Although EEG does have its place in the lab, it's generally not useful in psycholinguistic research. Your brain is the ultimate multitasker, and if we try to record the brain's

Figure 2.12 Participant Wearing an EEG Cap

Electroencephalography (EEG) measures electrical activity at the scalp. Event-related potentials (ERPs) can be extracted from the EEG as an indicator of the time course of cognitive functions.

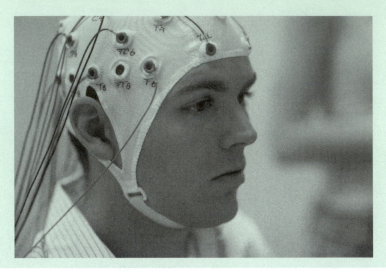

Source: iStockphoto.com/ annedde.

electrical activity for a particular function, we also get signals from all the other activities the brain is simultaneously performing. Consider the following sentence:

I take my coffee with cream and dog.

You were probably surprised to see the word *dog* in this context. One question a psycholinguist would like to ask is how long it takes the brain to recognize that this sentence ends in an unexpected way. Using a modified version of EEG, we can answer this question as well as others regarding the time course of cognitive events.

If you record the EEG while a participant listens to a hundred sentences with unexpected endings, the EEG waveform for each sentence will look completely different because of all the other activity that was going on in the brain at the same time. However, if you lay all of these waveforms on top of each other, time-locking each to the start of the unexpected word, you can calculate an average waveform that represents the cognitive processing involved in interpreting sentences with unexpected endings. This is the logic behind a technique known as ERP, or event-related potential (Luck, 2005).

An **event-related potential** is *a waveform extracted from the EEG that signifies a specific cognitive process.* ERP provides a millisecond-by-millisecond time line of cognitive processing as the balance of positive and negative charges in the brain shifts back and forth. *A specific ERP waveform that is tied to a particular cognitive process* is known as a **component**. Components are labeled N if they are negative-going and P if they are positive-going, followed by the time in milliseconds when the component peaks. For example, the P300 is a component tending toward the positive that peaks about 300 milliseconds after the presentation of an unexpected stimulus.

Many ERP components have been identified, but the one most relevant to psycholinguistic research is the N400. Like many important findings in science, it was discovered by accident. Kutas and Hillyard (1980) were investigating ERP responses to unexpected words at the ends of sentences, such as the *I take my coffee with cream and dog* example above. They were expecting to find the typical P300 response to unexpected stimuli, but instead they observed a negative-going waveform peaking around 400 milliseconds after the presentation of the unexpected word. Sentences with expected endings, such as *He returned the book to the library*, elicited no negative component, and sentences with unexpected changes in font, such as *She put on her high-heeled SHOES*, elicited the standard P300. This suggests that the N400 is a marker for the processing of **semantic anomaly**, *a condition in which a grammatically correct sentence does not make sense because of a mismatch between the meaning of one or more words and the sentence as a whole*. Thus, it appears that the N400 is specifically a marker of linguistic processing, as opposed to the more general P300.

ERP research is relatively inexpensive to conduct, and it has become an important tool in cognitive psychology laboratories. Within the subdiscipline of psycholinguistics, the discovery of the N400 has led to a fertile field of research, and a large literature on the N400 has accumulated over the last three decades.

"Watching" the Brain in Action

Your brain is a hungry organ. Even though it has no moving parts, the computations it routinely performs consume vast amounts of energy that need to be continuously replenished by the bloodstream. We have methods that allow us to monitor increases and decreases in blood flow in various regions of the brain. Working on the assumption that any part of the brain performing computations needs more blood, we infer that areas of high blood flow are also areas of high activity in the brain.

Two main functional imaging techniques are used in studying the relationship between language and the brain. One is PET, which stands for positron emission tomography. **PET** is *a brain imaging technique that produces a three-dimensional moving picture of blood flow by tracking gamma rays emitted from a mildly radioactive substance injected into the bloodstream*. One of the first PET studies looking at language processing in the brain was by Petersen and colleagues (1988). The researchers presented lists of words in either auditory or visual form to participants undergoing a PET scan and asked them to perform one of three tasks: (1) read or listen to the word; (2) repeat the word; or

(3) name a verb associated with the word, such as "eat" for "cake." Based on their findings, Petersen and colleagues developed a functional-anatomical model that has inspired functional imaging research for the last quarter century.

PET is especially suited to certain types of research, but it has a number of limitations. The most important of these is that it exposes participants to radiation, albeit in small doses. Still, potential risks to the participant must be weighed against the potential benefit to society of the research. Furthermore, an individual's participation in PET studies needs to be limited to keep radiation exposure within acceptable levels.

Another commonly used technique is functional magnetic resonance imaging. More generally known as **fMRI**, this is *a brain-imaging technique that makes use of differences in magnetic properties between oxygenated and deoxygenated hemoglobin to track blood flow.* Compared with PET, fMRI has a number of advantages, the most important of which is that it doesn't expose the participant to dangerous radiation. It's true that fMRI exposes the participant to a very strong magnetic field, but this in itself isn't known

Figure 2.13   An MRI Scanner

A common brain-imaging technique uses fMRI to track blood flow in the brain under the assumption that regions of heavy blood flow indicate regions of activity.

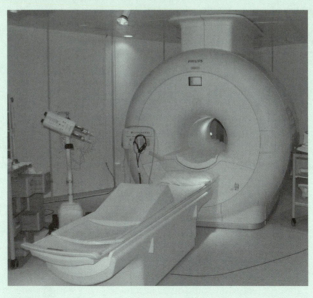

Source: Retrieved from http://en.wikipedia.org/wiki/File:MRI-Philips.jpg.

to be dangerous. However, all metal objects must be removed from the room because they can be pulled into the scanner by its powerful magnets. Also, people with metal implants or pacemakers may experience adverse effects. Still, the risks of fMRI are minimal compared with those of PET.

Like PET, fMRI produces a three-dimensional image of the brain, with a spatial resolution on the order of a few cubic millimeters. Each voxel, or three-dimensional pixel, is color-coded to represent degree of blood flow, and this level of resolution allows researchers to pinpoint activity to quite specific areas of the brain. Just as motion pictures are created by taking a series of snapshots in quick succession, fMRI produces a functional image of the brain by combining a series of MRI still pictures. In the movies, the industry standard is 24 frames per second, but fMRI sampling is much less frequent, generally on the order of once every few seconds.

The first fMRI studies to look at language processing in the brain mainly aimed to replicate earlier PET findings as well as the observations of patients with brain lesions over the last century (Binder et al., 1997; McCarthy et al., 1993). In addition to practical and safety advantages, fMRI produces sharper images because participants can stay in the scanner longer (Le Bihan & Jezzard, 1995), and so fMRI has become the premiere brain-imaging technique in psycholinguistics (Price, 2012).

With the advent of fMRI, our understanding of how the brain processes language has increased dramatically. But perhaps the most important thing we have learned is that there's still a lot we don't know, and it turns out that many of our initial assumptions about brain organization were simplifications at best.

In Sum

Two important language areas of the brain, Broca's area and Wernicke's area, are lateralized on the left hemisphere of the cerebral cortex in most people. Subcortical structures such as the hippocampus, amygdala, and basal ganglia also serve language functions. ERP and fMRI are often used in tandem to explore the relationship between brain and language. Each technique has its strengths and weaknesses, but when used together they provide a power set of tools for studying the brain in action. ERP has excellent temporal resolution but poor spatial resolution, whereas fMRI has good spatial resolution but poor temporal resolution. Thus, we can measure the time frame of a cognitive process using ERP, and we can determine what areas of the brain are involved in that process using fMRI. The results of these two approaches can then be combined to obtain a fuller picture of language processing as it unfolds in the brain.

Review Questions

1. Locate the four lobes and briefly describe the functions that occur in each. Involve your whole body in the learning of these terms by laying your hand on the appropriate area of your scalp as you do this.

2. Explain the six directional terms used in describing locations in the brain. Use your finger to point out these directions in your own head.

3. Point to Broca's and Wernicke's areas in your own head, and then name the lobe in which each is located. Describe the aphasia that results from damage to each of these areas.

4. What is EEG? What is ERP? What is a component? What is the N400, and what is it a response to?

5. What is the basic assumption behind functional brain imaging? What is PET, and how does it work? What is fMRI, and how does it work?

6. What are the relative strengths and weaknesses of ERP and fMRI?

Thought Questions

1. Two more directional terms you'll encounter are **dorsal**, meaning *toward the back*, and **ventral**, meaning *toward the belly*. These terms specifically refer to four-legged body structure. Consider carefully how a brain in a four-legged animal, such as your dog, is oriented within the body. Think also about how the human head repositioned itself with respect to the rest of the body as we rotated upward onto two legs from our four-legged ancestors. Dorsal and ventral are still used to identify parts of the human brain, especially when those parts are analogous to those in four-legged animals. However, they no longer necessarily orient toward the back or belly. Why? Which pair of direction terms most closely align with dorsal-ventral?

2. Occasionally, the corpus callosum is severed as a treatment of last resort for severe epilepsy. Such "split-brain" patients function normally in everyday life, but they are highly valued as research participants in certain lines of psycholinguistic research. Given what you know about the organization of the brain, what sorts of hypotheses might researchers be testing with these participants. Hint: There are ways to project images so that they are only received by one hemisphere or the other.

Google It! Brain Imaging

Search YouTube for videos demonstrating **event-related potential**, **positron emission tomography**, and **fMRI**. You can also find articles and videos about **split brain experiments**.

CONCLUSION

The scientific method provides us with a powerful tool for understanding the world that's unsurpassed by any other means. By cycling between theory and observations, scientists gradually unwind the great mysteries of the universe. In this chapter, we've seen how the experimental method is used to explore how humans acquire, comprehend, and produce language.

Although the cognitive processes aren't directly observable, psychologists employ a number of techniques to make inferences about them. Proven behavioral methods such as priming and the lexical decision task can be combined with more extensive procedures to test complex hypotheses about language processing. Likewise, neuroimaging techniques such as ERP and fMRI have greatly expanded our understanding of how the brain handles language.

In the chapters that follow, we'll learn more about the findings from half a century of psycholinguistic research. We start at the most basic level of language, speech perception, and from there we work our way up to higher levels of language structure—words, sentences, and discourse. We'll also consider reading and writing, bilingualism, and the signed languages used by deaf communities. While we keep in mind the social and cultural aspects of language throughout the book, we especially focus on these issues in the last three chapters. There, we'll consider language development across the lifespan as well as the three-way interplay of language, culture, and thought. In the last chapter, we look at how modern technology impacts the ways we use language in our daily lives.

CROSS-CULTURAL PERSPECTIVE: The Lexical Decision Task in Other Languages

In this chapter, we learned that the lexical decision task is a basic building block of many behavioral studies investigating the cognitive processes involved in language comprehension. Two sets of stimuli are needed for a lexical decision task. One is a set of real words in the language under investigation, such as MOVE and TRIM. The other is a set of nonwords, that is, letter sequences that are possible in the language but just happen not to be words, such as MOBE and TREM. In some cases, a third set of impossible words, such as PVRT and QWTR are also included.

Typically, nonwords are constructed by meshing the spelling patterns of two real words. For instance, both MOVE and LOBE are words in English, and when we put the beginning of the first word with the ending of the second word, we create the nonword MOBE. The other combination, LOVE, is also a word, but this fact strengthens our confidence that MOBE is a possible word. We can also have native speakers rate each item as possible words in the language.

Throughout the last half of the twentieth century, almost all psycholinguistic research has been performed in North America using English stimuli. However, in the last decade or so, much more research has been coming out of Europe and East Asia. The stimuli used in these studies typically come from European languages, such as German or French, or else from Asian languages like Chinese and Japanese.

Cross-linguistic research is vital if we want to gain a full understanding of language processing in humans. If our experiments only use English stimuli, we can't tell whether our findings are specific to that language or if they apply to other languages as well. Sometimes studies in other languages corroborate the findings in English, and sometimes they yield contradictory results. In either case, our understanding of language as a universal human phenomenon is deepened.

Imagine you've traveled with a companion to another country. Everyone around you is speaking a language you and your partner don't understand. Will this incomprehensible speech interfere with your ability to understand what your partner says in English? Gautreau, Hoen, and Meunier (2013) explored this situation using an auditory lexical decision task with native speakers of French. Instead of responding to printed words on a screen, the participants indicated whether items they heard were word or nonwords in French. (Background noise consisted of four voices speaking in either Irish or Italian. And yes, the other languages did cause interference, but in complex ways.)

Gautreau, Hoen, and Meunier created their French nonword stimuli in a similar fashion to that described above. All of the stimulus items consisted of two syllables, a common word structure in French. The nonwords were consistent with the patterns of French spelling, as in the nonword TROUCHET, which follows the patterns of the French words TROUVER and CROCHET.

Creating realistic nonword stimuli in East Asian languages, however, is more challenging. In Chinese, each character is pronounced as a single syllable, and each character also has a particular meaning associated with it. Some Chinese words consist of a single syllable and are written with a single character, but two-syllable (and hence, two-character) words are far more common. Chinese psycholinguists have taken two approaches to creating nonword stimuli.

One approach involves the creation of pseudo-characters. Although there are thousands of characters in use, they're all made up out of a limited number of components that are combined according to rules. Not all possible combinations are in use, so researchers can use these as nonwords. This is the approach taken by Yuan and colleagues (2012). These researchers combined a lexical decision task with fMRI to study the brain processes involved in reading Chinese characters.

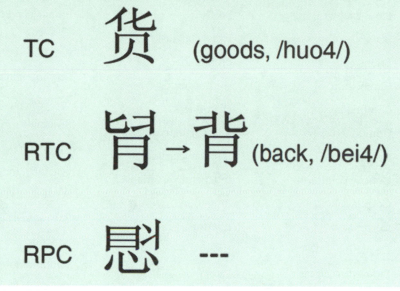

Figure 2.14 Pseudo-Characters in Characters

Examples of stimuli used in a Chinese lexical decision task. TC stimuli are "true characters"; RTC stimuli were created by rearranging the components of true characters; and RPC stimuli were created by combining a set of components that could not be rearranged to form a true character.

TC 货 (goods, /huo4/)

RTC 胃 → 背 (back, /bei4/)

RPC 慰 ---

Source: Deng et al. (2012).

The other approach takes advantage of the fact that many words in Chinese consist of two-character combinations. In many cases, these characters can occur in other words but not alone. (English has a number of combinable morphemes like this as well. Consider the words *consume* and *resume*. Although *con-*, *re-*, and *-sume* all occur in other words, none of them are words by themselves.)

Du, Zhang, and Zhang (2014) took this second approach. They investigated the time it takes for the brain to read Chinese words by combining ERP with a lexical decision task. All of their stimuli consisted of two-syllable words, and their nonwords were two-character combinations that just happened not to be words in Chinese. (We can take the same approach in English. Although *restore* is a word, *constore* is not.)

In Chapter 8, we'll learn more about reading processes, considering both languages that are written in alphabets as well as those, like Chinese and Japanese, that are written in meaning-based characters. The cross-linguistic research that has been published so far has challenged many of the assumptions that American psychologists have long held about how human languages are processed. As the world turns into a global village, our views about human nature will surely change as well.

KEY TERMS

Accuracy

Amygdala

Anterior

Basal ganglia

Between-subjects design

Brainstem

Cerebellum

Cerebral cortex

Component

Construct

Control condition

Corpus callosum

Correlation

Deduction

Delayed recall task

Dependent variable

Digit span task

Dorsal

Electroencephalography

Error rate

Event-related potential

Experiment

Experimental condition

Experimental method

Falsifiability criterion

Field study

Fixation

fMRI

Free recall task

Frontal lobe

Hippocampus

Hypothesis

Immediate recall task

Implicit learning

Independent variable

Induction

Inferior

Latency

Lateral

Lateralization

Lexical decision task

Medial

Model

Naturalistic observation

Nonword

Occipital lobe

Operational definition

Parietal lobe

PET

Phonological loop

Posterior

Primacy and recency effects

Priming

Psycholinguistics

Regression

Reliability

Saccade

Semantic anomaly

Serial recall task

Subcortical structures

Superior

Temporal lobe

Theory

Trial

Two-alternative forced-choice task

Validity

Ventral

Wernicke's aphasia

Wernicke's area

Within-subjects design

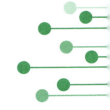

Speech Perception

The scientists at Haskins Laboratories had just invented a machine that could produce human-like speech. It didn't speak *like* a human. That is, it had no jaw or tongue or lips, and it didn't breathe either. Instead, it produced complex patterns of sound at different frequencies which, when combined together, resembled human speech. It didn't sound like natural human speech, but it was clearly understandable. They called the machine Pattern Playback (Liberman, 1996).

It was the late 1940s, and research was shifting from the war effort to solving more practical problems. The researchers thought they could use Pattern Playback as the basis for a machine that could read to the blind. The solution seemed obvious. All they had to do was discover the pattern of sound frequencies that represented each speech sound to create a sort of phonetic alphabet that Pattern Playback could read. A new age of talking machines seemed right around the corner.

Today we do live in an age of talking machines, but these weren't possible until cheap and powerful computers became available around the end of the twentieth century. This is because the sound patterns of speech are far more complex than researchers had once imagined. Although Pattern Playback never read a book aloud, it did provide psycholinguists with tremendous insights into the nature of speech. In fact, much of what you'll read about in this chapter is science we learned from a failed attempt to build a reading machine.

SECTION 3.1: AUDITORY PERCEPTION

- Sound is composed of waves; the frequency of the wave is perceived as pitch, and the amplitude of the wave is perceived as loudness.
- Vibrating objects produce a fundamental frequency as well as multiple overtones; the particular combination of fundamental frequency and overtones is perceived as timbre.

- Vibration events produce periodic sounds, which are composed of regularly recurring patterns; friction and collision events produce aperiodic sounds, which have no repeating pattern, and are generally perceived as noise.

- The organ of auditory sensation is the cochlea, or inner ear. The basilar membrane extends inside the length of the cochlea, and its hair cells are sensitive to particular frequencies; the basilar membrane exhibits tonotopic organization, with sensitivity to high frequencies at one end and low frequencies at the other end.

- The primary auditory cortex is located in the superior temporal lobe, and it has the same tonotopic arrangement as the basilar membrane; neighboring cortical regions, including Wernicke's area in the left hemisphere, do higher-level processing of the auditory input.

- We can recognize objects and events just by the way they sound; speech sounds are likewise auditory events and of extremely short duration, yet our ability to perceive them accurately is remarkable.

Imagine you're wading through a pool of still water. Notice how ripples form as you push ahead, spreading out as waves along the surface of the pool. The same thing happens when objects move in the atmosphere. They send out waves of high and low pressure as they bump against and pull away from the air molecules around them. You can't see these waves, but oftentimes you can hear them.

The Look of Sound

There are two properties you need to know to describe a wave. The first property is **frequency**, which is *the number of wavelengths that pass by a given point in a given amount of time*. Sound frequency is usually measured in *cycles per second*, also known as **Hertz**, abbreviated Hz. *The psychological perception of sound wave frequency* is **pitch**. High-pitched sounds have waves that are tightly packed together, while low-pitched sounds have waves that are stretched out.

The second property is **amplitude**, which is *the amount of change that a wave undergoes during one cycle*. In the case of waves through water, you can visualize the amplitude as the difference in height between its highest and lowest points. In the case of sound, which involves rapid alternations of air pressure, you can think of amplitude as the difference between the highest and lowest pressure. *The psychological perception of sound wave amplitude* is **loudness**.

These two properties describe a **sine wave**, so called because it's *a wave that can be described by a trigonometric sine function*. If you move very steadily through water, the ripples you create are roughly sine waves. We can produce sound sine waves with electronic equipment, but they rarely occur in the natural world. Real life is messy.

Figure 3.1   Examples of Sound Waves (G9.3)

Waveforms (a) and (b) have the same frequency but different amplitudes, as do waveforms (c) and (d). Waveforms (a) and (c) have the same amplitudes but different frequencies, as do waveforms (b) and (d). Waveform (e) is aperiodic noise, while waveform (f) is one cycle of a periodic musical note played on a clarinet.

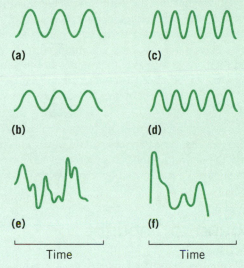

(a)   (c)

(b)   (d)

(e)   (f)

Time   Time

Take a rubber band and stretch it between your thumb and forefinger. You've just created a simple musical instrument. Run your finger across one of these strings and watch how it vibrates. If you hold it close to your ear, you can even hear it. If the string simply flexed back and forth along its entire length, it would produce a sine wave. But vibrating objects don't behave that way. They not only vibrate along their entire length, they also vibrate along half their length, a third of their length, a fourth, and so on.

Vibration along the entire length of the string generates the **fundamental frequency**, which is *the lowest frequency produced by a vibrating object*. Vibrations at half length, third length, and so on generate **overtones**, which are *frequencies higher than the fundamental that are also produced by a vibrating object*. Thus, naturally occurring sounds from vibrating objects are complex, as overtones are laid atop the fundamental frequency. *The psychological perception of sound wave complexity* is known as **timbre** (pronounced *TAM-ber*). A violin and a flute may play the same note (fundamental frequency), but they still sound different because they produce different patterns of overtones. Likewise, many speech sounds are distinguished by their patterns of overtones.

A vibrating object produces *a sound with a regularly repeating pattern*, which is known as a **periodic sound**. But not all sounds are periodic. Rub your hands together close to your ear. There's none of that ringing, twanging sound you got from the rubber band. Instead, you get the grating, hissing sound of friction. Two objects rubbing against each other produce *a sound with no regularly repeating pattern*, and this is known as **aperiodic sound**. Objects bumping into each other also produce bursts of aperiodic sound, or noise.

The distinction between periodic and aperiodic sound is very important in the science of speech perception. Speech sounds can be broadly categorized into vowels and consonants, roughly paralleling the distinction between periodic and aperiodic sounds. Vowels are periodic; they have a ringing, musical character to them. You can sing vowels, extending them for as long as you have breath. Consonants, on the other hand, are noisier. Some consonants, like "sh," are produced with friction, and like vowels you can extend them for as long as you have breath, but you can't sing them. Other consonants, like "p," are produced as puffs of air and can't be extended. (Go ahead. Try it. Say "sh........" until you run out of breath. Now say "p........" You can't do it.)

When we speak, we push sound waves out of our mouths, and they spread in all directions around us. If there's a listener nearby, those sound waves will enter that person's ear canal and press against the eardrum, setting off a process of auditory sensation and perception. Let's now turn to this process of converting sound waves into meaningful thoughts.

From Sound to Thought

Ask people what they hear with, and they'll say, "With your ears, of course." They'll probably also point to those gnarly bits of flesh and cartilage protruding from the sides of their head. They'll also be wrong.

If you were to cut off your outer ear (as Vincent van Gogh did), you wouldn't even notice a difference in hearing. (Please don't try this!) Instead, auditory sensation begins at the eardrum, where pressure waves in the air cause it to vibrate. On the other side, the middle ear mechanically amplifies these vibrations, which are then sent on to the inner ear, also known as the **cochlea**, which is *the organ of auditory sensation*. The cochlea is a fluid-filled tube that curls around itself like a snail shell. (In fact, cochlea is Latin for snail.)

Inside the cochlea is the **basilar membrane**, which is *a structure extending inside the length of the cochlea and dividing it in two*. As vibrations enter the cochlea, they are carried as waves through the fluid, traveling down one side of the basilar membrane and then back along the other side. The surface of the basilar membrane is covered with **hair cells**. These are *specialized cells of the basilar membrane that are sensitive to movements in the cochlear fluid*. The basilar membrane undulates in response to various passing frequencies, thus stimulating the hair cells.

Different hair cells are sensitive to different frequencies. Near the entrance to the cochlea are the hair cells sensitive to the highest frequency in the range of human hearing, about 20,000 Hz. As we proceed along the basilar membrane, we find hair cells sensitive to lower frequencies, down to the lower range of human hearing, around 20 Hz. Thus, the basilar membrane is configured like a piano keyboard going from

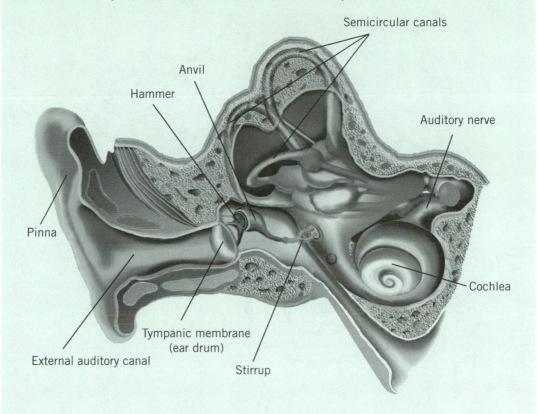

Figure 3.2 The Outer, Middle, and Inner Ear

The outer ear collects sound, the middle ear amplifies it, and the inner ear (cochlea) converts the sound waves into neural impulses that are sent to the brain via the auditory nerve.

right to left. *The progressive arrangement of cells sensitive to different frequencies* is known as **tonotopic organization**, and it is an organizing principle that extends all the way up to the primary auditory cortex.

When hair cells are activated, they produce electrical impulses that travel along the auditory nerve to the brain. Deafness due to damage of the hair cells can often be remediated by use of a **cochlear implant**, which is *an electronic device attached to an external microphone that directly stimulates the auditory nerve.* Cochlear implants do not restore hearing to normal levels; however, many cochlear implant recipients can learn to perceive speech using these devices (Szagun et al., 2012).

The amplitude of the sound wave, which we perceive as loudness, is encoded as neural signals in two ways. First, more hair cells are excited as the amplitude at their

Figure 3.3   Tonotopic Organization of the Basilar Membrane

Hair cells along the basilar membrane are organized according to the frequency they are sensitive to, with the highest frequency positioned at the opening of the cochlea.

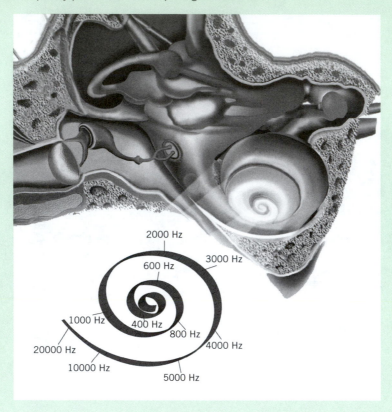

frequency increases. And second, these hair cells also fire neural impulses more rapidly when the amplitude is greater.

The transmission of auditory signals proceeds from the cochlea by way of the auditory nerve to the brainstem. There, the signals cross over to the other side, so that information from the left ear is first processed by the right side of the brain and information from the right ear is processed by the left side of the brain. This information, still organized tonotopically, is then transmitted to the primary auditory cortex in the temporal lobe.

The **primary auditory cortex**, also known as area A1, is *the region of the superior temporal lobe that does the initial processing of the input from the cochlea*. Like the basilar membrane, the primary auditory cortex is organized tonotopically, with higher frequencies being processed toward the back and lower frequencies toward the front.

Figure 3.4   Tonotopic Organization of the Auditory Cortex

The auditory cortex is tucked deep inside the lateral fissure on the surface that is still considered to be part of the temporal lobe. The primary auditory cortex is arranged in tonotopic fashion, just like the basilar membrane.

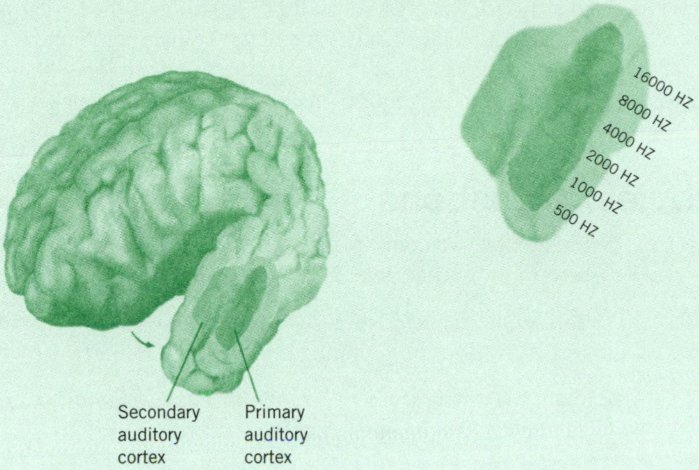

16000 Hz
8000 Hz
4000 Hz
2000 Hz
1000 Hz
500 Hz

Secondary auditory cortex

Primary auditory cortex

The secondary auditory cortex, which performs a more complex analysis, lies just below the primary auditory cortex. And in the left hemisphere, Wernicke's area, which processes incoming speech, is located just posterior to area A1.

The World of Sound

We live in a world awash with sound, waves of varying air pressure crashing into us from all sides. And yet from all this confusion we are able to extract a rich auditory impression of our surroundings. We recognize objects and events just by the way they sound (Gregg & Samuel, 2012), and we do so not just in pristine conditions but even when multiple sound sources are cluttering the "air waves." Likewise, we don't need quiet conditions for speech perception; rather, our brains are able to sift out speech sounds from other auditory input, even the speech sounds of other conversations we're not a part of.

Auditory perception unfolds along the dimension of time. Sounds are fleeting, with speech sounds being among the briefest of all auditory inputs that we can perceive. It is also the temporal nature of auditory perception that provides us with a sense of time (Iordanescu, Grabowecky, & Suzuki, 2013). Musicians use the beat of a drum or the strumming of a bass to mark time, and speech has its rhythms as well. As we'll see in the next section, one of the most difficult aspects of speech perception is that it takes place in real time, and in spite of the enormous complexity of the task, we humans proceed at a level of accuracy unparalleled by even our most powerful computers.

In Sum

Sound consists of pressure waves traveling through the air. The frequency of the sound wave is perceived as pitch, and the amplitude of the sound wave is perceived as loudness. Vibrating objects produce a fundamental frequency and several overtones, which combine to produce a complex but regularly repeating periodic sound wave. Friction and collision events produce aperiodic sound waves with no repeating patterns, and these are often perceived as noise. The organ of auditory sensation is the basilar membrane inside the cochlea, and the tonotopic organization of the basilar membrane is conveyed all the way to the primary auditory cortex in the superior temporal lobe. More complex auditory processing is performed in neighboring regions, including Wernicke's area.

Review Questions

1. What are the two components of a wave? How are these components of a sound wave perceived?

2. Describe the characteristics of a sound produced by a vibrating object. Why don't all vibrating objects sound alike?

3. Explain the difference between periodic and aperiodic sound. What kind of event produces each of these types?

4. Describe the process of auditory sensation. What is meant by tonotopic organization? How far up the auditory processing stream does this organization go?

5. Describe the cortical areas of auditory processing.

Thought Questions

1. In this section, you were presented with the simple story of auditory sensation, namely the theory that different locations along the basilar membrane encode different frequencies. However, the real world is more complex. There is also evidence that at least some sound frequencies are encoded by the firing rate of the hair cells. Given that the maximum firing rate of neurons, including the specialized hair cells, is about 1,000 cycles per second, explain why it is impossible for the nervous system to only encode sound frequency by firing rate. Speculate on why the nervous system might use both methods of encoding sound.

2. The region of the basilar membrane nearest the entrance to the cochlea codes for the highest frequencies we can hear. Given this fact, make some predictions about patterns of hearing loss as people get older or are exposed to extremely loud noises.

3. Given what you know about the auditory processing system, pinpoint the places where a breakdown could lead to hearing loss. In what circumstances might a hearing aid or cochlear implant be beneficial?

Google It! Sine Wave Speech

If you'd like to hear what a **sine wave** sounds like, search for clips on YouTube. You can also check out clips of **sine wave speech**, which is artificially produced speech composed entirely of sine waves. See if you can understand it. To find out what the world sounds like through a cochlear implant, search **cochlear implant simulation**.

SECTION 3.2: THE SPEECH STREAM

- Spectrograms allow us to visualize the structure of the speech stream.

- Prosody is the perceived modulation of a speaker's fundamental frequency; prosody serves a number of linguistic functions as well as conveying information about the speaker's emotional state.

- Vowels are identified by the relative distance of the first two formants, while consonants are largely identified by the formant transitions of preceding and following vowels.

- Speech sounds do not occupy discrete sections of the speech stream, but rather they overlap each other in a process known as coarticulation; speech sounds are perceived categorically, even though they are produced differently depending on the context.

- The speech perception system relies on context to fill in missing information from a speech stream that has been masked by ambient noise, in a process known as phonemic restoration.

- The McGurk effect illustrates how the speech perception system integrates auditory and visual information to decipher the speech stream.

In a written text, each letter is a discrete symbol, and each word is separated from its neighbors by spaces. The speech stream, however, doesn't consist of discrete phonemes and clear word boundaries. Instead, it comes at us as a continuous flow of ever-changing frequencies and amplitudes, and it's the job of the speech perception system to infer intended phonemes and word boundaries on the basis of multiple cues within the speech stream (Poeppel & Monahan, 2008).

The Speech Stream

Sound is fleeting, but we can study its structure systematically using a device called a spectrograph, which separates the sound wave into its component frequencies. Its output is called a **spectrogram**, which is *a chart displaying the pattern of frequencies in the speech stream and how those patterns change over time.*

When we look at a spectrogram of a speech sample, we see an alternation of aperiodic and periodic sounds. These roughly correspond to the consonants and vowels of the language. We also see brief sections of silence, but these aren't spaces between words. Rather, they're the marker of a particular type of consonant that's produced by momentarily blocking the air stream as it passes through the mouth. There are no spaces between words within an utterance. Somehow, the speech processing system interprets pauses in the speech stream as sounds and inserts pauses at word boundaries that aren't in the speech stream.

At the bottom of the spectrogram, we find the fundamental frequency of the speech. More accurately, this is the fundamental frequency of *the sound resulting from vibrations of the vocal folds as air is expelled from the lungs*. This **phonation** is the raw material that speech sounds are built from. Adult males generally have a fundamental frequency in the range of 75–150 Hz and adult females in the range of 150–300 Hz. If you are musically inclined, you'll have noticed that the average vocal range is about an octave, and that women's voices are roughly an octave higher than men's.

There's some leeway in the rate at which the vocal folds vibrate, resulting in *fluctuations of the fundamental frequency during an utterance*, and this variation in pitch is known as **prosody**, pronounced *PRAH-zuh-dee* (Komatsu, 2007). Both linguistic and emotional information is conveyed by prosody. For example, we modulate prosody to stress certain words, and we use intonational patterns to mark phrases in utterances. Furthermore, if you speak a language like Mandarin, you modulate your fundamental frequency on each vowel to produce tones.

Different languages have different rhythms and intonations, and we can often recognize a particular language by these characteristics even though we don't understand the language. In fact, newborn babies can distinguish their mother's language from other languages, presumably on the basis of prosody alone, since they can only hear the prosody of their mother's speech and not the individual speech sounds while in their mother's womb (Nazzi, Bertoncini, & Mehler, 1998).

We also convey emotion through prosody. When we speak with high levels of emotional arousal, such as when we feel fear, anger, or joy, the pitch of our voice increases, and when we experience a low level of arousal, such as when we are sad or tired, we speak with a lower pitch (Bachorowksi, 1999). Thus, the same expression can convey different meanings depending on the prosodic pattern accompanying it.

If we look at that periodic stretches of the speech stream, we see *bands of high-amplitude sound at certain frequencies above the fundamental frequency*. These bands are called **formants**, and they result from the fact that the shape of the vocal tract dampens certain harmonics and enhances others. The relative distance between the first and second formants in comparison with the fundamental frequency is what we use to distinguish vowels. Thus, the vowel "ah" sounds the same regardless of the speaker not because it is composed of the same set of pitches, but rather because it has the same pitch relationships regardless of the actual frequencies making up the formants (Ladefoged, 2001, 2006). We then use the higher formants to distinguish individual voices.

In addition to a vowel, a periodic stretch in the speech stream may also signal a **sonorant**. This is *a speech sound that usually serves as a consonant but sometimes as a vowel*, like *l*, *r*, *n*, and *m*. For instance, the first *l* in *little* acts like a consonant, while the second *l* acts like a vowel. (The final *e* is silent.) On the other hand, an aperiodic portion of the speech stream clearly indicates a consonant. We can divide these into two types. The first type is a **fricative**, which is *a consonant that is produced by constricting the airstream to create friction*. Hissing sounds like *s*, *sh*, and *f* are examples of fricatives, and they appear as broad bands of noise on the spectrogram. The second type is a **plosive**, which is *a consonant that is produced by momentarily blocking and then releasing the airstream*. Plosives are also known as stops. On the spectrogram, a plosive appears as a silence followed by a brief band noise that blends into the formants of the following vowel. Sounds such as *p*, *d*, and *t* are examples of plosives.

Table 3.1	Major Categories of Speech Sounds	
Periodic	Vowels	*I owe you a yo-yo.*
	Sonorants	bott*om*, butt*on*, bott*le*, butt*er*
Aperiodic	Fricatives	*sh*ow, *J*oe, *s*ue, *z*oo, *f*ew, *v*iew
	Plosives	*p*ot, *t*ot, *c*ot, bough*t*, *d*ot, go*t*

If you record the word *attitude* and analyze it with a spectrogram, you'll see three regions of periodic sound, each followed by a span of silence, with a brief pulse of noise at the end of the word. If you then play the recording while watching the cursor move across the spectrogram, you'll experience an interesting perceptual illusion. You'll hear the periodic stretches as the vowels *a*, *i*, and *u*. You'll also hear the first two silences as the two *t* consonants and the last silence as *d*. However, if you select one of these silent spaces and play it, you'll hear nothing. If you include just a snippet of the preceding or following vowel, though, you'll again hear the silence as a consonant.

In short, the speech processing system doesn't simply read out the sound patterns present in the speech stream. This is especially true in the case of consonants, which are recognizable not so much by the sounds they make but rather by the way they influence the quality of the surrounding vowels. *A modification of a formant due to a preceding or following consonant* is called a **formant transition**, and these transitions provide important cues for distinguishing consonants. Incidentally, if you just listen to a formant transition, all you'll hear is a chirp. In other words, the formant transition itself isn't the consonant; rather, it's the combination of brief silence followed by a transition into a steady-state formant that signals the consonant.

Figure 3.5 Spectrogram of the Word *Attitude*

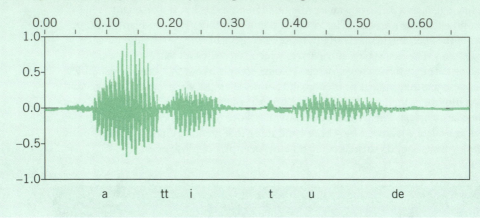

The high-energy segments are vowels, and the "silent" segments are consonants, which are only identified by the effects they have on the preceding and following vowels.

The Sound of Silence

Unlike printed letters on the page, which are clearly separated from each other, speech sounds smear into each other. This is known as **coarticulation**. This *process of overlapping phonemes in the speech stream* results from the fact that it takes time for the tongue, jaws, and lips to move from one position to another. However, coarticulation also increases the transmission rate of the speech signal; in other words, we can say more in less time by overlapping speech sounds.

Although they're nothing more than brief bits of silence, plosives are common consonants in English and in languages around the world. The plosive consonants in English are grouped into three pairs: *b* and *p*; *d* and *t*; and *g* and *k*. The three sets are distinguished from each other by the formant transitions they produce on neighboring vowels. For example, *b* and *p* produce similar formant transitions, and likewise with the other two pairs.

Now let's consider how consonant pairs like *b* and *p* are distinguished from each other. Hold your left hand against your throat and your right hand in front of your mouth. Slowly say *bah* and then *pah*. You should notice two things. First, there is more phonation, or vibration of the vocal cords, in the production of *bah* than *pah*. Second, you should get a greater puff of air with *pah* than with *bah*. *The puff of air accompanying the release of some plosives* is called **aspiration**. You'll get similar results if you try the pairs *dah-tah* and *gah-kah*. These two characteristics of phonation and aspiration—the buzz of the *b* and the puff of the *p*—are generally explained in terms of a phenomenon called **voice onset time**, which refers to *the difference in time between the release of a plosive consonant and the beginning of vocal fold vibration*. Voice onset time is often abbreviated as VOT.

When synthetic speech is used to create a continuum of voice onset times ranging from 0 to 50 milliseconds, native speakers of English do not perceive a series of syllables that gradually transition from *pa* to *ba*. Instead, they perceive a series of *pa* syllables followed by a series of *ba* syllables.

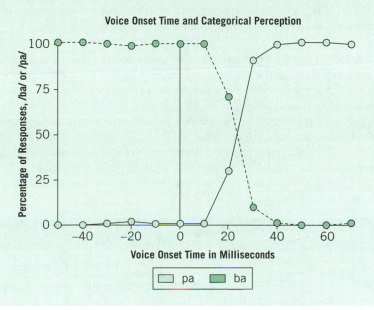

Voice Onset Time and Categorical Perception

Source: Wood (1976).

As bits of silence, plosives shouldn't be accompanied by phonation. And as stretches of periodic sound, vowels are expected to be accompanied by phonation. Yet the boundary between the consonant and the following vowel is fuzzy. The vocal folds can kick in right at the beginning of the formant transition, in which case you have early voice onset time, or else there can be a delay, in which case, at least in English, you can get a puff of air.

Using synthetic speech, it's possible to manipulate voice onset time, producing a continuum of syllables ranging from a clear *bah* with a zero millisecond voice onset time to a clear *pah* with a voice onset time of 100 milliseconds or more. Although the stimuli gradually transition from *bah* to *pah*, that's not how English speakers perceive the series. Instead of hearing a sequence going from *bah* to something in between and then to *pah*, they hear a set of perfectly good *bah*s followed by a set of perfectly good *pah*s. In other words, the speech processing system divides the VOT continuum into two discrete categories. Furthermore, the boundary between the two categories is quite consistent across speakers of English, although different languages place the boundary at different locations along the VOT continuum (Lisker & Abramson, 1964).

The process of experiencing continuously changing stimuli as belonging to two or more discrete sets is called **categorical perception**. Voice onset time is just one such characteristic of the speech stream that we perceive categorically, but there are also other dimensions along which we discriminate continuously changing speech sounds in categorical fashion (Liberman et al., 1961). Again using synthetic speech techniques, we can manipulate formant transitions to create a continuum of incrementally changing stimuli ranging from *bah* to *dah* to *gah*. In this case as well, we do not perceive any of the stimuli as being halfway between *bah* and *dah* or *dah* and *gah*. Rather, we hear a set of equally good *bahs* followed by a similar set each of *dahs* and *gahs*.

Originally, categorical perception was believed to be a unique characteristic of speech perception. However, it was soon understood as a general cognitive principle (Cross, Lane, & Sheppard, 1965). For example, we see a rainbow as a set of distinct bands of colors and not as a continuum, which in fact it is. Likewise, we perceive faces categorically, recognizing people as the same whether they are smiling or frowning or even if they've aged quite a few years (Hoonhorst et al., 2011; Keyes, 2012; Sauter, LeGuen, & Haun, 2011). Categorical perception is not restricted to the auditory and visual modes but extends to other modalities as well, such as touch (Gaißert et al., 2012). It even plays a role in higher-level processing, such as social perception (Sacco et al., 2011).

Figure 3.7   Formant Transitions

The steady-state portions of F1 and F2 represent the vowel sound *uh*. Consonants modify the shapes of the formants, creating the formant transitions we perceive as consonants. However, if you were to only listen to the formant transitions without the following vowel, you would hear a chirping sound instead of a consonant.

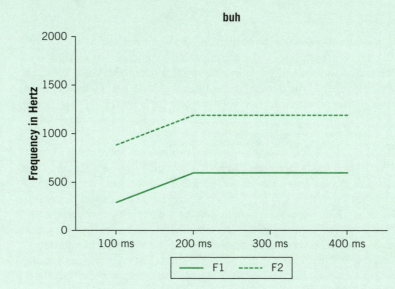

Simply put, categorical perception is one way our brains deal with the messiness of the real world. In actual speech, we don't have such precise control over voice onset time (Rothenberg, 2009), and so it's only reasonable that the speech processing system would impose categories on the messy input. And the input really is messy. We rarely speak to each other under pristine conditions, and there are plenty of occasions when the ambient noise overwhelms the speech signal. Just think about having a conversation at a large party, trying to talk over the din of clattering dishes and raucous laughter. When portions of the speech stream are blotted out by the noise, the speech processing system doesn't just leave these segments blank, it fills them in with its best guess of what should have been there. *The process of filling in missing segments of the speech stream with contextually appropriate material* is known as **phonemic restoration**.

Warren investigated the phonemic restoration effect with a series of experiments. In the first study (Warren, 1970), he recorded the sentence, splicing out the first s in *legislatures* to produce a gap:

> The state governors met with their respective legi*latures convening in the capital city.

When participants listened to this sentence, they noticed the gap and could tell which phoneme was missing. However, when Warren filled the gap with the sound of a cough, participants no longer noticed that the s was missing. Although they heard the cough, they couldn't identify its precise location, usually placing it either right before or right after *legislatures*.

In the second study, Warren and Warren (1970) modified the following sentence by splicing out the *wh* of *wheel*:

> It was found that the *eel was on the axle.

Again, when the gap was filled with a cough, participants said they heard the missing *wh*. The experimenters then cut off the word *axle* and replaced it with other words, such as *shoe*, to produce:

> It was found that the *eel was on the shoe.

But now they reported hearing the word *heel* when the gap was filled with a cough. The most surprising aspect of this result is that the context disambiguating the missing segment comes several words later. It appears that the speech processing system doesn't make phoneme-by-phoneme judgments of the speech stream. Rather, it seems to play a wait-and-see game, at least when the input is ambiguous or undecipherable.

Read My Lips

Until now, we've been discussing speech perception as if it operated strictly in the auditory mode. Sometimes we only have the auditory input available, as for example when we talk on the phone or around corners. But most speech is conducted face to face, and so it's only reasonable that the brain would also make use of visual input whenever available.

Psychologists used to assume that the senses operated independently of each other. But in recent years many researchers have come to agree with *the idea that the senses strongly interact with each other to produce our rich experience of the world*. This phenomenon is known as **multimodal perception**. One example of multimodal perception in the realm of speech perception is the McGurk effect.

The **McGurk effect** is *an artificially induced illusion in which the auditory information for one speech sound is combined with the visual information for another speech sound to produce the perception of a third speech sound* (McGurk & MacDonald, 1976). For example, we can audio record a person producing the sound bah and video record the same person producing the sound gah. If you only listen to the audio recording, you will perceive bah. And if you only watch the video recording, you will perceive gah. However, if you listen to the audio and watch the video at the same time, you will perceive dah. This is because dah is a speech sound halfway between bah and gah. Rather than relying solely on auditory input, the speech perception system apparently attempts to integrate the contradictory visual and auditory components to produce a compromise.

The McGurk effect demonstrates the importance of visual information in speech perception. Speech perception is a complex task that must be completed with split-second timing under less than ideal conditions. Hence, it only makes sense that the brain will make use of any and all information available to extract the speech stream from the surrounding noise and decipher it. What is also remarkable about the McGurk effect is that it continues to occur even when the perceiver is fully aware of what is going on. I have known about the McGurk effect since I was a graduate student, and yet, even after all these years, I still can't help but fall for the illusion. This suggests that the auditory and visual information are integrated at a very early stage in speech perception.

In Sum

Spectrograms provide a window to the structure of the speech stream. At the bottom we see the fundamental frequency of the vibrating vocal folds, and fluctuation in this frequency is perceived as prosody. Vowels appear on the spectrogram as parallel bands of high energy known as formants, and the relative position of the first two formants indicates the identity of that vowel. Consonants are largely detected by the effects they have on neighboring vowels. Speech sounds smear into each other in a process called coarticulation. The speech perception system employs a number of strategies to extract and decode the stream stream. Contextual cues are very important for filling in portions of the speech stream that were obliterated by ambient noise, and visual input about the movement of the speaker's lips and jaws is integrated into the processing of the speech stream.

Review Questions

1. What is prosody? What are the different kinds of information that prosody provides?

2. Describe the acoustic characteristics of vowels. How do we distinguish different vowels?

3. In this section, we met three classes of consonants: sonorants, fricatives, and plosives. What are the acoustic characteristics of each?

4. What is coarticulation? Why are formant transitions considered an example of coarticulation?

5. What is voice onset time? What is the role of aspiration and phonation in voice onset time?

6. What is categorical perception? What are some examples of categorical perception in language? What are some examples of categorical perception outside of language?

7. What is phonemic restoration? What is the McGurk effect? What do these two phenomena suggest about the workings of the speech perception system?

Thought Questions

1. In the McGurk effect, visual information overrides conflicting auditory information. Given that speech is an auditory phenomenon, why might the speech perception system give more credence to visual than auditory input when there is a discrepancy between the two?

2. If you are interested in trying out spectrograms for yourself, download Audacity, which is free, open source, cross-platform software for recording and editing sounds that includes a spectrogram function. Record different utterances and play back segments while looking at the spectrogram. Try the *attitude* example above to see how consonants can emerge from silence. If you have a good singing voice, or know someone who does, record the same utterance twice, once spoken and once sung. You can also record and analyze the sounds of animals and everyday objects. There's no end to the fun you can have with a spectrogram!

Google It! The McGurk Effect

Search YouTube for demonstrations of **phonemic restoration** and the **McGurk effect**. Recently, Discover Card ran a TV commercial based on the McGurk effect, which you can find by googling **frog protection**. Furthermore, **multimodal perception** is not limited to speech, nor is it limited to the auditory and visual modalities. Search online for other examples of multimodal perception, including the **rubber hand illusion**.

SECTION 3.3: DEVELOPMENT OF SPEECH PERCEPTION

- During the third trimester, a fetus can hear and respond to sounds in the environment, particularly its mother's voice; at birth, a newborn can already distinguish its mother's voice from other women's voices and its mother's language from other languages.

- Infant-directed speech is spoken with a higher fundamental frequency, a broader pitch range, and exaggerated intonation and stress patterns; these features attract the infant's attention and provide cues to speech stream segmentation.

- The prosodic bootstrapping hypothesis proposes that infants use intonation and stress patterns to infer phrase and word boundaries.

- According to the metrical segmentation strategy, both infants and adults tend to segment the speech stream at the onset of stressed syllables, at least in English.

- Transitional probabilities provide a fairly reliable cue to word boundaries that even young infants are sensitive to.

- Infants are born with the ability to discriminate most speech sounds, and through a process known as perceptual narrowing they acquire the phonetic categories of the language they are learning during the first year of life.

Imagine you were suddenly transported to an alien civilization on another planet. You observe that the inhabitants appear to communicate by producing sequences of sounds, and yet you have no idea what they are trying to say. Is there any way to decipher their code just by listening to it? This is exactly the situation every human infant is confronted with.

Language Learning in the Womb

Language learning begins in the womb, especially during the third trimester, which extends from week 28 until birth at week 38 or later. During this time, the fetus can hear and respond to sounds in the environment. The mother's voice dominates in the womb, but the voices of others around her also carry to the fetus. These voices are muffled, as the higher frequencies that we use to discriminate speech sounds are largely filtered out. However, the lower frequencies, which carry prosody, do reach the fetus. The fetus's experience is much like listening to a conversation in another room. You can distinguish male from female voices, and you can judge emotional content from intonational patterns, but you can't make out the words.

Much of the research on prenatal learning has used measurements of fetal heartbeat. Near-term fetuses tend to reduce their heart rate when they hear a novel auditory stimulus such as a male or female voice uttering the same sentence (Lecanuet et al.,

Figure 3.8   Photo of Newborn Infant

This newborn already knows a lot about the language it will speak one day.

Source: ©iStockphoto.com/arekmalang.

1992). Thus, we can use changes in heart rate to infer whether the fetus can distinguish between a familiar and a novel auditory stimulus. For example, near-term fetuses can discriminate between two low piano notes (D4 and C5) that are within the range of the fundamental frequency and first formant of the normal human voice (Lecanuet et al., 2000). The ability to discriminate low-frequency tones likely accounts, at least in part, for the ability of third-trimester fetuses to distinguish their mother's recorded voice from other women's voices and their mother's language (English) from another language (Mandarin) (Kisilevsky et al., 2009).

By observing changes in heart rate, we can also see that fetuses demonstrate recognition of previous auditory experiences during the last trimester (Krueger et al., 2004). For instance, when mothers recited a short nursery rhyme once a day during weeks 33 to 37, the fetuses exhibited cardiac deceleration to the familiar rhyme but not to a novel rhyme when tested in week 38 (DeCasper et al., 1994). Notice in this case that the deceleration was elicited by the familiar, not unfamiliar, stimulus. However, the key in interpreting fetal and infant research is not to focus on the response itself but rather whether the familiar and novel stimuli elicit different responses.

Furthermore, there's evidence that experiences within the womb are still remembered after birth. Fetuses that were repeatedly exposed to a particular melodic contour during weeks 35–37 demonstrated recognition of that melody six weeks later at one month after birth (Granier-Deferre et al., 2011). Likewise, we've already seen that fetuses can distinguish their mothers' voices from other women's, and they continue to do so as newborns, once again demonstrating that experiences in the womb affect behavior after birth (DeCasper & Fifer, 1980).

Experiences in the womb can even shape behavior after birth. Newborn babies cry in melodic and intensity contours that parallel those of their mother's language. For example, words in French are usually produced with a rising intonation and stress on the last syllable, while words in German are usually produced with a falling intonation and stress on the first syllable. Based on an acoustic analysis, researchers found that French newborns tended to cry with a rising melodic contour and German newborns with a falling contour (Mampe et al., 2009). Thus, fetuses not only remember auditory experiences in the womb, they also mimic them as newborns.

Born Yesterday

We can determine whether newborns perceive differences in auditory stimuli by using the **high-amplitude sucking technique**. This is *an experimental procedure that measures the frequency of an infant's sucking on a non-nutritive nipple*, and it is often referred to as HAS. If the sucking rate changes when a new stimulus is presented, we infer that the infant perceived the difference. Infants can also be trained to suck at particular rates to produce stimuli, and thus we can even determine which sounds infants prefer to hear. Once an infant is able to turn its head, the **conditioned head turn technique** is used instead. This is *an experimental method that trains the infant to turn its head in a particular direction when it detects a change in the auditory stimulus*. Using these and similar methods, developmental psychologists can explore what's going on in the minds of babies.

Overwhelmingly, newborns prefer the sound of their mother's voice and language to other voices and languages. To mimic the quality of sound in the womb, Spence and DeCasper (1987) filtered recordings of women's voices to remove higher frequencies. Newborns responded the same to filtered and unfiltered versions of their mother's voice but differently to filtered and unfiltered versions of another woman's voice. This suggests that the neonates recognize their mother's voice as the same one they heard in the womb, even though the sound quality is different.

Even when they're not listening to their mother's voice, newborns prefer listening to another woman speaking mom's language than a different language. Four-day-old French infants prefer hearing a woman speaking French to the same woman speaking Russian (Mehler et al., 1988). To demonstrate that the French utterances were not inherently more pleasing to listen to than the Russian utterances, the researchers performed the same experiment with a group of American infants, who showed no preference for either language sample.

Newborns also have a preference for speech passages that were familiar to them in the womb. DeCasper and Spence (1986) asked mothers to read a particular Dr. Suess story out loud each day during the last three weeks of pregnancy. After birth, the infants preferred hearing that story to a different story also read by their mothers. Presumably, the infants recognize the particular prosodic patterns of different stories.

In addition to prosodic patterns, fetuses also appear to be picking up on some of the phonetic qualities of their mother's language. Newborns within days of birth are already able to recognize the vowel sounds of their mother's language. When English and Swedish newborns heard similar vowel sounds, they produced more sucking for the vowel sound in their mother's language than for the one that was not (Moon, Lagercrantz, & Kuhl, 2013). These results also suggest that at least some of the higher frequency formants of the mother's voice are audible to the fetus.

Baby Talk

Prosody is the foundation on which spoken language is based, and this foundation is already laid before birth. The adults in the baby's life, especially the mother, take advantage of this and use prosody to teach the baby other aspects of the language.

Especially right after birth, mother and baby spend a lot of time together, gazing into each other's eyes and exchanging facial expressions and vocalizations. These behaviors are vital for building the tight emotional bond between mother and child, but they also convey lessons about language use (Snow, 1977). Even when the mother uses meaningless coos, she and the infant take turns, and in this way the infant learns the basic rules of conversation and social interaction (Rochat, Querido, & Striano, 1999). Cross-culturally, mothers use similar pitch contours in the same interactional caregiving

Figure 3.9   Mother and Baby

Language learning takes place in intimate interactions like this, in which a mother and baby engage in conversation-like behavior even before the child can speak.

Source: ©iStockphoto.com/kordovsky.

contexts, such as soothing, turn taking, and the modeling of new words and actions (Papoušek, Papoušek, & Symmes, 1991), suggesting a deep evolutionary history for these behaviors.

When talking with their infants, mothers tend to speak in short, repetitive utterances with exaggerated acoustic features. They speak with a higher fundamental frequency and use a broader range of frequencies than they do in normal conversation. Moms also exaggerate stress contrasts and vowel length (Fernald & Kuhl, 1987). As we learned in Chapter 1, the stylized speech that mothers use when talking with their infants is often referred to as motherese. However, mothers aren't the only ones to talk this way with infants. Other family members, including siblings, fathers, and grandparents, tend to speak to the infant this way, and even non-family members visiting the newborn will speak to the baby in motherese. Thus, motherese is also known caregiver speech or **infant-directed speech**, emphasizing the fact that it is *a manner of speaking to infants that attracts their attention and helps them learn language*.

Infant-directed speech has been observed in a wide range of languages, suggesting that it's universal, or at least nearly so (Grieser & Kuhl, 1988). While higher pitch and larger range may be universal characteristics of motherese, different languages exhibit particular intonational patterns. Recall that newborns are already able to distinguish their mother's language from other languages on the basis of prosodic cues, and they can distinguish infant-directed speech exhibiting the intonational patterns of their mother's language from that of a novel language (Mastropieri & Turkewitz, 1999). Incidentally, speech directed at dogs and other pets has essentially the same acoustic properties as motherese (Hirsh-Pasek & Treiman, 1982).

Infants are attracted to the acoustic qualities of infant-directed speech and prefer it to adult-directed speech (Fernald, 1985). Newborns will direct their gaze toward their mother's voice even when she is using adult-directed speech, but they prefer her to use infant-directed speech, and they'll only pay attention to other adults when they are talking in motherese (Cooper et al., 1997).

The higher pitch of the speaker's voice catches the newborn's attention (Fernald & Kuhl, 1987), but other features of infant-directed speech help the infant learn the language. Infant-directed speech provides the infant with a model of the language in which features are clearer and more exaggerated than in adult-directed speech, drawing the infant's attention to those aspects of the language that are important for learning. Research has shown a relationship between the consistent use of motherese and the infant's progress in developing speech perception skills (Liu, Kuhl, & Tsao, 2003). Furthermore, infants of depressed mothers who do not consistently use infant-directed speech with them show delays in speech perception (Kaplan et al., 2002). There is also evidence to suggest that newborns exposed to motherese before birth due to having an older sibling at home are better able to discriminate vowel sounds compared with newborns only exposed to infant-directed speech after birth (Tian et al., 2011).

The observation that prosodic features of a language provide cues to syntactic structure has led to the **prosodic bootstrapping** hypothesis (Fernald & McRoberts, 1996). This is *a hypothesis proposing that infants use intonation and stress patterns to infer phrase and word boundaries*. The term *bootstrapping* comes from the metaphor of lifting yourself up by your own bootstraps to describe the act of solving a difficult problem without help from others.

There's plenty of evidence to support the notion of prosodic bootstrapping, especially in connection with the exaggerated prosody of infant-directed speech. Infants are sensitive to indicators of phrase boundaries in motherese but not adult-directed speech (Kemler Nelson et al., 1989). By six months of age, infants can use prosodic patterns to infer phrase structure, and they prefer listening to speech with prosodic contours that match phrasal structure (Soderstrom et al., 2003). And in an ERP study, five-month-old German infants were found to be sensitive to acoustic cues to phrase boundaries, such as changes in pitch and vowel duration (Männel & Friederici, 2009). However, as Fernald and McRoberts (1996) point out, prosodic cues to syntax are not all that reliable, and prosodic bootstrapping is just one of many tools the infant brings to the task of segmenting the speech stream.

I've Got Rhythm

English has a characteristic rhythmic pattern of alternating stressed and unstressed syllables. Stressed syllables typically have long or complex vowel sounds, while unstressed syllables have reduced or shortened vowels. Notice how the vowel sounds change in the related words *photograph* and *photography* as the stress shifts from the first to the second syllable. Furthermore, most multisyllabic words in English begin on a stressed syllable. The **metrical segmentation strategy** is *a rule-of-thumb both infants and adults use in segmenting the speech stream by assuming English words begin on a stressed syllable* (Cutler & Norris, 1988; Norris, McQueen, & Cutler, 1995).

Using a conditioned head turning procedure, Morgan (1996) presented two-syllable sequences to six- and nine-month-olds. Half of these sequences were stressed on the first syllable, and half were stressed on the second syllable. The six-month-olds showed no preference for either pattern, but the nine-month-olds preferred the words with initial stress, suggesting they'd adopted the metrical segmentation strategy.

Stress in English combines the acoustic properties of falling pitch, vowel duration, and increased amplitude. This means that infants don't need to identify syllables to use the metrical segmentation strategy. Rather they can rely on prosody and vowel quality—which they're already sensitive to at birth—as a guide to dividing up the speech stream (Cairns et al., 1997; Cutler & Mehler, 1993). Results of experiments using resynthesized speech suggest that fundamental frequency variation and vowel quality are the acoustic cues for stress-based segmentation (Spitzer, Liss, & Mattys, 2007).

Further evidence that English-learning infants employ the metrical segmentation strategy comes from observations of language production in toddlers, who'll frequently impose a stressed-unstressed pattern on words that are exceptions. It's not uncommon for two-year-olds to render a name like *Amanda* as *Manda*, and for that matter, even adults will shorten the name to *Mandy*. Likewise, youngsters will often pronounce a word like *spaghetti* as *sketti*.

It's not at all clear to what extent the metrical segmentation strategy is universal. In stress-based languages like English, Dutch, or German, the metrical segmentation strategy is an effective guide to inferring word boundaries. French, on the other hand, tends to stress the last syllable of each word or phrase (Goetry & Kolinsky, 2000). Thus, infants cannot rely solely on this strategy, but instead they can only use it in conjunction with other segmentation cues in the speech stream.

What's Coming Next

The speech stream consists of regular, predictable patterns, especially in the case of highly repetitive motherese, and there are statistical cues that indicate likely word boundaries. Take, for example, the phrase *pretty baby*, something the infant no doubt hears a lot. Considering the limited vocabulary the infant is exposed to, it will soon learn that once it hears the syllable *pret*, the syllable *ty* is sure to follow. But what comes next is any infant's guess. It could be *baby*, *doggy*, *picture*, or a host of other pretty things. Yet, once the infant hears the syllable *ba*, it knows *by* is coming next.

The likelihood that a particular event will occur next given the current event is known as its **transitional probability**. In the realm of infant-directed speech, the transitional probability from *pret* to *ty* is very high, and likewise from *ba* to *by*. But the transitional probability from *ty* to *ba* is low. Thus, transitional probability provides a fairly reliable cue to word boundaries.

To test whether infants can use transitional probabilities to segment a speech stream, Saffran, Aslin, and Newport (1996) created a simple artificial language such that the transitional probabilities within words was 100% and between words was 33%. They produced a continuous monotone speech stream of this language, using a speech synthesizer to remove all other cues to word boundaries, such as stress, rhythm, and intonation. After just two minutes of exposure to this speech stream, eight-month-old infants were able to segment the speech stream on the basis of transitional probabilities.

Follow-up studies have shown that infants as young as six months use statistical cues to infer word boundaries and that they don't consider rhythmic cues until around nine months of age (Hay & Saffran, 2012). This suggests that syllable-level transitional probabilities help infants identify other cues to word boundaries (Sahni, Seidenberg, & Saffran, 2010). By nine months, English-learning infants will rely on rhythmic cues to segment the speech stream even when the transitional probabilities are contradictory (Thiessen & Saffran, 2003). In short, infants use transitional probabilities to make an initial segmentation of the speech stream, and then they detect rhythm patterns within those segments that become even more powerful cues to word boundaries.

It's also important to note that statistical learning is not language-specific (Saffran et al., 1999). Rather, it's a general-purpose learning mechanism that we use to detect regularities in both the auditory and visual modes (Baldwin et al., 2008; Saffran & Thiessen, 2007). Statistical learning probably underlies much of our ability to learn complex behaviors.

In addition to statistical and rhythmic cues, infants are also able to detect more complex patterns in the speech stream. When seven-month-old infants are exposed to an artificial speech stream consisting of a repeating pattern such as *lee lee fah*, they later showed a preference for a novel pattern like *boo dee boo* as opposed to the familiar pattern *boo boo dee* (Marcus et al., 1999). Note that it's not the syllable sequences per se but rather the abstract pattern that the infants have learned. Again, this ability to learn patterns is not limited to language but extends to other auditory and visual inputs as well (Saffran et al., 2007).

Narrowing Down

As adults, we perceive speech sounds in a categorical fashion, and so the intuitive view is that infants gradually develop an ability to discriminate speech sounds during the first year of life. However, research over the last four decades shows that this process instead runs in reverse. That is, infants come into the world with the ability to discriminate nearly all possible speech sounds, and as they interact with their caregivers they learn which distinctions are important for the language they're acquiring.

Infants as young as a month of age already exhibit categorical perception of consonants that differ on a number of dimensions (Eimas, 1974, 1975; Eimas et al., 1971). They're even sensitive to sound pairs that are perceived as the same consonant by adult speakers of the language they're learning (Streeter, 1976). For example, seven-month-old English-learning infants are able to discriminate two contrast pairs that occur in Hindi but not English, performing the same as Hindi-speaking adults. English-speaking adults, on the other hand, can't discriminate these sound pairs (Werker, Gilbert, & Humphrey, 1981). By four years of age, English speaking children can no longer discriminate these contrasts, even though four-year-old Hindi speaking children can (Werker & Tees, 1983).

Infants sort out vowel categories earlier than they do consonants. By six months of age, infants learning English or Swedish already categorize vowel sounds according to the phonetic categories of the language they are learning (Kuhl et al., 1992). At this same age, Japanese infants can still perceive the *l-r* contrast of English. However, by twelve months, they behave like Japanese-speaking adults and categorize *l* and *r* as the same phoneme (Kuhl et al., 2006).

Although tones are notoriously hard for adult learners of Chinese to master, four-month-old English-learning infants have no difficulty discriminating them, although they lose this ability by nine months of age (Yeung, Chen, & Werker, 2013).

Furthermore, infants learn the tonal categories of their language even earlier than they do the vowel categories. Although Mandarin and Cantonese are classified as dialects of Chinese, they are mutually unintelligible and have different tonal systems. By four months of age, Cantonese and Mandarin learners perceive tones according to the language they're learning.

Thus, it appears that infants acquire some native-language speech categories before others (Yeung et al., 2013). By five months of age, infants have worked out the stress and tonal patterns of their language. They sort out the vowel categories of their language by eight months and the consonant categories by the end of their first year.

In short, infants start out with the ability to discriminate speech contrasts in languages they've never heard before, but within the first year of life they lose this ability and can only discriminate the contrasts in the language they are learning (Werker & Tees, 2002). This phenomenon is an example of **perceptual narrowing**, which is *the process of transitioning from more universal or unconstrained perceptual abilities to those that are more narrow or constrained*. Perceptual narrowing is not limited to the development of phonemic categories in infants but rather is a more general learning mechanism (Cashon & DeNicola, 2011).

The perceptual narrowing of phonetic categories is aided by a process known as **distributional learning**, which is *the tracking of the frequency and location of various sounds in the speech stream* (Werker, Yeung, & Yoshida, 2012). As infants make note of how frequently and in what contexts various speech sounds occur, they reorganize their phonetic perception into the categories of the language they are learning (Yoshida et al., 2010). Distributional learning is also a domain-general process, and it isn't a uniquely human ability either, since even rats can be trained to distinguish human speech categories through distributional learning (Pons, 2006).

Putting the Pieces Together

A picture is now beginning to emerge of how infants learn to decipher the speech stream during their first year of life. It's not a simple or singular process, but rather it involves using various learning mechanisms to crack the code. For example, the statistical learning of transitional probabilities allows very young infants to make a rough-and-ready segmentation of the speech stream, and they can use distributional learning to detect stress and pitch patterns that can further help them to detect word and phrase boundaries (Thiessen, Kronstein, & Hufnagle, 2012).

Furthermore, it's now clear that language learning is a social process. Perceptual narrowing results from a reorganization of the brain as it adapts to local conditions, and social interaction is an essential factor driving this process (Kuhl, 2010). Through face-to-face interactions with caregivers, infants learn which categories are socially and ecologically relevant (Lewkowicz & Ghazanfar, 2009). Thus, gaze and infant-directed speech are best viewed as a joint experience between the infant and the caregiver that drives the development of social skills, including language (Guellai & Streri, 2011). Furthermore, visual experiences during face-to-face interactions with caregivers also play an important role in the perceptual narrowing of phonetic categories (Pons et al., 2009). Given that the acquisition of speech perception is a multimodal process involving both hearing and vision, it's not at all surprising that phenomena like the McGurk effect are so powerful. After all, we've been reading lips all our lives.

In Sum

Language learning begins in the womb as third-trimester fetuses listen and respond to sounds in the environment, especially their mother's voice. As a result, newborn babies can distinguish their mother's voice from other women's voices and their mother's language from other languages. Because infant-directed speech is spoken with a higher fundamental frequency, broader range of pitch, and exaggerated intonation and stress patterns, it attracts the infant's attention and provides cues to speech stream segmentation. The prosodic bootstrapping hypothesis proposed that infants pay attention to intonation and stress patterns to make inferences about word and phrase boundaries. Likewise, the metrical segmentation strategy proposes that both infants and adults tend to segment the speech stream before stressed syllables, at least in English. Even young infants are sensitive to transitional probabilities, which provide a fairly reliable cue to word boundaries. Although young infants can discriminate almost all possible speech sounds, they lose this ability by the first year of life as they learn the categories that are important for their language.

Review Questions

1. What can the fetus hear in the womb? What effect do these prenatal auditory experiences have on the newborn?

2. Describe the language perception abilities of newborns. How do they accomplish this?

3. What are the characteristics of infant-directed speech that help the newborn segment the speech stream? What is the prosodic bootstrapping hypothesis?

4. Explain the metrical segmentation strategy. In what sense is it a general language perception process and not just a language learning device?

5. What are transitional probabilities, and how do they help the infant segment the speech stream?

6. What is perceptual narrowing, and how does it guide the infant's formation of phonetic categories?

Thought Questions

1. The ability to detect transitional probabilities in sequences of events isn't limited to speech perception but rather is a general learning mechanism. Can you think of other complex human behaviors that could be learned by detecting transitional probabilities?

2. Perceptual narrowing through distributional learning is also a general process that isn't limited to language acquisition. Can you come up with some other examples of perceptual narrowing as the infant learns about the world? Is perceptual narrowing strictly a learning process for infants and children, or might even adults engage in this process? (Hint: If you've had a class in social psychology, try evaluating the research on stereotypes and biases in terms of perceptual narrowing.)

3. In what sense is spoken language acquisition a multimodal process? In what sense is it a social process?

Google It! Infant Speech Discrimination

If you're interested in learning more about the techniques that are used to study infant language development, search for articles and videos on **infant speech discrimination** and the **conditioned head turn technique**. You can also learn more about the experimental techniques used by developmental psychologists such as **Janet Werker**, **Pat Kuhl**, and **Jenny Saffran**, whose work we reviewed in this section.

SECTION 3.4: THEORIES OF SPEECH PERCEPTION

- Theories of speech perception need to explain the lack of invariance problem, meaning that there is no reliable correspondence between the acoustic signal and the perceived speech sound.

- Motor theory overcomes the lack of invariance problem by proposing that the object of speech perception is not the acoustic signal but rather the intended vocal gesture.

- Influenced by the theories of Chomsky and Fodor, motor theory argued that speech is special, in that it is processed by innate dedicated modules that are separate from general auditory perception.

- Ample research has shown that nonhuman animals perceive speech sounds in much the same way as humans do, forcing motor theorists to forsake the position that speech is special.

- General auditory approaches to speech perception overcome the lack of invariance by suggesting we make use of contextual cues, including information from other senses, to make reasoned inferences about the message conveyed in the auditory signal.
- The discovery of mirror neurons, which are active both when performing and perceiving an action, has lent support to a new version of motor theory known as direct realism.

Our conscious experience of the speech stream is a sequence of speech sounds grouped into words and phrases, but we've already seen that this is an illusion. There are no spaces between words, and the phonemes we perceive as separate entities are in fact overlapping and blurred into each other. Furthermore, the acoustic shape of a phoneme can be quite different depending the other phonemes surrounding it. *The observation that there is no reliable relationship between a phoneme and the acoustic signal* is known as **lack of invariance**, and so the problem that theories of speech perception need to explain is how we're able to extract the original speech sounds from the speech stream.

Motor Theory

After World War II, Alvin Liberman and his colleagues at Haskins Laboratories in Connecticut were trying to build a machine that could read to the blind (Liberman, 1996). The machine, known as Pattern Playback, failed to produce a synthetic speech stream at a rate that was intelligible, but in the process Liberman and his colleagues made important discoveries about the nature of speech. They quickly abandoned their naive notion of speech as consisting of an acoustic alphabet as they learned about coarticulation and the lack of invariance. And instead of using Pattern Playback as a reading machine, they used it to produce stimuli for experiments to test hypotheses about speech perception (Cooper, Liberman, & Borst, 1950).

These early experiments led Liberman and his colleagues to develop **motor theory** (Liberman, 1957). This is *a theory of speech perception that proposes people perceive speech by inferring the movements of the vocal tract that produced those sounds instead of by analyzing the speech stream into phonemes* (Galantucci, Fowler, & Turvey, 2006). In other words, we comprehend speech by imagining how we would make the sounds we're hearing. Thus, motor theory proposes a tight coupling between the perceptual and motor systems of speech.

The development of motor theory predates the advent of psycholinguistics as an independent field, and by tracing its history we can also get a good sense of how the science of language has progressed over the last half century. Liberman was trained in the dominant behaviorist paradigm of his day, and at first he assumed that this coupling between speech perception and motor systems developed as infants mimic the speech they hear around them (Liberman, 1957).

In the 1960s, psychology experienced a shift from behaviorism to cognitive psychology. The budding field of psycholinguistics was at the vanguard of the cognitive revolution, and Chomsky's (1959) review of Skinner's (1957) book *Verbal Behavior* is often seen as its opening shot. In this review, Chomsky demonstrated that Skinner's explanation of language acquisition in terms of operant condition was not supported by the data. Instead, Chomsky advocated for the position of **nativism**, which is *the view that behavior is mainly shaped by natural selection and thus encoded in our genes.*

In particular, Chomsky argued for a **language acquisition device**, which he viewed as *a specialized set of processing units in the brain that guides the rapid development of language in human infants.* The finding by Eimas and his colleagues that very young infants could already detect most phonetic contrasts lent credence to the nativist position (Eimas et al., 1971). Liberman and his partners at Haskins revised motor theory in line with the new cognitive paradigm (Liberman et al., 1967). In other words, the motor theory now viewed speech perception and speech production as linked not because of imitation in childhood but rather because the two processes had evolved together.

In the cognitive worldview, the brain-as-computer metaphor guided research. Computers are built out of processing modules, and so it was thought that the brain must be similarly structured. (Strictly speaking, cognitive psychologists study the mind, not the brain, but it's generally assumed that mind arises from brain activity.) In the 1980s, the concept of modularity gained currency. According to Fodor (1983), a **module** is *a dedicated neural system that has evolved to perform a specific function.* Fodor proposed that the brain was not a general purpose information processor but rather was built up from numerous modules, each performing its task independently of the others.

By this time, evidence from experiments was suggesting that speech perception operated differently from general auditory perception. For example, formant transitions, as produced in isolation using the Pattern Playback machine, sound like chirps. Yet, when produced in conjunction with the formants of following vowels, they sound like consonants (Mann & Liberman, 1983). Thus, Liberman and his colleagues revised motor theory again, this time to view the speech perception system as a phonetic module separate from the general auditory system. What made the phonetic module different from general audition was that speech perception operated through the motor system whereas the perception of other sounds did not.

Around this same time, Liberman (1982, 1996) and his associates began arguing that **speech is special**. This is *the view that speech perception is a distinct cognitive module that operates independently of and differently from other perceptual systems.* There were several reasons for taking this position. First, speech perception and production were viewed as uniquely human abilities, products of a long evolutionary history. Second, the speech perception module was believed to function separately from the auditory perception module, even though both processes started with the same acoustic input. Third, speech perception was viewed as special because it, unlike general auditory perception, was processed via the motor system. And fourth, the objects of speech perception were not the speech sounds themselves but rather the intended vocal tract gestures.

General Auditory Framework

The claim that speech was special was challenged by researchers working in the **general auditory framework**. These researchers proceed under *the assumption that speech perception operates by means of the same mechanisms that have evolved in humans and other animals to perceive environmental sounds* (Diehl, Lotto, & Holt, 2004). General auditory theorists argue against motor theory mainly by pointing out examples of speech perception without the ability to produce speech (Massaro & Chen, 2008).

The first line of evidence against motor theory is human infant speech perception. Human infants are born with the ability to discriminate nearly all possible speech sounds, yet they don't begin speaking until a year later. General auditory theorists argue that infants have this ability because human languages only make sound distinctions that the auditory system is already sensitive to (Diehl et al., 2004). We've already covered the evidence for human infant speech perception in Section 3.3, so there's no need to repeat it here.

Ironically, motor theorists also view human infant speech perception as support for their theory, especially the claim that speech perception involves an innate module. That is, motor theorists maintain that the speech perception-production system is hardwired into the brain and guides the development of language-specific skills in both perception and production during the first years of life. At this point, it's good to remind ourselves of the blind monks and the elephant. Evidence can only be interpreted within the framework of a theory, and so the facts on human infant speech perception are unlikely to resolve this debate.

The second line of evidence against motor theory comes from observations of speech perception in nonhuman animals. Kuhl and Miller (1975, 1978) found that chinchillas could be trained to respond differently to the syllables *da* and *ta*. When the chinchillas were presented with a set of synthetic speech stimuli ranging along a voice onset time (VOT) continuum from *da* to *ta*, they exhibited the same categorical perception as human infants. Since there's no reason to believe chinchillas have an innate speech perception module, their categorical perception of these two syllables must have resulted from general auditory abilities. And if general auditory processes are sufficient to produce categorical perception of speech sounds in chinchillas, then there's no reason to posit a special speech perception module in humans.

The chinchilla studies were soon followed by other reports of nonhuman animals exhibiting human-like speech perception. Kuhl and Padden (1982) found that macaque monkeys also perceived synthetic VOT continua categorically, showing the same phoneme boundary effect for the voiced-voiceless pairs *ba-pa*, *da-ta*, and

Figure 3.10   A Chinchilla

Chinchillas categorically perceive voice onset time just like humans. Does that mean that the categorical perception of speech sounds is innate, learned, or based on a more general cognitive principle?

Source: ©iStockphoto.com/ GlobalP.

ga-ka as do human infants. Birds such as parakeets and zebra finches also exhibit human-like categorization of speech sounds (Dooling, Best, & Brown, 1995; Kluender et al., 1998).

Perceptual compensation for coarticulation is another supposed function of the speech perception module, and yet Japanese quail perform similarly to humans on this task as well. Recall that consonants are pronounced differently depending on the sounds that precede and follow them. For example, the initial consonant of the syllable *dee* has different formant transitions from the initial consonant of *doo*, but we perceive the two as the same sound. Kluender and colleagues trained Japanese quail to peck different keys when they heard the consonants *b*, *d*, or *g* followed by four different vowels (Kluender, Diehl, & Killeen, 1987). The quail were then able to respond in the correct manner when they heard these consonants followed by eight other novel vowels. Since no invariant feature or pattern in the acoustic input could be used to identify these consonants, the researchers concluded that the quail perceived these consonants as abstract categories in the same way that humans do. Later research found that Japanese quail also compensate for the coarticulatory effects of preceding sounds in much the same way that humans do (Lotto, Kluender, & Holt, 1997).

Researchers working in the general auditory framework generally take the position that speech processing is such a complicated task that humans take advantage of whatever information is available, no matter how imperfect, to tackle the problem. In this view, speech perception doesn't just work like auditory perception, it works like

Figure 3.11 Japanese Macaques

Like humans, Japanese macaques perceive speech sounds categorically. And like humans, they also enjoy a good soak in the hot spring.

Source: ©iStockphoto.com/cameranew.

perception in general. One example of this approach is the **fuzzy-logical model of perception**, which is *a theory that proposes we arrive at perceptual decisions by matching the relative goodness of various sensory inputs against the values of particular prototypes stored in memory* (Massaro, 1989; Massaro & Chen, 2008; Oden & Massaro, 1978). In this approach, lack of invariance isn't a problem, because contextual cues are also taken into account. Information from other modalities is also considered when available. For example, the McGurk effect can be explained, in this view, as an averaging of the auditory and visual inputs.

Direct Realism

In recent years, motor theory has made a comeback, with Carol Fowler, also of Haskins Laboratories, as its main proponent. This new version of motor theory is also known as **direct realism**, because it's based on Gibson's (1979) *theory that we have direct awareness of the world because the sensory input is sufficiently rich for us to completely recover the object of perception.* Thus, direct realism is in complete opposition to general auditory approaches such as the fuzzy-logical model, which proposes that perception works by making inferences about the external world based on ambiguous sensory input.

One particular way in which direct realism differs from earlier motor theory is that it rejects the idea that speech is special (Galantucci et al., 2006). Thus, evidence of nonhuman speech perception is no longer a problem for the theory. Direct realism does keep the claim of motor theory that speech processing involves perceiving gestures, not acoustic signals. It's in this sense that the new motor theory is in line with Gibson's views on direct perception. However, there is a subtle theoretical distinction between the old and new versions of motor theory. In the original theory, the object of perception was intended gestures, but in the new theory it's the actual gestures. In either case, this position is intended to deal with the problem of invariance. Direct realism also holds on to the claim that the motor system is involved in the perception of speech. But now proponents can garner biological support for this claim.

The discovery of mirror neurons in monkey brains late in the twentieth century provided biological evidence for a tight linkage between perception and action (Rizzolatti et al., 1988; Rizzolatti & Craighero, 2004). **Mirror neurons** are *neurons in the brains of primates that fire not only when the primate performs an action but also when it observes somebody else performing that action*. Testing for mirror neurons involves inserting electrodes into the brain, which isn't ethical in humans; but indirect evidence for mirror neurons in humans has been found using brain imaging techniques (e.g., Iacoboni et al., 1999).

The implications of mirror neurons for motor theory were obvious to their discoverers (Rizzolatti & Arbib, 1998). Likewise, proponents of direct realism view mirror neurons as providing the mechanism for linking perception and action, not just in the case of speech but in perception generally (Galantucci et al., 2006). However, advocates of the general auditory framework disagree, maintaining that the existence of mirror neurons does not in itself imply that action drives perception (Massaro & Chen, 2008).

Direct realism aligns itself more generally with the notion of **embodied cognition**, *a point of view arguing that cognition is rooted in the body's interactions with the world around it* (Wilson, 2002). We aren't, after all, just brains in vats engaged in abstract thinking for its own sake. Rather, the essential purpose of a brain is to provide the organism with information about the environment in order to guide behavior. Thus, direct realism is less a model of speech perception than it is a philosophical stance on the nature of perception and cognition.

In Sum

Lack of invariance is what makes speech perception such a difficult problem, and the key requirement of any theory is that it needs to explain how speech perception occurs given the lack of correlation between features of the speech stream and the speech sounds we perceive. Motor theory solves the problem by proposing that the object of speech perception is intended vocal gestures, not the acoustic signal, thus maintaining that action drives perception. The general auditory framework takes the position that perception proceeds by taking advantage of all available information to make good guesses about the content of the message carried in the acoustic signal. Direct realism resurrects motor theory, bolstered by the discovery of mirror neurons, which may provide a biological mechanism for linking perception and action.

Review Questions

1. Explain the major tenets of motor theory. What is the evidence for each claim?

2. How is the concept of nativism related to the rise of cognitive psychology? What did Chomsky mean by a language acquisition device? What did Fodor mean by a module?

3. Explain the two lines of evidence that general auditory framework uses to argue against motor theory. How does the general auditory framework account for these data?

4. In what ways has direct realism diverged from the original tenets of motor theory? What other points does it align itself with?

5. What do mirror neurons do? How do they provide support for motor theory and direct realism? Are they problematic for the general auditory framework?

Thought Questions

1. Speech recognition technology has advanced rapidly in recent years. How might computer speech recognition help us understand human speech perception? How does the ability of computers to recognize speech impact the three theories of speech perception covered in this section?

2. Both motor theory and direct realism propose that the object of speech perception is vocal gestures, not the acoustic signal. However, direct realism proposes that speech perception is not special in this regard. Rather, it argues that perception generally speaking is about detecting distant events and objects. Think of examples of how we can identify objects and events just by sound. How might this general ability be related to speech perception?

3. Embodied cognition is a buzzword in many corners of psychology these days. What is really meant by the concept? In what sense is it in line with the principles of natural selection? How might it inform theories of speech perception?

Google It! Brain in a Vat

The philosophical concept of a **brain in a vat** has been around in various forms for centuries, and it's also made its way into popular culture. If you do an Internet search, you'll find examples of the concept in popular movies and TV shows that you may be familiar with (*The Matrix* and *Futurama* are just two examples.) If you're interested in the idea of **embodied cognition**, search for a fascinating TED Talk by neuroscientist Daniel Wolpert called "The Real Reason for Brains." Wolpert is a very engaging and thought-provoking speaker. You can find plenty of other videos on **embodied cognition**, including the idea of embodied cognition in robots. Finally, if you're interested in **computer speech recognition**, you can find videos on that, too. Also, don't forget to play with your own computer's speech recognition program. How well does it work?

CONCLUSION

Our ability to perceive events in the world by the sounds they make has evolved over hundreds of millions of years. Vibrating objects produce periodic sound waves with multiple overtones as they wobble in the air, and they have a ringing or musical quality to them. Friction and collision events, on the other hand, produce aperiodic sound waves with no recurring patterns, which we perceive as noise. From cochlea to cortex, our auditory system is designed to analyze sounds into their component frequencies and amplitudes and then to match those incoming patterns with samples stored in memory.

Speech comes at us as a continuous stream of complex and ever-changing sound waves. At the base of the speech stream is prosody, which is the fluctuating fundamental frequency of the speaker's vibrating vocal cords, and this undulating melody conveys both linguistic and emotional information. The periodic portions of the speech stream are perceived as vowels, which are distinguished mainly by their pattern of formants above the fundamental frequency. The aperiodic and silent portions of the speech stream are perceived as consonants, which are identified mainly by the ways they influence the surrounding vowels. The speech perception system relies on multiple sources of information, both auditory and visual, to decipher the speech stream, filling in gaps and making its best guess when the signal is unclear.

Language learning begins in the womb. During the third trimester of pregnancy, the auditory system comes online, and the fetus can hear sounds, especially its mother's voice. As a result, newborns can already recognize their mother's voice and language. After birth, mother and child spend a lot of face-to-face time, exchanging facial expressions and vocalizations. Infant-directed speech has exaggerated characteristics that babies find enticing and that may help them learn language. Babies employ statistical learning mechanisms to tease out the structure of the speech stream, such as tracking intonation and stress patterns as well as tracking the transitional probabilities of syllables. Although infants are born with the ability to discriminate most speech sounds, by the end of their first year they're only sensitive to the phonetic categories that are important to the language their learning.

Since there's no one-to-one correspondence between the acoustic signal and the perceived speech sound, this means that any theory of speech perception needs to account for the lack of invariance problem. Some theories argue that speech is special, proposing that language is quickly separated from the rest of the auditory input and processed by separate, dedicated systems. Other theories maintain that speech is perceived through general auditory processes just like any other sounds.

Current theories of speech perception emphasize the relationship between speech perception and production. This approach reflects the more general view among neuroscientists regarding the tight coupling of perception and action systems in the brain. No doubt speech perception and production systems co-evolved. In this chapter, we explored the process of speech perception. In the next chapter, we'll consider the mechanisms of speech production.

CROSS-CULTURAL PERSPECTIVE:
Tone Languages

As we speak, we vary the pitch of our voice, and variations in fundamental frequency convey important emotional information. Our voice tends to get higher in pitch when we're excited or uncertain about ourselves. On the other hand, a lower tone of voice conveys confidence or seriousness.

Changes in pitch can also be used to group words together. Typically, fundamental frequency over a phrase rises and then falls, and this pitch contour is one cue that helps listeners identify phrase boundaries. Roughly speaking, a rising pitch indicates that we still have more to say, while a falling intonation means we're finished. Listen carefully to the pitch of your voice as you read the following list out loud: *apples, peaches, cherries, bananas, and plums*. You should have heard the pitch of your voice rising with each item except the last, which has a falling pitch.

Rising and falling pitch at the end of an utterance can also be used to distinguish questions from statements. Imagine a flight attendant offering passengers a hot beverage: "Coffee?" This single word, spoken with a rising pitch, is clearly understood as meaning the question, "Would you like some coffee?" Now imagine a passenger asking the flight attendant, "What's in that pot?" The answer is "Coffee" with a falling pitch.

The use of rising intonation to indicate continuation or question and falling intonation to indicate completion or statement is a universal tendency among the languages of the world (Yuan, 2011). However, many languages also use pitch contours to make meaningful distinctions between words. This is known as tone.

About half of the world's languages use tone patterns to discriminate between otherwise identical words. Most of these tone languages are spoken in Asia and Africa, but they can be found in other parts of the world as well. Among these, Mandarin Chinese is the most widely spoken.

One way to think of tone is that it's the pitch at which a vowel is produced, much as it is when singing. If you've ever had voice lessons, you've learned how to sing vowels like *ah* on different notes up and down the music scale. In fact, there's some evidence suggesting that native speakers of tone languages also have enhanced perception of musical pitch (Bidelman, Hutka, & Moreno, 2013). Many tone languages, especially those in Africa, distinguish multiple pitch levels, such as low-medium-high, somewhat like musical notes. Other tone languages, especially those in Asia, distinguish multiple pitch contours. Mandarin makes use of four different tonal contours. The first tone is high and level, while the second tone starts at mid-level and rises. The third starts mid-low and dips to the lowest level before rising mid-high. The fourth tone falls sharply from high to low.

Tone is used to distinguish words in Mandarin that would otherwise sound alike. Consider the syllable *ma*. It means "mother" if you say it with the first tone as *mā*, and it's a common family name when pronounced with the second tone as *má*. Likewise, it means "horse" if you say it with the third tone as *mǎ* and "scold" if you say it with the fourth tone as *mà*.

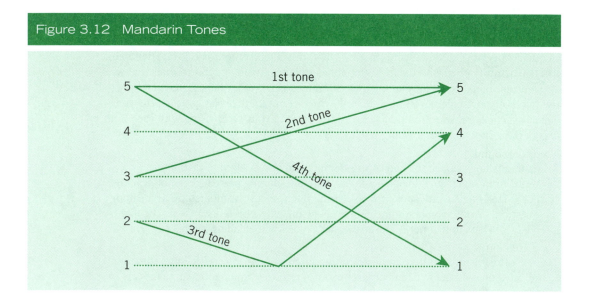

Figure 3.12 Mandarin Tones

Not all syllables in spoken Mandarin carry tone. Terms of address in Chinese are often doubled to produce familiar or intimate forms, as for example when Chinese children address their mother as *māma*. In cases like this, the second syllable is spoken with shorter duration and no distinct tone. The Chinese call this "light tone" (*qingsheng*), and it's essentially an unstressed syllable.

Mandarin also makes use of sentence-final particles as a sort of spoken punctuation. For example, attaching the syllable *ma* to the end of a statement turns it into a yes-no question. These particles are typically unstressed as well.

Altogether, there are five different ways to pronounce the syllable *ma*, each with a distinct meaning. Hence the tone-based tongue twister *má mā ma mà mǎ ma*, which means, "Does Mother Ma scold the horse?"

Mandarin also makes use of phrasal intonation, ending statements with falling pitch and questions with rising pitch, just like English. So how do speakers of tone languages reconcile intonation and tone contours? Chinese linguists often describe it this way: Syllable tones are like smaller ripples riding on larger waves of intonation (Yuan, 2011). Thus, a high first tone will have a somewhat lower absolute pitch when it occurs at the beginning or end of a sentence, where the intonation arc is low, compared with a first tone produced at the highpoint of the utterance.

You may also be wondering how Mandarin speakers deal with tone when they sing. The answer is simple. When we sing in English, we ignore the intonational patterns of natural speech and follow the melody instead. Likewise in Mandarin, singers disregard tones as well. Generally speaking, context is sufficient to make up for the lost tones. Unless, that is, you're singing about Mother Ma scolding a horse.

KEY TERMS

Amplitude	Cochlear implant	Formants
Aperiodic sound	Conditioned head turn technique	Frequency
Aspiration		Fricative
Basilar membrane	Direct realism	Fundamental frequency
Categorical perception	Distributional learning	Fuzzy-logical model of perception
Coarticulation	Embodied cognition	
Cochlea	Formant transition	General auditory framework

Hair cells

Hertz

High-amplitude sucking technique

Infant-directed speech

Lack of invariance

Language acquisition device

Loudness

McGurk effect

Metrical segmentation strategy

Mirror neurons

Module

Motor theory

Multimodal perception

Nativism

Overtones

Perceptual narrowing

Periodic sound

Phonation

Phonemic restoration

Pitch

Plosive

Primary auditory cortex

Prosodic bootstrapping

Prosody

Sine wave

Sonorant

Spectrogram

Speech is special

Timbre

Tonotopic organization

Transitional probability

Voice onset time

4

Speech Production

It seems that we humans spend most of our waking hours talking. We talk to each other, often just to pass the time. And when we're alone, we talk to ourselves, sometimes out loud, but perhaps more frequently as inner speech. We fill our lives with speech, and a fair number of us even make our livings by talking.

Think of your teachers—they get paid to stand in front of students and talk. For people in sales, their success depends mainly on how smoothly they can talk to their customers. And if you've got a good voice, you can make even bigger bucks in broadcast media, as news anchors, reporters, and talk show hosts do.

Film critic Roger Ebert was one such celebrity who made his living talking. Ebert was a noted film critic, with reviews syndicated in newspapers across the United States and abroad. He and fellow critic Gene Siskel also hosted a number of televised film-review programs such as *Sneak Previews* and *At the Movies*. Even if you've never seen a Siskel and Ebert review, you're probably familiar with their trademark phrase, "Two Thumbs Up!"

Losing the ability to speak would be devastating for anyone, no doubt even more so for those who make their livelihood by speaking. And yet that's exactly what happened to Roger Ebert when he lost his lower jaw to cancer.

We've already learned that Broca's aphasics suffer from impaired speech because the areas of the brain that program the motor plans for speech have been damaged. But Ebert's case was different. His brain was still intact, so he had no problem processing language. It's just that part of the physical apparatus for producing speech—his lower jaw—had been surgically removed. Thus, Ebert could still write, and he continued publishing written reviews until his death in 2013. But he never spoke again.

In this chapter we'll explore the production of speech. We'll start with an overview of the vocal tract, where speech is physically produced, and then we'll look at the processes in the brain that underlie speech production. We'll wrap up by considering how humans learn to speak, transitioning from speechless infants to nonstop talkers in just a few years.

SECTION 4.1: THE VOCAL TRACT AND THE PRODUCTION OF SPEECH

- The vocal tract consists of the oral and nasal cavities, and they serve as resonating chambers for the phonation produced by the vibration of the vocal folds.

- Consonants are produced by obstructing the flow of air through the oral cavity; the three factors that determine consonant quality are place of articulation, manner of articulation, and voicing (voice onset time).

- Place of articulation describes the location along the vocal tract where the obstruction occurs to produce a consonant; important places of articulation include the lips, teeth, alveolar ridge, hard palate, and velum.

- Manner of articulation describes the degree to which the airflow is obstructed in the production of a consonant; this obstruction can involve a complete stop, a constriction, or a diversion of the airstream.

- Vowels are produced by modifying the shape of the oral cavity; three factors influence this shape: the height of the jaw, the position of the tongue, and the shape of the lips.

- A diphthong is a vowel combination that is perceived as a single phoneme; English has three (as in *high*, *hoy*, and *how*), and Chinese has more, including some three-vowel combinations.

We humans perform an amazing feat. By blowing air out of our mouths, we communicate complex thoughts to other members of our species. The apparent ease with which we do this belies the underlying complexity of speech production, and in this section we'll just briefly survey how this process takes place.

Vocal Tract

The production of speech begins in the lungs, which provide the airstream for vocalization. This airstream flows up the trachea through the glottis, or voice box. The **vocal folds** consist of *a pair of membranes stretched across the opening of the glottis that can be vibrated to produce sound*. When the vocal folds are retracted, the airstream flows through unimpeded, as in the case of normal breathing. If the vocal folds are pulled across the opening of the glottis, the airflow is constricted, and the resulting air pressure causes them to vibrate, producing phonation. Recall from Chapter 3 that phonation is the buzzing sensation you can feel if you hold your hand to your throat while saying "Ahhh."

To see how phonation works, take a balloon and fill it with air. Pinch the stem of the balloon with the thumb and forefinger of each hand to hold in the air. As you release the pinch, the air comes rushing out. This is like normal breathing. Fill the balloon again, but this time stretch the neck sideways. As the air rushes through this constriction, it causes the two sides of the neck to vibrate, producing a high-pitched whine. You can even change the pitch within a certain range by adjusting how tightly you stretch the neck. The vocal folds work under the same principle.

Also recall from Chapter 3 that vibrating objects produce a fundamental frequency, which is perceived as pitch, plus a series of overtones. The vibrating vocal folds likewise produce a fundamental frequency and overtones, and this complex sound wave then is the phonation that serves as the raw material for speech production.

As we learned in Chapter 1, the open cavities of the throat, mouth, and nose that are situated above the vocal folds make up the vocal tract. The sound produced by the vocal folds resonants in the vocal tract, and we can change the shape of the vocal tract in various ways to create different sounds. For example, when we hum, we lead the vibrating air flow through the nose to resonate in the nasal cavity. Some speech sounds, like *m* and *n*, are also produced by resonation in the nasal cavity. In English, vowels are generally produced by directing the airflow through the mouth, producing resonation in the oral cavity. People that talk with a "twang" in their voice produce vowels through resonation in both the oral and the nasal cavities.

Figure 4.1 Vocal Tract

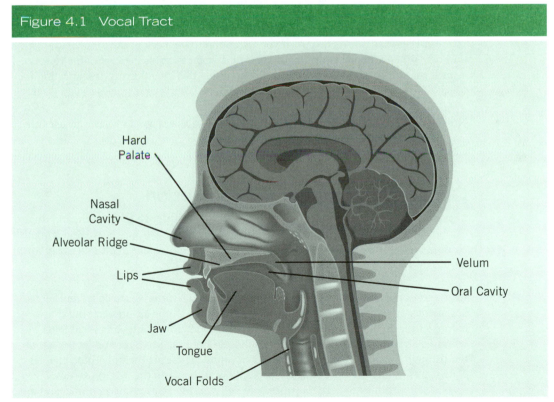

Hard Palate

Nasal Cavity

Alveolar Ridge

Lips

Jaw

Tongue

Vocal Folds

Velum

Oral Cavity

Source: ©Can Stock Photo Inc./alila

The vocal tract is shaped somewhat like an inverted saxophone, with the vocal folds acting as the reed and the oral and nasal cavities as the resonating tube. By pressing different keys on the saxophone, you modify the size of the tube to produce different notes. Similarly, you can use the tongue, jaw, and lips to change the size and shape of the oral cavity. You can also use the tongue, teeth, and lips to block or constrict the airflow, thus influencing the quality of the sound produced.

Now I'd like to take you on a tour of the inside of your mouth. Waggle your tongue, and notice how you can move it forward and backward, up and down, and side to side. Next, touch the tip of your tongue to your upper lip. (Go ahead and try it.) Slowly pull back your tongue, tracing the tip along your upper teeth and then against *the fleshy region of the mouth covering the bone where the upper teeth are anchored*. This is called the **alveolar ridge** (pronounced *al-VEE-lar*), and it's an important region for producing consonants. Behind the alveolar ridge, you should feel *the bony region along the roof of the mouth* called the **hard palate**. Curl the tip of your tongue, and you should be able to feel *the fleshy region behind the hard palate*. This is known as the soft palate, or **velum**.

You'll probably feel like you're gagging if you curl the tip of your tongue too far back, but there are two other regions of the tongue that you can move. Shift your focus now to the top surface of the tongue, which is known as the blade. You can raise the blade of your tongue against the hard palate. If you do this quickly, you can produce a snapping sound. (Go ahead and try it.) Some languages produce speech sounds in this way, but English doesn't. Next, turn your attention to the back of the tongue, known as the root. When you pull your tongue backward, you can press the root of the tongue against the velum. If you are having difficulty doing this intentionally, try repeating the syllables *kah* and *gah*, paying close attention to how your tongue moves as you do this.

Now that you're intimate with the parts of your mouth, let's see how you can use them to produce speech sounds.

Consonants: Place of Articulation

Consonants are produced by obstructing the flow of air through the mouth, and this can be done at a number of locations and in a number of ways. One way we distinguish consonants is by their **place of articulation**, meaning *the location in the oral cavity where the airflow is obstructed to produce a consonant sound*.

Let's start at the lips. *A consonant sound that is produced by bringing the upper and lower lips together* is called a **bilabial**. Purse your lips and let a little air pressure build up before letting go. You'll get the puff of a *p* sound. Do it again with your vocal folds vibrating and you'll get the buzz of a *b* sound. Or hold the lips tight and let the air go out through the nose to make a humming *m* sound. These are the only three bilabial consonants in English, but some languages blow air between the lips to produce a speech sound similar to *f*. The Japanese *f* of *Fuji-san* (Mt. Fuji) is one example, and a voiced version of this is the Spanish *v* sound. However, English *f* and *v* are produced somewhat differently. Repeat the syllable pair *few view*, paying attention to what you do with your lips and teeth. *A consonant that is produced by bringing the lower lip against the upper teeth* is called a **labiodental**.

Now for some tongue action. Press the blade of your tongue against your upper teeth and let some air come hissing through. You've just produced a *th* sound, which is known as an **interdental** because it's *a consonant that is produced by protruding the tongue between the upper and lower teeth*. In fact, there are two interdental consonants in English, both spelled *th*. The voiceless interdental can be found in words like *thick* and *thin*, while the voiced interdental can be found in words like *then* and *there*. You can also hear the difference in the minimal pair *thigh* and *thy*. In rapid speech, these sounds can also be produced by touching the tip of the tongue against the upper teeth. Try producing these sounds both ways and see if you can hear a difference.

Although many languages produce speech sounds by pressing the tip of the tongue behind the teeth, American English generally avoids this area, going for the alveolar ridge instead. *A consonant produced by pressing the tip of the tongue against the fleshy area behind the upper teeth* is called an **alveolar** consonant. Carefully articulate the series *new, dew, two, zoo, sue*, paying special attention to how the tip of the tongue strikes the alveolar ridge each time. Now repeat the list, trying to get a sense of how these sounds differ from each other.

Sliding the tip of your tongue along the alveolar ridge to just before the hard palate, you'll find another place of articulation. *A consonant produced by pressing the blade of the tongue against the region between the alveolar ridge and the hard palate* is called **postalveolar**. Play attention to the placement of your tongue as you say the words *gin, chin, shin*. There's also one more postalveolar in English. Although there's no consistent way to spell it, it's sometimes represented phonetically as *zh*. You can hear it in the middle of the word *version*, especially if you contrast it with *virgin*, which has a *j* sound in the middle. The *zh* sound is a voiced version of *sh*, and it's also the French *j* sound, as in *bonjour* and *soupe du jour*. Some American speakers use it as the final sound in *garage*.

Moving to the back of the mouth, we have a few more consonants to discuss. *Consonants produced by pressing the root of the tongue against the soft palate at the back of the mouth* are referred to as **velar** consonants, since the soft palate is also known as the velum. Pay attention the way you produce the final consonants in the series *sang, sag, sack*.

The glottis, which houses the vocal folds, can be used to make consonant sounds as well. The *h* sound of English is essentially a voiceless *ah* sound. If you alternate producing *hhh* and *aaa*, you'll see the only difference is that the vocal folds vibrate for *aaa*, but not for *hhh*. Finally, there's the **glottal stop**, which is *a consonant produced by constricting the vocal folds*. You can hear a glottal stop in the middle of the expressions *uh-oh* and *uhn-uhn*. Many English speakers also replace a middle *t* sound with a glottal stop, especially in rapid speech, as for example in the words *button* and *bottle*. Technically speaking, the glottal stop isn't a phoneme in English, but it is in some languages, such as Arabic (Ladefoged & Maddieson, 1996).

Consonants: Manner of Articulation

We've just seen how we can distinguish consonants by their place of articulation, but what we do at that location is important as well. *The degree to which airflow is obstructed in the production of consonants* is known as **manner of articulation**. Imagine running water through a garden hose. First, press your thumb against the mouth of the hose to stop the water flow and then release your thumb. Second, lift your thumb just a little to produce a spray. Notice that if you do this repeatedly, you'll produce a pulsating spray. Third, pull your thumb back just enough to produce a continuous spray. Fourth, press your thumb into the water stream just enough to divert it a little. And then finally, just let the water flow freely. Each of these actions corresponds to a manner of articulation in speech production.

Briefly pressing your thumb against a garden hose is like articulating a plosive or stop. As we learned in Chapter 3, a plosive is a consonant produced by momentarily stopping and then releasing the airflow. As we learned in Chapter 3, English and many languages use voice onset time (VOT) to distinguish between voiced (early VOT) and voiceless (late VOT) stops. You may recall that *b-d-g* is the series of voiced plosives in English and that *p-t-k* is the series of voiceless plosives. Additionally, English has a set of three nasal stops, *m*, *n*, and *ng*, which are produced by blocking the airflow in the oral cavity and releasing it through the nose instead.

Two manners of articulation create sound through friction. The first manner is like constricting the water hose with your thumb to produce a pulsating spray. *A consonant that is produced by momentarily blocking the airflow and then releasing it through a tight constriction* is called an **affricate**. English has only two affricate phonemes, *j* and *ch*. The second manner is like using your thumb on the garden hose to make a continuous spray. As we learned in Chapter 3, a consonant that is produced by passing the airflow through a constriction in the oral cavity is known as a fricative. English has four voiced-voiceless pairs of fricatives, the *v* and *f* of *view* and *few*, the two *th*s of *thy* and *thigh*, the *z* and *s* of *zoo* and *sue*, and finally the *zh* and *sh* of *fission* and *fishin'*. The glottal sound *h* is often included with the fricatives, even though it's produced with less friction than the others.

The last two manners of articulation don't produce a constriction of the airflow. An **approximant** is a *consonant that is produced by diverting the airflow without constricting it*. English has four approximants, *l*, *r*, *y* and *w*. Approximants are similar to vowels, which are produced without any turbulence of the airstream; thus, approximants are sometimes called semi-vowels. You may also recall from Chapter 3 that these approximants, along with the nasals, were classified as sonorants. From an acoustics perspective, sonorants are like vowels in that they're composed of periodic sound waves.

Returning to our garden hose analogy, vowels are like letting the water flow freely. This is because vowels are produced by simply letting the phonation resonate within the oral cavity without obstructing or diverting it.

Manner	Voicing	Bilabial	Labio-dental	Inter-dental	Alveolar	Post-alveolar	Palatal	Velar	Glottal
Table 4.1					English Consonant Inventory				
Nasal	Voiced	mat			new			wing	
Plosive	Voiced	bat			dew			gill	
Plosive	Voiceless	pat			two			kill	uh-oh
Affricate	Voiced					gin (virgin)			
Affricate	Voiceless					chin			
Fricative	Voiced		view	thy	zoo	(version)			
Fricative	Voiceless		few	thigh	sue	shin			hi
Approximant	Voiced				raw		yell	well	
Lateral	Voiced				law				

Vowels

Did you ever wonder why we say "cheese" when we get our picture taken? There's nothing funny about dairy products, but just saying "cheese" puts a smile on our face. That's because the *ee* sound is produced with the lips spread wide. In China they say the word for "eggplant" (*qiézi*), which sounds somewhat like "cheese." (Eggplant really is a funny vegetable.) Likewise, doctors ask you to say "ah" when they want to look down your throat. (Chinese doctors do this, too.) These examples show that the way we shape our mouth determines the vowel sound we produce.

Figure 4.2 An Eggplant

Naming this vegetable puts a smile on your face if you're speaking Chinese.

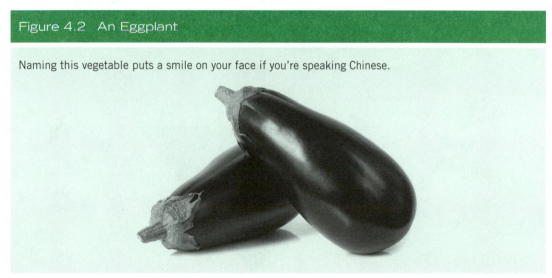

Source: ©iStockphoto.com/robynmac.

The jaw, tongue, and lips all get involved in the act of producing vowels. First, notice how your jaw moves up and down on a hinge, making the oral cavity inside your mouth larger or smaller. From a side view, we can also see that the rotating jaw produces a triangular vowel space. The vowel *ee* is said to be high because the jaw is positioned high, closing the mouth, and the vowel *ah* said to be low because the jaw lowers to open the mouth. Meanwhile, the tongue can move back and forth inside the mouth. The vowel *ee* is also said to be front because the tongue is pushed forward in the mouth, while the vowel *oo* is said to be back because the tongue is pushed backward in the mouth. Try alternating the vowels *ee* and *oo*, paying attention to the movement of the tongue. Now alternate the vowels again, this time paying attention to the shape of the lips. We also say that *oo* is a rounded vowel because the lips are rounded, and *ee* is an unrounded vowel because the lips are stretched wide.

The three vowels *ah*, *ee*, and *oo* mark the extremities of the vowel space, with *ah* at the bottom center, *ee* at the high front, and *oo* at the high back. All other vowel sounds fit in between these three (Ladefoged & Disner, 2012). Cycle through *ah-ee-oo* to get a sense of this vowel space.

English distinguishes vowels at five different levels of jaw height. Five front, unrounded vowels run in a series from high to low, as illustrated in the following examples:

- heed or he'd, as in: He'd better heed my advice.
- hid, as in: He hid in the closet.

Figure 4.3   Vowel Space of English

The hinged opening and closing of the jaw creates a triangular vowel space. The tongue can move forward and backward within this space, and the lips can be either rounded or unrounded.

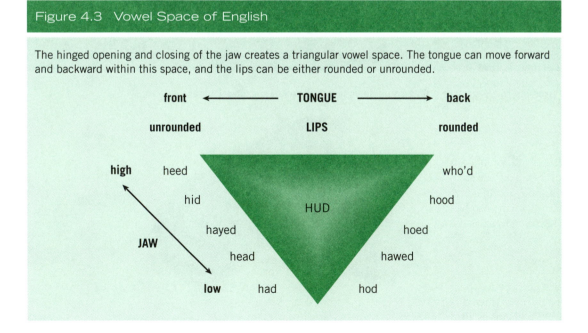

- hayed, as in: He hayed the horses, meaning that he fed them hay.
- head, as in: He hit his head.
- had, as in: He's had enough.

Cycle through these words, paying attention to the way the jaw lowers as you go down the list.

English also has a parallel series of five back, rounded vowels, running from high to low, illustrated in the following examples:

- who'd, as in: Who'd know?
- hood, as in: Who's the man in the hood?
- hoed, as in: He hoed the garden, meaning that he used a hoe.
- hawed, as in: He hemmed and hawed.
- hod, which, in case you didn't know, is a tool for carrying bricks on your shoulder.

Again, cycle through these words and focus on the movement of your jaw. By the way, if *hawed* and *hod* sound the same to you, you're not alone. Many Americans have lost this vowel distinction. (Your textbook author is one of them.)

As you ran through the series of front and back vowels, you should also have noticed that your lips were unrounded for the front vowels and rounded for the back vowels. English merges these two distinguishing features, but other languages separate them. For example, Chinese has four high vowels, a front unrounded *i*, a front rounded *ü*, a back unrounded *ï*, and a back rounded *u*.

English also has one or more phonemic vowels situated in the middle of the vowel space. The vowel of *HUD* (US Department of Housing and Urban Development) is classified as an unrounded mid-central vowel. There's also *a neutral mid-central vowel occurring in many unstressed syllables in English* known as **schwa**. The *a* in *about* or *sofa* is a schwa sound. Schwa often alternates with other vowels as stress shifts from one syllable to another. For example, in the word *photograph*, the first *o*, which is stressed, has the vowel of *hoed*, and the second *o* reduces to schwa. But in the related word *photography*, the stress shifts to the second syllable. Now the first *o* reduces to schwa, and the second *o* is pronounced as the vowel in *hod*. Other languages, such as Chinese and Russian, also have a tendency to reduce unstressed vowels to schwa. Some people perceive schwa as the same vowel as in *HUD*, and others perceive it as a separate phoneme (Heselwood, 2007).

We wrap up our discussion of the English vowel inventory with a brief mention of diphthongs. A **diphthong** is *a vowel combination that is perceived as a single phoneme.* English has three diphthongs, namely the vowels in *high*, *hoy*, and *how*. The vowel in *high* begins as an *ah* and ends as an *ee*, while the vowel in *hoy* begins as an *oh* and ends as an *ee*. Likewise, the vowel in *how* begins as an *ah* and ends as an *oo*. Not all languages have diphthongs. For instance, Japanese speakers tend to perceive English diphthongs as sequences of two separate vowels. Chinese, on the other hand, has many diphthongs as well as some three-vowel combinations.

In Sum

The oral and nasal cavities act as resonating chambers for the phonation produced by the vibrating vocal folds. Consonant sounds are made by constricting or diverting the airflow through the oral or nasal cavity, and they can be described in terms of their place and manner of articulation. Place of articulation refers to the location along the vocal tract where the airflow is obstructed, and manner of articulation refers to the degree of constriction. Vowel sounds are made by changing the shape of the resonating chamber created by the oral cavity. The position of the jaw and tongue and the shape of the lips can influence the strengthening or dampening of various overtones, thus producing the different vowel sounds. No language makes use of all possible consonant and vowel distinctions, but the consonant and vowel inventories of English are quite typical among the world's languages (Ladefoged & Maddieson, 1996).

Review Questions

1. Name and describe the major features of the vocal tract.

2. What places of articulation are used to produce consonants in English? Which sounds are produced at each place?

3. What manners of articulation are used to produce consonants in English? Which sounds are produced with each manner?

4. What are the three parameters for distinguishing vowels? How do they work together to produce the vowel inventory of English? What are diphthongs?

Thought Questions

1. According to the source-filter theory (Fant, 1970), speech production involves one or more mechanisms for producing sound (the source) and multiple mechanisms for modifying that sound (the filter). Based on your understanding of the structure and mechanics of the vocal tract, identify the source(s) and filter(s) of speech production in humans.

2. You learned in this section that English combines the features of lip rounding and tongue position in producing a vowel, so that front vowels are always unrounded and back vowels are always rounded.

But many languages separate lip rounding and tongue position. For example, a close front rounded vowel is common in many languages. You can produce it by saying *ee* while rounding the lips as if saying *oo*. Try making rounded versions of the English front vowels and unrounded versions of the English back vowels. Do they all sound different to you?

Google It! Click Languages

You can check YouTube to find videos of the **vocal tract** in action, using X-rays, fMRI, and even endoscopy (running a camera through the nasal passages and down into the throat).

All English phonemes are produced by pushing air out of the vocal tract. However, some languages in Africa also use phonemes that are produced by sucking air into the vocal tract. Check YouTube for videos of **click language**. Incidentally, we use clicks in English too, only not as phonemes. The *tsk! tsk!* sound used to express shame or pity is an alveolar click, and the *tchick!* sound used to get a horse moving is a lateral click. Then there's the bilabial click, which sounds like a lip-smacking kiss.

SECTION 4.2: SPEECH AREAS OF THE BRAIN

- According to the traditional Wernicke-Geschwind model, (1) Wernicke's area is responsible for speech perception; (2) Broca's area is responsible for speech production; and (3) the arcuate fasciculus, a band of fibers extending from Wernicke's to Broca's areas, connects speech perception and production.

- The Wernicke-Geschwind model explains three common forms of aphasia: expressive, or Broca's aphasia; receptive, or Wernicke's aphasia; and conduction aphasia, in which speech perception and production are preserved but the ability to repeat spoken language is lost.

- Other areas of the cerebral cortex are also implicated in speech production, including the somatosensory cortex in the parietal lobe, the primary motor cortex in the frontal lobe, the supplementary motor area and the anterior cingulate cortex in the lateral fissure, and the anterior insula in the lateral fissure.

- Many areas of the brain responsible for walking also play a role in the production of speech; these areas include the basal ganglia, which are involved in initiating movement, and the cerebellum, which is involved in coordinating movement.

- Dysarthria is a speech disorder that results from damage to motor areas of the brain; it is characterized by the poor articulation of phonemes, irregularities in prosody, and a slow rate of speech.
- While the higher levels of language processing are mainly lateralized to the left hemisphere, neuroimaging and clinical data indicate that wide regions of both hemispheres of the brain get involved in speech production.

Although we can talk about the functions that are performed in various regions of the brain, it's too simplistic to think in terms of particular brain areas being specialized for particular functions. Rather, in recent years we've come to understand that brain systems are highly interconnected. In other words, any particular function will recruit multiple brain areas, and likewise any particular brain area will take part in many different functions.

Wernicke-Geschwind Model

You were introduced to the classic model of language processing in Chapter 2. According to this model, speech production is processed in Broca's area in the left frontal lobe, and speech perception is processed in Wernicke's area in the left temporal lobe. Additionally, *a band of neural fibers extending from the temporal lobe to the frontal lobe* known as the **arcuate fasciculus** is thought to connect Wernicke's and Broca's areas, providing a link between speech perception and production. Known as the Wernicke-Geschwind model, it was first proposed by Carl Wernicke in the late nineteenth century and later refined by Norman Geschwind in the mid-twentieth century.

The model was based on evidence from aphasia, or loss of language abilities due to brain damage, which was the only evidence available at the time. As we've already seen, damage to Broca's area gives rise to **expressive aphasia**, which is *a condition in which brain damage leads to a loss of speech production without a loss of speech comprehension.* Likewise, damage to Wernicke's area gives rise to **receptive aphasia**, or *a condition in which brain damage leads a loss of speech comprehension and fluent but meaningless speech production.* Damage to the arcuate fasciculus can lead to **conduction aphasia**, which is *a language disorder characterized by preserved speech perception and production capabilities but with a marked difficulty in repeating spoken language.*

The Wernicke-Geschwind model guided research for much of the twentieth century, and it also fit well with the modular view of the brain that was prevalent in the last third of that century. However, brain imaging research over the last couple of decades has shown that this model is an oversimplification. Although our understanding of how the brain processes language is still incomplete, we now have some viable models that are supported by data and are useful in guiding research. What these models tell us is that many regions of brain that serve other functions are also recruited for language processing.

Figure 4.4 Wernicke-Geschwind Model

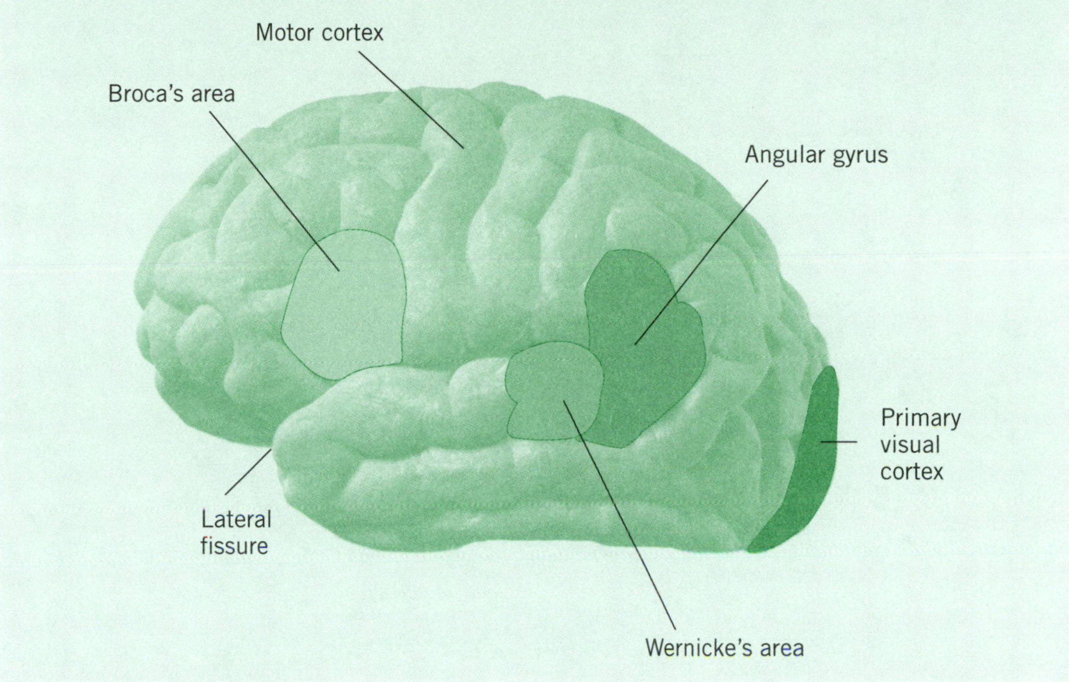

Motor cortex

Broca's area

Angular gyrus

Primary
visual
cortex

Lateral
fissure

Wernicke's area

Source: ©iStockphoto.com/robynmac.

Cerebral Cortex

The cerebral cortex is the thin outer covering of the brain where most of the computations that give rise to our conscious experience and interaction with the world take place. If you were to spread the cerebral cortex flat, it would be larger than a party-sized pizza, clearly too big to fit in your head. Take a piece of paper and wad it into a ball. Evolution has used the same approach to fitting your huge cerebral cortex into your head, and that's why the brain looks so wrinkled from the outside.

The folding of the cerebral cortex leads to a series of ridges and furrows, known by the Latin terms as gyri and sulci in the plural or gyrus and sulcus in the singular. In other words, a **gyrus** is *a protruding region of the cerebral cortex*, and a **sulcus** is *a region of the cerebral cortex that is folded inward*. The gyri may appear to be distinct structures of the brain, but as you already know from your wadded paper, the surface of the cerebral cortex continues into the sulci. Instead, it's better to think of the gyri and sulci as geographical features, the hills and valleys of the cortex, that are convenient landmarks for locating functional regions of the brain.

The names of the gyri are pretty straightforward. The temporal lobe exhibits three roughly horizontal gyri running in parallel, named the superior, medial, and inferior

Figure 4.5   Regions of the Cerebral Cortex

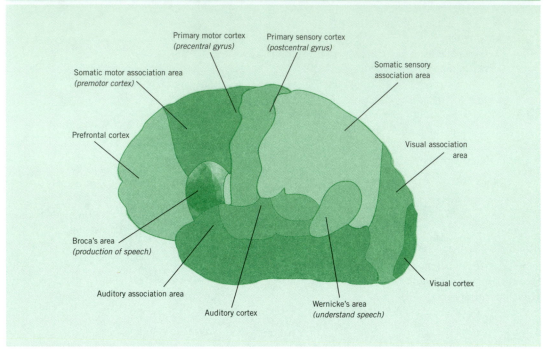

Primary motor cortex
(precentral gyrus)

Primary sensory cortex
(postcentral gyrus)

Somatic sensory
association area

Somatic motor association area
(premotor cortex)

Prefrontal cortex

Visual association
area

Broca's area
(production of speech)

Visual cortex

Auditory association area

Auditory cortex

Wernicke's area
(understand speech)

Source: Blausen.com staff. "Blausen gallery 2014." *Wikiversity Journal of Medicine.* DOI:10.15347/wjm/2014.010. ISSN 20018762

temporal gyri, going from top to bottom. Wernicke's area is located in the posterior superior temporal gyrus, in other words, toward the back. The frontal lobe also has three horizontal gyri called the—you guessed it—superior, medial, and inferior frontal gyri. Broca's area is in the posterior inferior frontal gyrus.

The frontal and parietal lobes are separated by the central sulcus, which is flanked by two vertical gyri known as the precentral and postcentral gyri. The postcentral gyrus, on the parietal side of the divide, is **somatosensory cortex**, *the region of the brain that processes the body senses to keep track of what the various body parts are doing, including the articulators for speech.* The precentral gyrus, on the frontal side of the divide, is the **primary motor cortex**, *the region of the brain that programs commands to move the body, including the articulators for speech.* Because of the tight integration between somatosensory and primary motor cortices in guiding behavior, the two parallel regions are often treated as a single functional region called sensorimotor cortex.

The deep groove separating the left and right hemispheres is called the **longitudinal fissure**, and its inner surfaces are covered with cerebral cortex. Included in this region is the **supplementary motor area**, which is *a brain region that is believed to be responsible for* *programming intentional actions*, as opposed to responses to sensory input. Nearby is the **anterior cingulate cortex**, which is *a region deep inside the longitudinal fissure that is believed to be involved in error detection and monitoring conflict* (Bush, Luu, & Posner, 2000).

The deep fold in the cerebral cortex that separates the temporal lobe from the frontal and parietal lobes is called the **lateral sulcus**. This is where the primary auditory cortex, which we learned about in Chapter 3, is located. The lateral sulcus runs deep and contains its own convolutions and structures. *A region deep within the lateral sulcus that has been implicated in language processing* is the **anterior insula** (Shuster & Lemieux, 2005). The lateral sulcus is also known as the Sylvian fissure, and for this reason *the region inside of and surrounding the lateral sulcus* is referred to as **perisylvian cortex**. The perisylvian cortex is a busy area for language processing. At this point, make sure you're familiar with the geography of the cerebral cortex before you continue reading.

Talking Is Like Walking

When you walk, you do much more than just move your feet. Rather, your whole body gets into the act. As you move your right foot forward, your left arm swings back, and your hips twist as you shift your weight. You step, and then your left foot moves forward while your right arm swings back and your hips twist in the other direction. This pattern repeats over and over again at a rate of up to a hundred steps per minute. Thus, walking is a rhythmic and highly coordinated behavior that unfolds over time, and it is in this sense that talking is like walking.

Talking, like walking, is rhythmic, with its repeating pattern of consonants and vowels producing a sequence of syllables, just as walking can be broken down into a sequence of steps (Grimme et al., 2011). It also requires the exquisite coordination of many muscles to move the articulators just the right amount at just the right time. When we think of speech in this way, it's not surprising to find that many of the brain structures involved in controlling locomotion are also enlisted for the production of speech.

Based on neuroimaging studies as well as clinical evidence from aphasic patients, Riecker and colleagues (2008) have identified what they call the "minimal network for overt speech production" (p. 102). This network is composed of three functional systems encompassing both cortical and subcortical structures on both sides of the brain.

The first functional system consists of starting mechanisms involved initiating and maintaining a continuous, fluent speech stream (Ackermann, 2008). This system centers on the supplementary motor cortex, which is believed to play a role in initiating voluntary actions, particularly those involving locomotion (Graziano, 2008; Graziano & Aflalo, 2007). The neighboring anterior cingulate cortex is also involved in the initiation and maintenance of speech. More generally, the anterior cingulate cortex is implicated in error detection and motivation from rewards and punishments (Bush et al., 2002; Taylor et al., 2006). Both of these areas become active in experimental conditions in which participants are asked to produce utterances as opposed to simply repeating them. Patients with damage to the supplementary motor area or the anterior cingulate cortex tend not to produce utterances on their own, even though they're capable of repeating what they hear (Riecker et al., 2008). Thus, your decision to get up and walk across the room and your decision to utter a sentence may both originate in the same brain regions.

The second functional system is composed of premotor components that are responsible for generating phonetic plans (Riecker et al., 2008). Broca's area, the traditionally recognized site for language production located in the left inferior frontal lobe, is included in this premotor system. Also included is the anterior insula, located deep within the lateral fissure. So many different cognitive functions have been linked to the anterior insula that it's hard to say exactly what its function is, but current thinking is that it's somehow involved in the experience of self-awareness (Craig, 2009). Some clinical evidence indicates that damage to the anterior insula is a better predictor of motor speech impairment, but neuroimaging studies confirm the importance of Broca's area in speech production (Richardson et al., 2012).

An additional component of the premotor system is the bilateral precentral gyrus, where primary motor cortex is located (Ackermann, 2008). The primary motor cortex contains a map of the body, with the head at the bottom and the feet at the top, so motor cortex for the vocal tract is adjacent to Broca's area (Simonyan & Horwitz, 2011). This is likely the area where the motor plans for the articulators are assembled. It's also important to notice that both the left and right primary motor cortexes are involved. Higher levels of speech production planning may be lateralized, but the lower levels need to be bilateral because both sides of the vocal tract have to be moved to speak.

The third functional system extends from the bilateral primary motor cortex down into a number of subcortical structures (Ackermann, 2008), and the system as a whole is responsible for coordinating the movements of more than one hundred muscles in the respiratory system, vocal tract, and face that are involved in the production of the speech stream (Simonyan & Horwitz, 2011). These subcortical structures are more typically associated with locomotion, and they link back up with the sensorimotor cortex, creating a number of motor loops (Ackermann, 2008). Apparently, brain systems that originally evolved for the temporal sequencing and muscle coordination of locomotion have been enlisted for the same purposes in producing speech.

One motor loop for speech production involves the cerebellum, which, we learned in Chapter 2, is responsible for coordinating movement. The cerebellum doesn't initiate behavior, but it does regulate behaviors that require the precise timing of muscle movements (Ivry et al., 2002). Walking is a good example of the type of behavior that requires cerebellar input to be performed smoothly, and damage to the cerebellum leads to a jerky, awkward gait but not paralysis.

Since speech production involves the precise timing of articulatory gestures, it's not surprising that the cerebellum is important for producing a fluent speech stream. Damage to the cerebellum can lead to a condition known as **dysarthria**, which is *a motor speech disorder due to neural injury that is characterized by poor articulation of phonemes and prosody* (MacKenzie, 2011). Based on clinical and neuroimaging evidence, it's believed that the role of the cerebellum in speech production is to sequence syllables within the rhythmic organization of larger utterances, in particular at speaking rates above three or four syllables per second (Ackermann, 2008). This is consistent with the clinical data, since dysarthric patients can still speak, only at a notably slower than normal rate.

Another motor loop for speech production runs through the basal ganglia, a set of subcortical structures that we learned about in Chapter 2. The basal ganglia regulate the motor system by selecting appropriate and inhibiting inappropriate behaviors to achieve the intended task (Kurata, 2005). Two diseases of the basal ganglia help illustrate their function. Parkinson's disease is characterized by tremor at rest, rigidity, and slowness of movement, while the most notable symptom of Huntington's disease is uncontrollable swaying motions. In either case, the patient experiences difficulty initiating appropriate movements and inhibiting undesired ones. It's believed that the basal ganglia serve a similar role in speech production by selecting the most appropriate motor program from competing alternatives given the particular context (Bohland, Bullock, & Guenther, 2010).

The thalamus is another subcortical structure that's often observed to be active during brain imaging studies of speech production. The **thalamus** is *a midbrain structure traditionally thought of as a sensorimotor relay from various brain structures up to the cerebral cortex*, and it forms part of the speech motor loop that includes the basal ganglia. In addition to relaying information from the basal ganglia to the sensorimotor cortex, clinical and experimental evidence suggests that the thalamus plays a role in coordinating motor programs for producing speech (Johnson & Ojemann, 2000).

In Sum

The traditional Wernicke-Geschwind model is a useful approximation of the higher-order organization of speech processing in the brain, but the full story is far more complicated and still not completely understood. Abstract language processing may be left-lateralized, but the actual planning and implementation of muscle movements to produce speech clearly engage both sides of the brain. Because talking and walking share certain temporal and rhythmic characteristics, it's not surprising to find that motor circuits involved in regulating the timing and rhythm of locomotion also modulate the timing and rhythm of the speech stream.

Review Questions

1. Explain the Wernicke-Geschwind model of speech processing and the three types of aphasia it predicts. What are the symptoms of each of these aphasias, and how are they explained by the model?

Figure 4.6   Subcortical Regions

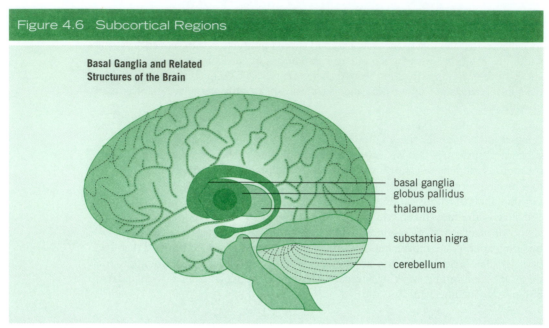

Basal Ganglia and Related Structures of the Brain

- basal ganglia
- globus pallidus
- thalamus
- substantia nigra
- cerebellum

Source: Henkel, John (July-August 1998). "Parkinson's Disease: New Treatments Slow Onslaught of Symptoms." FDA Consumer: p. 17. ISSN 0362-1332. Retrieved on 2009-07-23.

2. Describe the location of each of the cortical regions involved in speech production. Not all of these regions are visible on the surface of the brain, yet all of them are part of the cerebral cortex. Explain.

3. Ackermann (2008) proposed three functional systems in the speech production network. What are they, and what does each do?

4. What are the original functions of the cerebellum, basal ganglia, and thalamus. Relate these original functions to the roles they play in speech production.

Thought Questions

1. We've seen that many of the brain structures regulating locomotion are also involved in speech production. How is talking like walking? To answer this question, you need to observe carefully all of the movements you engage in when you walk and likewise when you talk. In what ways are timing and rhythm important for both?

2. Noted Dutch psycholinguist Willem Levelt maintains that articulate speech is the most complex motor skill performed by humans (Levelt, 1989). Given that we seem to speak without effort, why would he make such a claim?

Google It! Expressive and Receptive Aphasia

If you're interested in speech disorders, you can find example videos of these on YouTube. Google expressive aphasia and receptive aphasia for demonstrations. You can also find videos of patients with other forms of aphasia as well. Compare these symptoms with those of a patient with dysarthria.

SECTION 4.3: MODELS OF SPEECH PRODUCTION

- Current models of speech production are built on recent findings in neuroimaging research as well as on clinical data; many areas of the brain in both cerebral hemispheres as well as subcortical structures are involved in speech production.

- Speech production recruits many brain areas involved in moving the limbs; the motor system is organized into feedforward and feedback control systems, with the feedforward system generating the overall movement plan and the feedback system providing information so that adjustments can be made.

- Jaw perturbation studies and auditory perturbation studies show that somatosensory feedback is already available during the current articulation but that auditory feedback can only influence the production of subsequent utterances.

- Forward models propose that the motor system, in addition to generating a motor plan, also generates an expected sensory consequence of that motor plan. If the actual sensory input matches the expectation, the sensory experience is attenuated, and if there is a mismatch, it is intensified.

- The dual stream model of language processing proposes that a ventral stream from auditory cortex to the temporal lobe interprets the meaning of the incoming speech signal while a dorsal stream from auditory cortex to the frontal lobe links the incoming speech signal with speech motor programs.

- DIVA is a computational model that incorporates the latest neuroimaging data. It conceptualizes Broca's area as a speech sound map linking perception and production. It can also account for infant speech development and adult speech production with the same mechanism.

Perhaps you have a container of your favorite beverage in front of you as you read this text. Reach out and grab that container. (If you don't have a beverage, act out the motion anyway.) Repeat this several times, paying special attention to the way your arm moves.

Moving a limb toward a target typically involves a three-step process (Houde & Nagarajan, 2011). First, a burst of muscle activity propels the limb toward the target. Then, as the limb approaches its destination, opposing muscles act as a brake, bringing to limb to a stop just before the target. Finally, a weaker burst of muscle activity brings the limb into the proper configuration for contacting the target.

Moving the speech articulators involves a similar three-step procedure, in that the tongue, jaw, and lips are thrust into various positions. However, the process is also more complicated because the movements are so rapid, and they require the coordination of many more moving parts.

Feedforward and Feedback Control

A general property of the motor system is that it includes both feedforward and feedback control processes (Houde & Nagarajan, 2011). **Feedforward control** is *the process that provides the general motor plan for moving a body part toward a goal position.* Meanwhile, **feedback control** is *the process that adjusts the forward trajectory based on real-time information about the likely success of the movement.* In the case of reaching for an object, the motor system receives rapid feedback from the somatosensory system about the dynamic state of each of the muscles, tendons, and joints involved in the movement. In addition, visual feedback plays an important role in modifying actions in progress.

Current models of speech production generally assume a feedforward-feedback system as well, although there's still debate about about the some of the sources of feedback. In the case of speech production, the somatosensory system provides continuous feedback on the movements of the articulators. Feedback through the auditory system may be useful as well.

The **jaw perturbation technique** can be used to test the hypothesis that the motor speech system uses somatosensory feedback to make corrections during articulation (Golfinopoulous et al., 2011). This is *a procedure that involves attaching a robotic arm to the jaw of the research participant, who articulates syllables as the robot applies an upward or downward force.* The robotic arm is under the control of the experimenter, and it can be used to perturb the participant's jaw movement during vowel articulation.

Suppose the participant is asked to say *bet*. If the jaw is nudged upward during the articulation, the resulting utterance would be *bait*; and if nudged downward, it would be *bat*. However, these studies show that people are able to compensate for unexpected jaw perturbations during vowel production, moving the jaw in the opposite direction of the perturbation to produce the intended syllable. These findings suggest that the goal of a speech motor plan is not the production of a particular gesture but rather of a particular acoustic signal. Intuitively this makes sense, as we've all had the experience of talking with our mouth full or after dental surgery, when we have to modify the way we articulate.

The exact role of auditory feedback in speech production is less clear. Sensorimotor feedback loops provide rapidly available information for course corrections during articulation. However, there's a much larger time lag with auditory feedback, since the sound wave needs to travel from mouth to ear to be processed by the auditory system before being sent on to motor cortex (Houde & Nagarajan, 2011). This time lag is too great to provide useful feedback during the articulation of a particular syllable. However, it may have an influence on subsequent speech.

The **auditory perturbation technique** can be used to explore the role of auditory feedback in speech production (Shum et al., 2011). This is *a procedure in which participants repeat syllables into a microphone and listen through headphones as their voice is modified by a computer*. This technique uses a computer program that can shift the first formant of the vowel up or down so quickly that there's no discernible time lag.

Suppose the participant is asked to repeat the syllable *bet* multiple times. If the computer then shifts the first formant to sound like *bat*, the participant will gradually compensate by raising the jaw, as if to produce *bait*. When the computer stops filtering the input, the participant gradually returns to producing *bet*. This finding suggests that we use auditory feedback not to make course corrections of articulatory gestures in progress but rather to adjust subsequent articulatory movements (Cai et al., 2011).

Auditory Suppression During Speech

Another way to study the role of auditory feedback in speech production is to introduce an auditory delay. The **delayed auditory feedback technique** is *a procedure in which research participants speak while listening through headphones to their own voice, which is delayed a fraction of a second*. A delay of even fifty milliseconds can severely disrupt a person's ability to speak (Houde & Jordan, 2002). This effect isn't simply due to auditory interference, since hearing another voice while speaking doesn't have the same disruptive effect. These effects have been known since the mid-twentieth century (e.g., Fairbanks, 1955), but more recent electrophysiological and neuroimaging studies have shown that speech interference due to delayed auditory feedback is related to a process known as auditory suppression (Heinks-Maldonado, 2005; Houde & Jordan, 2002; Takaso et al., 2010).

Auditory suppression is related to a general principle of the sensorimotor system in which the expected sensory effects of a self-initiated action are attenuated (Heinks-Maldonado, 2005). For example, it's virtually impossible to tickle yourself, at least intentionally. Such observations are generally explained in terms of a **forward model**. This is *a model that explains sensory suppression by proposing that each time the sensorimotor system generates a motor command it also generates a predicted sensory consequence for comparison against the actual sensory input*. If the prediction and the input match, the sensory experience is dampened. A mismatch between prediction and input signals a production error, and input without prediction signals an external event; but in either case the sensory system intensifies the perceived experience. Numerous animal studies of birds, bats, and monkeys show that auditory suppression of self-vocalizations is the norm across species.

Auditory suppression is strictly a response to an immediately prior speech event. Houde and Nagarajan (2011) used a technique known as magnetoencephalography to investigate auditory suppression during speech. **Magnetoencephalography** is *a technique for recording brain activity by measuring subtle changes in the magnetic field surrounding the head produced by the electrical currents arising from neural events in the brain.* The researchers found reduced activity in the auditory cortex when participants heard themselves speaking in real time but not when they heard a recording of their own voice. Furthermore, when tone pips were added to the auditory input, there was suppression of the speech signal but not of the tone pips, showing that auditory suppression is specific to one's own voice.

Houde and Nagarajan (2011) suggest that auditory suppression prevents feedback interference during speech production. By the time that auditory feedback reaches the speech motor system, the command for the next articulatory gesture has already been sent, so it provides no useful information about the current state of the speech production system. However, this doesn't mean that auditory feedback provides no useful information, since speakers will modify subsequent articulations to compensate when they hear their voice altered in an unexpected way.

Because speaking our native language is such a highly practiced skill, we produce articulatory gestures with such a high degree of accuracy that auditory feedback simply isn't that important most of the time. Speaking in a non-native language, on the other hand, may require more feedback, and this hypothesis was tested by Jones and colleagues (2013). Using fMRI, these researchers observed activity in the auditory and articulatory regions of the brain while native and non-native speakers of English were engaged in a picture-naming task.

Both native and non-native speakers exhibited auditory suppression, in that increased activity in articulatory regions led to decreased activity in auditory regions. However, both groups also showed evidence of auditory feedback, in that increased activity in the auditory regions led to increased activity in the articulatory regions. The important difference between the two groups was that native speakers had more auditory suppression and the non-native speakers more auditory feedback. Furthermore, the degree of English fluency in the non-native speakers correlated with the degree of auditory suppression they experienced. These results suggest a flexible speech production system that incorporates auditory input when it's needed and disregards it when it's not.

Dual Stream Model

It's been recognized for several decades that visual processing in the brain involves two separate pathways (Ungerleider & Mishkin, 1982). The ventral stream flows from the primary visual cortex to association areas of the temporal lobe and is involved in object recognition. The dorsal stream flows from the primary visual cortex in the occipital lobe to association areas in the parietal lobe and is responsible for processing spatial relations, thus enabling the organism to navigate through the environment. In the original model, the dorsal stream was conceptualized as the "where" pathway and the ventral stream as the "what" pathway.

We now know that dual stream processing is a general organizing principle of the sensorimotor system. Alain and colleagues (2001) mapped out the dual processing stream for audition, while Dijkerman and de Haan (2007) did the same for the body senses. Furthermore, the dorsal stream has been reinterpreted as the "how" rather than the "where" pathway, in that it helps the organism decide *how* to navigate its surroundings (Rizzolati, Fogassi, & Gallese, 1997; Scott, 2005). It's the dorsal stream, then, that integrates the sensory and motor systems, creating a tight coupling between perception and action.

Since speech processing also involves a high degree of sensorimotor integration, it seems reasonable that the speech perception-production system would also be organized into "what" and "how" streams. This is exactly what Hickok and Poeppel (2007) proposed, and their dual stream model of speech processing has been quite influential in guiding research over the last few years. According to this model, the **ventral stream** is *a bilateral processing pathway that interprets the meaning of the incoming speech signal*, and the **dorsal stream** is *a left-hemisphere processing pathway that links the incoming speech signal with speech motor programs*. In other words, the ventral stream is the "What does it mean?" pathway and the dorsal stream is the "How do you say it?" pathway.

The traditional view has been that language is lateralized on the left side of the brain, but neuroimaging studies have shown that both hemispheres of the cerebral cortex and a number of subcortical structures are recruited for speech processing. The dual stream model proposes that there are parallel ventral streams in the left and right hemispheres. However, there is some degree of specialization, with the right hemisphere processing meaning over longer time scales and hence more holistically, and the left processing over shorter time scales and hence more analytically.

The dorsal stream originates in the speech perception area in the lateral fissure at the juncture of the parietal and temporal lobes (roughly speaking, Wernicke's area), and it extends to the posterior inferior frontal gyrus (roughly speaking, Broca's area) as well as to the primary motor cortex. Unlike the ventral stream, the dorsal stream is strongly lateralized to the left hemisphere.

The dual stream model is important because it ties together many different observations of language processing. In this model, the ventral stream provides an interface between processing below the level of the word (such as phonemes, syllables, and prosody) and processing at the word level and above (such as sentences and discourse). These two levels have mostly been studied separately, with little more than an assumption that somehow they are integrated. Furthermore, the ventral stream helps account for clinical and neuroimaging data regarding the retrieval of words from memory (Hickok &

Figure 4.7   Dual Stream Model

According to the dual stream model, the dorsal "how" stream processes the articulation of speech while the ventral "what" stream processes the meaning of the speech. Both streams are active in speech production and speech perception.

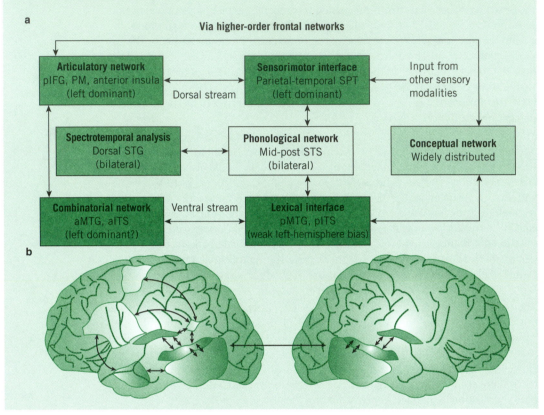

Source: Hickok and Poeppel (2007).

Poeppel, 2007). It's generally believed that semantic information is widely distributed throughout the cortex, but the left middle temporal gyrus seems to play a role in integrating meaning with spoken word forms.

The dorsal stream, integrating auditory and motor representations, incorporates a number of earlier ideas about language processing. You may have already noticed that the dorsal stream looks a lot like the traditional Wernicke-Geschwind model. What the dual stream model does, then, is integrate the earlier standard theory into a newer and more detailed model of language processing. Likewise, the dorsal stream provides a mechanism for motor theory, which proposes that the object of speech perception is the gestures that produced the acoustic signal. The tight coupling of speech perception and production provided by the dorsal stream provides an account as well for the development of speech production as the infant learns how to speak from hearing the speech of others. Finally, Hickok and Poeppel (2007) propose that the dorsal stream also provides a mechanism to account for phonological short-term memory.

DIVA

Cognitive scientists often create computational models to test their theories and to generate new hypotheses for research. A **computational model** is *a computer program that simulates a cognitive process in a manner that is consistent with what is currently known about human cognition*. A working model provides proof of concept for a theory, demonstrating that the proposed mechanism is plausible, and it also helps researchers find unexpected consequences of the theory. Many models of speech production have been proposed over the years, but one that's currently quite influential in the field is DIVA, developed by Frank Guenther and his colleagues (Bohland et al., 2010; Ghosh, Tourville, & Guenther, 2008; Guenther & Vladusich, 2012; Tourville & Guenther, 2011).

The DIVA model incorporates all of the functional brain regions described in this chapter, organizing them into feedforward and feedback control systems. The feedforward control system includes the supplementary motor area, Broca's area, and the motor cortex, which programs the motor commands for speech. Meanwhile, somatosensory and auditory targets (i.e., the expected sensory consequences) are sent to the feedback control system, where these targets are compared against the actual sensory inputs. Any detected somatosensory or auditory errors are sent to the feedback control map, which sends feedback commands to the motor cortex instructing it to modify its motor commands to the articulators. Incidentally, DIVA stands for "Directions Into Velocities of Articulators," in case you were wondering.

DIVA is an influential model for a number of reasons, only two of which we'll consider here. First, it proposes a new way of thinking about the role of Broca's area (Guenther & Vladusich, 2012). Traditionally, Broca's area is thought of as the speech production center. However, neuroimaging studies have indicated that the region is also involved in the perception and production of gestures. Furthermore, the mirror neurons that have been studied in monkeys are located in a brain region analogous to Broca's area. Recall that mirror neurons represent actions, whether performed by the self or observed in another. Thus, Guenther and his colleagues propose that Broca's area serves as a speech sound map where mirror neurons representing speech sounds, whether perceived or produced, are located. Research in the next few years should clarify whether this conceptualization of Broca's area is accurate or not.

By the way, the idea of a speech sound map is consistent with motor theory, which proposes that we perceive speech by activating the speech production system. The reverse should be true as well. That is, when we produce speech, the goal is to produce

Figure 4.8   DIVA Model

The DIVA model can account for both speech production and speech acquisition. Standard abbreviations are used for the brain areas involved. See how many of them you can decipher based on the the discussion of brain locations and directions in this chapter and in Chapter 2. For example, *pIFG* stands for posterior Inferior Frontal Gyrus—roughly speaking, Broca's area.

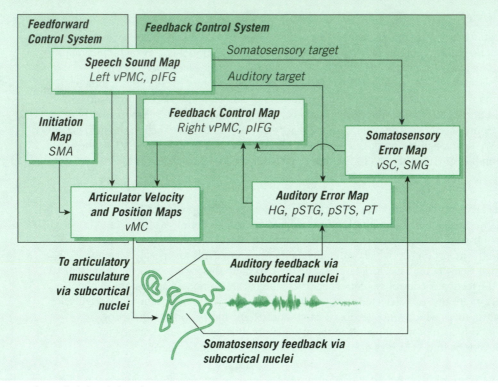

Source: Guenther and Vladusich (2012).

a particular acoustic signal. Thus, the coupling between perception and production runs in both directions.

The second important contribution of the DIVA model is that it explains both adult speech production and infant speech development in the same framework (Guenther & Vladusich, 2012). The model proposes that an infant's early babbling will be random and repetitive, because it is driven only by the feedforward control system. But as the infant babbles, it receives sensory feedback that it can compare against speech samples it has already experienced. When the DIVA model is begun in a random state, it will organize itself, over multiple trials, into a system that mimics an adult speaker. In the next section, we'll look at the development of speech production in more detail, considering whether the data are consistent with the DIVA model.

In Sum

Recent findings from neuroimaging studies have led to the development of new models of how the brain implements the production of speech. It's now known that many regions of the brain are recruited in speech production, including those regions whose original function was locomotion. Areas on both the left and the right side of the brain are involved, as are a number of subcortical structures. The motor system, which is recruited for speech production, consists of both feedforward and feedback control systems. The speech production system receives both somatosensory feedback, which can influence the articulation of the current utterance, and auditory feedback, which can influence the articulation of the next utterance. Forward models propose that the motor system generates an expected sensory consequence for each motor plan, which it compares against the actual sensory input as a means of detecting errors in motor execution. The dual stream model posits a ventral stream that interprets the meaning of the incoming speech signal and a dorsal stream that links auditory and motor representations of speech. The DIVA model views Broca's area as a speech sound map coupling production and perception.

Review Questions

1. Distinguish between feedforward and feedback control processes in the motor system. How are these terms applicable to speech production? What sort of feedback does the speech production system receive, and how does it use it?

2. Explain how forward models work. Why does auditory suppression during speech production support the notion that speech production can be described by a forward model?

3. Describe the dual stream model of speech processing. What does each stream do? What parts of the brain are involved in each stream? In what sense is the dual stream model an extension of the traditional Wernicke-Geschwind model?

4. Describe the components of the DIVA model and how they work together. What are some important contributions of the model?

Thought Questions

1. Broca's area is also involved in the production of signed language (Horwitz et al., 2003; Kassubek, Hickok, & Erhard, 2004). How would the DIVA model account for these findings?

2. Dual stream processing seems to be a general organizing principle of the sensorimotor system. Generally speaking, what is the function of each stream? What do these two functions tell us about the primary purpose of a brain?

Google It! Speech Jammer

If you'd like to experience **delayed auditory feedback** for yourself, search online for a DAF program. (There's even a DAF app for the Android phone!) If you're interested in wacky inventions, look up **speech jammer**, a device that uses delayed auditory feedback to shut up those annoying people who love to dominate conversations. (You can also find instructions for building your own speech jammer.) Finally, if you are interested in speech disorders, look into a surprising use of delayed auditory feedback on people who **stutter**.

SECTION 4.4: DEVELOPMENT OF SPEECH PRODUCTION

- During the first six months, infants produce a variety of speech-like sounds, but with the onset of canonical babbling, the child begins producing clearly perceivable consonant-vowel syllables.

- The frames-then-content model views babbling as driven by the motor system without auditory input coupling of jaw movement with phonation; as a result, some consonant-vowel pairs are more likely to occur in canonical babbling.

- Caregivers imitate their baby's babbling, and this social feedback helps the infant refine its production of the phonemes used in the language it's learning; caregivers' attempts to match baby's babbles with the names of objects helps the infant learn its first words.

- Delays in babbling or first words can indicate an underlying disorder such as hearing loss or apraxia of speech. Infants with hearing loss will show some signs of babbling but fail to progress toward clearly articulated canonical syllables.

- Childhood apraxia of speech is a condition in which children have difficulty producing speech despite having cognitive and motor functioning in the normal range; these children often need help from a speech language pathologist.

- Some children develop expressive language more slowly than receptive language but eventually catch up with their peers; other children have mostly normal language development except for particular speech sound errors that can persist well into elementary school or later.

Infants come into the world screaming, and for the next few months, crying is their main form of communication. However, they also produce speech-like sounds that, over the course of the first year, become their first words.

Stages of Babbling

During the first six months of life, infants progress through predictable stages of vocalization (Oller & Eilers, 1988). The first is the **phonation stage**, *the period from birth to two months when infants produce vowel-like sounds by vibrating the vocal folds.* While these sounds have some of the qualities of vowels, the infant still has little control over the articulators, so they aren't recognizable as any particular vowels. It's rare during this time for the infant to produce anything resembling a consonant. Next comes the **gooing stage**, *the period from two to four months when infants produce syllable-like sounds in the back of the vocal tract.* These sounds are often perceived as "coo" or "goo," hence the name of this period, but both the consonant and the vowel portions of these utterances are poorly formed and highly variable.

As the infant gains some control over the lips, tongue, and jaw, its vocal repertoire increases (Oller & Eilers, 1988). The **expansion stage** is *the period from four to six months when infants produce a variety of different sounds.* Sounds like the "raspberry," made by protruding the tongue and vibrating the lips, are common during this time. The infant will also produce well-formed vowels such as "ee" and "ah," with occasional consonant-like sounds mixed in, and the resulting syllable-like sounds are referred to as marginal babbling. It often appears as though the infant were vocalizing in order to attract the attention of the caregiver (Locke, 2006). In response, caregivers will often mimic the infant's vocalizations, and this social feedback encourages the infant to babble more (Goldstein & Schwade, 2008). Prelinguistic infants may also use feedback from caregivers to hone their vocalizations.

Between six and ten months, the infant's vocalizations become more speech-like (Nathani, Oller, & Neal, 2007). This marks the onset of **canonical babbling**, which is *prelinguistic vocalization characterized by sequences of clearly formed consonant-vowel syllables.* These syllables are first produced in isolation, such as "ba," but they are

Table 4.2 Stages of Babbling

Infants go through predictable stages of babbling during the first year, regardless of the language spoken around them and even if they have a profound hearing loss.

Stage	Months	Infant produces
Phonation	0–2	Vowel-like sounds made by vibrating the vocal folds.
Gooing	2–4	Syllable-like sounds in the back of the vocal tract.
Expansion	4–6	A variety of different sounds.
Canonical babbling	6–12	Sequences of clearly formed consonant-vowel syllables.

Source: http://training.seer.cancer.gov/head-neck/anatomy/overview.html.

soon followed by reduplicated syllables like "mama" and then variegated syllables like "daddy" (Harold & Barlow, 2013). Early canonical babbling has similar features regardless of the ambient language, with the consonants consisting mainly of oral and nasal stops produced with the lips or tongue tip (mainly *b, d, m,* and *n*) or glides like *w* and *y* (von Hapsburg & Davis, 2006). However, before the infant's first year, babbling takes on the characteristics of the ambient language.

Caregivers respond to canonical babbling as if it were intentional speech (Nathani et al., 2007). For example, if baby says "bah," mom or dad might look around for an object with a "bah"-like name, such as *ball* or *bottle,* holding it up and repeating "bah." This kind of behavior may help the infant associate names with objects, but it also works in the opposite direction, since families will also adopt "baby words" like "wawa" for *water* or "goggie" for *doggie,* even using these in speech not directed at the baby. Furthermore, the baby's first words typically develop out of babbling sequences that have been reinforced by caregivers (Morris, 2010).

The development of infant vocalizations follows a consistent pattern, even when the infant is profoundly deaf (Iyer & Oller, 2008). Canonical babbling is delayed in infants with hearing loss, but it still often occurs within the normal range. As a result, many infants with hearing loss aren't identified until well after their first year.

Frames-Then-Content Model

Two observations suggest that early vocalization is strictly driven by the motor system and not dependent on auditory feedback (von Hapsburg , Davis, & MacNeilage, 2008). The first is the universal nature of early infant vocalizations, which are markedly similar across cultures, both in the time they begin and in the types of sounds produced. The second is that even deaf children go through the same stages and produce just as much sound as hearing infants do.

Davis and MacNeilage (1994) proposed *a theory that explains babbling in terms of repeated jaw movements,* which they called the **frames-then-content model**. According to this model, babbling begins around six to eight months because this is when the infant gains control of the jaw. During this time period, the infant will make jaw movements without vocalizing (Harold & Barlow, 2013), but sometimes it will also produce phonation, which it has already been doing for several months. The result of this jaw oscillation accompanied by vocal fold vibration is a sequence of vocalizations that sounds like simple consonant-vowel syllables. After all, vowels are produced with the vocal tract open, and stop consonants are produced with the vocal tract closed.

The frames-then-content model also stipulates that certain speech sounds are more basic than others, and it is these consonants and vowels that will first appear in the infant's canonical babbling. In surveying the sound systems of the world's languages, Maddieson (1984) reports that nearly all languages make use of consonants produced at three particular places, namely the lips (such as *b* and *m*), the tip of the tongue (such as *d* and *n*), and the back of the tongue (such as *g* and *ng*). Furthermore, virtually all languages distinguish at least three vowels based on tongue position, specifically front (such as *ee*), central (such as *ah*) and back (such as *oo*).

It used to be believed that the early babbling of infants featured all possible speech sounds and that later these were narrowed down to the phoneme inventory of the language the child was learning (Jakobson, 1968). However, the modern view is simply that infant speech sound production is highly variable but centered on the most basic sounds common to all the world's languages. The frames-then-content model includes this assumption as well (von Hapsburg et al., 2008).

At the onset of canonical babbling, according to the model, the infant still has little control over the lips or tongue, and so their contribution to the vocal output will essentially be random (von Hapsburg et al., 2008). Furthermore, lip shape and tongue position are likely to remain constant through one or more cycles of jaw movement, thus influencing both the consonant and the vowel portion of the syllable. In other words, there should be predictable patterns of consonant-vowel pairs in babbling, as opposed to a random mixture of consonants and vowels.

Specifically, the model predicts that three patterns will prevail. First, if the tongue happens to be in a central position during babbling, the lips will constrict the vocal tract when the jaw closes, producing a consonant like *b*, *m*, or *w*, followed by a central vowel such as *ah* or *uh*. Second, if the tongue is in a front position, its tip will constrict the vocal tract by meeting the teeth or alveolar ridge, producing a consonant like *d*, *n*, or *y*, followed by a front vowel like *ee* or *ay*. Third, if the tongue is in a back position, the back of the tongue will meet the velum, producing a sound like *g* or *ng*, followed by a vowel like *oo* or *oh*. Although all consonant-vowel combinations occur in babbling, the three patterns just described tend to occur more often than would be expected by chance. Cross-linguistic studies have shown that similar babbling patterns occur in other languages as well, such as Italian (Majorano & D'Odorico, 2011) and the Ecuadorian indigenous language Quichua (Gildersleeve-Neumann, Davis, & MacNeilage, 2013).

Table 4.3   Frames-Then-Content Model

The frames-then-content model predicts that some syllables are more frequent than others in canonical babbling because the tongue position and resulting vocal tract configuration remain constant throughout the production of the syllable.

Tongue Position	Vocal Tract Configuration	Typical Syllables
Central	Mouth open, lips rounded	*baa, buh, mah, muh, wah, wuh*
Front	Tip of tongue strikes alveolar ridge	*dee, day, nee, nay, yee, yay*
Back	Root of tongue strikes velum	*goo, go, ngoo, ngo*

The frames-then-content model explains these data by postulating that the infant gains control of jaw movements before tongue movements, but it's also possible that the infant is simply mimicking the sound patterns it hears in its caregiver's language. Analyses of caregiver speech have yielded contradictory results (Whalen et al., 2012). The predicted patterns were found in French caregiver speech, meaning that the babbling patterns of French babies could be imitations of what they hear. However, in Mandarin the predicted patterns occur no more frequently than would be expected by chance, and to make matters worse, they occur less frequently in English than would be expected. Nevertheless, the early canonical babbling of French, Chinese, and English babies each follows the predicted patterns. Furthermore, infants with hearing impairment also display the same predicted patterns in their babbling (von Hapsburg et al., 2008). The reasonable conclusion from these findings is that these babbling patterns are driven by motor and not auditory processes.

Social Aspects of Babbling

Although the onset of canonical babbling may be driven by the developing motor system without auditory input, social interaction with the caregiver plays an important role in shaping babbling into the baby's first words. Parents are keenly attuned to the beginning of their infant's babbling, which they intuitively interpret as an attempt to speak (Oller, Eilers, & Basinger, 2001). Babbling babies are cute, and they attract the attention of both caregivers and other adults, who respond to babbling as if it were an invitation to conversation (Locke, 2006).

When babies babble, their parents imitate them, although within the confines of their language (Ramsdell et al., 2012). This auditory feedback then helps the infant home in on the sound categories of the language that it's learning. Goldstein and Schwade (2008) observed mothers who either imitated their infants' babbles (contingent feedback) or else responded without imitating (noncontingent feedback) during a thirty-minute play session. Infants whose mothers provided contingent feedback modified subsequent vocalizations to sound more like the ambient language. However, when the feedback was noncontingent (i.e., not imitation), the infants' babbling didn't become more like their mothers' speech. In short, infants use immediate feedback to adjust the character of their utterances.

As infants approach their first year, they begin to use babbling to elicit responses from their caregivers. One example is **object-directed vocalization**, which is *babbling uttered as the infant approaches and manipulates a novel object* (Goldstein et al., 2010). As we've already seen, parents will often respond by naming the object with a word that resembles the babble. Goldstein and his colleagues found that infants who received this kind of feedback to their object-directed vocalizations had larger vocabularies than infants whose parents habitually named objects with words that didn't sound like what the baby babbled. The researchers interpreted these findings as suggesting that object-directed vocalizations indicate the infant's heightened

Figure 4.9   Parent Playing With Infant

Parents often treat babbling as meaningful speech.

Source: ©iStockphoto.com/Lili_Bond.

attention and readiness to learn. In other words, parents' intuition that baby is asking "What's that?" may be correct.

Speech Delays and Disorders

Because infants with hearing impairment go through the same early stages of speech development as infants with normal hearing, their hearing impairment often goes undetected until the second year of life. However, a careful analysis of vocalizations in deaf and hearing infants reveals subtle differences (Koopmans-van Beinum, Clement, & van den Dikkenberg-Pot, 2001). Specifically, the ability to control the vibration of the vocal folds and the movement of the jaw develops in a similar fashion in both hearing and deaf infants, indicating that development of the phonation and articulation is an issue of motor development. However, the coupling of phonation and articulation is impaired in infants with hearing loss, suggesting that the ability to coordinate the two systems depends on auditory feedback. As a result, infants with hearing impairment will show some signs of babbling, but they don't show the normal progression toward making clearly articulated canonical syllables with features of the caregiver's language, which should occur around the end of the infant's first year of life.

Because early detection can lead to successful intervention, it's important to identify hearing loss as soon as possible. Routine hearing tests during pediatric exams are helpful, but Oller and colleagues point out that a simple diagnostic tool is also available (Oller et al., 2001). These researchers have found that parents, regardless of education or socioeconomic status, have a keen intuitive sense of when their children have started babbling. Since a delay in the onset of babbling may indicate a hearing problem or speech disorder, Oller and colleagues recommend that health care providers routinely ask parents if their infants have started babbling yet as a means of screening for speech delays.

Many children who start babbling late catch up with their peers by three years of age, and so late babbling onset per se isn't cause for alarm (Fasolo, Majorano, & D'Odorico, 2008). However, late babble onset can indicate a speech or language difficulty, and so late developers need to be examined more closely.

A hearing impairment isn't the only reason for a delay in babbling or first words. Some children display **slow expressive development**, meaning they experience *a delay in babbling or talking in spite of developing receptive language and social interaction skills at a normal rate*. When they do start to babble, these late talkers produce a narrower range of syllables and a smaller ratio of consonants to vowels. Because they have a smaller set of canonical syllables, late talkers are limited in the building blocks they have for producing their first words, and as a result their productive vocabularies are smaller. This observation suggests that even normally developing children are more likely to learn words that they can pronounce, as opposed to first learning the names of the objects and people that are most familiar to them. As we've already seen, family members will often adopt the words that baby uses to refer to people and objects (Oller & Eilers, 1988).

Delayed or infrequent babbling can also be a sign of **childhood apraxia of speech**, *a condition in which children experience severe difficulty in producing speech even though their cognitive, perceptual, and motor skills are otherwise in the normal range* (Highman et al., 2012). Unlike children with slow expressive development, who eventually catch up with their peers, children with apraxia of speech continue to have difficulties speaking well into the middle years of childhood. Oftentimes, long-term intervention by a trained speech language pathologist is necessary for the child to develop speaking ability within the normal range.

Finally, some children begin babbling and talking at the normal age, but they mispronounce certain phonemes. This is *a condition in which a child can clearly hear a distinction between two phonemes but uses only one of them when speaking*, and it is often referred to as the **fis phenomenon**, based on an incident reported by Berko and Brown (1960). A child they were studying had an inflatable toy fish that he called a "fis," but he objected when the adults said "fis" instead of "fish."

Phoneme substitutions are common in early speech, as the child uses the consonants and vowels of canonical babbling in place of those that are more difficult to pronounce.

Figure 4.10   Toddler With Fish

She may call these "fis," but she'll correct you if you call them that.

Source: ©iStockphoto.com/fishwor.

However, children with **residual speech sound errors** exhibit *misarticulations that persist into the elementary school years* (Preston et al., 2012). A common type of speech sound error involves the sounds *l* and *r*, which are typically replaced with *w*, as for example when the cartoon character Elmer Fudd says to Bugs Bunny: "I've got you now, you wascawy wabbit!" Other typical speech sound errors involve the fricatives and affricates made with the tip of the tongue, such as *s* and *sh*, in which case the child often uses one phoneme for both, as in the "fis" example. In other cases, bilabial fricatives are used instead of the two *th* sounds, as in "wif" for "with" and "bruvver" for "brother." Most of the time, there's no known reason for the residual speech sound error. Children and adolescents with a history of speech sound errors tend to perform more poorly than their peers on reading and spelling tasks, suggesting a deeper problem than just difficulty articulating. While most of these errors are eventually resolved, occasionally one will persist into adulthood, becoming part of that person's idiosyncratic way of speaking.

In Sum

From shortly after birth, infants make various speech-like vocalizations, but sometime after six months the infant begins babbling in canonical consonant-vowel syllables that caregivers respond to as if it were intentional speech. The frames-then-content model proposes that early babbling results after the infant has gained motor control over the vocal folds and jaw and that it isn't the product of imitation. This model explains why some consonant-vowel sequences occur more frequently than others, and furthermore it accounts for the observations that early babbling is remarkably similar across languages and that even hearing-impaired children babble. Social feedback from caregivers helps infants shape their babbling into their first words. Some infants initially develop speech at a slower rate but eventually catch up with their peers. However, a delay in babbling can signal an underlying disorder, such as a hearing impairment or apraxia of speech. A few children experience residual speech sound errors that can persist into the school years or later.

Review Questions

1. Give the typical age ranges and characteristics of each of the prelinguistic stages of speech development: phonation, gooing, expansion, and canonical babbling.

2. How does the frames-then-content model explain canonical babbling? What is the evidence to support this model?

3. Describe the experiment by Goldstein and Schwade (2008) on the effect of contingent feedback on babbling. What do the results suggest?

4. What is an object-oriented vocalization, and how does it facilitate word learning?

5. Explain the fis phenomenon and residual speech sound errors.

Thought Questions

1. In languages around the world, the words for mother and father are remarkably similar, typically some variant of *mama* and *papa,* respectively (Jakobson, 1962). Based on what you have read in this section, explain why this finding is not surprising.

2. What are the similarities and differences between slow expressive development and childhood apraxia of speech? What kind of intervention is needed in each case? (You'll need to do some more research online to answer this question.)

3. Consider possible reasons why adolescents with a history of speech sound errors tend to have poorer literacy skills. In responding to this question, it might help to introspect a while on what sort of mental operations you perform when you read.

Google It! Babbling Babies

There are countless hours of **babbling baby** videos on YouTube. Notice the language-like quality of babbling. But more important, pay attention to the way adults respond to the babbling as if it were intentional speech. In addition, you can find videos of

childhood apraxia of speech to get a sense of this disorder. You can also learn more about the therapies used to treat this disorder.

CONCLUSION

Speech is produced in the vocal tract, consisting of the oral and nasal cavities, which serve as resonating chambers for the phonation produced by the vibrating vocal folds. Consonants are produced by obstructing the flow of air through the oral cavity, while vowels are produced by moving the jaw, tongue, and lips to change the shape of the mouth. Coordinating the rapid movement of articulators to produce speech is one of the most complex motor tasks we perform, and yet we do it with seeming effortlessness.

Broca's area in the left frontal lobe has traditionally been viewed as the neural region responsible for speech production. The evidence for this view comes mainly from the symptoms of patients suffering from Broca's aphasia, who have great difficulty producing fluent speech. More recent neuroimaging and clinical studies have found that both hemispheres get involved in speech production, particularly at the level of articulation. In addition to the traditional language areas, sensorimotor regions of the brain are recruited for programming speech articulation. Furthermore, subcortical structures that play a role in regulating motor functions are also recruited for speech production. These structures include the cerebellum, the basal ganglia, and the thalamus.

Sensory and motor systems interact as speech is produced. The motor systems program the movements of the articulators, while somatosensory systems monitor those movements for errors. The auditory system also provides monitoring feedback, but this information comes too late to influence ongoing articulation. However, it can influence the subsequent production of speech. The dual stream model proposes that a ventral stream from the auditory cortex to the temporal lobe interprets the meaning of the incoming speech signal while a dorsal stream from the auditory cortex to the frontal lobe links the incoming speech signal with speech motor programs. In this way, speech perception and speech production are related and interactive processes.

During the first year of life, infants go through predictable stages in the development of speech production. Infants produce a variety of speech-like sounds that gradually converge on canonical babbling, which has characteristics similar to the ambient language. Caregivers treat babbling as if it were meaningful speech, and in this way the prelinguistic child learns the rules of discourse and social interaction. Delays in babbling or first words may be a sign of a language disorder. On the other hand, even profoundly deaf infants babble, which can lead to delays in identifying the hearing loss.

Once children have mastered the rudiments of speech articulation around their first birthday, they begin producing their first words. In the next chapter, we turn our attention to words, considering how they're learned, stored, and retrieved.

CROSS-CULTURAL PERSPECTIVE:
Click Languages

All speech sounds in English are produced by blowing air out of the mouth or nose. And in all languages around the world, the vast majority of speech sounds are produced with outward airflow. But a few languages also include speech sounds that are made by sucking air into the mouth. Speech sounds produced with inward airflow are known as clicks.

Clicks aren't difficult to make, and even native English speakers know how to produce them. It's just that they don't use them as speech sounds. Think about the sound you make when you disapprove of someone else's behavior. As part of our culture, we know that a sucking sound made by pressing the tongue against the back of the teeth is a signal of contempt or pity. This sound—often written as *tsk! tsk!*—is a click, and it's used as a phoneme in some languages of southern Africa, particularly among several speech communities collectively known as Khoisan.

Two other common clicks were very much a part of English-speaking culture until the advent of the automobile. These are horse-related sounds, but they're still part of our cultural heritage. Ask any four-year-old what sound you make when you want your horse to start moving, and she'll tell you: *tchick! tchick!* This sound is a lateral click, produced by sucking in air from the side of your mouth. Next ask your young informant what sound a horse's hooves make when it walks, and again she'll tell you: *clip! clop!* This sound is an alveolar click, made by pressing the tip of the tongue against the alveolar ridge or even the roof of the mouth. Both lateral and alveolar clicks can be used as speech sounds as well. Yet another click that's easy to produce is the labial click, which you make when you smack your lips in a fake kiss.

Perhaps the greatest mystery surrounding clicks is why they're limited to languages in a fairly restricted region of Africa. Because clicks occur in languages spoken closest to the original homeland of human beings, some researchers believe that they're evolutionarily ancient, part of the phoneme inventories of the first languages spoken by humans (Pennisi, 2004). According to this theory, languages spoken by peoples who have remained in the region where humans first arose still retain characteristics of primeval speech, but as bands of humans left southern Africa, the languages they spoke lost many of those features.

Other researchers believe that click phonemes are a fairly recent invention (Güldemann & Stoneking, 2008). First of all, it's not at all clear that the modern Khoisan peoples have always lived where they do now. In other words, there's no particular reason to believe that the Khoisan language today is in any sense representative of what the first human languages were like. Furthermore, both linguistic and genetic evidence shows that certain Bantu languages, which also have clicks, borrowed them from the Khoisan in the last few thousand years (Barbieri et al., 2013). Thus, clicks could be a recent linguistic phenomenon that's spreading as opposed to an ancient language feature that's been largely lost.

Clicks aren't difficult to learn, and children learning nonclick languages master them even before some of the more difficult but more common speech sounds such as *r* and *th*. However, when outsiders first encounter speakers of click languages, they perceive these sounds as bizarre and hence difficult to produce. While producing clicks in isolation isn't difficult for a native English speaker, integrating them into the rapid speech stream is more challenging. But that's mainly due to lack of practice.

You can try making clicks together with vowels to get a sense of what they sound like—and what it's like to produce them—within speech. Here are some exercises you can try:

1. Practice the following series of vowels: *ah, ay, ee, oh, oo*.

2. Practice the following series of consonant vowel sequences: *tah, tay, tee, toh, too*.

3. Practice alternating between the non-click consonant *t* and the click consonant *tsk!*, which we'll shorten to *!t*.

4. Now try alternating between *tah* and *!tah*.

5. Finally, practice the sequence *!tah, !tay, !tee, !toh, !too*.

You can practice other clicks with this vowel series as well.

At the end of Section 4.1, you were urged to google click languages and watch some of the videos about them. If you didn't follow that advice then, you might want to do so now. Can you imagine clicks catching on in modern American English, perhaps as part of some new slang? What if rap artists or other popular performers started incorporating clicks into their lyrics for special effects?

KEY TERMS

Affricate	Anterior cingulate cortex	Arcuate fasciculus
Alveolar	Anterior insula	Auditory perturbation technique
Alveolar ridge	Approximant	
		Bilabial

Canonical babbling

Childhood apraxia of speech

Computational model

Conduction aphasia

Delayed auditory feedback technique

Diphthong

Dorsal stream

Dysarthria

Expansion stage

Expressive aphasia

Feedback control

Feedforward control

Fis phenomenon

Forward model

Frames-then-content model

Glottal stop

Gooing stage

Gyrus

Hard palate

Interdental

Jaw perturbation technique

Labiodental

Lateral sulcus

Longitudinal fissure

Magnetoencephalography

Manner of articulation

Object-directed vocalization

Perisylvian cortex

Phonation stage

Place of articulation

Postalveolar

Primary motor cortex

Receptive aphasia

Residual speech sound errors

Schwa

Slow expressive development

Somatosensory cortex

Sulcus

Supplementary motor area

Thalamus

Velar

Velum

Ventral stream

Vocal folds

CHAPTER

5

Words

Before you read this chapter, first try the following vocabulary quiz. Read the definition and then name the word. The first letter of the word is given in parentheses after the definition in case you get stuck. Write your answers on a separate piece of paper so you can check them later.

1. A material prepared in ancient Egypt and used for writing or painting on. (p)

2. A medical condition in which the ability of the blood to clot is severely reduced. (h)

3. A person who explores and studies caves as a hobby. (s)

4. A recurrent urge to steal, typically without regard for need or profit. (k)

5. A person who dislikes, despises, or is strongly prejudiced against women. (m)

6. A lizard with a highly developed ability to change color. (c)

7. A person who undertakes law enforcement without legal authority. (v)

8. A grotesque carved figure projecting from the roof of a building. (g)

9. A political leader who appeals to popular desires and prejudices. (d)

10. A slender threadlike object that glows inside a light bulb. (f)

You can check your answers at the bottom of the next page, but first consider this question: Were there any words that you felt you knew but couldn't name, even when you were given its first letter? If so, you experienced a tip-of-the-tongue state, a feeling of knowing without being able to recall.

Tip-of-the-tongue experiences are common in everyday life. We get stuck for a word and end up using another that's not as good. Later, when we're no longer thinking about it, that word may suddenly come to mind, almost as if it were taunting us.

As frustrating as these experiences may be, the tip-of-the-tongue phenomenon tells us a lot about how words are stored and retrieved in the brain. Psychologists can even induce tip-of-the-tongue states in the laboratory by giving participants the definitions of uncommon words like the ones you just responded to. Although the researchers can never predict which definitions will induce a tip-of-the-tongue experience, they can still expect the phenomenon to occur on about 10% of the trials (James & Burke, 2000).

The tip-of-the-tongue phenomenon suggests that word retrieval works in stages. That is, you may be able to access the meaning of a word without accessing its pronunciation. In this chapter we'll first consider the two-sided nature of words—form and meaning—and then we'll look at some models of how words are retrieved from long-term memory.

So, did you experience a tip-of-the-tongue state while responding to the definitions above? Check your answers below and see if you really did know the word without being able to say it.

SECTION 5.1: ANATOMY OF WORDS

- Words are minimal units of meaningful speech that can be produced in isolation; however, words usually occur within larger utterances, and their form is influenced by the context in which they occur. Words also exhibit a dual nature, having both an outward phonological form and an underlying semantic representation.

- Content or open-class words convey the bulk of meaning in utterances, while function or closed-class words regulate syntax; content words include nouns, verbs, and adjectives, while function words include prepositions, determiners, and conjunctions.

- Words change their shape according to the context in which they are used; the process of word form change is called morphology.

- Words spoken in isolation consist of phonemes grouped into one or more syllables; however, when words are spoken within utterances, the phonemes of neighboring words often regroup to form new syllables across word boundaries.

- The question of how words acquire meaning is known as the symbol grounding problem; the traditional cognitive approach proposes that words acquire meaning through their relationships with other words, while the embodied cognition approach proposes that words acquire meaning through the perceptual and motor experiences those words evoke.

Answers: 1. papyrus; 2. hemophilia; 3. spelunker; 4. kleptomania; 5. misogynist; 6. chameleon; 7. vigilante; 8. gargoyle; 9. demagogue; 10. filament.

- Words are largely arbitrary symbols for concepts; however, languages also employ systematic word form patterns to classify words into grammatical categories.

As a skilled reader of English, you probably have some intuitions about words that aren't quite accurate. On the printed page, words appear as strings of letters separated by spaces, distinct entities of meaningful language. Yet, as you've learned, the primary mode of language is speech, not writing, and the speech stream is a continuous flow of sound, phonemes blending one into another and with no silences between words. To extract words from the speech stream, the infant needs to learn the statistical regularities of the language; and even as adult speakers, we rely on the patterns we've learned to make guesses about what the other person is intending to say. Thus, words exist as discrete entities in the minds of speakers and listeners but not in speech stream itself.

Words Are Labels for Concepts

Generally speaking, we can define a **word** as *a minimal unit of meaningful speech that can stand alone*. We can point to an object and name or describe it with a single-word utterance, such as "apple," "red," or "yummy." But we rarely do this, even when speaking to infants. Rather, we embed words within larger utterances, and the context can change the way the word is pronounced. For example, if you say the pronoun *her* in isolation, you will clearly pronounce the initial *h* sound. But in certain contexts, such as following a verb, the *h* is dropped, such that *tell her* sounds just like *teller*.

At a more abstract level, we can think of words as labels for concepts. A **concept** is *a mental representation of some sort of statistical regularity in our experience*. For example, you have a concept for things that can contain liquid, can be held in the hands, and are easy to drink from. And since you speak English, you also have a label for that concept, namely *cup*. In other words, concepts are representations of classes of objects (*spaghetti* and *meatballs* with *cheese*) or events (*shake*, *rattle*, and *roll*), and they provide us with expectations that guide our response to new instances of those objects or events.

You don't have word labels for all the concepts you have. Take, for example, the gadget down at the bottom of your kitchen drawer that you inherited years ago from your great aunt Josephine. You have no idea what it's called or what it's used for, but you saw a similar gadget at a yard sale once, so clearly you have a concept, though not a word, for it.

In short, words have a dual nature. On the one hand, a word has a phonological form, which is the way it sounds when produced in isolation or within an utterance. On the other hand, a word has also a semantic representation, namely the concept associated with that word.

Types of Words

Words can be grouped in a number of different ways. As we learned in Chapter 1, one useful distinction is the division between content words, which are words that convey meaning, and function words, which are words that serve grammatical purposes. Content words are the labels for concepts, and because we continue to learn new concepts and the labels for them, they're also called open-class words. New content words enter the language all the time while old content words fade from use. They also form the bulk of a language's vocabulary. Function words, however, are much more limited in number, and they remain fairly stable across generations and even centuries, so they're also known as closed-class words.

Content words can be divided into different classes depending on the type of concept they represent and the role they can play in sentences. The most basic division is between nouns and verbs, which seems to be universal among the languages of the world and may reflect an innate perceptual distinction between objects and events. Many languages also have a class of words called adjectives that describe the properties of objects or our perceptual experience of them. (The function of adjectives can be taken over by nouns or verbs even in English, as for example in the roughly synonymous phrases *a beautiful thing* and *a thing of beauty*.)

The boundary between content words and function words is fuzzy, and the class of words known as prepositions stands in this gray area. Prepositions are clearly closed-class words, since new ones are rarely introduced into the language. Furthermore, some prepositions, like *of*, have little meaning and are only used for grammatical purposes. However, other prepositions, like *over* and *under*, clearly have meaning and contribute to the semantics of the sentence in which they occur.

Two additional types of function words need to be mentioned. One class consists of determiners, which are used to help link nouns with the people or things they refer to. In English, *a* introduces a new noun to the discourse, while *the* indicates that the following noun has already been mentioned.

Consider how *a* and *the* work with the nouns *princess* and *frog* in the following short narrative:

> A princess was walking by a pond when she saw a frog. The frog said, "Princess, kiss me and I will turn into a handsome prince." The princess carefully considered the proposition.

Notice how the first mention of *princess* and *frog* is each preceded by *a* and subsequent mentions by *the*. You can see that the other nouns in the story (*pond* and *prince*) are also introduced with *a*, but can you figure out why the noun *proposition* is preceded by *the*? (Hint: Which proposition are we talking about?)

The other class is conjunctions, words like *and*, *but*, and *because*, that combine phrases or sentences into larger units. Can you identify the conjunctions in the story of the princess and the frog?

Shapeshifters

Many words, especially those in the open classes of noun, verb, and adjective, change their shape depending on the context in which they're used. English nouns have a different form depending on whether they're singular or plural. For instance, we say *one duck* but *two ducks* and *one goose* but *two geese*. Likewise, English verbs shift shape to indicate present or past tense. For example, we say *I walk every day* but *I walked yesterday*, and *I run every day* but *I ran yesterday*. English verbs also have two or three additional forms, such as *walks* or *walking* and *runs* or *running*. The grammar regulating the use of these forms is complex.

As we learned in Chapter 1, the set of processes involved in changing the shape of a word to fit its grammatical context is known as the morphology of that word. English nouns and verbs have fairly simple morphology compared to some languages. For instance, nouns in Spanish are not only marked as singular or plural but also as either masculine or feminine, and any determiner or adjective associated with a particular noun must also be marked for gender and number. Thus, "the tall boy" is *el chico alto* but "the tall girl" is *la chica alta*. In Russian, nouns also change their shape depending on the role they play in the sentence (in addition to being marked for number and gender). As the subject of the sentence, "book" is pronounced *kniga*, but as the object of the sentence, it's *knigu*. On the other hand, Chinese nouns have no morphology, and you need to rely on context to tell whether a word like *péngyou* is singular or plural, masculine or feminine, or subject or object of the sentence.

The most basic form of a word is called its **lemma**, and *the set of all forms a word can take* is called its **lexeme**. For example, *run* is the lemma for the lexeme that includes *run, runs, ran,* and *running*. You can think of the lemma as the naked word and the lexeme as the word dressed up for a particular occasion.

Phonology of Word Forms

At an abstract level, we can think of words as being composed of a string of phonemes organized into one or more syllables. For instance, the word *cat* is composed of three phonemes, *c-a-t*, organized as a single syllable, *cat*. On the other hand, the word *begin* is composed of five phonemes, *b-e-g-i-n*, organized as two syllables, *be-gin*.

Many words in English are monosyllabic, and we can see in them a complex syllabic structure. Take the single-syllable word *cash* as an example. This word can be divided into an onset *c*, which is the initial consonantal portion of syllable, and a rime *ash*, which is the second half of the syllable, consisting of a vowel and any following consonants. Onsets are what we match when we make alliterations, such as *the bold and the beautiful* or *then and there*. Rimes are, well, rhymes. *Cash* rhymes with *hash* but not with *hatch*, with *dash* but not with *dish*. A rime can be further subdivided into a nucleus, which is the middle vowel portion of a syllable, and a coda, which is the final consonant portion of a syllable.

Figure 5.1   Structure of a Syllable

A syllable can be divided into the onset, which is the initial consonantal portion, and the rime. This can be further subdivided into the nucleus, which is the vowel at the middle of the syllable, and the coda, which is the final consonantal portion. Not all syllables have an onset or a coda, but they all have at least a nucleus. The structure of the one-syllable word *speech* is shown here.

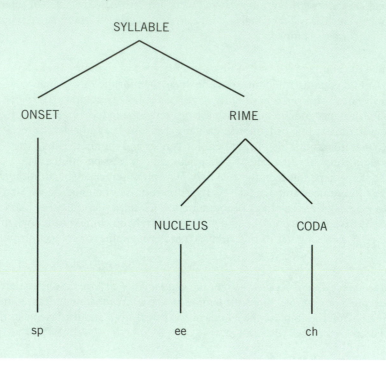

Words uttered in isolation consist of a whole number of syllables. However, when words are spoken within utterances, the phonemes of neighboring words often regroup themselves so that syllable boundaries no longer line up with word boundaries. For example, you can clearly articulate each word in the sentence *It's an elephant*, but in normal speech this will come out as *It-sa-NEL-e-phant*.

Phonemes are the building blocks of phonological word forms, but not all combinations of phonemes are possible words. Rather, each language has a set of *rules for combining phonemes into sequences to form words*, and these are known as **phonotactic rules**. As a native speaker, you have implicit knowledge of your language's phonotactic rules, and you use them as one cue for determining word boundaries in the speech stream. For example, if you hear the string *a sealed letter*, you know not to parse it as *a seal dletter* at least in part because you know that *dl* is not a legal onset in English. Likewise, phonotactic rules help you distinguish possible words, such as *treb*, from impossible words, such as *tneb*.

Words as Symbols

Words are sound symbols that stand for concepts. Many concepts are universal, but languages use different words to represent those concepts. For instance, nearly all cultures have the concept of a furry, four-legged animal that wags its tail and makes a good pet, and we can notate this concept as DOG in all capital letters to indicate that we are referring to the concept and not the word. In English, the concept DOG is symbolized with the word *dog*, but in Chinese with *gŏu* and in Japanese with *inu*. As a general rule, words are arbitrary sound symbols of the concepts they represent, although we'll discuss some exceptions to this observation before we end this section.

In a sense, the meaning of a word is the concept it symbolizes. However, concepts are also symbols, since they are mental representations of classes of objects or events, so we still have *the question of where the meaning of a symbol comes from*. This is known as the **symbol grounding problem**.

In the traditional cognitive approach, symbols are believed to acquire meaning through the relationships they have with other symbols (Glenberg et al., 2003). Look up any word in the dictionary, and you will see that it's defined in terms of other words without any of those words being grounded in the real world. Dictionaries work because you already know the meanings of many words.

However, philosopher John Searle (1980) in his **Chinese Room argument** gives *a demonstration of why meaning cannot arise solely from the relationships among symbols*. Suppose you have just landed in Beijing and are trying to decipher the signs. If all you have is a Chinese dictionary, you'll never be able to figure out what the signs mean. You may find the characters in the dictionary, but their definitions will be strings of other characters you don't know. And if you look up those characters, you'll find them defined by other characters. You could even memorize the whole dictionary, and you still wouldn't understand any Chinese. We'll discuss the symbol grounding problem and the Chinese Room argument in more detail in Chapter 13.

One way to solve the symbol grounding problem is to have a set of *innately meaningful concepts that are used to define all other concepts* (Goddard, 2002). These **semantic primes**, then, would be the building blocks of meaning, much as atoms are the building blocks of physical matter. However, there's no consensus on just how many semantic primes there are or which concepts should count as semantic primes. So far, this approach has largely taken the form of a philosophical debate that has produced few testable hypotheses.

Another approach to the symbol grounding problem proposes that a concept is an **embodied representation**, meaning it's *a symbol that is understood in terms of the perceptual and motor experiences it evokes* (Glenberg et al., 2003). For example, you understand the word *apple* because it evokes the perceptual experience of interacting with an apple—its shape, texture, smell, and taste. Likewise, you

Figure 5.2   Symbol Grounding Problem

A Chinese dictionary won't help you understand the meaning of this symbol if you don't already know Chinese. At least some of the words we use must be grounded in our real-world experiences.

Source: ©iStockphoto.com/ photo168.

understand the word *eat* because you know the muscle movements involved in performing the act of eating. Results from behavioral and neuroimaging studies show that areas of the brain involved in perceiving objects and performing actions are also involved in processing the meaning of words referring to those objects and actions.

The embodied cognition approach has intuitive appeal. Maybe we really do imagine an apple when we hear the word. However, it's more difficult to explain how we understand abstract concepts. One way we do this is through metaphor (Lakoff & Johnson, 2003). Consider how we understand the words *temperature* and *rise* in the statement *the temperature's rising*. Although *temperature* is an abstract concept, it can be understood in terms of perceptual experiences of hot and cold things. The word *rise* is understood in terms of motor experiences of upward motion, but there is no actual motion in this case. Rather, the statement uses the concept of MOTION as a metaphor for CHANGE and the concept of UP as a metaphor for HOT.

Sound Symbolism

Hockett (1960) made *the observation that the sound of a word gives virtually no information about its meaning*. This is known as the **arbitrariness of the sign**, and it's considered to be a universal property of human languages. Nevertheless, word forms in languages are more systematic than would be expected if they were truly arbitrary (Monaghan, Christiansen, & Fitneva, 2011). For instance, many words in English beginning with *gl* have to do with the perception of light, such as *glow, gleam,* and *glitter*. There are also plenty of words with a *gl* onset that don't have to do with light (*gloat, glob,* and *glide*, to name just a few). Still, systematic sound symbol patterns are found in many languages.

In fact, it's not immediately obvious why there isn't more sound symbolism in language, since this should be an aid in learning and remembering words. You might expect similar concepts, such as DOG and WOLF to have similar words to label them. However, Monaghan and his colleagues propose that arbitrariness of the symbol, while taxing memory, aids in discriminating similar concepts (Monaghan, Mattock, & Walker, 2012). On the other hand, the role of systematic forms among words is to help sort them into grammatical categories. For example, practically all Spanish nouns ending in *-o* are masculine and *-a* are feminine. Thus, according to this view, regularities in word forms mainly serve grammar and not semantics.

Finally, we need to consider the case of **onomatopoeia**, which is *a word that represents a sound*, such as *thud* and *bang*. That is, an onomatopoeia really is a sound symbol, and yet sound words vary widely from language to language. For instance, pigs say *oink* in English but *bubu* in Japanese. Thus, while these words bear some resemblance to the sounds they symbolize, they are also shaped by the cultures in which they are used.

Figure 5.3 Bouba-Kiki Effect

More than 95% of adults agree on which is the *bouba* and which is the *kiki*. What do you think? Search online for the answer.

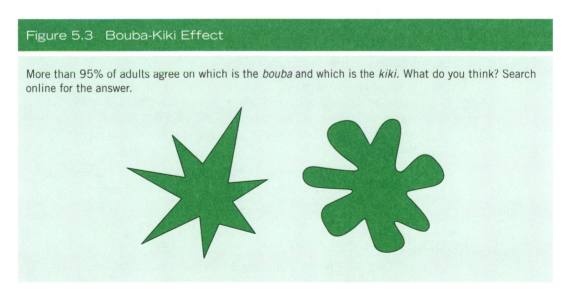

Source: ©Andrew Dunn / Wikimedia Commons / CC-BY-SA-3.0 / GFDL.

In Sum

Although we can easily produce words in isolation, we usually do so within larger utterances. Words are symbols for concepts, and as such they have both a phonological form and an underlying semantic representation, or meaning. Content words such as nouns, verbs, and adjectives carry most of the meaning in an utterance, while function words such as prepositions, determiners, and conjunctions mostly serve grammatical roles. New content words are constantly being added to the language while old ones die out, and so they are also called open-class words. The set of function words, on the other hand, remains fairly stable across generations and even centuries, and for this reason they are also known as closed-class words. There is still debate about how words acquire meaning. The traditional cognitive approach asserts that words derive meaning through their associations with other words, but the embodied cognition approach proposes that motor and perceptual experiences give words meaning. Although words are arbitrary symbols for concepts, languages do make use of word form patterns to organize words into grammatical categories.

Review Questions

1. What is the difference between a word and a concept? Can you have one without the other? Why do we say that words have a dual nature?

2. Explain the difference between content words and function words. Why are they also referred to as open-class words and closed-class words? What are the major categories of words in each class?

3. What is morphology? What is the difference between a lemma and a lexeme? Work out the morphology of the following English nouns: *hand, foot*. See if you can also work out the morphology of the following English verbs: *talk, speak*.

4. What is the symbol grounding problem? What is the traditional cognitive approach to the problem? How does the Chinese Room argument demonstrate the weakness of this approach? Explain the semantic prime and embodied representation approaches to solving this problem.

5. What is meant by the expression "arbitrariness of the sign"? In what ways do languages make use of sound symbolism? In what sense is onomatopoeia arbitrary?

Thought Questions

1. See if you can label the grammatical category of each of the words in the story about the princess and the frog. Use the following notation: N = noun, V = verb, A = adjective, P = preposition, D = determiner, and C = conjunction. You will need two additional categories to

complete this task. Adverbs (Adv) describe the manner in which an action takes place, and they are usually derived from adjectives, in the case of English by adding the suffix *-ly*. Auxiliary verbs (Aux) are verbs that help express the tense of the main verb (V).

2. Do you think in terms of words or in terms of concepts? If you're like most people, you probably keep a running monologue going on inside your head. This suggests that thought is internalized speech. But what about animals that don't have language? For example, chimpanzees improvise tools, navigate a complex social life, and even engage in cooperative hunting and warfare. The behaviors certainly suggest underlying thought processes. What advantages might thinking in words (and language more generally) provide over thinking solely in concepts?

Google It! Bouba Kiki and the Chinese Room

Searle's (1980) **Chinese Room** thought experiment is somewhat different from the way it's presented here, but there are plenty of sites on the Internet that discuss it. You'll find that the Chinese Room argument is related to artificial intelligence and the question of consciousness. A similar thought experiment known as the **Turing test** is relevant here. The **embodied cognition** approach has been gaining currency not only in psychology but also in the field of **robotics**. Find out how giving robots human-like bodies may lead them to think and behave like humans. Neuroscientist Vilayanur Ramachandran gives a fascinating **TED Talk** in which he discusses the **bouba-kiki** effect in terms of **synesthesia**.

SECTION 5.2: HOW WORDS ARE LEARNED

- Vocabulary acquisition through the lifespan follows an S-shaped curve, with slow learning during the first couple of years, followed by a vocabulary spurt that starts to taper off by school age; however, learning to read additionally boosts vocabulary, and adults continue to learn new words and new meanings for familiar words throughout their life.

- Word learning is a complex task involving three processes: (1) constructing a concept, (2) learning a phonological word form, and (3) creating a link between the word form and the concept.

- Children learn at least some aspects of words very quickly in a process known as fast mapping; however, complete mastery of a word requires many exposures in varying contexts.

- A challenge for word learning is referential uncertainty, or knowing what aspect of the current situation a novel word refers to; several cognitive constraints help children overcome referential uncertainty, and these include the whole object, taxonomic, and mutual exclusivity assumptions.

- Referential ambiguity can also be resolved by cross-situational word learning, in which the child tracks the co-occurrence of novel words and possible referents, eventually homing in on the appropriate word-concept mapping; furthermore, caregivers often help by naming an object while the child is paying attention to it.

- Various characteristics of a word form, such as word frequency, neighborhood density, phonotactic probability, and stress patterns, can influence how easily it is learned.

It's generally believed that the best time to learn another language is in early childhood, and this is probably true when it comes to phonology and syntax. Adult learners of a second language almost always speak with an accent and struggle with subtle aspects of grammar. But vocabulary is a different issue. Although you master the phonology and syntax of your first language in early childhood, you continue learning new words for your entire life.

On a Curve

Vocabulary acquisition follows an S-shaped learning curve. During the first year and a half of life, word learning is slow. By their first birthday, many infants can recognize dozens of words but only produce half a dozen or so (Junge, Cutler, & Hagoort, 2012). As we learned in Chapter 1, eighteen months marks the beginning of a time period in which children learn words rapidly. This is known as the vocabulary spurt. During this time, children pick up half a dozen or more words each day, so that by the time they reach school age at around six years old, they have a vocabulary in the neighborhood of 14,000 words (Li, Zhao, & MacWhinney, 2007). At this point, the rate of word learning tapers off somewhat, although learning to read does drive further vocabulary expansion. We continue learning new words throughout our life as we have new experiences and as technology presents us with novel objects and behaviors.

Researchers have offered a number of explanations for the vocabulary spurt (Li et al., 2007). A traditional account of this phenomenon is that children acquire a naming insight at around this age. In other words, they suddenly come to the understanding that everything has a name. However, in recent decades many researchers have begun seeking explanations for psycholinguistic processes in terms of more general principles. One explanation is that efficient word learning can't take place until the infant has mastered the phonology of the language, which isn't complete until about a year and a half. Another explanation accounts for the vocabulary spurt in terms of improved memory abilities. A third explanation is that children become much more socially engaged at this time, and hence it's social interactions that provide the scaffolding for rapid vocabulary growth. All of these processes may have some role to play in the vocabulary spurt, yet none of them alone is sufficient to account for the rapid word learning of early childhood.

There's also some disagreement on exactly what it means to learn a word. For example, some researchers will show an infant a novel object and name it with a nonword such as *blick*. If the child can then pick out another *blick* from a group of familiar objects, the researcher judges that the child has learned the word. A more stringent test of word learning involves seeing whether the child still recognizes the word some days or weeks later. These methods test children's **receptive vocabulary**, which is *the set of words a person is able to recognize and understand the meaning of*. Other research on word learning has focused on the child's **productive vocabulary**, that is, *the set of words a person is able to produce in appropriate contexts* (Singleton, 2012). Measures of vocabulary size are usually assessments of productive vocabulary (Junge et al., 2012). This lack of consistency in measuring word learning has led to considerable confusion in the field (Gupta & Tinsdale, 2009).

Word learning is a complex process involving at least three different skills (Junge et al., 2012). First, the learner has to construct a concept. As we have already seen, this is a general cognitive process, and we all have concepts that we have no names for. Second, the learner needs to learn a phonological word form. This means extracting a sound sequence from the speech stream and storing it in memory as an abstract phonological form that can be reproduced. Finally, the learner needs to create a link between the phonological word form and the underlying meaning of the concept. This link needs to go in both directions, from phonological representation to semantic representation in word recognition and in the other direction for word production (Gupta & Tinsdale, 2009).

In the Fast Lane

One of the most notable aspects of word learning in children is how rapid it is. Children have *the ability to learn a new word after only one or a few exposures* in a process known as **fast mapping**. This ability is typically demonstrated in receptive word learning tasks, and there's some debate about the depth of learning in fast mapping (McMurray, Horst, & Samuelson, 2012). For example, Gupta and Tinsdale (2009) argue that there are two kinds of learning involved in vocabulary acquisition. They propose that fast mapping is facilitated by the hippocampus, a brain structure of the medial temporal lobe that is involved in the initial encoding of memories and the regulation of long-term memory consolidation. Thus, fast mapping is like remembering where you parked your car while you shop at the mall, in that you keep the information in memory for just as long as it's useful. But the permanent learning of a word requires consolidation in long-term memory, which requires slow learning over repeated exposures to the word in various contexts (Bion, Borovsky, & Fernald, 2012).

An additional challenge for the word learner is the problem of **referential uncertainty** (Quine, 1960). This is *the observation that there is no direct link between the word and the*

Figure 5.4   Model of Word Recognition, Production, and Repetition

Word recognition starts with speech perception and accesses a phonological representation before a semantic representation. Word production begins with a semantic representation and accesses a phonological representation for speech production. Word repetition accesses a phonological representation but not necessarily a semantic representation, since we can repeat words we don't have meanings for.

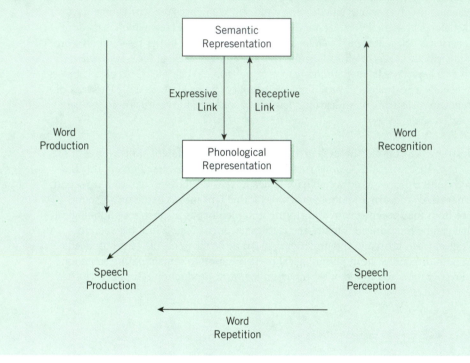

Source: Gupta and Tinsdale (2009).

object or event it refers to. When a mother points and says, "Look at the doggie," her baby has no idea—at least in principle—precisely what "doggie" refers to. It could be the furry, four-legged animal as a whole, or it could be the waggly tail or the floppy ears. Yet somehow the baby does know what mom is referring to and attaches the word *doggie* to the correct concept.

One approach to solving the problem of referential uncertainty is to propose that cognitive constraints guide the child in narrowing down the possible range of referents for new words (Mayor & Plunkett, 2010). One constraint is the **whole object assumption**, which is *the assumption that a new word refers to the entire object and not just a part of it.* Thus, baby assumes *doggie* means the whole animal and not just its tail. Furthermore, children don't interpret the new word as a name for that specific object. Rather, they make *the assumption that a newly learned word extends to other similar* *referents*. This is known as the **taxonomic assumption**. In other words, children seem to understand that words are labels for concepts, not things. The only exception to this is in the learning of proper names, in which case the word is a label for a specific individual. (However, little tykes have been known to point out strange men and call them "Daddy," creating considerable embarrassment for all involved.) Finally, children overcome referential uncertainty by making *the assumption that no two words mean exactly the same thing*. This is called the **mutual exclusivity assumption**. So, if baby already knows the word *doggie* and hears mom say, "Look, the doggie's wagging its tail," baby assumes *tail* isn't just another word for *doggie* but instead means something else, perhaps that thing moving around on the dog's rear end. Cognitive constraints of this sort can also account, at least in part, for fast mapping because they greatly reduce the difficulty of the task.

Not So Fast

Other researchers point out that resolving referential ambiguity is not the same as establishing a permanent link in memory between a word form and a concept (McMurray et al., 2012). Consider a typical word learning experiment, in which a youngster is shown a novel object such as a garlic press and told it's a *dax*. Later, the youngster is shown two objects, say a bottle and a different garlic press. The experiment asks which one is the *dax*, and since the infant knows the word for *bottle*, it can assume, based on mutual exclusivity, that the novel object is the dax. Perhaps the child has learned that *dax* refers to garlic presses, or perhaps she was just making a reasonable guess in the moment without establishing a connection between the word *dax* and the concept of garlic press.

If we define word learning as being able to produce the word in appropriate contexts, then fast mapping is just the first step in a slow process of associative learning (McMurray et al., 2012). Referential ambiguity is only a problem if we assume words are learned quickly. However, Vouloumanos and Werker (2009) found that eighteen-month-old infants have *the ability to learn to associate novel words with novel objects even in cases of referential ambiguity by tracking co-occurrence statistics*. This process known as **cross-situational word learning** (Smith, Smith, & Blythe, 2011). On a single trial, the infant may not know which of several novel objects is the *dax*, but if on multiple trials there's always a garlic press in the set, then *dax* probably refers to the garlic press.

Keeping all possible referents of the novel word in memory may be too taxing for young children (or even adults), but Trueswell and colleagues found evidence for what they called the propose-but-verify strategy (Trueswell et al., 2012). When encountering a novel word in an ambiguous context, both children and adults make a guess about what the word refers to. Let's say their attention was focused, by chance, on the melon baller when they heard *dax*, and so they tentatively associate the two. But on the next trial, there's no melon baller among the set of objects, and so they make a new guess, perhaps the cucumber slicer this time. Eventually, they'll pick the garlic press, and every time after that, they'll find

Figure 5.5   Cross-Situational Word Learning

By hearing the word *ball* in several situations where a ball and other objects are present, the infant can gradually infer the meaning.

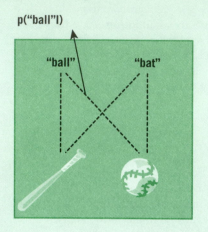

Cross-modal Statistical Learning

Source: Chen and Smith (2012). Modeling cross-situational word-referent learning: prior questions. *Psychological Review, 119,* 21-39.

the garlic press is always present when they hear the word *dax*. In this way, the learner gradually converges on the correct mapping between word and object. Furthermore, it's this repeated co-occurrence of word and referent in different contexts that solidifies the connection between word form and concept in long-term memory (Jones, Johns, & Recchia, 2012).

Caregivers can also help reduce referential ambiguity when they interact with their children. Imagine a situation in which a dad and a toddler are playing with a set of toy farm animals. Dad picks up the horse and moves it around, saying: "Look at the horsie! The horsie's running! Here comes the horsie!" And then he hands the horse to the child. Dad has just created **joint attention**, *a situation in which all participants in an interaction have focused their attention on the same object or event.* Although there are several other farm animals in view, the child is paying attention to the horse as the dad repeatedly says "horsie" because the dad is moving it. And when the child holds the horse to look at it, virtually everything else in the visual field is occluded or out of focus. Thus, there really is no referential ambiguity in this case. Research shows that children learn words faster when their parents regularly name objects under conditions of joint attention (Samuelson et al., 2011; Yu & Smith, 2012a).

Nouns may be easier to learn than verbs because their referents are concrete objects that the child can look at and interact with. But verbs, as names for events, are by nature more abstract, and so cross-situational learning probably is necessary to acquire their full meaning. An important aspect of an event is that it involves one or more participants playing different roles. Some events, such as sleeping, involve only one participant role, namely the person or animal that's sleeping. But other events, such as eating, involve two participant roles, one that does the eating and another that gets eaten. These participant roles are reflected in language as subjects and objects of verbs, and an integral part of the meaning of a verb is the number of participant roles associated with it.

Gleitman (1990) found that young children make *use of syntactic information to infer the meaning of verbs*. This process is known as **syntactic bootstrapping**, and when it's employed in conjunction with contextual cues, it provides valuable information about the meaning of the verb. Even in the absence of contextual cues, young children are sensitive to the grammatical characteristics of verbs. Yuan and Fisher (2009) found that two-year-olds remembered the grammatical characteristics of a novel verb like *gorp* in a conversation they overheard that provided no contextual cues to meaning. For example, they may hear a conversation about John gorping and Mary gorping, or else about John gorping the dog and Mary gorping the cat. Afterwards, the children saw only one of two scenes, either of a person performing a novel act, such as waving one arm in the air, or else of a person performing a novel act on another person, such as pulling a leg. The children looked longer at the scene that was consistent with the conversation they'd previously overheard, suggesting that they'd remembered the grammar of the verb even though they didn't yet know the meaning.

In the Neighborhood

Characteristics of the words themselves affect how easily they're learned. One of these is **word frequency**, which is *a measure how often a particular word in all its forms occurs in the language*. Corpus studies use computers to count the occurrences of words in large bodies of texts, and now we have fairly accurate lists of word frequencies in the major languages of the world. An important finding in these studies is that a small number of words are extremely frequent, while most words are relatively, or extremely, rare. Not surprisingly, the most common are function words like *the* and *of*, while content words are less common.

Traditionally, it was assumed that children learned the most frequent words of the language first, but in fact recent studies have shown that the active vocabularies of young children contain mostly words of low frequency (Stokes et al., 2012). Traditional corpus studies count word frequencies in printed documents, which may not be a good measure of word frequencies in speech. However, even corpus studies of child-directed speech don't line up well with the productive vocabularies of typically developing children. The only exception is nouns, in which case frequencies in child-directed speech are reflected in children's productive vocabularies. These results make sense when you consider that children tend to learn nouns first,

Figure 5.6   Syntactic Bootstrapping

Infants use their partial knowledge of syntax to make inferences about the meanings of newly encountered words. Given the frame *The X is Y*, the child knows that *X* is probably a noun phrase and *Y* a verb phrase.

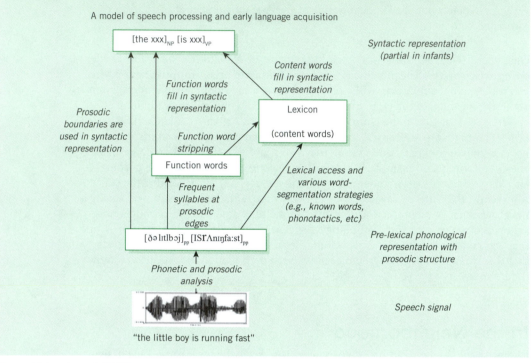

A model of speech processing and early language acquisition

Source: Christophe et al. (2008).

followed by verbs and adjectives, and furthermore that children don't regularly use function words until later.

Another factor that influences how easily a word will be learned is its similarity to other words. **Neighborhood density** is *a measure of how many other words differ from a particular word by substitution of a single phoneme.* For example, neighbors of *hat* include *cat* and *rat* by substitution of the first phoneme, *hot* and *hit* by substitution of the second phoneme, and *ham* and *have* by substitution of the third phoneme (Stokes et al., 2012). Some words, like *hat*, reside in dense neighborhoods, while other words, like *juice*, reside in sparse neighborhoods.

A related concept is **phonotactic probability**, which measures *the likelihood that a particular sequence of phonemes will occur in a language.* Words in high density neighborhoods also

Figure 5.7   Neighborhood Density

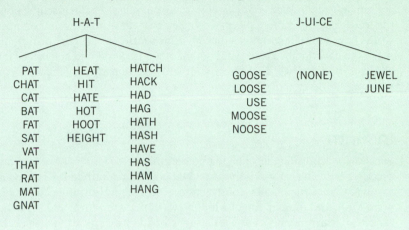

A neighbor differs from a particular word by only one phoneme. Some words, like *hat*, reside in dense neighborhoods. Other words, like *juice*, reside in sparse neighborhoods.

tend to have high phonotactic probability. However, it's possible to create nonwords that contrast in these two measures, and word learning studies have found that both children and adults more easily learn nonwords that are low in phonotactic probability and high in neighborhood density (Storkel et al., 2010). Perhaps this is because the unusualness of low phonotactic probability make these words more memorable while the familiarity of high neighborhood density provides a scaffold for recall.

Stress patterns can also influence word learning in youngsters. Most two-syllable nouns in English have a **trochaic** or *strong-weak stress pattern*. Examples of the trochaic pattern include nouns like *basket* and *pillow*. Some nouns exhibit an **iambic** or *weak-strong stress pattern*, although they're less common. Examples of the iambic pattern include nouns like *guitar* and *amount*. (As an aside, there's a set of words in English, such as *record* and *produce*, that are trochaic as nouns and iambic as verbs.) We've already seen how infants learning English use the metrical segmentation strategy to infer word boundaries before stressed syllables.

Estes and Bowen (2013) investigated whether stress patterns can help or hinder word learning in infants. They created a set of two-syllable nonwords that were either high or low in phonotactic probability and exhibited either a trochaic or iambic stress pattern. For example, *MOE-dike* is trochaic and has high phonotactic probability, while *gay-FOUTH* is iambic and has low phonotactic probability. Using these nonwords as labels for novel objects, they found that nineteen-month-old infants only learned the trochaic, high-probability labels. This suggests that, at least at this age, infants need support both from stress and phonotactic regularities to learn new words.

Finally, we need to keep in mind that word learning is a lifelong process. Furthermore, most words have multiple meanings, and we continue to learn new meanings of familiar words as we go through life. For instance, the advancement of social media has forced us all to learn new meanings for familiar words such as *tweet* and *like* (as in *like us on Facebook*). Some words have multiple meanings that are semantically related. For example, *virus* can refer to a microscopic organism that causes disease or to a piece of software that can damage your computer. Other words have multiple meanings that are semantically unrelated. For instance, *bark* can mean the covering of a tree or the sound of a dog. Rodd and colleagues found that adults learn a new word meaning faster when it's semantically related to the familiar meaning (Rodd et al., 2012).

In Sum

Vocabulary acquisition is a lifelong process that proceeds slowly at first but accelerates during early childhood and tapers off in adulthood. Knowing a word involves three components: construction of a concept, learning of a phonological word form, and the creation of a link between the word form and the concept. Some aspects of learning can occur after a single or a few exposures of a word, but full mastery requires multiple experiences in different situations. Cognitive constraints help children overcome the referential ambiguity inherent in word learning situations, but caregivers help as well by engaging children in joint attention as they teach the names of objects. Furthermore, children are statistical language learners, and they can infer the meanings of words by keeping track of the contexts in which they occur. The characteristics of the word form also have an effect on how readily the word is learned.

Review Questions

1. Explain the processes involved in learning a word. What is the difference between receptive and productive vocabulary. Which is a better measure of word learning? (Hint: This is a trick question.)

2. What is fast mapping? Is it a learning process that is specific to language, or is it more general? What brain structures seem to be involved?

3. Explain the problem of referential ambiguity and the three cognitive constraints that have been proposed to deal with it. How do cross-situational learning, joint attention, and syntactic bootstrapping also help overcome referential ambiguity?

4. Explain word frequency, neighborhood density, and phonotactic probability. How does each affect word learning? Also explain the effect of stress patterns on the learning of English words.

Thought Questions

1. A neighbor is any word that differs from the target word by a single phoneme, whether by substitution, addition, or deletion. See how many neighbors you can find for the word *cat*. Remember to work with phonemes, not letters. This means *chat* is a neighbor because *ch* is a phoneme, but *what* is not because the vowel sounds are different as well as the initial consonants.

2. Word frequencies in child-directed speech are quite different from those in the language in general. Why would caregivers spend so much time teaching their children words that aren't very common?

3. Is the distinction between receptive and productive vocabulary only relevant to children, or does it apply to adults as well? Explain.

4. Most words in a language have multiple meanings. If words are so ambiguous, how are we able to understand each other?

Google It! Culturomics

If you're curious about which words in English are most common, look up **word frequency**. What sources do corpus studies use to calculate these frequencies? Do you think these sources are a good sample of the language as a whole? **Culturomics** is a project that tracks the frequencies of words in Google books over the last two centuries. Use the **Ngram Viewer** to see how English (or any other common language) has changed. You can also watch a **TED Talk** about this program called "What We Learned From 5 Million Books." If you're curious about word frequencies or types of words that occur in child-directed speech, look up **CHILDES**, the Child Language Data Exchange System.

SECTION 5.3: HOW WORDS ARE STORED

- The words you know are permanently stored in long-term memory; this mental lexicon contains information about how words are pronounced, what they mean, and how they are related to other words.

- Traditional models of the lexicon assume that only base word forms are stored, with other inflected forms generated by rule, while connectionist models assume all word forms are stored in the lexicon.

- The mental lexicon is envisioned as a network of words; words are connected by both taxonomic (categorical, such as *dog-cat*) and thematic (associative, such as *dog-bone*) relations.

- Evidence from word association, semantic priming, and picture-word interference tasks suggest that word activation spreads to related words; this spreading activation causes semantic interference for categorically related words and semantic facilitation for associatively related words.

- Neuroimaging data suggest that the brain processes words along two pathways, a dorsal sound-to-action route and a ventral sound-to-meaning route; traditional models propose that the mental lexicon is located in the posterior temporal lobe, a part of the ventral stream.

- Embodied semantics proposes that we understand words by simulating their meanings in the motor and perceptual areas of the brain.

When you were young, you may have had a book called a dictionary that you could use to look up the meaning of words. It had tens of thousands of entries organized in alphabetical order, and you had to leaf through the pages to find the word you were looking for. Nowadays, all you have to do is type the word into your web browser, and various online resources will offer a definition. You know tens of thousands of words, so in a sense you have a dictionary in your head as well. This **mental lexicon** is *the storage of information about words in long-term memory*, but it's most definitely not organized in an alphabetical list. Instead, you search for words in your head much as you do on the Internet, in that you find their meaning almost immediately. Dictionaries provide both phonological information (how the word is pronounced) and semantic information (what the word means), and your mental lexicon also stores this kind of information about the words you know.

Phonological Forms

Conventional models of lexical processing tend to make two assumptions about how phonological word forms are stored in the mental lexicon (Bürki & Gaskell, 2012). The first assumption is that word forms are stored as a set of phonemes. Recall that phonemes are the basic speech sounds of the language, represented in an abstract form that provides a template for speech recognition and a target for speech production. This assumption is motivated by research on speech errors in which individual phonemes of words in a phrase are either transposed, as in *keep your foot meeving* for *feet moving*, or else repeated, as in *bake my bike* for *take my bike* (Fromkin, 1971). However, some researchers have proposed that at least very common words may be stored as syllables rather than phonemes (Levelt & Wheeldon, 1994).

The second assumption is that only the most basic form of the word is stored in memory, and the other forms the word can take are generated by rule as an utterance is being constructed (Bürki & Gaskell, 2012). For example, you wouldn't have two separate entries, one for singular *book* and another for plural *books*. Rather, you store the lemma *book* and generate the plural form as needed. Evidence for this view of the lexicon comes from the fact that we can easily generate plurals for nonwords such as *dax* and *blicket*. However, irregular forms such as singular *man* and plural *men* are presumed to be stored separately. (But then again, we can also make new irregular plurals by analog, such as the facetious plural of *meese* for *moose*.) Reduced forms of words, such as shortened *int'rest* for the full form *interest* may have to be stored separately as well.

Experimental evidence also suggests that the mental lexicon stores only the base form of the word and attaches suffixes as needed during word recognition and production. *A suffix that is added to words for the purposes of grammar* is known as an **inflectional suffix**, and it's the set of inflected forms that make up the lexeme of a word, such as (*toy, toys*) and (*play, plays, played, playing*). However, we can also add *a suffix that changes the meaning and grammatical category of a word*. This is known as a **derivational suffix**. For example, we can add the suffix *-able* to the verb *agree* to change it into an adjective or the suffix *-ment* to change it into a noun. Psycholinguists don't agree on whether words like *agreeable* and *agreement* are stored together with or apart from the lemma *agree*.

We know that more frequent words are recalled more quickly than their less frequent counterparts (Vannest et al., 2011). In addition, we find a **base frequency effect**, by which we mean *the observation that the frequency effect of the base form extends to its inflected forms*. Thus, words like *agrees* and *agreed* exhibit the same frequency effect as the base form *agree*. This evidence provides support for the assumption that all forms of a lexeme are stored together as a single unit. Traditionally, the lexeme is viewed as the set of inflected forms, that is, changes in the word form due to the requirements of grammar. However, words can also take suffixes that change their meaning, and the base frequent effect sometimes extends to these derived forms as well. Although *agreeable* and *agreement* are less frequent than *agree*, reaction times for these words are similar to that of the base word. This suggests that these derived forms may also be part of the lexeme.

On the other hand, not all derived word forms exhibit the base frequency effect. For instance, the derivational suffix *-ity* turns adjectives into nouns, but slower reaction times for words like *serenity* compared with those for their base forms (*serene*) suggest that they are stored as two separate items, not one (Vannest et al., 2011). There are two explanations for this observation, both of which may be valid. First, the semantic relationship between *serene* and *serenity* may not be as obvious as that between *agree* and *agreeable*. Second, the base *seren-* changes its pronunciation when the *-ity* suffix is added, further muddying the relationship between the two.

The connectionist approach solves this problem by proposing that all word forms, both inflectional and derivational, have separate entries in the mental lexicon (Gonnerman, Seidenberg, & Andersen, 2007). In this model, each word in the lexicon is connected to every other word that has a similar pronunciation or meaning, and when one word is activated, all other related words are activated as well. Thus, the base frequency effect is greater for *agreeable* because is related both phonologically and semantically to *agree*, while the base frequency effect is less for *serenity* because it is only related semantically, but not phonologically, to *serene*.

Exploring the Mental Lexicon

What's the first word that comes to mind when you hear the word *dog*? If you said *cat*, you're like many people. If you said *bone*, you're also in good company. One of the most basic tools we have for exploring the organization of the mental lexicon is the **word association task** (Sheng & McGregor, 2010). This is simply *a procedure in which the participant is asked to produce a word in response to a prompt*. Each participant can be asked to give a single response, in which case the goal is to see what response is most common. Likewise, the participant can be asked to give as many responses as possible, to get a sense of how many associations the prompt word has in the mental lexicon.

Evidence from word association tasks suggests that words in the mental lexicon are semantically associated in two different ways. On the one hand, the word pair *dog-bone* is an example of a **thematic relation**, meaning *a relationship between two words based on frequency of co-occurrence*. That is, the words *dog* and *bone* often appear together in the same contexts. Thematic relations are also called associative relations. On the other hand, the word pair *dog-cat* is an example of a **taxonomic relation**, which is *a relationship between two words that belong to the same semantic category*. In other words, *dog* and *cat* are both *animals*. Taxonomic relations are also known as categorical relations. Children and adults build both kinds of relations in their mental lexicon, but there is a developmental shift in the frequency of the two kinds of semantic association (Sheng, McGregor, & Marian, 2006). Younger children tend to produce more thematic than taxonomic word associations, but by age nine they already show the adult bias of taxonomic relations.

Observations such as these have lead psycholinguists to *a conceptualization of the mental lexicon as a network of words or concepts connected to each other by semantic links*. Depending on the **network model**, the links between nodes may or may not be labeled with the type of relationship between the two concepts. For example, the ISA label (as in, "X is a Y") marks category membership, as in *a canary ISA bird*. Two other common semantic relationships are HAS and CAN, as in *a bird HAS wings* and *a canary CAN sing*.

The most influential of the network models is the **spreading activation model** proposed by Collins and Loftus (1975). This is *a model of the mental lexicon that proposes activation of one node spreads out to other nodes linked to it*. Thus, the prompt word *dog* activates the *dog* node, and this activation then spreads to neighboring nodes, such as *cat* and *bone*, enabling a response. The spreading activation model accounts for the findings from word association tasks, and it also accounts for the data from semantic priming tasks.

Recall from Chapter 2 that priming is an effect of implicit memory in which a response to a stimulus is affected by prior exposure to a similar stimulus. For example, if you read a list that contained words such a *tree, flower*, and *leaf* and then were asked to complete the word *PLA__* , you'd likely say *plant*. On the other hand, if the prior list had contained words like *cup, bowl*, and *saucer*, you'd likely say *plate*. Priming can also be used to measure the strength of association between words.

Figure 5.8   Hierarchical Network Model

The hierarchical network model proposes that semantic memory was organized in terms of hierarchical categories. Attributes at a higher level are inherited by categories at a lower level. For example, we know that a canary has skin, because a canary is a bird, and a bird is an animal, and an animal has skin.

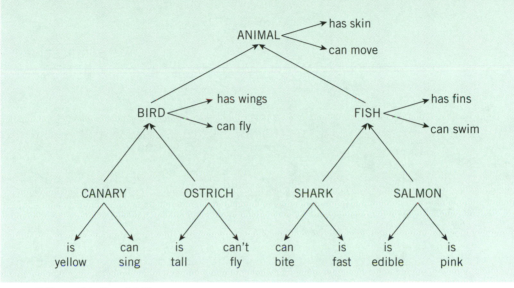

Source: Collins and Quillian (1969).

The **semantic priming task** is *an experimental technique that presents a pair of words and measures the participant's reaction time.* Typically, the semantic priming task is used in conjunction with the lexical decision task, as we learned in Chapter 2. For example, the participant may see the word DOCTOR on the computer screen followed by the word NURSE. The participation needs to decide as quickly as possible whether the second stimulus is a word or not. In this case, the correct response is "yes," but if the second stimulus had been NARSE, the correct response would have been "no." People rarely make a mistake in performing the lexical decision task. However, their reaction time is influenced by the semantic relatedness of the two words. In other words, people respond faster to NURSE when it follows DOCTOR than when it follows BUTTER. *The observation that target words are recognized faster when they are preceded by related primes than unrelated primes* is known as the **semantic priming effect** (Yap, Balota, & Tan, 2013).

The mental lexicon has also been explored using the **picture-word interference task**. This is *an experimental procedure in which the participant is asked to name a picture while ignoring a simultaneously presented distractor word.* For instance, you may see a picture of a *cat* above the word *door*, and your task is to say "cat" as quickly as possible.

Figure 5.9   Spreading Activation Model

The spreading activation model proposes that semantic memory acts as concept nodes with links to related concepts. The prompt RED also activates other nodes that are linked to it, such as FIRE ENGINE, APPLE, or ROSE. This model can be used to explain priming effects as well as semantic facilitation and interference.

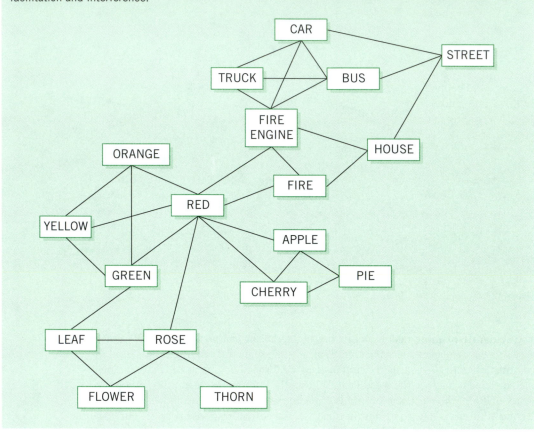

Source: Collins and Loftus (1975).

The picture-word interference task yields consistent patterns of results that help us understand how words in the mental lexicon are organized (de Zubicaray, Hansen, & McMahon, 2013). First, when the distractor word is categorically related to the picture, such as *horse-cat*, reaction time is increased compared with a nonrelated distractor. *The observation that taxonomic relations lead to slower naming times* is called the **semantic interference effect**. Second, when the distractor word is associatively related to the target picture, as in *whiskers-cat*, reaction time is decreased compared to a nonrelated distractor. *The observation that thematic relations lead to faster naming times* is called the **semantic facilitation effect**.

Results from picture-word interference tasks provide support for spreading activation models (de Zubacaray, Hansen, & McMahon, 2013). On the one hand, semantic interference for taxonomic relations occurs because when you attempt to produce a word, such as *cat*, other categorically related words like *dog* and *horse* also become activated and compete for selection. On the other hand, semantic facilitation occurs because associatively related words like *whiskers* and *fur* don't compete for lexical selection but rather increase activation for the target word *cat*.

Cortical Organization of the Mental Lexicon

Hickok and Poeppel's (2007) dual stream model of speech processing has been influential in guiding recent studies on how the mental lexicon is organized in the brain. According to this model, the dorsal stream extends from the speech perception area of the posterior temporal lobe, roughly speaking Wernicke's area, to the posterior frontal lobe, roughly speaking Broca's area. The dorsal stream is responsible for

Figure 5.10   Picture-Word Interference Task

On each trial, a picture and a word appear on the screen. The participant is instructed to ignore the word and name the picture as quickly as possible. When the word is categorically related to the picture (HORSE and a picture of a CAT), reaction time is delayed due to semantic interference. When the word is thematically related to the picture (the word WHISKERS and a picture of a CAT), reaction time is sped up due to semantic facilitation. Unrelated word-picture pairs (the word DOOR and a picture of a CAT) serve as a control condition to provide a baseline for comparison against the other two groups.

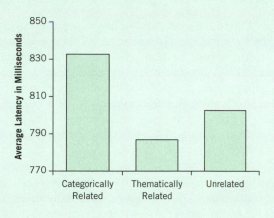

Source: de Zubicaray, Hansen, and McMahon (2013).

converting the acoustic signal of the speech stream, and so we can think of it as going from sound input to motor output. On the other hand, the ventral stream extends from to the same speech perception area into the superior and middle regions of the temporal lobe, and it is responsible for translating the acoustic signal into meaning. Although the dorsal sound-to-action stream is dominant in the left hemisphere, the ventral sound-to-meaning stream is bilaterally organized, although left and right functions may vary somewhat.

Building on the dual stream model, Gow (2012) developed a **dual lexicon model**, which is *the proposal that there are two mental lexicons, one for the dorsal sound-to-action stream and another for the ventral sound-to-meaning stream.* In this model, the ventral lexicon is located in the posterior temporal lobe, part of the ventral stream from sound to meaning. However, the ventral lexicon is not where word meanings are stored. Rather, it consists of word forms that link up with semantic representations elsewhere in the brain. This interpretation of the ventral lexicon is based on neuroimaging studies that show this region to be sensitive to nonwords as well as words, suggesting that phonological but not semantic representations are processed in this region (Graves et al., 2008).

According to the dual lexicon model, the dorsal lexicon is located in the **supramarginal gyrus**, *a region of the inferior parietal lobe that is adjacent to the lateral fissure* (Gow, 2012). The role of the dorsal lexicon is to hold representations of phonological word forms for translation into articulatory codes for speech production. Not all researchers agree on Gow's interpretation of the supramarginal gyrus as the dorsal lexicon. However, evidence from several sources suggests that word forms are stored in this region. For example, speakers are sensitive to neighborhood effects and tend to modify their pronunciation of easily confused words, such as *coat* and *goat*, when there is no context to help disambiguate them, as when reading words from a list. Brain imaging studies show the locus of this effect to be in the left supramarginal gyrus. Clearly more research is needed to help resolve this issue.

The traditional Wernicke model viewed language processing as strictly lateralized to the left hemisphere, and the dual stream model also views the dorsal sound-to-action stream as left-hemisphere dominant. However, the dual stream model proposes that the ventral sound-to-meaning stream is bilaterally organized, although their functions are somewhat different. This proposal is still controversial, but some evidence supports the view that the two hemispheres differ in terms of the timeframe in which they operate (Gow, 2012). Specifically, processing cycles in the left hemisphere are closer to the duration of individual phonemes, while those in the right hemisphere are more like the duration of syllables.

Another way in which the left and right hemispheres seem to differ is in the processing of semantic relationships. Brain imaging studies show activity in the left temporal lobe during the processing of direct semantic relations such as *acorn-squirrel* (de Zubicaray et al., 2013). However, when participants are asked to consider indirect semantic relationships such as *lion-stripes* (i.e., *lion-tiger* and then *tiger-stripes*), the right hemisphere gets involved (Weltman & Lavidor, 2013). Findings such as these lead researchers to believe that the left hemisphere does fine-grained semantic processing focused on tightly linked concepts while the right hemisphere does coarse-grained processing by spreading its activation wider but more weakly.

While there is general agreement that the left posterior temporal lobe mediates between sound and meaning, there is less agreement about where—or how—the word meanings themselves are stored. Traditionally, concepts have been viewed as abstract mental representations. However, there's a growing body of evidence supporting the idea of **embodied semantics**, which is *the proposal that we understand the meaning of a word by simulating it in the sensorimotor cortex.*

To test the hypothesis that the motor system is engaged in the understanding of action verbs, Glenberg and Kaschak (2002) had participants perform tasks that were meant to interfere with the comprehension of those verbs. Participants heard a series of sentences and were asked to judge as quickly as possible whether each made sense. For example, *Shut the door* is sensible, but *Boil the air* is not. On half the trials, the participants had to move their hand toward their body to respond yes, and on the other half they had to move away for a positive response. Some sentences, such as *Open the drawer,* had an implied movement toward the body, while other sentences, such as *Close the drawer*, had an implied movement away from the body. As predicted by the hypothesis, a response movement that conflicted with the implied movement led to a longer reaction time. Thus, participants were quicker to respond yes to *Open the drawer* when they moved their hand in the same direction as they would to open a drawer, that is, toward their body, than when they had to move their hand in the opposite direction.

As we've already seen, the embodied semantics approach provides a possible solution to the symbol grounding problem. However, it's still unclear how abstract words like *freedom* or *academic* would be embodied.

In Sum

The mental lexicon is a permanent store of all the words you know, and it contains information about how those words are pronounced, what they mean, and how they are related to other words. Because of base frequency affects, traditional models of the lexicon assume that only the base form of the word is stored. However, connectionist models assume all word forms are stored but are grouped together according to similarity of pronunciation and meaning. Words in the mental lexicon are arranged as a network with both categorical and associative relations linking them to other words. When a word is activated in the network, the activation spreads to other words that are related to it. Spreading activation causes semantic interference for taxonomic relations (*dog-cat*) and semantic facilitation for thematic relations (*dog-bone*). The dual stream model proposes a dorsal sound-to-action stream from auditory cortex to the inferior frontal lobe and a ventral sound-to-meaning stream from auditory cortex to the posterior temporal lobe. A ventral lexicon is well established by the data, but some evidence suggests a separate dorsal lexicon as well. Embodied semantics hypothesizes that we understand the meanings of words by simulating them in the relevant motor and perceptual regions of the brain.

Review Questions

1. What two assumptions do conventional models of lexical processing tend to make about how phonological word forms are stored in the mental lexicon? What is the evidence for each assumption? How do connectionist models organize the mental lexicon to account for the data?

2. What is the word association task, and what do its results suggest about the organization of the mental lexicon? Clarify the distinction between thematic and taxonomic relations, illustrating with examples.

3. Explain the semantic priming task and how its results provide support for the spreading activation model. Describe the picture-word interference task and the pattern of results it yields. How does the spreading activation model account for these results?

4. Describe the dual stream model of speech processing and the dual lexicon model based on it. What regions of the brain seems to be involved in processing phonological word forms, and what seems to be the processing goal in each location? How does the functioning of the ventral stream differ in the left and right hemispheres?

5. Describe the design and results of Glenberg and Kaschak's (2002) experiment. How do the researchers interpret these results?

Thought Questions

1. Use the word association task to develop a small semantic network. Select a random word and then try to generate as many associated words as you can. Or better yet, perform the word association task on friends and family members, and use these data to build your network. Do you find more taxonomic or thematic associations in your network?

2. Mind mapping is a technique for brainstorming and organizing information. Perhaps you were taught how to make a mind map in school, but if you're unfamiliar with the technique, google it. Based on what you know about the organization and mechanics of the mental lexicon, explain the underlying cognitive processes that are engaged when you build a mind map.

3. Popular psychology has made a big deal out of differences between the "left brain" and the "right brain." What sorts of things have you heard about the way the left and right hemispheres process information? How do these pop "facts" compare with the experimental observations?

Google It! Mind Maps

If you'd like to get some idea of how the kinds of stimuli used in the **picture-word interference task**, search for images online. If you're interested in the **mind map** technique for brainstorming, you can find articles about it online as well as many image examples of completed mind maps.

SECTION 5.4: HOW WORDS ARE RETRIEVED

- Word recognition involves extracting phonological word forms from the speech stream and linking them by way of the mental lexicon to their semantic representations, while word production entails finding a phonological word form in the mental lexicon to match a semantic representation.

- Spoken word recognition involves three stages: (1) lexical access, or matching the acoustic signal to candidate word forms; (2) lexical selection, or choosing the best candidate based on context or expectations; and (3) lexical integration, or linking the word with its meaning within the larger context.

- The cohort model of word recognition proposes that a cohort of candidates is generated from the speech stream in a bottom-up fashion and that lexical selection occurs when a recognition point is reached.

- Models of word production generally feature at least two stages: (1) lexical selection, or choosing an abstract word form, or lemma, to represent a concept; and (2) phonological encoding, which transforms the lemma into a phonological word form.

- In feedforward models of spoken word production, information flows in one direction only from lexical selection to phonological representation, although the Levelt model allows feedback by means of self-monitoring.

- The Dell interactive model consists of three layers (semantic, word, and phonemic) with spreading activation in both directions between layers; processing between semantic and word layers regulates lexical selection, while processing between word and phoneme layers is responsible for phonological encoding.

Now for a pop quiz.

(1) True or False: Symbols that are understood in terms of the perceptual and motor experiences they invoke are called embodied representations.

(2) Fill in the Blank: The _____ is an experimental procedure in which the participant is asked to name a picture while ignoring a simultaneously presented distractor word.

You probably found the first question easier than the second. This is because the first question only requires **recognition** of the correct answer. That is, you only need to do *a search of long-term memory to find a stored match with the current stimulus*. The second question was probably harder because it requires *the intentional retrieval of information from long-term memory*, otherwise known as **recall**. In other words, recognition is a passive form of memory retrieval, while recall is active. The concepts of recognition and recall are important in word processing as well.

We spend most of our waking hours talking with other people. As listeners, we engage in repeated cycles of **word recognition**, which is *the process of extracting phonological word forms from the speech stream and linking them by way of the mental lexicon to their semantic representations*. As speakers, we run through repeated cycles of **word production**, which is *the process of finding phonological word forms in the mental lexicon to express underlying semantic representations or thoughts*.

These processes are largely automatic. It's virtually impossible to tune out speech in your native language, and in our daily chit-chat words flow from our mouths with little conscience effort. These processes are also remarkably fast, given a normal speaking rate of two or three words per second (Levelt, Roelofs, & Meyer, 1999). And finally, these processes are remarkably accurate. Although both recognition and recall errors occur, they rarely impede communication.

In this section, we'll first review the dominant model of spoken word recognition, and then we'll consider two competing models of spoken word reduction.

Spoken Word Recognition

Going from hearing a spoken word to understanding what that word means involves three stages (Marslen-Wilson, 1987). The first stage, called **lexical access**, involves *the process of matching the acoustic signal of the speech stream to candidate phonological representations stored in the mental lexicon*. Since the speech stream is noisy and ambiguous, there will always be multiple ways of parsing it, and evidence shows that listeners briefly entertain multiple candidate word forms. There's also no consideration of meaning at this point. The second stage is known as **lexical selection**, and it's *the process of choosing the best-fitting word match to the acoustic input*. At this point, both context and expectations such as knowledge of word frequency have an effect. The last stage is called **lexical integration**, and it consists of *the process of linking the selected word form to the overall semantics and syntax of the utterance*. Not only must listeners link phonological word forms to their semantic representations, they need to link those concepts to the other concepts expressed in the sentence as regulated by the syntax. In other words, you don't just understand the individual words of a sentence, you also understand how those word meanings are related to each other.

Most researchers in the field of word recognition favor some form of cohort model. A **cohort** is *the set of all words that begin with the same sequence of phonemes*. For example, the *e-l-e* cohort contains words like *elephant, elevator, elegant,* and *elementary,* to name a few. As more phonemes are added to the sequence, the cohort gets smaller. If we follow *e-l-e* with an *f,* the cohort reduces to the single word *elephant.* (Unless you're a jazz fan, in which case you'll still be considering *Ella Fitzgerald* as a possibility.) *The point at which a string of phonemes provides enough evidence for identifying a word* is known as that word's **recognition point**. Short words with many neighbors, such as *hat* or *coat,* may not have a recognition point until the end of the word. However, longer words, like *elephant* or *thermometer,* typically have recognition points well before the end.

The **cohort model** is a *model of word recognition proposing that listeners initially consider all possible word matches to the incoming speech stream but identify the word as soon as a recognition point is reached* (Marslen-Wilson, 1987). The standard cohort model argues that this initial process of extracting possible words from the speech stream is strictly a **bottom-up process**, meaning that it is *a process that is driven solely by the input without consideration of context or expectations*. This means that even when the context strongly biases one member of the cohort, all members will initially be activated. Thus, even if you hear the start of a sentence like *The other day at the zoo I saw elef . . . ,* you will still momentarily entertain the possibility of having seen Ella Fitzgerald in addition to the far more likely elephants. And why not? Maybe your friend really did see Ella Fitzgerald at the zoo.

Evidence for the cohort model comes from several different experimental paradigms (Marslen-Wilson, 1987). One technique is the **shadowing task**, *a procedure in which the participant is asked to repeat a continuous flow of speech out loud and as quickly as possible.* This task requires a lot of attention, but it can typically be performed with a lag of about 200 milliseconds, suggesting that participants start shadowing a word before they've completely heard it. Another technique is the **gating task**. This is *a procedure in which participants are presented increasingly longer increments of a word and asked to guess what they think the word will be.*

On average, participants can identify a word after about 200 milliseconds when it occurs within a sentence, but they take more than 300 milliseconds when the word is presented in isolation. *The improved ability to identify a word within a sentence as opposed to by itself* is known as the **sentence superiority effect**. This effect suggests that lexical selection is influenced by context and expectations, as opposed to the strictly bottom-up process of accessing the cohort (Zhang et al., 2011). In addition, word frequency also influences lexical selection, with common words being recognized more quickly than less common words. This word frequency effect has been demonstrated in eye-tracking studies. As listeners hear sentences describing a visual display, they tend to move their eyes to look at the objects that are being mentioned.

In a set of experiments done in German, Weber and Crocker (2012) examined the competitive effects of context and frequency on lexical selection. For example, they looked at the cohort pair *Blume* (flower), which is a high-frequency word, and *Bluse* (blouse), which is a low-frequency word. Each was preceded by one of two sentence beginnings. When the sentence began *The woman found . . .* , participants were more likely to look at the picture of the flower, indicating that when the context is neutral, listeners assume to more frequent cohort member. However, when the sentence began *The woman ironed. . . .* , eye gaze was mostly fixated on the picture of the contextually appropriate blouse but with occasional glances at the high-frequency flower. This result suggests that context influences lexical selection but doesn't completely exclude high-frequency candidates.

Word frequency has a greater impact on word selection as listeners get older. Even when their hearing is still in the normal range, older adults struggle more with spoken language comprehension than do young adults. To test the hypothesis that older adults relied more on word frequency in word selection than younger adults, Revill and Spieler (2012) tested both groups using a **visual world paradigm**, *a task in which participants are asked to interact with objects or pictures in the visual environment according to spoken instructions.* Specifically, participants were asked to click on named objects projected on a computer monitor, and their eye movements were tracked during the task. The words naming the pictures were from the same cohort but differed in frequency. Although both groups were quite accurate in their responses, older adults were more likely to look at or select the high-frequency picture when the low-frequency picture was named. Perhaps because older adults have more difficulty overall with spoken language comprehension, they rely more on their knowledge of word frequencies than on the context present in the speech stream.

Spoken Word Production

Psycholinguists generally agree that there are two basic stages in spoken word production (Jaeger, Furth, & Hilliard, 2012). The first step, known as **lexical selection**, is *the process that goes from a particular concept to an abstract word form, or lemma.* Any particular concept, say DOG, can be expressed by a number of different words, for example *dog, puppy, hound, pooch, poodle, Rover,* and so on. So the goal of lexical selection is to make the best choice given the situation. Notice that the same term, lexical selection, is used both in theories of word recognition and word production to mean somewhat different processes. Yet in both cases the goal is to choose one word from among a number of candidates. The second step, called

phonological encoding, is *the process that goes from abstract word form, or lemma, to its phonological representation*.

By describing spoken word production as a two-stage process, we can account for two observations. First, there's no systematic relationship between meaning and sound, and it's difficult to create a workable computational model of word production with an intermediate level linking the two (Dell, 1986). Second, evidence from the tip-of-the-tongue (TOT) experience clearly suggests the existence of an abstract lemma level. When we're in a TOT state, we know that we know the word, but we can't produce a full phonological encoding of that word. Thus, TOT occurs when lexical selection is successful but phonological encoding is not.

Psycholinguists are divided on the issue of how information flows through these two stages. Some researchers advocate for a **feedforward model** of word production, arguing that the evidence supports *a model in which each process is performed in a serial fashion*. In other words, later levels of processing have no influence on earlier levels, so the flow of information goes in one direction only. Other researchers argue for an **interactive model**, pointing to evidence for *a model in which higher and lower levels of processing influence each other*. That is to say, the flow of information goes in both directions.

The Levelt Feedforward Model

The most influential of the feedforward models in the one proposed by Levelt and his colleagues (Levelt et al., 1999). This model fleshes out what happens before, between, and after the two basic stages of lexical selection and phonological encoding, beginning with a wordless thought and ending with a sound wave.

There are six stages in the model altogether, with the output of one stage serving as the input for the next stage. Although the flow of information through the system is strictly feedforward, the ability to self-monitor the end production does provide feedback to the beginning of the system. The Levelt model is similar in many respects to earlier models based on observations of speech errors, such as the one by Fromkin (1971), but the details of the model are based on the results of various reaction time experiments.

In the Levelt model, word production begins with conceptual preparation (Levelt et al., 1999). You can think without language, but to share your thoughts, you need to put them into words. Thus, the output of conceptual preparation is a **lexical concept**, that is to say, *a concept that can be expressed by a word*. However, there's no one-to-one correspondence between concepts and words, and so you still have to select a particular word to express the concept you're thinking about. This is the job of the second stage, lexical selection. In this model, lexical selection involves choosing a lemma, which is an abstract word form. You can think of a lemma as the name of a word, its most basic form as you would find it in the dictionary.

If you think of the lemma as the naked form of the word, then the next two processes dress up the word so it can go out into the world. Let's say you've selected the lemma *KITTEN* to express the newborn offspring of the family pet. First, the shape of the word may have to be modified to find the overall syntax and semantics of the sentence. Since there's more than one *KITTEN*, you'll need to add the plural suffix -*S* to make *KITTEN+S*. This process is called morphological encoding, and its output is a set of morphemes, or minimal units of meaning.

Next, this set of morphemes needs to be encoded as a series of phonemes, and this is the job of the next stage, phonological encoding. In this case, the morphemic sequence *KITTEN+S* needs to be converted into the phonemic sequence *k-i-t-uh-n-z*. Notice, for example, that phonological encoding realizes the *s* of the plural suffix as *z* in this case. This stage also organizes the phonemes into syllables and assigns stress, such that the output is the phonological word *KIT-uhnz*.

You can think of the phonological word as the word the way it sounds in your head, and so the next two stages convert that inner sound into a physical sound wave. The role of phonetic encoding is to program a phonetic gestural score. The term *gesture* here is being used much as it is in motor theory, to refer to the general motor plan for articulating a phoneme. The gestural score, then, is like a musical score. In other words, it's a read-out of the gestures that need to be programmed to produce the spoken word. These gestures need to be specified according to current circumstances, such as coarticulation effects of neighboring phonemes and interference from ambient noise. This is the job of the final stage, articulation, which produces a sound wave, in other words, a speech stream.

The Dell Interactive Model

Among interactive models of word production, the one developed by Dell and colleagues is perhaps the most notable (Dell, 1986; Dell et al., 1997). The model is designed mainly to account for speech errors in healthy people as well as those with brain damage, as obtained through picture naming and other word production tasks.

The Dell model consists of three layers. At the top is the semantic layer, where concepts are distributed across a network of feature nodes. Thus, **semantic neighbors**, or *concepts with related meanings*, such as DOG and CAT, have overlapping feature nodes. Notice that the idea of semantic neighbors at the meaning level is parallel to the idea of phonological neighbors at the phonological level.

In the middle is the word layer, which contains one node for each lemma. Keep in mind that lemmas are abstract representations of words, not the word forms as they're spoken. At the bottom of the model is the phoneme level, which contains different nodes for each speech sound. In order to properly sequence the phonemes in words, the model assumes that each phoneme is tagged with its syllable position (onset, nucleus, coda). Thus, the first *p* in *pop* is *p(ONSET)*, while the second *p* is *p(CODA)*.

Figure 5.11 Feedforward Word Production Model (Levelt, Roelofs, & Meyer, 1999)

In a feedforward model, the output of one process provides the input for the next process. Feedback only occurs at certain points where self-monitoring occurs. In the feedforward model proposed by Levelt, Roelofs, and Meyer (1999), self-monitoring occurs at the Phonological Word output (where you hear the word in your head) and at the Sound Wave output (where you hear the word through your ears).

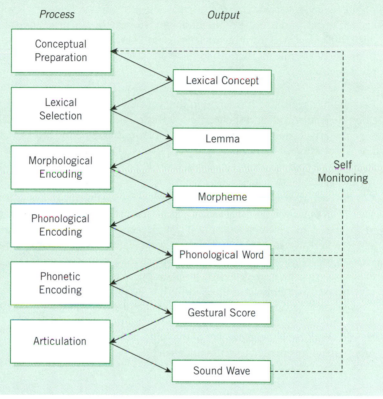

Source: Levelt, Roelofs, and Meyer (1999).

The two processing stages between these layers are the standard lexical selection and phonological encoding processes common to word production models. However, interactive models view word production not as a step-by-step process but rather as a process of spreading activation. In other words, information flows both from top to bottom and from bottom to top. Thus, activation in the phoneme layer can influence activation in the word layer, and likewise activation in the word layer can influence activation in the semantic layer.

Let's walk through the model with an example. Suppose I show you a picture of a cat. The picture activates feature nodes in the semantic layer relevant to the concept of CAT, such as fur, four legs, long tail, whiskers, and so on. Some activation will also occur for related concepts as well, like DOG and RAT, but only on rare occasions will they win out over CAT. This activity will spread down to the word layer, mainly exciting the *cat* lemma but with some excitement of the *dog* and *rat* lemmas as well. The focusing of excitement on the *cat* lemma feeds back to the semantic layer, further activating the feature nodes related to the CAT concept.

Back at the word level, the lemmas *cat, dog,* and *rat* are sending activation down to the phoneme layer. Because *cat* has the strongest activation in the word level, *k* is the most excited onset, and because of the phonemic overlap between *cat* and *rat,* the nucleus *a* is far more excited than the nucleus *o,* and likewise for the coda *t.* The activity at the phoneme level spreads back up to the word layer, further enhancing the activation of the *cat* lemma.

Eventually, a threshold is reached in the word layer, a lemma is selected, and a phonological encoding is spelled out, in this case *cat* going to *k-a-t.* Random noise in the network accounts for speech errors. Noise in the semantic layer can lead to the lexical selection of the *dog* lemma by mistake, and noise in the phoneme layer can result in *cat* being pronounced *cag* in error.

Whether word production is a feedforward or interactive process is still an unresolved question, with even the most recently published reports finding evidence for one model or the other. In a picture description task, Jaeger et al. (2012) found that participants selected verbs so as to avoid alliteration. That is, they tended to avoid the verb *gave,* selecting a verb like *handed* or *passed* in a sentence from like *Patty _____ the gauge to Simon.* This result suggests that lower-level phonological information can affect higher-level word selection, thus supporting an interactive model. However, Geng, Kirchgessner, and Schnur (2013) tested competing hypotheses, and their results were more consistent with feedforward models than interactive models. At this point, we should think back to the parable of the blind monks and the elephant. Clearly, a lot more research is needed to settle this issue.

In Sum

Words are retrieved from the mental lexicon during the process of word recognition in listening as well as word production in speaking. Spoken word recognition involves three steps: (1) identifying possible word forms in the speech stream, (2) choosing the most likely among these based on context or expectations, and (3) integrating the word with its meaning. The cohort model proposes that a cohort of candidate word forms is extracted from the speech stream in a bottom-up fashion and that lexical selection occurs when a recognition point is reached. Models of word production typically include a minimum of two stages: (1) lexical selection of a lemma to represent a concept, and (2) phonological encoding of that item for speech production. In feedforward models of speech production, information flows in one direction only, from lexical selection to phonological encoding, although the Levelt model allows

Figure 5.12 Interactive Word Production Model (Dell et al., 1997)

Interactive word production models work by spreading activation. In a picture-naming task, seeing a picture of a cat excites concept nodes related to cat-ness (the dark circles). Activation in these nodes spreads to the word *cat*, but some activation also spreads to the related words *dog* and *rat*. Meanwhile, activation from *cat, dog,* and *rat* spreads to the phoneme layer. Activation can also feed back, from phonemes to words and from words to concepts. A word is selected when a certain threshold is reached. Noise in the system accounts for word-choice and pronunciation errors.

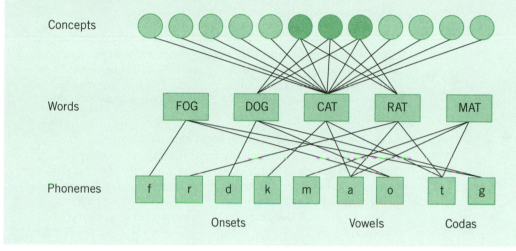

Source: Dell et al. (1997).

feedback through self-monitoring. Interactive models allow information to flow in both directions between lexicon selection and phonological encoding. The Dell interactive model views lexical selection as spreading activation between semantic and word layers, and it views phonological encoding as spreading activation between word and phoneme layers.

Review Questions

1. Explain the distinction between recognition and recall in memory retrieval. Explain how the processes of word retrieval (word recognition and word production) are parallel to these general memory retrieval processes.

2. Explain the three processes involved in spoken word recognition. Describe how the cohort model handles these three processes. What kinds of experimental evidence support the cohort model?

3. What are the two basic stages of spoken word production common to word production models, and what evidence supports the assertion that there needs to be an intermediate lemma level between the semantic and phonological levels? Distinguish between feedforward and interactive models.

4. Describe the Levelt and Dell models, illustrating with an example for each.

Thought Questions

1. Cohort models have applications beyond spoken word recognition. Predictive text technologies used in cell phones and search engines also operate in terms of cohorts. What are the parallels between cohort models of word recognition and predictive text in typing? In the case of predictive text, who is the word producer and who is the word recognizer?

2. A tip-of-the-tongue state can be thought of as memory retrieval failure in word production, specifically at the stage of phonological encoding. What would be the experience of a retrieval failure at the stage of lexical selection? What would the experience of a retrieval failure in spoken word recognition be like? Have you ever had such an experience? If so, explain the circumstances under which it occurred.

Google It! Tip of the Tongue

The development of **speech recognition** and **speech synthesis** software is advancing rapidly. By finding ways to get computers to recognize and produce words, we gain insight into how humans might be accomplishing these tasks. You can also find articles and videos about the **tip-of-the-tongue** phenomenon.

CONCLUSION

Words are minimal units of meaningful language that can be uttered in isolation. They also exhibit a dual nature in that they have both of an outward phonological form as well as an underlying semantic representation. Words are arbitrary symbols for concepts, but the question of how words acquire meaning, which is known as the symbol grounding problem, still isn't well understood.

We learn words throughout our entire life. At first, children's word learning progresses slowly. Then at about a year and a half of age, a vocabulary spurt occurs that continues into the early school years as children master tens of thousands of words. As we learn to read, we continue to expand our vocabulary, and even adults who rarely read take on new words that they encounter in their daily lives.

The dual nature of words is reflected in neuroimaging studies. The dual stream model of word processing proposes that phonological word forms are processed in the dorsal stream, which provides a sound-to-action route. The ventral route, on the other hand, is conceived of as a sound-to-meaning route that links phonological word forms with semantic representations.

We need to retrieve words from memory as both listeners and speakers. Word recognition involves finding a matching word form in memory, accessing its meaning, and then integrating it into the ongoing utterance. Word production involves linking a concept with a phonological word form to represent it. Researchers debate whether word production involves a feedforward or an interactive process.

We rarely utter words in isolation. Instead, we combine them into sentences that we speak at a rapid rate. Thus, in the normal course of conversation, we cycle through the processes of lexical retrieval two or three times per second. In the next chapter, we'll explore how we accomplish the task of retrieving and integrating words into sentences with such split-second accuracy.

CROSS-CULTURAL PERSPECTIVE: May I Have a Word With You?

In this chapter, we defined a word as a minimal unit of speech that can stand alone. This definition suggests that determining whether a stretch of speech is a word or not should be a straightforward process. In other words, if it can stand alone and if it means something, then it's a word. However, real language is messy, and oftentimes even native speakers can't agree on where the boundaries in the speech stream should go.

As an educated speaker of English, you have pretty good intuitions about what constitutes a word in English based on your experience with reading, since we use white space to mark boundaries between written words. However, you learned in Chapter 3 that there are no spaces between words in speech. Instead, we infer word boundaries on the basis of statistical regularities and prosodic cues such as stress and intonation patterns.

We all agree on the boundaries for most words, but we don't always agree when it comes to rare or novel expressions. For instance, if you did research on the Internet, would you write that you got your information *online* or *on-line*? (I just checked online/on-line and got both spellings.)

Sometimes the conventional placement of word boundaries is inconsistent. For example, we write *highway* but *high school*. In terms of prosody, both should be considered compound words. This is because compound words are stressed on the first element, whereas adjective-noun sequences are stressed on the second element. Compare the stress patterns in these two sentences: (1) *Barack Obama lives in the WHITE-house*; (2) *Barry O'Brien lives in the white-HOUSE on the corner*. Since *HIGH-school* has the same stress pattern as *HIGH-way*, it should be written as one word.

Educated Chinese speakers have different intuitions about what constitutes a word based on their reading experience. Chinese is written in characters, or logograms, that represent meaningful syllables. While some Chinese words are one-syllable long and hence are written with a single character, most are composed of two or more syllables and are written with an equal number of characters. Furthermore, Chinese is written as a continuous line of characters, with no spaces between words.

Experiments have shown that Chinese readers mentally insert word boundaries as they scan text. However, experiments have also shown that they don't all put those word boundaries at the same places (Liu et al., 2013). That is, native Chinese speakers have differing intuitions about what constitutes a word in their language. The issue isn't so much with picking out the content words as it is deciding whether characters that serve grammatical functions should be treated as suffixes or separate function words.

In one sense, Chinese speakers treat the character as the minimal meaningful unit that can stand alone, at least in writing. After all, each character does have a meaning in isolation even if it's mostly used in combination. Thus, while your instructor may assign a 500-word essay, a Chinese teacher would ask you to write 500 characters, and no one would even think to ask how many "words" that is.

Chinese text has several distinctive features. Each character occupies the same amount of space and is separated from each of its neighbors by a small gap. A common misunderstanding is that each Chinese character stands for a word, and it's easy to see why people would think that way. It's also clear why the Chinese perception is that the character is the minimal unit of stand-alone meaning, at least in writing.

In some ways, written Chinese better represents the speech stream than does written English. Each character takes up the same amount of space in the printed line, just as each syllable takes up a similar amount of time in the speech stream. And word boundaries aren't marked in either the spoken or written language, but major phrase and sentence boundaries are. Notice that Chinese has adopted the use of the comma to separate phrases and a period, in the form of a small circle, to mark the ends of sentences.

As with most constructs in language, the concept of a word is fuzzy. And in the end, words have more psychological reality than they do clear-cut physical characteristics. Somehow, though, we manage to succeed remarkably well at communicating with each other despite the fuzziness in language.

Figure 5.13 Sample of Chinese Text

The following is a Chinese translation of the opening paragraph of this section, beginning "In this chapter." Notice how each character, which stands for a meaningful syllable, occupies the same amount of square space. In the twentieth century, Chinese writers adopted Western-style punctuation, including the comma and the period (represented by a small circle). Translation by the author using the software Google Translate.

在本章中，我们定义了一个字作为讲话中可以独立的最小单元。我们还了解到，一个字是一个概念的象征。以这种方式思考的话使我们的假设，即确定一个舒展讲话是否是一个词或不应该是一个简单的过程。换句话说，如果它可以独立并且如果它意味着什么，那么它是一个字。然而，真正的语言是凌乱，甚至常常母语不能同意的地方在语流的边界应该去

KEY TERMS

Arbitrariness of the sign

Base frequency effect

Bottom-up process

Chinese Room argument

Cohort

Cohort model

Concept

Cross-situational word learning

Derivational suffix

Dual lexicon model

Embodied representation

Embodied semantics

Fast mapping

Feedforward model

Gating task

Iambic

Inflectional suffix

Interactive model

Joint attention

Lemma

Lexeme

Lexical access

Lexical concept

Lexical integration

Lexical selection

Mental lexicon

Mutual exclusivity assumption

Neighborhood density

Network model

Onomatopoeia

Phonological encoding

Phonotactic probability

Phonotactic rules

Picture-word interference task

Productive vocabulary

Recall

Receptive vocabulary

Recognition

Recognition point

Referential uncertainty

Semantic facilitation effect

Semantic interference effect

Semantic neighbors

Semantic primes

Semantic priming effect

Semantic priming task

Sentence superiority effect

Shadowing task

Spreading activation model

Supramarginal gyrus

Symbol grounding problem

Syntactic bootstrapping

Taxonomic assumption

Taxonomic relation

Thematic relation

Trochaic

Visual world paradigm

Whole object assumption

Word

Word association task

Word frequency

Word production

Word recognition

CHAPTER 6

Sentences

If evolutionary psychologist Robin Dunbar (1998) is right, language evolved for gossip. At any rate, we certainly do enough of it. Think of how many hours a day you spend in idle chit-chat, mostly talking about who did what to whom. We really can't help it, because language compels us to organize our thoughts in sentences, which are basically tidbits of gossip. Every sentence has a subject—who or what, but mostly who—the sentence is about. Every sentence also has a verb—what the subject did, or will do, or is doing right now. And most sentences also have an object—who or what the subject performed the action on.

Even a science lecture takes the form of gossip. We talk about neurons firing action potentials and the substantia nigra producing dopamine, as if neurons and the substantia nigra were animate beings with minds of their own. There's just no other way to talk about things, which is one reason why scientists resort so often to explaining their ideas in math instead.

We just seem born to gossip. Infants are attuned to it and learn their language through chit-chat with their caregivers. In this chapter, we first learn about the basic structure of sentences. We then look at the strategies we use for extracting meaning from the speech stream. Following that, we examine how we convert our thoughts into messages our listener can understand. We wrap up the chapter by considering how infants learn to comprehend and produce sentences so that they, too, can spend their days chatting about who did what to whom.

SECTION 6.1: SENTENCE STRUCTURE

- Sentence processing involves three levels: (1) a conceptual level representing the intended message; (2) a syntactic level, where the structure of the sentence is composed; and (3) a phonological level, which produces the spoken sentence form.

- At the conceptual level, sentences are descriptions of events, and the nature of the event determines the types of participants, or thematic roles.

- At the syntactic level, the basic components of a sentence are its subject, verb, and object; an event at the conceptual level is mapped onto the verb, but the assignment of thematic roles to subject and object is complex.

- At the phonological level, the spoken form of the sentence is produced; this entails programs for syllabification, assignment of stresses, and intonational contours of the sentence for the articulatory system.

- A noun phrase consists of a noun plus any determiners, adjectives, or other modifiers. A verb phrase consists of a main verb plus any auxiliary verbs, adverbs, or object noun phrases. A clause is a simple sentence consisting of a verb and its arguments; clauses can be combined to form complex sentences.

- Certain syntactic structures have been the focus of psycholinguistic research, and these include reversible versus irreversible sentences, active versus passive voice, subject versus object clefts, subject versus object relative clauses, the dative construction, and agreement.

As we learned in Chapter 1, vervet monkeys use different vocalizations to warn other members of their group about an approaching leopard, eagle, or snake (Seyfarth et al., 1980a, 1980b). But they can't talk about leopards, eagles, or snakes, and there are no vervet stories about leopards or discussions about what to do the next time an eagle swoops overhead. Unlike our primate cousins, we're not limited to uttering single words in isolation. Rather, we combine words together to express complex ideas and relationships. We do this by using **syntax**, which is *a set of rules for ordering words in a sentence*.

Mind Meld

Language enables us to transfer thoughts from one mind to another in the form of spoken sentences. Psycholinguists generally agree that there are at least three stages in the process of producing a sentence.

The first stage is the conceptual level, where the intended message is formulated. We can think without language, but to produce a sentence we need to organize our thoughts into concepts that we have names for. Thus, we search the mental lexicon for words to match up to those concepts, but recall that the lexicon is generally assumed to store abstract word forms, or lemmas. Also, there's no particular order to the concepts in our intended message at this point. Let's say I see a clown riding a unicycle, and I want to tell you about it. At the conceptual level, my message consists of the following set of three lemmas, {RIDE, CLOWN, UNICYCLE}. This thought can be visualized as a concept map.

Figure 6.1   Concept Map of a Clown Riding a Unicycle

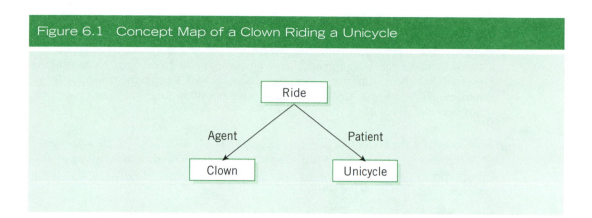

A sentence provides a description of some kind of event or state of affairs, and the nature of the event determines the kinds of participants that can be involved in that event. In our example, the event is RIDE, which requires two participants, someone that does the riding and something that gets ridden. *The entity that causes the event portrayed in a sentence to occur* is called the **agent**, and *the entity that is acted upon in the event that is portrayed in a sentence* is called the **patient**. In our example, CLOWN is the agent and UNICYCLE is the patient. *The various types of participants involved in an event portrayed in a sentence are called its* **thematic roles**. Agent and patient are the most common thematic roles, but there are others.

Table 6.1   Common Thematic Roles

Thematic Role	Example
Agent	**The strong man** twisted the iron bar.
Patient	The lion chased **the clown.**
Recipient	The lion tamer fed **the lion** a steak.
Instrument	The bearded lady charmed the strong man **with her beauty.**
Goal	The clown jumped **onto the unicycle.**
Source	The elephants rushed **out of the tent.**

We have all experienced our thoughts running in multiple directions, but when we speak, we can only say one word at a time. Thus, language forces us to put our thoughts in order. That's the job of the syntactic level. Each language has its own *typical sequence of sentence elements*, but the **canonical word order** for English is subject-verb-object.

The subject is what the sentence is about, and so it typically goes at or near the beginning. Since I want to make a statement about a clown, I'll make CLOWN the subject. *The mapping of thematic roles onto syntactic positions such as subject and object is called* **thematic role assignment**. There's a tendency to assign the agent to the subject position, but there are plenty of exceptions to this as well. I assign the remaining the remaining thematic role, UNICYCLE, to the object position simply because I have nowhere else to put it.

We now have the kernel of a sentence, namely CLOWN RIDE UNICYCLE. Although we can understand what this proto-sentence means, it still needs some dressing up to be proper English. In particular, we need to add some inflectional suffixes and function words to satisfy the rules of grammar.

Let's start with the subject. In English, we need indicate whether nouns are singular or plural. There's just one CLOWN in this case, so I select the word form *clown*. We also are required by the rules of English grammar to indicate whether this is a noun we've mentioned before or a new noun in the discourse. Let's suppose we've already introduced the clown into the conversation, so I select the determiner *the* and insert it before *clown* to make the subject noun phrase *the clown*. My sentence so far is *The clown. . . .*

Next let's deal with the verb. English grammar requires that we specify when the event took place, and furthermore the verb form must agree with the subject in number. Let's keep things simple and use the present tense. Because the subject is singular, I need to attach the singular suffix *-s* to the verb to make *rides*. (That's right, *-s* on a noun means plural, but *-s* on a verb means singular.) Now I have the sentence fragment *The clown rides. . . .*

Table 6.2 Sentence Tree Abbreviations	
S	Sentence
NP	Noun Phrase
VP	Verb Phrase
D	Determiner
N	Noun
Pro	Pronoun
A	Adjective
V	Verb
PP	Prepositional Phrase
Triangle	Indicates that detail has been omitted

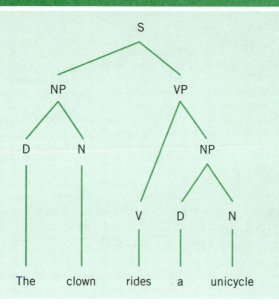

Figure 6.2 Sentence Tree for *The clown rides a unicycle*

```
                            S
                   ┌────────┴────────┐
                  NP                 VP
              ┌────┴────┐        ┌────┴────┐
              D         N        V        NP
              │         │        │      ┌──┴──┐
              │         │        │      D     N
              │         │        │      │     │
             The      clown    rides    a  unicycle
```

I go through the same process with the object as I did with the subject. There's just one *unicycle*, but it's new to the conversation, so I make the object noun phrase *a unicycle*. My sentence is now syntactically complete as *The clown rides a unicycle*.

It's important to note that syntactic positions such as subject, verb, and object are phrases, not words. The subject and object are noun phrases, which include not only the noun but also a determiner if needed and any adjectives or other modifying expresses as desired. For example, I could expand the subject to *That crazy clown with the fuzzy red wig*. . . . Likewise, the verb phrase includes not only the main verb but also any auxiliary verbs that help the main verb express its meaning. For instance, if I wanted to emphasize a current, ongoing state of affairs, I would change *rides* to *is riding*.

This syntactic sequence now goes to the phonological level, where it's spelled out in terms of syllables and stresses so that it can be articulated. My sentence, with syllables separated by hyphens and stresses in capital letters, becomes *the-CLOWN-RIDE-za-U-ni-cy-cle*. An intonational contour is assigned as well. Because the sentence is short, it will likely be spoken as a single prosodic phrase. I start my sentence with the fundamental frequency of my voice at a medium level, and it rises through the course of the sentence until I reach the word *unicycle*, which I want to emphasize, and after that my voice falls. A drop in pitch is an important cue to phrase boundaries in speech (Anderson & Carlson, 2010).

Now you, my listener, need to extract my intended meaning from this spoken sequence. Hearing the phonological string *the-CLOWN-RIDE-za-U-ni-cy-cle*, you

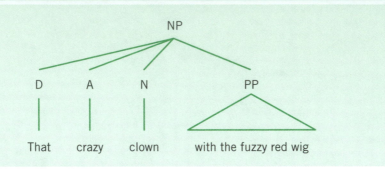

Figure 6.3 Noun Phrase Tree of *That crazy clown with the fuzzy red wig*

interpret it as the syntactic sequence *The clown rides a unicycle*. From this, you extract the event RIDE, the agent CLOWN, and the patient UNICYCLE, and in your own head you recreate the conceptual message {RIDE, CLOWN, UNICYCLE}.

The entire process of formulating a thought in my head to reconstructing that same thought in your head takes place in a matter of seconds. Furthermore, it's essentially effortless and takes place largely outside of awareness. In short, humans have developed an efficient means of thought transfer, without resort to supernatural devices like extrasensory telepathy or Vulcan mind melds, simply by blowing air at each other.

Syntactic Structures

The grammar of English, like all languages, is exceedingly complex and still not fully understood by linguists. However, there are some common syntactic structures that psycholinguists frequently use in their studies because of the potential they have for shedding light on how sentences are processed. Here we present an overview of these structures, and in the following sections of this chapter we'll examine some of the studies that have used these structures.

There are multiple approaches to analyzing a sentence, and we've already considered two. The first approach considers the way that thematic roles at the conceptual level are mapped onto syntactic categories at the syntactic level. The second approach considers canonical word order, which in English consists of a subject noun phrase followed by a verb phrase and ending with an object noun phrase.

We can also analyze a sentence as consisting of two main components, a subject and a predicate. The subject, of course, is the topic of the sentence, and the predicate makes a comment about the subject. When I told you *The clown rides a unicycle*, I was making a statement about the clown. In other words, *the clown* is the subject, and *rides a unicycle* is the predicate.

When I told you about the clown and the unicycle, my focus of attention was on the clown, and so I selected it as the subject of my sentence. This is normal, since animate entities, especially other humans, tend to grab our attention (Altmann & Kemper, 2006; Tanaka et al., 2011). On the hand, let's say we're inspecting the circus equipment and I want to tell you something about the unicycle, I could select it as the subject instead. Of course, I can't just say *The unicycle rides the clown*, since that doesn't match my intended meaning. Instead, I need to use a syntactic structure that will let you, my listener, know the subject is not the agent but the patient. This structure is called passive voice, and it looks like this: *The unicycle is ridden by the clown*. In contrast, the sentence *The clown rides the unicycle* is in the active voice. Putting it in simple terms, **active voice** is *a sentence structure in which the agent is mapped onto the subject position*, and **passive voice** is *a sentence structure in which the patient is mapped onto the subject position*.

Syntactic structures provide meaning to sentences above and beyond the sum of the meanings of each of the content words, in that they tell us who did what to whom. But we can often rely on our real-world knowledge to infer thematic roles. If you heard me say, "The unicycle rides the clown," your likely response would be, "Don't you mean, 'the clown rides the unicycle'?" Because our example is *a sentence that no longer makes real-world sense if the agent and patient swap subject and object positions*, it's called an **irreversible sentence**. On the other hand, if I told you *The clown chased the lion*, you'd have no reason to think I really meant that the lion had chased the clown. That's because this example is a **reversible sentence**, meaning that it's *a sentence that still makes sense, but with a different meaning, if the agent and patient swap subject and object positions*. As we'll see later in this chapter, reversible passives like *The clown was chased by the lion* can be especially difficult to process.

Adding Complexity

Recall from Chapter 1 that one of the features of human language that gives it such expressive power is recursion. In other words, we can do more than just speak simple sentences. Rather, we can build complex sentences by inserting one sentence inside of another. *A simple sentence that is part of a larger complex sentence* is known as a **clause**.

One way to build complex sentences is through the use of conjunctions. For example, we can say: *The clown rides the unicycle while the bearded lady stands atop the horse*. We could continue this sentence indefinitely. In this case, *the clown rides the unicycle* is the main clause, and *while the bearded lady stands atop the horse* is a subordinate clause that is inserted into the main clause. If you're not convinced that the *while*-clause is inside of the main clause, as opposed to simply continuing as a separate sentence, consider the fact that it can be replaced with the single word *then*, as in: *The clown rides the unicycle then*.

Sometimes we turn a simple sentence into a complex one in order to focus attention on a particular participant in the event. For example, some folks are saying that the elephant chased the clown, but I know the truth: *It was the lion that chased the clown*. This kind of structure is called a **cleft sentence**, and it's *a syntactic structure that attaches*

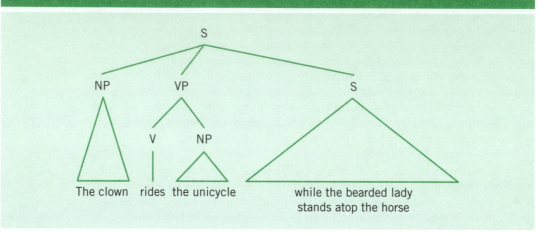

Figure 6.4 Sentence Tree of *The clown rides the unicycle while the bearded lady stands atop the horse*

an introductory clause to the beginning of a sentence for the purpose of highlighting one of the participants in the event. This cleft sentence means essentially the same thing as the simple sentence *The lion chased the clown*, but notice how *the lion* has been "moved" out of its position before *chased* and into the introductory clause.

In a subject cleft, the order of subject and object remains the same. However, we can also make cleft sentences that focus the object, as for example: *It was the clown that the lion chased*. Now the object *the clown* precedes the subject *the lion*, and, as you've probably already guessed, object clefts like these are a lot harder to process, especially when the original sentence is reversible.

We can also create complex sentences by inserting clauses inside of other sentences. One way we do this is through the use of a **relative clause**, which is *a sentence that is placed inside of another sentence for the purpose of describing a noun*. For example, if I want to specify which clown the lion chased, I could say: *The lion chased the clown that rides the unicycle*. Roughly speaking, this is equal to the sentence pair *The lion chased the clown* and *The clown rides the unicycle*. However, the relative clause construction emphasizes the fact that it's the same clown in each of the two simple sentences. Since relative clauses are noun modifiers, they're considered part of the noun phrase, not a separate clause outside of the main clause.

As with cleft sentences, we can distinguish between subject and object relative clauses. In the case of a subject relative clause, the noun in the main clause that's being described is the subject of the relative clause. Thus, in the sentence *The lion chased the clown that rides the unicycle*, the subject of *rides* is *the clown*. However, the object of a relative clause can also be matched up with a noun in the main clause. Consider the

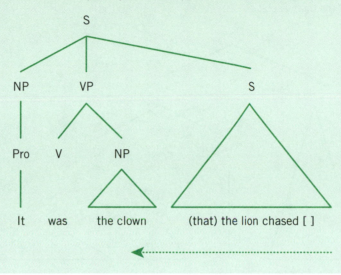

Figure 6.5   Sentence Tree of *It was the clown that the lion chased*

In this cleft sentence, *the clown* is moved forward from its position as the object of *chased*. The conjunction *that* can be deleted, especially in casual speech.

following sentence, which ends with an object relative clause: *The lion mangled the unicycle that the clown rides.* In this case, the object of *rides* is *the unicycle*, but it occurs in the sentence before the subject *the clown*. As you have probably already guessed, object relative clauses tend to be more difficult to process, especially when the relative clause is reversible, as in: *The strong man rescued the clown that the lion chased.*

At the heart of every clause is a verb, but verbs can vary in the number and type of objects they take. Some verbs don't take an object, but most do, and some take more than one. For example, there's a class of verbs that can be used in the **dative construction**, which is *a syntactic structure that entails the meaning of doing something for the benefit of someone else.* Some examples would be *The clown fed the lion a steak* and *The strong man baked the bearded lady a cake.*

In English, the dative construction comes in two versions. In the double object version, the two objects are simply lined up one after the other, with the recipient coming first and the patient coming second, as in the two examples we just looked at. However, we can also put the patient before the recipient, but only if we insert a preposition like *to* or *for* between them, as in *The clown fed a steak to the lion* and *The strong man baked a cake for the bearded lady.* This version is called a prepositional dative construction. A number of psycholinguistic studies have examined differences in the comprehension, production, and acquisition of the two dative constructions.

The noun phrase *the clown* is the object of the verb *rescued* in the main clause and also the object of the verb *chased* in the relative clause.

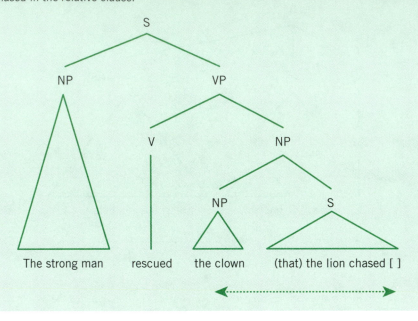

Finally, we need to look at syntactic agreement in more detail. **Agreement** is *a set of syntactic devices for linking related elements within and between sentences.* Some languages have complex systems of agreement, but English agreement is fairly simple, if a bit quirky. We already encountered agreement when we were constructing the sentence *The clown rides a unicycle* and noted that, if there were multiple unicycle riders, we'd have to say *The clowns ride.* . . . This is an example of subject-verb agreement, which English syntax enforces to a limited degree. If the subject is in the third person (not me and not you but somebody else), and if the verb is in the present tense, then the subject and the verb agree in number. The present singular *-s* is a historic relic from a time many centuries ago when English had rich system of subject-verb agreement, but nowadays it's a quirk of grammar that vexes even eloquent native speakers.

English also has a system of agreement between nouns and pronouns. That is to say, English third person pronouns (*he, she, it, they*) agree with the noun they refer to in gender and number. Again, the system is a bit quirky, as gender is only an issue if the referent is singular. Thus, if I say *My friends (blah blah), they* . . . , you don't know if they're men or women or even a mixed group. But if I mention just one friend, I'll give that person's gender away as soon as I use a pronoun. Unless, that is, I resort to the singular *they*, which is widely accepted now in everyday speech despite the vain protests of English teachers.

Table 6.3   Subject-Verb Agreement in English and German

English and German are both descendants of a language that was once spoken in northern Europe about two thousand years ago. English has mostly lost subject-verb agreement, but what remains parallels the intact system of German. English has lost the singular second-person pronoun *thou* (except as the "God" pronoun), but the German equivalent *du* is still in general use.

Number	Person	English	German
Singular	First	I love	ich lieb**e**
	Second	thou love**st**	du lieb**st**
	Third	he love**s**	er lieb**t**
Plural	First	we love	wir lieb**en**
	Second	you love	ihr lieb**t**
	Third	they love	sie lieb**en**

In Sum

Models of sentence processing generally incorporate three levels. At the conceptual level, abstract word forms (lemmas) are selected to represent the intended message. This message consists of an event and the participants (thematic roles) of that event. At the syntactic level, the abstract word forms are ordered and modified according the rules of grammar. In addition, thematic roles are assigned to syntactic positions such as subject and object, and function words are also inserted as required by the grammar. At the phonological level, syllable organization, stress assignment, and intonation contours are programmed for production by the articulatory system. Canonical word order in English is subject-verb-object; however, these syntactic positions are phrases, not individual words. Subject and object are noun phrases, and they include determiners, adjectives, and other modifiers as well as the noun, while the verb phrase includes not only the main verb but also any auxiliary verbs. A simple sentence is also known as a clause, and clauses can be combined to form complex sentences. Cleft sentences focus attention on one of the participants in the event by means of an introductory clause. Relative clauses modify nouns and are considered part of the noun phrase. Other variations on canonical word order include the passive voice and the dative construction. Syntactic agreement binds related elements within and between sentences.

Review Questions

1. Describe the three basic stages in producing a sentence.

2. Explain the thematic roles of agent and patient. Explain the syntactic positions of subject and object. What is thematic role assignment, and how does it affect the syntactic structure of the sentence?

3. What is the difference between a reversible and an irreversible sentence? Give an example of each.

4. What is a cleft sentence? What is the difference between a subject cleft and an object cleft? Give an example of each.

5. What is a relative clause? What is the difference between a subject relative clause and an object relative clause? Give an example of each.

6. What is the purpose of syntactic agreement? Why kinds of agreement does English grammar employ?

Thought Questions

1. Make a subject cleft and an object cleft out of the sentence *The strong man is in love with the bearded lady*. (Hint: Treat *is in love with* as the verb.)

2. Consider the following state of affairs: (1) The strong man is in love with the bearded lady. (2) The bearded lady does a handstand on the horse. (3) The strong man rescued the clown. Make a sentence containing a relative clause that answers the question: The strong man is in love with which bearded lady? Then answer the question: Which strong man is in love with the bearded lady?

3. Two thematic roles, agent and patient, were explicitly discussed in this section, but a third thematic role, recipient, also came up in the discussion of the dative construction. Consider the intended message {BAKE: STRONG MAN, BEARDED LADY, CAKE}. Construct three sentences that convey this intended message, one with the agent as the subject, another with the patient as the subject, and a third with the recipient as as subject. Put the verb in the past tense.

Google It! Yoda Translator

If you're a *Star Wars* fan, you're no doubt familiar with master Yoda's quirkish grammar. Usually, second language learners quickly adjust to the canonical word order of their new language, and it's only the finer points of grammar that continue

---

Answers:

1. (1) It is the strong man that is in love with the bearded lady. (2) It is the bearded lady that the strong man is in love with.

2. (1) The strong man is in love with the bearded lady that does a handstand on the horse. (2) The strong man that rescued the clown is in love with the bearded lady.

3. (1) The strong man baked the bearded lady a cake. Or: The strong man baked a cake for the bearded lady. (2) A cake was baked for the bearded lady by the strong man. (3) The bearded lady was baked a cake by the strong man.

to vex them. However, master Yoda is 900 years old and set in his ways. Presumably, he imposes the canonical word order of his native language on English. You can find a **Yoda translator** online. Enter some sample sentences into the translator and see if you can figure out Yoda's canonical word order. (Hint: Focus on the main verb and the auxiliary verb you must!)

SECTION 6.2: COMPREHENDING SENTENCES

- Models of sentence comprehension can be divided into two-stage and one-stage models; two-stage models assume that syntactic analysis proceeds prior to semantic interpretation, while one-stage, or constraint-based, models argue that syntactic analysis and semantic interpretation work in tandem.

- Heuristics are mental shortcuts that often, but not always, lead to a correct solution; both heuristics and expectancy play an important role in sentence comprehension.

- Two important heuristics in syntactic parsing are late closure and minimal attachment. Late closure assumes sentences will have a subject-verb-object structure, and minimal attachment organizes phrases according to the simplest possible structure. These heuristics can lead us astray in the case of garden path sentences.

- Many sentences are structurally ambiguous, but syntactic priming can bias the listener toward a particular structural interpretation; syntactic priming effects can be found even without lexical overlap between sentences, but they get a lexical boost when the verbs of the two sentences are the same.

- Two important ERP components in the study of sentence processing are the N400 and P600; the N400 is elicited by a semantic violation and the P600 by a syntactic violation.

- Based on clinical evidence, it has long been believed that Broca's area plays a role in syntactic processing, but recent clinical and neuroimaging calls this view into question; instead, new theories suggest that the function of Broca's area may instead be involved in working memory, executive control, or action planning.

Language comes at us as a speech stream, and as we learned in Chapter 3, the first step in processing that stream is to find the boundaries so that we can parse the sentence into words and phrases. Prosodic phrase boundaries give us some clues to syntactic structure (Luo, Yan, & Zhou, 2013). However, many sentences are structurally ambiguous, meaning that more than one syntactic structure may be possible. This is especially true given that we attempt to assign a syntactic category to each new word that comes in (Loncke et al., 2011). While real-time processing speeds up the pace of communication, it can lead us astray. However, it's the errors we make in interpreting sentences that give us insights into how sentence comprehension takes place.

Down the Garden Path

Psycholinguists generally agree that comprehending a sentence involves the integration of two processes, a syntactic analysis of the sentence's structure and a semantic interpretation based on the meanings of the individual words and the way that structure relates them together. However, what they don't agree on whether this occurs in one stage or two (Tooley, Traxler, & Swaab, 2009). A two-stage model proposes that a sentence is first analyzed for its syntactic structure and then the lexicon is consulted to interpret the meaning of the sentence. On the other hand, a **constraint-based model** (or one-stage model) makes *the proposal that syntactic analysis and semantic interpretation occur simultaneously and influence each other* (Tanenhaus & Trueswell, 1995). In other words, syntax and semantics constrain each other as the listener interprets the intended meaning of the sentence.

Consider a sentence like *While Sarah bathed her baby played on the floor*. You probably assumed at first that *the baby* was the object of *bathed*, following canonical subject-verb-object word order in English. But when you then encountered the verb *played*, your syntactic processor had no idea what to do with it. You had been led astray, down the garden path to a dead end. Now all you can do is go back and try a different path. *A sentence that deviates significantly from expected structure, making it difficult to process*, is known as a **garden path sentence**.

Frazier and Rayner (1982) tracked eye movements while people read sentences, some of which were structurally ambiguous. Not surprising, the participants were slower at reading the ambiguous sentences and they were more likely to go back and reread portions of them. Based on data like these, the researchers proposed *a two-staged model of sentence processing in which syntactic analysis precedes semantic interpretation*. This is commonly known as the **garden path model**.

According to the garden path model, we first build a syntactic structure based on the apparent syntactic category (noun, verb, etc.) of each incoming word. Only after we've constructed a syntactic structure do we then look up the meanings of the words and integrate them into the sentence. Because spoken language goes at a rate of two or three words per second, we have to identify syntactic categories quickly. Furthermore, working memory limitations prevent us from holding more than a few words at a time, so we can't just wait to see how the rest of the sentence turns out. Instead, we have to make quick decisions based on limited information and our expectations of what's coming next. This means we have to rely on heuristics. A **heuristic** is *a mental shortcut to problem solving that usually, but not always, gives the correct answer*.

Late Closure

The garden path model proposes that we use two heuristics when assigning sentence structure. The first heuristic is **late closure**, which is *a syntactic parsing strategy that continues to add new words to the current structure unless there is sufficient evidence that a new structure should begin*. When you first read the sentence *While Sarah bathed her baby played on the floor*, you almost certainly thought *her baby* was the object of *bathed*. This is because you used the late closure heuristic. Because you know that the canonical sentence in English has a subject-verb-object structure, and moreover because you know that *bathe* usually takes an object, late closure tells you not to end the clause until after *baby*. This is a reasonable assumption, but it's just not the correct way to parse this sentence.

At this point, you should be protesting that there's something wrong with the sentence. And you are correct. In writing, a comma after *bathed* would disambiguate this sentence, as would a falling-pitch prosodic phrase boundary in speech. But writers don't always use commas where they should, and speakers don't always clearly mark phrase boundaries either. In fact, listeners and speakers are often unaware of the errors they make, and since the conversation must go on, listeners may not have time to do a reanalysis when they suspect they've misunderstood (Slevc & Ferreira, 2013).

Even if listeners do recover from a parsing error, it's often the initial structure that is retained. Thus, participants who heard sentences like *While Sarah bathed her baby played on the floor* tend to later respond "yes" to the question, "Did Sarah bathe her baby?" (Christianson et al., 2001). They also tend to paraphrase the sentence as *Sarah bathed her baby and then it played on the floor* (Patson et al., 2009). These findings suggest that listeners often take a "good enough" approach to parsing sentences, at least when the stakes aren't very high, as is the case in daily conversation (Ivanova et al., 2011).

The late closure heuristic can also lead us to closing a structure too early. For example, try to make sense of the following sentence: *The horse raced past the barn fell*. Strictly speaking, this sentence is grammatically correct (but see McKoon & Ratcliff, 2003, for an opposing view). However, this sentence makes use of an oddity of English grammar known as a **reduced relative clause**, which is *a kind of embedded syntactic structure that allows for economy of expression but can be extremely difficult to process in some cases*. The full relative clause version of this sentence is: *The horse that was raced past the barn fell*. Granted, this is still a clunky sentence, but it basically means: *The horse was raced past the barn and then it fell*. If I had used the verb *ridden* instead of *raced*, you wouldn't have had a garden path experience. The sentence *The horse ridden past the barn fell* should make sense to you.

The listener is led down the wrong garden path because the word *raced* is syntactically ambiguous. It could be a past tense, as in *I raced the horse*, or it could a past participle, as in *The horse was raced*. On the other hand, the verb *ride* has different forms for the past tense and past participle: *I rode the horse* and *The horse was ridden*. Because the minimal attachment strategy assumes canonical subject-verb-object structure, it interprets *raced* as the verb, hence signaling the closure of the subject noun phrase *The horse*. On the other hand, *ridden* cannot be a main verb, and so we interpret it as the beginning of a reduced relative clause, which is still part of the subject noun phrase.

Table 6.4 Some Examples of Garden Path Sentences

How would you rewrite these sentences to make them easier to read?

Because he runs a mile is nothing.

We painted the wall with cracks.

He knew her as a young boy.

I told the girl the cat scratched Bill would help her.

The cat returned home was hungry.

Minimal Attachment

The second heuristic of the garden path model is known as **minimal attachment**. This is *a syntactic parsing strategy that assumes the simplest possible sentence structure*. The great twentieth-century comedian Groucho Marx used minimal attachment to comic effect in his famous line: *One morning I shot an elephant in my pajamas. How he got into my pajamas I'll never know.*

The joke revolves around the question of who was wearing the pajamas, Groucho or the elephant. At the syntactic level, the question is where the prepositional phrase *in my pajamas* should be attached. The minimal attachment strategy assumes the prepositional phrase attaches to the main verb *shot*, and thus, since *I* (referring to Groucho) is the subject of *shot*, Groucho was also wearing the pajamas. As we learn in the next sentence, though, *in my pajamas* attaches to the object noun phrase *an elephant* instead.

The parsing strategy of attaching a prepositional phrase to the verb is called **high attachment**, and *the parsing strategy of attaching a prepositional phrase to the object* is called **low attachment** (Pickering, McLean, & Branigan, 2013). In syntactic theory, the verb is considered higher in the sentence structure that the object, hence the names. High attachment results in a somewhat simpler structure, and that's why it's favored by the minimal attachment strategy, according to the garden path model.

Recall that the garden path model says we do a syntactic analysis first before we consider the meaning of the sentence. If this is correct, then we should expect listeners to always use the minimal attachment strategy, in other words to attach prepositional phrases high with the verb instead of low with the object. But this isn't the case. Listeners can and do use context to parse syntactically ambiguous sentences. For example, the sentence *The thief opened the safe with the stick of*

Figure 6.7   Two Sentence Trees of *I shot an elephant in my pajamas*

Notice that high attachment, which is the default interpretation, has a simpler structure than low attachment.

(a) High attachment

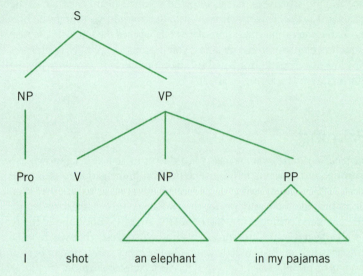

(b) Low attachment

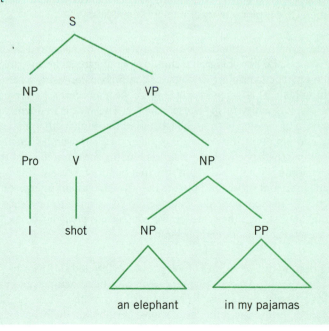

dynamite calls for high attachment, since *with the stick of dynamite* describes how the safe was opened. On the other hand, the sentence *The thief opened the safe with the rusty lock* calls for low attachment, since *with the rusty lock* describes the safe, not how it was opened.

Listeners can also be biased toward a particular interpretation based on previously encountered structures. For example, if you first heard the high-attachment sentence *The thief broke the window with the crowbar*, you might be biased toward a high-attachment interpretation of *The thief opened the safe with the rusty lock*. Unlike Groucho's elephant in his pajamas, you'll probably quickly reinterpret the sentence with low attachment, but you'll still be more likely to consider the high-attachment interpretation (Pickering et al., 2013).

Priming

The tendency to repeat a previously heard sentence structure is known as **syntactic priming**, and it occurs in both sentence comprehension and sentence production tasks (Bock, 1986). There's some debate in the literature as to whether syntactic priming effects provide more support for the two-stage or one-stage model. On the one hand, pure syntactic priming, in which only the structure but none of the words is repeated, is well attested in the literature. This finding suggests that we do in fact process sentences first at the syntactic level. On the other hand, researchers find *an increase in syntactic priming when the verb is repeated between the prime and target sentences*, also known as a **lexical boost**. This finding suggests an early role for semantics, thus providing support for one-stage interactive models.

Syntactic priming in sentence comprehension can be measured through a number of behavioral and physiological techniques. Branigan, Pickering, and McLean (2005) tested for syntactic priming in sentence comprehension using a **sentence-picture matching task**. This is *a procedure in which the respondent selects from a set of pictures the one that is described by the prompt sentence*. This task is frequently used as a test of sentence processing both in the lab and in the clinic with aphasic patients. For example, the prompt *The waitress is prodding the clown with the umbrella* is presented with two pictures, one with the waitress holding the umbrella and the other with the clown holding the umbrella. Thus, the first picture represents the high-attachment interpretation and the second picture the low-attachment interpretation. In this ambiguous situation, participants tended to go with the same structure as in the previous trial, such as the sentence *The policeman is prodding the doctor with the gun* and a picture of a policeman holding a gun.

In addition, both ERP studies (Tooley et al., 2009) and fMRI studies (Segaert et al., 2013) have found evidence that repeated syntactic structures are processed more easily, and this is especially the case when the verb is repeated. Thus, physiological evidence for syntactic priming and the lexical boost corroborate the behavioral evidence.

Figure 6.8 Sentence-Picture Matching Task

An experimental item from a syntactic priming task, disambiguated for a high-attached prime.

The policeman is prodding the doctor with the gun.

The waitress is prodding the clown with the umbrella.

Source: Pickering, McLean, and Branigan, 2013.

Anticipation

As listeners in a conversation, we don't just process each word as it comes in, quickly deciding how it fits into the sentence structure we're building. We also try to predict what's coming next. We all have the experience of being able to complete each other's sentences, and humor, at least in part, is based on a violation of expectations. *The likelihood that a person will complete a sentence with a particular word* is known as that word's **cloze probability** (Wlotko & Federmeier, 2012). For instance, if I gave you the sentence fragment *I take my coffee with cream and . . .* , the cloze probability of *sugar* is nearly 100%.

One way we can observe listeners as they anticipate upcoming words is by using a visual world paradigm (Tanenhaus et al., 1995). As we learned in Chapter 5, this is an experimental technique that tracks eye-movements across a visual display as the participant listens to sentences. In one study, participants saw a display that included a cake and several non-edible items (Rommers et al., 2013). When participants heard the sentence *The boy ate . . .* , they were more likely to move their eyes to the cake than when they heard the sentence *The boy moved. . . . .* In general, listeners look around their environment for visual cues to aid in comprehension.

Event-related potential (ERP) research has shed light on the time course of sentence processing as well as the role of expectancy in language comprehension. Recall from Chapter 2 that an ERP component is a predictable waveform extracted from the EEG signal that correlates with a specific cognitive process. As your brain performs its various functions, its total electrical activity shifts back and forth from positive to negative. (Keep in mind that we're talking about electrical charges, so it's important not to interpret positive and negative in any other way.) The results of numerous ERP studies show that we anticipate not only upcoming words but also upcoming structures.

Suppose you're a participant in an ERP study and hear the sentence *She spreads her toast with socks*. I'm sure you weren't expecting to hear the word *socks*, but how long did it take your brain to detect the semantic inconsistency in this sentence? By matching up the waveform of electrical activity in your brain as you listen to this and similar sentences, we find it takes less than half a second. That is, roughly 400 milliseconds after you hear the word *socks*, the electrical activity of your brain shifts toward the negative to produce a component called the **N400**, so called because it's *a negative-going ERP waveform that begins about 400 milliseconds after a semantically inconsistent stimulus is presented*. Since the magnitude of the N400 is correlated with cloze probability, the waveform is interpreted as an index of expectations about upcoming lexical items (Hunt et al., 2013).

One way to think about a garden path sentence is that it violates our expectation about sentence structure. When we hear the sentence beginning *While Sara bathed . . .* , we have no expectation for a particular word, but we do expect an object noun phrase, that is, a particular syntactic structure. Garden path sentences typically elicit a **P600**, which is *a positive-going ERP waveform that starts about 600 milliseconds after a syntactically inconsistent stimulus is presented* (Osterhout & Holcomb, 1992). All kinds of syntactic violations can elicit a P600, including number and gender agreement errors (Szewczyk & Schriefers, 2013).

As a general principle, expectation guides perception. We look for something where we expect to see it, and when we see something we didn't expect, our attention is drawn to it. Generating predictions and comparing them against the sensory input is how the brain deals with noisy evidence from a messy world. In real life, speakers mumble and make mistakes, environmental noises interfere, and our attention strays. But by making predictions about upcoming words and structures, our brains are often able to fill in the gaps and recover from errors (Gibson, Bergen, & Piantadosi, 2013).

Broca's Area Revisited

It's generally believed that patients with damage to Broca's area are impaired in their ability to process syntactic structures. When given a nonreversible passive sentence like *The fence is kicked by the horse*, Broca's aphasics have little difficulty selecting the right picture, presumably basing their decision on semantics and real-world knowledge. But

Figure 6.9 N400 and P600

According to the traditional view, the N400 is elicited by semantic anomaly while the P600 is elicited by syntactic error.

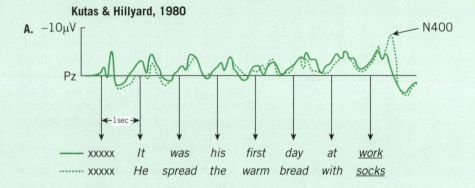

Kutas & Hillyard, 1980

A. −10µV

Pz

←1sec→

——— xxxxx   It   was   his   first   day   at   work
········· xxxxx   He   spread   the   warm   bread   with   socks

N400

B.   **Osterhout & Holcomb, 1992**

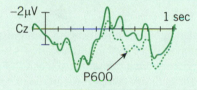

−2µV

Cz

1 sec

P600

——— The broker hoped <u>to</u> sell the stock.   ········· The broker persuaded <u>to</u> sell the stock.

Source: Kuperberg (2007).

when these patients are given reversible sentences like *The cow is kicked by the horse*, they seem to select a picture at random. This sort of clinical evidence suggests that Broca's area plays some role in syntactic processing. However, a new line of evidence is emerging that calls for a reinterpretation the role played by Broca's area in sentence comprehension.

Recall from Chapter 5 that a visual world paradigm tracks participants' eye movements as they listen to sentences and look at pictures (Spivey et al., 2002; Tanenhaus et al., 1995). Under normal conditions, participants tend to look toward the object that is currently being mentioned, and in cases of syntactic ambiguity, they rely on context cues.

Chance performance for Broca's aphasics on a sentence-picture matching task may reflect guessing, but it could also be the result of a syntactic processor that sometimes works and sometimes doesn't (Burchert, Hanne, & Vasishth, 2013). When Broca's aphasics are tested with a visual world paradigm they show normal eye movements for the sentences they correctly comprehend and abnormal eye movements for the sentences they get wrong. This suggests that Broca's aphasics are still able to process syntactic structures and that their poor performance is due to some other kind of cognitive impairment. This view is supported by the observation that the performance of these patients improves when sentences are presented at slower than normal rates.

Recent neuroimaging evidence also questions the role of Broca's area in the processing of syntax (Rogalsky & Hickok, 2011; Thothathiri, Kimberg, & Schwartz, 2011). Instead, the data suggest Broca's area plays a role in working memory or executive functioning, consistent with its location in the frontal lobe. This view of the function of Broca's area is consistent with the dual stream model of language processing that is currently gaining wide currency among neuroscientists (Bornkessel-Schlesewsky & Schlesewsky, 2013).

Recall that dual stream processing is a general organizing principle of perceptual systems in the brain. In the case of vision, the ventral stream processes information about object identification, and so it's also known as the "what" stream. The dorsal stream processes information about how to navigate through the world, and so it's also known as the "how" stream.

In terms of sentence processing, the function of the ventral stream, running from the primary auditory cortex through the temporal lobe to the frontal cortex, seems to be involved in the unification of concepts, that is, what the sentence means. On the other hand, the dorsal stream, running from the auditory cortex through the parietal lobe to the frontal cortex, seems to be involved in the ordering of elements, or how the sentence is put together.

If this model is correct, both syntactic and semantic analysis will have been completed by the time the information reaches Broca's area, which is probably responsible instead for regulating resources or planning action. In short, recent evidence is challenging traditional views of how language is processed in the brain.

In Sum

Listeners use various strategies or heuristics to quickly interpret sentences as they are being spoken, and they also build expectations about what is coming next. One important heuristic in sentence processing is late closure, which continues building on the current syntactic structure until evidence suggests a new structure should be started. Another heuristic is minimal attachment, which assumes the simplest possible structure. Because many sentences are ambiguous, these heuristics can lead us down the garden path to the wrong interpretation. Some models of sentence comprehension propose that we perform syntactic analysis before semantic integration, while other models propose that the two processes occur at the same time and interact with each other. Syntactic priming effects occur when structures are repeated, but they get a lexical boost when the verb is also repeated. Two ERP components are implicated in sentence processing. The N400 is considered an index of semantic expectation, and the P600 is considered an indicator of syntactic expectation. Although it is traditionally believed that Broca's area plays a role in syntactic processing, new clinical and neuroimaging evidence suggests that the function of Broca's area is more general, perhaps playing a role in cognitive control.

Review Questions

1. What is the garden path model of sentence comprehension, and how does it explain why garden path sentences are difficult to parse?

2. What is late closure? How does it explain why the following sentences are difficult to parse? (1) *While Sarah bathed her baby played on the floor.* (2) *The horse raced past the barn fell.*

3. What is minimal attachment? How does it explain the ambiguity of the sentence *One morning I shot an elephant in my pajamas*? Distinguish between high and low attachment, giving example sentences of each.

4. Explain syntactic priming and the lexical boost.

5. What are N400 and P600?

6. What is the recent evidence suggesting that Broca's area is not responsible for syntactic processing, as previously believed? How does this view of the function of Broca's area fit within the dual stream model of language processing?

Thought Questions

1. Certain syntactic structures in English are prone to garden pathing. One such structure is the reduced relative clause, as in the sentence *The horse raced past the barn fell*. This complex sentence is derived from two simple sentences, *The horse was raced past the barn* and *The horse fell*. Can you work out the rules for generating a reduced relative clause? Here are a couple more examples to help you: (1) *The barge floated past the pier sank.* (2) *The dog walked around the block found a bone.* Based on the rules you've devised, can you create your own garden path sentences with reduced relative clauses?

2. Another structure prone to garden pathing is the optional object construction. Some verbs that normally take objects can omit those objects under certain circumstances. Actions that can either be performed on another person or on one's self often fall in this category, with the verbs *dress* and *bathe* being good examples. This

happens in the complex sentence *While Sarah bathed her baby played on the floor*, which is made up of the two simple sentences *Sarah bathed (herself)* and *Her baby played on the floor*. Can you create some new garden path sentences on this model? Here's another example to help you: *As the barber shaved his customer read the newspaper*.

Google It! Elephant in My Pajamas

There are many examples of **garden path sentences** on the Internet. Some follow the reduced relative clause and optional object patterns, but there are other syntactic structures that can also lead listeners or readers down the garden path. See if you can work out what these patterns are, and then see if you can generate new ones based on these models. Also, can you think of ways to paraphrase these sentences to avoid ambiguity?

If you're curious about **event-related potential** research, you can find plenty of videos demonstrating it on YouTube. See for yourself what it's like to be part of an ERP study.

Finally, you can find a video clip of the **elephant in my pajamas** skit on YouTube. Groucho was a master at manipulating linguistic expectations to create humor. The last joke in this scene is a real groaner!

SECTION 6.3: PRODUCING SENTENCES

- As we produce a sentence, information flows along two dimensions: the vertical dimension represents the processing of individual words, from conceptual activation through lexical selection to phonological encoding; and the horizontal flow refers to the linked processes of producing words and phrases in the right sequence.

- Sentence production is incremental. We don't plan the entire sentence, nor do we plan and produce one word at a time; rather, as the processing of the first part of the sentence is under way, the activation of the next part begins. Incremental processing involves a trade-off between fluency and efficient use of resources.

- The data are inconsistent about the scope of planning in sentence production; some evidence suggests we plan clause by clause, while other evidence suggests the scope of planning is the phrase or content word.

- Inconsistency in the scope-of-planning data can be explained in a number of ways: (1) the experimental procedure may bias the participant toward one scope or another; (2) planning scope may vary according to processing demands; and (3) different levels of processing may have different scopes of planning.

- Visual attention plays an important role in sentence production. Eye movements across the visual display are correlated with the order in which items are mentioned in a sentence; furthermore, visual attention plays an important role in subject selection, at least in English.

- Syntactic priming biases speakers toward producing a particular sentence structure; fMRI studies show that syntactic priming is correlated with the suppression of activity in the left temporal and frontal lobes.

There's a scene in the movie *Raiders of the Lost Ark* (Lucas & Spielberg, 1981) in which the Nazis have just snatched the ark from Indiana Jones.

> "Get back to Cairo," Indy tells his friend Sallah. "Get us some transport to England: boat, plane, anything. Meet me at Omar's. Be ready for me. I'm going after that truck."
>
> "How?" Sallah asks.
>
> "I don't know," Indy replies. "I'm making this up as I go."

When we produce sentences, we're like Indiana Jones. We have a general idea of what we want to say, but we haven't thought out the entire sentence before we begin to speak it.

Vertical and Horizontal Flow of Information

In Chapter 5, we learned about models of word production. You should recall that these models generally propose three broad levels of processing. The first stage of word production is the concept or semantic level, where the language processor searches the mental lexicon for a concept that can be represented by a word in the language. The second is the lemma level, where an abstract word form is selected along with syntactic and morphological information, that is, which structures it can fit in and which shapes it can take. The third stage is the phonological level, where the word is arranged as a series of phonemes for the articulators to produce. You should also recall that these models fall into two classes. Feedforward models propose that the flow of information is strictly sequential, while interactive models allow for information to flow in both directions.

Whichever version you prefer, if you want to extend your model from word production to sentence production, it has to be able to repeat the word selection procedure for each content word in the utterance. Furthermore, sentences aren't just strings of random words but instead are composed of words in tightly constrained orders. Consider the event of Indiana Jones chasing the Nazis. By selecting one of the participants in the event, say Indiana Jones, you constrain your options downstream in the sentence. Since you selected the agent as the subject, the verb has to be in the active voice, and furthermore it has to agree with the subject in number, while the patient has to take the object position, thus producing the sentence: *Indiana Jones is chasing the Nazis.* Had you selected the patient as the subject, you would have committed the verb to passive voice and plural number while relegating the agent to a prepositional phrase with *by*, that is: *The Nazis are being chased by Indiana Jones.*

As we produce a sentence, information flows in two dimensions, vertical and horizontal (Smith & Wheeldon, 2004; Yang & Yang, 2008). The vertical dimension represents the flow of information from conceptual to phonological levels for each content word. We've already seen that the various models of word production differ on whether they envision the flow of information as feedforward, going only from top to bottom, or else interactive, going bottom-up as well as top-down. Models of sentence production also differ in terms of whether they conceptualize the horizontal flow of information as serial or parallel.

A **serial model** is *a model in which all of the processing at one step needs to be completed before moving on to the next step*. A strictly serial model would require the speaker to go from the concept activation through lemma selection to the phonological encoding of *Indiana Jones* before it could move on to forming the concept for *chase*. Such a model would produce halting speech, and none of the models in the literature suggest that sentence production works this way. However, it's easy to imagine that something like this is at work in the labored speech of Broca's aphasics.

At the other extreme is a **parallel model**. This is *a model in which the processing at one step occurs simultaneously with the same processing at other steps*. In a strictly parallel model, the three concepts—INDIANA JONES, CHASE, and NAZIS— would all be activated at the same time, and after that the three lemmas would be selected and their phonological forms encoded. As the speaker, you would already have the entire sentence planned in your head before you began speaking. Such a model would produce very fluent speech, at least within a sentence, although there would likely be a substantial pause before the next sentence as a new sequence is programmed up. Even then, the model would be very demanding in terms of cognitive resources. None of the sentence production models are strictly parallel, either.

Instead, the various models of speech production lie somewhere between the two extremes of strictly serial and strictly parallel. That is, it's generally agreed that uttering a sentence is incremental (Lee & Thompson, 2011; Sass et al., 2010). An **incremental model** is *a model in which the processing at one step is still under way when the processing at the next step begins*. For example, you might activate the concept for INDIANA

JONES and retrieve its lemma before activating the concept for CHASE. Subsequently, phonological encoding of *Indiana Jones* may proceed in parallel with the lexical selection of *chase* and the concept activation of NAZIS. In other words, incremental models are partially serial and partially parallel, striking a balance between the limited cognitive demands of a serial model and the relative fluency of a parallel model. Incremental models have intuitive appeal because our speech is generally fluent but with occasional breaks in the flow, as in: *Indiana Jones is chasing the, uh, Nazis*. All of the major models of sentence production are incremental, but the debate centers on the exact mix of serial and parallel components.

Figure 6.10 Parallel, Incremental, and Serial Models of Sentence Processing

The sentence *Indiana Jones is chasing the Nazis* as processed (a) in parallel, (b) incrementally, and (c) serially. Conceptual level in capitals, lexical/syntactic level in italics, and phonological level in plain text.

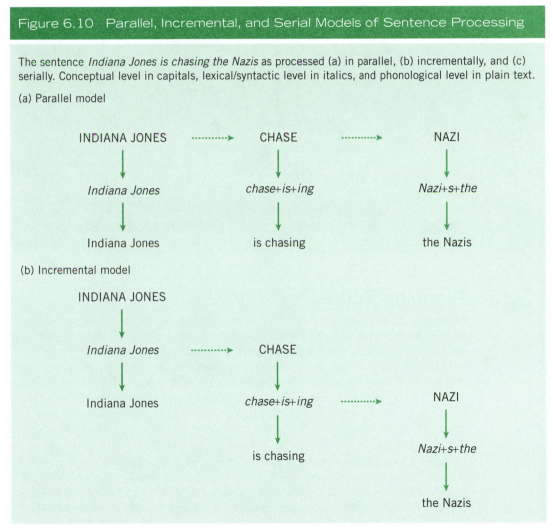

(a) Parallel model

(b) Incremental model

(Continued)

(Continued)

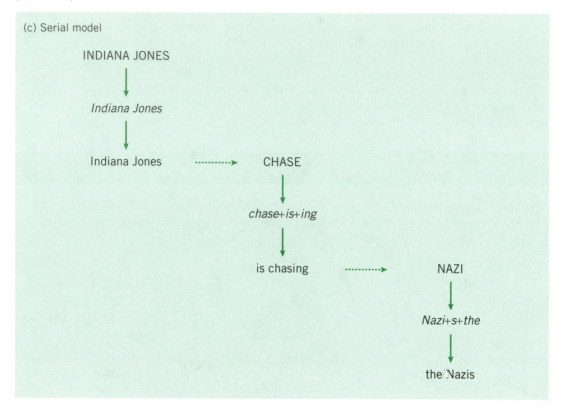

(c) Serial model

INDIANA JONES

Indiana Jones

Indiana Jones ┄┄┄→ CHASE

chase+is+ing

is chasing ┄┄┄→ NAZI

Nazi+s+the

the Nazis

Planning Scope

Given that spoken sentence production is incremental, psycholinguists disagree on how far ahead we plan. The results of some experiments suggest that we plan sentences one content word at a time, while others point to the phrase or clause level (Allum & Wheeldon, 2007). In our example sentence about Indiana Jones chasing the Nazis, the subject, verb, and object are each composed of a single content word. (That is, assuming *Indiana Jones*, as a person's name, is a single concept.) The question of how far ahead we plan becomes a theoretical issue when we consider more complex structure.

In the sentence *Venomous snakes completely covered the floor of the chamber*, for example, there are two content words in each phrase: *venomous snakes* in the subject noun phrase, *completely covered* in the verb phrase, and *the floor of the chamber* in the object noun phrase. If we plan our sentence one content word at a time, we need to start the lexical retrieval of *venomous* before we can activate *snakes*. On the other hand, if we plan our sentence one phrase at a time, we'll activate the concepts for *venomous* and *snakes* and start lexical retrieval for both of them, before moving on to the verb phrase.

It may not be too cognitively demanding to process a short noun phrase like *venomous snakes* in parallel, but it's harder to argue in favor of the phrase as the scope of planning when the subject noun phrase is considerably longer. Take for example the sentence: *The date that the monkey ate was poisoned*. Here, the subject noun phrase includes a relative clause, and it could be that the sequence *the date that the monkey ate* is too complex be processed in parallel.

The data point in all directions regarding how far in advance we plan our sentences. No doubt part of the reason for this is that different researchers use different procedures, and it could be that the experimental design has an effect on planning scope (Allum & Wheeldon, 2007). A typical way to get participants to produce sentences of interest is to ask them to produce one-sentence descriptions of pictures or short videos. Typically, the range of lexical items and sentence structures is tightly constrained. This allows the researchers to test hypotheses about how particular structures are processed, but it's also likely to reduce processing demands for the participant. In such a situation, the speaker may be able to plan larger units than would be the case in normal speech.

Cognitive demands on sentence production can vary even in natural speech. Idle chit-chat, with its formulaic expressions and low cost for errors, is no doubt easier to process that a formal conversation in which the participants need to pay careful attention not only to what they're saying but also how they say it. It could then be that the scope of planning in sentence production isn't some fixed unit but rather is flexible, depending on the complexity of the sentence and what other cognitive tasks the speaker may currently be engaged in (Wagner, Jescheniak, & Schriefers, 2010).

Other processes that the brain engages in, such as motor performance, make use of **hierarchical structure in advance planning**, which is *a programming approach that makes a general plan at the highest level while restricting the scope of planning at lower levels* (Martin et al., 2010). Sentence production is, after all, a kind of motor performance, and so it could be the case that different levels of sentence production processing have different scopes of advance planning.

The scope of planning at the conceptual level may be the clause, while the scope of planning at the lexical/syntactic level may be the phrase or content word. Thus, the sentence *Indiana Jones recovered the ark while his friend secured transport to England* may be planned out conceptually as two units, {INDIANA JONES, RECOVER, ARK} and {FRIEND, SECURE, TRANSPORT TO ENGLAND}. But then lexical retrieval and phonological encoding for INDIANA JONES would already be under way before these processes were started for RECOVER. Also, depending whether the speaker was planning by phrase or by content word, TRANSPORT TO ENGLAND could involve one step or two.

Visual Attention and Sentence Production

In Chapter 5, we saw how researchers combine the visual world paradigm with eye-tracking to examine how listeners comprehend spoken sentences. As participants listen to descriptions of events portrayed in pictures, their eye gaze tends to shift to the item currently being mentioned, and it will also shift in anticipation of an upcoming word. In the case of a picture description task, participants tend to fixate their gaze toward the center of the picture for a fraction of a second, and after that they shift their gaze to each item before they mention it (Allum & Wheeldon, 2007). This pattern of eye movements suggests that some sort of initial planning is taking place, perhaps at the conceptual level, followed by more sequential planning at either the phrase or the content word level. In fact, eye movements in picture description tasks provide strong evidence that sentence planning, at least at a lexical/syntactic level, proceeds one content word at a time (Martin et al., 2010).

Much of our everyday conversation concerns people and objects engaged in events at the present time (Myachykov, Garrod, & Scheepers, 2012). Imagine teaching someone how to bake an apple pie or giving your guest a tour of the house. As you speak, your visual attention will likely be focused on the objects you mention, and your listener's attention will be drawn to them as well. Joint attention is a fundamental aspect of human interaction, going all the way back to early exchanges between babies and their caregivers.

Figure 6.11 Picture Description Task

Example of a complex scene used for a picture description task with words not allowed for the description.

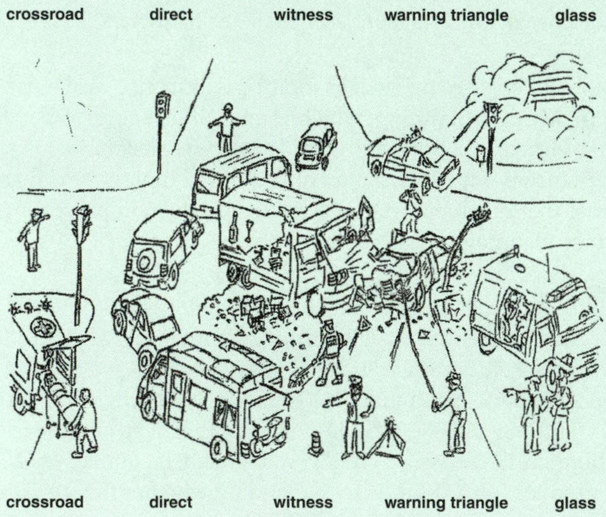

Source: Grande et al. (2012).

Visual attention plays an important role in sentence production, and in fact the two share structural parallels (Coco & Keller, 2012). When we open our eyes, a wide visual scene appears before us. But we can't take in the whole scene at once. Instead, we move our eyes across the visual scene in a series of saccades and fixations, our gaze jumping from one point to another as we take in the image. Think about it: If I show you a picture for a fraction of a second before taking it away, you won't be able to tell me much about it. But if I let you study the picture for a minute or two, you'll be able to describe it in great detail. Thus, visual attention proceeds in sequential fashion, just like sentences do.

An understanding of visual attention processes also sheds light on how we decide which participant of an event will be the subject of our sentence (Myachykov et al., 2011). Roughly speaking, the subject is the focus of our attention and what we want our listener to pay attention to. In the lab, we can direct the participant's attention to a particular item in a visual display by using **referential priming**. This is *an experimental procedure in which the participant is first shown only one of the items of a visual display before the full display is presented*. Referential priming tends to direct the participant's attention toward the primed item in the visual display, and in a picture description task, the primed item tends to be selected as the subject of the sentence.

A number of other factors can also influence subject selection. We're especially drawn to other humans, and humans are more likely to be selected as subjects than nonhumans. More generally, animate things are more likely to be subjects than inanimate things (Tanaka et al., 2011). Also, a recently mentioned item is more likely to be named the subject of the current sentence, indicating a role as well for memory processes in subject selection.

There's a strong tendency across languages to select the agent as the subject (Myachykov et al., 2011). However, languages also need ways to allow patients and other thematic roles to serve as subject when they're the focus of attention. In English, this is done by using the passive voice. If for some reason the focus of my attention is on the bad guys, I can say *The Nazis are being chased by Indiana Jones*. Not all languages use passive voice this way. Although Russian does have a passive voice structure, it's not widely used in everyday conversation. So in Russian there's a much tighter binding between agent and subject on the one hand and between patient and object on the other hand. Instead of using the passive voice, Russian speakers employ **scrambling**. This is *the syntactic process of putting the object before the subject*. In other words, they would say the equivalent of *The Nazis Indiana Jones is chasing*. Since nouns in Russian are clearly marked for their role as subject or object, changing the word order doesn't create any confusion about who did what. Occasionally, English speakers will use scrambling as well, for example in the sentence *Now **that** I like!*

Sentence Production and the Brain

Brain imaging studies of sentence production are difficult to set up for a number of reasons, but the few that have been performed so far have yielded results that are consistent with current models of language processing. The temporal lobe is implicated in lexical selection, and the left inferior frontal gyrus (roughly speaking, Broca's area) is implicated in syntactic processing (Grande et al., 2012).

In Section 6.2, we learned that syntactic priming can lead to a particular structure being processed more easily. In comprehension tasks, prior exposure can bias listeners toward one interpretation of an ambiguous sentence, as evidenced by anticipatory eye movements and picture matching choices (Segaert et al., 2013). Likewise, prior exposure can bias speakers toward a particular structure as well. For example, participants that have just heard several sentences in the passive voice are more likely to use the passive voice in a picture description task than they would otherwise. Syntactic priming can even be observed in the brain using fMRI. In both comprehension and production tasks, **repetition suppression** occurs. In other words, there's *a reduction in brain activity when a syntactically primed sentence is processed.*

Findings such as these are in line with the dual stream model of language processing, and they also suggest that the same or similar areas of the brain are involved in both comprehension and production. Clearly more research is needed, but with the development of new experimental procedures and more powerful brain imaging techniques, this is a field that is ripe for study.

In Sum

Like Indiana Jones, we make up sentences as we go. Cognitive limitations prevent us from fully planning our sentences before we speak them, and instead we use incremental processing to trade off fluency and efficient use of resources. The clause, the phrase, and the content word have all been proposed as planning units in speech production, but how far ahead we plan may depend on current cognitive demands. Also, different levels of processing may have different scopes of planning. Like the motor performance system, the sentence production system may employ hierarchical structure in advance planning. Visual attention plays an important role in sentence production, and eye movements across the visual scene predict the order in which items will be mentioned. Visual attention also plays a role in subject selection; however, other factors also play a role in which item we focus our attention on. Neuroimaging studies show that syntactic priming at the behavioral level is linked to repetition suppression at the neural level.

Review Questions

1. Explain the distinction between vertical and horizontal flow of information in sentence production.

2. Explain how serial, parallel, and incremental models work. In what sense is an incremental model a mix between serial and parallel?

3. What is meant by scope of planning? What three sentential units have been proposed as potential scopes of planning? What are three explanations for why the data are so inconsistent on scope of planning? Are these three explanations mutually exclusive?

4. Explain what is meant by the assertion that visual attention is sequential. How is visual attention related to sentence production?

5. What is syntactic priming? What happens in the brain during syntactic priming?

Thought Questions

1. Hierarchical structure in advance planning is a general principle in the motor system. At the highest level, a general plan is produced, such as reaching for a coffee mug. The details of how this action will be carried out are relegated to lower levels, where specific plans for flexing muscles, avoiding obstacles, and responding to feedback are prepared and carried out. Complex human organizations, such as corporations and governments, also employ hierarchical structure in advance planning. Can you come up with one or two hypothetical scenarios to illustrate this? Now, can you come up with a model of sentence production that involves hierarchical structure in advance planning? Illustrate with an example sentence or two.

2. Imagine a situation in which visual attention is essential to sentence production. Carefully think out how your eye gaze would move through the visual scene as you thought about what to say.

3. The Malagasy language, spoken in Madagascar, has a canonical word order of object-verb-subject. In a referential priming task, Malagasy speakers consistently assigned the primed item to the final subject position (Rasolofo, 2006, as cited in Myachykov et al., 2011). What does this finding suggest about the relationship between visual attention and sentence production? More specifically, does visual attention influence the structure of language, or is it the reverse?

Google It! Sentence Production and Aphasia

Patients suffering from Broca's, or expressive, aphasia may still be able to produce words in isolation, but they have considerable difficulty producing sentences in a fluent fashion. If you would like to learn more about **sentence production and aphasia**, google it! You can find videos on YouTube that demonstrate the difficulties these patients experience in producing sentences, and you can also learn about therapies that have been developed to help them communicate more effectively.

SECTION 6.4: LEARNING SYNTACTIC STRUCTURE

- Infants use prosodic patterns to group words into phrases in a process called prosodic bootstrapping, which provides them with insights into sentence structure; as children become more familiar with syntactic patterns, they also become more sensitive to prosodic cues.

- Vocabulary and syntax develop in parallel during the early years of childhood, and they reinforce each other; children use syntactic bootstrapping to infer the meaning of new words and lexical bootstrapping to infer the meaning of new structures.

- The generativist approach argues that language acquisition is driven by innate, language-specific abilities, while the usage-based framework argues that children use general cognitive mechanisms to gradually construct a grammar of their language.

- Children often learn collocations like *brush your teeth* before they understand the grammar of the individual words making up the language chunk; they also use partial structures they hear in adult speech, like *Eat yet?* to build up canonical structures, like *Did you eat yet?*

- Specific language impairment involves a deficit in the use of grammatical morphemes. Children with late language emergence exhibit a delay in development but a normal trajectory, and they usually end up within the normal range; dyslexia, though considered a reading disorder, also has effects on spoken language perception and production.

- Recent neuroimaging studies show that language processing is bilateral in infancy but gradually lateralizes to the left hemisphere by the early school years; the ventral stream matures before the dorsal stream, consistent with the behavioral evidence that meaning drives syntax in the early years.

In Chapter 3 we found that language learning begins in the womb and that infants come into the world already familiar with the pitch and rhythm patterns of their mother's language. These prosodic cues serve as the key that infants use to crack the syntax code.

Cracking the Code

Adult speech, and especially that directed at infants, flows in arcs of rising and falling pitch that stretch across groups of words. Each **intonational phrase boundary** is *a prosodic cue consisting of a change in pitch, usually downward, and a lengthening of the final* *syllable that signals the end of a syntactic phrase* (Männel & Friederici, 2011). In adult-directed speech, intonational phrase boundaries are not always followed by a pause, but in infant-directed speech they usually are. Thus, just as infants use transition probabilities to detect word boundaries, they use intonational phrase boundaries to group words together. *The use of prosodic patterns to identify syntactic structure* is called **prosodic bootstrapping**.

Young children's sensitivities to prosody and syntax grow together, and they reinforce each other (Männel & Friederici, 2011). At first, infants only use pauses to detect phrase boundaries. But as they get more familiar with the syntactic structure of their language, they begin to associate drops in pitch and preboundary lengthening as additional cues to phrase boundaries. By three years of age, they're sensitive to intonational phrases even when there's no pause, just like adults.

The Terrible Twos

Productive language ability develops slowly during the first year and a half of life, but in the following years children experience a language spurt as their vocabularies increase and their sentence-building skills improve.

As we learned in Chapter 5, two-year-old children have the ability to use syntactic structure to infer the meaning of words. This is known as syntactic bootstrapping. For example, when two-year-olds heard a conversation about a boy *moop*ing, they later preferred a scene of a person performing a novel act alone when they heard *moop* again. But when they heard a conversation about a boy *moop*ing a girl, they later preferred a scene of a person performing a novel act on another person (Arunchalam & Waxman, 2010). Even as adults, we encounter novel words and have to infer their meaning from context, including syntactic structure. However, young children with their limited vocabularies are constantly encountered new words they have to deal with. Children at this age also have *the ability use word meanings to make inferences about syntactic structure*, which is known as **lexical bootstrapping**.

Between the second and third year of life, children's vocabulary and understanding of syntax grow rapidly and in tandem (Pérez-Leroux, Castilla-Earls, & Brunner, 2012). *The standard measure of children's syntactic complexity* is the **mean length of utterance**, or MLU. An utterance is a continuous piece of speech bounded by pauses, but it needn't be a complete or grammatically correct sentence, and its length is calculated as the number of morphemes, or meaningful units, not words. For example, the utterance *doggie running* has an utterance length of 3, since *run* and *-ing* are separate morphemes. *A common measure of the child's productive vocabulary* is the **number of different words**, or NDW, that a child actively uses. MLU and NDW are positively correlated, such that one is a good predictor of the other.

During this time, children's ability to produce sentences progresses rapidly, although disruptions in their spontaneous utterances are common (Rispoli, Hadley, & Holt,

2008). These speech disruptions are of two types. A **stall** is a *disruption of speech that does not change the syntactic structure of the utterance*, and it can consist of either silence or fillers such as *uh* or *um*. The frequency of stalls remains stable between the ages of two and three, but it does increase with sentence length. Thus, stalls are believed to be the result of a processing logjam in either lexical retrieval or phonological encoding as the child incrementally builds a sentence. A **revision**, on the other hand, is *a disruption of speech that changes the syntactic structure of the utterance*. Revisions increase with age but not with sentence length, and for that reason they're viewed as evidence of children's developing ability to monitor their own speech.

Models of Syntax Acquisition

In the last third of the twentieth century, psycholinguists were largely influenced by Chomsky's (1957, 1980) transformational-generative grammar. Chomsky took *the position that the linguistic input children receive is insufficient for them to learn the language*, and this is known as the **poverty-of-the-stimulus argument**. In Chomsky's view, adult speech is too full of errors to be a good model for learning. Instead, as we learned in Chapter 3, he proposed that children have a language acquisition device, or LAD, which is a hypothetical module of the brain containing a universal set of grammar rules that guides language development. Researchers no longer talked about language learning but rather about language acquisition, to distance themselves from the earlier behaviorist movement, which assumed virtually all behavior was learned.

There were always those who disagreed with Chomsky's generativist approach, but with the transition into the twenty-first century, a new generation of researchers has shifted the focus away from innate language-specific abilities. Instead, they emphasize complex interactions between general cognitive abilities and the rich learning environment of childhood. In the new **usage-based framework**, psychologists take *the position that the child uses general cognitive mechanisms like pattern detection and categorization to gradually build an understanding of the grammar of the language* (Theakston et al., 2004). Instead of acquiring rules, in this view, the child stores examples in memory that gradually converge on the adult grammar. Thus, the child is seen as building a grammar over time, and for this reason the usage-based framework is also known as the constructivist account to distinguish itself from Chomsky's generativist account.

The debate between these two approaches centers on children's developing abilities to use inflections, especially the past tense (Kidd, 2011). As far as languages go, the English inflectional system is fairly simple. Nouns are marked for plural with the *-s* suffix, except for a handful of nouns that make an internal vowel change instead, such as *man-men, foot-feet,* and *mouse-mice*. Likewise, verbs are marked for the past with the *-ed* suffix, except for several dozen verbs that change their vowel, like *come-came, run-ran,* and *eat-ate*. Irregular nouns and verbs tend to be among the most frequent in the language, so children learn them early.

As children's vocabulary and grammar develop during the second and third years, they exhibit a U-shaped learning curve for the plural and past-tense inflections. At first, they produce both regular and irregular inflections correctly, as in *walk-walked* and *go-went*. Then they begin an **overgeneralization** phase characterized by *the treatment of irregular words as if they were regularly inflected*. That is, they tend to say *mans* and *foots*, *comed* and *goed*. Eventually, they sort out regular and irregular inflection as their speech becomes more adult-like.

The generativist approach views overgeneralization as evidence for the acquisition of a rule (Pinker, 1999). However, a **connectionist network**, which is *a computer program that models statistical learning*, exhibits both overgeneralization and a U-shaped learning curve when trained on plural or past tense inflection (Rumelhart & McClelland, 1986). A connectionist network doesn't learn rules but only organizes examples by pattern, and so researchers in the usage-based framework argue that children do the same (Keren-Portnoy & Keren, 2011).

Incremental Structure Building

Stronger evidence for the usage-based framework comes from children's acquisition of another English inflection, the third-person singular -*s* suffix on verbs. Two-year-olds are more likely to use the -*s* inflection when the verb is at the end of the utterance than when it's in the middle (Sundara, Demuth, & Kuhl, 2011). For example, a child might say *There he goes* but *He go now*. Children at this age are also less sensitive to a missing -*s* in middle of a sentence compared with at the end.

This finding is difficult to reconcile with a rule-based account. Instead, it suggests that children are accumulating examples. Moreover, these stored examples are subject to perceptual limitations. It seems that children are less likely to produce sentence-medial -*s* because they are less likely to hear it. Thus, instead of extracting abstract rules, children at this age seem to be basing their productions on examples as they perceived them.

Further evidence for the usage-based approach is garnered by considering the contexts in which key words occur. *A sequence of words that frequently go to together* is called a **collocation**, and these predictable phrases are likely learned as chunks (Arnon & Clark, 2011). For example, we say *disappearing ink* but *vanishing cream*, *strong coffee* but *a powerful computer*. Young children do interesting things with irregular inflections when they occur in collocations. Although they overgeneralize plurals like *tooths* and *mouses* in other situations, they produce them correctly in collocations like *brush your teeth* and *three blind mice*. Thus, familiar patterns can serve as a scaffolding for building more complex grammar.

A premise of the poverty-of-the-stimulus argument is that adult speech is filled with grammatical errors and incomplete sentences. Usage-based theorists don't disagree with this premise, but they argue that this supposedly faulty input is a boon to language learning (Estigarriba, 2010). A good example of this is the learning of yes/no question structure, which is quite complex in English. The basic pattern involves inverting the subject and auxiliary, so that the statement *It is raining* becomes the question *Is it raining?* Likewise, the statement *You can see me* becomes the question *Can you see me?* When there is no auxiliary, we use *do*, as in: *He wants to come* → *He does want to come* → *Does he want to come?* That's a lot for a two-year-old to handle!

Even in adult speech, we don't always follow these rules. Instead of *Do you want your lunch?* we'll say *You want your lunch?* or even *Want your lunch?* These noncanonical question forms are structurally simpler than the canonical form, and they provide examples that children can understand and produce (Estigarriba, 2010). In this way, children learn syntax in an incremental fashion, gradually building on simpler forms to produce more complex structures.

The Primacy of Meaning

Researchers working in the usage-based framework emphasize the primacy of meaning in the development of syntax (Bloom, 1993). In other words, children don't just learn patterns, they learn syntactic structures that are meaningful to them. Verbs are especially important in driving the development of syntax, since it's their meaning that determines the structure of the sentence. Children learn action verbs early, and the agent-patient relationship they express helps youngsters learn canonical word order and what it means (Lempert, 1989). Likewise, children learn early how to link action sentences together using conjunctions like *and*, as in: *Mommy's sleeping and Daddy's sleeping and doggie's sleeping and . . .*

We learned in Chapter 1 that one of the hallmarks of human language is recursion, or the ability to embed one sentence inside of another sentence, like Russian nested dolls. Linking two sentences with a conjunction like *and* isn't recursion but rather concatenation, like putting beads on a string. Mental state verbs such as *think* and *know* provide semantic scaffolding for creating complex sentences with embedding (Klein, Moses, & Jean-Baptiste, 2010). Mental state verbs can act like action verbs, fitting into the canonical subject-verb-object format, as in *I know that* and *I think so*. But mental state verbs are about the contents of our minds, which we express as sentences, and so their meaning supports the syntactic process of embedding a sentence in the object position to form sentences like: *I know Mommy likes flowers* and *I think Daddy's sleeping*.

The passive voice is another area of language development where we see a complex interaction between form and meaning. Children's ability to understand and properly use the passive voice develops slowly, and it's not until around nine years of age that normally developing children can reliably use the passive construction correctly (Messenger, Branigan, & McLean, 2012). The meaning conveyed by a

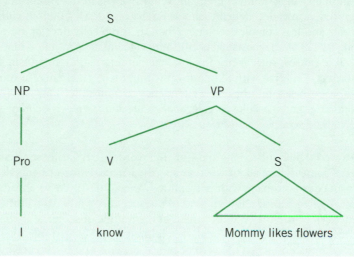

Figure 6.12 Sentence Tree of *I know Mommy likes flowers*

Young children learn first about recursion through the use of mental-state verbs such as *think* and *know*, which typically take sentence complements instead of noun-phrase objects.

particular passive sentence influences how likely it is that a child will comprehend or produce it correctly.

Recall that the passive construction poses a number of conceptual challenges for language users, whether children or adults. One challenge is the strong tendency to equate subject with animate agents. Thus, a sentence like *The window was broken by the boy* violates expectations by putting an inanimate patient in the subject position. Especially for a young child who's relying mostly on the meanings of the content words to understand the meaning of the syntactic structure, such sentences are difficult to process and don't even begin to appear in children's speech until seven or eight years of age (Kidd, 2012a). However, truncated passives like *The window was broken*, in which the agent is left unexpressed, appear much earlier in children's speech. This pattern of development supports the argument that children learn sentence structure incrementally, using simpler familiar forms to facilitate the development of more complex syntax.

Another challenge posed by the passive construction is reversible sentences. In a passive sentence like *the cat was chased by the dog*, both participants in the event are potential agents. Preschool children tend to interpret this sentence as meaning *the cat chased the dog* (Messenger et al., 2012). They'll also sometimes produce passives of this type, but again with the active, not passive meaning. This suggests that children learn the passive form before they learn what it means, interpreting it instead according to canonical word order. Children are in the second or third grade before they fully master passive sentences.

Language Impairments

There's wide variation in the timeline for normally developing children, but some children exhibit a marked delay in language development. As we learned in Chapter 1, specific language impairment, or SLI, is a developmental disorder characterized by difficulty in acquiring grammatical morphemes in the absence of any other cognitive or physical deficit (Schuele & Dykes, 2005). Children with SLI produce shorter and less complex sentences than their typically developing peers (McGregor et al., 2012). A diagnosis of specific language impairment must first rule out other possible causes, such as hearing loss, mental retardation, or autism spectrum disorders. Children with SLI perform within the normal range at other cognitive and motor tasks, but they have a tendency to omit inflections and function words, producing sentences like *He going to the store* and *We play yesterday* well into the early grade school years (Owen, 2010).

Because English inflections and function words are typically short and unstressed, there's some debate about whether specific language impairment is truly a deficit in syntax or a problem with perception (Owen, 2010). We've already seen that typically developing children tend to produce the *-s* inflection at the ends of sentences before they produce them in the middle of sentences, where they're also more difficult to perceive. Similarly, children with SLI are more likely to produce the *-ed* inflection when the verb occurs at the end of the sentence rather than the middle (Dalal & Loeb, 2005). Thus, it could be that children with specific language impairment don't reliably produce grammatical morphemes because they don't consistently perceive them.

It's important to distinguish specific language impairment from **late language emergence**, which is *a condition in which children are initially delayed in language development but eventually catch up with their peers* (Domsch et al., 2012). Children with SLI continue to exhibit language difficulties long after these have been resolved in late talkers (Schuele & Dykes, 2005). We also need to briefly mention dyslexia. Although dyslexia is generally viewed as a reading disorder, it's now widely recognized that it has effects on spoken language perception and production as well (Altmann et al., 2008). School-age children and even young adults with dyslexia produce more grammar errors and exhibit more dysfluencies in spoken language that do their peers.

Language Development and the Brain

Language development in childhood stems from changes in brain structure during the first years of life. Friederici and her colleagues have recently outlined three behavioral milestones associated with changes in the organization of the young brain (Friederici, Brauer, & Lohmann, 2011; Friederici, Oberecker, & Brauer, 2012). During the first year, statistical learning drives language development, and these processes are performed by auditory and association cortices in the temporal lobe. In the second and third years, children begin developing syntax, but, as we have seen, their understanding of sentence structure relies heavily on individual word meanings. The ventral stream from the temporal lobe to the inferior frontal gyrus is already developed and likely subserves the semantic-based syntax of this period.

The ability to handle complex syntax such as passive and scrambling doesn't fully come online until around seven to nine years of age, and this is probably due to the fact that the dorsal stream, which is believed to process complex syntactic structure, doesn't mature until around this time. Furthermore, during the first few years, both hemispheres seem to engage in language tasks, but language functions gradually become more lateralized to the left hemisphere as the brain matures. Although brain development during early childhood still isn't well understood, the neuroimaging data so far are at least consistent with the well-documented behavioral trajectory.

In Sum

Prosody is a key to cracking the syntax code. While infants use transition probabilities to find word boundaries, they use prosodic cues to find phrase boundaries, in a process known as prosodic bootstrapping. In the second and third years of life, children go through a language spurt in which their vocabulary and understanding of syntax develop rapidly. The traditional generativist approach argues that language development is driven by innate language-specific abilities. However, the usage-based framework, which has gained currency over the last two decades, argues that children use general cognitive mechanisms, like pattern detection and categorization, to incrementally build up a grammar of the language. The overgeneralization of inflectional morphemes is seen as evidence for the usage-based approach. Further

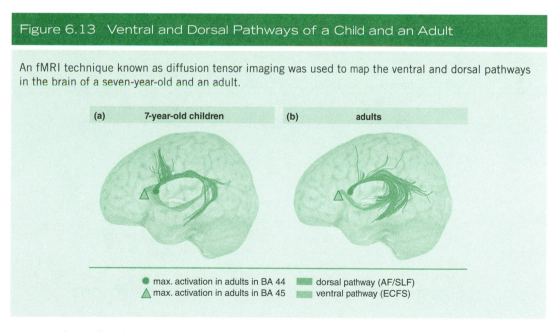

Figure 6.13 Ventral and Dorsal Pathways of a Child and an Adult

An fMRI technique known as diffusion tensor imaging was used to map the ventral and dorsal pathways in the brain of a seven-year-old and an adult.

(a) 7-year-old children   (b)   adults

● max. activation in adults in BA 44   dorsal pathway (AF/SLF)
△ max. activation in adults in BA 45   ventral pathway (ECFS)

Source: Friederici, Oberecker, and Brauer (2012).

evidence for the usage-based approach comes from children's learning of collocations and their use of partial structures to gradually build full structures. During the preschool years, children rely on semantic relationships to infer syntactic relations, and abstract syntactic structures such as passive and scrambling are generally beyond the abilities of children until around age seven to nine. Neuroimaging studies show that brain development during this time is consistent with behavioral milestones. Some children do not show normal language development. Children with specific language impairment have persistent difficulties with grammatical morphemes, as do children who are later diagnosed with dyslexia. Other children experience late language emergence but eventually reach language abilities within the normal range.

Review Questions

1. Explain how infants use prosody to crack the syntax code.

2. Describe the standard measures of vocabulary size and syntactic complexity. Explain what syntactic and lexical bootstrapping are and how they illustrate the interaction of meaning and form.

3. Compare and contrast the generativist and usage-based framework approaches to syntax acquisition. What is the evidence for each?

4. Explain how the learning of collocations and yes/no question structure provide evidence for the view that children incrementally develop an understanding of syntactic structure.

5. How does children's understanding of passive constructions demonstrate that they primarily depend on semantic relationships to interpret sentences until a fairly late age?

6. Describe the characteristics of specific language impairment and late language emergence. What is the relationship between dyslexia and spoken language processing?

7. Explain why the neuroimaging data are consistent with behavioral milestones.

Thought Question

1. Compare young children's comprehension of passive sentences with the performance of Broca's aphasics on sentence-picture matching tasks. Based on what you've read in this chapter, speculate on the behavioral and neurological reasons for their performance.

Google It! Specific Language Impairment

If you're interested in learning more about **specific language impairment**, there are plenty of educational and demonstration videos on YouTube. You can also find videos about other language impairments such as **expression language disorder**. You can learn how these disorders differ from other impairments such as **apraxia of speech**, and you can also learn how the speech of children with SLI differs from that of children with autism.

CONCLUSION

Our thoughts seem to flow in a random stream and scatter in multiple directions, but when we speak, we need to impose order on our thoughts. This is because speech unfolds along the single dimension of time—that is, you can only say one thing at any given instant. Our speech needs to be ordered for our listener to understand. And to the extent that we think in terms of internalized speech, our thoughts are ordered by the syntax of our language as well.

Syntax does more than just provide a consistent word order. It also adds meaning to the sentence in addition to the joint meanings of all the words that the syntax ties together. The words in a sentence may name the event and the actors in it, but syntax tells us who did what to whom.

Traditional models of language acquisition viewed syntactic structure as part of our cognitive makeup. Rather than learning grammar from scratch, according to this model, children's innate knowledge is activated as they hear a particular language spoken around them. The idea of universal grammar also accounts for the fact that languages around the world all have very similar structures with only minor variations. More recent studies of language development suggest a different process, though. Rather than activating fully formed structures, children seem to build up their grammar gradually as they learn patterns in the language.

Much of the psycholinguistic research of the twentieth century focused on the sentence as the fundamental unit of language. However, we don't go around uttering sentences in isolation. Instead, we mainly use language to engage in conversations and to tell stories. That is, we combine related sentences into coherent structures. This higher level of language, known as discourse, is the topic of the next chapter.

CROSS-CULTURAL PERSPECTIVE:
Canonical Word Order Around the World

Canonical word order for simple declarative sentences in English is subject-verb-object. This word order seems natural to native English speakers, and it is a frequent word order among the world's languages. Even more common is the word order of languages like Japanese and Korean, which structure their sentences as subject-object-verb.

Logically, there are six possible ways to order the three major components of a sentence. In reality, though, just two patterns—the English type and the Japanese type—account for word order in 85% of the world's languages (Gell-Mann & Ruhlen, 2011). This strong bias in the distribution of word orders suggests that canonical word order isn't just due to chance but rather is motivated by either psychological or historical reasons.

As Greenberg (1963) pointed out in his pioneering research on language universals, the two most common canonical word orders both place the subject (S) in the initial position. The only remaining question then was the order of verb (V) and object (O). In Greenberg's data, based on thirty-five languages, SOV and SVO occurred with about equal frequency.

We can think of the subject noun phrase as the topic of the sentence. Likewise, we can think of the following verb phrase, which includes both the verb and the object noun, as a comment on that topic. In the sentence *The clown rides the unicycle*, the topic is *the clown* while *rides the unicycle* makes a comment about it. If we think of declarative sentences in this way, then it only makes sense that the subject should come first.

Still, 15% of the world's languages have a canonical word order in which the subject doesn't come first. However, as Greenberg (1963) noted, in all such cases there's also a subject-first option in the language. Thus, subject-first word order does seem to be a universal tendency. If we think of spoken language as an activity of joint attention, this pattern of pointing something out and then making a comment about it makes sense.

Table 6.5 Canonical Word Order in Languages Around the World

Subject-Object-Verb	1,072	47%	Japanese, Korean	The clown the unicycle rides.
Subject-Verb-Object	864	38%	English, Mandarin	The clown rides the unicycle.
Verb-Subject-Object	215	9%	Hawaiian, Hebrew	Rides the clown the unicycle.
Verb-Object-Subject	85	4%	Malagasy	Rides the unicycle the clown.
Object-Verb-Subject	31	1%	Hixkaryana	The unicycle rides the clown.
Object-Subject-Verb	31	1%	Warao	The unicycle the clown rides.
Total	2,298	100%		

Source: Gell-Mann and Ruhlen (2011).

The question of whether VO or OV is a more natural order is still open to debate. As we already mentioned, Greenberg's (1963) data showed a roughly even split, suggesting the order was an arbitrary decision each speech community makes. However, Bickerton (1981) argued that VO was more natural and probably reflects an innate cognitive tendency. He based this assertion on the observation, as we already noted in Chapter 1, that all known creoles have SVO word order.

Recent anthropological evidence suggests that all existing human languages may have a common ancestor about 50,000 years ago in Africa (Gell-Mann & Ruhlen, 2011). This evidence also suggests that the ancestral language had SOV order. According to this theory, as humans dispersed out of Africa, the language each group spoke gradually changed in syntax and vocabulary from the original, with SVO order appearing first, followed by VSO. Only later, and much farther away from the ancestral homeland, did the other orders emerge.

How can a language change its canonical word order from one type to another? It's important to keep in mind that "canonical" means typical, not absolute. Even English, which is strongly SVO, makes use of other word orders, especially in colloquial speech. If you pay careful attention, you'll hear all sorts of noncanonical utterances like *Chocolate I love, but peanut butter I can't stand.*

Some languages have so-called free word order in that two or three orders are commonly used. Russian is one such language, with SVO and SOV occurring with roughly equal frequency. Furthermore, when there's no object in the sentence, either the subject or the verb can come first.

Over many generations, the balance of one word order over another can shift. This is what happened in English over many centuries. In fact, relics of the old SOV word order remain in certain ceremonial expressions such as the wedding vow *With this ring, I thee wed.*

Further evidence for Gell-Mann and Ruhlen's (2011) "Out-of-Africa" hypothesis comes from the fact that object-before-subject word orders only occur in languages spoken in the last regions to be populated by humans. Malagasy, spoken on Madagascar, uses VOS word order. Although the island lies off the east coast of Africa, it was populated by way of the Pacific islands, where verb-first languages are common. Likewise, object-first languages are exceedingly rare and are only found in South America, which was one of the last regions of the Earth that humans migrated to.

In brief, both psychological and historical reasons can account for the different word orders of the various languages around the world. While subject-first sentence structures seem to be psychologically motivated, historical accidents probably account for the rest of the variation we see.

KEY TERMS

Active voice

Agent

Agreement

Canonical word order

Clause

Cleft sentence

Cloze probability

Collocation

Connectionist network

Constraint-based model

Dative construction

Garden path model

Garden path sentence

Heuristic

Hierarchical structure in advance planning

High attachment

Incremental model

Intonational phrase boundary

Irreversible sentence

Late closure

Late language emergence

Lexical boost

Lexical bootstrapping

Low attachment

Mean length of utterance

Minimal attachment

N400

Number of different words

Overgeneralization

P600

Parallel model

Passive voice

Patient

Poverty-of-the-stimulus argument

Prosodic bootstrapping

Reduced relative clause

Referential priming

Relative clause

Repetition suppression

Reversible sentence

Revision

Scrambling

Sentence-picture matching task

Serial model

Stall

Syntactic priming

Syntax

Thematic role assignment

Thematic roles

Usage-based framework

CHAPTER 7

Discourse

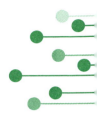

Riding an elevator with someone you don't know is awkward for most people. On the one hand, we're taught as children not to talk to strangers. But on the other hand, occupying the same space with other people and not speaking to them just doesn't feel right. Talking is simply what we humans do when we're around each other, and we spend many of our waking hours chatting and swapping stories with other people. As we talk, we share information with each other, and as our common knowledge expands, so also does our sense of connectedness.

Discourse is the technical term we use to refer to speech structured at its highest level. All the speech sounds, words, and sentence structures we learned as children are put to use in the construction of conversations and narratives, the two basic forms of discourse. As we engage in spoken interaction with others, we shift between periods of turn-taking as listener and speaker (conversation) and other periods when one speaker dominates (narrative). The development of discourse abilities encompasses the acquisition of all speech skills, starting in the womb as the fetus learns the prosodic patterns of its mother's tongue and continuing well into adolescence, when the finer points of adult-like chit-chat and storytelling are honed.

SECTION 7.1: CONVERSATION

SECTION 7.2: NARRATIVE AND REFERENCE

SECTION 7.3: ANAPHORA AND INFERENCE

SECTION 7.4: DEVELOPMENT OF DISCOURSE ABILITIES

SECTION 7.1: CONVERSATION

- Discourse is a set of sentences that cohere about one or more related topics; conversation is the most common form of discourse, and it has the added feature of being a collaborative process between two or more participants who take turns in an orderly fashion.

- Conversation is replete with ill-formed sentences and vague references; conversation partners understand each other because they have recourse to pragmatics, or the way context lends meaning to a discourse, and common ground, which is a body of knowledge that is shared among the participants.

- Participants in a conversation take turns speaking. Each turn is composed of one or more turn-constructional units, and a new speaker can only begin a turn at a transition relevance place; participants observe the principle of no gaps/no overlaps at turn transitions.

- The listener plays an active role in the conversation by providing the speaker with backchannels that indicate points of understanding and confusion, thus helping to establish common ground and encouraging the speaker to continue.

- Turn allocation proceeds stepwise through three rules: (1) the current speaker selects the next speaker, (2) a listener self-selects, and (3) the current speaker self-selects; the process then cycles through steps 2 and 3 until a new turn begins.

- Participants in a conversation tend to match each other in terms of body movements, breathing rates, and speech patterns in a process known as entrainment; it is believed that endogenous oscillators, or neural circuits with regular firing rates, are responsible for entrainment.

Imagine a pair of figure skaters gliding across the ice. Their motions are completely synchronized, their bodies moving as one as they proceed through their tightly choreographed routine. Sometimes the male takes the lead, sometimes the female, but their turns transition gracefully from one to the other, never missing a beat. Such a performance takes thousands of hours of strenuous practice and a dedication to perfection that few of us can ever muster. And yet every time we have a conversation with another person, we go through a choreographed routine with our partner that's also complex, and we execute it with the skill that comes from a lifetime of practice.

Anatomy of a Conversation

Conversation is what language is all about. **Talk-in-interaction**, or *the spontaneous speech people use as they engage in joint activities*, is the main function of language, far outweighing all other forms of discourse. As we learned in Chapter 1, discourse is a set of sentences that cohere about one or more related topics, and the term includes not only conversations and narratives but also written texts. However, a conversation is far more than a set of sentences produced by alternating speakers.

Incomplete and ill-formed utterances are the norm in spontaneous conversation (ten Bosch, Oostdijk, & Boves, 2005). In part this is because, as we saw in Chapter 6, we don't plan out our sentences before we begin speaking them. As a result, we often experience processing delays, during which we buy time with **conversational fillers**, *words like "uh" and "um" that are semantically empty but are used to signal planning difficulties* (Beňuš, Gravano, & Hirschberg, 2011). Although they seem to disrupt syntactic structure, conversational fillers are actually beneficial to both

Figure 7.1   Photo of Two People Conversing

Talk-in-interaction, the spontaneous use of speech as people engage in joint activities, is the main function of language.

Source: ©iStockphoto.com/ skynesher.

speakers and listeners, giving speakers more time to plan their intended messages and listeners more to time to anticipate what's coming next. In fact, words in conversations are better recalled later on when they followed a conversational filler. Thus, speakers can also use conversational fillers intentionally to highlight important information.

Ill-formed utterances in conversation also result from planning errors. Oftentimes, speakers will simply drop a structure in mid-sentence and start anew. Other times, speakers will persevere with an errant sentence, attempting to steer it back to the intended message by tacking on additional phrases and clauses. As a result, transcripts of conversations can be difficult to read, as for example in this exchange recorded by Lee-Goldman (2011):

> Aaron: For instance, I mean I wouldn't expect that it was very com-
> mon overall, that when two people were talking at the same
> time, that it would — that it really was lower, although
> sometimes, as you say, it would.
>
> Megan: Yeah, no, that was—That was a joke.

Notice Aaron's use the conversational filler *I mean* near the beginning of his turn. He seems to be having difficulty planning his utterance, and at one point he abandons a newly started clause, *that it would*, repairing it with *that it really was lower*. Megan starts her turn with the *yeah, no* combination filler (the *no, yeah* combination is common as well), and she also breaks off in mid-clause—*that was*—only to repeat the same beginning as she completed the sentence.

Although Aaron and Megan seem to understand each other just fine, you probably don't have a good idea of what they're talking about. This is because most of the meaning of a conversation resides not in the semantics of the individual words but rather in the pragmatics of the situation in which the conversation is taking place. The term **pragmatics** refers to *the various ways that context contributes to the meaning of a discourse*. Furthermore, many of the content words in a conversation serve as indices to entities and events that the participants all know about. This *pool of information that all participants of a conversation share* is known as **common ground**. Because of common ground, the **interlocutors**, or *the participants in a conversation*, can be brief and vague in their references. In Section 7.2, we'll learn more about how common ground is established and maintained.

Turn Construction

A hallmark of conversation is the seamless transition from one speaker to another as the interlocutors take turns. Naïve intuition suggests that the listener waits for the current speaker to finish before starting a turn, but this can't be true. Although there is some variability due to speaking rate, the average gap between turns is about a quarter of a second, shorter than the human reaction time to verbal stimuli (Stivers et al., 2009; Wilson & Wilson, 2005). In other words, listeners predict when the current speaker will end his or her turn and begin planning their response before the speaker's turn ends.

Conversations are composed of turn-constructional units. A **turn-constructional unit** is *a syntactic structure, ranging from a single word to a sentence, that can make up a turn in a conversation*. Turns can consist of more than one turn-constructional unit, but turn transitions generally occur between and not during them (Oloff, 2013; Wilson & Wilson, 2005). Hence, psycholinguists treat them as units of conversation.

The end of each turn-constructional unit constitutes a transition relevance place. A **transition relevance place** is *a point in the conversation where the listener can expect the current speaker to end a turn*. Syntax, semantics, and prosody all signal approaching transition relevance places as the current sentence comes to a meaningful conclusion and the speaker's intonation falls (Stadler, 2011). At a transition relevance place, a new speaker might start a turn, or the current speaker might continue. If instead a brief silence ensues, either participant may pick up the conversation, perhaps with a new topic, yet it's rare for both interlocutors to start speaking at the same time (Wilson & Wilson, 2005). Rather, if there's an overlap in speakers, it's more likely to take place at the transition relevance place (Oloff, 2013).

Turn Transition

Turn transition from one speaker to the next generally follows the **principle of no gaps/no overlaps** (Beňuš et al., 2011). This refers to *the tendency to avoid leaving a noticeable silence between turns of conversation and beginning a new turn before the current turn is finished.* As we've already seen, the typical gap between turns is about a quarter of a second, but this is perceived as no gap. Longer gaps are perceived as silences, and they can be interpreted as hesitancy or awkwardness on the part of the speaker (Wilson & Wilson, 2005). If you ask someone to do you a favor and that person hesitates, you'll probably prepare yourself for an excuse or refusal. On the other hand, overlaps can be interpreted as aggressiveness and an attempt to dominate the conversation (ten Bosch et al., 2005).

However, overlaps are not always considered rude. During a speaker's turn, it's common for the listener to make noises or nod the head to indicate understanding or agreement. These **backchannels** are *signals like "mmhmm" and "uhhuh" from the listener that indicate engagement and encourage the speaker to continue* (Beňuš et al., 2011). Without backchannels, speakers tend to stop, apparently interpreting this silence as lack of interest on the part of the listener (ten Bosch et al., 2005). In face-to-face conversations, speakers may even turn their gaze toward the listener looking for visual cues of understanding if no vocal backchannels are forthcoming (Gupta, Duff, & Tranel, 2011). Backchannels can overlap the speaker's speech, but listeners often time them to fall within pauses during the speaker's turn (Wilson & Wilson, 2005).

Overlaps, or *instances when multiple interlocutors speak at the same time*, are interpreted negatively or positively, depending on the context. Overlaps that involve competition for control of the conversation topic are viewed negatively, but overlaps in which the listener signals solidarity with the speaker are viewed positively (ter Maat, Truong, & Heylen, 2011). For example, interlocutors often overlap turns when they greet each other as a way of expressing heightened emotion. Likewise, when listeners engage in collaborative turn completions, finishing the turn along with the speaker, they signal engagement and affiliation (Wilson & Wilson, 2005).

Interlocutors use a number of visual and vocal cues to signal their interest in taking or maintaining a turn, and they monitor these in their partners as they continuously adjust their stance toward approaching or withdrawing from a possible turn (Oloff, 2013; Wilson & Wilson, 2005). The smoothness with which interlocutors negotiate turns suggests an underlying set of procedures for allocating turns and resolving conflicts (Beňuš et al., 2011).

Turn-Taking Rules

Sacks, Schegloff, and Jefferson (1974) proposed a simple model of turn allocation. This model has since received considerable empirical support and is now generally accepted as the standard model of conversational turn-taking (Wilson & Wilson, 2005). The model consists of three simple rules that are applied in strict sequential order.

1. Current selects next. At a transition relevance place, the current speaker explicitly passes the turn to the listener. For example, the speaker might ask a question, which clearly hands the turn over to the listener. In the case of multiparty conversations, the speaker may look at the next speaker or say that person's name.

2. Listener selects self. If the current speaker doesn't select the next speaker, any listener may take a turn. This does raise the possibility of overlapping turns, but usually all but one will quickly drop out (Wilson & Wilson, 2005).

3. Current selects self. If no listener steps up for a turn, then the speaker can start a new turn. If the speaker chooses not to take a turn, the process cycles between steps 2 and 3 until someone takes a turn.

It's important to understand that the steps in this process are played out in real time, with each cycle extending the length of the silence. In other words, each step takes up a certain interval of time, known as a **beat**, which the interlocutors seem to be tracking.

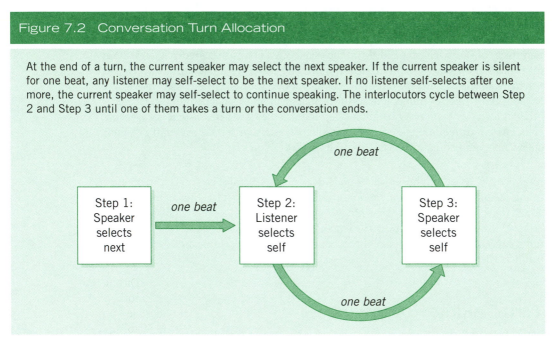

Figure 7.2   Conversation Turn Allocation

At the end of a turn, the current speaker may select the next speaker. If the current speaker is silent for one beat, any listener may self-select to be the next speaker. If no listener self-selects after one more, the current speaker may self-select to continue speaking. The interlocutors cycle between Step 2 and Step 3 until one of them takes a turn or the conversation ends.

Source: Sacks, Schegloff, and Jefferson (1974).

This beat is generally thought to be *the average time it takes to produce a syllable, as set by the speaking rate of the last turn* (Wilson & Wilson, 2005; for a somewhat different interpretation of beat, see Beňuš et al., 2011).

Participants in a conversation synchronize their behaviors at a number of levels. They tend to sway their bodies in unison, and listeners match their breathing rate to that of the speaker, especially at transitional relevant places (Beňuš et al., 2011). It seems as though the listener is preparing to pick up the next turn at the same speaking rate, much as runners in a relay race match their gait just before passing the baton (Wilson & Wilson, 2005). Alternating speakers also tend to match each other in terms of pitch, rhythm, and loudness (Beňuš et al., 2011). *The synchronization of rhythmic behavior in social interactions* is known as **entrainment** (Wilson & Wilson, 2005).

It's believed that entrainment results from the activation of **endogenous oscillators** in the brains of the interlocutors (Beňuš et al., 2011; Wilson & Wilson, 2005). Endogenous oscillators are *neural circuits that fire at regular intervals and thus serve as internal timekeepers for the brain.* A number of endogenous oscillators running at different rates have been discovered, and they're known to play important roles in perception and motor control as well as memory and attention. Entrainment occurs when the firing rate of endogenous oscillators in the listener's brain match those of the speaker, as communicated through various visual and vocal signals. Once listeners have picked up the speaker's rhythm, this beat continues after the end of the speaker's turn, which then guides both parties through the turn-taking steps and keeps both interlocutors from attempting to begin a turn at the same time. After an extended silence, though, the listener's and speaker's endogenous oscillators fall out of sync, and then it's possible for both parties to take a turn at the same time (Wilson & Wilson, 2005).

In Sum

Conversation is the most common form of discourse, and it is a collaborative process in which two or more interlocutors take turns in an orderly fashion. Although conversation is filled with incomplete and run-on sentences, the participants understand each other because of pragmatics, which is the information provided by the context, and common ground, which is the information that the interlocutors share. Each turn in a conversation is composed of one or more turn-constructional units, and a new turns can only start at transition relevance places. During turn transitions, participants avoid perceivable gaps or overlaps between turns. Turn allocation occurs through a sequence of steps that alternate between the right of way of the current speaker and the current listener until one of them takes up a turn. During a conversation, and especially around transition relevance points, the interlocutors become entrained, matching breathing and speech rhythms. Entrainment is believed to result from the synchronization of neural circuits known as endogenous oscillators in the brains of the speaker and listener.

Review Questions

1. What is discourse? In what sense is a conversation more than a set of sentences produced by alternating speakers? What two sources of information do interlocutors use to make sense of a conversation?

2. Explain the elements of a conversational turn, specifically turn-constructional unit and transition relevance place.

3. What is the principle of no gaps/no overlaps? How are gaps and overlaps often perceived? Under what circumstances are overlaps not only allowed by expected?

4. Explain Sacks et al.'s (1974) model of turn allocation. How does the model prevent interlocutors from speaking at the same time?

5. What is entrainment? What are endogenous oscillators, and how do they account for entrainment?

Thought Questions

1. The smooth turn transitions typical of conversation are likely due to entrainment. What are some other social activities that likely involve entrainment?

2. Endogenous oscillators are internal timekeepers that mark beats at regular intervals. Besides speech, what sorts of activities do humans engage in that would require timekeeping?

3. Over the next few days, pay attention to the use of backchannels, both by you and by other people. Once you have a heightened awareness of their use, experiment with them in casual conversations with your friends. Try withholding backchannels and see if this has an effect on the speaker. On a different occasion, make ample use of backchannels and see what kind of effect that has. Do your observations match up with what you read in this section?

4. In their paper "Passenger and Cell Phone Conversations in Simulated Driving," Drews, Pasupathi, and Strayer (2008) found that when drivers talked on a cell phone, they were four times more likely to have an accident (similar to a blood alcohol level of .08.) However, when drivers conversed with an adult passenger in the vehicle, their risk of accident was lower than driving alone. Given what you've learned in this section about conversation, consider some possible explanations for these data.

Google It! Cell Phone Versus Drunk Driving

Mythbusters Adam Savage and Jamie Hyneman (Discovery Channel) tested the **cell phone versus drunk driving** "myth." You can find video clips from the episode online.

How do their results compare with those of Drews et al. (2008)? Carefully observe the behavior of the drivers while talking on a cell phone. Do you think there would be a difference in performance if they used a hands-free device?

SECTION 7.2: NARRATIVE AND REFERENCE

- Conversations and narratives form two ends of a discourse continuum. In the case of conversation, interlocutors take turns constructing the discourse. In the case of narrative, one interlocutor dominates as narrator, although listeners still play an important role as co-narrators.

- Storytelling is cognitively demanding because the speaker and listener need to distance themselves from the here and now (decontextualization) as well as create and maintain a situation model of the narrative; thus, producing and comprehending narratives require executive functions such as memory allocation, planning, and inhibition.

- Story grammar provides the framework for narratives; a story consists of one or more episodes that depend for their construction and comprehension on the schemas we have about how the world works.

- Reference is the process of using a word or phrase to represent an entity; speakers need to judge what is in common or privileged ground when crafting referring expressions, and likewise listeners consider common and privileged ground in the interpretation of those referring expressions.

- Relevance theory proposes that speakers strike a balance between too much and too little information in selecting referring expressions; likewise, listeners assume that referring expressions are optimally relevant when interpreting them.

- Interlocutors collaborate to hone referring expressions; clinical evidence suggests that implicit learning plays a more important role in building common ground than does explicit learning.

A conversation is a form of discourse in which all participants contribute to its ongoing construction. In contrast, a **narrative** is *a form of discourse in which one participant dominates as the active speaker while the other participants assume passive roles as listeners*. The most extreme example of narrative would be a speech or lecture where the audience sits quietly while the speaker talks. However, most day-to-day narratives, such as the telling of stories, jokes, or personal experiences, still includes an important role for the listeners.

Narrative

We can think of narratives within conversations as multiturn units (Norrick, 2011). The would-be narrator typically indicates the beginning of a narrative with a formulaic expression such as "You'll never believe what happened to me this morning" or "Did you hear the one about. . . . ?" In response, the other interlocutors show their willingness to yield the floor, perhaps with an expression like "What happened?" or "Go on." But this doesn't mean the listeners become passive. Rather, listeners signal their engagement in the developing narrative by gazing at the speaker and providing appropriate backchannels. When speakers sense their listeners aren't paying attention, they'll often wait for them to look back again before resuming their story (Bavelas, Coates, & Johnson, 2000).

As the narrative progresses, the listeners take on a more active role (Bavelas et al., 2000). They provide vocal and facial expressions, such as gasps and winces, adding an emotional layer to the story's content. Listeners will also interject brief comments like "Yikes!" and "Oh no!" at appropriate places in the narrative, and they may even supply words or phrases when it appears the speaker is struggling for the right expression. In this sense, listeners are active collaborators in the building of the narrative.

Conversation partners will often exchange narratives, taking turns as storytellers. Shop talk is a good example of this (Norrick, 2011). When people engage in shop talk, they exchange news items and how-to instructions pertinent to their shared profession or mutual interests. But shop talk is more than just an exchange of

Figure 7.3   Photo of Coffee Break Chat

Although one speaker does most of the talking in storytelling, the listeners play an active role in constructing the narrative through their use of backchannels, facial expressions, and body postures.

Source: ©iStockphoto.com/ biffspandex.

expertise information, it's also a way for participants to demonstrate that they have access to privileged knowledge. Thus, shop talk helps the participants build rapport and create a group identity.

Sometimes narratives don't involve the exchange of any new information. A good example of this is what Sacks (1992) called spouse talk, in which couples recount their past experiences together as a way to reminisce and bond. The retelling of familiar stories is an important vehicle for creating a sense of solidarity and group membership, and it occurs at the family level as well as in clubs and churches and other organizations. Politicians will often retell familiar historical events to evoke a sense of national identity in the audience. The next time you attend a holiday dinner or family reunion, pay attention to the way your relatives retell family stories and the emotional impact it has on those present.

Storytelling is a cognitively demanding task. Unlike a lot of talk-in-interaction, storytelling requires **decontextualization**, or *the distancing of thought, language, and behavior from the current situation* (Green & Klecan-Aker, 2012). To tell a story, you need to be able to relate events in the correct order and suppress unrelated thoughts while detaching yourself from the present moment. In other words, telling a story taps into the **executive functions** of *memory allocation, planning, inhibition, and other cognitive processes necessary for guiding intentional behavior* (Lê et al., 2011).

Evidence for the position that narrative involves higher cognitive functioning and not just linguistic abilities comes from developmental and clinical observations. Young children, whose executive functions are not yet fully developed, are notoriously poor at telling coherent stories. Likewise, adults who've experienced certain types of brain damage may have difficulty comprehending or producing narratives even though they exhibit no other signs of language disorder (Mozeiko et al., 2011). In these cases, the damage is typically in the **prefrontal cortex,** which is *the most forward area of the frontal lobe, known to be responsible for executive functioning* (Ash et al., 2012).

Story Grammar

Storytelling may be a highly demanding cognitive task, but we can perform it with such seeming ease because narrative is so tightly structured. When we tell a story, we relate a sequence of events in a temporal or logical order (Norrick, 2011). But not just any series of events can make up a good story. Rather, those events have to be fitted into a conventional framework that includes a setup to provide background information followed by a sequence of events that leads to a dramatic or amusing resolution (Bavelas et al., 2000). *The framework guiding the presentation of events and characters in a narrative* is known as **story grammar** (Lê et al., 2011).

The fundamental building block of a story is the **episode**, and story grammar explains how an episode is structured. An episode begins with the setting, which is an introduction of the main characters and the location where the episode takes place. This is followed by an initiating event, which is a problem or challenge the protagonist must face. The protagonist then attempts to solve that problem, and at this point the internal thought processes of the protagonist are often revealed as well. As a consequence of this attempt, the protagonist may either succeed or fail, but whatever the outcome, the protagonist will have a reaction to this consequence.

Table 7.1 Story Grammar	
Common elements of story grammar, with examples.	
Setting	One day, a princess was walking by a pond when she saw a frog.
Initiating Event	"Fair maiden," croaked the frog. "Kiss me and I'll turn into a handsome prince."
Internal Response	The princess thought carefully about the proposition.
Attempt	She shut her eyes and leaned over to give the frog a kiss.
Consequence	"Hah, hah, fooled you!" croaked the frog as it leaped back into the water.
Reaction	The princess swore never to kiss another prince or frog again.

Story grammar is related to the more general concept of **schema** (Lê et al., 2011). A schema is *a mental framework for organizing our understanding of how some aspect of the world works*. We have schemas for all sorts of social behaviors that we engage in, such as eating at a restaurant or going out on a date. Since we all know what events are supposed to occur and in which order as well as who's responsible for initiating each event, we can smoothly perform the rituals that make up our lives, even when we're engaging with total strangers. Stories are built on the schemas we all share. After all, even fairy tales about frogs and princesses have relevance to our personal lives, since we can empathize with the characters in the stories.

Reference

As the speaker relates a story, the listener makes sense of it by building a **situation model** (Arnold, 2008). A situation model is *a mental representation of the entities and events in a story and how they are related*. You can think of a situation model as the imagery you create in your head as you listen to a story. But situation models are more than just imagery, as they draw on schemas already stored in long-term memory. Suppose your friend begins a joke with the line, "A priest, a minister, and a rabbi walk into a bar." You immediately call up schemas about priests, ministers, and rabbis, which include information about how these people typically look and behave. You also activate a bar joke schema, which suggests the bartender may play a role in the punchline. All this information goes into the situation model you construct as you listen to the story. (Oh yes, and as for the punchline: The bartender looks at them and says, "What is this, a joke?")

The speaker also has a situation model and uses it to construct the narrative. Thus, the purpose of the narrative is to transfer the situation model from the mind of the speaker to the mind of the listener. To do this successfully, the speaker needs to choose words carefully. Words and phrases stand for, or refer to, entities and events in the world (real or imagined), but any particular entity or event can be referred to by many different words. *A word or phrase that is used to represent a particular entity or event* is known as a **referring expression** (Brown-Schmidt, 2012). *The entity that is represented by a particular word or phrase* is called the **referent**, and *the process of using a word or phrase to represent an entity* is known as **reference**. Make sure you understand the distinctions and relationships among these three terms before moving on.

I want to tell you a story about someone I know. To do this, I need to consider how much you know about that person as I select a referring expression. If I know you've met the guy and know his name, I'll probably use his name, *Brian*, as the referring expression, especially when I introduce him into the story. Or, if I know you've met him but probably don't know his name, I might refer to him as *that guy I introduced you to at the party Saturday night*. And if I know you've never met him, I'll probably choose a referring expression that explains something about his relationship to me, such as *my best friend from college*. In other words, when speakers select referring expressions, they consider what's in the common ground, that is, knowledge they share with the listener, and **privileged ground**, that is, *information that one interlocutor knows but the other one doesn't* (Brown-Schmidt, Gunlogson, & Tanenhaus, 2008).

How speakers distinguish what's in common ground versus privileged ground is a matter of some debate. Some researchers argue that speakers make inferences about listeners' mental states (Gupta et al., 2011). But other researchers maintain that speakers rely mainly on their memories of shared experiences with their listeners to gauge common ground (Arnold, 2008). At any rate, speakers often overestimate common ground (Svennevig, 2010). Some experimental evidence suggests the speakers are initially egocentric in their selection of referring expressions, but then they use feedback from their listeners to make adjustments (Yoon, Koh, & Brown-Schmidt, 2012). For example, if I start telling you a story about Brian and you give me a puzzled look, I'll add, "You know, that guy I introduced you to at the party Saturday night."

Relevance theory is *the proposal that speakers strive for a balance between providing too much and too little information in choosing referring expressions* (Gibbs & Bryant, 2008). Providing more than enough information, especially when an entity is first introduced into a narrative, may help the listener identify the referent faster, although overly specific referring expressions later in the narrative can hinder comprehension (Arts et al., 2011). Thus, speakers tend to aim for a happy medium that minimizes production effort on their part while maximizing comprehension effect on the part of the listener. Where that happy medium lies, however, depends on the situation.

To test the hypothesis that speakers aim for optimal relevance—neither too precise nor too vague—in crafting referring expressions, Gibbs and Bryant (2008) approached people and asked the time. They noted whether the person was wearing a digital or analog watch, and in some cases they also explained that their watch had stopped, thus implying that the exact time was needed. Overall, analog watch wearers were more likely to give rounded answers, such as "about a quarter till two," than were the digital watch wearers, and both groups were more likely to give exact answers when the experiment said his watch had stopped.

What's noteworthy about these results is that nearly two-thirds of the digital watch wearers gave approximate time, unless there was an obvious need for the exact time (Gibbs & Bryant, 2008). In other words, the digital watch wearers went through the effort of converting the exact time of their watch into an approximate time for their response. Furthermore, those who did give the exact time took longer to respond than those who gave an approximate time. The researchers suggest that these respondents took longer because they were trying to decide whether a precise or ambiguous response was appropriate. In other words, they were striving for optimal relevance in their response.

Figure 7.4 Optimal Relevance in Time Expressions

Random pedestrians were approached and asked the time, either as a general question or with the explanation that the interviewer's watch had stopped. Analog watch watch wearers were more likely to give approximate time in both conditions. However, most digital watch wearers gave approximate in response to the general question even though they had access to the exact time.

Source: Gibbs and Bryant (2008).

In resolving a referring expression—that is, deciding what it means—listeners also have a tendency to be egocentric (Brown-Schmidt et al., 2008). Listeners do make use of common ground in identifying referents, and they can also make use of situational cues, including the speaker's eye gaze. Hanna and Tanenhaus (2004) examined how listeners resolve references by engaging research participants in a joint activity in which they made a cake together with the experimenter. At a critical point in the task, the experimenter said, "Hand me the cake mix." There were two cake mix boxes on the table, one nearer the experimenter and one nearer the participant. When the experimenter's hands were full, the participants more often picked the box nearer the experimenter, but otherwise they more often picked the box nearer themselves. Although the referring expression *the cake mix* was ambiguous in both cases, participants interpreted it according the relevance of the situation. Incidentally, the experimenter wore reflective sunglasses during the task so that there would be no cues from eye gaze.

Over time, speakers and listeners work together to hone referring expressions. Thus, when Grandma says to Grandpa, "Get me the thingamajig from the whatchamacallit," Grandpa knows exactly what Grandma means. Implicit learning from subtle social cues plays a more important role in the building of common ground than any sort of explicit memory, and this impacts the ways speakers craft referring expressions as well as the ways listeners resolve them (Gupta et al., 2011). Patients with damage to the amygdala, a subcortical structure that plays a role in social and emotional processing, have difficulty establishing common ground with interlocutors and tend to use the same overly specific referential expressions again and again. On the other hand, patients with damage to the hippocampus, a subcortical structure that plays a role in explicit memory consolidation, have no difficulty negotiating economical referring expressions with their interlocutors.

In Sum

Conversations and narratives are two common types of spoken discourse, and we often shift from one to the other during everyday talk-in-interaction. All interlocutors contribute to the building of conversation, but listeners play an important supporting role during narrative as well. Telling stories requires good control over executive functions like memory allocation, planning, and inhibition, and understanding stories involves the creation of situation models to represent them. We are guided in our production and comprehension of stories by our implicit knowledge of narrative structure. Story grammar outlines narratives as consisting of one or more episodes, and these episodes are structured according to schemas we have about how the world works. Reference is the link between the words of the discourse and the entities in the world, or more precisely, the situation model. Speakers and listeners distinguish between common ground and privileged ground in resolving referring expressions. Relevance theory proposes that interlocutors strike a balance between too much and too little information as they negotiate referring expressions. Clinical evidence suggests that implicit learning plays more of a role in the building of common ground than does explicit learning.

Figure 7.5   Collaborative Referencing Task

Two participants facing each with a low barrier between them were asked to arrange a set of cards in a specified order. Each card displayed an abstract triangular image known as a tangram. Since they could not see each other's cards, the participants at first used detailed descriptions, but over time they settled on brief referring expressions such as "praying guy" or "kneeler."

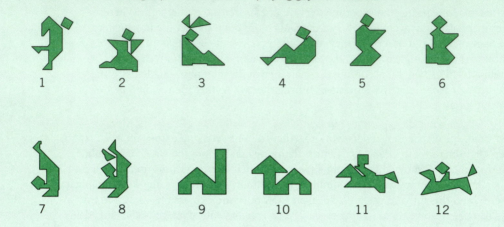

Source: Gupta, Duff, and Tranel (2011).

Review Questions

1. What are the similarities and differences between conversations and narratives? Why do we say they exist along a continuum as opposed to seeing them as two separate categories?

2. What characteristics of storytelling make it such a cognitively demanding task? What sorts of cognitive functions are called on in the production and comprehension of stories?

3. What are the elements of story grammar? Illustrate these elements with a simple story example.

4. Explain the concepts of referring expression, referent, and reference, considering how they are related to each other.

5. What is relevance theory? How do the results of Gibbs and Bryant (2008) provide evidence for relevance theory?

Thought Questions

1. Conversation and narrative are two forms of spoken discourse that are common in everyday talk-in-interaction. Can you think of some other forms of spoken discourse? How do these forms

differ from conversation and narrative? Can you place them along the same discourse continuum with conversation and narrative? What do you think this continuum is a measure of? In other words, what feature or features distinguish the different forms of discourse?

2. Try analyzing a familiar story or joke in terms of story grammar. Can you divide it into one or more episodes? Can you identify all the elements of each episodes? If an element is missing, can you make a reasonable guess about what it is? (For example, the internal response is often missing, but can you infer what the protagonist is thinking at this point?)

Google It! Teaching Reading With Story Grammar

The concept of story grammar has become very influential in reading education in recent years. YouTube has videos demonstrating techniques for developing reading comprehension by teaching **story grammar**. You will find that, while all children can benefit from explicit story grammar instruction, it's especially helpful for those with communicative disorders, who typically don't develop good intuitions about narrative structure.

SECTION 7.3: ANAPHORA AND INFERENCE

- An anaphor is a word or phrase that refers back to an antecedent in the discourse. Anaphors are memory retrieval cues, and the proper use of anaphora considerably eases the listener's comprehension of the discourse.

- The type of anaphor that a speaker chooses depends in part on the antecedent's givenness, or the degree to which it is likely to be within the memory and attention span of the listener.

- Cohesion refers to the use of linguistic devices such as anaphors to bind the sentences of a discourse. Coherence refers to the use of schemas and logical relations to connect different parts of the discourse. A bridging inference is the use of logic or real-world experience to fill gaps in a discourse.

- Speech act theory proposes that the value of an utterance should be judged not by its literal meaning (the locution) but rather by the intention of the speaker (the illocution) and the effect it has on the listener (the perlocution).

- An indirect speech act is an utterance whose literal and intended meanings are different; indirect speech acts are often used to express politeness or to save face.

- Grice's cooperative principle provides guidelines for when the listener should take an utterance at face value or consider possible alternative meanings.

Consider the following story:

> One day, a princess was walking along a pond when the princess saw a frog. The frog told the princess that the frog was really a handsome prince. If the princess kissed the frog, the frog said, the evil spell would be broken. . . .

You probably find this story difficult to read. The two characters in the story, the princess and the frog, are always referred to by the same referring expressions, so you always know exactly who is doing what. However, when participants are asked to read stories like these, researchers find *a delay in processing when the same referring expression is used on multiple consecutive occasions in a narrative* (Almor & Eimas, 2008). This is known as the **repeated name penalty**. You already understand the repeated name penalty if you were thinking that some of those *princess*es and *frog*s need to be turned into pronouns.

Anaphora

Pronouns are one example of an **anaphor** (pronounced *AN-a-phor*), which is *a word or phrase that refers back to a previously mentioned entity in the discourse*. Let's rewrite the first sentence of our story as:

> One day a princess was walking by a pond when she saw a frog.

We call *the entity in a discourse that an anaphor refers back to* the **antecedent**. In the above example, princess is the antecedent. *The process of an anaphor referring back to an antecedent* is known as **anaphora** (pronounced a-NAPH-o-ra) or anaphoric reference. Notice how the terms anaphor, antecedent, and anaphora parallel the terms referring expression, referent, and reference. Whereas reference links the discourse and the real-world or situation model, anaphora links later portions of the discourse with earlier portions. In other words, the pronoun *she* serves as a memory cue to the previously mentioned princess, which elicits the concept of PRINCESS and its schema in the mind of the listener.

Anaphors come in various degrees. For example, let's rewrite the second sentence of our story as follows:

> The frog told the girl that it was really a handsome prince.

Notice the choice of the noun-phrase anaphor *the girl* as an anaphor for *the princess*. Although the pronoun anaphor *her* would work, the listener may need a stronger memory cue for the antecedent, given the intervening discussion about the frog. We avoid the repeated name penalty by using a **category anaphor**, which is *a noun phrase anaphor that names the category that the antecedent is a member of* (Ditman, Holcomb, & Kuperberg, 2007). Incidentally, we don't get a repeated noun penalty for the second occurrence of *frog* because its repetition is meaningful. It tells the listener that we're shifting from the perspective of the princess to that of the frog. (Also notice the switch from *a* to *the*, which we'll get to later.)

Noun-phrase anaphors that are more general in meaning are typically easier to process than those that are more specific. Consider this rewrite of the first two sentences from our story:

> One day a girl was walking by a pond when she saw a frog. The frog told the princess that it was really a handsome prince.

It's quite likely, in this case, that you initially interpreted *the princess* as referring to somebody other than the girl mentioned in the first sentence. In other words, we're not making effective use of anaphora here.

The next degree of anaphora is the pronoun. Theories of anaphor resolution generally propose that the more semantic content there is in an anaphor, the more mental resources it takes to resolve it (Dopkins & Nordlie, 2011). Thus, speakers have an incentive to use pronouns as often as possible, and listeners assume that a noun-phrase anaphor where they'd expected a pronoun signals something important, such as the introduction of a new entity into the narrative or else a shift in focus (Almor & Eimas, 2008).

Pronouns convey minimal semantic content. English pronouns, like those of many European languages, provide nothing more than gender and number information about their antecedents. Chinese pronouns are even more semantically sparse, providing only number information, with *ta* meaning 'he', 'she', or 'it', and *tamen* meaning 'they'.

The last degree of anaphora is, well, nothing. **Zero anaphora** is *the case in which no overt anaphor is used even though anaphoric reference can easily be inferred.* Consider the following sentence about the princess and the frog:

> She leaned over and gave the frog a kiss.

Recall that every verb has a subject. In this sentence, there are two verbs, *leaned* and *gave*, but only one overt subject, the pronoun anaphor *she*, which refers back to the princess. Of course, we known that *she* is also the subject of *gave*, since we can rewrite the sentence as:

> She leaned over and she gave the frog a kiss.

Some languages make far more extensive use of zero anaphora than English does. If you've ever taken a Spanish course, you know there's no "I" in "I love you." When you say *te amo*, the ending on the verb lets your sweetheart know who's doing the loving, so the subject is reduced to a zero anaphor.

Table 7.2   Degrees of Anaphora

Various anaphoric expressions can be used to refer back to an antecedent. The degree of anaphora speakers use reflects their estimate of how strong a retrieval cue their listeners will need.

Antecedent	A princess
Noun-phrase anaphor	The frog told <u>the girl</u> . . .
Pronoun anaphor	<u>She</u> felt sorry for the frog.
Zero anaphor	She leaned over and Ø gave the frog a kiss.

Another aspect of the discourse that guides speakers in the selection of anaphors is the givenness of the antecedent. **Givenness** refers *the degree to which an antecedent is likely to be within the memory and attention span of the listener* (Kitzinger, Shaw, & Toerien, 2012). When an entity is first introduced into a discourse, it's new (i.e., not given). Once an entity has been introduced, it's given for the rest of the discourse. However, an entity that hasn't been mentioned in several sentences will be less accessible to memory than one that was just mentioned in the same sentence. Thus, there's a tendency for more recently referred-to antecedents (i.e., those that are more given) to be represented by more reduced anaphors, like a pronoun or zero. But when the antecedent hasn't been referred to in a while, it's more likely to be reintroduced with a noun-phrase anaphor or even a repetition of the original antecedent.

English tends to mark newly introduced entities with indefinite determiners like *a, an,* and *some,* while it marks given noun phrases with the definite determiner *the.* Notice the alternation of *a* and *the* as the two characters (as well as the pond) are introduced into our story:

> A princess was walking by a pond when she saw a frog. The frog told the girl . . .

The first mention of each entity is marked with *a,* and each time it's mentioned after that, it's marked with *the.* In other words, *a* means something like, "Here's something new," while *the* means something like, "Remember the one I mentioned before."

Pronoun and zero anaphors tend to be used when the antecedent is highly given, that is, easily accessible in memory. However, in talk-in-interaction, we'll often use an

unheralded pronoun, that is, *a pronoun without an antecedent*, at the beginning of a discourse (Kitzinger et al., 2012). One reason we use unheralded pronouns is because the referent of the pronoun is unimportant, as for instance if I tell you, "They're raising our taxes again!" The exact referent of *they* is unimportant, but what is important is that we'll soon be paying more. Another reason we use unheralded pronouns is because the antecedent, though not mentioned, is clearly on everyone's mind. When the nurse announces to the new father, "It's a girl," we all know what *it* refers to.

Making Inferences

In Section 7.1, we defined discourse as a set of sentences that cohere about one or more related topics. To cohere means to stick together, and there are two ways that discourses can cohere (Ditman et al., 2007). One way is through **cohesion**, which refers to *the use of linguistic devices to tie together the sentences of a discourse*. Anaphora plays an important role in providing cohesion for a discourse by providing retrieval cues for previously mentioned entities. The other way is through **coherence**, which refers to *the use of schemas and logical relations to bind the sentences of a discourse together*. Unlike cohesion, which is overtly marked in the discourse, coherence must be inferred by relying on our understanding of how the world works.

Oftentimes, what is left unsaid is even more important than what is actually said in the discourse. Consider the following alternative ending to our story about the princess and the frog:

> The frog said, "Kiss me, and I'll turn into a handsome prince." The princess carefully considered the proposition. That night, she had frog legs for supper.

There's a lot that's left unsaid between the second and third sentences, and if you can span the gap here, you've just made a bridging inference (Valencia-Laver & Light, 2000). A **bridging inference** is *the use of logic or real-world experience to fill in gaps in a discourse*. Bridging inferences play an important role in the production of humor. (And I hope you found the alternative ending above at least mildly amusing.) Making bridging inferences is costly, at least as measured by reading times of written texts, but content linked with bridging inferences is also better recalled later on, probably due to the fact that it was more deeply processed.

The area of the brain responsible for processing discourse coherence is the prefontal cortex (Kim et al., 2012). This makes sense, given that the prefrontal cortex is generally involved in planning and organizing events and behaviors. However, when discourse coherence is weak and bridging inferences need to be made, the left medial temporal gyrus becomes active. This is a semantic processing region, and these data suggest that the brain is searching for meaningful ways to connect sentences that are not obviously related.

Figure 7.6 Prefrontal Cortex and Medial Temporal Gyrus

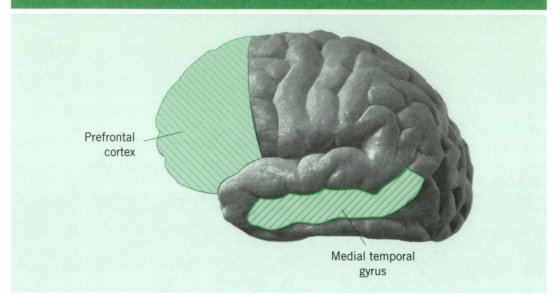

Prefrontal cortex

Medial temporal gyrus

When we make a bridging inference, we focus on the logical or commonsense structure of the discourse. This is also the case when we make a **predictive inference**, in other words, when we generate *an expectation of what comes next in a discourse based on the sequence of events so far*. However, as listeners we also make inferences that go beyond the discourse.

The ability to make inferences about the mental states and intentions of others is known as **theory of mind**. Note that this isn't a scientific theory of mental processes. Rather, the expression comes from the idea that we are constantly generating explanations, or theories, for why other people behave the way they do. Or, to put it another way, when we interact with other people, we assume they have minds of their own with perspectives and intentions that may be different from ours. As a result, we tend not to rely on the literal meaning of utterances but rather on what we believe the speaker intended (Goodman & Stuhlmüller, 2013).

It's theory of mind, for example, that enables us to distinguish between a joke and a lie (Champagne-Lavau & Joanette, 2009). Clinical data show that patients with damage to the right hemisphere often have difficulty assessing the mental states of others. They also tend to interpret all utterances literally, missing out on figurative aspects of language such as irony and metaphor. Thus, the general ability to take the perspective of others is also regularly employed as part of language comprehension.

Speech Acts

Three philosophers of language active during the middle of the twentieth century—John Searle, J. L. Austin, and Paul Grice—were influential in shifting the then common view of language as primarily a mechanism for transmitting information to a new perspective of language as a social activity. Together, they developed **speech act theory**, which is *the position that the value of an utterance lies not in the literal meaning of its words but rather in the intention of the speaker and the effect it has on the listener* (Holtgraves, 2008).

Imagine a family dinner with Mom, Dad, teenage Daughter, and school-age Son. Dad looks at teenage Daughter and says, "Could you pass me the salt?" Teenage Daughter replies, "Yes, I could," and continues eating. Mom casts an angry glance at teenage Daughter and gives a disapproving grunt. School-age Son rolls his eyes and hands poor Dad the salt.

If we judge utterances by their literal truth value, this father-daughter exchange should be deemed a communicative success. Dad inquired about daughter's ability to pass the salt, and the daughter responded truthfully. However, if we think in terms of speech acts, this exchange carried an entirely different set of meanings. Dad's intention behind his utterance was a request, even though there's nothing in the literal meaning of *Could you pass the salt?* to suggest this. By choosing to respond to the literal as opposed to intended meaning of her dad's utterance, the daughter has communicated something about her current emotional state (Dad's a dolt, this family is stupid, or something like that).

Speech act theory provides a framework for connecting the literal meaning of utterances with their intended meaning. Austin (1962) argued that every utterance has three layers of meaning:

- The **locution** is *the literal meaning of the utterance*.
- The **illocution** is *the speaker's intended meaning behind the utterance*.
- The **perlocution** is *the listener's perception of the speaker's intended meaning*.

Since, in Austin's view, the purpose of speaking was to cause things to happen, he thought of an utterance as having force. The locutionary force of Dad's utterance *Could you pass the salt?* is an inquiry into his daughter's ability. However, the illocutionary force of the utterance is to make a request. Judging from the daughter's behavior, the perlocutionary force of her dad's utterance was an inappropriate demand. (Here's a memory tip: illocution and intention, perlocution and perception.)

Table 7.3 Speech Act Theory

The three layers of meaning of the question *Do you know what time it is?* uttered by a mother to her teenaged daughter as she arrives home well after her curfew.

Locution	Literal meaning	"What's the time?"
Illocution	Intended meaning	"You're late."
Perlocution	Perceived meaning	"Mom's angry at me."

According to Searle (1969), when the locution and illocution of an utterance do not match, the result is an indirect speech act. In simpler terms, an **indirect speech act** is *an utterance whose literal and intended messages are not the same*. Although it seems counterproductive to say one thing and mean another, we are often put in this position by social constraints.

As a general rule, indirect requests are considered more polite, because instead of asking directly, you give the listener a way out. Furthermore, since indirect requests are more polite, the listener may feel more compelled to comply. In recent years, social psychologists and psycholinguistics have begun thinking of indirect requests as face-saving devices, borrowing the East Asian concept of **face** as *the personal need to be viewed as competent and to have one's actions unimpeded by others* (Pfister, 2010). The concept of face ties in notions of self-esteem and respect, and although the idea derives from East Asian philosophy, it's now considered to be a universal concept (Feeney & Bonnefon, 2012).

In the family dinner table example, Dad politely used an indirect request, which gives Daughter a way out by interpreting the utterance literally. Of course, social norms dictate interpreting an indirect request according to its illocutionary, not locutionary, force, but Daughter flouts the norm. Given the social dynamics in this family, Dad may have gotten better results from a direct request, like "Pass the salt."

Grice (1975) then added to speech act theory by proposing the **cooperative principle**, which, in a nutshell, is *the proposal that speakers should follow social norms to tailor their utterances to fit the current needs of the conversation*. It's important to understand that Grice isn't describing how conversation actually works or making prescriptions for improving communication. Rather, what he means by the cooperative principle is that any violation of the principle is meaningful (Davies, 2007). That is, as listeners we take what the speaker says at face value unless we have reason to suspect the locutionary and illocutionary forces of the utterance don't match. This triggers theory of mind processes, in which we begin making inferences about what the speaker really meant.

Paul Grice is one of the rare men in history who has had so much influence on his field that he has his own adjective, and his cooperative principle is fleshed out in terms of four **Gricean maxims** (pronounced *GRI-shin*), which are *aspects of a speaker's utterance that the listener attends to in deciding whether to accept the statement at face value* (Breheny, Ferguson, & Katsos, 2013). Grice worded the maxims in terms of what the speaker should strive for, and in brief they are:

- Quality: Be truthful.
- Quantity: Give just enough information, not too much or too little.
- Relevance: Stay on topic.
- Manner: Be clear and unambiguous.

When Dad politely asked, "Could you pass the salt?" he violated the Gricean maxim of manner. This doesn't mean he violated the rules of conversation. Rather, it cues the listener to look for an underlying intended meaning instead of relying on the literal meaning of the utterance. Speech act theory and the cooperative principle have generated a considerable amount of research over the years, far more than we can cover in this book.

Table 7.4 Gricean Maxims	
Philosopher of language Paul Grice proposed four maxims of conversation. These maxims are rules of thumb, not absolute rules. Furthermore, the violation of a maxim implies that the speaker's meaning is different from the literal meaning of the utterance. It's up to the listener to guess what that intended meaning is.	
Quality	Make your contribution as informative as required; don't say too much or too little; make the strongest statement you can.
Quantity	Don't say what you believe to be false; don't say something that you lack adequate evidence for.
Relation	Be relevant; stay on topic.
Manner	Avoid obscurity of expression; avoid ambiguity; be brief and orderly.

Source: Grice (1975).

In Sum

Anaphors serve as memory retrieval cues that refer back to antecedents earlier in the discourse. The type of anaphor used, whether full noun phrase, pronoun, or zero, depends in part on the givenness of the antecedent, that is, how likely it is to still be in the listener's memory and attention span. Linguistic devices like anaphors provide a discourse with cohesion, binding its sentences together. Likewise, schemas and logical relations give discourses their coherence, and when there are gaps in the discourse, the listener must make bridging inferences to span them. Speech act theory views language as social interaction and asserts that the intended meaning of an utterance (its illocution) and its effect on the listener (its perlocution) are more important than its face value (its locution). When the locution and illocution of an utterance don't match, it's considered an indirect speech act. According to Grice's cooperative principle, violations of conversational norms are meaningful and lead the listener to make inferences about the speaker's intentions. For example, indirect speech acts are often used to be polite or to avoid threatening the listener's face, or self-esteem.

Review Questions

1. Explain the concepts of anaphor, antecedent, and anaphora, and how they are related. What are the parallels and differences between anaphora and reference? What is the repeated name penalty, and how is it relevant to anaphora?

2. What is givenness, and how is it marked in discourse? What is the relationship between anaphora and givenness? Illustrate with a short example discourse.

3. Distinguish between cohesion and coherence. How is each achieved? What are bridging and predictive inferences, and how are they related to coherence?

4. What is speech act theory? Explain Austin's three layers of utterance meaning (locution, illocution, and perlocution), illustrating with an example. In terms of speech act theory, what is an indirect speech act? What are indirect speech acts commonly used for?

5. Discuss Grice's cooperative principle and the four Gricean maxims. Are these guidelines for the speaker or for the listener? Explain.

Thought Questions

1. Find two or three humorous stories on the Internet or in a popular magazine like *Reader's Digest* and analyze the anaphoric structure of each text. First, underline each newly introduced entity. Next, circle each anaphor and draw an arrow from it to its antecedent. What seems to be determining whether the writer chose a noun-phrase or pronoun anaphor?

2. Consider the punchlines of the humorous stories you just analyzed. Do these stories lead you to make bridging or predictive inferences? If so, how did these inferences affect the humor of the story.

Google It! Flouting Gricean Maxims

If you're interested in learning more about the **Gricean maxims**, you can find plenty of sites of the web that discuss these. Remember that a **violation of Gricean maxims** implies that the literal meaning and the speaker's intention are not the same, and you can find plenty of examples of **flouting Gricean maxims** online, some of them quite humorous.

SECTION 7.4: DEVELOPMENT OF DISCOURSE ABILITIES

- The turn-taking behavior of conversation is learned in infancy during face-to-face interactions with the caregiver, who treats the infant's vocalizations as conversational turns; around a year of age, when the child begins producing words, the caregiver starts responding to the content of the child's utterance with repetitions and elaborations.

- Some children with developmental language delay eventually catch up with their peers, but many experience disruption of their socialization process. Although their turn-taking behavior is normal, their utterances are brief, marked by ellipsis and formulaic expressions, and they provide little content for caregivers to elaborate on.

- There are two types of cospeech gesture: indexical gestures are used to point to objects in the environment as referents in conversation, while iconic gestures are used to imitate actions. Iconic gestures tend to line up at the clause level in adult speech, and children do not master language-specific gesture patterns until grade school years.

- Although children are sensitive to the emotional content of prosody when heard in isolation, they tend to ignore it when it conflicts with the semantics of an utterance. As a result they are prone to interpreting utterances literally; they are, however, adept at inferring speaker intentions from context cues.

- Use of the Gricean maxims sometimes leads adults to make inferences that are not logically valid (although they are pragmatically sound); because it takes years for children to learn the Gricean maxims, there are some cases, as in the interpretation of quantity words like *some* and *all*, where child think more rationally than do adults.

- In specific language impairment, deficits in syntax and expressive vocabulary affect the ability to construct coherent discourse; in pragmatic language impairment, the child displays no structural language difficulties but struggles with the social and pragmatic aspects of discourse, which can lead to various behavioral disorders.

The family dinner is winding down. "Can I be excused?" the son asks. "You mean, 'May I be excused'," his mother chides him. "OK," says the son, "*May* I be excused?" His mother reminds him of the importance of proper English, and when she's done, the son asks, "Now can I be excused?"

Parents may think they teach their children how to speak, but in fact they don't, at least not in such an explicit fashion. Rather, caregivers play a supporting role in the language development process as their children venture out into the terrain of social language interaction.

Conversational Turn-Taking

In Section 7.1, we compared the seamless turn-taking of everyday conversation to the graceful moves of a pair of figure skaters. Like figure skating, conversation is a skill that takes years of practice to develop, and we begin the learning process shortly after birth.

By two months of age, infants already coordinate their behaviors with those of their caregiver during face-to-face interactions (Henning & Striano, 2011). Caregivers often imitate their baby's vocalizations and facial expressions, thus providing a framework for the development of turn-taking skills. Because caregivers respond in a timely and predictable fashion, infants experience these exchanges as something they caused. In other words, the beginnings of turn-taking behavior are in the natural reactions of the infant, which the caregiver treats as meaningful turns (Berducci, 2010). This means that it is the infant, and not the caregiver, that drives the interaction, with the caregiver serving the role of facilitator.

Infants seem to be attracted to adult faces that mimic their current emotional state (Henning & Striano, 2011). Thus, when caregivers respond in kind to their infants' natural reactions, they engage and hold their attention. This process of infant engagement through caregiver imitation is studied by using a **perturbation paradigm**, which is *an experimental procedure that disrupts normal infant-caregiver interaction to observe the infant's response*. One example is the still-face paradigm, in which the caregiver interrupts a normal interaction by suddenly shifting to a neutral facial expression while maintaining eye contact with the infant. Another example is the replay paradigm, in which the infant interacts with the caregiver via video screen. After a certain period of time, the original session is replayed so that the caregiver's responses no longer line up with the infant's current behaviors. In both cases, the result is the same, with the infant averting eye gaze and becoming agitated or disinterested.

Conversational turn-taking behavior develops from prelinguistic interactions between the infant and the caregiver. At first, the caregiver responds to nonlinguistic vocalizations and gestures; but when the toddler begins producing words, the caregiver starts responding to the content of the child's utterances instead (van Balkom, Verhoeven, & van Weerdenberg, 2010). Again, it's largely the infant who leads the interaction, with the caregiver serving as facilitator by providing repetitions and elaborations. For instance, when the child points and says "doggie," the mother responds with something like, "Yes, that's a doggie! Look at the doggie! What's the doggie doing?"

Late Talkers

The process of learning conversation through the facilitation of caregivers is disrupted when the child experiences a **developmental language delay**. This is *a condition marked by slower than normal development of expressive language during the first few years of life even though hearing, motor, and cognitive functions are otherwise in the normal range* (van Balkom et al., 2010). Sometimes these so-called late talkers catch up with their peers and progress normally after that. But others descend into a downward spiral that negatively impacts their overall socialization process. Because they speak less, they provide their caregivers with less to respond to.

Children with developmental language delay understand the basic mechanics of conversational turn-taking, since that's learned during prelinguistic infancy. As a result, their overall pattern of conversational turn-taking doesn't differ from that of normally developing children. However, the content of their turns is considerably reduced, as these children have a tendency to speak in single words or short phrases as opposed to complete sentences. Of course, in everyday conversation we often speak in sentence fragments, such as in an exchange like "Eat yet?" "Not yet." However, children with developmental language delay are far more likely to use **ellipsis**, or *the deletion of sentence elements that can be inferred from context*. They also make more use of pointing to indicate referents.

It's important to understand that children with developmental language delay are clearly aware of themselves as a partner in a two-way interaction and know the general rules of turn-taking (van Balkom et al., 2010). For example, they become quite adept at backchannels, using them even more than normally developing children do. It appears that children with developmental language delay adopt a strategy of encouraging their partner to talk so they don't have to. Thus, their difficulty with conversation doesn't seem to stem from theory of mind issues, as is believed to be the case in autism spectrum disorders. Rather, they seem to be suffering from a lack of expressive vocabulary, as evidenced, for example, by their over-reliance on formulaic utterances and set expressions.

Because children with developmental language delay talk less, caregivers have less to respond to (van Balkom et al., 2010). Mothers of these children employ various coping strategies, which, although well-meaning, are not always beneficial to the child's long-term development. Some mothers adopt a high-control strategy, directing the flow of topics and commenting more on the child's meager utterances. However, these mothers don't just simply have a controlling personality, since they interact with their other children in a normal fashion. Other mothers become less responsive to the content of the child's attempts at utterances, shifting the topic instead toward their own interests.

The best results are seen in cases where the mother displays high sensitivity to the interests of the child and follows up on conversation topics the child proposes. These children tend to be more engaged in conversation and the flow of topics is smoother than when the mother takes a more directive or less responsive style. In other words, children with developmental language delay benefit most from additional facilitative support as opposed to direct guidance.

The importance of letting the child take the lead applies as well to the initial learning of turn-taking behavior in infancy. Preterm infants are generally less active or vocal than full-term infants (Reissland & Stephenson, 1999). As a result, some mothers of preterm infants try to compensate by becoming even more active and vocal with their babies. However, this just overstimulates the infant, making it even quieter. Instead, when mothers only imitate the behaviors and vocalizations of their infants, these babies in turn become more active and engage in more eye contact with their caregivers.

Gesture

When people speak they also gesture, and we can identify two different types of meaningful gestures. The first is an **indexical gesture**, which is *a movement of an upper limb to point out a referent in a conversation*. For example, the question "What's that?" is often accompanied by an indexical gesture toward the thing referred to as *that*. The second is an **iconic gesture**, which is *a movement of one or both upper limbs to imitate an action*.

Caregivers often use indexical gestures as they interact with their children (So & Lim, 2012). For example, parents will often play a sort of naming game with their infants, pointing out objects and then naming them: "Oh, what's that? Yes, that's a balloon. And what's this? Oh, this is a flower." As the child's language skills develop, the caregiver continues to use indexical gestures, pointing out newly introduced entities in the discourse. Young children seem to be sensitive to these discourse cues and appear to use them in learning to associate words with the things they refer to. Children also learn to use indexical gestures when they're unsure of the name for an object. We've already seen that children with developmental language delay rely heavily on indexical gestures, at least in part to compensate for their lack of expressive vocabulary.

Iconic gesture seems to be a universal phenomenon, but it is also shaped by the specific language it's used with (Özyürek et al., 2008). Iconic gestures are often used in conjunction with descriptions of motion events, with the speaker making hand or finger movements to mimic the manner and path of the action. A common example is two dangling fingers waggling across the space in front of the speaker to representing walking along a path. Languages differ in the way they represent motion events that describe a manner of movement along a trajectory. Some languages, like English, encode the manner with a verb and the path with a preposition, as in the sentence *Jack and Jill rolled down the hill*. Thus, in English this event is expressed in a single clause consisting of a verb plus prepositional phrase. However, other languages, like Turkish, express the same event in two clauses, with one clause describing the path and the other describing the manner. Such a language would describe the Jack and Jill incident as *Jack and Jill descended the hill while rolling.*

Cospeech gestures, or *hand movements that speakers make while they talk*, tend to be lined up at the clause level (Özyürek et al., 2008). Thus, an English speaker would likely describe Jack and Jill's tumble with a single rolling gesture in downward motion, while a Turkish speaker would likely use two separate gestures, one accompanying the downward path verb (*descend*) and the other accompanying the manner verb (*rolling*). Language-specific aspects of cospeech gesture are not fully developed until at least nine years of age. When younger English-speaking children employ cospeech gestures while describing motion event, they tend to use two separate gestures, one for the manner and the other for the path, just as Turkish-speaking children (and adults) do. Only later do the English-speaking children learn to combine manner and path into a single cospeech gesture.

Figure 7.7 Iconic Gestures

In a study of the role of iconic gestures in speech perception, participants watched brief videos of a man and a woman talking and gesturing about common actions, such as cutting or stirring. Their task was to indicate whether the man or the woman was speaking. Reaction time was slower when the gesture was incongruent with the speech, especially when the gender of the person and the voice were the same. Furthermore, the incongruent conditions also elicited an N400, indicating that iconic gestures are interpreted as meaningful.

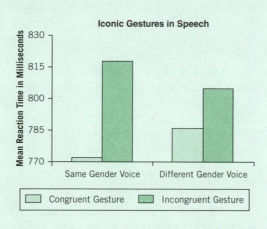

Source: Kelly, Creigh, and Bartolotti (2010).

Figure 7.8   Cospeech Gestures

Cospeech gestures are an important part of talk-in-interaction, and they often provide visual aids to accompany speech.

Source: ©iStockphoto.com/ Photodjo.

Prosody

Recall that prosody refers to the fluctuations in pitch, intensity, and syllable duration over the extent of an utterance, and it's perceived as tone of voice or "the way" a sentence is said. You should also remember that prosody conveys both emotional and syntactic information. Adults and even young children can distinguish a "happy" from a "sad" tone of voice, even in a foreign language (Hupp & Jungers, 2013). Preschoolers, like adults, can also use prosodic cues to phrase boundaries to interpret ambiguous sentences, although it takes them longer to process this information (Zhou, Crain, & Zhan, 2012).

Prosody can also be used as a form of sound symbolism (Hupp & Jungers, 2012). Try saying the phrase *a tiny mouse and a great big elephant*, using your voice to convey a sense of the relative sizes. You probably said *tiny* with a high pitch and *great big* with a low pitch. In the real world, small things tend to make high-pitched noises and large things low-pitched noises, and so we can use pitch prosody to convey information about size. We also use speaking rate to convey a sense of speed in describing fast or slow actions. Even preschoolers are sensitive to this kind of sound-symbolism prosody and use it in their own speech.

Since fetuses can hear, and are sensitive to, the prosody of their mother's voice during the last trimester of pregnancy, and since neonates can distinguish their mother's language from another language on the basis of prosody shortly after birth, it's no surprise that even young children have nearly adult-like mastery of it. What is surprising, though, is the degree to which children under the age of nine tend to disregard prosodic information when inferring a speaker's intention. In what is known as the **lexical bias**, there's *a tendency among children to rely on the literal meaning of an utterance even when prosody strongly suggests a nonliteral meaning* (Aguert et al., 2010). For example, when a speaker says "I like it" but does so with an "unhappy" tone of voice, adults infer that she doesn't really like it, but children infer that she does. However, when the utterance is low-pass filtered so that the language is unintelligible and only the prosody remains, the children correctly infer the speaker doesn't like it.

Prosody is also an important cue in detecting irony and sarcasm. The utterance "That's great!" spoken with a negative tone of voice is easily recognized as sarcastic by adults but not by children until they are into their school years (Aguert et al., 2010). However, this doesn't mean that children this age don't understand irony and sarcasm, since they are able to use situational context to infer nonliteral meanings of utterances.

Gricean Maxims

The lexical bias exhibited by children doesn't mean that they take every utterance at face value. Rather, it seems that children have difficulty interpreting prosody when it conflicts with semantics and context (Aguert et al., 2010). In fact, preschoolers are already quite adept at using the Gricean maxims to make inferences about speakers' intentions (Eskritt, Whalen, & Lee, 2008). Before they're three years old, children have a grasp of the Gricean maxim of quantity and can infer how much information a speaker is asking for (Ferrier, Dunham, & Dunham, 2000). By thirty-three months, children will respond to the general query "What?" with a complete repetition of their previous utterance, but they will respond to the specific query "Piggy is in what?" with a specific response, such as "In the barnyard." On the other hand, twenty-seven-month-olds tend to respond to both types of questions by repeating what they'd said.

The Gricean maxims have generated a lot of research on a topic known as **scalar implicature**. This term refers to *a listener's inference that the speaker's use of a weaker term means that a stronger term is not true* (Politzer-Ahles et al., 2013). Research on scalar implicature most commonly examines listener inferences about the quantity terms *some* and *all*, but other weaker-stronger pairs such as *or-and* have been studied as well.

Imagine your professor announces, "Some of the students passed the test." Do you think this statement necessarily means that not all of the students passed? Perhaps your reasoning goes like this: If all of the students passed, he would have said *all*. But he said *some*, so that must mean *not all*. This is exactly what is meant by scalar implicature. Yet your reasoning is not logical. If it's true that all of the students

Figure 7.9   Scalar Implicature

If it is true that *all* of the faces are smiling, then it is also true that *some* of the faces are smiling.

Some of the faces are smiling.

All of the faces are smiling.

passed, then the statement *some of the students passed* is necessarily true. But if your professor said *some* when he meant *all*, you probably feel he was lying or at least being facetious.

By adulthood, the Gricean maxims have become so ingrained in us that it's hard for us to understand that the inferences we draw from them are not always logical. Preschoolers are certainly not known for their logical thinking, but they do understand that *all* logically entails *some* (Foppolo, Guasti, & Chierchia, 2012). For example, when presented with a statement such as *Some elephants have trunks*, many adults will respond false, since *all* elephants have trunks. Preschoolers, on the other hand, generally reply that the statement is true. When asked follow-up questions, these children demonstrate that they know all elephants have trunks. Therefore, they aren't making the scalar inference that *some* means *not all*. It's generally not until well into the school years that children start thinking like adults when it comes to scalar terms.

Discourse Impairments

In Chapter 6, we learned that children with specific language impairment (SLI) have difficulties with sentences because they tend to omit grammatical suffixes and function words. SLI is not due to perceptual, motor, or cognitive deficits, and hence it's a disorder that is considered specific to language.

Although the symptoms of SLI are most evident in sentence structure, children with the disorder also exhibit considerable difficulty constructing narratives (Colozzo et al., 2011). Not only do they produce narratives with more grammatical errors than do normally developing children, they also produce stories with less content and fewer story grammar elements. Children with diagnosed language impairment display varying degrees of difficulty with narrative form and content, often exhibiting a greater deficit in one than the other; but underlying these problems seems to be a basic deficit in syntactic structure and a lack of expressive vocabulary.

Sometimes the narrative difficulties of children with SLI go unnoticed. These children produce stories with simple vocabulary and sentence structure, and so on the surface their productions appear to be relatively error free; but they are also much less complex than the narratives produced by their peers. In other words, these children seem to have some intuitions about their language limitations and "play it safe."

Children with SLI often have difficulties making bridging inferences, suggesting that they may not be adequately representing story elements in memory (Karasinski & Weismer, 2010). These children often show deficits in working memory tasks, and neuroimaging studies suggest that they may have abnormalities in brain areas involved in verbal working memory. Thus, memory constraints seem to be limiting their ability to make inferences, especially when those narrative elements linked by the inference are some distance apart.

While the ability to make bridging inferences requires adequate working memory capacity, the ability to make inferences about the speaker's intentions relies on theory of mind abilities; and some children with language impairment experience difficulty with this as well (Spanoudis, Natsopoulos, & Panayiotou, 2007). It's easy to see how the sentence-level impairments of SLI impact the production of narrative, since sentences are the building blocks of discourse. However, some children who show no evidence of sentence-level difficulty nevertheless exhibit problems in both the perception and production of discourse. In particular, they seem to have difficulty inferring the mental states of others, but they also have problems using context cues to infer nonliteral interpretations of utterances.

Pragmatic language impairment, then, is *a developmental disorder in which the child has structural language skills intact but still experiences difficulties with the social and contextual aspects of discourse, such as inferring nonliteral meanings of utterances* (Ketelaars et al., 2010). A problem with pragmatics, in particular theory of mind, is a symptom of autism spectrum disorders. However, children with pragmatic language disorder do not show the other typical symptoms of autism, suggesting that these are separate disorders.

Pragmatic language impairment often leads to behavioral problems such as hyperactivity, aggression, or excessive shyness. These children are also frequently given a diagnosis of attention deficit hyperactivity disorder (ADHD). Although more research is needed, the evidence so far suggests that it could be that pragmatic language impairment leads to these other problems because of the way it disrupts the child's socialization process.

In Sum

From their first days, infants develop deep emotional bonds with their primary caregivers, typically their mothers, by engaging in mutual eye gaze and face-to-face interactions. Mothers treat their infants' vocalizations as conversational utterance, thus facilitating the development of turn-taking behavior. When infants start speaking, their mothers respond with repetitions and elaborations. However, children with developmental language delay begin talking late and are less expressive than their peers, so their caregivers have fewer opportunities to facilitate the development of their conversational skills. Children use cospeech gestures from early on, using indexical gestures along with their caregivers to point out intended referents. Preschoolers also use iconic gestures, but they don't master language-specific patterns until school age. Although preschoolers are sensitive to emotional prosody, they tend to disregard it when inferring a speaker's intention, relying instead on the literal meaning of the utterance and cues from context. It's also not until the early school years that children use Gricean maxims to infer speaker intent in an adult-like manner. Children with specific language impairment also have trouble constructing coherent discourse because of their syntactic and vocabulary deficits. On the other hand, some children with no discernable syntax or vocabulary deficit still experience difficulty with the social and pragmatic aspects of language. Pragmatic language impairment can lead to behavioral problems and may be associated with other disorders such as attention deficit hyperactivity disorder and autism spectrum disorders.

Review Questions

1. Describe how infants learn conversational turn-taking behavior. What role do caregivers play in this process? How is the perturbation paradigm used to study infant-caregiver interactions?

2. Describe the characteristics of children with developmental language delay. Also discuss the various coping strategies caregivers engage in and the effects they have on these children. What seems to be the best approach?

3. Discuss the development of cospeech gesture. What is the difference between an indexical and an iconic gesture? Is there a difference in the development of these two kinds of gesture?

4. Discuss the perception of emotional prosody and the lexical bias in young children. Also discuss the use of sound-symbolism prosody in children and adults.

5. Distinguish between specific language disorder and pragmatic language disorder. What other conditions may be associated with pragmatic language disorder?

6. What is scalar implicature? How does it derive from the Gricean maxims? How do children perform differently from adults in this regard?

Thought Questions

1. The "pushy parent" industry provides all sorts of products for ambitious parents who want to accelerate their baby's language development, whether it be by teaching them sign language, how to read, or a second language like Spanish or Chinese. Given what you've read about language development, do you think these products are likely to be helpful? Might they even be harmful? Explain. Based on what you know about child language development, what sorts of things should parents do to help children learn language?

Google It! Still Face Experiment

If you're interested in learning more about the **still face experiment**, you can find video clips of it on YouTube. You can see how the experiment is performed and the way the baby reacts when her mother suddenly stops responding.

CONCLUSION

One of the characteristics of human language that distinguishes it from animal communication systems is its hierarchical structure. At the bottom we have meaningless speech sounds. At the next level, we combine phonemes to produce meaningful words. After that, we combine words to generate sentences that express our thoughts. And at the top level, we combine sentences to build conversations and narratives. Thus, discourse is the highest level of language analysis. In other words, discourse is what language is all about. The machinery of phonology, morphology, and syntax all work toward its production. And in turn, the function of spoken discourse is to serve as the social glue that binds members of our species together.

In the next chapter, we'll be looking at another form of discourse, the written text, and how we interact with it. We've engaged in spoken discourse, chatting and swapping stories, since the dawn of our species, but written text is a fairly recent invention in terms of the history of *Homo sapiens*. However, the ability to preserve discourse has radically changed the nature of our species and its place in the world.

CROSS-CULTURAL PERSPECTIVE: "Hey, you!"

In most respects, English is a fairly normal language, but it does have one characteristic that makes it highly unusual among the languages of the world, namely its second-person pronoun. We use the same word, *you*, whether we're addressing one person or a million, and whether our addressee is our most intimate friend or the president of the United States.

In English, the first- and third-person pronouns have different singular and plural forms—*I* versus *we*, *he/she/it* versus *they*. But not *you*. In Chinese, for example, the second-person pronoun *nĭ* is made plural by adding the plural suffix *-men*; in other words, *nĭ* means 'you, just one' while *nĭmen* means 'you, more than one', sort of like the plural pronoun *yous* that can still be heard among Irish immigrant populations along the eastern seaboard of the United States.

Many languages also use different pronouns depending on the level of familiarity between the speaker and hearer. In French, *tu* is 'you, singular' and *vous* is 'you, plural'. However, you can only use *tu* with someone you're fairly intimate with, such as a family member, close friend, or lover, or else with someone whose social status is far beneath yours, such as young children. Otherwise, you need to address your listener as *vous*, even if there's only one. Other European languages have similar formal/informal distinctions in their second-person pronouns. Even the non-European language Chinese makes this distinction, with *nín* meaning 'you, formal'.

It gets even more complex among the languages of East and Southeast Asia, where both first- and second-person references change depending on the exact relationship between speaker and listener. As a result, there are dozens of ways to refer to yourself and the other member of the conversation, depending on the situation. Since I know Japanese, I'll describe how the system works in that language. However, many other languages in the region work in a similar fashion, including Burmese, Javanese, Khmer, Korean, Malay, and Vietnamese (Jaszczolt, 2013).

Let's sample the byzantine Japanese pronoun system by tracing the developing relationship between a typical Japanese man we'll call Yoshi and a typical Japanese woman we'll call Yoko. Yoshi and Yoko encounter each other for the first time at a formal business meeting. Each addresses the other with the standard formal pronouns *watashi* for 'I' and *anata* for 'you'. There's a mutual attraction, and through the first few dates they awkwardly continue with the formal pronouns, or else they avoid using pronouns altogether, which is easy to do in Japanese.

As Yoshi and Yoko become intimate, there's a shift in referring expressions. Yoshi now uses "intimate" pronouns, referring to himself as *boku* and his girlfriend as *kimi*. Yoko, however, can't use these forms, as they're mainly reserved for male speakers. Instead, she uses "reduced formal" pronouns, referring to herself as *atashi* and her boyfriend as *anta*.

Ten years and two kids later, Yoshi and Yoko have settled into the "old married couple" system of pronouns. Yoshi now uses the "arrogant" pronouns, referring to himself as *ore* and his wife as *omae*. But even after all these years, Yoko still defers to her husband and uses the reduced formal pronouns *atashi* and *anta* with him. Such is the lot of a married woman in Japan.

There are many other relationships a Japanese person navigates on a daily basis, and each of them has its own set of first- and second-person referring expressions. Using the wrong forms can cause offense and damage the relationship. Yet by adulthood the speakers of the language have internalized the system, and they negotiate its complexities with relatively few errors.

KEY TERMS

Anaphor	Cohesion	Endogenous oscillators
Anaphora	Common ground	Entrainment
Antecedent	Conversational fillers	Episode
Backchannels	Cooperative principle	Executive functions
Beat	Cospeech gestures	Face
Bridging inference	Decontextualization	Givenness
Category anaphor	Developmental language delay	Gricean maxims
Coherence		Iconic gesture
	Ellipsis	

Illocution

Indexical gesture

Indirect speech act

Interlocutors

Lexical bias

Locution

Narrative

Overlaps

Perlocution

Perturbation paradigm

Pragmatic language impairment

Pragmatics

Predictive inference

Prefrontal cortex

Principle of no gaps/no overlaps

Privileged ground

Reference

Referent

Referring expression

Relevance theory

Repeated name penalty

Scalar implicature

Schema

Situation model

Speech act theory

Story grammar

Talk-in-interaction

Theory of mind

Transition relevance place

Turn-constructional unit

Unheralded pronoun

Zero anaphora

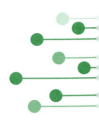

CHAPTER 8

Reading and Writing

With but a few exceptions, we all learn to speak our native language. However, it wasn't until modern times that most people learned to read and write. Over evolutionary time, our brains have adapted to the needs of processing spoken language, but natural selection hasn't had time to meet the demands of reading. Instead, we recycle brain systems originally designed to serve other functions, training them instead to take visual inputs and hook them up with the language system. As a result, all writing systems have common features that enable them to be processed by the same brain areas.

It takes many years of training to turn a brain into a reading machine, and not all of us succeed. A significant percentage of the population struggles with reading throughout their lives, even though they're intelligent and well educated. However, an ability to read well is essential in our modern society. Thus, a great amount of research has been devoted to understanding the underlying causes of dyslexia and to finding effective interventions for helping those who suffer from reading impairment to develop the literacy skills they need to be successful in life.

SECTION 8.1: WRITING SYSTEMS

- Because the brain has evolved dedicated systems for processing speech, we all learn spoken language effortlessly as we grow up; however, reading is a recent invention that requires years of effortful training with varying degrees of success.

- There are three types of writing systems: logographic systems use symbols to represent words or morphemes; syllabaries represent each possible syllable of a language with a different symbol; and alphabets represent language at the phoneme level.

- Orthography is the set of rules for writing the words of a language; the orthography of a language is said to be shallow when there is a close match between spelling and pronunciation (as in Spanish), and it is said to be deep when spelling and pronunciation are poorly matched (as in English).

- Homophones are words with the same pronunciation but different meanings and often with different spellings (as in *to, too,* and *two*); homographs are words with different pronunciations and meanings but the same spelling (as in *read* or *lead*).

- The visual word form area is a region at the boundary between the left inferior temporal and parietal lobes that processes the shapes of written words regardless of the language or type of script.

- The observation that all writing systems are processed the same way in the brain is explained in terms of the neuronal recycling hypothesis, which proposes that brain areas designed for one function can be recruited to perform another, somewhat similar function.

Humans have likely been speaking since the dawn of the species a quarter million years ago, and, as we saw in Chapter 1, their predecessors may have used pidgin-like proto-language for many millennia before that. Over evolutionary time, the human brain has been molded for language as regions like Broca's and Wernicke's areas have become specialized for speech production and perception. We've also seen how language has encroached on other functional areas of the brain as well. For example, the cerebellum, which coordinates the rhythmic movements of the limbs when walking, also guides the rhythmic production of syllables when talking. In short, natural selection has re-engineered the human brain for speech.

Reading, on the other hand, is an entirely different matter. Almost all of us learn our mother tongue effortlessly as a normal part of growing up. Learning to read, however, is hard work, and many of us struggle with the task even in adulthood. In fact, reading is a very unnatural act for humans. Writing is a recent invention, going back only a few thousand years, a mere blink of the eye in evolutionary terms. Hence, there are no predesignated areas of the brain for processing the written word. Instead, we make use of areas originally intended for other functions and retrain them to process reading and writing. Consequently, all writing systems have certain features in common that enable them to be learned by the brain.

Writing Systems of the World

For most of our existence as a species, we humans have lived in small bands hunting game and gathering the fruits of the forest. Hunter-gatherers have no need for writing, as their societies are small and tightly knit, their possessions are few, and they maintain their accumulated folklore through oral transmission from one generation to the next. But as humans shifted their lifestyles to agrarian city-states within the last 10,000–15,000 years, they learned to keep careful records. Farmers needed accurate calendars to know when to sow their crops, and businessmen needed to keep accounts of commercial transactions.

Full-fledged writing systems evolved out of these early calendars and tally sheets. Civilizations in the Middle East started keeping written records about 5,000 years ago, and the Chinese followed suit a couple thousand years later. Historians still debate whether the Chinese came up with the idea of writing on their own or picked up the idea from the Middle Easterners (Fischer, 2001). However, rising civilizations in Central America also developed writing systems somewhat later and clearly without any knowledge of writing in the Old World (Gnanadesikan, 2009). Until the fairly recent past, few people ever learned to read and write, and it was a skill mainly reserved for priests and bureaucrats.

All writing systems of the world fall into one of three types. However, these categories are fuzzy, and many writing systems straddle the boundaries. The first writing systems were all logographic. A **logogram** is *a written symbol that represents a word or morpheme*. The early Middle Eastern and Central American scripts were logographic, but none of these are in use today. The Chinese, however, still use essentially the same logographic script they invented 3,000 years ago. To fully represent a language in a logographic script requires thousands of logograms, one for each morpheme in the language. Obviously, such systems are taxing on memory and take years to learn.

Figure 8.1   Sample of Ancient Egyptian Hieroglyphic Writing

Sample from the Ani Papyrus, dating back more than 3,000 years. Egyptian hieroglyphs were logograms, but they could also be used for their phonetic value, much like Chinese script today.

Source: Bridgeman Art Library v. Corel Corp.

Foreign names and loanwords pose a particular problem for logographic systems, and the general solution is to use logograms for their pronunciation value only. For example, the Chinese call the US capital *huá-shèng-dùn*, written with the characters 华盛顿. Literally, these three logograms mean something like "flowery-abundant-pause," but they're used solely as a pronunciation guide and not as an indication of meaning. Other logographic systems, such as Egyptian hieroglyphics, also used otherwise meaningful characters for their phonetic value only (Gnanadesikan, 2009).

This practice was taken to its logical conclusion in Japan. A millennium and a half ago, Buddhist missionaries began arriving in Japan from the mainland, bringing with them not only their religion but also the Chinese writing system. At first, educated Japanese simply wrote in Chinese when they wanted to compose a text. This situation was similar to that of medieval European scholars who wrote in Latin even though it wasn't their mother tongue. In the beginning there seems to have been a psychological connection between the script and the language, and it was only later generations that saw how a foreign script could be used to write their native tongue.

Over time, the Japanese began using Chinese characters to represent Japanese words. But many of their words and morphemes had no direct equivalents in Chinese, so they would also use characters for their sound values only. Early in this transitional period, writers were free to choose any character that sounded like the syllable they wanted to represent, but eventually the Japanese agreed on a set of about fifty symbols that could stand for all possible syllables in the language. Thus, in Japan the Chinese logographic system evolved into a native **syllabary**, which is *a writing system that represents each syllable with a different symbol.* Over time, these syllable characters were simplified to the point that they bear little resemblance to the original logograms.

In fact, the Japanese invented not just one syllabary but two. While the bureaucrats favored an angular style known as katakana, the Buddhist monks preferred the rounded hiragana style (Gnanadesikan, 2009). In modern times, the two syllabaries have been merged, such that hiragana is used to write native words while katakana is for foreign loanwords or for emphasis, serving much the same purpose as italics do in English. However, the Japanese didn't give up on Chinese characters altogether. In a typical Japanese text, the content words—nouns, verbs, and adjectives—are written with logograms while the function morphemes are written in hiragana and the loanwords (mostly from English) in katakana. This arrangement no doubt makes Japanese the most complex writing system currently in use.

A similar process occurred on the other side of Asia. As the logographic writing of the early Middle Eastern empires spread to the developing civilizations of the Mediterranean region, the logograms were generally used for their phonetic values (Gnanadesikan, 2009). In some cases, such as Hebrew and Arabic, only consonants are written and vowels must be inferred from context. In these languages, most of the meaning is carried by consonants while vowels are highly predictable, so this arrangement isn't as strange as it sounds. The Greeks were the first to invent a full **alphabet**, which is *a writing system that represents each phoneme with a different symbol.*

The Roman alphabet, which English speakers use, and the Cyrillic alphabet, which the Russians use, are descendants of the first Greek alphabet.

Table 8.1 Scripts Around the World	
A sample written English sentence with its equivalent in several other languages that use different scripts from the Latin alphabet. Translations by the author using Google Translate.	
English	Although humans have been speaking since the beginning of the species, writing is a fairly recent invention.
Chinese	尽管人类一直在讲，因为物种的开始，写作是一个相当新的发明。
Japanese	人間が種の初めから話してきたが、書き込みは比較的最近の発明である。
Korean	인간 종의 초부디 말하는되었지만, 기입은 비교적 최근의 발명이다.
Arabic	على الرغم من أن البشر قد تحدث منذ بداية الأنواع، والكتابة و هو اختراع حديث نسبيا.
Bengali	মানুষরে পরজাতরি শুরুতে থকেে বলতে হয়ছে,ে যদিও লখেঁার একটিমি টিামুটি সিাম্পরতকি আবষিকার.
Armenian	Չնայած մարդիկ արդեն խոսում սկզբից տեսակների, գրելու բավականին վերջերս գյուտը.
Greek	Παρά το γεγονός ότι οι άνθρωποι έχουν μιλώντας από την αρχή του είδους, το γράψιμο είναι μια αρκετά πρόσφατη εφεύρεση.
Gujarati	મનુષ્યો આ જાતિના શરૂઆત પછીથી બોલતા કરવામાં આવી છે, તેમ છતાં, લેખન એકદમ તાજેતરની શોધ છે.
Hebrew	למרות בני אדם רבב מדברים מאז מחילת עמין ,האנושית, הבית היא האצמה השדח חיסתי.
Hindi	मनुष्य पुरजाति की शुरुआत के बाद से बोल रहा है, लेखन एक काफी हाल ही आविष्कार है.
Kannada	ಮಾನವರು ಜಾತೀಯ ಆರಂಭದೊಂದಲೂ ಮಾತನಾಡುವ ಮಾಡಲಾಗಿದೆ ಆದಾಗ್ಯೂ, ಬರವಣಿಗೆ ತಕ್ಕಮಟ್ಟಿಗೆ ಇತ್ತೀಚೆನ ಆವಿಷ್ಕಾರವಾಗಿದೆ.
Russian	Хотя люди говорили с начала вида, письмо является довольно недавнее изобретение.
Tamil	மனிதர்கள் இனங்கள் தொடக்கத்தில் இருந்து பேசும் போதும், எழுத்தும் ஒரு மிகவும் சமீபத்திய கண்டுபிடிப்பு.
Thai	แม้ว่ามนุษย์ได้รับการพูดตั้งแต่จุดเริ่มต้นของสายพันธุ์เขียนเป็นสิ่งประดิษฐ์ล่าสุดอย่างเป็นธรรม

Shallow Versus Deep Orthography

The Roman alphabet is no doubt the most widely used writing system in the world. Most of the languages of Europe use it, and many non-European languages, such as Turkish, Swahili, and Vietnamese, have adopted it in modern times. The invention of the typewriter and the QWERTY keyboard solidified its place as the world's premier writing system. Even the Chinese and Japanese type on a QWERTY keyboard, letting the computer convert the keystrokes into their native writing systems. This doesn't mean that the Roman alphabet isn't without its faults.

Although we use the Roman alphabet to write English, it's not an especially good fit. Latin had about two dozen phonemes, but English has over forty, so many of its speech sounds, like *ch* and *sh*, need letter combinations to represent them. Other languages that adopted the Roman alphabet have faced similar problems. Furthermore, spoken English has undergone a number of major sound shifts over the last few centuries, but its spelling has remained virtually unchanged, with the result that there's often a mismatch between a word's spoken and written forms.

The term **orthography** refers to *the set of rules for writing the words of a language,* and English orthography is certainly complex. But some languages, like Spanish, have much simpler spelling systems. *The situation in which spelling and pronunciation are closely matched* is called **shallow orthography**, and *the situation in which spelling and pronunciation are poorly matched* is called **deep orthography**. Thus, highly regular Spanish has shallow orthography while highly irregular English has deep orthography.

We can think of shallow and deep orthography as two ends of a continuum. Scholars generally recognize Korean as having the shallowest orthography of any written language (Gnanadesikan, 2009). Originally the Koreans, like their Japanese neighbors, wrote in Chinese characters. But instead of adapting the Chinese system, they intentionally invented an alphabet, known as Hangul, to precisely write their language. You could say that Hangul is the rare example of a writing system being intelligently designed instead of having evolved for the task.

Among European languages, Spanish, Italian, and German are considered to have shallow orthography. Their spelling systems are easy to learn, and with minimal training you can "read" these languages out loud well enough for a native speaker to understand, even though *you* don't understand what you're reading. Two European languages considered to have deep orthography are French and English. In these languages, the mapping between written and spoken forms is complex and riddled with exceptions, and even educated readers get tripped up on spelling from time to time.

One way shallow and deep orthographies differ is in their treatment of **homophones**, which are *words with the same pronunciation but different meanings.* For example, the English word *sound* has three unrelated meanings, "noise" as in *the Sound of Music,* "healthy" as in *safe and sound,* and "body of water" as in *Puget Sound.* In speech, we have to rely on context to decide which meaning of *sound* was intended, and this is likewise the case when the orthography is shallow, as it is with the word *sound.* But many homophones in English are spelled differently, as for example in the following triplets: *to, too, two; for, four, fore;* and *there, their, they're.* Multiple spellings of homophones pose no particular problem when reading them but they do when writing them, and even your humble textbook writer depends on the spell checker to decide which spelling variant to use. More troublesome for readers are **homographs**, which are *words that are spelled the same but pronounced differently*. For example, the words *lead* and *read* rhyme with either *heed* or *head* depending on their meaning.

At the deep end of the orthography pool is Chinese. It's often thought, at least in the West, that each Chinese logogram is an arbitrary symbol, but if this were true, few people could learn the 5,000-plus characters needed to read everyday texts in China. There are a couple hundred basic characters for common words, such as 人 for "man," 女 for "woman," 日 for "day/sun," and 月 for "moon/month," which are fairly simple in shape and derived from ancient picture writing.

However, the vast majority of Chinese characters are composed of two parts, typically with the left side suggesting the meaning and the right side suggesting the pronunciation. For example, the simple character for "tree/wood" is 木 (pronounced *mù*), and it occurs on the left side of most characters representing the names of trees. Likewise, the character 公, which means "public" and is pronounced *gōng*, often occurs as a phonetic component in characters. In Chinese, the word for "pine tree" is *sōng*, and it's written 松. In other words, the character tells the reader that it's the name of a tree that rhymes with *gōng*. Granted, the system is convoluted, but it's patterns like these that make Chinese logograms learnable.

Homophones and homographs add to the complexity of reading and writing Chinese. For instance, the word *cháng* means "long" when written 长, "often" when written 常, and "taste" when written 尝. Moreover, the character 长 is a homograph, meaning "long" when pronounced *cháng* and "chief" when pronounced *zhǎng*. Thus, homophones and homographs aren't unique to English or even to alphabetic scripts.

English orthography bears some similarity to the Chinese writing system, with its combination of semantic and phonetic components (Dehaene, 2009). Part of the reason why English orthography is deep is that it preserves the history of words. Thus, the semantic relationship between words like *sign* and *signature* is apparent in writing even though the connection has been lost in speech. Likewise, we would lose the semantic relationship between *photograph* and *photographer*, which have different vowel sounds, if we wrote them as they're pronounced.

In the end, whether a language has a shallow or deep orthography has more to do with historical and social factors. In the case of China, a unified national identity has been maintained for more than two millennia because its people, who speak dozens of mutually unintelligible dialects, all use the same logographic script that they can read the way they speak. English orthography, on the other hand, belies a history of conquest and subjugation, revealing it as a Germanic language mixed with French, Latin, ancient Greek, and numerous contributions from other languages as well.

The Brain's Letterbox

Writing systems may represent language at the word, syllable, or phoneme level, but they are all alike in terms of the symbols they use. That is, all writing systems consist of characters that are composed of lines and curves in contrasting orientations (Changizi & Shimojo, 2005). In other words, letters are line drawings. This is true whether the language is written with stylus on clay tablet, pen on parchment, or ink brush on paper; and it's not due to limitations of the writing instruments, since all of these media can be used to produce other kinds of visual designs.

Because the brain isn't hardwired for reading, writing systems must conform to the way the brain processes visual information. The primary visual cortex is in the occipital lobe at the back of the head. An early process in visual perception is edge detection, and it's one of the brain's first steps in distinguishing the various objects in the visual array. This is why line drawings are often easier to interpret than photographs—they highlight the edges of objects so you brain doesn't have to. Thus, the brain first interprets letters as visual, and not linguistic, objects.

The brain also needs a place to store information about the writing system it's learned. At the boundary between the inferior temporal and occipital lobes is a region known as the fusiform gyrus, which serves as a processing area for complex visual stimuli. The fusiform face area, where we store representations of the faces of the thousands of people we know, is located there. Nearby is the **visual word form area**, *a region between the occipital and temporal lobes where the symbols of the writing system are stored, regardless of the language or the type of script* (Perfetti & Tan, 2013). The visual word form area is informally known to language researchers as the brain's letterbox (Dehaene, 2009).

Figure 8.2   QR Code

Your smartphone can read this QR code, but your brain cannot. A matrix of black and white squares is not the kind of visual input your brain has evolved to process. Although QR codes pack lots of information into a concise space, no writing system used by humans could work this way.

Source: ©iStockphoto.com/ franckreporter.

Figure 8.3 Visual Word Form Area

The visual word form area is located in the left hemisphere on the underside of the brain at the border between the occipital lobe and the temporal lobe.

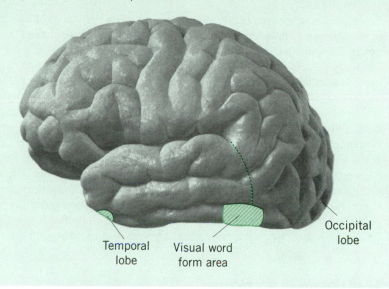

Temporal lobe

Visual word form area

Occipital lobe

Since the brain hasn't evolved to process written language, the discovery of the visual word form area was a bit of a surprise. More surprising was the finding that all writing systems, including logographic Chinese, are processed in this same area (Zhang et al., 2013). Research suggests that the visual word form area begins with the component strokes (lines and curves) of written words and then reassembles them into familiar combinations (Dehaene, 2009). These would be letters in the case of an alphabetic script or commonly recurring stroke patterns in the case of Chinese. The visual word form area then searches for higher-level patterns, such as recognizing the sequence -*ough* as representing the same sound in words like *rough, tough,* and *enough* or identifying semantic and phonetic components in Chinese characters. In brief, the visual processing of written words works in essentially the same way regardless of whether it's written in an alphabet, syllabary, or logographic system.

It's not quite clear what humans were doing with their visual word form area for hundreds of thousands of years before they started reading. Perhaps our hunter-gatherer ancestors used that portion of the brain for "reading" animal tracks and distinguishing edible from inedible plants (Dehaene, 2009). This recruitment of a specific brain region for use as the visual word form area is generally explained in terms of the **neuronal recycling hypothesis**, which is *the proposal that brain areas designed for one function can be reorganized to perform another, somewhat similar function* (Dehaene & Cohen, 2011).

Neuronal recycling gives us the ability to learn all sorts of novel complex behaviors, such as driving a car or playing the piano, that our brains were not preprogramed to perform.

In Sum

Evolution has shaped our brains for speech, and so we learn to speak as a normal part of development. But writing is a recent human invention, and universal literacy an even newer phenomenon, so the brain hasn't evolved mechanisms to handle the written word. The neuronal recycling hypothesis proposes that we reorganize a region of the fusiform gyrus known as the visual word form area to process written symbols. Presumably this region originally processed some other type of visual input, and so writing systems also had to adapt to the functional limitations of this area. As a result, all writing systems have certain common features despite their different approaches to representing words. Logographic systems represent words at the morpheme level, while syllabaries do so at the syllable level and alphabets at the phoneme level. The set of rules for writing the words of a language is known as its orthography. Some languages have shallow orthography, meaning that the relationship between spoken and written forms of words is simple, while other languages have deep orthography, meaning that the relationship between spoken and written forms is complex. Differently spelled homophones and differently pronounced homographs are hallmarks of deep orthography.

Review Questions

1. What are logograms? How do logographic systems handle foreign words and names? How did this practice lead to the development of syllabaries and alphabets?

2. What is orthography? What is the distinction between shallow and deep orthography? What is the issue with homophones and homographs in a language with deep orthography? In what sense does a logographic system like Chinese also have orthography?

3. Where is the visual word form area, and what is its function? Given the fact that the brain hasn't had time to evolve dedicated reading processors, how do we explain the fact that all writing systems are processed in the same visual word form area?

Thought Questions

1. In this section, we learned about homophones and homographs in the context of deep orthographies like English and Chinese. Strictly speaking, homophones (same sound, different meaning) are a feature of all spoken languages, and as listeners we rely on context to infer the speaker's intended meaning. In the case of written languages, the real issue is with heterographic homophones (different spelling, same sound) and heterophonic homographs (different sound, same

spelling). Create a two-by-two table crossing same and different sound with same and different spelling, and then come up with example word sets to illustrate each of the four conditions. What is particular about the different sound, different spelling category?

2. Do we make use of any logograms in written English? (Hint: Look at the top row of your computer keyboard.) Can you think of other logograms we sometimes use in writing? (Search through the symbol set on a word processor for ideas if you need to.) It's important to distinguish between logograms, which represent words, and ideograms, which represent concepts. No writing system uses ideograms, but we do make use of them in our culture. Collect some examples of commonly used symbols in our culture and determine whether each is a logogram representing a word or an ideogram representing a concept.

3. It is thought that the fusiform area is involved in distinguishing complex visual stimuli that belong within particular categories (Price & Devlin, 2003). Thus, the fusiform face area doesn't recognize faces in general but rather distinguishes one familiar face from another. In what ways is distinguishing written words like distinguishing faces? Consider that we recognize familiar faces from multiple angles, in various lighting conditions, and in spite of changes of facial expression or hairstyle. In what ways can a written word form change and still be recognized as the same word?

4. Dyslexia is a reading disability that cannot be attributed to visual or cognitive impairment. How do you think this disability is influenced by shallow or deep orthography? In other words, would you expect any differences in frequency of diagnosis in a country depending on its language's orthography? What sorts of symptoms would you expect, depending on whether the orthography was shallow or deep?

Google It! History of Writing

If you're curious about the **history of writing** or the **history of the alphabet**, you can find some interesting and informative videos on YouTube.

SECTION 8.2: COGNITIVE PROCESSES IN READING

- The eyes move across the page in a series of saccades and fixations. Skilled readers saccade from one content word to the next, but novice readers tend to fixate on every word. Most saccades are forward, but some saccades are regressive, reviewing previously fixated words.

- Visual acuity is limited to a small region of the retina directly behind the pupil known as the fovea; the area surrounding the fovea, known as the parafovea, provides only a blurred image.

- The range of letters that can be taken in during one fixation is known as the perceptual span. Skilled readers of English have a greater perceptual span to the right than to the left; the perceptual span is measured by the gaze contingency paradigm, which uses eye-tracking technology to restrict the amount of readable text around the fixation point.

- Fixation duration is influenced by characteristics of the currently fixated word, such as frequency and predictability, but similar characteristics of the previous and following words, which appear in the parafovea, can also affect the fixation duration of the current word.

- The dual route model proposes that lexical access in reading can occur through a direct route linking the written word to its meaning or else through an indirect route in which the word's phonology is accessed first; clinical data from acquired dyslexia and from the neuroimaging of skilled reading support the dual route model.

- As we read, we hear an inner voice that reconstitutes the pronunciation of the words and the intonations of the phrases; thus, processing written text is similar to processing spoken narrative, in that it proceeds through cycles of memory retrieval and integration that operate at the level of the prosodic phrase.

When you read, it feels as though your eyes are moving smoothly along the line of text, taking in each letter and word in turn. But this is an illusion. Sometimes your eyes do move smoothly, as for example when you "keep your eye on the ball" when playing a sport like tennis or baseball. But when you look at something, say a person's face, your eyes jump from location to location, going from the eyes to the nose to the mouth and back to the eyes, taking snapshots. Your brain then combines these images into a continuous visual experience. You use this same process of visual inspection when you read, your eyes jumping from one location to the next, taking snapshots of the printed line that your brain will merge into a coherent text.

Eye Movements

As you read, your eyes move along the line of text in a series of saccades and fixations. As we learned in Chapter 2, a saccade is a rapid movement of the eyes from one fixation point to another, while a fixation is a period of time during which the eyes remain stationary, focusing on a particular point in the visual scene. The average duration of a fixation is about 200 milliseconds, but it can vary widely depending on a number of factors (Kliegl et al.,

2012). The brain processes visual input during fixations and ignores it during saccades, when it would be just a blur anyway (Paterson, McGowan, & Jordan, 2013). Most saccades are progressive, moving forward in the text, but some are regressive, going backward in the text to a previously fixated point or a point that was missed during the first pass.

In skilled readers, the target of a saccade is a point just left of the center of next fixated word (Li et al., 2014). Beginning readers tend to fixate on every word, but as they gain experience in reading, they learn to skip highly predictable function words and saccade from content word to content word (Miller & O'Donnell, 2013). If you don't believe that you don't actually fixate on every word, try counting the *F*s in the following sentence while reading at a normal rate:

> FINISHED FILES ARE THE RESULTS OF YEARS OF SCIENTIFIC
> STUDY COMBINED WITH THE EXPERIENCE OF MANY YEARS.

If you counted fewer than six Fs, you experienced the **missing letter effect**, which *is the observation that skilled readers skip over predictable words and thus cannot track the letters in those words* (Newman et al., 2013).

The amount of information that can be taken in during one fixation is limited by the structure of the retina at the back of the eye. The **fovea** is *the region of the retina directly behind the pupil where vision is most acute.* This is the only region of the retina where the image is in focus. *The area surrounding the fovea, where vision is less acute,* is called the **parafovea**. You can clearly discern only letters that fall on the fovea, and *the range of letters that can be processed during one fixation* is known as the **perceptual span**.

In skilled readers, the perceptual span is lopsided, extending approximately fifteen characters to the right of the fixation point and about four characters to the left (Kliegl et al., 2012). However, perceptual span can decrease as the reading material becomes

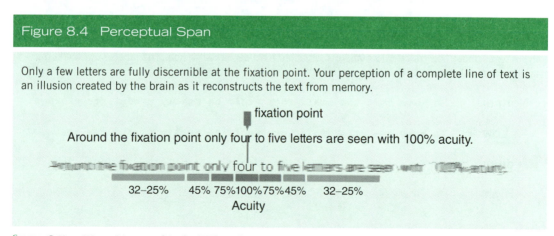

Figure 8.4 Perceptual Span

Only a few letters are fully discernible at the fixation point. Your perception of a complete line of text is an illusion created by the brain as it reconstructs the text from memory.

fixation point

Around the fixation point only four to five letters are seen with 100% acuity.

Around the fixation point only four to five letters are seen with 100% acuity.

32–25%   45% 75%100%75%45%   32–25%
Acuity

more complex, and likewise beginning readers and readers with dyslexia have smaller perceptual spans (Paterson et al., 2013). Skilled readers of scripts such as Arabic and Hebrew, which run from right to left, have a greater leftward than rightward perceptual span (Velan, Deutsch, & Frost, 2013).

The perceptual span is measured by using the **gaze contingency paradigm**. This is *an experimental procedure in which a narrow window of text surrounding the fixation point is displayed on a computer screen* (Paterson et al., 2013). In a typical gaze contingency experiment, the display window is determined by feedback from an eye-tracking device and changes with each saccade to the new fixation point, while the rest of the letters in the text are replaced with *X*s. Since the parafoveal image is blurred, participants in these experiments generally don't notice that the rest of the text is masked and that only the portion they are currently looking at is displayed. By varying the width of the display window, the participant's perceptual span can be measured.

The gaze contingency paradigm has also enabled researchers to investigate how visual text is processed, in particular how eye movements are related to visual word recognition (Miller & O'Donnell, 2013). While the currently fixated word is squarely within foveal vision, the preceding and following words will typically fall in the parafovea. Although they can't be seen clearly, some information about them can be extracted, and this can influence the fixation duration of the current word.

Fixation duration is influenced both by characteristics of the currently fixated word as well as by features of the preceding and following words in the left and right regions of the parafovea. Currently fixated words exhibit a **frequency effect**, referring to *the observation that low-frequency words are fixated longer than high-frequency words*. Likewise,

Figure 8.5   Gaze Contingency Paradigm

By restricting how much text is available on either side of the fixated word, researchers can test hypotheses about how much information is extracted from parafoveal vision. The labels Low, Medium, and High refer to how much visual information is removed from the text.

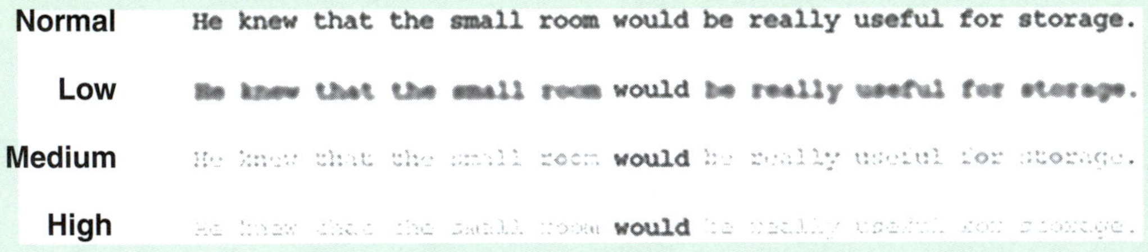

Normal	He knew that the small room would be really useful for storage.
Low	He knew that the small room would be really useful for storage.
Medium	He knew that the small room **would** be really useful for storage.
High	He knew that the small room **would** be really useful for storage.

Source: Paterson, McGowan, and Jordan (2013).

they also show a **predictability effect**, referring to *the observation that less predictable words are fixated longer than more highly predictable words*.

However, it's important to keep in mind that fixation duration isn't a measure of total processing time. Rather, once the eyes have taken in enough information to get the word recognition process going, the next saccade is executed, and this can lead to a **spillover effect**, which is *the case in which processing difficulties of the preceding word cause the fixation duration of the current word to be extended* (Kliegl et al., 2012). The spillover effect provides strong evidence for the idea that word access isn't completed during the fixation period. That is to say, the word you're currently aware that you're reading isn't the word your eyes are currently fixated on. As a skilled reader, your eyes are saccading in advance of word recognition, confident that the word will eventually be recognized; but processing difficulties can affect later fixations, and if word recognition fails, your eyes will make a regressive saccade back to the trouble spot.

There is also *the case in which characteristics of the following word affect the fixation duration of the current word* (Dimigen, Kliegl, & Sommer, 2012). Because *the following word is in the parafovea while the current word is in the fovea,* this is known as the **parafovea-on-fovea effect**. More specifically, when the word in the parafovea—which, remember, cannot be seen clearly—is high in frequency or predictability, it can shorten the fixation duration of the current word. It's still unclear why this effect occurs, and it's also not consistently found in experiments, unlike the spillover effect. In other words, the parafovea-on-fovea effect is still an unresolved question in reading research.

In brief, only unskilled readers read one word at a time. As we gain skill in reading, our eyes learn to saccade ahead before the processing of the current word is complete. Skilled readers use top-down knowledge of word frequency and predictability to speed up the reading process, and they also make use of whatever information can be extracted from the parafovea. Thus, skilled reading involves a combination of bottom-up word detection and top-down word prediction processes.

Models of Lexical Access in Reading

Various models have been proposed to describe how we go from the written word form to retrieving that word's meaning from memory. The models differ in the details of the mechanisms they propose and the predictions they make, but they all agree that there are two routes for processing written words (Jobard et al., 2011).

A **dual route model** makes *the proposal that readers can either first access a word's meaning and then its pronunciation or else first access a word's pronunciation and then its meaning*. You can think of these two routes as different reading strategies (Moseley et al., 2014). When you read words that are very familiar, such as *is* or *of*, or when you encounter irregular words, such as *yacht* or *colonel*, you use the **direct route**, which is *the process of going straight from the written word to its meaning*. Only after the word's meaning is accessed does its pronunciation also become available.

On the other hand, when you encounter a word you don't know, such as the pseudoword *antriscoldate*, you can sound it out because you know the orthographic rules of English. In this case, you use the **indirect route**, which is *the process of accessing the meaning of a written word by first reconstructing its pronunciation*. That is, you first convert the written word into a spoken format (whether you say it out loud or silently to yourself), and then you search your memory to see if it's a word you know the meaning of (Moseley et al., 2014).

Evidence that the dual route model reflects actual brain processes first came from clinical data. A condition known as **acquired dyslexia** involves *an impairment in reading ability due to brain damage in a person who had previously been a skilled reader* (Levy et al., 2009). Depending on the exact location of the brain lesion, different abilities are lost. Patients with **surface dyslexia** have *a condition in which the ability to read regularly spelled words and pseudowords is spared while the ability to read irregularly spelled words is lost*. According to the dual route model, their indirect route is intact but their direct route has been disrupted by the lesion. The opposite pattern also occurs. Patients with **phonological dyslexia** exhibit *a condition in which reading is relatively spared with the exception that the ability to sound out unfamiliar words is lost*. In other words, they can read via the direct route but not the indirect route.

Patients with surface dyslexia tend to have lesions in the left temporal lobe, where word meanings are believed to be stored, while those with phonological dyslexia

Figure 8.6   Dual Route Model and Acquired Dyslexia

The direct route goes straight from spelling (orthography) to meaning (semantics). The indirect route passes through pronunciation (phonology) first. If the direct route is disrupted, the patient can still read regularly spelled words because they can sound them out (surface dyslexia). If the indirect route is disrupted, the patient can still read familiar words but can't sound out unfamiliar words (phonological dyslexia).

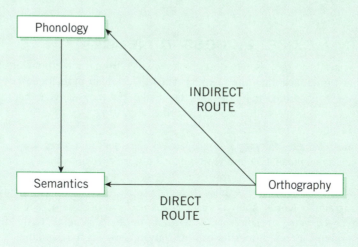

tend to suffer from damage to the left inferior parietal and frontal regions, which are believed to play a role in recognizing and producing spoken word forms (Levy et al., 2009). These areas also show up in fMRI studies of normal skilled reading (Welcome & Joanisse, 2012). Thus, both clinical and neuroimaging data match up with our intuitions about reading.

You should recall from earlier chapters that a general organizing principle of the brain's sensorimotor systems is that it processes "what" information along a ventral stream and "how" information along a dorsal stream. In spoken word perception and production, the meaning of the word is processed along a ventral stream from the primary auditory cortex to the left temporal lobe while its pronunciation is processed along a dorsal stream through the left parietal cortex into the inferior frontal lobe. Written word recognition hooks into these two streams to access the word's meaning and pronunciation (Moseley et al., 2014). In other words, the direct route of the dual route model maps onto a ventral stream from the visual word form area in the left fusiform gyrus into the left temporal lobe. Likewise, the indirect route corresponds to a dorsal stream through the left parietal cortex in the inferior frontal lobe.

One important way in which reading models differ has to do with the question of whether the two routes work exclusively of each other or in parallel (Jobard et al., 2011). According to some accounts, each word is processed through either the direct or indirect route depending on its characteristics. Specifically, irregular words and highly familiar words go through the direct route, which is assumed to be more efficient, while less familiar words, which are assumed to be regular, go through the indirect route. However, other models propose a sort of "horse race" in which both routes process each word (Seidenberg, 2005). The indirect route will win the race when the word is highly familiar or if the indirect route fails to find a recognizable spoken word form. In the case of novel words, the direct route will fail to access a word meaning, but the indirect route may still succeed in producing a pronounceable word form.

More recent evidence suggests that the relative use of the direct or indirect route depends not just on the characteristics of the word but also—perhaps even more so—on the characteristics of the reader. Skilled readers tend to rely more on the direct route even when the orthography is shallow (Moseley et al., 2014). On the other hand, novice readers mainly depend on the indirect route, sounding out each word, which works as long as the orthography is shallow but leads to reading difficulties when the orthography is deep (Jobard et al., 2011).

Text Comprehension

As you read this passage, you may hear your voice pronouncing the words in your head. This is perfectly normal, and most people report hearing an "inner voice" when they read (Perrone-Bertolotti et al., 2012). It may be that this inner voice is merely an extension of the inner monologue we all maintain throughout most of our waking hours. It's also possible that this experience is merely a remnant of the way we all learned to read, that is, by pronouncing the words out loud. According to this view, we internalize the process of reading aloud as we become more proficient speakers.

There's some evidence to support the idea that people rely more on phonological processes as the difficulty of the text increases (Perrone-Bertolotti et al., 2012). Novice readers, who find all texts difficult, read out loud. But even proficient readers tend to read aloud when the text is hard to understand, as for example when reading the instructions for filling out your tax forms or assembling a piece of furniture. If this is the case, we can imagine there are people so skilled at reading that they no longer depend on even subvocalized speech as they read but rather access the meaning of the text directly from the written words without considering how those words are pronounced.

On the other hand, neuroimaging data suggest that integrating speech with written text is an important aspect of becoming a skilled reader (Shankweiler et al., 2008). That is, activity in the left inferior frontal lobe, which is active during speech perception and production, is also active during silent reading, but only for skilled readers. Perhaps, then, the endpoint of the reading process isn't just an access of the word's meaning but also its pronunciation. This suggests that the inner voice may be an essential component of reading comprehension.

Furthermore, there's evidence that this inner voice involves more than just the pronunciation of individual words but extends to the prosodic features of speech as well. The **implicit prosody hypothesis** is *the proposal that skilled readers organize the material they read into prosodic phrases similar to the way they would when they speak* (Roll et al., 2012). In speech, utterances tend to be organized around prosodic phrases lasting two to three seconds, and this is believed to be associated with short-term memory limitations. An ERP component known as the closure positivity shift is associated with the detection of phrase boundaries in speech, and it's believed to reflect the processes of memory storage and redirection of attention. The closure positivity shift is also elicited in readers as they reach phrase boundaries in the text, occurring roughly every two to three seconds, just as they do when listening to speech.

Reading and comprehending a text is a dynamic process built on cycles of memory retrieval and memory storage (Rapp & van den Broek, 2005). As each word is read, its meaning and all related concepts are retrieved from memory. This information is somehow integrated with the current context and with previous information to construct a situation model of the text, which then must be stored in long-term memory. Rather than waiting until the end of the text, the reader builds up this situation model in an incremental fashion, presumably phrase by phrase. After all, if you're interrupted half way through a story, you can still tell what you've read up to that point. In the end, it appears that processing written discourse is very much like processing spoken narrative.

In Sum

When we read, our eyes skip across the line of text in a series of saccades and fixations, taking in the content words and skipping over the predictable function words. Since acute vision is limited to the narrow region of the fovea, the perceptual span can usually only take in one or two words at a time. Still, information from the parafovea can influence how quickly we process words in a text, as can the frequency and predictability of the current word. When we read, we need to access both the meaning and the pronunciation of each word. Familiar words and irregularly spelled words are processed through the "direct" ventral route, which accesses meaning before pronunciation, while regular and unfamiliar words are processed through the "indirect" dorsal route, which accesses pronunciation before meaning. Reading a text is much like listening to a spoken narrative, in that it involves processing cycles of memory retrieval and memory integration at the phrasal level.

Review Questions

1. Explain how reading a line of text proceeds by saccades and fixations. How do we account for the missing letter effect in terms of eye movements during reading? How is the perceptual span of a given fixation limited by the structure of the retina?

2. Describe how the gaze contingency paradigm works. How is it used to measure perceptual span? Explain the spillover effect and the parafovea-on-fovea effect.

3. Explain the dual route model, being explicit about how the direct and indirect routes are supposed to work. Describe the clinical evidence from acquired dyslexia that supports the dual route model. What is the evidence from neuroimaging studies that supports the dual route model?

4. What is the implicit prosody hypothesis? In what sense is reading a text similar to listening to a spoken narrative? What cognitive processes are common to both?

Thought Questions

1. Given what you know about eye movements during reading and the acuity of the fovea and parafovea, what do you think about claims that you can learn to speed read?

2. How does skimming or scanning a text differ from actually reading it? Speculate on the sorts of eye movements involved in these tasks.

Google It! Acquired Reading Disorder

There are a number of articles about **acquired dyslexia** on the Internet. You can also see a video about it on YouTube in which a patient describes his experience and a researcher explains the brain areas involved. Search for **acquired reading disorder**.

SECTION 8.3: DEVELOPMENT OF READING SKILLS

- Reading skill involves not only quickly accessing the meaning and pronunciation of visual word forms, it also includes the ability to move quickly through a text while maintaining good comprehension.

- Reading skills are normally distributed among the population, with most people being average readers while some excel and others struggle; the cutoff for diagnosing a reading disorder depends on what society considers an acceptable level of reading ability.

- Developmental dyslexia is a reading disability in children that is not due to a lack of intelligence, motivation, or educational opportunity; it affects about 5%–17% of schoolchildren, and those with a family history of dyslexia are at elevated risk.

- Phonological awareness, or sensitivity to the sound structure of words, is an essential prerequisite to learning to read; the deep orthography of English poses special problems for a child with reading impairment, but rates of dyslexia are similar worldwide.

- Brain imaging studies show structural differences in the brains of dyslexic individuals compared with skilled readers, and even in the brains of preliterate children with a family history of reading impairment; both the gray matter of functional regions involved in reading and the white matter tracts connecting those regions are affected.

- The personal and social costs of developmental dyslexia are considerable. Behavioral tests that screen preschoolers for risk of reading disorder are now available though not yet widely used; techniques for improving phonological awareness are generally effective, but we still lack adequate methods for helping dyslexic children become fluent readers.

Until recently, few people needed to read, but the skill has become essential for success in modern society. As a college student, you probably don't experience reading as an especially difficult task. But the ease with which you read now is built on many years of practice and hard work. As you read this chapter, think about how fortunate you are, since there are many people who still find reading difficult even though they've put in just as much effort as you have.

Learning to Read

An obvious first step in developing reading skill is learning the letters of the writing system. But this is complicated by the fact that each letter comes in a variety of fonts, sizes, and styles (Perea, Abu Mallouh, & Carreiras, 2013). For example, upper and lower case letters, like A and a or G and g, often bear little resemblance to each other, and the shapes of print and cursive letters are usually dissimilar as well. Even Chinese characters can have considerably different shapes depending on the font and whether they're written in a print or cursive style. Nevertheless, most novice readers quickly develop a set of abstract representations for each letter and for visual word forms more generally. In other words, they learn to recognize words regardless of font or case or style.

Novice readers sound out the words as they read aloud, relying heaving on phonological processes to extract meaning from the text; but as they become more skilled, they learn to read familiar words as a whole without sounding them out. That is, novice readers mainly use the indirect route, accessing pronunciation before meaning, but they gradually shift to greater reliance on direct route, accessing meaning before pronunciation, as their reading skill improves. This shift can be observed in neuroimaging studies, which show more activity in the dorsal stream of early readers but more activity in the ventral stream of skilled readers (Schlaggar & Church, 2009). Recall from Section 8.2 that the dorsal stream from the visual word form area to the parietal and frontal lobes is believed to process the conversion of written symbols into phonological word forms, and thus is the biological analog of the indirect route. On the other hand, the ventral stream from the visual word form area to temporal lobe is considered the analog of the direct route, accessing meaning directly.

Figure 8.7   Different Fonts and Styles of the Letter A

Although each of these shapes is different, the visual word form area learns to identify all of them as the letter A.

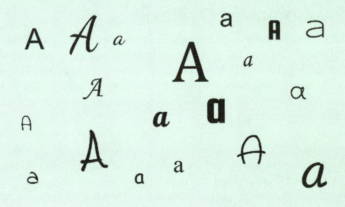

Skilled reading involves not only the rapid conversion of visual word forms into their phonological equivalents, it also requires an appropriate prosodic rendering of the text (Valle et al., 2013). Unskilled readers often read aloud with flat intonation and pauses at inappropriate locations, while skilled readers learn to read with a natural intonation and pausing at prosodic phrase boundaries. Studies find that readers who use proper prosody when reading aloud also have better comprehension of what they read. This is in line with the implicit prosody hypothesis (Section 8.2), which proposes that prosody guides comprehension even in silent reading by breaking the text into short, meaningful phrases that fit within the limits of short-term memory.

Silent reading speed depends both on the difficulty of the text and on the skill of the reader (Korinth, Sommer, & Breznitz, 2013). Experienced readers tend to read faster, suggesting that reading for them has become a largely automatic process. However, there is wide variability in reading speed even among readers with equivalent amounts of training. Measurable differences in reading speed and reading comprehension can already be detected in the first grade of elementary school, when reading is first taught (Goldman & Manis, 2013). These differences among schoolchildren only increase in the following years, as strong readers continue to read and gain experience while poor readers fail to keep pace with the ever more challenging materials they are asked to read.

Since reading is a learned skill, it's only reasonable to expect a wide range of outcomes, just as we do with other forms of expert learning such as playing a sport or a musical instrument. In fact, measurements of reading ability reflect a normal distribution, with most people in the middle range, a small percentage of strong readers at the high end and another small percentage of poor readers at the low end (Pugh et al., 2013). For educational purposes, we set a cut point and label those lowest in the reading skill continuum as having a reading disability (Goldman & Manis, 2013). However, whatever criterion we select will be arbitrary and doesn't reflect a categorical distinction between those with or without a reading disorder (Gebauer, Fink, et al., 2012).

Developmental Dyslexia

It's often thought that people with dyslexia confuse the order of letters in words, for example reading *top* as *pot*, or spelling *it* as *ti*. In fact, **letter position dyslexia** is *a rare form of reading disorder in which readers mix up the order of letters in words* (Perea et al., 2013). In most cases, people with dyslexia experience problems with reading accuracy and fluency. That is, they read slowly, frequently misidentify words, and have difficulty understanding what they read.

A reading disability in children that cannot be attributed to a lack of intelligence, motivation, or educational opportunity is known as **developmental dyslexia** (Lebel et al., 2013). About 5%–17% of the school-age population is considered to suffer from this specific reading disorder, with the actual percentage depending on how the cutoff between acceptable and unacceptable reading ability is defined. Children who have a family

Figure 8.8   Normal Distribution of Reading Abilities

Reading abilities, like many human characteristics, are normally distributed. This means that most people have abilities close to the average, while some have considerably stronger or weaker abilities than average. In a normal distribution, about 16% of the population will have a score that is one standard deviation or more below the mean. If this is the cutoff criterion for diagnosing a reading impairment, then about 16% of the population will be considered dyslexic.

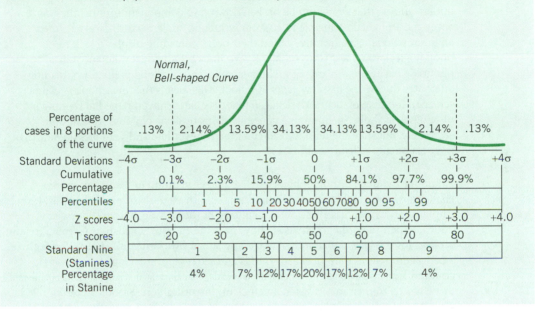

Source: Jeremykemp / Wikimedia Commons / Public Domain.

history of reading disability are at high risk for developing dyslexia (Hosseini et al., 2013). This suggests a genetic component to dyslexia, although environmental factors, such lack of reading materials at home, also put the child at risk for developing a reading disorder (Cope et al., 2012). Even with remediated reading instruction, dyslexic readers often fail to attain acceptable levels of reading speed and accuracy (Stoodley & Stein, 2013).

Although the symptoms of developmental dyslexia first become apparent when the child starts learning to read, the roots of the disorder can be found in spoken language deficits. In part through experience with nursery rhymes and language games, preschoolers begin to acquire *an understanding that words can be broken down into smaller sound structures*, and this insight into the nature of language is known as **phonological awareness** (Pugh et al., 2013). For example, they begin to notice that some words start with the same sound, like *tic, tac, toe,* and that other words end the same way, as in *cat, sat, mat.* They also become sensitive to the syllable structure of words and can clap to the rhythm of syllables in speech and especially in song.

Phonological awareness is a necessary precursor to reading. Without sensitivity to the sound structure of words, novice readers can't make sense of the **alphabetic principle**, *the process by which readers associate written symbols with speech sounds* (Pugh et al., 2013). It's this insight that enables young readers to learn the orthographic rules of their language. In other words, children are only successful at learning how to read if they can see the consistent ways that written words map onto spoken word forms.

When children receive reading instruction before they have developed an understanding that words can be broken down into component sounds, they can't apply the alphabetic principle to go from written to spoken word. Overwhelmed, children who fall significantly behind their peers in reading display a lack of phonological awareness (Pugh et al., 2013). In fact, individual differences in phonological awareness among preliterate children is a strong predictor of reading outcomes during the first few years of school. This means that preschoolers can be screened for developmental dyslexia so that they can be given remedial training in phonological skills. Such training generally helps dyslexic children to read more accurately, but they still tend to read at a much slower rate and with less fluency than their classmates (Zhang et al., 2013).

No doubt the deep orthography of English makes learning to read even more challenging for a child with a reading disorder. However, the prevalence of dyslexia is similar worldwide, regardless of the language or the writing system (Shaywitz et al., 2006). When the orthography is shallow, as is the case for Spanish or German, reading accuracy is less of a problem than is reading speed (Korinth et al., 2013). Since there's a consistent relationship between sounds and letters in these languages, dyslexic children learn how to sound out written words, but they still struggle with connecting those words to their meanings in an efficient, fluent fashion (Stoodley & Stein, 2013). This is especially true when reading instruction includes a **phonics-based approach**, which is *a method of teaching reading that explicitly trains children to recognize consistent relationships between letters and sounds* (Gómez-Velázquez, González-Garrido, & Vega-Gutiérrez, 2013).

Since Chinese uses a logographic writing system, you might expect that an understanding of the sound structure of words isn't important for young Chinese readers. Nevertheless, measures of phonological awareness among Chinese preschoolers are a strong predictor of reading performance during the first few years of school, just as it is in countries that use an alphabetic writing system (Wang et al., 2012). However, you should remember from Section 8.1 that Chinese characters encode a fair amount of phonetic information, and novice readers need phonological awareness to make good use of these pronunciation cues.

A version of the alphabetic principle is important in learning to read Chinese as well. The structure of Chinese characters is complex but fairly predictable, as there are rules for how basic elements can be combined (Wang et al., 2012). Most Chinese readers learn these rules intuitively and can easily distinguish possible from impossible characters, just as English readers can distinguish possible words, such as *tervid*, from impossible words, such as *trvdei*. Dyslexic readers of Chinese often have difficulty with this task, suggesting that they haven't internalized the rules for constructing characters.

In addition to assessing phonological awareness, researchers and educators can screen for potential reading impairments by using a **rapid automatized naming** task (Raschle, Zuk, & Gaab, 2012). This is *a diagnostic for dyslexia in which the child is asked to name written letters, numbers, or other familiar symbols as quickly as possible*. The rapid automatized naming task is a good predictor of later reading performance (Gómez-Velázquez et al., 2013). Presumably, this test taps into connections between visual and phonological areas in the brain, which are essential for fluent reading.

Developmental Dyslexia and the Brain

It's now generally accepted that developmental dyslexia is a disorder of the brain that can lead to a variety of problems not obviously related to reading (Stoodley & Stein, 2013). Since reading is a new skill in terms of human history, it has no dedicated brain systems. Rather, reading processes hitch a ride on brain systems originally designed to do other tasks, and variation in any of these systems can lead to a reading disorder (Vogel et al., 2013).

Brain imaging studies show that dyslexic readers use different brain areas while reading compared with normal readers (Cope et al., 2012). The standard reading areas of the brain in the left temporal-parietal region (the dorsal stream) and the left occipital-temporal region (the ventral stream) are less active during reading tasks in dyslexic individuals compared with skilled readers (Hosseini et al., 2013). As reading skill develops, the cerebral cortex in the reading areas becomes thicker, and so some of these differences in brain structures are likely due to experience with reading (Goldman & Manis, 2013). However, structural abnormalities in the reading areas can be found in preliterate children with a family history of reading impairment (Raschle et al., 2012). Furthermore, these differences can't be attributed to differences in the socioeconomic status of the child's family nor can they be explained in terms of the child's early experiences with printed materials, such as having books in the home or being read to by family members (Raschle, Chang, & Gaab, 2011). In other words, these findings indicate a genetic or early developmental basis for reading impairment in these children.

As normally developing children gain experience with printed material, the reading process becomes automatic. However, reading continues to be an effortful experience for children with dyslexia. This difference is also reflected in patterns of brain activity. Older children and adults who have been diagnosed with a reading disorder exhibit greater activation in the left and right frontal lobes compared with skilled readers (Raschle et al., 2012). This kind of frontal lobe activity is typically associated with effortful control over cognitive processes, and in this case dyslexic readers are likely attempting to compensate for a poorly functioning reading system.

Brain tissue can be divided into gray matter and white matter. **Gray matter** is *brain tissue that is mainly composed of neuron cell bodies and whose function is to process information*. The cerebral cortex is composed of gray matter. Different functional areas communicate with each other by means of **white matter tracts**, which are *bundles of fibers that connect various regions of the brain and whose function is to transmit information*. White matter tracts run beneath the cerebral cortex, much like the wires under an instrumental panel. Traditional fMRI techniques measure activity in the gray matter regions of the brain, and scientists could only make inferences about how these regions were connected. However, this has changed since the development of **diffusion tensor imaging**, which is *an fMRI technique that enables researchers to trace the pathways of white matter tracts*.

Diffusion tensor imaging has provided researchers with a number of insights into how the different language areas are connected. For example, studies using this technique have demonstrated that the arcuate fasciculus, the white matter tract extending from the temporal through the parietal to the frontal lobe, plays an important role in language processing, as was hypothesized by Carl Wernicke over a century ago (Lebel et al., 2013). Furthermore, the size and distribution of the arcuate fasciculus and other white matter tracts are correlated with reading ability in adults and with phonological awareness in preliterate children (Wandell & Yeatman, 2013). The white matter tracts

Figure 8.9   White Matter Tracts as Shown by Diffusion Tensor Imaging

White matter tracts are the neural pathways that connect one functional area of the brain with another. Differences in the location or density of white matter tracts can have a major impact on ability to learn how to read.

Source: © Thomas Schultz / Wikimedia Commons / CC-BY-SA-3.0 / GFDL.

are laid out early in development, and variations in their size and positioning may set the stage for reading impairment.

It's generally accepted nowadays that children can't learn to read until they've developed phonological awareness, but this may depend on an even more basic processes. The **auditory processing deficit hypothesis** is *the proposal that dyslexia stems from an underlying difficulty in accurately detecting and remembering rapid sound changes* (Johnson et al., 2013). According to this view, reading impairment is just one symptom of a more general disorder that's not specific to language. This hypothesis predicts that an auditory processing impairment is a risk factor for both specific language disorder and developmental dyslexia (McArthur, Atkinson, & Ellis, 2009). There's also some evidence that a dysfunction of the cerebellum may play a role in developmental dyslexia (Stoodley & Stein, 2013). The cerebellum is involved in coordinating both motor and cognitive tasks, and some individuals with dyslexia also show impairments on other tasks involving the cerebellum. Yet another risk factor for reading impairment is premature birth (Feldman et al., 2011). Preterm babies have a higher risk of developing all sorts of cognitive impairments, including language and reading disabilities, and they generally have more difficulty in school compared with children born full term.

Early Intervention

Until recently in human history, few people learned to read or even needed to. But in the modern world, reading is an essential skill, and developmental dyslexia imposes heavy costs both for those who suffer from it and for society at large. Children with a reading disability are less likely to complete high school or enter college compared with their peers, and they're more likely to enter the juvenile justice system (Raschle et al., 2011). Too often, reading disability isn't diagnosed until mid-elementary school, only after the child has fallen noticeably behind peers. However, at this late stage the dyslexic child has already been negatively impacted in a number of ways, including poor vocabulary skills and a dampened motivation to learn. Furthermore, the child's repeated failures in the classroom can lead to frustration and low self-esteem.

Instead of taking a "wait and see" approach to the slow reader, early intervention is essential (Fielding-Barnsley & Hay, 2012). As we've seen, there are simple diagnostic tests, such as phonological awareness and rapid automatized naming tasks, that can be used to screen preschoolers at risk of developing a reading impairment (Wandell & Yeatman, 2013). These children can then be given explicit training in the sound structure of words and the alphabetic principle. Slow readers who don't receive explicit instruction rarely catch up with their peers, and instead they rely on compensatory strategies to avoid having to read.

We now have good intervention techniques for helping at-risk children overcome the initial challenge of converting letters into speech sounds (Lebel et al., 2013). However, we still don't have good techniques for helping children with dyslexia develop fluent reading skills. Given the high personal and social costs of reading impairment, developmental dyslexia has become a major focus of research for language scientists.

In Sum

Learning to read is a two-stage process. First, novice readers need to learn how to break the code, transforming visual symbols into spoken words; and phonological awareness is essential for developing this skill. Second, readers need to learn how to move rapidly through a text while maintaining good comprehension; and as young readers gain experience, they rely less on sounding out words as they are able to access word meanings directly. Reading skill is highly variable among individuals, and those who perform below a given criterion are considered to have reading impairment. When measured in terms of reading fluency and not just single word recognition, rates of dyslexia are similar worldwide, regardless of how complex the writing system is. Brain imaging studies indicate structural abnormalities in the brains of individuals with dyslexia, and these include both the gray matter of cortical areas involved in reading and the white matter tracts connecting those regions. Because the personal and social costs of reading impairment are so high, early detection and intervention are essential. We now have effective methods for helping dyslexic children attain acceptable levels of single-word recognition, but effective techniques for improving reading fluency have not yet been developed.

Review Questions

1. Explain why it's simplistic to categorize individuals into normal readers and those with a reading disorder. How does the prevalence of dyslexia in the United States compare with that in other countries?

2. Explain how developmental dyslexia is related to phonological awareness and an understanding of the alphabetic principle. What kinds of behavioral tasks can be used to screen preschoolers for risk of developing a reading disorder?

3. Describe the structural differences between the brains of individuals with reading impairment and those of skilled readers. Is it better to interpret these differences as a cause of reading impairment or an effect of reading experience? (Hint: This is a trick question.)

4. What are the personal and social costs of reading impairment? Why is early intervention essential?

Thought Question

1. For more than a century, scholars in the United States and Great Britain have advocated for a spelling reform of the English language to make learning to read easier. Given what you've learned about developmental dyslexia, do you think spelling reform would help individuals with reading impairment? Carefully explain your reasoning.

Google It! Phonological Awareness

If you are interested in early childhood education, you can find plenty of videos on YouTube that discuss **phonological awareness**. You can also search for the related concepts of **phonemic awareness**, which is one aspect of phonological awareness, and **phonics**, which is a method for teaching phonological awareness. One commercial product for improving phonological awareness through computer activities is known as **Fast ForWord**. You can find demonstrations of this product on YouTube.

SECTION 8.4: COGNITIVE PROCESSES IN WRITING

- Learning to write the letters of a writing system involves changes in two areas of the brain: the visual word form area at the occipital-temporal junction stores visual features of the letters, while Exner's area in the frontal lobe stores motor plans for handwriting those letters.

- Learning to spell requires integrating three types of information: the phonological structure of words, the orthographic rules for converting spoken words into written form, and morphological information about how word forms can change when prefixes or suffixes are added.

- As schoolchildren progress through primary and secondary school, the texts they write show a developmental trajectory from a loose structure with no unifying topic toward hierarchically organized texts built on a set of subtopics arranged under a common theme.

- The Hayes model is a theory of the cognitive processes involved in the writing task, and it has guided writing research for more than three decades; it is designed to explain how writing processes are dependent on more general cognitive processes and on support from the environment.

- Individuals with dyslexia or specific language impairment perform much worse on writing tasks than do their peers; although they put as much effort into the task and produce similar content compared with normally developing writers, they write less, have more spelling and grammatical errors, and use more limited vocabulary.

- The visuospatial aspects of the text are important to skilled writers, who organize paragraphs based on how they are laid out on the page and use spatial memory to locate information during revision.

Reading and writing are complementary tasks, just as are listening and speaking. However, there are also differences. Most of us learn to listen and to speak with seeming effortlessness. Furthermore, we spend roughly equal times listening and speaking, taking turns with others in our group. Reading and writing, on the other hand, are solitary tasks. Reading takes years of effort to learn, and not all of us succeed at the task. Learning to write well is an even more challenging task, perhaps one of the most cognitively demanding behaviors humans engage in (Alves et al., 2008). It's also a skill that takes decades to master, starting with learning the letters of the alphabet in the preschool years and extending well beyond our college writing courses (Hayes, 2012). Even though they are complementary tasks, all of us read far more than we write, and few of us ever master the art of writing.

Learning the ABCs

We can think of learning how to write as involving three overlapping stages. In the first stage, children learn the symbols of the writing system. Writing letters soon becomes an automatic process in alphabetic languages, but learning new letters continues into adulthood for readers and writers of Chinese. In the second stage, novice writers learn how letters combine to form words. This is true even for logographic Chinese, in which most words consist of two or three characters. In the third stage, developing writers learn how to compose texts. Writing coherent texts is a process that takes years of practice, with quite variable results.

In modern society, most children begin learning their letters in preschool. Children not only need to learn how to recognize letters by sight, they also have to learn how to write those letters. In fact, learning to write letters is also an important part of learning how to read them. As we already learned in Section 8.1, the abstract form of letters is stored in the visual word form area of the left occipito-temporal region of the brain, but practice in handwriting letters helps train this area to recognize the symbols of the writing system (Nakamura et al., 2012).

Learning to write letters also requires the building and storage of motor programs. Exner's area is *a brain region located in the left frontal premotor cortex just above Broca's area that stores the motor programs for handwriting gestures* (Perfetti & Tan, 2013). Neuroimaging studies find that Exner's area is activated when reading handwritten letters, suggesting that a process similar to the motor perception of speech takes place when we read handwritten words.

Writing letters may be essential for learning how to read them, but at least in the case of alphabetic systems, letter perception and production soon become automated processes. However, in a more complex writing system like Chinese, learning to read characters is much more dependent on learning how to write them. When researchers trained non-native adult learners on a set of Chinese characters, those who had practiced writing them out could recognize them faster than those who had spent a similar amount of time visually studying the characters (Cao et al., 2012). Furthermore, the researchers found greater activation in Exner's area during a reading task among those who had learned the characters by writing them rather than by just looking at them. In brief, we learn to read letters at least in part by learning how to write them.

Figure 8.10 Exner's Area

Exner's area contains the motor plans for handwriting. It is located just above Broca's area, anterior to the primary motor cortex in the frontal lobe.

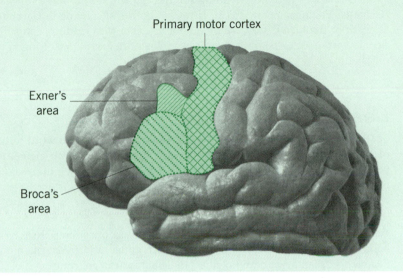

Learning to Spell

Learning how to spell words is a more challenging task than learning how to read them because it requires coordinating information about word forms at three different levels (Bahr et al., 2012). At the phonological level, the young writer has to be able to analyze the spoken word form into smaller units, such as syllables and phonemes. In other words, the writer needs to have phonological awareness. At the orthographic level, the novice writer has to understand the rules for representing spoken words in a written format. That is, the child needs to know how phonemes are translated into letters or letter combinations. Finally, at the morphological level, the developing writer needs to understand how the structure of words, including suffixes and prefixes, interacts with spelling patterns. For example, the young writer can't simply tack the *ing* suffix onto the root word *write*, since the silent *e* has to be dropped. Likewise, the final consonant of *plan* has to be doubled to add *ed* but not *s*. It's not until late in the elementary school years that children master spelling at all three levels.

Especially in a language with such deep orthography as English, learning to spell is a significant challenge, and all of us struggle with spelling from time to time. However, people with dyslexia experience persistent problems with spelling (Morken & Helland, 2013). Since they generally have poor phonological awareness, the spellings they produce are frequently not even good reflections of the way the words sound. Some people even exhibit an **isolated spelling disorder**, which is *a specific and significant impairment in spelling skills even though reading ability is in the normal range* (Gebauer, Fink, et al., 2012). This disorder is mainly reported in languages like German that have shallow orthography. In such cases, children with a reading disorder who receive appropriate interventions can sometimes develop sufficient skill to raise their reading abilities to the low end of the normal range (Gebauer, Enzinger, et al., 2012). However, quirks of spelling in German, such as silent or doubled letters, which do not interfere with reading, can still trip up people with poor orthographic awareness when they write, resulting in frequent misspellings.

Learning to Compose Texts

Spelling represents the interface between spoken and written word forms, and most of us master the orthographic rules of our language during our elementary school years. Composing written texts, on the other hand, is a much more daunting task because the rules of written discourse diverge considerably from those of spoken narrative.

Written texts produced by schoolchildren can be categorized into three types on the basis of their structure (Hayes, 2012). Children in the early grades often produce flexible-focus texts that have no global topic but instead are composed of sentences chained together by loose associations. Rambling narrative is common in the speech of young children and not that uncommon even in adults, but we expect written text to be organized around a single topic. As children pick up on this convention, they start producing fixed-topic texts, in which each statement relates to the core topic, but there's still no elaboration of these statements. It's not until after the sixth grade that we see most children producing topic-elaboration texts, which exhibit a set of subtopics arranged about a common theme.

Figure 8.11   Development of Text Organization in Elementary School

Text organization in children's writing follows a developmental trajectory as they learn conventions of writing that differ from spoken language.

Flexible-focus text

(1) I like coloring because it's not boring
(2) I like coloring cats
(3) I have a black cat at home
(4) His name is Inky

Fixed-focus text

(1) I like Erin because she is my sister
(2) and she shares things with me
(3) and she plays with me
(4) and we go places together
(5) she also is a twin sister with me
(6) and she likes to go to the store and buy candy and toys

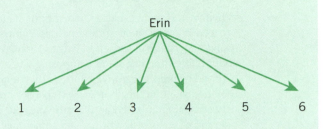

Topic-eleboration text

(1) I like dinosaurs because they are big
(2) and they are scary.
(3) I like Rex.
(4) He was very big.
(5) He ate meat.
(6) Triceratops is a very nice dinosaur.
(7) He ate plants.
(8) He had three horns on his face.
(9) He had a shield on his neck.
(10) Stegosaurus was a plant eater too.
(11) He had(unfinished)

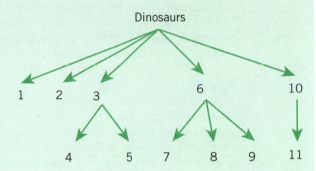

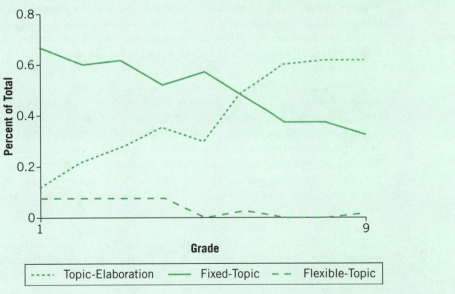

Source: Hayes (2012).

The Hayes Model

When writers compose texts, whether by hand or on the keyboard, they tend to proceed in cycles of bursts and pauses. A **burst** is *a period of active text composition bounded by pauses at both ends*. Pauses lasting two seconds or more typically make up about half of the time spent composing a text (Alves et al., 2008). Pause times are believed to reflect cognitive effort, as they tend to increase in length with the size of the linguistic unit they border, with pauses between sentences being shorter than those between paragraphs (Leijten & van Waes, 2013). During pauses, writers sometimes plan the next burst of writing, and sometimes they evaluate what they've already written for possible revision (Quinlan et al., 2012).

Writing is a complex task that involves the interaction of both long-term and working memory with language, problem-solving, and sensorimotor processes. The so-called **Hayes model** is *an influential theory of the writing process that has guided research since the 1980s* (Quinlan et al., 2012). The strength of this model lies in its fertile ability to generate testable hypotheses, and it has been adopted by most researchers who study cognitive processes in writing (Morken & Helland, 2013). Since it was first proposed in 1980, it has undergone a number of revisions as experiments based on the model have yielded new data.

In its current form, the Hayes (2012) model consists of four core writing processes. The proposer generates ideas, while the translator converts the proposed ideas into spoken language strings. This doesn't mean that writers actually say the sentences out loud, but rather they produce them with the same inner voice they use in silent reading. The third process is the transcriber, which converts the spoken language strings into the motor plans to handwrite the words or type them on a keyboard. The final process is the evaluator, which scans for errors and initiates revisions of the output from the other three processes. In other words, the writer can revise proposed ideas, spoken language strings, or already transcribed text. These writing processes interact with the task environment, which includes the text-produced-so-far, source materials, and collaborators.

The model also has three levels of interacting cognitive processes (Hayes, 2012). The writing processes and task environment are situated on the processing level. Above this is the control level, where motivation, goals, plans, and writing schemas exert top-down control over the writing process. Supporting the writing process is a resource layer that includes long-term memory, working memory, attention, and reading. The process of reading is included because it's necessary for both accessing resource materials and revising the text-produced-so-far. In addition, writers often read over the text-produced-so-far to generate new ideas. The complexity of the Hayes model reflects the multitude of cognitive processes that interact in the writing task.

To get a feel for the model, let's walk through it with an example. Suppose your instructor asks you to write an essay describing the Hayes model. At the control level, you're motivated by your desire to get a good grade on the assignment, and so you work up a general plan for the essay based on the writing schemas you've acquired through years of writing lessons.

Figure 8.12 The Hayes Model

The Hayes model has guided writing research for more than three decades. As new data come in, it has undergone numerous revisions. The most recent version (Hayes, 2012) attempts to account for developmental data as well as that from skilled writers.

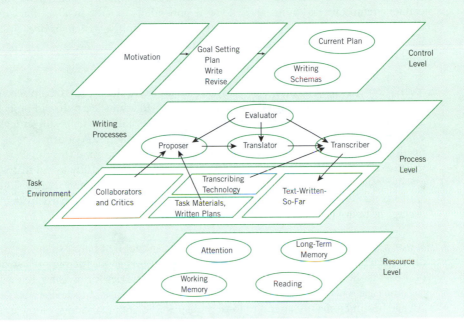

Source: Hayes (2012).

As you begin the writing process, you may reread this section of the textbook or go online for additional materials. The proposer draws from these materials in the task environment to begin generating ideas, which the translator converts into the sentences you hear in your head. The transcriber guides your fingers across the keyboard as you type while the evaluator monitors for errors and makes revisions. After you've written a few sentences, you may go back and read the text-produced-so-far to see if you need to add more information.

All of these processes depend on general cognitive resources. The amount of text you can produce in a single burst is likely limited by working memory constraints, and you need to keep referencing long-term memory as you come up with ideas to write (Leijten & van Waes, 2013). You also depend on attention to bring your mind back to the writing task whenever you start daydreaming about things more pleasant than writing an essay.

Modeling the Development of Writing Skills

The original Hayes model was much simpler, and it was designed to describe how skilled adult writers produce texts (Morken & Helland, 2013). However, it had serious shortcomings as a model for developing writers. For example, transcription is largely an automated task for adults, but young children struggle with the task of putting letters on paper or typing on a keyboard, and this impinges on other writing processes (Hayes, 2012). Thus, the transcriber was put into the model to account for developmental data, but it also suggested that transcription could be an issue for skilled adults under certain circumstances. For instance, if you require adults to write in all capital letters, the effort of transcription puts as much stress on the cognitive system as does ordinary handwriting in children. Likewise, typing can either be a boon or a burden compared with handwriting, depending on the writer's keyboarding skills.

Motivation is another cognitive process that was added to the model to help account for developmental data. Although the majority of educated adults learn to read proficiently and come to find it an enjoyable activity, many of these skilled readers still struggle with writing. While some people learn to excel at writing and keep journals or blogs just for the joy of it, most adults have little motivation to write, and this can have a negative effect on the texts they do produce. For example, one study found that when a college offered supplemental activities aimed at improving students' writing skills, students that had been admitted as "basic" writers were less likely to participate than average or honors students (Hayes, 2012).

Writing schemas are also a new component to the model that help explain developmental data. Skilled writers have solid intuitions about the required structure of the texts they write, and they also have effective strategies for revising; but this isn't the case with less skilled writers. For instance, when asked to revise a text, college freshmen mainly attend to local problems like grammar and spelling and disregard global text issues like organization, while skilled writers attend to both local and global problems (Hayes, 2012). However, when the freshmen are given instruction on how to attend to global text issues, the quality of their revisions improves significantly.

Children with dyslexia or specific language impairment perform much worse on writing tasks compared with their peers (Morken & Helland, 2013). Although they put as much effort into the writing task and produce similar content as do their peers, the end product is of lower quality (Koutsoftas & Gray, 2012). Their writing is riddled with misspellings and grammatical errors as well as with limited choice of vocabulary. The Hayes model predicts that the bottleneck for dyslexic and language-impaired students is transcription, that is, converting spoken language into written form via the rules of orthography, and this drain on cognitive resources impacts these writers' ability to attend to grammar and vocabulary (Morken & Helland, 2013). Evidence in support of this hypothesis comes from the observation that the bursts of language-impaired children are briefer and contain fewer words compared with those of typically developing peers (Connelly et al., 2012).

Visuospatial Aspects of the Text

Unlike speech, which is fleeting and invisible, written language is relatively permanent and laid out in two-dimensional space. This means that the writer has a different relationship with a text than a speaker has with a narrative. For example, when we give a speech, we may forget whether we've already made a particular point, or we may inadvertently skip over information we meant to tell. But when we write, we don't have this kind of memory limitation. Since we can always review what we've written, the text-produced-so-far serves as a sort of auxiliary memory (Olive & Passerault, 2012). Furthermore, we usually know about where in the text to search for a piece of information.

To some extent we rely on our memory for the sequence of ideas in the text to find information, but we rely on spatial memory as well. That is, we often know about where on a page to find the information we're looking for. Spatial information is especially important for revising texts, as writers are more efficient at detecting errors when page boundaries are visible in the text presentation mode than when the boundaries are not visible (Olive & Passerault, 2012).

Skilled writers also rely on visuospatial information for organizing and revising their texts. For instance, experienced writers rely on both linguistic information and spatial properties of the text when deciding where to place paragraph breaks (Olive & Passerault, 2012). In other words, writers organize paragraphs not just in terms of common topic but also by length. Thus, the writing schemas of skilled writers also include visuospatial information about how a paragraph should look.

In Sum

Writing is one of the most cognitively demanding tasks that humans engage in, and it's a skill that takes decades to master. While the visual word form area stores visual information about the shape of letters and words, Exner's area in the frontal lobe stores motor plans for handwriting. Texts written by young schoolchildren are often structured as free-association chains, but as they progress through primary and secondary school, they produce more texts structured around themes and subtopics. The Hayes model has been very influential in the field of writing research since the 1980s. The model attempts to account for how the writing process interacts with general cognitive factors and with the environment. Although individuals with language disorders put as much effort into producing texts compared with their peers, their end product is deficient in terms of quality, spelling, grammar, and vocabulary choice. Skilled writers make use of the spatial layout of text on the page as they make decisions about paragraph structure and to search for information within the text as they make revisions.

Review Questions

1. What are the three stages in learning how to write? What skills need to be learned at each stage?

2. Describe the Hayes model. Include a discussion of the four core writing processes and the three interacting levels. What role does each of these levels play in the writing process?

3. Why does the revised Hayes model include a role for motivation and for writing schemas? Why did Hayes and his colleagues add transcription as a fourth writing process?

4. What is the evidence that suggests skilled writers encode visual and spatial information about the text they are writing?

Thought Questions

1. Imagine that your school asked you to design a program to help college students improve their writing. What sorts of skills would you want to teach them? How would you go about recruiting participants for the program? Support your argument with evidence from this chapter.

2. The Hayes model has undergone many revisions since it was first proposed in 1980. Given that it is constantly changing, what good is it as an explanation of the writing process? You may want to refer to Chapter 2 as you consider the purpose and value of a theory.

Google It! The Cursive Controversery

In recent years, many schools have phased out the teaching of cursive and replaced it with instruction in keyboarding. However, many education experts argue that being able to read and write cursive is still an important part of literacy. You can learn more about the **cursive controversy** on the Internet. Articles and videos on the subject can also be found by searching for the **importance of teaching handwriting**.

CONCLUSION

Congratulations! You've just performed an amazing task. Taking squiggles on a page and transforming them into thoughts in your head is an incredibly complex task, and it took you years of training to learn how to do it. In the process, you rewired your brain to perform a task it was never designed for.

We think of writing as language in a visual mode, but in fact the relationship between writing and language is more complex. Writing not only differs from speech in modality—that is, vision or hearing—it also differs in the dimension of time. Speech is ephemeral—it is cast into the air and quickly dissipates. But writing is eternal—or at least much more lasting than speech. Furthermore, reading doesn't always involve vision. For example, Braille is a writing system for the blind in which readers trace their fingers across a page, converting raised bumps into meaningful language. So reading can work through the sense of touch as well as sight (Gnanadesikan, 2009).

In Chapter 10, we'll learn about another visual form of language that has much more in common with speech. Deaf people, who cannot hear spoken language, instead learn to talk with their hands. Signed languages are not charades or gestures. They are full-formed languages with all the features of spoken languages even though they're conveyed in a visual mode.

But first we return to the realm of speech in Chapter 9. There, we'll learn about the world of bilinguals, those people that have somehow fit two languages into one brain.

CROSS-CULTURAL PERSPECTIVE:
Writing in a Different Language

When we read, we convert visual symbols into spoken language. However, writing is more than just speech on paper. Young schoolchildren write the way they speak, and it takes years to train them in the art of written prose.

Written language has a different set of conventions than speech, because the circumstances in which the two are produced differ considerably. Generally, when we speak, we do so to a live audience, and our listeners provide us with feedback in the form of facial expressions and backchannels to let us know whether they understand us or not. Since we're performing in real time when we speak, our audience cuts us slack when we make errors or omissions. And if we mess up completely, we're allowed to start over.

Speech is a social act, but writing is a solitary one. When we write, we imagine an audience, but our readers can't give us any real-time feedback on how well we're conveying our message. And since our writing is laid out in a permanent format, our readers expect it to be error-free. Of course, we revise and rewrite, but our audience only sees the final polished product. So we write in complete, grammatical sentences, and we organize them into paragraphs based on common topic and logical flow. We're also more careful about our use of referring expressions, and skilled writers think carefully about how much common ground they have with their potential audience.

Thus, we learn to write in a language that's not quite like our mother tongue. For speakers of Standard American English (SAE), the difference between spoken and written forms is not that great. But for speakers of regional and ethnic dialects, learning to compose texts in formal written English is more challenging.

African American English (AAE) is a dialect of North America that diverges considerably from SAE. For many years, educators disparaged AAE as ungrammatical or sloppy English. However, linguists have studied AAE extensively and have found it to be a fully formed linguistic system governed by complex rules (Ivy & Masterson, 2011). In other words, AAE—and any dialect, for that matter—isn't bad English, it's just different English.

The grammar of AAE is often different from SAE. For example, AAE has lost that pesky -s suffix on the end of third-person singular verbs: *I go, you go, he go*. Like Chinese, AAE doesn't mark the plural of nouns, especially when it's clear from context: *one shoe, two shoe*. And like Russian, AAE drops linking verbs like *is* and *are* in the present tense: *He my brother*.

Since early grade schoolers write the way they speak, African American children write in AAE. Especially when the teacher is not a speaker of AAE, this can lead to misunderstanding and problems. It's important for elementary teachers to be sensitive to dialect differences and to be able to recognize the features of spoken AAE in the writing of their students (Ivy & Masterson, 2011). In particular, the teacher needs to be careful not to convey the sense that there's a problem with the student's language. Rather, teachers need to help all of their students understand that the language they are expected to write in is different from the language they speak.

KEY TERMS

Acquired dyslexia

Alphabet

Alphabetic principle

Auditory processing deficit hypothesis

Burst

Deep orthography

Developmental dyslexia

Diffusion tensor imaging

Direct route

Dual route model

Exner's area

Fovea

Frequency effect

Gaze contingency paradigm

Gray matter

Hayes model

Homographs

Homophones

Implicit prosody hypothesis

Indirect route

Isolated spelling disorder

Letter position dyslexia

Logogram

Missing letter effect

Neuronal recycling hypothesis

Orthography

Parafovea

Parafovea-on-fovea effect

Perceptual span

Phonics-based approach

Phonological awareness

Phonological dyslexia

Predictability effect

Rapid automatized naming

Shallow orthography

Spillover effect

Surface dyslexia

Syllabary

Visual word form area

White matter tracts

Bilingualism

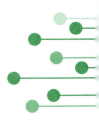

British linguist David Crystal (2000) tells the story of a Johannesburg taxi driver who could speak eleven languages. Crystal was impressed, but the driver saw nothing remarkable about his linguistic abilities—nor any great value in them, either. Instead, his goal in life was to earn enough money so that his children could learn English, the only language worth knowing in his opinion.

Native speakers of English tend to be monolingual, and they also tend to assume one person–one language is the norm. But this assumption is false. Most people in the world speak more than one language, and they do so out of necessity. Immigrants to a new country need to learn a new language, and people living in multiethnic societies, like the South African taxi driver, have to know the languages of their fellow citizens.

In the twenty-first century, English has become the world language of business and science, and today one in four people around the globe speaks English, most of them as a second language (Crystal, 2003). By exploring the experience of being bilingual, we can gain deeper insights into what it means to be human.

SECTION 9.1: THE BILINGUAL EXPERIENCE

- Most people in the world are bilingual, meaning that they speak two or more languages; however, they rarely speak all of their languages with equal proficiency, and typically one language is preferred or dominant.

- The distinction between language and dialect is based more on political than linguistic considerations; two languages or dialects are said to be mutually intelligible when their speakers can understand each other.

- Language shift among immigrants to the United States follows a predictable three-generation pattern; the first generation speaks the heritage language and some English, the second generation speaks the heritage language but prefers English, and members of the third generation grow up as monolingual English speakers.

- In multilingual societies, one of the languages is often dominant and is used for communication in government, education, and business; in some cases, communication between ethnic groups proceeds through a lingua franca, which is a second language that members of different ethnic groups can also speak.

- Bilinguals engage in codeswitching to select the language that best suits the pragmatics of the situation; codeswitching can occur between or within turns of conversation. Bilinguals will also engage in language negotiation, tentatively trying different languages until the best fit for the current situation is mutually agreed upon.

- Language is a vital component of a person's identity, and bilinguals modify their language use to assert their membership in various social groups; language also influences the emotional recall of memories, with those memories being more vivid and arousing when recalled in the language in which the events were first experienced.

If you're an American, you probably speak English and no other language. You may also assume that most people are **monolingual**, or *able to speak only one language*, just like you. But you would be wrong. In fact, most people in the world today are **bilingual**, meaning they're *able to speak two or more languages*, and monolinguals are the exception (Dixon, Wu, & Daraghmeh, 2012). Two-thirds of the children in the world are growing up in bilingual environments, and even in the United States, one in five school children speaks a language other than English at home (Brito & Barr, 2012).

The Bilingual World

People grow up learning more than one language for a variety of reasons. Globalization has led to an increase in immigration, which usually means learning the language of the new country (Dixon, WU, et al., 2012). There are also regions of the world where bilingualism is the norm because those societies consist of multiple ethnic groups. In such circumstances, people need to be able speak more than one language in order to be able to fully participate in home and social life; for them bilingualism is a necessity, not a choice (Kay-Raining Bird, Lamond, & Holden, 2012). In addition, the emergence of English as the global language of business and science means that many educated people in most parts of the world have at least some command of English.

Bilingualism comes in varying degrees. *A person who grows up speaking two languages and can communicate equally well in either language* is considered a **balanced bilingual** (Hsu, 2014). However, few bilinguals are truly balanced, and in most cases the person will have a preferred or dominant language. Although we learn the foundation of our language at home as children, school is also an important environment for language development, especially vocabulary and literacy. Thus, the language the child is educated in will usually become the dominant language in adulthood. Furthermore, people who learn a second language after early childhood rarely develop native speaker proficiency in that language, and in this case the first language learned will usually be the dominant language. Finally, some people will be counted as bilingual or not depending on whether you view the linguistic systems they're familiar with as distinct languages or rather as different dialects of the same language.

Languages and Dialects

Look at a map of Europe and you'll see a patchwork of nations, each with its own language. They speak French in France, Spanish in Spain, Italian in Italy, German in Germany, and so on. But this view of language is simplistic. If you were to travel from Amsterdam to Berlin, sampling the language of each town and village along the way, you would find the standard Dutch of Amsterdam gradually become more German-like until you encountered the standard German of Berlin. Furthermore, people living on either side of the Dutch-German border can understand each other! You'll find a similar transitioning of dialects as you cross many of the other borders in Europe.

Figure 9.1 Map of Europe

Although there are clear-cut political borders in Europe, the linguistic boundaries are blurred.

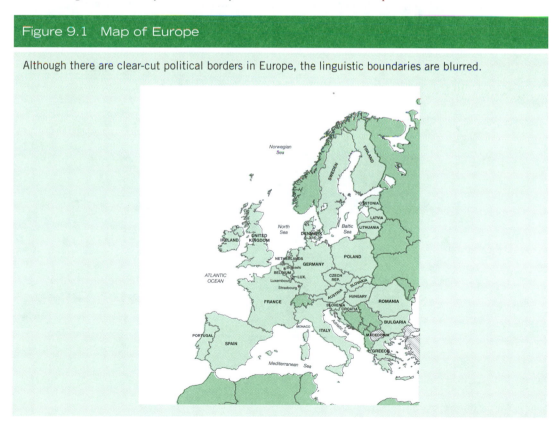

Because the Netherlands and Germany are different countries, their linguistic systems are treated as different languages. However, you find the same transitioning of dialects from one region to another in China as well. A native of Beijing cannot understand the local dialect of Shanghai, but as you travel from one city to the next, you find that people in adjacent towns can always understand each other. Since China is a single nation-state, the various regional linguistic systems are considered dialects. In other words, the difference between two languages and two dialects is based more on political than on linguistic considerations.

Linguists avoid the language-dialect conundrum altogether by assessing **mutual intelligibility** instead, meaning that they consider *the degree to which speakers of two different languages or dialects can understand each other* (Hsu, 2014). American and British English are mutually intelligible even though there are obvious differences between them. On the other hand, the various major regional dialects of China are not mutually intelligible.

Figure 9.2   Map of Major Chinese Dialects

Although mainland China is a single political unit, its people speak a dozen mutually unintelligible dialects.

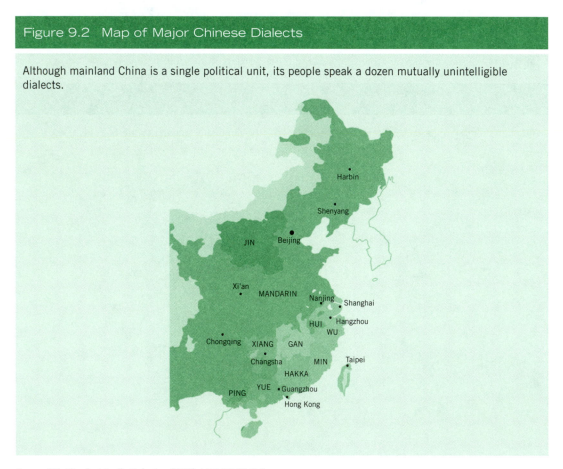

Source: Wu Yue (original); Gohu1er (SVG) / CC-BY-SA-3.0.

You might assume that if a speaker of Language A can understand a speaker of Language B, the reverse should be true as well. But this is not always the case. For example, the Scandinavian languages of Swedish and Danish are closely related and generally considered to be mutually intelligible (Schüppert & Gooskens, 2011). However, adult Swedes find Danish difficult to understand while adult Danes can easily understand Swedish. Sweden is the dominant country in Scandinavia, and attitudes seem to play a role. In surveys, adult Danes report favorable attitudes about Sweden while adult Swedes indicate less positive attitudes toward Denmark. Considering that preschool Danes and Swedes are equally capable of understanding the other language, it appears that adult Swedes are less willing to understand Danish because of social bias.

Immigration to the United States

Immigration accounts for most instances of bilingualism in the United States, and there's also a very predictable pattern of language shift across generations in immigrant families (Shin & Alba, 2009). The first generation, of course, speaks the **heritage language**, which is *the language spoken in an immigrant's country of origin.* They may also learn English to varying degrees of proficiency, but English rarely becomes their dominant language. The second generation, which was either born in the United States or came to this country at a very early age, generally grows up bilingual, learning the heritage language at home and English at school. Because of the strong economic and social pressure in this country to assimilate to American culture, English becomes

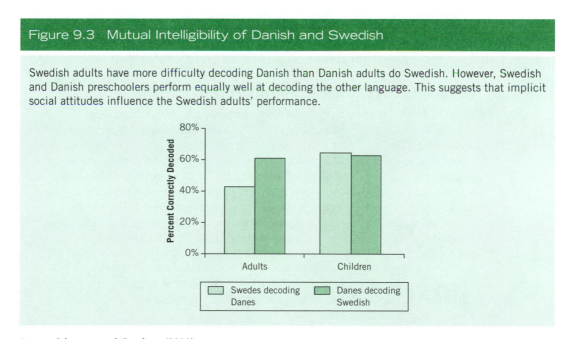

Figure 9.3   Mutual Intelligibility of Danish and Swedish

Swedish adults have more difficulty decoding Danish than Danish adults do Swedish. However, Swedish and Danish preschoolers perform equally well at decoding the other language. This suggests that implicit social attitudes influence the Swedish adults' performance.

Source: Schüppert and Gooskens (2011).

the dominant language of this generation. Furthermore, because they are educated in English, the children of immigrants may not learn to read and write the heritage language without explicit training, and many immigrant communities in the United States maintain after-school or weekend heritage language programs for their children. This second generation grows up with a strong preference for English and frequently marries outside the heritage ethnic group. As a result, their children, who constitute the third generation, typically grows up as monolingual English speakers.

This pattern of language shift is accelerated in the case of older children or young adolescents who immigrate to this country. These children are still in the process of learning their first language when they are thrust into a new environment, and English soon becomes their dominant language (Rothman, 2009). As a result, they often experience **incomplete first-language acquisition**, referring to *the failure to attain full native speaker proficiency of the first language*. In other words, these young first-generation immigrants have language abilities more like those of second-generation immigrants. And likewise their children typically grow up as English monolinguals.

It's important to point out that incomplete first-language acquisition doesn't mean that these bilinguals are deficient in any way (Cabo & Rothman, 2012). People learn languages to the extent that they need to use them. Young immigrants may need to speak enough of the heritage language to communicate with family members about day-to-day matters, but they need to have native speaker proficiency to fully participate in American society. For that matter, the heritage language of adult immigrants also changes over time, since they no longer participate in the society of the country of origin and are inevitably influenced by the language and culture of their new homeland. Again, we see that languages are not categorical linguistic systems but rather exist along a continuum, varying from region to region and even speaker to speaker.

Multigenerational Bilingualism

In many areas of the world, multiple ethnic groups with different languages live side by side. In this case, bilingualism becomes the norm, and each new generation grows up bilingual. One such example is the city-state of Singapore in southeast Asia. Three ethnic groups—Chinese, Malay, and Tamil—live together in this society, and all three languages are spoken there (Dixon, Wu, et al., 2012). As a former British colony, English is the **lingua franca**, which is *a second language in common to all ethnic groups in a given region*. In other words, while the three ethnic groups may not speak each others' languages, they can generally communicate with each other in English. This is especially true of educated Singaporeans, since English is the main language of instruction. English is also the **dominant language** of Singapore, meaning that it is *the language of political and economic power within a bilingual society*. The three ethnic languages are also arranged in a pecking order, with Chinese and Malay having higher status than Tamil. Of course, language status reflects the social status of the various ethnic groups within the community.

Another example of a multilingual society is the Grand Duchy of Luxembourg, a tiny country on the border between France and Germany. Luxembourg is officially a trilingual nation (Engel de Abreu, 2011). The citizens of the Grand Duchy grow up speaking Luxembourgish, but they learn both French and German in school. Although Luxembourgers continue to speak Luxembourgish among themselves, many of them also need to interact on a regular basis with French and German speakers, since Luxembourg City is an international center of politics and finance. In this case, Luxembourgish can't be considered the dominant language, since government and business are mostly conducted in French and German. Rather, the ability to speak Luxembourgish serves as a marker of identity separating locals from foreigners. In fact, it's not uncommon for ethnic minorities included within larger political structures to fiercely maintain their ethnic language across generations as a way to provide an identity separate from that of the dominant society.

Codeswitching

Among bilinguals, their different languages are often associated with different environments or contexts. On the one hand, the heritage language may be used at home with family members, and topics pertaining to home and family life may be more easily expressed in that language. On the other hand, the **societal language**, which is *the language spoken by the majority of people in a given society*, may prove easier to use when discussing topics relevant to issues outside of the home. This may even be the case for first-generation immigrants, whose command of the societal language is relatively weak. Thus, bilinguals will often engage in **codeswitching**, which is *a change from one language to another within a single interaction* (Rontu, 2007). Codeswitching can occur between sentences in a conversation or even within sentences, and it's observed even in young bilingual children.

Codeswitching reflects a deep pragmatic knowledge on the part of the speakers (Angermeyer, 2010). When bilinguals engage in codeswitching, they're not only aware of their interlocutor's language abilities, they also have a good sense of which language will best convey the intended message. In other words, codeswitching is not the result of a language failure but rather arises from the skillful crafting of language to the appropriate context (Greer, 2013).

A more formalized type of codeswitching occurs in the case of translation (Angermeyer, 2010). When persons who speak different languages need to interact, they rely on translators, who are by definition bilingual. In many cases, such as in the United States, native speakers of the dominant language are typically monolingual, and it's the bilingual speakers of the heritage or ethnic language who are called upon to do the translating. The social dynamics of translation are complex, as they involve interactions between members of the dominant and subordinate social classes, and the translator, though able to speak both languages, is still viewed as a member of the subordinate group.

Bilingual speakers' choice of language depends more on pragmatic factors than their own competence (Angermeyer, 2010). First, there's strong pressure to use the local language whenever possible. As a result, immigrant families to the United States tend to speak more English at home the longer they've been in the country. Second, bilingual speakers tend to use the native language of their interlocutor because it increases the likelihood that their intended message will be understood. Finally, in interactions between speakers of the dominant and minority languages, the burden of being understood falls squarely on the speaker of the nondominant language. Thus, minority speakers will take great pains to express themselves in the majority language, knowing full well that the majority language speaker isn't likely to make a similar effort to be understood.

Although young bilingual children sometimes codeswitch due to limitations in one of the languages they're speaking, they also learn the pragmatics of codeswitching at an early age (Khattab, 2013). By the time they're two years old, bilingual children show *sensitivity to the identity or ethnic background of the interlocutor in selecting a language to use*, and this awareness is known as **bilingual accommodation**.

Young bilinguals also become skillful at **language negotiation**, which is *a process in which bilingual interlocutors work together to decide which language to use* (Cromdal, 2013; Lehti-Eklund, 2012). Immigrants and visitors to the United States often need to negotiate language when meeting fellow members of their ethnic group for the first time. As we've seen, ethnic minorities in this country typically lose their heritage language by the second or third generation after immigration; and so the initial exchange is usually in English, with a switch to the ethnic language only after it's been established that both interlocutors are more comfortable with it.

Receptive language abilities generally outpace productive abilities, and this is true for monolinguals as well as bilinguals. For example, although you can understand your teachers' lectures, you probably can't speak with the same level of vocabulary and structural complexity. In the case of immigration, members of the second or third generation may still have *the ability to understand a second language without being able to speak it*, and this capacity is known as **receptive bilingualism** (Herkenrath, 2011). In this situation, the interlocutors each speak in their dominant language but still manage to understand each other.

Mutual intelligibility, as in the case of Danes understanding Swedish, is one example of receptive bilingualism, and it stems from the fact that the two languages are very similar in vocabulary and structure. However, receptive bilingualism can also occur between two languages that are not closely related. For example, French and German are not mutually intelligible, but both are official languages of Switzerland. Most Swiss speak one of these as their native language but can still understand the other language, and sometimes they engage in conversations where one interlocutor speaks French and the other responds in German. Receptive bilingualism also often occurs within immigrant families, in which case the parents or grandparents speak to the children in the heritage language while the children respond in their preferred English.

Language and Identity

Language is an integral part of a person's identity, and bilinguals use language to establish their identity, which may vary as they move from one social group to another (Khattab, 2013). First-generation immigrants typically strive to maintain their heritage identity, and they speak the societal language with an accent that reveals their country of origin. Members of the second generation, however, strive to assimilate to the new culture, and they speak the societal language with the local accent. However, they may opt to speak the local language with a heritage language accent when interacting with members of their ethnic group, especially those who are older.

Language can also have an impact on the emotions experienced when recalling memories, as for example in the case of bilingual psychotherapy (Frie, 2013). Early childhood memories are recalled more vividly and with greater emotion when bilingual clients present them in their native language. Thus, it's often easier for clients to first discuss early traumatic events in their second language, since the emotional experience is dampened. Later in the course of therapy, when clients have already achieved some healing, they may opt to revisit those memories with the therapist in their native language to resolve the meaning of those memories in their lives.

In Sum

Most people in the world speak two or more languages, but in almost all cases they have one preferred or dominant language that forms part of their personal identity. Sometimes speakers of different languages can still understand each other, not because they speak each other's language but because the two languages are similar enough to be mutually intelligible. Immigration language shift in the United States typically occurs across three generations, with the first generation bilingual but dominant in the heritage language, the second generation bilingual but dominant in English, and the third generation monolingual English speaking. In multilingual societies, such as Singapore or Luxembourg, citizens need to be multilingual in order to fully engage in society. Bilinguals engage in codeswitching to maximize communication, taking into account multiple pragmatic factors, such as context, topic, and the language abilities of their interlocutors. Bilinguals also switch languages to identify themselves as members of various social groups as well as to modulate the emotional impact of memories.

Review Questions

1. What does it mean to say that two languages are mutually intelligible? On the one hand, Danish and Swedish are mutually intelligible, yet they are considered different languages. On the other hand, Shanghainese and Cantonese (spoken in Hong Kong) are mutually unintelligible, yet they are considered dialects of Chinese. What then is the distinction between language and dialect?

2. Describe the language shift that occurs across generations among immigrant populations in the United States. Why does this shift occur?

3. What is a lingua franca? In what sense has English become a global lingua franca?

4. Describe the various ways in which bilinguals engage in codeswitching. What sorts of pragmatic and social factors do bilinguals consider as they negotiate language?

Thought Questions

1. How is the language you speak related to your sense of personal identity? Even if you're a monolingual English speaker, do you modify the way you speak to convey different aspects of your personal identity in different situations? Do you ever modify the way you speak in order to conform to the social group you are interacting with?

2. It used to be thought that bilingualism had mostly negative consequences because bilinguals rarely perform as well as monolinguals on single-language tasks. However, it's now well understood that monolingual language performance is not a good measure for language competence for bilinguals. Explain why this is so, given what you have read in this section.

Google It! Codeswitching

If you're interested in **codeswitching**, you can find a number of videos on YouTube that explain the phenomenon in more detail and provide examples.

SECTION 9.2: ORGANIZATION OF THE BILINGUAL MIND

- Both languages are activated in the brains of bilinguals every time they speak, regardless of which language they are currently using; evidence for this assertion comes from cross-language priming, eye-tracking, and electrophysiological studies.

- Translation equivalents are words in two languages that refer to the same concept. Closely related languages share cognates, which are words that have similar forms and meanings in both languages; however, interlingual homographs are "false friends" in that their forms are similar but their meanings are different.

- Bilinguals have smaller vocabularies in each of their languages and more difficulty retrieving words compared with monolinguals; while this bilingual disadvantage is measurable in the laboratory, it has no discernible impact on the day-to-day activities of the bilingual person.

- The weaker links hypothesis explains the bilingual disadvantage by suggesting that bilinguals are less practiced at using the words they know since they need to split their time between two languages; the interference hypothesis proposes that translation equivalents create interference that slows down lexical access.

- The revised hierarchical model proposes a separate lexicon for each language with links to a common conceptual level; translation occurs either by passing through the conceptual level or via direct links between the two languages.

- The sense model takes into account the fact that most words have multiple meanings that do not fully overlap across languages; extensions of this model also take into account cultural differences in the imagery evoked by words.

Since bilinguals rarely confuse their two languages, it seems logical to assume that the bilingual mind houses each language separately (Bialystok, Craik, & Luk, 2012). However, the empirical evidence clearly shows that balanced bilinguals activate both languages every time they speak, even when using their dominant language or in strictly monolingual situations where only one of the languages would be appropriate (Bialystok, 2011). This parallel activation of the two languages in bilinguals occurs at all levels of speech production (Festman, 2013).

It's less clear whether this is also the case with an **unbalanced bilingual**, that is, *a person who has limited ability in a second language*. However, immersion in the second-language context, as happens for example during study abroad, does have a temporary impact on the speaker's ability to access words and structures in the dominant language (Gutierrez et al., 2012). This second-language interference soon dissipates, though, once the speaker has returned to the environment where the dominant language is used.

Two Tongues in One Head

Evidence for the joint activation of both languages in a bilingual comes from a number of different approaches. The lexical decision task, in which participants decide as quickly as possible whether a letter string is a word or not, shows that bilinguals cannot simply shut off one language when making word judgments in the other language (Poulin-Dubois et al., 2012). For example, the letter string NOCHE is not a word in English, but the reaction time of a Spanish-English bilingual will be slowed down in this case, because it is a word in Spanish.

Additional evidence for joint activation comes from **cross-language priming** (Bialystok et al., 2012). This is *the situation in which a word in one language aids the retrieval of a word with a related meaning in another language*. For instance, in the case of English monolinguals, the word DOCTOR primes the word NURSE, meaning that reaction time in a lexical decision task is reduced when NURSE follows DOCTOR compared with when it follows an unrelated word. However, in the case of a German-English bilingual, the German word ARZT, which means "doctor," also primes the English word NURSE.

Eye-tracking studies have also found evidence for joint activation in bilinguals. Imagine you're a participant in the following experiment. On each trial, four pictures appear on the computer screen, and you hear a single English word. Your job is to look at the picture named by the word. So, for example, if the visual array contains pictures of a postage stamp, a flag, a marker, and a dog, and you hear "marker," your eyes will quickly move to the picture of the marker. However, it's more complicated for a Russian-English bilingual because the Russian word for "postage stamp" is *marka*. Since we often identify words before they're completely spoken, a Russian-English bilingual is just as likely to look first at the postage stamp as at the marker (Marian, Spivey, & Hirsch, 2003).

Even more evidence for joint activation in bilinguals comes from clinical and neuroimaging studies (Bialystok et al., 2012). Although bilinguals frequently engage in codeswitching for pragmatically appropriate purposes, bilingual patients suffering from language-related brain disorders will often make inappropriate language switches or mix words from their two languages. Furthermore, bilinguals in event-related potential (ERP) studies exhibit semantic priming in both languages, as indicated by a reduced N400 component, even when only one of the languages is being used (Martin et al., 2012). Thus, even when bilinguals are merely listening, both languages are active.

Links Between the Two Languages

Although simultaneous interpreters, such as those employed at the United Nations, are highly trained professionals, any bilingual can do a rough-and-ready translation from one of her languages to the other. This observation suggests that the vocabularies of the two languages are linked at the conceptual level. Put simply, whatever you can talk about in one language, you can also talk about in another language. *Words in two different languages that refer to the same concept* are called **translation equivalents**. Thus, *dog* and *chien* are translation equivalents in English and French.

An interesting issue with translation equivalents is how they are learned in the first place, especially in the case of bilingual children who were exposed to both languages from an early age. As we learned in Chapter 5, young children learning the vocabulary of their first language operate according to the principle of mutual exclusivity, meaning that they assume a new word must refer to a novel concept. Suppose a young child growing up in a bilingual home has heard her English-speaking mother refer to the family pet as *dog*, and then later she hears her French-speaking father utter *chien* while talking about the dog. According to the principle of mutual exclusivity, the child should assume *chien* refers to something else, such as the dog's droopy ears or wagging tail. But bilingual children don't act this way and instead readily accept two different words for the same concept (Poulin-Dubois et al., 2012). This suggests that even at a very young age, children growing up in bilingual environments have some awareness that separate linguistic systems are in use.

Sometimes there are *words in two languages that have similar form and meaning*, and these are known as **cognates**. Cognates occur for two reasons. One reason is that some languages are related to each other and thus share a certain amount of vocabulary. For example, all of the Romance languages, including Spanish, French, and Italian, developed out of the Latin spoken in the Roman empire two thousand years ago. Likewise, the Germanic languages, including German, Dutch, English, and the Scandinavian languages, developed out of a common tongue spoken in central Europe a few thousand years ago. Hence, German and English share a number of cognates, such as *Mann-man*, *Fisch-fish*, *Wein-wine*, and *Bier-beer*. The other reason for cognates is that languages often borrow the names for concepts they acquire from other cultures. For instance, the German-English cognates *Kaffee-coffee* occur because both languages borrowed the name along with the beverage from the Turks.

Cross-language priming studies yield a different pattern of results for cognates and noncognates (Wang, 2013). Recall that most bilinguals have one language (L1) that is stronger than the other language (L2). In the case of cognates, robust priming effects occur in either direction, that is, whether from L1 to L2 or from L2 to L1. For example, either KAFFEE or COFFEE primes TEA for a German-English bilingual. In the case of noncognates, however, priming effects are asymmetrical. If German is the speaker's dominant language, then ARTZ ("doctor") will prime NURSE, but NURSE may not prime ARTZ.

Table 9.1 Some English Cognates With German and French

English has many cognates with German because both languages have a common ancestor. English has many cognates with French because of widespread borrowing after the Norman Conquest of 1066.

English	German	English	French
house	Haus	reason	raison
God	Gott	season	saison
land	Land	beef	boeuf
friend	Freund	biscuit	biscuit
sun	Sonne	bouquet	bouquet
moon	Mond	robe	robe
mother	Mutter	gourmet	gourmet
brother	Bruder	lingerie	lingerie
son	Sohn	pardon	pardon

Appearances may be deceiving, and there are *words in two languages that have similar form but different meanings.* These are technically known as **interlingual homographs**, but they are often called "false friends" in the literature. For example, never accept a *Gift* from a German because it's *poison.* Likewise, *Chef* means "boss" in German, not a person who's skilled at cooking. Bilinguals know these "false friends" have different meanings in each of their languages. Nevertheless, both meanings of an interlingual homograph are temporarily activated, as measured by the event-related potential (ERP) component N400, which is elicited when a semantic expectation is violated. For example, the word pair *Gift-deadly* should elicit a stronger N400 component in an English monolingual, because the meanings are unrelated, compared with a German-English bilingual, who finds a meaningful relationship across the two languages. Again, such results indicate that both languages are activated regardless of which language the bilingual is speaking.

The Bilingual Disadvantage

While fears that raising a child bilingual will only lead to confusion are ungrounded, speaking two languages does have an impact on language abilities. The term **bilingual disadvantage** refers to *the observation that bilinguals have smaller vocabularies in each of their languages and more difficulty retrieving words compared with monolinguals* (Bialystok et al., 2012). This is true for both receptive and expressive vocabulary, and at all ages, from elementary school to adulthood, as measured by standardized tests (Poulin-Dubois et al., 2012).

The bilingual disadvantage can be measured using a variety of laboratory tasks. Bilinguals make slower responses and are less accurate on picture naming tasks (Festman, 2013). They're also slower and come up with fewer items in a **semantic categorization task**, which is *an experimental procedure that asks participants to name members of a given category* (Gutierrez et al., 2012; Wang, 2013). Thus, bilinguals can typically name fewer kinds of bird or pieces of furniture than a monolingual can, and it takes them more time to do so.

The lexical decision task is also more difficult for bilinguals than monolinguals (Martin et al., 2012). Monolinguals can discriminate words from nonwords without considering the meanings of the words, as evidenced by N400 modulation. However, bilinguals show semantic processing for both words and nonwords. It appears that bilinguals perform the lexical decision task by considering whether each letter string is meaningful while monolinguals do so by considering the surface form of the string.

Compared with monolinguals, bilinguals experience more tip-of-the-tongue states (Wodniecka et al., 2010). The tip-of-the-tongue phenomenon, when you know that you know a word or name but can't say it at the moment, is generally interpreted as a temporary difficulty in lexical retrieval, and it's more common with words that are used less frequently. Since bilinguals split their time between two languages, they'll use any given word less often than a monolingual would. Hence, some researchers have made *the proposal that the bilingual disadvantage can be explained in terms of lower word frequencies* (Gollan & Goldrick, 2012). This is known as the **weaker links hypothesis** (Poulin-Dubois et al., 2012). According to this view, bilinguals are less practiced at using the words they know compared with monolinguals, and so they have more difficulty accessing them.

An alternative explanation for the bilingual disadvantage in lexical retrieval is the **interference hypothesis**. This is *the proposal that the bilingual disadvantage can be explained in terms of interference from translation equivalents in the unused language* (Gollan & Goldrick, 2012). Since bilinguals can never simply turn off the other language when they're speaking, the two languages will always compete for activation, and this competition leads to interference in lexical access that slows the process down (Festman, 2013). In other words, bilingual speakers need to be constantly inhibiting intrusions from the unintended language, thus making lexical access more effortful (Poulin-Dubois et al., 2012). We'll revisit the inhibition in the next section.

While the bilingual disadvantage is clearly measurable in the laboratory, it's also important to note that it doesn't lead to any noticeable language problems in real life. In fact, bilinguals rarely experience overt intrusions of the unintended language, and instead they skillfully navigate between their two languages with a high degree of accuracy (Bialystok et al., 2012). Furthermore, when the two languages are closely related, the bilingual disadvantage can be reduced. For example, Spanish and Catalan are closely related and share many cognates. While Catalan-Spanish speakers still exhibit the bilingual disadvantage, they also experience a boost in performance in the case of cognates (Kamat et al., 2012).

Models of the Bilingual Lexicon

Several models have been proposed to explain how the vocabularies of the two languages are organized in the bilingual mind. Perhaps the most influential has been the **revised hierarchical model**, first proposed by Kroll and Stewart (1994). This is *a theory of bilingual language processing that assumes separate lexicons for each language connected by a common underlying conceptual level*. The two lexicons are connected directly by lexical links and indirectly by conceptual links that run through the conceptual level (X. Luo et al., 2013). The strength of each link depends on the proficiency of the bilingual. In the case of the truly balanced bilingual, all links will be strong, and the speaker should be able to translate words just as quickly from L2 to L1 as from L1 to L2. Likewise, cross-linguistic priming should occur in either direction.

In the case where one language is dominant, the revised hierarchical model proposes that some of the links are weaker than others. First, the lexical link from L1 to L2 is weaker than in the opposite direction. This arrangement represents the observation that it's usually easier to translate words from the weaker to the stronger language than from the stronger to the weaker language. If you've ever studied a foreign language, you should have some intuitions about this. It should be easier for you to give the English translations for a list of common words in the foreign language than it is to give the foreign language

Figure 9.4 The Revised Hierarchical Model

The revised hierarchical model proposes separate lexicons for each language with an underlying common conceptual layer. Solid links are strong, and dotted links are weak, reflecting data from translation and cross-language priming tasks.

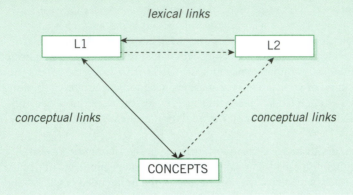

Source: Kroll and Stewart (1994).

equivalents for a list of common English words. As second-language learners become more proficient, they also create conceptual links between L2 and the conceptual core, but these links are weaker because they are less practiced than the L1 conceptual links.

The revised hierarchical model explains asymmetrical cross-language priming by assuming that priming takes place at the conceptual level (Wang, 2013). Since the links from L1 conceptual links are strong, they induce priming that spreads to L2. However, the weaker L2 conceptual links produce less activation in the conceptual level, and as a result there's less priming. The lexical links in the revised hierarchical model are there to account for translation data, but it's unclear why priming can't proceed through the lexical links, in which case priming from L2 to L1 should be stronger, which is not what we find.

Another weakness of the revised hierarchical model is that it doesn't take into account the fact that so-called translation equivalents rarely have exactly the same meaning (Jared, Poh, & Paivio, 2013). For example, the Russian translation equivalent for *cup* is *chashka*, and the translation equivalent for *glass* is *stakan*. In English, if a drinking vessel is made of glass, it's called a *glass*, otherwise it's a *cup*. But in Russian, the distinction is whether the vessel has a handle or not. Thus, a paper coffee cup is a *stakan*, not a *chashka*.

The more abstract the concept, the more the meanings of translation equivalents diverge. Verbs are more abstract than nouns, and they're notoriously difficult to translate. Take for instance the English-Chinese translation equivalents *open-kāi*. While the Chinese verb *kāi* can be used in virtually any context that you would use the English verb *open*, such as open a door, a window, a bank account, or a book, it's also the verb that's used in expressions such as "turn on a light" (*kāi dēng*) and "drive a car" (*kāi chē*).

Figure 9.5   Chashka or Stakan?

Even translation equivalents for common objects often have non-overlapping meanings. Compare the English words *cup* and *glass* with the Russian words *chashka* and *stakan*.

(a)
English *cup*
Russian *chashka*

(b)
English *cup*
Russian *stakan*

(c)
English *glass*
Russian *stakan*

Source: (a) ©iStockphoto.com/RTimages. (b) ©iStockphoto.com/inkit. (c) ©iStockphoto.com/ fcafotodigital.

The **sense model** is *a theory of bilingual language processing that takes into account the fact that most words have multiple meanings that do not fully overlap across languages* (Wang, 2013). According to the sense model, priming activates all senses, or meanings, of a word. Cross-language priming, then, depends on how many shared senses there are between the translation equivalents (X. Luo et al., 2013). Because the bilingual will likely know only a few senses of the L2 word, almost all of which will map onto meanings of the L1 equivalent, cross-language priming from L2 to L1 is more likely to occur. However, the bilingual knows many more senses for the L1 word, many of which will not map onto the senses of the L2 equivalent; hence cross-language priming from L1 to L2 is less likely to happen. Another strength of the sense model is that it can account for the observation that bilinguals are faster at translating concrete words, which tend to have more overlapping meanings, than they are at abstract words (Kauschanskaya & Rechtzigel, 2012).

Words don't just link with abstract concepts, they can also elicit powerful imagery that can vary by culture (Jared et al., 2013). Thus, even very close translation equivalents can be associated with different prototypical images in the two languages. For instance, the English-Chinese translation equivalents *dragon* and *lóng* closely overlap in meaning, in that both refer to a mythological fire-breathing reptile. However, there are subtle differences between the prototypical image of a dragon in the East and West. In a

According to the sense model, translation priming from L2 to L1 is strong because all L2 senses map onto L1 senses. However, translation priming from L1 to L2 is weak because only a few L1 senses map onto L2 senses. The model predicts that, for a native speaker of Chinese, priming for *open-kai* should be stronger than that for *kai-open* because *kai* has other senses that don't map onto *open*.

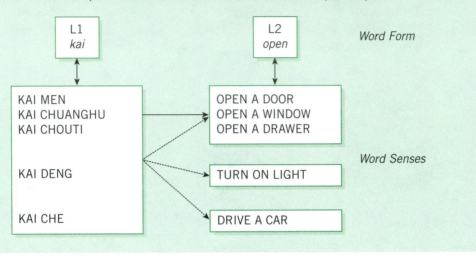

Source: Finkbeiner et al. (2004).

picture naming task, Chinese-English bilinguals named Chinese-typical pictures faster when they responded in Chinese and named Western-typical pictures faster when they responded in English. These results provide clear evidence that word meaning is more than just abstract conceptual knowledge but also includes visual and probably other sensory information. This interpretation is also consistent with the notion of embodied cognition, which proposes that we understand language by activating the relevant perceptual and motor areas of the brain.

In Sum

Whenever bilinguals speak, both of their languages are activated, even in situations that highly bias only one of those languages. Joint activation in bilinguals has been measured through a number of experimental techniques, including both behavioral and brain imaging methods, and it has also been ascertained through clinical data. Pairs of words in two languages that have the same meaning are known as translation equivalents. When they also share a similar form, they're known as cognates. On the other hand, interlingual homographs are false friends, since they have the same form but different meanings. Bilinguals experience a disadvantage in terms of reduced vocabulary size for each language and also slower lexical retrieval,

Figure 9.7 Dragons

In a picture-naming task, Chinese-English bilinguals are faster to respond *lóng* when they see the Chinese-typical image, and they're faster to respond *dragon* when they see the Western-typical image.

(a) Chinese-typical image of a dragon

(b) Western-typical image of a dragon

Source: ©iStockphoto.com/ Tomboy2290.

even in their dominant language. Although the bilingual disadvantage is measurable, it causes no discernable detriment to the daily activities of bilingual speakers. In part the bilingual disadvantage may be due to lack of practice, since bilinguals split their time between two languages. The disadvantage may also result from interference or competition from the unintended language. The revised hierarchical model views the bilingual mind as composed of two separate lexicons united by an underlying common conceptual level. Conversely, the sense model recognizes that words have multiple meanings, not all of which will match up across languages. Extensions of the sense model also consider cultural differences in the imagery evoked by words.

Review Questions

1. Review the evidence for the joint activity of both languages of a bilingual. Consider the results from the lexical decision task, cross-language priming, and eye-tracking, as well as clinical and electrophysiological data.

2. Explain the concepts of translation equivalents, cognates, and interlingual homographs.

3. What is the bilingual disadvantage? How is it explained in terms of the weaker links hypothesis and the interference hypothesis?

4. Describe the revised hierarchical model. How does it explain translation and cross-language priming effects? What are its weaknesses? Describe the sense model and how it accounts for translation and priming effects.

Thought Questions

1. Young children growing up bilingual need to override the mutual exclusivity principle in order to learn translation equivalents in their two languages. What sorts of linguistic or pragmatic cues might enable them to do this?

2. If you know another language in addition to English, perhaps you can come up with some examples of translation equivalents with non-overlapping senses, such as the English-Russian pairs *cup-chashka* and *glass-stakan*.

Google It! Myths About Bilingual Children

In English-dominant North America, it's often believed that raising children to be bilingual can have a negative impact on their development. On YouTube, you can found informative videos by professionals in the field that dismiss common **myths about bilingual children**.

SECTION 9.3: COGNITIVE BENEFITS OF BILINGUALISM

- Bilinguals' ability to quickly and accurately switch from one language to another carries over to other nonverbal cognitive tasks; living with two languages also leads to a better understanding about the nature of language (metalinguistic awareness), and this has a positive impact on creative thought processes as well.

- The bilingual advantage in nonverbal tasks is based on three cognitive skills: interference inhibition, selective attention, and mental flexibility; these three processes work together to produce executive control, which manages cognitive resources to yield efficient performance.

- Lifelong bilinguals generally outperform monolinguals on tests of executive control, but the bilingual advantage is more robust in early childhood and also in later adulthood; those who learn a second language later in life tend to perform more like monolinguals on these tasks.

- Structural brain differences between lifelong bilinguals and monolinguals account for the bilingual advantage; these include increased activity in the executive control centers in the prefrontal and inferior parietal regions, greater white matter integrity, and increased gray matter volume in the classical language areas as well as in the auditory cortex.

- The term *cognitive reserve* refers to the ability to resist the debilitating effects of dementia in old age; regularly engaging in stimulating mental or physical activity throughout the lifespan helps develop cognitive reserve, as does lifelong bilingualism.

- Despite the concerns of many practitioners, raising children with language disorders as bilinguals causes no additional delays in development; furthermore, the social isolation that results from denying these children access to the heritage language can lead to cognitive and behavioral problems.

As we saw in Section 9.2, bilinguals experience some disadvantages in processing their languages, especially with regard to lexical decision and semantic categorization tasks, which rely on efficient lexical retrieval from a large vocabulary (Hsu, 2014). However, at a more global level, bilinguals exhibit superior language processing abilities relative to their monolingual peers.

Compared with monolinguals, bilingual children display heightened **metalinguistic awareness**, which allows them to use their *understanding about how language works* to make effective choices regarding how to communicate with other people (Lauchlan, Parisi, & Fadda, 2012).

In addition, a number of studies have found a bilingual advantage for tasks involving creativity and problem-solving skills (Lee & Kim, 2011; Leikin, 2012). This is especially true when those tasks require symbolic flexibility or concept formation (Lauchlan et al., 2012). For example, bilinguals are better than monolinguals at learning arbitrary names for objects. This skill no doubt stems from their metalinguistic awareness that words are arbitrary symbols, a fact that may not be intuitively obvious to monolinguals.

Executive Control

Recall that bilinguals experience joint activation whenever they use language, and so they need to carefully monitor the language they're using to avoid intrusions from the other language. The **adaptive control hypothesis** is *a proposal suggesting that bilinguals' constant need to monitor and control their languages leads to benefits in nonverbal cognition* (Bobb, Wodniecka, & Kroll, 2013). For example, bilinguals are better than monolinguals at multitasking, which involves quickly switching attention from one cognitive task to another (Engel de Abreu, 2011). In other words, it appears that bilinguals use general purpose mechanisms as they switch from language to language, and so the constant practice they get in the linguistic realm carries over to other perceptual and cognitive functions as well.

Three basic cognitive processes underlie the bilingual advantage. The first is *the ability to ignore distracting or misleading information*, which is known as **interference inhibition** (Lauchlan et al., 2012). From an early age, bilinguals hone their skills at inhibiting interference from the unintended language. The second is **selective attention**, which is *the ability to direct and focus attention on the current task* (Hsu, 2014). Since bilinguals need to take into account pragmatic factors such as which language is appropriate in the current context, they also are highly practiced at selective attention. The third is **mental flexibility**, or *the ability to rapidly switch from one cognitive task to another* (Nicolay & Poncelet, 2013). Bilinguals regularly change from one language to another according to pragmatic demands, and mental flexibility is especially important in the case of code switching, where language shifts occur within sentences.

These three abilities are components of a larger system known as **executive control**, which involves *the management of cognitive resources to perform tasks efficiently* (Wodniecka et al., 2010). Executive control can be measured in a number of ways, and generally bilinguals outperform monolinguals, especially on tasks that don't have a verbal component.

One measure of executive control is the **Simon task**, which is *an experimental procedure that requires participants to respond to the color of a stimulus regardless of its location* (Nicolay & Poncelet, 2013). Imagine you're seated before a computer screen and a keyboard with two buttons. You're told to press the right key when you see a red target and the left key when you see a green target. If the red target appears on the right side of the screen or the green target on the left (the congruent condition), your reaction time will be faster than if the targets are on the opposite side of the screen (the incongruent condition). However, bilinguals show less reduction in speed during the incongruent trials compared to monolinguals.

Another measure of executive control is the **flanker task**. This is *an experimental procedure in which participants respond to the direction of the central arrow in an array, regardless of the direction the other arrows are pointing* (Nicolay & Poncelet, 2013). For example, if you see the array >>>>>, you'll press the right key because the central arrow is pointing to the right. On congruent trials, all arrows point either left or right, but on incongruent trials, the flanker arrows point in the opposite direction of the central, as in >><>>. This time, you need to press the left key. As with the Simon task, participants respond faster during congruent than incongruent trials, but bilinguals are less affected by incongruent trials than monolinguals are (Hsu, 2014).

Bilinguals generally exhibit greater executive control than age-matched monolinguals, but the bilingual advantage is more pronounced among some age groups than others (Bialystok et al., 2012). In monolingual populations, executive control develops late in childhood, peaks in young adulthood, and then declines in middle age. However, bilingual children develop executive control early through their constant need to negotiate language use, and likewise they have to maintain a high level of executive control throughout their life as they balance their two languages. Thus, children and older adults show a clear bilingual advantage in executive control, but the advantage isn't always found in bilingual young adults. This is because they are competing with

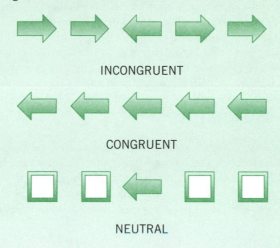

Figure 9.8   Flanker Task

The flanker task is a common test of executive control. The participant responds by pressing the left or right button, according to the direction of the middle arrow. Lifelong bilinguals typically outperform monolinguals in the Incongruent condition of this task.

INCONGRUENT

CONGRUENT

NEUTRAL

Source: Janessaaag / CC-BY-SA-3.0.

monolinguals that are also at their peak cognitive functioning, and only when the task is extremely demanding does a bilingual advantage emerge.

The cognitive benefits of bilingualism are evident in those who've grown up speaking both languages and are more or less balanced in their language proficiency as adults. In the case of nonbalanced bilinguals, who clearly have greater proficiency in one of the languages than the other, the circumstances in which the second language was learned has an impact on the type of cognitive advantages that develop (Salvatierra & Rosselli, 2010).

On the one hand, a high level of proficiency in the second language leads to better performance on tasks requiring metalinguistic awareness; on the other hand, length of time using the second language is a better predictor of executive control (Bialystok & Barac, 2012). Thus, the Spanish major who spends a year abroad in Mexico and then gets a job where she uses her Spanish on an occasional basis may enjoy increased metalinguistic skills, but her performance on executive control tasks will likely be no different from that of a monolingual. Conversely, the immigrant who has spent most of his life in the host country but has only developed basic proficiency in the societal language, which he uses on a daily basis, may exhibit increased executive control while performing more like a monolingual on metalinguistic awareness tasks.

The Bilingual Brain

Neuroimaging studies show structural brain differences between bilinguals and monolinguals. Since bilingualism is not a choice, it's clear that these changes in the bilingual brain are due to the experience of living with two languages. It was already known that the brain center for executive control is in the frontal lobe, so it's not at all surprising to find greater activation in the frontal lobes of bilinguals engaged in tasks requiring executive control (Bialystok et al., 2012). More specifically, the **dorsolateral prefrontal cortex** is known to be *an area of the brain involved in executive control*, and this area becomes active during language switching tasks (Bialystok et al., 2012). The frontal lobe is involved in nonverbal switching tasks as well, but the pattern of activation is different, with more right-side activity for monolinguals and more left-side activity for bilinguals, perhaps because of greater activity of this system for managing their languages (Garbin et al., 2010).

The frontal cortex, as the center for executive control, exerts its influence on other brain regions through a system of white matter tracts running front to back (Bialystok et al., 2012). Neuroimaging studies of young bilinguals show that they recruit a more diverse array of brain regions, compared with their monolingual peers, when they engage in nonverbal tasks requiring executive control (Luk et al., 2011). Presumably,

Figure 9.9   Dorsolateral Prefrontal Cortex and Heschl's Gyrus

Bilinguals exhibit greater activation in the dorsolateral prefrontal cortex, which is responsible for executive control, compared with monolinguals. They also have larger Heschl's gyri, the structure deep inside the lateral fissure where the auditory cortex is located.

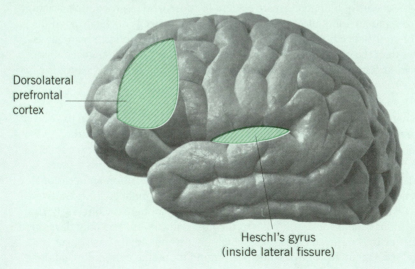

Dorsolateral prefrontal cortex

Heschl's gyrus (inside lateral fissure)

these various regions are connected to the executive control center in the frontal lobe. Executive control of language-related tasks have been found to involve two distinct networks (Christoffels, Kroll, & Bajo, 2013). One network involves white fiber tracts extending from the frontal lobe to the basal ganglia and back, and this system seems to be involved in the inhibition of the unintended language during speech. The other network involves white matter tracts extending from the frontal to the parietal lobes, and this system is implicated in switching tasks, whether language related or not.

Lifelong bilingualism leads to increases in gray matter density not only in the classical language areas but also in regions involved in executive control (Kruchinina et al., 2012). In addition to the executive control center in the prefrontal cortex, which is predominantly responsible for inhibition of inappropriate responses, the left inferior parietal region is recruited for tasks that require selective attention, and brain imaging studies show increased density of gray matter in this area in bilinguals compared with monolinguals (Bialystok et al., 2012). Furthermore, this increase in parietal gray matter density was positively correlated with second-language proficiency and negatively correlated with the age at which the bilinguals acquired the second language (Luk, De Sa, & Bialystok, 2011). In other words, it was the lifelong balanced bilinguals who exhibited the increase in brain mass.

Auditory perception is also affected by bilingualism (Ressel et al., 2012). Recall from Chapter 3 that the auditory cortex is located deep in the lateral fissure on a structure known as Heschl's gyrus. Typically, Heschl's gyrus is larger in lifelong balanced bilinguals than it is in monolinguals, even when other potential factors, such as socioeconomic status, education, or musical experience, are controlled for. Furthermore, the size of Heschl's gyrus is correlated with the ability to quickly learn new consonantal or tonal contrasts not in either of the bilingual's two languages. You should remember that young infants are able to discriminate all possible speech sound contrasts, losing all but those relevant to their native language by their first birthday. However, it seems that lifelong bilinguals maintain some of this neural plasticity from infancy.

Cognitive Reserve

The saying "use it or lose it" applies just as much to your brain as it does to your body. Ample research supports *the notion that engaging in stimulating mental or physical activity on a regular basis helps maintain cognitive functioning as we age and protects against dementia* (Bialystok et al., 2012). A number of factors contribute to **cognitive reserve**, including level of formal education and occupational status, which typically lead to higher socioeconomic class and better health overall. Likewise, regular physical exercise and stimulating leisure activities as well as social engagement all boost cognitive reserve. In addition to these various factors, lifelong bilingualism has been shown to provide cognitive reserve (Bialystok, 2011).

At the level of the brain, cognitive reserved is based on maintaining white matter integrity and gray matter volume (Luk et al., 2011). As we age, the white matter tracts, which connect different functional areas, tend to deteriorate, and the volume of gray matter, which performs those functions, tends to shrink. However, older bilinguals show less reduction of white and gray matter compared with monolinguals, suggesting that living with two languages is sufficiently stimulating mentally to provide some protection against brain atrophy and dementia.

Even when aging bilinguals do develop dementia, they still fare better than their monolingual peers. One study looking at clinical records found that lifelong bilingual patients were, on average, four years older than monolingual patients when symptoms of Alzheimer's disease were first diagnosed (Bialystok, 2011). It could be that balancing two languages for a lifetime provides cognitive reserve that gives bilingual brains additional time before they succumb to the disease, but brain imaging studies tell a more complex story. When the brains of bilingual and monolingual patients at similar stages of Alzheimer's disease were studied using a neuroimaging technique called computed tomography, it was found that the bilingual brains had incurred far more atrophy than the monolingual brains (Schweizer et al., 2012). In other words, the bilinguals were still functioning at a higher level than were the monolinguals even though they had experienced more advanced deterioration of the brain areas typically affected by Alzheimer's disease. It's believed that the greater white matter connectivity and increased gray matter in other areas of the bilingual brain were compensating for the areas affected by the disease.

Bilingualism is one source of cognitive reserve, but it doesn't confer any additional benefit beyond that provided by physical or intellectual stimulation (Gollan et al., 2011). In other words, well-educated individuals will not show any additional benefit for being bilingual, but among those with lower levels of education, bilingualism does provide protection against dementia in old age. Moreover, bilingualism provides cognitive reserve for younger populations, too. Bilingual children growing up in poverty conditions perform better on nonverbal cognitive tasks than do their monolingual peers living in similar conditions (Engel de Abreu et al., 2012).

Bilingualism and Language Disorders

Children with specific language impairment (SLI) or autism spectrum disorder experience developmental delays in both language and cognition. When such a child is born in an immigrant family, there's additional concern about how the bilingual environment will affect language development, and many educational and clinical professions advise the family to speak only English to simplify the language environment (Bialystok et al., 2012). However, this attitude is based on the unwarranted fear that bilingualism will cause further delays for the child.

Studies comparing bilingual and monolingual children with autism spectrum disorder found no differences in cognitive functioning or language development (Valicenti-McDermott et al., 2013). Similar findings are reported for children with SLI (Kay-Raining Bird et al., 2012). In other words, children with these disorders growing

Figure 9.10 Cognitive Reserve

Engaging in stimulating mental or physical activity on a regular basis helps maintain cognitive functioning and protect against dementia as we age. Lifelong bilingualism confers cognitive reserve as well.

Source: ©iStockphoto.com/ kali9.

up in a bilingual home learn both languages to the same extent that monolingual children with these disorders learn their single language. Thus, there's no evidence that bilingualism is detrimental either to autism spectrum disorder or SLI.

In fact, enforcing an English-only policy in the bilingual household may be problematic for a number of reasons (Korkman et al., 2012). On the one hand, if the parents or grandparents don't speak English well, they are limited in how much they can communicate; furthermore, they may provide a poor model for the child. On the other hand, not teaching the child the heritage language limits his or her engagement with the family and the larger immigrant community, and this social isolation may exacerbate developmental and behavioral problems. Furthermore, the child may even benefit from the cognitive advantages, such as increased interference inhibition and selective attention that accrue from balancing two languages in daily life (Yu, 2013).

In Sum

Because bilinguals live with two languages, they have greater metalinguistic awareness, and this can lead to improvements in creativity and problem solving. Furthermore, their need to juggle two languages yields increases in executive control, which is the general ability to manage cognitive resources such as attention for efficient performance. Lifelong bilinguals generally outperform monolinguals on tasks requiring executive control, but the bilingual advantage is more evident in early childhood and later adulthood. Underlying the bilingual advantage are structural brain differences that include increased activity in prefrontal and inferior parietal areas, which are known to be responsible for executive control, as well as increased white matter integrity and gray matter volume. These structural differences in bilingual brains also yield greater cognitive reserve, which is the ability to fend off dementia in old age. Many practitioners fear that raising children with language disorders as bilinguals will lead to developmental delays, but research shows that these concerns are unfounded. Furthermore, these children may benefit from the enhanced executive control and extended social networks that bilingualism provides.

Review Questions

1. What is metalinguistic awareness, and what sorts of knowledge would it include? How might metalinguistic awareness improve problem solving and creativity?

2. What is executive control, and what are its three component processes? Describe some of the ways executive control is measured. How does the adaptive control hypothesis explain why lifelong bilinguals tend to have better executive control than their monolingual peers?

3. Describe the various differences in brain structure between lifelong bilinguals and monolinguals that account for the bilingual advantage in executive control.

4. What is cognitive reserve? What is the evidence that lifelong bilingualism confers cognitive reserve? What other factors contribute to cognitive reserve?

5. Discuss the issues surrounding bilingualism and children with language disorders. Why might an English-only policy be detrimental to the child?

Thought Questions

1. The adaptive control hypothesis can explain why lifelong bilingualism confers cognitive reserve, but consider some of the reasons why regular physical and social activity provide protection from dementia. In particular, think about how the brain is engaged during these activities.

2. Marc and Suzie are a monolingual English-speaking American couple who want to provide their newborn daughter with the cognitive advantages of being a lifelong bilingual. So they've purchased audio recordings of French nursery songs and videos of French-language programs for children. They also plan to enroll her in Saturday

morning French school as soon as she turns three years old. Given what you've read in this section, what will be the result of all these efforts? Explain your reasoning.

Google It! The Bilingual Advantage

If you're interested in learning more about the cognitive benefits of bilingualism, google it! Another useful search term is bilingual advantage. You can find informative articles and videos that discuss the unexpected benefits of speaking another language.

SECTION 9.4: SECOND-LANGUAGE ACQUISITION

- Ultimate attainment in a second language acquired before puberty is largely predicted by two factors, age of arrival and length of residence in the country where the second language is spoken; after puberty, other factors better account for ultimate attainment.

- The critical period hypothesis explains the effect that age of arrival has on ultimate attainment in second-language acquisition by proposing that children have a biological predisposition to learn languages, which they lose after puberty due to a reduction in cerebral plasticity.

- The speech learning model explains ultimate attainment in a second language in terms of the time spent using the two languages in communicative contexts; under the right conditions, a near native speaker accent can be acquired at any age.

- Some bilingual children grow up in homes where each parent speaks a different language. Others grow up with one language at home and a different language outside. And still others grow up in a bilingual environment where both languages are mixed freely. The key to success in raising bilingual children is to make both languages meaningful.

- There are two approaches to bilingual education. Transitional programs aim to assimilate heritage language students into the mainstream language and culture, while two-way immersion programs aim to develop fully bilingual and biliterate individuals. Transitional programs run the risk of first-language attrition.

- While children are better than adults at acquiring native-like skill at pronunciation and grammar, adults are faster at learning vocabulary. In the early stages of second-language acquisition, adults outperform children, but the adults typically stall while children develop into native speakers.

It's widely believed that children learn languages faster and better than adults. When a family moves to a new country, the kids pick up on the new language on the streets as they play with other children, while the parents need special classes, and even then they rarely master the language. This scenario has some truth to it, but the reality is far more complex (DeKeyser, 2013). Although children have some advantages when it comes to learning language, adults can also master a second language under the right conditions.

Ultimate Attainment

Monolinguals virtually always achieve native speaker mastery of their language in terms of pronunciation, grammar, and vocabulary, but the final outcome for second-language learners is more variable. Adult immigrants tend to learn some amount of the new language and then reach *the endpoint of second language acquisition that typically falls short of full mastery*. This is known as the language learner's **ultimate attainment** (Hayashi & Murphy, 2013). In other words, individuals vary widely in how successful they are at learning a second language, ranging from basic survival level with a heavy accent to nearly native speaker proficiency.

The most difficult aspect of a second language to master is its pronunciation (Hopp & Schmid, 2013). Because of subtle differences between languages in terms of consonant and vowel quality as well as prosodic and stress patterns, second-language learners almost always speak with a foreign accent, unless they learned the second language in very early childhood (Saito & Brajot, 2013). As a general rule, those who learn the language before puberty develop native or near native proficiency, while those who learn the language after puberty will speak with a foreign accent even if their ultimate attainment is very high in all other aspects (Serratrice, 2013).

Many factors contribute to the ultimate attainment of a second-language learner, but two in particular have been the focus of research (Saito & Brajot, 2013). The first factor is **age of arrival**, which is *the time when the learner receives the first intensive exposure to the second language in the country where it is spoken*. Immigrants often have some formal training in the second language before leaving their home country, especially when they're adults, but it's usually not until after arrival in the new country that they use the second language for communication. The second factor is **length of residence**, referring to *the number of years the learner has lived in the country where the second language is spoken*. Regardless of age of arrival, it takes many years to master a language.

For those who come to the new country before puberty, age of arrival and length of residence are very good predictors of ultimate attainment, including whether the individual will speak with a detectable foreign accent (Saito & Brajot, 2013). Thus, even a young child living in the new country less than year can't be expected to speak like her peers just yet, but she probably won't have a noticeable foreign accent in a few years' time. Likewise, the individual that arrived just before puberty will likely still speak with a slight accent even after living in the new country for decades (Hopp & Schmid, 2013).

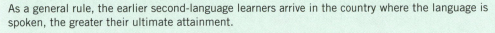

Figure 9.11   Age of Arrival and Ultimate Attainment in a Second Language

As a general rule, the earlier second-language learners arrive in the country where the language is spoken, the greater their ultimate attainment.

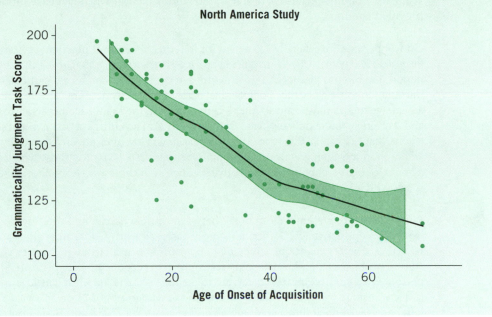

North America Study

Source: Vanhove (2013).

After puberty, age of arrival and length of residence are no longer good predictors of ultimate attainment (Saito & Brajot, 2013). Virtually all adult second-language learners speak with a foreign accent even if they have excellent mastery of the language. Perhaps you've had a professor from another country who has a far better command of English vocabulary than you do but speaks with a foreign accent. On the other hand, many adult second-language learners fall short—often far short—of full mastery, even though they've lived in the new country for decades. The factors that influence the ultimate attainment of later language learners are complex and not well understood. Since many immigrants live in heritage language enclaves, it may be that they learn the second language only to the extent that they need it in their daily lives.

Critical Period Hypothesis

The effect that age of arrival has on ultimate attainment in second-language acquisition provides evidence for the **critical period hypothesis** (Lee & Kim, 2011). This is *the idea that children have a biological predisposition to learn languages that they* *lose around puberty* (Amengual, 2011). Several arguments favor the critical period hypothesis. For example, critical periods are commonly observed in the development of a wide range of species for various learned behaviors. Moreover, the critical period hypothesis pertains not just to second-language acquisition but to language acquisition in general, since children who are deprived of language input in their first years, for example because of deafness, rarely fully recover when language input is provided later on.

Critical periods are generally accounted for in terms of **cerebral plasticity**, referring to *the brain's ability to modify its structure in response to new experiences*. During the critical period, the brain is plastic, and its structure can be reformed to process particular information more efficiently. For example, cerebral plasticity accounts for the bilingual advantage in executive control. After a certain period, the brain becomes less plastic, and learning is more difficult (Saito & Brajot, 2013). The critical period hypothesis asserts that cerebral plasticity for language learning is lost after puberty, especially where pronunciation is concerned (Hopp & Schmid, 2013). Hence, those who learn a language before puberty become native speakers, but those who learn after puberty speak with a foreign accent.

Puberty doesn't present a clean break between those who can and those who can't learn a second language. Rather, it's simply easier to learn before than after, and you have a better chance of achieving native speaker proficiency the earlier you start. This observation has led some researchers to reconceptualize the critical period as a **sensitive period**, referring to *the time early in life when language learning is more likely to be successful* (Barreña & Almgren, 2012). In this view, language-learning abilities gradually decrease as we get older, and there's nothing special about puberty other than it's about the time when language learning shifts from being relatively easy to relatively difficult. The idea of a sensitive period, as opposed to a critical period, also leaves open the possibility that the age of arrival effect may not be due to a loss of cerebral plasticity but rather to other factors, such as motivation to learn, attitude toward the second language or its speakers, and the degree to which learners identify themselves with either the heritage or target culture (DeKeyser, 2013).

Speech Learning Model

The critical period hypothesis emphasizes age of arrival as the most important factor in determining ultimate attainment in second-language acquisition. Some researchers, however, focus on the length of residence factor, making *the proposal that a foreign accent is the result of an imbalance between the amount of time spent using the first and second languages* (Saito & Brajot, 2013). According to the **speech learning model**, there are no maturational constraints on language learning. However, late bilinguals have far more lifetime experience using their first language, whose sound system has become entrenched and thus influences pronunciation in the second language, resulting in a foreign accent (Hopp & Schmid, 2013).

A number of observations provide support for the speech learning model. For example, immigrants who assimilate well into their new society and maintain relatively little contact with their heritage community often eventually develop pronunciation in the second language that is close to that of a native speaker (Saito & Brajot, 2013). In other words, as lifelong experience with active use of the second language increases, the influence of the first language decreases. Likewise, even early bilinguals may speak one of their languages with an accent, as is often the case in second- or third-generation immigrants who speak some of the heritage language but predominantly use the societal language in their daily lives (Mora & Nadeu, 2012). Researchers have also observed cases in which bilinguals develop a foreign accent in their first language after spending many years in the new country speaking the second language almost exclusively (de Leeuw, Mennen, & Scobbie, 2011).

A final observation that lends support to the speech learning model and provides evidence against the critical period hypothesis, at least in its strong form, is the fact that foreign accents are learnable (Mora & Nadeu, 2012). Actors routinely undergo phonetic training to learn convincing foreign or dialectal accents for the roles they play. Perhaps willingness or need to learn plays a role in ultimate attainment of second-language pronunciation. Another factor may be self-concept. It could be that bilinguals who still identify themselves as members of the heritage society maintain a foreign accent to signal that identity, while those who see themselves as assimilated members of the new society show their affiliation by achieving near native speaker pronunciation in the second language. Much more research is needed to tease out these internal variables.

Bilingual Home Environment

Parents wishing to raise their children bilingually take different approaches, depending on their circumstances. One type of bilingual home environment is known as the **one-parent–one-language approach**, which is *a strategy for raising bilingual children that has one parent speaking the heritage language and the other parent speaking the societal language* (Byers-Heinlein, 2013). This is commonly used in cases where each parent speaks a different native language. (Of course, they do have at least one language in common.) Let's take the example of a French woman married to an American man raising their children in the United States. The children speak French with their mother and English with their father; but because their English is also supported by the larger society, they run the risk of not fully developing as native French speakers without support outside the home (Cantone, 2013).

In the case of an immigrant couple raising their children in a new country, the **one-language-at-home–one-language-outside approach** is typical. This is *a strategy for raising bilingual children in which the heritage language is learned from family members and the societal language is learned at school* (Cantone, 2013). This approach is more likely to produce a balanced bilingual because the child gets heritage language support from more than one adult. Furthermore, the child acquires a solid foundation in the heritage language before exposure to the societal language that will likely be dominant in his or her life.

Some parents use a mixed approach in which they speak both languages interchangeably at home. Recall that codeswitching is a normal part of bilingual talk-in-interaction, and children learn from a young age the pragmatic rules for when to use each language. Despite this apparently confusing situation, research shows that children raised in a bilingual home are able to separate the two languages from early on (Meisel, 2012). The real key to raising bilingual children is to make sure that both languages play important roles in their lives (Cantone, 2013). This is usually only possible if there is some sort of support for the heritage language outside the home or else a compelling reason to frequently speak it such as needing to communicate with family members that only speak the heritage language (Dixon et al., 2012.)

Raising bilingual children requires sustained effort over many years. If the heritage language isn't valued or supported in the larger community, bilingual children will favor the dominant language (Dixon et al., 2012.) This is especially true when the parents also speak the dominant language well and have shifted to using it at home. This may lead to incomplete first-language acquisition, in which case the child shifts from the heritage to the dominant language during the early stages of learning the first language (Cuza, 2012). There is also *the situation where a bilingual favors the second language to the extent that first-language ability is lost*, known as **first language attrition** (de Leeuw et al., 2011). In either case, these people are essentially monolingual, and the language they speak is not the first one they were exposed to. This is the normal course of language development for a child adopted from another country.

Bilingual Education

In the United States, over five million **English language learners** are enrolled in the public school system (Han, 2012). These are *children entering school whose native language is not English*, and they come from over 350 heritage language backgrounds, with the majority from Hispanic or Asian families. Since these children don't have sufficient language proficiency to succeed in an English-only classroom, some sort of bilingual instruction is in order.

Various forms of bilingual education are being implemented in the United States and other countries with sizeable immigrant or ethnic minority populations, but these programs can be classified into two main types (Leikin, 2012). A **transitional program** is *a form of bilingual education that is intended to assimilate heritage language students into the mainstream language and culture*. Consider as an example a school district with a sizable Hispanic population. In the first grade, English language learners may receive

Figure 9.12   Bilingual Education

Many schoolchildren in the United States speak a language other than Standard American English at home. Bilingual education is essential for helping these children reach their full potential.

Source: ©iStockphoto.com/CEFutcher.

90% of their instruction in Spanish and 10% in English. In each successive grade, the ratio of English- to Spanish-language instruction is increased until students reach a point where they can perform successfully in English-only classrooms. This transition generally takes five to seven years (García & Nánez, 2010).

The other approach is known as a **two-way immersion program**, which is *a form of bilingual education that is intended to develop fully bilingual and biliterate students* (Leikin, 2012). By necessity, two-way immersion starts out, like a transitional program, with the bulk of the instruction in the heritage language; but instead of a transition to full English instruction, the end state is a fifty-fifty split between subjects taught in the heritage and societal languages.

Both approaches develop students who are socially and academically proficient in English (García & Nánez, 2010). However, students in transitional programs run the risk of first-language attrition (Han, 2012). As a result, these students feel less solidarity with their families and ethnic communities, leading to lower self-esteem, poorer academic performance, and higher incidence of behavioral problems (Han &

Huang, 2010). On the other hand, students in two-way immersion programs maintain their heritage language and thus enjoy closer relationships with their families and ethnic communities, which leads to higher self-esteem and fewer behavioral problems. Furthermore, by high school they outperform their monolingual English peers in all academic subjects.

The End Game

Let's wrap up this section on second-language acquisition with a consideration of what it means to be bilingual. It's important to understand that a bilingual is not a double monolingual (Hopp & Schmid, 2013). That is, the two languages are not separate but rather overlap and interact with each other (de Leeuw et al., 2011). Since all languages share a core set of features, much of what is learned in the first language will transfer to the second language. For example, we only need to learn how to read once, since the basic skills will automatically transfer to a newly learned language (Rauch, Naumann, & Jude, 2011). Where there are differences between the two languages, there is bound to be interference, mainly from the dominant to weaker language, but still going in both directions (García & Nánez, 2010). Thus, bilinguals can't be expected to perform like monolinguals in either of the languages they speak.

We also need to revisit the received wisdom that children are better language learners than adults. We've seen that children are more likely to acquire a second language without a foreign accent, and they may also do better on subtle aspects of grammar. However, adults also have advantages when it comes to learning a second language. Studies of immigrant families show that, at least in the early stages of language acquisition, the parents outperform the children (DeKeyser, 2013). The difference is that the adults tend to plateau before full mastery while the children go on to become native speakers. Adults also have an advantage when it comes to learning vocabulary (Barreña & Almgren, 2012). No doubt this is because the learning mechanisms for vocabulary are different from those for learning pronunciation and grammar. After all, we learn the phonology and syntax of our native language within a few years, but we continue to learn new words for our entire life. The same is true for a second language as well.

In Sum

Before puberty, age of arrival and length of residence are the best predictors of ultimate attainment in a second language. After puberty, internal factors such as aptitude, attitude, motivation, and self-concept have more influence on ultimate attainment. The critical period hypothesis explains age of arrival effects in terms of early cerebral plasticity. That is, young brains are receptive to new languages and readily adapt to them, but after puberty cerebral plasticity is reduced, making it more difficult to learn a new language. The speech learning model focuses instead on the amount of time spent using each language. Since most late bilinguals continue using their first language throughout their lives, it inevitably impacts the second language. However, when learners assimilate to the new culture, they may speak the second language with near native speaker pronunciation. In such cases, they may lose their first language altogether. Bilingual education programs take one of two approaches. Transitional programs attempt to assimilate heritage language students into the new culture, while two-way immersion programs strive to produce balanced bilingual speakers and readers. Although children are better than adults at acquiring the finer points of pronunciation and grammar, adults are better at learning vocabulary. In the end, native speaker pronunciation may not be the best way to evaluate ultimate attainment in a second language. Rather, we need to consider overall how effective individuals are in the second language at meeting their communication needs.

Review Questions

1. Explain the concepts of ultimate attainment, age of arrival, and length of residence. Discuss how well age of arrival and length of residence predict ultimate attainment before and after puberty.

2. Compare and contrast the critical period hypothesis and the speech learning model in terms of how they account for ultimate attainment. Which variable (age of arrival or length of residence) does each approach emphasize? Explain.

3. Describe the different bilingual home environments. What are the circumstances that determine which approach parents are likely to take? What are the advantages and disadvantages of each approach?

4. Describe the phenomena of incomplete first-language acquisition and first-language attrition. Under what circumstances might these occur?

5. Describe the two approaches to bilingual education. What is the goal of each approach? Which approach is generally considered more successful? Why?

Thought Questions

1. Many students in the United States study a foreign language, but few become competent speakers. If you were designing a foreign language program for a high school or university, what sorts of programs would you want to implement to help your students become successful language learners? Explain your rationale in terms of what you've read in this section.

2. Imagine you are an administrator of a school district with a sizable immigrant population. What factors would you need to take into

consideration as you developed a plan for implementing a bilingual education program?

Google It! Foreign Accent Training

If you're interested in how actors learn foreign and dialectal accents, search YouTube for videos on **foreign accent training**. For a humorous take on the subject, google **Indianapolis Academy of the French Accent**.

CONCLUSION

A *New Yorker* cartoon by noted artist Victoria Roberts shows a middle-aged couple sitting in their living room. Out of the blue, the wife declares: "I'm not wasting this year. I'm learning Catalan." While resolving to spend the year learning a new language may be a noble idea, this learner is unlikely to be successful unless she immerses herself in the society that speaks the language and uses it on a daily basis. For most adults occupied with their work-a-day lives, learning a new language just for the fun of it simply isn't an option.

Few of us have the luxury of choosing which language to learn. As children, we have one or more languages foisted upon us, learning to speak whatever is spoken around us. As adults, we might find ourselves in a position where we need to learn a new language, for example if we study abroad or immigrate to a new country.

Learning a language takes time and effort—a whole lot of both, in fact. So adults, in their busy lives, only learn as much of a second language as they need to get on with their lives, whether that be haggling in the marketplace, chatting with passengers in their taxicab, or attending college in another country. In short, bilingualism isn't a choice but a necessity, and for most people on the planet it's a way of life.

CROSS-CULTURAL PERSPECTIVE:
You Are What You Speak

Your personality is unique to you. It's the set of traits and characteristics that make you different from other people. It's also what's consistent about you from one situation to another. So it's only reasonable to assume that your personality would stay the same no matter what language you speak. But that's not what personality researchers have found.

Although there are many theories of personality, the most commonly used model in personality research nowadays is the Big Five model, originally proposed by McCrae and Costa (1990). As the name implies, the model describes personality in terms of five core traits:

- How *open* or imaginative you are
- How *conscientious* or self-disciplined you are
- How *extraverted* or outgoing you are
- How *agreeable* or trusting and helpful you are
- How *neurotic* or emotional you are

These five traits are considered universal, but different cultures value or emphasize different traits. For example, when researchers administered personality tests to Americans who spoke only English and to Mexicans who spoke only Spanish, they found the Americans to be more conscientious, extraverted, and agreeable than the Mexicans on average (Ramírez-Esparza et al., 2006). This finding suggests that people tend to shape their personalities to fit cultural norms or stereotypes.

The researchers then asked Spanish-English bilinguals living in Texas to take the personality test twice, once in each language. When they took the test in English, their scores were similar to those of the American monolinguals, and when they took it again in Spanish, their scores were more like those of the Mexican monolinguals. In other words, the bilinguals' personalities changed somewhat depending on the language they were tested in. The researchers interpreted these findings in terms of cultural frame shifting, analogous to codeswitching between languages.

These results have been replicated a number of times, even with bilinguals who had learned their second language as adults. In one study, researchers administered personality tests to German-Spanish bilinguals (Veltkamp et al., 2012). Regardless of which was their first language, they all tended to have different traits when tested in Spanish than when tested in German. In particular, both groups were more extraverted and neurotic in Spanish and more agreeable in German. These findings provide additional support for the idea of cultural frame shifting as bilinguals switch from one language to another.

Similar results were also found among Chinese-English bilinguals living in Hong Kong (Chen & Bond, 2010). As expected, these bilinguals reported personality traits closer to Chinese cultural norms when tested in Chinese and more like American norms when tested in English. Furthermore, the ethnicity of the interviewer (Chinese or American) also had an influence, as these bilinguals yielded personality scores tending toward the cultural norms of the person they were talking to.

Language and culture are inextricably linked, and when a person speaks a particular language, the norms and stereotypes of that culture are brought to mind as well. Studies like these show us that our personalities are not as stable as we'd like to think. Rather, we modify our behavior, and even our thought processes, depending on the group we're currently associated with. Thus, when bilinguals switch from one language to another, they shift their personalities as well.

KEY TERMS

Adaptive control hypothesis

Age of arrival

Balanced bilingual

Bilingual

Bilingual accommodation

Bilingual disadvantage

Cerebral plasticity

Codeswitching

Cognates

Cognitive reserve

Critical period hypothesis

Cross-language priming

Dominant language

Dorsolateral prefrontal cortex

English language learners

Executive control

First-language attrition

Flanker task

Heritage language

Incomplete first-language acquisition

Interference hypothesis

Interference inhibition

Interlingual homographs

Language negotiation

Length of residence

Lingua franca

Mental flexibility

Metalinguistic awareness

Monolingual

Mutual intelligibility

One-language-at-home–one-language-outside approach

One-parent–one-language approach

Receptive bilingualism

Revised hierarchical model

Selective attention

Semantic categorization task

Sense model

Sensitive period

Simon task

Societal language

Speech learning model

Transitional program

Translation equivalents

Two-way immersion program

Ultimate attainment

Unbalanced bilingual

Weaker links hypothesis

Signed Language

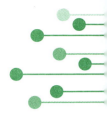

Perhaps you've seen a group of deaf people communicating with their hands. Or else you might have seen a sign language interpreter on TV. Although we call this communication system sign language, it appears to have little in common with the spoken languages we're accustomed to. In fact, hearing people have a lot of misconceptions and false intuitions about the way that deaf people communicate with each other. Test your sign language awareness with the following quiz. Just answer "True" or "False" to each question.

1. Sign language is universal, so all deaf people everywhere in the world can understand each other.

2. Sign language communicates through pantomime and acting out intended meanings.

3. Sign language is a gestural form of English.

4. Sign language is easier to learn than spoken language.

5. Sign language is a fairly recent invention.

If you answered "True" to any of the questions above, you need to work on your sign language awareness. Read the chapter, and then try the quiz again. What you read in this chapter is likely to challenge your assumptions and intuitions about sign language and what it means to be deaf.

SECTION 10.1: SIGN LANGUAGE COMMUNITIES

- Sign languages are full-fledged languages with the same range of expression as spoken languages; they are perceived visually, and they are produced through hand movements and facial expressions.

- Homesign is a kind of pidgin sign language that hearing families develop to communicate with a deaf family member; village sign languages arise in communities with a high incidence of deafness, and they are learned and used by both deaf and hearing members of the community.

- A deaf community sign language naturally arises whenever a group of unrelated deaf individuals is brought together to form a community, as for example in the case of residential schools for the deaf; many of the national sign languages began as deaf community sign languages.

- American Sign Language is the sign language used by many deaf communities in the United States and Canada; a quarter-million people use ASL as their primary language, and another quarter-million use ASL as a second language.

- Spoken and signed languages have the same underlying structure, but their modality of transmission is different; spoken languages are transmitted through the oral-aural mode, meaning from mouth to ear, while signed languages are transmitted through the manual-visual mode, meaning from hand to eye.

- ASL is not just English in signed format; rather, it is an independent language with its own vocabulary and grammar; however, a hybrid system known as Signed English, consisting of ASL signs in English word order, is sometimes used in classrooms.

In 1977, the government of Nicaragua established the nation's first school for the deaf (Senghas & Coppola, 2001). Twenty-five deaf children came to the capital, Managua, to enroll in the residential school. None of them could speak, and none of them had ever learned sign language. The teachers didn't use sign language either, and they focused instead on trying to teach the children to speechread and to speak Spanish, with little success. Instead, the children invented their own sign language, which they used with each other as a secret code the adults couldn't understand.

At first, the sign language was simple, more like the examples of pidgin we looked at in Chapter 1. However, as each new cohort entered the school and learned the language from their peers, they increased the complexity of the grammar and added new words to the vocabulary. In about two decades, this signed pidgin developed into Nicaraguan Sign Language, a fully formed language just as expressive as Spanish or English, although it's articulated with the hands, not the mouth (Meir et al., 2010). Many sign languages have arisen among deaf communities throughout history, but this is the first time that researchers have been able to observe and document the genesis of a sign language as it was being created.

Clearly, we humans have a drive to communicate and the ability to create languages as needed. Mainly we communicate through speech, but when this channel is blocked, as in the case of deafness, we talk with our hands instead. This isn't really surprising, considering that we often gesture when we speak and naturally resort to gesture for communication when speech is impractical (Senghas & Monaghan, 2002). Although languages, whether spoken or signed, can arise out of nothing, they are not born fully formed but rather take time to develop (Meir et al., 2010). Furthermore, innovation is driven not by the adults but rather by the children who are still learning the language (Senghas & Coppola, 2001).

How Sign Languages Arise

Just as there are thousands of spoken languages, many different sign languages are in use among various deaf communities around the world. A **sign language** is *a linguistic system that is perceived visually and produced through hand movements and facial expressions* (Kouremenos et al., 2010). Sign languages are used not only by deaf people but by hearing people who wish to communicate with them. More than simple gesture or pantomime, sign languages are structured communication systems with all the features of spoken languages, although their manual-visual mode of transmission lends them some unique features as well (Senghas & Monaghan, 2002). Some researchers reserve the term *sign language* to refer a particular language, such as Nicaraguan Sign Language or American Sign Language, while using the term **signed language** in reference to *the expression of language in the manual-visual mode* (Quinto-Pozos, Forber-Pratt, & Singleton, 2011). For example, in the next section we'll talk about qualities of signed language, as opposed to spoken language, that are consistent across sign languages in general.

Children usually learn their language from their caregivers and other family members. However, when deaf children are born into hearing families, they have no opportunity to learn language from the speech around them. Nowadays in developed countries

Figure 10.1 Boy Signing "Mom" in American Sign Language

Source: ©iStockphoto.com/ Lokibaho.

there are ample opportunities for deaf children to learn the national sign language or else to receive training in speechreading. But this wasn't always the case, nor is it even today in less developed regions of the world.

When there's no opportunity to learn an established sign language, the hearing family and the deaf child often communicate by **homesign** (Senghas & Coppola, 2001). This is *a gestural communication system for interactions with a deaf family member*. Homesign generally has a simple grammar and a limited vocabulary. Furthermore, each family develops its own form of homesign, so deaf persons from different families wouldn't be able to understand each other (Senghas & Monaghan, 2002).

Homesign is similar to the kind of pidgin that forms when speakers of different languages come into contact (Meir et al., 2010). The hearing family members don't learn it as a native language and can only communicate with the deaf child at a simple level. While homesign is the only communication system the deaf child knows, it's better to view this as a case of incomplete first-language acquisition, since the child never develops the ability to communicate at a complex, abstract level.

Although we said that Nicaraguan Sign Language arose from nothing, this is strictly speaking not true. In fact, the first cohort of deaf children brought with them the homesigns of their individual families. Of course, each homesign system was different, but they did provide the material out of which these schoolchildren built their language (Meir et al., 2010).

Congenital deafness can be caused by illness during pregnancy, as is often the case among child born deaf to hearing parents. However, genetic factors also play a role in about half of the cases (Centers for Disease Control, n.d.). Thus, deafness can run in families, which will then have multiple members of different generations who are deaf. Since there's a high degree of intermarriage in small rural villages, sometimes a sizable portion of the population can be deaf. In such situations, a **village sign language** is likely to form. This is *a sign language used by both deaf and hearing members of a community with a high incidence of deafness*.

A number of "deaf" villages have been studied, but an especially well-documented case existed on the island of Martha's Vineyard in the nineteenth century (Meir et al., 2010). Two villages in particular had a high rate of hereditary deafness, and in one neighborhood a quarter of the population was deaf. In these villages, all children grew up learning the village sign language as well as spoken English if they were hearing. The deaf were fully integrated into the life of the community, owning land and businesses and even holding public office. In fact, little distinction was made between deaf and hearing in the minds of the villagers. This situation continued for several generations until the collapse of the whaling industry forced many people on the island, both hearing and deaf, to seek new lives on the mainland.

Unlike homesign, which is made up to communicate with one or a few deaf members of a single family, village sign is used by an entire community and is passed down from generation to generation (Meir et al., 2010). In other words, homesign dies with the person it was used to communicate with, but village sign continues beyond a single human lifespan. As a result, homesign doesn't have time to grow into a full language. However, this isn't the case with village sign, which over several generations develops a complex grammar and rich vocabulary. Thus, we can think of "deaf" villages as bilingual communities where both spoken and signed language are used.

A **deaf community sign language** is *a sign language that naturally emerges whenever a group of unrelated deaf individuals is brought together to form a community* (Meir et al., 2010). This occurs, for example, when a residential school for the deaf is established, as happened in Nicaragua in the 1970s. The first known schools for the deaf were established in Europe in the late eighteenth century and in North America in the early nineteenth (Aronoff, Meir, & Sandler, 2005). Deaf clubs and associations also serve as centers for meeting and communicating with other signers and thus play an important role in maintaining the sign language within the community.

The Rise of National Sign Languages

The established sign languages of the world today seem to have all had their origins in residential deaf schools within the last century or two. Compared with the major spoken languages of the world, which have long histories, the sign languages in use today are all fairly young.

Nicaraguan Sign Language (NSL) provides a fascinating case study in how quickly a language can develop. Unlike hearing children, who receive linguistic input in the form of a fully developed language, the first students at this school had no linguistic input other than the pidgin-like homesigns of their peers (Senghas & Coppola, 2001). NSL didn't arise as a full-fledged language overnight. Rather, it took about two decades for its grammar and vocabulary to become systematized. In other words, it required multiple cohorts to build the language, and this fact has repercussions today. Adults that were students in the first years of the school use a form of NSL that is less grammatically complex than that used by younger Nicaraguan signers. In fact, the time period involved, about two decades, roughly corresponds with the time it takes for a pidgin to develop into a creole, namely one human generation.

A similar process occurred in the case of Israeli Sign Language (ISL), which arose as a deaf community sign language in Israel less than a century ago (Meir et al., 2010). Four generations of signers live in the Israeli deaf community today, totaling around 10,000 members. The oldest members of the community use a simpler form of ISL that is more pidgin-like, and younger members employ a much greater degree of grammatical and lexical complexity in their production of ISL. Thus, by comparing the signing of younger and older members of the community, we can see how the language has evolved across generations.

Figure 10.2   Nicaraguan Sign Language

Examples of signs in Nicaraguan Sign Language. (a) "I see" and "s/he sees"; (b) "I pay" and "s/he pays." Notice how space is used to indicate who did what.

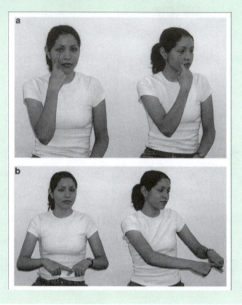

Source: Senghas, A., & Coppola, M. (2001). Children Creating Language: How Nicaraguan Sign Language Acquired a Spatial Grammar. Psychological Science (Wiley-Blackwell), 12(4), Figure 1.

American Sign Language, or ASL, is *the sign language used by many deaf communities in the United States and Canada* (Meir et al., 2010). Approximately a quarter of a million people use ASL as their primary language, and perhaps a similar number sign as a second language. It developed at the American School for the Deaf in Hartford, Connecticut. This school was founded in 1817 by French immigrant Laurent Clerc, who had learned French Sign Language (FSL) as a student at a school for the deaf in Paris (Aronoff et al., 2005). Thus, ASL evolved from a mixture of French Sign Language and the various home and village sign languages already in use in the New World. Nevertheless, some 50% or 60% of the vocabulary in ASL and FSL is identical or similar.

This brings us to the important observation that the geographical distributions of signed and spoken languages don't always match. For example, the spoken languages of the United States and Great Britain (English, that is) are mutually intelligible, but the signed languages (ASL and British Sign Language) are not (Sutton-Spence & Napoli, 2012). This is because the two sign languages have different origins. Likewise, Nicaraguan Sign Language and Mexican Sign Language are separate languages, even though Spanish is spoken in both countries.

Figure 10.3 American Sign Language

The signs for "American Sign Language" in American Sign Language.

AMERICAN   SIGN   LANGUAGE

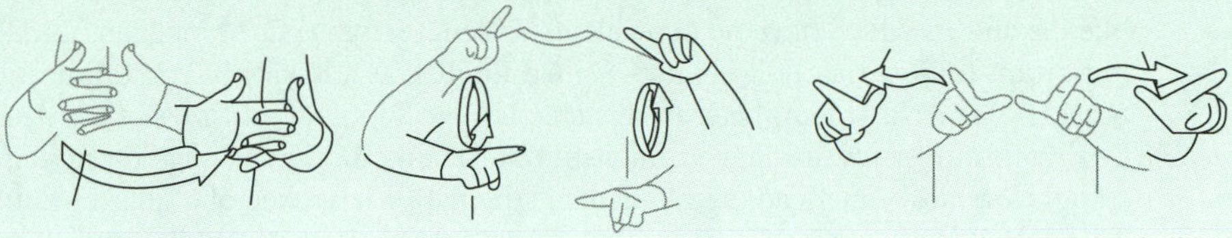

Source: Gallaudet University.

Signed Versus Spoken Languages

Signed languages are also not related to the spoken languages of the same region. For example, the grammar and vocabulary of ASL weren't modeled on spoken English but rather were independently developed by the American deaf community (McKee, Schlehofer, & Thew, 2013). In other words, ASL isn't just English in a signed format.

We can see that ASL and English are different languages by comparing vocabulary items. For instance, the English word *right* has two meanings, either the opposite of *left* or the opposite of *wrong*. If ASL were just signed English, we'd expect the same ASL sign to be used for both meanings, but instead we find two different signs (Perlmutter, n.d.). The mismatch between the vocabulary of ASL and English shows that they are different languages. Furthermore, the grammars of ASL and English are radically different, although counterparts of ASL syntax can be found in other languages. That is to say, ASL grammar isn't deficient in any way. It's just different from English.

Signed languages have all the same features as spoken languages and are fully capable of expressing the same level of complex thought (Senghas & Monaghan, 2002). Rather, the fundamental distinction between the two is the mode in which each is produced and perceived. The articulators for spoken languages consist of the lips, teeth, tongue, and other structures of the vocal tract, whereas the articulators for signed languages consist of the hands, torso, and face. Likewise, spoken languages are perceived through the auditory system, while signed languages are perceived through the visual system. Hence, spoken languages are conveyed through the **oral-aural mode** (meaning *transmission from mouth to ear*), and signed languages are conveyed through the **manual-visual mode** (meaning *transmission from hand to eye*). As we'll see in Section 10.2, the two modes present somewhat different constraints on the structure of spoken and signed languages. However, in all other respects, both signed languages and spoken languages are natural human languages.

ASL and English are completely different languages. However, deaf people in the United States need to at least be able to read written English, and some master speechreading as well. To help deaf students bridge the gap between ASL and English, educators have created *an artificial sign language for use in the classroom that uses ASL signs in English word order* (Wilbur, 2009). This hybrid system is known as **Signed English**. To get this system to work, additional signs had to be created for words like *the* and *is*, which have no equivalents in ASL (Senghas & Monaghan, 2002). It's important to note that nobody uses Signed English as a means of communication outside of the classroom. Later in this chapter, we'll look at attitudes of the American Deaf community toward Signed English, but the take-home message for now is straightforward: American Sign Language, the native language of a quarter-million Americans, is not simply English in a gestural format. Rather, ASL is a full-fledged language that is unrelated to English.

In Sum

Sign languages are linguistic systems that are perceived visually and produced with hand movements and facial expressions. They are full-fledged languages with the same range of expression that spoken languages have. Hearing families of deaf children often develop a rudimentary sign language known as homesign. Village sign languages also arise in communities with a high incidence of deafness. In each case, it's important to note that the sign language is used by both hearing and deaf members of the group. The national sign languages that are established today have their roots in the deaf community sign languages that arose as residential schools for the deaf were created within the last century or two. While spoken and signed languages are conveyed in different modalities, their underlying structures are essentially the same. We say that spoken languages are expressed in the oral-aural mode and signed languages are expressed in the manual-visual mode. American Sign Language is used by about half a million people in the United States and Canada. It is not just a gestural form of English but rather an independent language with its own lexicon and syntax.

Review Questions

1. Describe the characteristics of homesign, village sign language, and deaf community sign language. In particular, consider the circumstances under which each develops.

2. What is the relationship between American Sign Language and other national sign languages? How many people use ASL today? Where?

3. It is often thought that ASL is a gestural form of English. What evidence can you provide to show that this is not the case?

4. It is often thought that sign language is a universal language. How do you respond to this statement?

Thought Questions

1. We have seen that sign languages develop through the interactions of children and not the efforts of adults. Speculate on why this is the case.

2. Because of the structural similarities between signed and spoken language, some researchers believe that the first human languages were signed, not spoken. Can you think of some advantages of signed over spoken languages? What are the advantages of spoken languages compared with signed languages?

Google It! Signed English

If you are interested in learning some ASL, there are plenty of video dictionaries and tutorials available online. You can also learn more about the differences between ASL and Signed English, also known as Signing Exact English, or SEE.

SECTION 10.2: CHARACTERISTICS OF SIGNED LANGUAGES

- Although signed language makes use of visual gestures instead of speech sounds, it is structured in ways that very much parallel the phonology of spoken language; duality of patterning, which is the process of combining a small set of meaningless units into a large set of meaningful units, is a quality of both signed and spoken language.

- The three basic components of a sign are handshape, location, and movement. Handshape refers to the configuration of the fingers on the signing hand, location refers to the part of the upper body where the sign is produced, and movement refers to the way the signing hand is moved during the sign.

- Sign language has visual prosody in terms of the timing and rhythm of signs, and this conveys both emotional and syntactic information just like the auditory prosody of speech; nonmanual markers are conventionalized expressions of the face and movements of the head that convey both syntactic and semantic information.

- Because signed language is produced in the three-dimensional signing space in front of the signer, it has some properties that are not possible in spoken language; in discourse, the signer designates different regions of signing space as referential loci that serve the same role as pronouns in speech.

- The combination of signing space with nonmanual markers allows signers to layer multiple morphemes into a single sign; in particular, a sign for a verb will often include information about its subject, object, and aspect, while simultaneous nonmanual markers convey information about syntax and the manner in which the action takes place.

- The visual nature of signed language allows for a far greater degree of iconicity than is possible in spoken languages; although signs are often suggestive of their referents, the decision about which aspects of the referent to include in the sign is arbitrary; hence, signs for the same referent differ from sign language to sign language.

In Chapter 1, we learned that duality of patterning is what gives language such expressive power. Spoken languages are composed of a limited set of meaningless speech sounds that are combined according to rules to form meaningful words. This process then repeats itself, with words combining to form phrases, phrases combining to form sentences, and sentences combining to form discourse. Although signed languages are built from visual gestures instead of speech sounds, they still exhibit the same duality of patterning as spoken languages (Wilcox, 2004). The discovery that signed languages also have phonology was unexpected, and it tells us that duality patterning is a fundamental feature of language, regardless of the mode in which it's transmitted (Sandler, 2003). More research has been done on American Sign Language than on other sign languages, so ASL will be the focus of this section. However, data from other sign languages suggest that they too have the properties we're about to discuss.

It had long been assumed that the signed languages of the deaf consisted of holistic gestures and pantomime (Sandler, 2003). However, the groundbreaking work of linguist William Stokoe (pronounced *STOW-key*) demonstrated that the meaningful word-signs of American Sign Language were built from a small inventory of meaningless handshapes that were made at particular parts of the body and with specific movements (Stokoe, 1960). In other words, ASL exhibited duality of patterning just like spoken languages (Wilcox, 2004).

The Structure of Signs

Word-signs in American Sign Language can be distinguished on the basis of three components: handshape, location, and movement (Sandler, 2003). **Handshape** refers to *the configuration of the fingers during the production of a sign*. For example, one common handshape has the index finger extended with the thumb across the remaining closed fingers, just as you do when you point at something. If you extend both the index and the middle finger but keep the rest of the configuration the same, you have a different handshape. Another variation on this theme is to hook the index finger instead of extending it, which produces a third handshape.

Signs are made in front of the body within a region extending from the forehead to the torso. Hence, location refers to the region of the body where the sign is produced. The same handshape produced at a different location results in a different sign. For instance, the hooked index finger produced at the cheek means APPLE, but it means ONION when produced next to the eye.

One way signed languages are different from spoken languages is that signers have two hands but speakers have only a single vocal tract. This means that you can only speak one word at a time, but you can simultaneously sign two different words, one on each hand. Although signers use this ability for special effect, it's much more common to produce one sign at a time.

Typically, signs are made with the signer's dominant hand while the nondominant hand either rests or mimics the dominant hand. For example, the sign for TRY is made by moving both fists in parallel away from the torso. The nondominant hand can also serve as a location for the sign, as in the case of the sign for YEAR, in which the fist of the dominant hand rotates on the palm of the nondominant hand.

In addition to handshape and location, a sign always involves some kind of movement. Both the APPLE and the ONION signs include a twisting motion of the fist, the first one at the cheek and the second one at the side of the eye. Sometimes the handshape remains constant during the movement. For instance, to make the sign meaning LOOK AT, you use the two-extended-fingers handshape held at eye level with a movement

Figure 10.4   ASL Signs Contrasting Only in Handshape, Location, or Movement

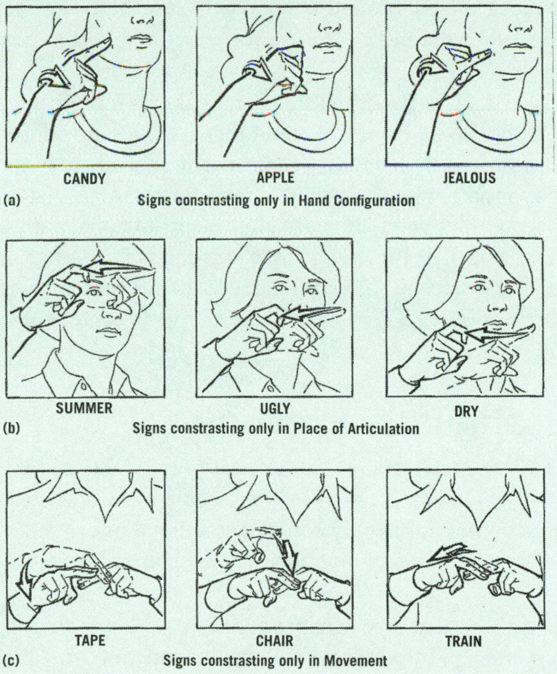

(a) CANDY   APPLE   JEALOUS
Signs contrasting only in Hand Configuration

(b) SUMMER   UGLY   DRY
Signs contrasting only in Place of Articulation

(c) TAPE   CHAIR   TRAIN
Signs contrasting only in Movement

Source: Reprinted by permission of the publisher from THE SIGNS OF LANGUAGE by Edward Klima and Ursula Bellugi, pp. 42, Cambridge, Mass.: Harvard University Press, Copyright © 1979 by the President and Fellows of Harvard College.

away from the eyes. Other times, the handshape changes during the movement. An example of this is the sign for DRY, in which the handshape changes from extended to hooked index finger as it moves across the chin.

Location is important in determining the meaning of a sign, since the same combination of handshapes and movement, when executed at different locations, have different meanings. For example, the signs for DRY, UGLY, and SUMMER are identical in handshape (extended index finger) and movement (across the face, hooking the index finger) but differ only in location (chin, nose, and forehead respectively). Thus, they make up a minimal triplet in ASL, just like the words *pop*, *top*, and *cop* make up a minimal triplet in English.

The duality of patterning in signed languages is evident in the way that meaningless handshapes, locations, and movements combine to form meaningful signs. However, the parallel between signed and spoken words goes even deeper. Signs within a sign stream are produced in rhythmic fashion much the same way that syllables are produced in a speech stream. In fact, this observation has led sign language researchers to argue that signs *are* syllables (Aronoff et al., 2005). The vast majority of words in ASL consist of a single sign-syllable, but two-syllable words also occur. For example, the signed expression for BOOTS is made in two parts, first by bringing the two fists together and then by placing the open palm of the dominant hand into the crook of the nondominant elbow. Notice that both the handshape and the movement change between the two parts, suggesting that these are two separate syllables.

An even closer look at the structure of signs shows more similarities to spoken syllables (Sandler, 2003). Recall from Chapter 4 that syllables are composed of consonants, which are produced by blocking or constricting the airflow, and vowels, which are produced by modifying the airflow. This comparison has led researchers to argue that handshapes are the signed language equivalents of consonant manners of articulation (such as nasal, stop, or fricative), while location is like consonant place of articulation (such as bilabial, alveolar, or velar). Finally, the movements within signs serve the function of vowels in speech, namely the energetic centers of syllables.

Sign Language Prosody

Recall that we use the term *prosody* to refer to the fluctuations of intonation, stress, and rhythm in speech. Prosodic cues help us segment the speech stream into words and phrases. Furthermore, prosody conveys emotional information, allowing us to infer nonliteral interpretations of utterances. Signed languages have prosody as well.

We've already seen that signs are produced in a syllabic rhythm, and the tempo of this rhythm conveys important emotional information, just like the tempo of speech (Meir et al., 2010). Similarly, there's a tendency in spoken languages to lengthen the duration of the last syllable of a phrase, and in fact this is an important cue to phrase boundaries. Signers also tend to lengthen the duration of phrase-final signs. Likewise, signers can emphasize or stress certain words by extending the duration of the sign or by producing it in a more energetic manner, just as speakers do.

Acoustic prosody, or intonation, provides information about syntactic structure as well as the speaker's emotional state, and this has its counterpart in signed languages too. **Visual prosody** refers to *the facial expressions and body movements that convey an extra layer of meaning in a signed language*. Facial expression and body movements carry meaning in spoken languages as well. However, there are *conventionalized expressions of the face and movements of the head that convey specific meanings in signed languages*, and these are known as **nonmanual markers** (Wilbur, 2009).

Nonmanual markers produced in the upper part of the face mainly convey syntactic information (Fenlon et al., 2007). In American Sign Language, movements of the eyebrows provide very important cues to syntactic structure. For instance, the English sentence *If it rains, class is canceled* can be expressed in ASL with the sequence of RAIN CLASS CANCEL. In English, the function word *if* signals a conditional clause, but in ASL a conditional is signaled by raising the eyebrows for the duration of the clause, which happens to be the single sign RAIN in this case (Wilbur, 2009). The rest of the sentence is produced with the eyebrows in normal position.

Lowered eyebrows are also syntactically meaningful in ASL (Wilbur, 2009). For example, the English sentence *How many siblings does she have?* is expressed in ASL as the sequence MANY SIBLING SHE HAVE. With the eyebrows in normal position throughout, the meaning of this sequence would be a comment about somebody having a lot of siblings. However, by lowering the eyebrows during the signing of MANY, a *wh*-question is produced.

Figure 10.5   Visual Prosody in Israeli Sign Language

Notice the use of visual prosody as she signs the sentence *If the goalkeeper had caught the ball, they would have won the game.*

Source: Dachkovsky and Sandler (2009). Visual intonation in the prosody of sign language. *Language & Speech, 52,* 287–314.

Figure 10.6   ASL Grammatical Nonmanuals

Notice the use of nonmanuals to mark topics ("as for . . ."), conditionals ("if . . ."), and phrase boundaries. Also notice that the English word *picnic* is fingerspelled as a loanword in ASL.

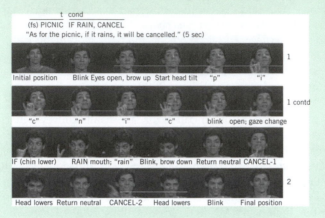

Source: Wilbur (2009).

Figure 10.7   ASL Nonmanuals for Conditionals and *Wh*-Questions

(a) Raising the eyebrows while signing RAIN means "if it rains." (b) Lowering the eyebrows while signing MANY means "how many."

Source: Pyers and Emmorey (2008).

Nonmanual markers such as brow movements are believed to be derived from natural facial expressions that are produced while speaking (Pyers & Emmorey, 2008). However, they've become exaggerated, and they're also produced in strict alignment with syntactic structures, unlike the facial expressions produced during speech. Furthermore, neuroimaging studies show that signers process the grammatical facial expressions of ASL in the left-hemisphere language areas of the brains, whereas nonsigners process these expressions in nonlanguage areas of the right hemisphere (Brentari et al., 2010).

In contrast, nonmanual markers in ASL that are produced in the lower part of the face are mainly used to modify nouns and verbs (Fenlon et al., 2007). For example, letting the tongue protrude between the lips as if making a *th* sound indicates that something is done carelessly. Thus, signing DRIVE while protruding the tongue means *drive carelessly*. Pursing the lips carries the opposite meaning; for example, pursing the lips as if making an *mm* sound while signing STUDY means *study carefully* (Wilcox, 2004).

Since semantic information is often conveyed by the hands, you might think that signers mostly look at each other's hands. However, signers maintain eye contact just as speakers do (Sutton-Spence & Napoli, 2012). This means that the handshapes and movements of signs are mostly perceived through peripheral vision, and the nonmanual markers on the face become the center of attention. Clearly the nonmanual markers convey important information, just as intonation does in speech.

Language in 3-D

Spoken language unfolds along the single dimension of time, phonemes and morphemes strung together one after another. Likewise, sign language unfolds over time, but it also plays out in *the three-dimensional space within arms' reach in front of the signer*. This region where signs can be produced is known as **signing space**, and the fact that signers have three spatial dimensions available to them leads to some interesting linguistic phenomena that are characteristic of all mature sign languages (Meir et al., 2010).

One use of signing space is to establish a system of referring expressions. In Chapter 7, we learned about anaphors, which are words and phrases that serve as memory cues to previously mentioned entities in the discourse. If you want to tell a story about two people, say Mike and Megan, you won't just keep repeating their names through the whole narrative. Instead, you'll start off the story by naming the characters and then shifting to the use of pronouns to refer back to them as your story unfolds: *Mike . . . Megan. . . . he. . . . her. . . . she . . . him. . . .*

In signed language, separate signs for pronouns are generally not used. Instead, the signer will designate *a region of the signing space that serves as a referring expression during a discourse* (Aronoff et al., 2005). Each designated space is known as a **referential locus** (or **loci** if plural). For instance, the narrator might sign MIKE on the left side of signing space to establish a referential locus for him while establishing a referential locus for MEGAN on the right side. After that, the narrator will simply point to the left to refer back to Mike, and to the right to refer back to the Megan. These third-person referential loci are reassigned with each new discourse. In a similar fashion, pointing to the self while signing serves the role of first-person pronoun (*I, me, my*), while pointing to the interlocutor serves as the second-person pronoun (*you, your*).

The incorporation of referential loci in the signing of verbs is known as **verb agreement**, and it's used to convey information about who did what to whom (Quinto-Pozos et al., 2011). For example, the sign for SEE is made with the V handshape (index and middle fingers extended in a V-shape). Moving this sign from the signer's face out toward the interlocutor means *I see you*, while moving it from the interlocutor toward the signer means *you see me*. Furthermore, moving this sign from the referential locus for MIKE to the referential locus for MEGAN means *he sees her*. Thus, execution of a sign for a verb can also incorporate information about its subject and object.

Verbs represent events, and events play out over time. Languages often have ways to describe *the temporal flow of the event expressed by a verb*, and this is known as **verb aspect**. For instance, English distinguishes simple actions (*I ate breakfast*), ongoing actions (*I was eating breakfast when the phone rang*), and completed actions (*I've eaten breakfast, but I will have another cup of coffee*).

ASL and other mature sign languages have rich verb aspect systems. However, instead of adding extra words to mark aspect, as spoken language do, signed languages typically mark aspect by modifying the movement part of the sign. For example, in ASL a straight movement denotes a simple event, while a circular motion indicates an ongoing or repeated event (Sandler, 2003).

The combination of a three-dimensional signing space with the nonmanual markers of the upper and lower face in signed languages allows for *the expression of multiple morphemes within a single sign* (Aronoff et al., 2005). This process is known as **layering** (Wilbur, 2009). Consider the sign for HELP, which is made by placing the right fist atop the left palm. By moving this sign in a circular motion from the MIKE space to the MEGAN space while protruding the tongue, the signer can express the sentence *Mike was carelessly helping Megan*. In other words, the execution of this sign layers five morphemes: *Mike, Megan, help, carelessly*, and *ongoing action*.

Since signed language is articulated with the large muscles of the upper limbs as opposed to the small muscles of the vocal tract, signs take more time to produce than do syllables. Nevertheless, layering gives signed languages great economy of expression. As a result, equivalent passages of spoken English and American Sign Language take about the same amount of time to produce (Wilbur, 2009).

In Chapter 1, we learned that a defining feature of language is that it makes use of arbitrary symbols. However, you may have noticed that the handshapes and movements of signs are often suggestive of their meaning. A special feature of signed languages is their **iconicity**, which refers to *the degree to which a symbol resembles its referent*. The visual nature of signed languages simply allows for more iconicity than is possible in spoken languages (Wilcox, 2004). Still, this doesn't mean that iconic symbols aren't arbitrary, since different signed languages select different features

Figure 10.8 Verb Aspect in ASL

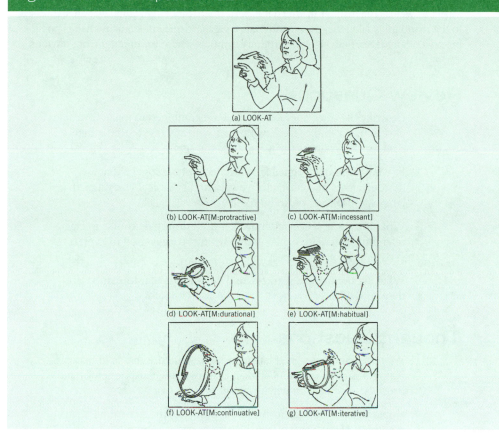

(a) LOOK-AT

(b) LOOK-AT[M:protractive]

(c) LOOK-AT[M:incessant]

(d) LOOK-AT[M:durational]

(e) LOOK-AT[M:habitual]

(f) LOOK-AT[M:continuative]

(g) LOOK-AT[M:iterative]

Source: Reprinted by permission of the publisher from THE SIGNS OF LANGUAGE by Edward Klima and Ursula Bellugi, pp. 293, Cambridge, Mass.: Harvard University Press, Copyright © 1979 by the President and Fellows of Harvard College.

of objects or events to represent in their signs. For instance, while American Sign Language expresses SEE with the V-handshape moving from the eyes, Nicaraguan Sign Language expresses the same meaning by pointing the index finger at the eye (Senghas & Coppola, 2001). While both signs are iconic, they're still arbitrary symbols.

In Sum

Signed language has phonology just like spoken language, and duality of patterning is a common feature of both modes of language. Sign language researchers analyze the handshapes and locations of signs as the equivalents of consonants, and the movements as vowels. Signed language also has visual prosody that fulfills the same functions as does the auditory prosody of speech, conveying emotional as well as syntactic and semantic information. In discourse, the three-dimensional signing space is divided into referential loci that serve as pronouns. The structure of verb signs is layered to simultaneously express information not only about the basic action of the verb but also its subject, object, and aspect as well as the manner in which it is performed. Since sign languages are expressed in the manual-visual mode, they incorporate a greater degree of iconicity than is possible in spoken languages. Still, signs are arbitrary symbols whose meanings are not obvious.

Review Questions

1. Describe the three components that are combined to make up a sign. Give some examples to show how varying any one of these three components changes the meaning of the sign.

2. In what sense does signed language have phonology? What are its equivalents of consonants, vowels, and syllables? Does signed language also have prosody? Explain.

3. What is signing space, and how is it used during discourse to create referential loci? Also explain how signing space is used to express verb agreement and aspect.

4. What are nonmanual markers, and what kinds of information do they convey?

Thought Questions

1. We have seen that signed language has a structure that is in many respects parallel to that of spoken language, such as phonology and prosody. Speculate on why this might be the case.

2. How can signs be both iconic and arbitrary at the same time? Can you think of any ways in which spoken language employs iconicity?

Google It! Singing in Sign Language

Since ASL has prosody, it can also be "sung." Check YouTube for videos of **ASL songs**. In what sense can deaf people still perceive music? How do the performers fit their signs to the music?

SECTION 10.3: LANGUAGE ACQUISITION IN DEAF CHILDREN

- Deaf children of deaf parents learn sign language from their environment just as hearing children naturally learn speech; however, the vast majority of deaf children are born to hearing parents, who neither know sign language nor have good intuitions about how to interact with their deaf child.

- Children acquiring a sign language from birth engage in manual babbling around the same time that hearing children engage in vocal babbling; signing children produce their first word slightly earlier than speaking children; however, both groups produce their first two-word sentences at about the same time.

- Deaf children of hearing parents often experience a significant delay before they are exposed to language since they cannot hear their parents' speech and the parents do not know how to sign; most of these children do not get significant language-learning experience until they enter a residential or day program for the deaf.

- Hearing children of deaf parents grow up in a situation similar to second-generation immigrants in that they learn the minority sign language at home and the societal spoken language in the community; because they know two languages in different modalities, they are referred to as bimodal bilinguals.

- The oralist approach to deaf education emphasizes speechreading and speaking, often in conjunction with a cochlear implant; conversely, the manualist approach emphasizes the use of sign language for both informal communication and formal instruction.

- Literacy is an essential skill in modern society for both hearing and deaf people; many deaf children have difficulty learning to read English because they have poor phonemic awareness of English and because ASL is so different from English; fingerspelling is a way of representing English words by assigning a particular handshape to each letter of the alphabet.

About one in a thousand children is born with a profound hearing loss (Meir et al., 2010). Congenital deafness can be caused by various diseases during pregnancy, but about half of the cases are due to genetic factors (Centers for Disease Control, n.d.) For many years it was believed that 10% of deaf children were born to deaf parents, but more careful studies in recent years have put the figure at closer to 4% (Miller, 2010).

When deaf children have deaf parents who communicate in sign language, they too will learn to sign just as hearing children learn to speak. Likewise, hearing children of deaf parents will learn signed language, but they'll also learn spoken language from other hearing and speaking family members.

Deaf parents communicating with their children in sign language need to adopt special strategies for getting their children's attention (Harris & Chasin, 2005). Hearing children are sensitive to speech coming at them from any direction, but deaf children are largely unaware of anything happening outside of their field of vision. Deaf parents will walk into the child's line of sight before signing, and they'll also use hand waving and shoulder tapping to get their child's attention. In fact, deaf adults commonly use these techniques as well to get each other's attention.

Since deaf parents know what it's like to be deaf, they have good intuitions about how to engage their children. However, this is often not true for hearing parents of deaf children (Harris & Chasin, 2005). Studies show that deaf mothers are more proactive in garnering their deaf children's attention—and more often successful at it—compared with hearing mothers. Hearing mothers, on the other hand, were more likely to wait for their children to look in their direction before engaging them in sign.

Deaf Children of Deaf Parents

Infants exposed to signed language from birth pass the typical milestones of language development at the same age as hearing children learning spoken language (Krentz & Corina, 2008). Furthermore, these children grow up to become native signers, outperforming deaf adults who learned sign language later, as measured by a variety of language tasks (Morford et al., 2008). This is true whether the child is deaf or hearing.

At around six months of age, infants growing up in a signing environment engage in **manual babbling**, which involves *the repeated movements of the hands and arms in ways that mimic the components of signed language* (Quinto-Pozos et al., 2011). This behavior, of course, mirrors the vocal babbling of hearing children. However, it's important to point out that even hearing infants engage in the manual babbling of cospeech gestures. This fact is often overlooked, however, because the caregivers'—and researchers'—attention is usually focused on the development of speech.

Figure 10.9   Manual Babbling

Infants growing up in a signing home engage in manual babbling. Even hearing infants engage in the manual babbling of cospeech gestures.

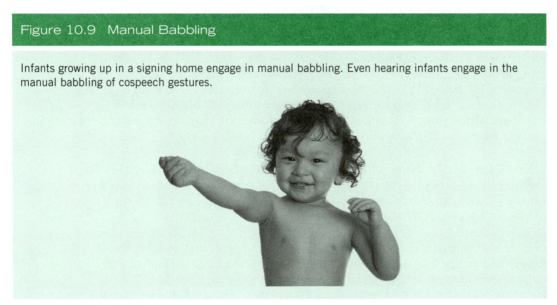

Source: ©iStockphoto.com/ Anetta_R.

Children acquiring a sign language from birth typically produce their first sign before their first birthday (Quinto-Pozos et al., 2011). The so-called **sign language advantage** refers to *the observation that infants can produce their first signed word earlier than they can produce their first spoken word*. It's generally believed that this advantage stems from the fact that muscle control of the hands and arms develops before muscle control of the vocal tract. At any rate, the sign language advantage is soon lost, as both hearing and deaf children produce their first two-word utterance around the same time, at a year and a half to two years of age.

Deaf children learning signed language make the same types of errors that hearing children do as they learn speech (Quinto-Pozos et al., 2011). For example, young hearing children will often simplify the pronunciation of words, such as saying *ba* for *ball* or *fis* for *fish*. Likewise, young signers will often simplify their signs by replacing a difficult handshape with an easier one. In fact, handshape errors are far more common than errors of location or movement, which don't require as much fine motor control.

We know there's something about speech that infants find attractive, as they usually prefer to look in the direction of a source emitting human language as opposed to nonlanguage sound. This preference extends to human sign languages as well (Krentz & Corina, 2008). Six-month-old hearing infants with no previous exposure to American Sign Language prefer watching an adult sign in ASL as opposed to performing pantomime. However, this interest in signed language is lost in ten-month-olds, who are now biased toward spoken language. Duality of patterning may underlie infants' fascination with language, whether spoken or signed. Both modalities of language are composed of a small number of elements, either phonemes or gestures, which are combined according to rules into predictable patterns. In other words, it's the predictable patterns, and not the sounds or gestures per se, that engage the infant and thus make language learnable.

Deaf Children of Hearing Parents

The vast majority of deaf children grow up in hearing families, and as a result they don't get the same kind of consistent exposure to full-fledged language as do hearing children or children of deaf parents (Aronoff et al., 2005). Since these children can't hear, they get no exposure to spoken language. And since their parents don't know how to sign, they have no opportunity to learn signed language, either.

In fact, these children may be several years old before their first exposure to sign language (Quinto-Pozos et al., 2011). One reason is that their hearing loss may not be detected right away, although mandatory hearing tests for newborns are now far more common than they once was. Whether detected at birth or later, it still takes time for parents to fully understand the implications of having a deaf child. Many parents attempt to learn sign language, either by taking evening classes or through books, but these resources are not always available. Even when hearing parents do learn how to sign to their deaf children, the linguistic input they provide is poor, since the parents aren't native signers.

Most deaf children of hearing parents aren't exposed to full-fledged sign language until they enter a residential school or day program for the deaf (Aronoff et al., 2005). Even if the child is enrolled at three or four years of age, a significant span of the critical period for language acquisition has passed. Poor advice from doctors and therapists as well as a lack of access to services for the deaf can delay the child's first exposure to language by several more years. Thus, there's considerable variability in age of initial exposure to sign language among deaf children, and this has noticeable impact on ultimate attainment in sign language (Morford et al., 2008).

Late learners of sign language often fail to develop into native signers (Boudreault & Mayberry, 2006). As adults, they have a reduced ability to produce and comprehend sign language compared with adults who had learned it as infants. Late learners are more likely to confuse similar signs or to substitute an inappropriate handshape when making a sign. They also tend not to include agreement or aspect in the signing of verbs. That is to say, late learners exhibit incomplete acquisition, much like second-language learners. The situation may be even more dire for late learners compared with hearing adults learning ASL as a second language. In tests of grammatical recall, second-language learners of ASL outperformed late first-language learners.

Deaf children learning sign language from hearing parents are very much in the same situation as children learning language from pidgin-speaking parents (Senghas & Coppola, 2001). As we saw in Chapter 1, these children turn the pidgin into a fully developed language known as a creole. Although the signing of hearing parents is inconsistent, their deaf children are able to extract regularities in the input, and the children quickly surpass their parents' signing ability (Senghas & Monaghan, 2002).

Hearing Children of Deaf Parents

Hearing children of deaf parents grow up in a situation similar to that experienced by second-generation immigrants (Quinto-Pozos et al., 2011). At home, they learn sign language and use it to communicate with their parents. However, the rest of society speaks a different language, which the child must also learn in order to be successful in life. Thus, hearing children of deaf parents grow up to be **bimodal bilingual**, meaning that they're *able to communicate in both spoken and signed language*.

We learned in Chapter 9 that both languages are activated whenever a bilingual speaks, and the same is true for bimodal bilinguals (Pyers & Emmorey, 2008). As a result, we can expect to see the signed and spoken languages influencing each other. For example, a **unimodal bilingual**, who is *able to communicate in two spoken languages*, will often engage in codeswitching, changing from one language to another, when speaking with other bilinguals who know the same languages. However, bimodal bilinguals rarely codeswitch. Instead, they engage in **code blending**, or *discourse in which signed and spoken language are produced simultaneously*.

In Chapter 9, we learned that bilinguals exhibit a cognitive advantage for tasks involving executive control, such as selective attention and inhibition of distractors. It's generally believed that the source of this enhanced executive control stems from the bilingual's need to constantly inhibit the currently unused language. This proposal gains support from studies that compare unimodal and bimodal bilingual performance on various cognitive tasks (Pyers & Emmorey, 2008). In these tests, bimodal bilinguals perform more like monolinguals. Because bimodal bilinguals can, and often do, produce both languages simultaneously, they simply don't need to develop the level of cognitive control required of unimodal bilinguals.

ASL is not just English in signed form, but rather it has its own lexicon and syntax. This means that ASL signs and English words won't line up exactly during discourse, and so the simultaneous English that bimodal bilinguals produce when they sign is often modified to fit the constraints of ASL. Conversely, ASL also influences their production of English. For example, ASL-English bilinguals often produce nonmanual markers, such as raised eyebrows for conditionals and furrowed eyebrows for *wh*-questions, even when speaking English (Pyers & Emmorey, 2008). Of course, speakers often use facial expressions to accompany their speech. However, bimodal bilinguals use ASL-specific expressions and synchronize them exactly to the syntax of their spoken English, unlike monolinguals.

Learning to Speak

Signed language provides an effective means of communication within deaf populations. However, deaf individuals also need to interact with the larger hearing community on a daily basis, and some access to spoken language is necessary. Since the beginning of formal deaf education two centuries ago, there has been a debate about whether deaf children should be taught signed or spoken language (Lindgren, 2012).

An approach to deaf education that emphasizes spoken language instruction is known as **oralism**. This is contrasted with **manualism**, which is *an approach to deaf education that emphasizes signed language* (Cook, 2011). We've already seen that deaf children readily learn a sign language, even when it's discouraged or forbidden by adults. However, learning to perceive and produce speech without the benefit of hearing is an entirely different matter.

Central to the oralist approach is teaching deaf children the skill of **speechreading**, which is *the perception of spoken language by observing the movements of the face, lips, and tongue* (Suh et al., 2009). All of us have some ability to read lips, and the McGurk effect, which we learned about in Chapter 3, demonstrates that visual information is integrated into the process of speech perception. However, you only need to watch a TV program with the sound turned off to get a sense of the challenges involved in speechreading. While some deaf individuals become competent enough at speechreading to interact regularly with hearing people, many struggle with the task and fail to meet educators' expectations. Individuals who lose their hearing later in life, after they've learned spoken language, are generally more successful at speechreading than those who are **prelingually deaf**, *having lost hearing before learning language*.

Learning to speak without the aid of auditory feedback is also a difficult task for the prelingually deaf child (De Raeve et al., 2012). As is the case with speechreading, some students with profound hearing loss learn to produce comprehensible speech, but many more do not. We learned in Chapter 4 that auditory perturbation studies show how important auditory feedback is to the production of fluent speech. Without feedback, there's no way for the speech production system to fine-tune output or to monitor for errors. However, the development of the cochlear implantation technique over the last couple of decades has helped many prelingually deaf children develop competent levels of speech perception and production.

As we learned in Chapter 3, a cochlear implant is an electronic device that is surgically implanted in the cochlea to provide a sense of hearing for deaf individuals. The cochlea, or inner ear, is the organ that converts sound waves into neural signals for processing by the brain. It's important to note that cochlear implants don't restore hearing to normal levels, and some people adapt to them better than others (Suh et al., 2009). Children implanted before two years of age are more likely to develop sufficiently good speech perception and production to attend mainstream schools (De Raeve et al., 2012). Even then, however, these children tend to underperform in their schoolwork compared with their hearing classmates. Training in speechreading along with intensive speech therapy are often necessary to help children with cochlear implants become fully integrated into hearing society.

Figure 10.10   Infant With Cochlear Implant

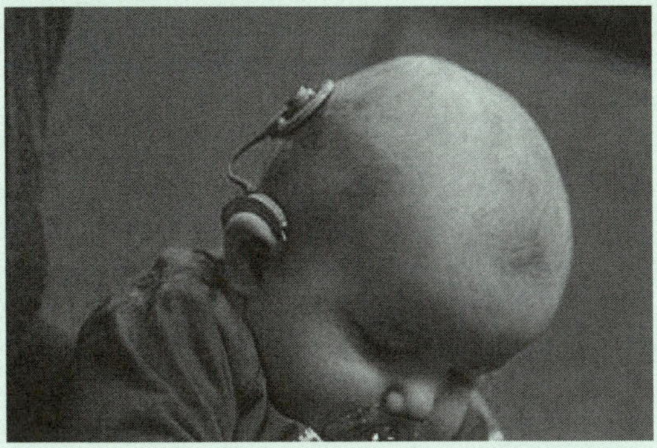

Source: National Institutes of Health.

Learning to Read

Literacy is an essential skill in modern society, and whether they learn to sign or to speak, deaf children also need to learn how to read and write in English. In addition to providing access to the vast amounts of printed information available in modern society, reading and writing serve as another means for deaf people to communicate with members of the hearing community.

The reading skills of deaf students typically lag several years behind those of same-age hearing children (van Staden, 2013). There are many reasons for this developmental gap. One reason is that many deaf children get a late start on learning sign language, and this negatively impacts ultimate attainment in their first language. The same is true for deaf students instructed in an oralist approach, in which case their spoken language skills are underdeveloped compared with their hearing peers. Another reason is that neither signing nor speaking deaf children have sufficient phonological awareness in English. As we learned in Chapter 8, sensitivity to the sound structure of words is an essential prerequisite to literacy. Still another reason is that ASL and English have considerably different vocabulary and structure, so the words on the printed page don't line up well with the way deaf readers express themselves in sign language.

One way to bridge the gap between signed and spoken languages is through **fingerspelling**, which is *a method for representing the letters of the alphabet with hand gestures* (Quinto-Pozos et al., 2011). Fingerspelling is different from signing in that it's executed as a sequence of rapidly changing handshapes without changes in location or movement. Thus, it has a quicker rhythm than signing does. Moreover, children don't pick up fingerspelling through exposure the way they learn sign. Instead, it has to be explicitly taught as a two-stage process in which the child first learns to equate the handshapes with printed letters and then learns to recognize and understand English words as they're fingerspelled. Literacy attainment is strongly linked to mastery of this second stage. Signed English, which we read about in Section 10.1, is another means that educators use to help signing students bridge the gap between ASL and English.

In Sum

Deaf children of deaf parents learn sign language in the same way that hearing children of hearing parents learn speech. Both groups of children go through similar milestones at similar times, although there's a slight sign language advantage for producing the first word. Most deaf children, however, are born to hearing parents who can't sign, and as a result their language acquisition is delayed until they enter an environment where sign language is consistently used, such as a residential school for the deaf. Hearing children of deaf parents are like second-generation immigrants in that they learn sign language at home and speech outside of home. Because their two languages are in different modalities, these bimodal bilinguals exhibit some characteristics that are different from unimodal bilinguals. The oralist approach to deaf education focuses on speaking and speechreading with the aid of a cochlear implant.

The manualist approach to deaf education focuses on the use of sign language both inside and outside the classroom. Many deaf children struggle with reading because they have underdeveloped phonemic awareness in English and because English vocabulary and syntax are quite different from those of ASL. Fingerspelling provides an interface between English and ASL.

Review Questions

1. Describe language acquisition in the following three groups: (1) deaf children of deaf parents, (2) deaf children of hearing parents, and (3) hearing children of deaf parents. How does language acquisition in each group compare with that of hearing children of hearing parents?

2. Discuss the following three milestones of language acquisition in hearing and deaf infants: babbling, first word, and first two-word sentence. Compare the typical language errors of hearing and deaf children.

3. What are bimodal bilinguals? In what ways do they differ from unimodal bilinguals? What is code blending?

4. Compare and contrast the oralist and manualist approaches to deaf education. What are the advantages and disadvantages of each approach?

5. What issues are involved in teaching deaf children to read English?

Thought Questions

1. Watch a TV program or video with the sound turned off. Imagine you've been trained in speechreading. Take note of when you think speechreading is likely to be successful or not. What special challenges does the speechreading deaf person face that a hearing person doesn't?

2. Do you favor an oralist or manualist approach to educating deaf children? Justify your position by weighing the advantages and disadvantages of each approach.

Google It! Cochlear Implants and Speechreading

In Chapter 3, you were prompted to search the Internet for videos of **cochlear implant simulation**. You can find more videos like these that demonstrate what **cochlear implant sound like**. You can also find videos that demonstrate **speechreading**, as known as **lip reading**.

SECTION 10.4: DEAF CULTURE

- The term *deaf* with a lowercase "d" refers to the state of profound hearing loss, while the term *Deaf* with an uppercase "D" refers to the culture associated with the use of sign language and includes both deaf and hearing signers.

- Learning of language and culture through interactions with parents and elders is known as vertical transmission, while learning these from peers is called horizontal transmission; most deaf children acquire sign language and Deaf culture via horizontal transmission, that is, from other deaf children.

- The medical model views deafness as a disability or defect that needs to be corrected whenever possible; conversely, the cultural model views deafness as being within the normal range of human variation and as providing an alternative experience of the world that is visually oriented and centered on signed language.

- The Deaf community views the medical model, which prevails in hearing society, as a threat to its continuing existence as a cultural entity; thus, they advocate strongly for a manualist approach to deaf education. They also oppose cochlear implantation on the grounds that deaf children can have a more meaningful life within the accepting Deaf community than in a hearing society that views them as disabled.

- The Deaf community has a rich tradition of storytelling; these stories serve as an important vehicle for the horizontal transmission of Deaf culture and sign language; stories also help bind the Deaf community by relating shared experiences unique to Deaf people.

- Humor is often used to build in-group cohesion; common themes in Deaf humor include the rejection of deafness as a disability, a deaf person getting the upper hand over a hearing person, and a deaf person experiencing the negative consequences of rejecting his or her Deaf identity.

Language and culture are two sides of the same coin. If we think of **culture** as *a system of learned behaviors and thought processes shared by a group*, then language provides the means for expressing culture as well as a way of transmitting it from one generation to the next. Likewise, any particular language reflects the culture of the people who use it, and this is just as true for signed languages as it is for spoken ones.

About half a million people in the United States identify themselves as members of an ethnic and linguistic minority group that is proud to be Deaf (Hamill & Stein, 2011). In its meaning as the name of a cultural entity, Deaf is capitalized. Members of the American Deaf culture communicate with each other through American Sign Language, and the ability to sign is the defining feature for membership in the Deaf community.

This means that not all people with profound hearing loss (deaf with a lowercase "d") are Deaf. Conversely, hearing individuals who can sign may also consider themselves Deaf, even though they're not deaf (Lindgren, 2012).

The Deaf community in the United States is tightly knit and politically active in advocating for issues of importance to the group, such as recognition of ASL as a legitimate language and equal treatment of deaf and hearing people (Hamill & Stein, 2011). Deaf users of ASL share a unique set of experiences and attitudes that are quite different from those of hearing nonsigners, whose intuitions about what it's like to be deaf are often contrary to reality (McKee et al., 2013; Senghas & Monaghan, 2002). Members of the Deaf community live in a visually oriented culture centered on the use of ASL, which provides access to a multitude of social activities as well as the transmission of a rich signed literature and folklore.

Horizontal Transmission

You're probably very similar to your parents. No doubt you speak the same language, like the same kinds of food, follow the same customs, and practice the same religion. *The learning of language and culture through interactions with parents and elders* is known as **vertical transmission** (McKee et al., 2013). When a hearing family has a deaf child, however, vertical transmission of language and culture is interrupted. In fact, the driving factor in cochlear implantation is the desire of hearing parents to be able to raise their deaf child as one of them (Mauldin, 2012).

The vertical transmission of language and culture also occurs with deaf children of deaf parents, and these people, as adults, often take on leadership roles in the Deaf community as stewards of the culture (Sutton-Spence, 2010). However, most members are integrated into the Deaf community via **horizontal transmission**, which is *the learning of language and culture through interactions with peers* (McKee et al., 2013). The case of students at the Nicaraguan school for the deaf, who taught each other sign language, is an excellent example of horizontal transmission.

Most members of the Deaf community learn their language and culture through horizontal transmission (McKee et al., 2013). Residential schools for the deaf have long been important centers for maintaining and transmitting sign language and Deaf culture (Miller, 2010). Ironically, oralism was the dominant approach to deaf education until the 1980s, and as educators began recognizing the legitimacy of ASL as a language and the value of manualist instruction, there was also a social movement toward mainstreaming deaf children into the local schools in an attempt to integrate them into hearing society (Sutton-Spence, 2010).

Adult members of the Deaf community often gather at deaf clubs, where experienced signers serve as mentors for new members (Senghas & Monaghan, 2002). Deaf individuals who had had cochlear implants or oralist education as children may find, as adults, that they have more in common with the Deaf community, and so they may

Figure 10.11   Girls Learning Sign Language

Deaf children often learn sign language from each other instead of from parents and teachers.

Source: iStockphoto.com/Figure8Photos.

not learn ASL until relatively late in life (Sutton-Spence, 2010). In the hearing world, the deaf are treated as disabled and often discriminated against, but in the Deaf world, members learn to embrace deafness as a positive and meaningful element of their identity.

Medical Model

The fact that Deaf individuals take pride in their deafness and view it as a positive attribute is counterintuitive to those of us who take our hearing for granted. Rather, the hearing community generally holds *the view that deafness is a disability that needs to be remediated or eliminated whenever possible*. This is known as the **medical model** of deafness (Senghas & Monaghan, 2002). In contrast, the **cultural model** takes *the position that deafness is within the normal range of human variation and provides an alternative experience that is visually oriented and centered on signed language*. In other words, the cultural model refutes the idea that deafness is a deficiency that needs to be corrected, seeing it instead as a physical attribute that defines a particular cultural identity, much as other ethnic groups can be identified by physical attributes.

The Deaf community views the medical model, which is so prevalent in hearing society, as a threat to its cultural existence (McKee et al., 2013). Hence, the Deaf community takes a strong position on a number of issues that make no sense in terms of the medical model but make perfect sense from the cultural model point of view. For example, the Deaf community strongly objects to the idea of genetic testing or prenatal screening for deafness, based on the legitimate concern that hearing parents would terminate pregnancies to avoid giving birth to a deaf infant. If this were to become standard practice, the long-term viability of Deaf culture would be threatened.

Education is another issue that the Deaf community takes a strong stand on. As we've already seen, hearing educators of deaf children often advocate for an oralist approach, teaching the students to speechread and speak with the goal of integrating them into hearing society. We've also seen that the success rate for the oralist approach isn't very good. In a survey of Deaf blogs, researchers found two themes regarding the oralism-manualism debate (Hamill & Stein, 2011). One is the view that oralism is a form of child abuse, making impossible demands of students and setting them up for failure. The other is that oralism prevents deaf children from achieving linguistic competency by denying them the signed language that they could easily learn.

Another important issue for the Deaf community is cochlear implantation. Deaf scholars argue that cochlear implantation is unethical because parents put their young children at considerable risk for an uncertain outcome (Mauldin, 2012). According to this view, these children would be much better off growing up within the supportive Deaf community than living a marginalized life in hearing society, where they'll always be seen as disabled or defective (Hyde & Power, 2005). Furthermore, not all children respond well to the implants and the long years of speech therapy that are required. Although Deaf scholars cite anecdotal evidence of cochlear implant patients who eventually give up trying to live in the hearing world and join the Deaf community instead, careful studies on this issue are still needed (Mauldin, 2012).

Cochlear implantation in infants raises an important ethical question, namely who has the right to decide, on behalf of the child, whether the procedure should be done or not. Ordinarily, the parents have the right to decide what's in the best interest of their child, and this position is generally supported by the legal system (Hyde & Power, 2005). Thus, hearing parents of deaf children typically view Deaf objections to cochlear implantation as an inappropriate intrusion on their rights as parents. On the other hand, the Deaf community argues that it has more in common with the deaf child than do the hearing parents, and thus it knows better what's in the child's best interest. While both sides have legitimate concerns, they should also agree that the most important issue is making sure the child doesn't fall into a language-less state, having failed to learn either spoken or signed language (Mauldin, 2012).

Storytelling in Sign Language

Humans are storytellers. Every culture in the world has a tradition of oral storytelling, which provides a means for passing on to the next generation the collective knowledge of the group. In this way, shared stories help build the group identity of a culture (Cook, 2011). Many of the classic tales of Western literature, from ancient Greek poems like the *Iliad* and the *Odyssey* to the English tales of Beowulf and King Arthur, were originally oral stories transmitted across generations, only to be written down centuries

Figure 10.12   Adults in ASL Class

Adults and older siblings often take ASL classes to learn how to communicate with a deaf child in their family.

Source: ©iStockphoto.com/ Lokibaho.

later. Even at an informal level, stories are important for molding group identity. Just think about the family stories that are told at special gatherings like Thanksgiving and Christmas—often the same stories every year.

Storytelling is likewise an important vehicle for cultural transmission in the Deaf community. Since American Sign Language has no written form, all of its stories are told live in sign language (Lindgren, 2012). Whether these are informal stories exchanged by children at a school for the deaf or rehearsed performances on stage at a Deaf club, these narratives provide the glue that unites the community and the material that defines Deaf culture (Sutton-Spence, 2010).

Many Deaf persons receive no formal training in sign language, so signed stories also provide language-learning opportunities (Sutton-Spence, 2010). By experiencing these stories, especially those told by talented storytellers, both children and adults can expand their sign vocabulary as well as learn good models for discourse. In Deaf culture, plot is not considered an important element of narrative, and Deaf stories are often little more than a sequence of events. Rather, what is valued is the ability of the storyteller to engage the audience through vivid characterizations and creative use of signs in novel expressions.

Signed stories teach children valuable lessons about life and what it means to be a Deaf person. A common theme in signed stories is the nature of Deaf identity (Sutton-Spence, 2010). Being Deaf isn't defined in terms of a hearing loss but rather as the ability to sign. In other words, the Deaf worldview divides people into two categories, those who can sign and those who cannot. Hearing ability, in this view, is an irrelevant issue.

Language oppression is a common topic in Deaf stories (Sutton-Spence, 2010). Many Deaf people can relate to stories about the teacher who forbade them to sign or the speech therapist who humiliated them. Likewise, all Deaf people have experienced misunderstanding and discrimination in their interactions with hearing society. Since these narratives relate shared experiences, they serve to bind the Deaf community. These stories also serve to validate Deaf identity by assuring members, especially those new to the community, that their experiences are not unique. Furthermore, these narratives teach lessons about effective ways to interact with the dominant hearing society.

Another common topic in signed narrative is the personal discovery of deafness (Sutton-Spence, 2010). Especially in the case of congenitally or prelingually deaf children, there's no immediate reason for them to think they are different in any way. For example, Sutton-Spence relates the story of the deaf man who grew up in a signing household. Until he was school-age, he assumed that signing was normal and that his grandmother, who couldn't sign, had something wrong with her. Each individual experience is different, but all such stories have one common element, namely the moment when each Deaf person comes to realize that he or she is somehow different from other people. This is an important common experience that helps define Deaf identity.

Deaf Humor

Humor is often used to build support for the in-group by mocking the out-group (Sutton-Spence & Napoli, 2012). This is especially true in the case of culturally oppressed societies, where humor often involves a member of the minority in-group getting the upper hand over a member of the out-group (Hamill & Stein, 2011). Deaf humor frequently involves a Deaf person getting an advantage on account of his or her deafness, and usually at the expense of a hearing person. Thus, the collective self-esteem is raised by turning a negative attribute (unable to hear) into a positive attribute (being Deaf).

Deaf jokes and humorous sign language games spread rapidly through the Deaf community (Sutton-Spence & Napoli, 2012). They even cross international borders and are translated into the sign languages of other countries, where they're adapted to local conditions. New jokes and funny stories are passed along from person to person, but in recent years YouTube has become an important platform for disseminating Deaf humor.

A common theme in Deaf humor is the rejection of deafness as a disability (Sutton-Spence & Napoli, 2012). Many jokes of this type involve three characters, a blind man, a man in a wheelchair, and a deaf man. As the joke unfolds, it's revealed that the first two characters really do have disabilities while the deaf man has an advantage. The purpose of these jokes isn't to mock disabled people but rather to reject the disability label that hearing society imposes on the Deaf, as seen in the following example:

> A blind man, a man in a wheelchair, and a deaf man are having a drink in a bar. Just then, God walks in and comes over to their table. God turns to the blind man and says, "Be healed!" The blind man looks around at everything he can see, shouting, "Praise the Lord!" Then God turns to the man in the wheelchair and says, "Be healed!" The man in the wheelchair stands up and runs from the bar shouting, "Praise the Lord!" Finally, God turns to the deaf man, but before He can speak, the deaf man signs, "No, please don't heal me! I don't want to lose my disability benefits!" (Modified from Sutton-Spence & Napoli, 2012, p. 314)

This joke reflects both themes that we just mentioned. First, it rejects the notion that deafness is a disability. And second, it gives an example of a deaf person gaining an advantage over the hearing society that pathologizes and discriminates against him by publicly accepting a disability benefit while privately rejecting the disability label.

Yet another common theme in Deaf humor is that of the deaf person who rejects his or her Deaf identity and suffers negative consequences as a result. The story of the Deaf man and the genie illustrates this point:

> A Deaf man finds a teapot, and when he polishes it, a Deaf genie appears. "You can have three wishes," the genie signs. The man asks for a cochlear implant, and the genie grants him his wish. Next, the man asks for the ability to speak so he won't have to sign any more, and the genie grants him his wish. "Third wish?" the genie signs. "What?" the man says. But the genie doesn't understand speech, so the man loses his last wish. (Modified from Sutton-Spence & Napoli, 2012, pp. 333–334)

This joke conveys an important message about group solidarity by emphasizing the importance of embracing deafness and the folly of rejecting the Deaf identity.

Other jokes play on tensions between the Deaf and hearing worlds. Cochlear implants are the frequent butts of jokes, as are incompetent translators and menacing oralist teachers (Sutton-Spence & Napoli, 2012). Cross-linguistic puns are also a favorite, especially playful mistranslations of English, such as signing BEE

WRITE BACK for *be right back*. Puns in ASL also occur. For example, extending the little finger from the fist is an insulting gesture in Deaf culture, much like extending the middle finger is in English-speaking culture. Thus, incorporating an extended pinky into a handshape while signing TEACHER expresses disdain for that person.

Deaf studies is a new field that's ripe with research opportunities. It's only been within the last two or three decades that the hearing world has realized there was such a thing as a Deaf culture. In the next few decades, new research into signed languages and their Deaf cultures will provide fresh insights into the dynamic interrelationship between language and culture.

In Sum

The Deaf culture is associated with the use of sign language, and it includes both deaf and hearing signers. Most people learn their language and culture vertically through interactions with parents and elders, but most Deaf people acquire sign language and Deaf culture horizontally through interactions with their peers. The medical model, which prevails in hearing society, views deafness as a disability to be corrected or eliminated if possible. This position contrasts with the cultural model, which views deafness as being within the normal range of human diversity and providing a different experience of life that's oriented toward the visual sense and centered on sign language. The Deaf community sees the medical model as a threat to its existence as a unique culture. Thus, most Deaf people oppose cochlear implantation in children, arguing that their life will be more fulfilling within an accepting Deaf community as opposed to living in hearing society as a disabled person. Deaf culture has a rich tradition of storytelling and humor. These narratives encourage in-group cohesion by sharing common experiences that are unique to Deaf people.

Review Questions

1. Explain the difference between *deaf* and *Deaf*.

2. Discuss vertical and horizontal transmission of language and culture. Why do most deaf children acquire their language and culture through horizontal transmission?

3. Compare the medical model of deafness with the cultural model. Why does the Deaf community feel threatened by the medical model? How are Deaf views on education and cochlear implantation motivated by the medical model?

4. What are some common themes in Deaf stories and Deaf humor? How do these narratives help create Deaf identity?

Thought Question

1. Imagine you know a couple with a deaf infant. They can't decide whether to give their child a cochlear implant and mainstream her in the local schools or to send her to a residential school for the deaf that takes a manualist approach to education. What advice would you give them? Be sure to support your reasoning.

Google It! Deaf Blogs

YouTube has become an important center for maintaining Deaf culture. Here you can find vlogs (video weblogs) discussing various aspects of **Deaf culture**. If you enjoyed the **Deaf humor** in this section, you can find many more on YouTube. Pay attention to the visual portrayal of the characters and their actions in these videos, as this is an important aspect of good storytelling in sign language.

CONCLUSION

The discovery that signed languages have phonology just like spoken languages has radically changed the way we understand the nature of language. This means that duality of patterning is a feature of language in general and doesn't depend on the modality. However, sign languages aren't just gestural versions of spoken languages. Rather, the mode of transmission, whether oral-aural or manual-visual, does impact the structure of the language in other ways.

Since spoken language is restricted to the single dimension of time, it needs to sequence its phonemes and morphemes one after another. In contrast, sign languages are produced in three-dimensional signing space, and this fact permits signers to produce multiple phonemes and morphemes at the same time. That is to say, while the handshape, location, and movement of a sign are separable elements, they are produced simultaneously, not sequentially, to make up the sign. Furthermore, grammatical morphemes, such as verb agreement and verb aspect, can be layered on top of the base sign to express a wide range of subtle distinctions in meaning.

While signs are produced in a syllabic rhythm one after another, each sign packs more information than does a spoken word. This makes sign language more compact, so even though it takes more time to produce a sign than a spoken syllable, equivalent discourses in sign and spoken languages take about the same amount of time.

Language and culture are inseparable. Native signers, whether deaf or hearing, are part of a Deaf culture that defines their identity, influences their thinking, and even shapes the way they perceive the world. In the next chapter, we'll explore this relationship between language and culture in more detail.

CROSS-CULTURAL PERSPECTIVE: Are There Foreign Accents in Sign Languages?

People that learn a second language as an adult usually speak that language with a foreign accent. But suppose a native signer of ASL moved to England as an adult and learned British Sign Language. (Recall that ASL and BSL are unrelated languages.) Would native signers of BSL perceive a foreign accent in her signing? Some evidence from cross-linguistic comparisons of sign languages suggest that there can be foreign accents in sign languages.

Although all spoken languages have a set of phonemes as their building blocks, no spoken language makes use of the entire range of speech sounds that is possible. Rather, each language selects several dozen speech sounds as its phonemes and simply ignores the rest. Thus, each language has a different phoneme inventory. For instance, English has two *th* sounds, as in *thigh* and *thy*, but German has neither of these. On the other hand, German has two vowels that don't occur in English, as in the words *Tür* ("door") and *hören* ("hear").

In addition, no language allows all possible combinations of phonemes, and in fact their phonological rules tightly constrain which combinations are possible. However, each language has a different set of rules for stringing phonemes together. In the German word *Knabe*, each letter represents a separate phoneme that is pronounced: *k-n-ah-b-uh*. The word means "boy," and it's a cognate with the antiquated English word *knave*. In English, the phoneme sequence *k-n* is no longer allowed, although it used to be, which explains the spelling.

Even when two spoken languages make use of the same phoneme, its pronunciation may vary. For example, the initial sound in the German word *Land*, which means the same thing as its English counterpart, is produced with the tongue farther back in the mouth than in English. These differences in phonology lead to foreign accents in adult second-language learners, who tend to pronounce the second language with the phoneme inventory of the first language.

If we just study the structure of ASL, we have no way of knowing whether these characteristics of spoken languages also apply to sign languages. In their seminal work on ASL, Klima and Bellugi (1979) also undertook a comparison of signs in ASL and Chinese Sign Language (CSL). Their findings show that sign languages, just like spoken languages, don't make use of the entire inventory of possible phonemes or combinations.

First, they found that the forms of some signs in ASL and CSL were identical, even though their meanings were different. For example, touching the thumb of the closed fist handshape to the chin means SECRET in ASL but FATHER in CSL. This case is just like the so-called false friends of spoken languages, such as the word *Gift*, which means "poison" in German.

Second, they found that some signs in one language were possible forms in the other language, even though they had no meaning. For instance, the CSL sign for OFTEN shares a handshape with ASL HORSE and a location with ASL CARELESS, but this combination of handshape and location has no assigned meaning. This happens in spoken languages too, as in the case of the German word *Blick*, which means 'glance'. Although *blick* isn't a word in English, it could be.

Third, and most important, they found that some signs in CSL were simply impossible in ASL, in that they used either a handshape, location, or movement that wasn't part of the ASL phoneme repertory. Thus, sign languages, just like their spoken counterparts, only make use of a limited number of possible phonemes.

Finally, Klima and Bellugi (1979) made an unexpected discovery. Although ASL and CSL had many handshapes in common, they weren't always made in exactly the same way. One example is the closed fist handshape. The knuckles are rounded in ASL handshape but kept square in CSL. Likewise, the ASL thumb is held close, but the CSL thumb protrudes somewhat. Just as spoken phonemes, such as the German and English *l*, can vary slightly, so can signed phonemes.

The linguistic analysis of the world's sign languages is still in its infancy. However, there's no doubt that as it progresses, it will broaden our understanding of the nature of language. We may even find that native signers do perceive a foreign accent in the signs of non-native signers.

Figure 10.13 Closed Fist Handshape in American and Chinese Sign Language

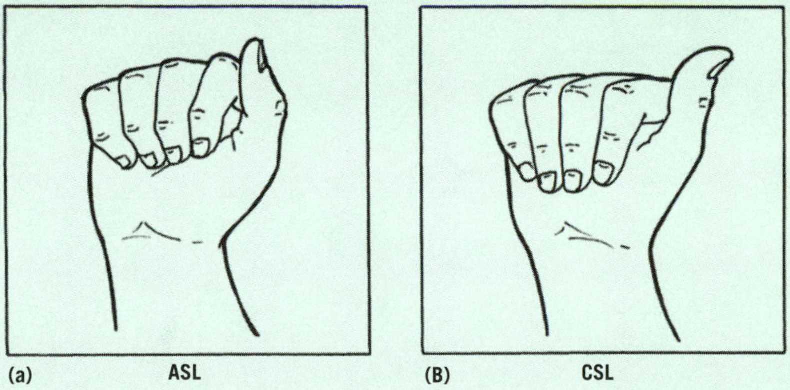

(a) ASL   (B) CSL

Source: Reprinted by permission of the publisher from THE SIGNS OF LANGUAGE by Edward Klima and Ursula Bellugi, pp. 161, Cambridge, Mass.: Harvard University Press, Copyright © 1979 by the President and Fellows of Harvard College.

KEY TERMS

American Sign Language

Bimodal bilingual

Code blending

Cultural model

Culture

Deaf community sign language

Fingerspelling

Handshape

Homesign

Horizontal transmission

Iconicity

Layering

Manual babbling

Manual-visual mode

Manualism

Medical model

Nonmanual markers

Oral-aural mode

Oralism

Prelingually deaf

Referential locus

Sign language

Sign language advantage

Signed English

Signed language

Signing space

Speechreading

Unimodal bilingual

Verb agreement

Verb aspect

Vertical transmission

Village sign language

Visual prosody

CHAPTER

11

Language Development Across the Lifespan

It takes a lifetime to learn a language. Although your knowledge of English pronunciation and grammar may have been set by grade school, you kept on learning new words at a prodigious rate. And you'll keep on learning new words till the end of your life.

Think about your parents for a minute. When they were your age, there were no cell phones or GPS devices, and there was no email, Internet, Facebook, or Wi-Fi either. And yet they certainly understand these concepts today and know what to call them. Who knows what as yet uninvented things you'll have to learn the names of by the time you get to be your parents' age.

Now think about how you and your friends talk. You guys, like, probably use a lot of, you know, conversational fillers. Most likely, your parents don't talk this way anymore, but they probably did when they were your age. So why did they change? And when? And will it also happen to you?

As you read this chapter, you'll get to see how you've developed up to this point in your life. And you'll also get to see what the future has in store for you. It'll likely be a happy ending for most of us.

SECTION 11.1: INFANCY

- Language development is tied to all other areas of development, and early developmental processes in one area can have cascading effects that impact later development; early delays in development can have lasting effects into later childhood and even adulthood.

- Children do not learn language simply by listening to others speak; instead, they learn through active engagement in communicative interactions with caregivers and other family members. However, cultures vary in the degree to which they direct speech at prelinguistic infants.

- Infant-directed speech provides a good model for language learning. Its exaggerated prosody makes content words salient, or easy to pick out from the speech stream; moreover, frequent repetition of limited vocabulary makes word forms familiar and easy to identify in novel contexts.

- Walking is a developmental event that sets off a cascade of language development. The motor and rhythmic control needed for walking is also important for coordinating the speech articulators; furthermore, walking allows the child to engage with the environment and with other people in ways that encourage further language development.

- Adult–child interactions are important for language development; business talk consisting of instructions and prohibitions may be necessary for shaping behavior, but what drives vocabulary development is descriptive talk in which the caregiver names objects of joint attention and comments on them.

- Reading storybooks to toddlers is important not only for vocabulary development but also for later literacy skills; passive viewing of TV programs or videos is detrimental to language development, but electronic media can be beneficial when parents use the programs as opportunities for joint attention and verbal interaction.

Every baby is unique. Still, infants follow a predictable pattern of language development, even though the time they reach each milestone varies considerably (Nelson, White, & Grewe, 2012). In other words, each baby passes through the stages of development in the same order, but some will progress more quickly than others. Infants generally engage in babbling around five to ten months of age. At around eight to ten months, they can already understand a number of words, and they usually produce their first words around their first birthday. Some toddlers begin producing two-word utterances as early as fourteen months, while others don't reach this benchmark until their second birthday.

Table 11.1 Some Milestones in Early Language Development

Months	Milestone
2–3	Turn-taking and protoconversation
5–10	Babbling
8–10	Comprehension of words
10–12	Production of first words
14–24	Production of two-word utterances
18–30	Symbolic play

Developmental Cascades

The first two or three years set the pace for language and cognitive development during the rest of childhood and can even affect ultimate abilities as an adult (Vaala et al., 2010). As we learned in Chapter 9, there's a critical period for learning a second language as a native speaker, and this observation holds for first-language acquisition as well. In spite of wide variations in language exposure, almost all children learn to speak, but both the quality and the quantity of language they're exposed to has a direct impact on higher-order language skills, such as vocabulary size, expressive language use, and even literacy. However, simple exposure to language isn't enough. Rather, the most important predictor of ultimate language attainment is the amount of time the infant spends in social exchanges with caregivers and other older family members.

Infants who get a poor start at language development frequently experience social, behavioral, academic, and even psychological problems later in life, so early intervention is essential. It's estimated that 2%–19% of children experience early language difficulties (Määttä et al., 2012). However, the wide time frames for reaching key milestones make it difficult to identify potential problems. For example, an infant who's still not speaking at eighteen months may very well catch up and even excel, but the child may already be showing signs of a developmental disorder. The best approach involves frequent assessments of multiple prelinguistic skills to identify those that are falling below the normal range.

Language development is intertwined with all other aspects of development, including areas such as motor skills and visual object recognition (Smith, 2013). For example, word learning is dependent on the ability to sit upright. Until they are able to support themselves upright, infants are unable to manipulate objects. By holding objects and turning them about in their hands, babies develop an understanding of characteristics of solid objects that's essential for category formation. Since words are labels for categories, children can't learn words until they've developed categories. *The observation that early developmental processes in one area have an impact on later developmental processes in other areas* is known as the **developmental cascade**.

Another example of the developmental cascade involves the relationship between working memory and language development (Smith, 2013). Working memory in infants is very limited, but this actually turns out to be an advantage for young language learners. The **less-is-more hypothesis** is *the proposal that working memory constraints help infants focus on the relevant cues to segmenting the speech stream* (Newport, 1990). In other words, infants would be overwhelmed with the task if they had adult-like working memory, so an immature system is actually a boon to development.

Advances in language development also have their impact on other types of behavior (Smith, 2013). Although toddlers will play with objects as soon as they're mobile, they begin making object substitutions in their play sometime between eighteen and thirty months. That is, they'll use a banana as a telephone or wear a pot as a hat. This form of symbolic play is tied to children's understanding of words as labels for categories and not

Figure 11.1 Developmental Cascade

Language development is dependent on particular motor and cognitive skills already being in place. Development unfolds as a cascade of new abilities, each coming online only after the preceding ability has matured.

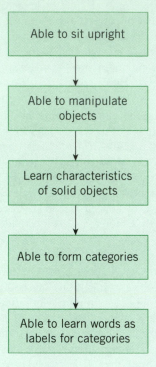

specific objects. For example, infants often first interpret the word *doggie* as a referent for the family pet and only later extend the term to dogs in general. A lack of symbolic play during this period is considered a sign of a possible developmental disorder.

Babytalk

Children don't learn language simply by listening to others speak. Rather, they actively engage in communicative interactions with their family members (Wankoff, 2011). As early as two to three months, infants will engage in **protoconversation** with a caregiver. This involves *social exchange in which an infant and a caregiver convey emotions through facial expressions and mutual gaze while taking turns gesturing and vocalizing* (Oller et al., 2013). These nonverbal conversations appear to be quite pleasurable to both parties, but when the infant expresses a negative emotion, the caregiver is quick to offer comfort or distraction. These interactions provide the infant with early lessons in social behavior such as turn-taking and reading the emotions of others.

During these protoconversations, infants generally look at the caregiver's face, but they shift their attention between the caregiver's eyes and mouth. The region around the eyes yields important information about the caregiver's emotional state, but the movements of the mouth demonstrate how speech sounds are produced (Lewkowicz & Hansen-Tift, 2012). At four months of age, infants mainly look at their caregiver's eyes, but in the following months they shift their attention more toward the mouth, only to shift back to the eyes sometime after their first birthday. However, twelve-month-olds shift their attention back to the mouth when they interact with a speaker of a language they don't recognize. Adults are also more likely to look at the speaker's mouth when they don't understand the language. In other words, both infants and adults look more at the speaker's mouth when they're having difficulty comprehending; but otherwise they look at the eyes to garner information about the speaker's emotional state.

Figure 11.2 Proportion of Total Looking Time

At four months of age, infants look more at their interlocutors eyes than mouth, but in the eight-to-ten-month range they focus mainly on the mouth, presumably observing articulatory gestures to aid speech perception. But by twelve months of age, they're tending to look more at the eyes, as adults do. When faced with a speaker of a foreign language, both infants and adults look more at the mouth than the eyes.

a. English speaker

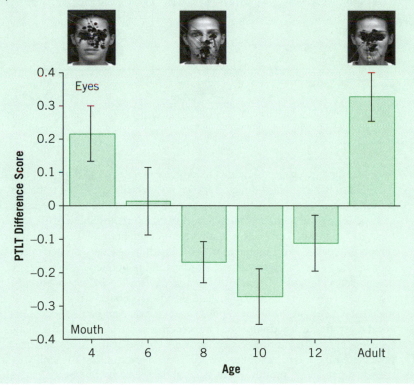

(Continued)

(Continued)

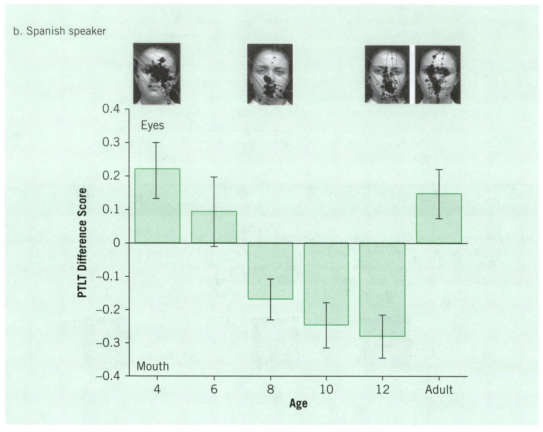

b. Spanish speaker

Source: Lewkowicz and Hansen-Tift (2012).

As we learned in Chapter 3, adults tend to use an exaggerated form of language when they talk to babies. Infant-directed speech is especially appealing to babies, who prefer it over adult-directed speech. Several characteristics of infant-directed speech make it an especially good model for language learning (Bortfeld, Shaw, & Depowski, 2013). First, its exaggerated prosody not only captures infants' attention, it also provides important cues to word boundaries. Second, adults use very limited vocabulary when they talk to babies, and they repeat words far more frequently than they do in adult-directed speech: *Look at the baby! What a pretty baby! Look at the pretty baby!* By repeating words like *baby* and *look* and *pretty* and using exaggerated stress, the adult speaker makes them **salient**, or *prominent and easy to notice*. And finally, because of the limited vocabulary, frequently used word forms soon become familiar to the infants, making them easier to recognize in new contexts. Of course, at this stage the infant doesn't understand the meanings of these word forms. Nevertheless, the ability to segment the speech stream at ten months predicts vocabulary size at two years of age, suggesting a developmental cascade from early speech stream segmentation to later word learning.

Theories of language development emphasize the importance of infant-directed speech and social engagement between infants and caregivers, as this is the pattern that's generally observed in the industrialized countries of Europe, North America, and East Asia. However, there are also reports of traditional societies where caregivers don't use infant-directed speech or engage their infants in protoconversations. For example, Schneidman and Goldin-Meadow (2012) studied Mayan families living in several villages on the Yucatan peninsula of Mexico. In this culture, infants aren't viewed as viable conversation partners, and caregivers rarely address them directly. Furthermore, because of the distribution of labor in these villages, infants are mostly cared for by older siblings, who also rarely talk to them. However, adults and older siblings do begin speaking to infants after they produce their first words, and from this point onward infant-caregiver exchanges are more similar to the model observed in developed countries. Thus, infant-directed speech, while helpful, may not be necessary for language development. It's also important to note that the pattern observed among Yucatan Mayans may also be prevalent among families of lower socioeconomic status or of certain ethnic groups in the United States as well.

Learning Words

To learn words, infants first need to extract them from the speech stream (Gonzalez-Gomez & Nazzi, 2013). We saw in Chapter 3 that infants use a variety of cues to accomplish this task. As infants begin to recognize stretches of the speech stream as recurring sequences, they develop abstract representations of these word forms. At first, infants associate speaker's voice, accent, and emotional inflection as part of the word form, but by seven to eight months they're capable of recognizing familiar word forms across different speakers and prosodic contexts (Singh, Reznick, & Liang, 2012).

Shortly after this, infants also develop an understanding of the structure of typical word forms in the language they are learning. As we learned in Chapter 5, most two-syllable words in English follow a trochaic, or stressed-unstressed pattern, as in *PAN-cakes*, *BUT-ter*, and *SYR-up*. There are of course plenty of exceptions, as in *be-GIN* and *a-GAIN*, which follow an iambic, or unstressed-stressed pattern. When English-learning toddlers begin to speak, they often impose a trochaic structure on their first words, pronouncing *spaghetti* as *SKET-ti* or *banana* as *NA-na*.

The observation that young children produce the strong-weak stress pattern earlier and with more ease than the weak-strong stress pattern is known as the **trochaic bias** (van Rees et al., 2012). This bias is likely due to their familiarity with the prominent stress pattern of the language, since in English over 90% of nouns, which make up the bulk of a toddler's vocabulary, have a trochaic structure. Furthermore, children learning Hebrew, which has a predominant weak-strong stress pattern, show an iambic bias instead (Segal & Kishon-Rabin, 2012).

As they approach their first birthday, infants begin associating familiar word forms with particular meanings (Lany & Saffran, 2011). During their second year, toddlers experience a vocabulary spurt as their productive vocabularies expand to over a hundred words, and the pace of learning quickens over the next couple of years as they improve their word-learning skills (Junge, Kooijman, et al., 2012). Pointing is also an important form of communication for toddlers, since they still don't know the names for many familiar objects (Esseily, Jacquet, & Fagard, 2011). Toddlers point or gesture to indicate a desired object, but they will also do so to gain the attention of an adult. Prelinguistic infants point and gesture with either hand, but once they're mobile, toddlers tend to accompany their gestures with vocalizations, and they also begin to display a right-hand bias for pointing. By the end of their second year, most children are already combining words into multiword utterances and engaging in simple conversations with family members (Wankoff, 2011).

Walking and Talking

As we've already seen, early developmental milestones can set off a cascade of later development in other areas. This is especially true of motor control, which sets the stage for psychological development in various cognitive, social, and emotional realms (Walle & Campos, 2014). For instance, the ability to shake a rattle emerges at about the same time as reduplicated babbling, suggesting a common capacity for rhythmic movement that underlies both the arms and the speech articulators. Even more important for the development of speech is the ability for self-locomotion, whether by crawling or walking, and it's been frequently noted that babies tend to starting walking and talking at about the same time. Walking enables the toddler to actively explore the environment from different viewpoints with hands free to manipulate objects. Furthermore, walking enables toddlers to assert their will and challenge the authority of their caregivers, which can lead to rich sociolinguistic interactions. Studies show that parents increase the amount of speech they direct at their infants once they begin walking. These increasingly complex verbal interactions between caregivers and toddlers are no doubt important factors driving the vocabulary spurt that begins in the middle of the child's second year.

Adult–child interactions take various forms during this time. **Business talk** is *caregiver speech that consists mainly of instructions and prohibitions*. This kind of caregiver speech focuses on influencing the child's behavior, with instructions like *pick up your toys* and *drink your milk* and prohibitions like *no* and *stop that* (Vaala et al., 2010). It's believed that children are at greater risk of developing language disorders when business talk is the main form of engagement with caregivers.

What drives the development of higher-order language skills is the extra talk that seems to accomplish no immediate task. Parents frequently engage their children in **descriptive talk**, which is *caregiver speech that involves labeling objects of joint attention and commenting on them*. Mothers tend to tailor their descriptions to their infant's level of comprehension, perhaps simply remarking "That's a wagon" to their child at one year of age but "That's a red wagon just like yours" to their two-year-old. Caregivers also engage their children by asking questions and elaborating on their answers. Children are found to have larger vocabularies when their parents engage them in descriptive talk.

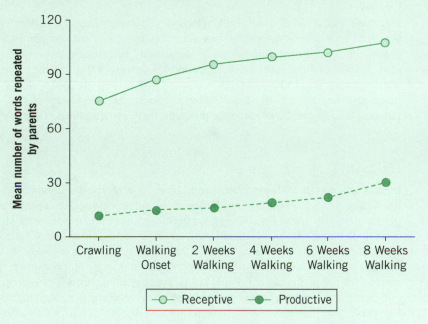

Children show much more similar developmental trajectories when receptive and productive vocabularies are plotted with respect to the onset of walking than to absolute age.

Source: Walle and Campos (2014).

Story Time

Early literacy activities such as book reading and storytelling are also important for vocabulary development throughout the preschool years and even have a significant impact on later academic success (Song et al., 2012). Although reading to children is the norm in middle-class American families, literacy activities vary considerably by socioeconomic status. Low-income parents are less likely to read to their infants, either because they don't value reading or because they don't have the time to do so. Unfortunately, youngsters that don't get literacy experience at home are unlikely to catch up with their peers when they're introduced to reading in school, and this sets off a cascade of developmental problems throughout the school years.

In recent years, there's been some concern about the negative impact of electronic media on early language development (Ferguson & Donnellan, 2014). In the United States, most children under two years of age watch TV or videos for more than an hour a day (Vaala et al., 2010). Some research has found that the passive viewing of non-educational programs is detrimental to language development, but under certain conditions electronic media can be helpful. This is especially true if caregivers watch the program with their child and talk about the content on the screen. This type of coviewing shares many characteristics with storybook reading, in which the parent uses the content in the book or on the screen to create joint attention and engage the child in conversation (Mendelsohn et al., 2010).

Electronic media can also support language development when the performers on screen directly address the viewer, give time for a response, and provide feedback or praise, thus creating joint attention and simulating face-to-face conversation (Vaala et al., 2010). Children who watch educational programs of this sort have larger vocabularies at two and a half years compared with those who don't watch such programs. However, not all media labeled as educational have these features, and so parents should carefully monitor the programs they let their children watch.

In Sum

Infants progress through predictable milestones in language development, although the timing varies somewhat from child to child. All aspects of development are tied, and a delay in one area can impact development in other areas. Likewise, early developmental events have cascading effects on future development. Children don't learn language just by listening to adults talk. Rather, it's active engagement with caregivers that drives language development. Cultures differ on how much speech adults direct at prelinguistic infants, but rich verbal interactions between caregivers and newly speaking toddlers is probably universal. Walking is an important precursor for speech development: (1) the same motor and rhythmic control may underlie both walking and talking; (2) walking enables the toddler to explore the environment in active ways that drive the development of cognitive abilities required for language; and (3) enhanced mobility enables the toddler to engage in a "battle of wills" with the caregiver, leading to rich verbal interactions. While caregivers use language to shape the child's behavior, vocabulary growth depends on interactions in which the caregiver labels and comments on objects of joint attention. Reading story books and watching educational media, when coupled with descriptive talk, help the toddler develop vocabulary and literacy skills.

Review Questions

1. Explain the concept of developmental cascade and relate it to the idea of a critical period in first-language acquisition. Give some examples from the text that illustrate the concept of developmental cascade.

2. What is protoconversation? How is it similar to, and different from, infant-directed speech? What are the characteristics of infant-directed speech that make it a good model for language learning?

3. Discuss the kinds of information are provided by the speaker's eyes and mouth during face-to-face conversations. How do infants and adults use these two sources of information?

4. What sorts of verbal interactions with toddlers are most beneficial for their vocabulary development? How does joint storybook reading or coviewing of videos with caregivers enhance the youngster's language development?

Thought Questions

1. In recent years, there's been a popular trend toward teaching sign language along with spoken language to infants and toddlers with normal hearing (Nelson et al., 2012). Based on what you know about sign language and early child development, consider what might be the pros and cons of such an approach. Be sure to look at this issue from the perspective of both the infant and the caregiver.

Google It! Developmental Milestones

YouTube has plenty of short videos on **developmental milestones**. You can also specify age range, such as **infants** or **toddlers**.

SECTION 11.2: THE PRESCHOOL YEARS

- Children's first words consist of simple syllable structures and easy-to-pronounce consonants such as stops and nasals. But as their vocabularies expand, they need to produce words with more complex structures and difficult sounds; during this period, children's output gradually approaches adult norms.

- English-learning children develop a trochaic bias because of the dominant strong-weak stress pattern in the language. During the preschool years, they need to overcome this bias as they learn alternative stress patterns; children are in their early school years before they fully master lexical stress.

- Although preschool children are quick to learn new words in situations of joint attention (fast mapping), it takes multiple experiences with each word to fully integrate it into the lexicon (slow mapping); children can also use cross-situational word learning to gradually associate a word form with a meaning.

- Children have no difficulty learning multiple meanings for a given word form, but they do not learn all meanings at once; rather, they gradually add new meanings to familiar word forms, and sometimes they overextend the meanings of words in ways that are logical but not in accord with adult usage.
- Preschool children gradually learn the grammatical markers of their language, and at first they apply noun and verb suffixes inconsistently; mastery of grammatical markers such as plural and past tense depend on two factors: (1) consistency of the adult input and (2) ease of pronunciation for the child.
- Preschool children learn the syntax of their language first as predictable sequences of words and then later abstract the underlying rules of the grammar from these patterns; while the emphasis during the preschool years is on oral language development, the skills that will support literacy in school are laid down during this time.

Expressive language development is slow during the first two years of life, but by their second birthday most children have entered into a period of rapid development. Three- and four-year-olds are effective communicators, especially with family members and other children (Wankoff, 2011). They use grammatical markers in their sentences, although not always consistently, and they can tell simple stories in sequential order. As children progress through the preschool years, their pronunciation also improves, and people other than family members can usually understand them.

Phonology

A baby's first words are generally simplified versions of adult pronunciations, such as saying *ba* for *ball* or *wawa* for *water*. During the third year, the child's phonology improves considerably, but we can still observe simplifications of word forms (Zanobini, Viterbori, & Saraceno, 2012). In the previous section we saw that young children often struggle with lexical stress patterns and will often drop weak syllables that don't fit in the dominant trochaic (strong-weak) pattern, such as saying *sketti* for *spaghetti* or *Manda* for *Amanda*.

Toddlers can also have difficulty with consonant clusters, either dropping a phoneme, as in saying *monter* for *monster*, or else by spreading the cluster across two syllables, as in *horsie* for *horse*. Some phonemes are consistently hard for youngsters to pronounce, and so sound substitutions are common. The English *r* sound, especially at the beginning of a word, poses difficulties for many children, who tend to replace it with *w*, as in *wabbit* and *wunning* for *rabbit* and *running*. The voiced and voiceless *th*-sounds are challenging as well, and *brother* often comes out as *bruvver* while *birthday* comes out as *birfday*.

Simplifications to syllable structure are more common during the earlier preschool years, whereas phoneme substitutions tend to occur more often in the later preschool period (Zanobini et al., 2012). Phoneme substitutions are less common in the early stage because baby's first words are typically structured as simple consonant-vowel syllables with easy to pronounce phonemes like stops and nasals. In short, these first words have the sounds and syllable structures of babbling, like *mama*, *dada*, and *ba* (which could mean *ball* or *bottle*). However, as children's vocabularies increase, they need to start using words with more difficult phonemes, and when they haven't yet mastered a particular phoneme, they're likely to substitute a similar sound that's easier to pronounce.

As children overcome the trochaic bias, they become more adept at producing other lexical stress patterns, and so syllable structure simplifications become less common. During the third year, children become less likely to drop unstressed syllables that don't find into the dominant trochaic pattern (Ballard et al., 2012). At the same time, they begin to produce more lexical stress errors. Children at this age have a tendency to equalize the stress across multisyllabic words, perhaps because they're unsure where to place it. Difficulties with stress patterns in long and less frequent words continue well into the early school years. In other words, the refinement of lexical stress is a gradual process that likely depends both on the amount of language exposure and also the development of the motor control system for speech.

Sometimes children who make speech-sound substitutions can clearly hear the distinction even though they have trouble distinguishing the two sounds in production. As we learned in Chapter 4, this case is known as the fis phenomenon because of a child who said *fis* for *fish* but objected when adults said *fis*. Other times, children have difficulties hearing the difference between two sounds that they can't distinguish in their speech. For example, some children that say *wabbit* for *rabbit* have difficulty perceiving the difference between word pairs like *won* and *run* (Byun, 2012). It's important to keep in mind that children are learning the phonology of their language at the same time that they're developing their vocabularies (Storkel, Maekawa, & Aschenbrenner, 2013). As a result, children's phoneme categories are likely be in flux through the preschool years, gradually becoming more adult-like as they move into the early school years.

Lexicon

As we learned in Chapter 5, preschool children have the remarkable ability to learn words after hearing them only once or a few times. This rapid word-learning process is known as fast mapping. Word learning isn't an all-or-nothing process but rather unfolds gradually over time (Gray, Brinkley, & Svetina, 2012). Although a child may be able to hear a word once and then use it correctly right after that, the word is also likely to fade from memory if it isn't heard and spoken in other situations. *The extended process of consolidating the pronunciation and meaning of a word through multiple encounters* is known as **slow mapping**. Fast and slow mapping aren't just two ends of a learning continuum, but rather they're distinct processes. Fast mapping leads to **lexical configuration**, which is *the process of associating a sound sequence with a particular meaning.*

Building a vocabulary requires more than just learning a list of words. Instead, every word you know has links to many other words in terms of synonyms, antonyms, class membership, and frequency of co-occurrence. For instance, you know that *fire* often co-occurs with *smoke* but not with *cotton*. Slow mapping is what's responsible for **lexical engagement**, which is *the process of associating a newly learned word with other items that are already stored in the mental lexicon*.

Fast mapping occurs during instances of joint attention, when the new word and its referent are both obvious. This is most likely to occur when the caregiver has engaged the child in descriptive talk. Children can also pick up words by overhearing them, even though fast mapping is less likely in this case. Instead, the child will make use of cross-situational word learning, as we discussed in Chapter 5 (Yu & Smith, 2012b). For example, the child may hear the word *ball* in a context where both a ball and a bat are possible referents. On a different occasion, the child might hear *ball* in the context of a ball and a dog. In either individual situation, it's impossible to tell which object *ball* refers to. However, if you compare across situations, the referent is clear. There's plenty of experimental evidence showing that both adults and children make use of cross-situational word learning.

Categories tend to be arranged in hierarchies. For example, a dalmatian is a kind of dog, and a dog is a kind of animal. Likewise, a recliner is a kind of chair, and a chair is a kind of furniture. Young children tend to learn words in the middle, like *dog* and *chair*, before they learn specific words like *dalmatian* or general words like *furniture*. A word like *dog* or *chair* refers to a **basic level category**, which is *a class of objects or events that is cognitively salient and is neither too specific nor too general*. Adults use words that refer to basic level categories unless they have good reason to be more specific or more general, and these are the words that youngsters first learn. However, as children pass through their third and fourth years, they begin picking up words referring to higher- and lower-level categories as well (Gray et al., 2012). Thus, basic level categories provide scaffolding for the learning of categories at higher or lower levels.

As children's vocabularies expand, they begin to encounter homonyms, also known as homophones. We learned in Chapter 8 that a homophone is a single word form that has multiple unrelated meanings. For example, *bank* can refer to the side of a river or a place to keep your money, and *bark* can mean the outer surface of a tree or the sound of a dog. All languages are replete with homonyms, and they provide the grist for puns, which may well be a universal form of humor. Even older preschoolers pick up on the humor of homonyms, as in the following example:

> *What are you eating under there?*
>
> *Under where?*
>
> *Ah, you're eating underwear!*

As literate adults, we often struggle with homophones when they're spelled differently, as in *there, their, they're* and *its, it's*. However, youngsters learning new words experience

Figure 11.4 Basic Level Categories

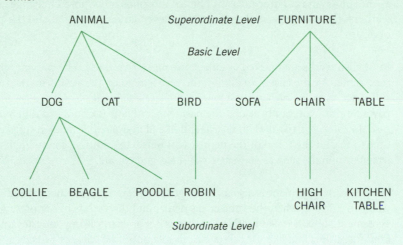

Children tend to learn words at the basic level before more general superordinate terms or more specific subordinate terms.

ANIMAL   *Superordinate Level*   FURNITURE

Basic Level

DOG   CAT   BIRD   SOFA   CHAIR   TABLE

COLLIE   BEAGLE   POODLE   ROBIN   HIGH   KITCHEN
CHAIR   TABLE

Subordinate Level

a **homonym advantage**, referring to *the observation that children learn a new word faster when it sounds like a familiar word* (Storkel et al., 2013). Children get a boost in learning a homonym because they only have to learn the meaning, since the word form is already familiar.

In Chapter 9, we learned that it's difficult to translate from one language to another because many words have multiple meanings that don't overlap across languages. *A word that has multiple related meanings, or senses,* is known as a **polyseme**. For example, the word *line* has a number of related meanings, among which are (1) "a long, narrow mark" and (2) "a length of string or wire." While the various meanings of *line* have a common underlying semantic component, the two meanings of *bark* given above are unrelated, and so they are considered homonyms, not polysemes. Most of the frequent words in a language are polysemes, oftentimes with numerous meanings. The distinction between a homonym and a polyseme is subtle, but as a general rule, dictionaries list homonyms as separate entries and polysemes as single entries with multiple numbered senses.

Older preschool children seem to be aware that words can have multiple senses, but they don't learn all senses of a polyseme at one time. Furthermore, they'll often extend the meaning of a word in a way that's reasonable but nevertheless not what an adult would do (Rabagliati, Pylkkänen, & Marcus, 2013). For instance, an older preschooler might accept a question like *Can a movie be round?* by explaining that a movie can be on a DVD. Although an adult is unlikely to point at a DVD and call it a *movie*, it's a reasonable inference for a child to make in a situation where an adult asks such a question.

Morphosyntax

During the preschool years, children learn thousands of words, and they learn how to arrange those words into grammatical sentences. They also learn *the ways that a word changes its form according to the role it plays in a sentence*. This is known as **morphosyntax**. Three areas of English morphosyntax pose challenges to young learners: the past tense and subject agreement markers on verbs and the plural form of nouns.

In English, verbs are marked as either present or past tense. The present tense is represented by the base form, and if the verb is regular, the past is marked with the suffix *-ed*, as in the present-past pairs *play-played, talk-talked,* and *want-wanted.* If you pay attention, you can hear that the past tense suffix is pronounced differently in each case, like *d* in *played*, like *t* in *talked*, and like *id* in *wanted*. It takes youngsters some time to master the rules for the regular past tense. In addition, many English verbs have irregular plurals, such as *go-went, come-came,* and *eat-ate*.

Subject-verb agreement is also a challenge for children (and sometimes adults as well). In English, when the subject is singular and the verb is in the present tense, the agreement suffix *-s* or *-es* is added to the verb. For example, a youngster might hear *Birds fly* but *Big Bird flies*, or *Bert and Ernie talk* but *Ernie talks*, or *Miss Piggy and Kermit watch* but *Kermit watches*. If you pay attention to the pronunciation of these plural-singular pairs, you'll notice that the agreement suffix is pronounced like *z* in *flies*, like *s* in *talks*, and like *iz* in *watches*.

Two-year-olds sometimes mark their verbs for tense and agreement, but they aren't consistent about it until at least age four (Fitzgerald, Hadley, & Rispoli, 2013). Although French, Italian, and Spanish all have more complex tense and agreement systems, children learning these languages master verb morphosyntax faster than children learning English. The reason is that tense and agreement are much less consistently marked on verbs in English than in other languages. For example, in questions, negative sentences, and commands, the tense and agreement markers move off the verb. Consider:

> Kermit sings. Does Kermit sing? Kermit doesn't sing. Sing, Kermit!

> Miss Piggy laughs. Did Miss Piggy laugh? Miss Piggy didn't laugh. Laugh, Miss Piggy!

When parents mostly use business talk, such as *eat your food* or *pick up your toys*, children get little exposure to tense or agreement markers (Fitzgerald et al., 2013). Rather, the best examples of English verb morphosyntax occur in descriptive talk, in which the caregiver talks about the focus of joint attention:

> Kermit is singing. He likes to sing.

This is no doubt part of the reason why children exposed to descriptive talk develop language faster than children who mainly hear commands and questions.

One reason why English-learning youngsters are inconsistent in their use of morphosyntax has to do with ease or difficulty of pronunciation (Ettlinger, Lanter, & Van Pay, 2013). Children consistently use the plural suffix first on words that end in a vowel, such as *key-keys* and *pie-pies*. Consonant clusters at the ends of words are already difficult for young children to pronounce, and so adding the plural marker to a word ending in a consonant doesn't come until later. The *iz* pronunciation of the plural suffix, as in *lunches* and *roses*, isn't mastered until later preschool years. Not only are the rules for when to use this form complex, but also the suffix adds an extra syllable, changing the rhythm of the word. Similar issues of pronunciation likely arise with the verb tense and agreement markers as well.

Syntax

Preschool children construct sentences, but they seem to rely more on familiar patterns than abstract rules (Kidd, 2012a). For example, children ages two to three can repeat a frequent four-word sequence like *sit in your chair* more easily than a similar but less

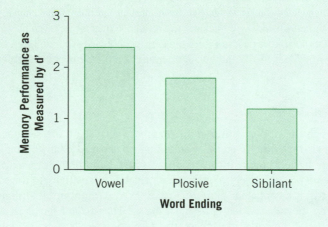

Figure 11.5   Memory for Singular and Plural

Children can better remember whether a previously seen stimulus consisted of one or two identical objects if they can pronounce the plural form of the word signifying that object. The dependent variable *d'* (pronounced *dee-prime*) is a measure of sensitivity. Children are most sensitive to the singular-plural distinction when the word ends in a vowel, less sensitive when the noun ends in a stop consonant (plosive), and least sensitive when the noun ends in a *s*-like sound (sibilant).

Source: Ettlinger, Lanter, and Van Pay (2013).

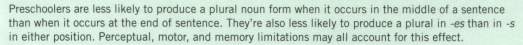

Preschoolers are less likely to produce a plural noun form when it occurs in the middle of a sentence than when it occurs at the end of sentence. They're also less likely to produce a plural in *-es* than in *-s* in either position. Perceptual, motor, and memory limitations may all account for this effect.

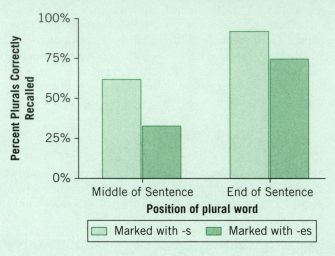

Source: Mealings, Cox, and Demuth (2013).

frequent sequence like *sit in your truck*. It's not until later that preschoolers tease out the rules of their language from the patterns they've learned.

Young children often fail to take plausibility into account when interpreting an ambiguous utterance (Rabagliati et al., 2013). Based on familiar frames like *chop the vegetables with the knife*, three-year-olds will interpret the sequence *chop the tree with the leaves* to mean *use the leaves to chop the tree*. It's not until the early school years that children have enough real-world knowledge to disambiguate utterances on the basis of believability.

Literacy

Although the emphasis during the preschool years is on oral language development, this is also the time when the road to literacy is paved. Many of the language activities that youngsters engage in with caregivers help build preliteracy skills. As we learned in Chapter 8, phonological awareness, which is a sensitivity to the sound structure of words, is essential for mastering reading. Also important is **alphabet knowledge**, which is *an understanding of the name of each letter and the sounds associated with it* (Vaala et al., 2010). In addition to these, the development of strong oral language abilities during the preschool years provides the foundation for successful reading achievement later in school (Cabell et al., 2011).

In Sum

During the last half of an infant's first year, meaningless babbling morphs into the child's first meaningful words. As a result, these first words have simple syllable structures and contain mostly stop and nasal consonants, which are easy to pronounce. It takes several years for children to master the phonology of their language. English-learning infants make use of the dominant trochaic (strong-weak) stress pattern to find word boundaries, but this also leads to a trochaic bias in which young children impose a strong-weak stress pattern on multisyllabic words even when not appropriate. While children can learn words through fast mapping in cases of joint attention, repeated exposure is needed to fully integrate words into the lexicon (slow mapping). Children can also use cross-situational word learning to associate a word form with a meaning through repeated exposures in different circumstances. The homonym advantage enables children to quickly acquire new meanings for familiar word forms. While children understand that one word can have multiple senses, they often overextend word meanings in ways that are reasonable but not based on adult usage. Preschool children gradually learn to modify the shapes of words to fit the syntax of a sentence, but mastery of morphosyntax depends both on the consistency of the adult input and the ease of pronunciation for the child. Children learn syntax first as predictable patterns and only later abstract the underlying rules. Although few children enter school knowing how to read, the groundwork for successful literacy is laid during the preschool years.

Review Questions

1. What is the trochaic bias? How does this bias influence the way young children produce words in English? If you've had experience with a preschooler, perhaps you can cite some examples of the trochaic bias in that child's speech.

2. Distinguish the circumstances under which fast mapping and slow mapping occur. Explain the difference between lexical configuration and lexical engagement as well as which word learning process is necessary for each.

3. What is morphosyntax? What factors influence the development of morphosyntax in the language of preschoolers?

4. What sorts of language skills learned during the preschool years help children become successful readers after they enter school?

Thought Questions

1. What's the difference between a homonym (homophone) and a polyseme? How do dictionaries distinguish the two? Consider the following two Japanese words: (1) *hana* means either "flower" or "nose"; (2) *ao* is an inclusive color term referring to both "green"

and "blue." Classify each of these words as either a homonym or a polyseme, and explain your reasoning.

2. Add the past-tense *-ed* suffix to each of the following verbs, paying special attention to whether the pronunciation of the suffix is *d*, *t*, or *id*. Then, see if you can provide a rule that explains the pattern: rob, nod, hug, live, bathe, fizz, judge, hop, hit, bake, laugh, lace, latch, hush.

3. For an extra challenge, work out the rule for agreement suffix *-(e)s*, which can be pronounce *z*, *s*, or *iz*. (Note: the plural suffix for nouns works the same way.)

Google It! Fast Mapping

In this section you learned that preschool children can often learn a new word after hearing it only once or just a few times. This process is known as **fast mapping**, and you can find video clips on YouTube of researchers engaging youngsters in fast mapping tasks in the laboratory.

SECTION 11.3: THE SCHOOL-AGE YEARS

- An important predictor of a child's later academic success is oral language skills in kindergarten, because the ability to produce a coherent narrative depends on a mastery of phonology, vocabulary, syntax, and discourse, all of which underlie literacy.

- Reading involves the process of decoding printed symbols into a spoken word format; in addition to oral language skills and pre-literacy skills such as print knowledge, alphabet knowledge, and phonological awareness, readers need to have well-developed phonological short-term memory and the ability to rapidly access words from long-term memory.

- Around the third or fourth grade, schoolchildren no longer struggle with learning how to read but instead use reading to learn; children learn tens of thousands of words during the school years, most of them learned incidentally through reading.

- Schoolchildren employ two strategies for learning the meanings of new words while reading: (1) contextual abstraction, in which they use the surrounding text to infer meaning; and (2) morphological analysis, in which they use their knowledge of prefixes, suffixes, and word roots to infer meaning.

- The construction-integration model explains a reader's ability to make bridging inferences based on the information in the text, the reader's real-world knowledge, and working memory constraints; deficiencies in any of these three can impair the reader's ability to make inferences.

- Schoolchildren also learn how to produce both oral and written discourse. They are expected to master the literate language used in academic situations; in addition to developing the microstructure and macrostructure of narratives (stories), they are also expected to learn a new style known as expository discourse.

During the school years, the focus of language development shifts from listening and speaking to reading and writing. While the first few school years are dedicated to learning how to read, the remainder is dedicated to the task of learning by reading. Children also learn to express themselves through writing, using grammar and vocabulary that are more formal than everyday speech. Without a solid foundation in reading and writing skills, academic success is unlikely, and yet many children struggle with literacy. This is why educational researchers have put so much effort into finding ways to detect language and reading disabilities early in the hope that effective intervention can be made.

Children entering kindergarten are not expected to already know how to read, but they are expected to have **print knowledge**, such as *familiarity with how to hold a book and turn pages as well as how print is organized on a page* (Wankoff, 2011). They should also know the names and sounds of the alphabet letters (alphabet knowledge), and they should be able to recognize common logos, such as the golden arches of McDonald's. These skills combined with phonological awareness are the foundations for learning how to read. Although most middle-class children enter kindergarten with these skills, many children from poorer families do not, and hence they are already disadvantaged from the first day of school.

Oral Language and Literacy

Research shows that an important predictor of a child's later academic success is oral language ability in kindergarten (Terry et al., 2013). Particularly important is a child's ability to produce oral narratives, which researchers often assess by asking children to tell a story based on a series of pictures. Since constructing a coherent narrative depends on *the ability to produce accurate pronunciation, appropriate vocabulary, sophisticated syntax, and discourse structure*, all levels of language production can be assessed at the same time. **Oral language skills** are not only an important precursor to the development of reading and writing skills, they're also necessary for the development of mathematical abilities.

Oral language skills underlie literacy because even highly skilled readers can't access the meaning of a printed word without also activating the speech production system (Scott et al., 2013). Novice readers read out loud, but they develop silent reading skills as they mature. Even when you read silently, though, you can still hear your voice in your head sounding out the words, reflecting the fact that the speech production system is still being activated in order to retrieve word meanings.

Decoding is *the process of converting printed symbols into a spoken word format* (Scott et al., 2013). It not only involves print knowledge, alphabet knowledge, and phonological awareness but also depends on both short- and long-term memory processes. Phonological short-term memory is important because the reader needs to hold on to a developing phonological representation as it is being extracted from the text. Poor readers often struggle to sound out words and may forget the beginning of the word by the time they get to the end, suggesting that they have exhausted working memory capacity.

Readers also need to be able to quickly access meaning from long-term memory before the current spoken word representation in short-term memory has faded. These phonological memory processes develop during the school years as literacy skills increase, and they can be assessed by asking children to repeat novel words, which measures short-term memory, or to rapidly name familiar objects, which measures speed of lexical access. Children who perform poorly on these tasks generally also exhibit reading disabilities.

Oral language skills play an important role in decoding (DeThorne et al., 2010). This is especially true in a language like English, which has deep orthography. Since the spelling of a word may not reflect its pronunciation, novice readers need to rely on their spoken word vocabulary to make reasonable guesses about what an unfamiliar written word might be. Let's say a first-grade reader encounters the word *knight*. She may attempt to sound it out, perhaps as *kuh-nig-hit*, but if she has good oral language skills, she'll know that there's no such English word. Furthermore, if she encounters this word in the context of other words like *castle, horse,* and *armor*, she might be able to infer the meaning of the word, which, she already knows, sounds like the word *night*, meaning the opposite of *day*. Without strong oral language skills, this kind of sophisticated detective work would be impossible.

The trochaic bias that English-learning preschoolers exhibit continues in the early school years as novice readers tend to impose a strong-weak stress pattern on unfamiliar written words (van Rees et al., 2012). At the same time, English orthography includes spelling patterns that give hints as to whether the stress pattern should be strong-weak or weak-strong. For instance, most two-syllable words beginning with *be-* are iambic, as in *begin, before,* and *believe*. Likewise, most two-syllable words ending in *-oon* are also iambic, as in *saloon, platoon,* and *cartoon*. Over years of text experience, readers internalize these sorts of patterns. Thus, a first-grader encountering a pseudoword like *bedoon* will probably pronounce it *BE-doon*, whereas a sixth-grader will be more likely to pronounce it as *be-DOON*.

Although early reading is slow and deliberate with frequent errors and corrections, by the third or fourth grade, most children are reading fluently (Wankoff, 2011). They're able to decode unfamiliar words, make predictions about what comes next, and even draw inferences. Fluent reading involves automatic processing at multiple levels of language, from lexical access to parsing syntactic structure (O'Brien et al., 2011). While novice readers struggle to decode text, word recognition becomes automatic in practiced readers, and it's essential for reading to become fluent. Around this time, children also become fluent oral readers such that they're able to read aloud with the same prosodic and stress contours of speech, coordinating pauses with phrase and sentence boundaries.

Vocabulary Growth

People continue to learn new words throughout their lifespan. However, the most intense period of vocabulary growth is no doubt during the school years. It's been estimated that children learn upwards of 40,000 words between the first and twelfth grades (Lewis et al., 2011). Vocabulary size is crucial for developing literacy. Children entering school with a large oral vocabulary quickly become proficient readers, while a small oral vocabulary often leads to reading and other cognitive disabilities.

Schoolchildren learn vocabulary through direct instruction, as for example when they're given lists of words and definitions to memorize. However, direct instruction alone cannot account for the tens of thousands of words that students learn during the course of their education (Ram et al., 2013). This means that most of the words they learn are picked up incidentally through reading.

Figure 11.7 Photo of Elementary School Students

In the middle grade school years, children shift from the task of learning to read toward the task of reading to learn.

Source: ©iStockphoto.com/ CEFutcher.

During the school years, reading becomes the vehicle for word learning. Schoolchildren who read frequently have larger vocabularies than classmates who don't read as often (Ram et al., 2013). The more children read, the more opportunities they have to encounter new words in various contexts. In this way, new words gradually become familiar as the reader builds up knowledge about how they're used. As the child's reading vocabulary expands, word recognition becomes more automatic, increasing reading speed. You should also notice the vicious cycle for underprepared students. Those who enter school with poor vocabulary become poor readers, and as a result they read less and so have fewer opportunities to learn new words.

As we saw in the previous section, preschoolers can often learn a new word form with its meaning in one or two exposures, but it takes multiple exposures in various contexts for the word to become fully integrated into the lexicon (Wagovich, Pak, & Miller, 2010). Word learning through reading works in a similar fashion. When good readers first encounter a new word, they can apply their knowledge of English orthography to construct an approximate phonological representation, and they can use context to infer the word's meaning. Future encounters with the word in different contexts then lead the reader to build a more complex understanding of the word's meaning, its various senses, and its relationships with other words.

Research shows that schoolchildren make use of two different strategies to infer the meanings of novel words when reading (Ram et al., 2013). The first word-learning strategy is **contextual abstraction**, which involves *the use of surrounding text to determine the meaning of a word.* Children's ability to use contextual abstraction depends on several factors, including the difficulty and length of the target word as well as the proportion of unfamiliar words in the text. The second word-learning strategy is **morphological analysis**, which is *the tactic of breaking down a word into its component parts to determine its meaning.* Even in the early school years, children are able to use their knowledge of suffixes to infer word meanings, for instance recognizing that a *violinist* must be someone who plays the violin.

The ability to do morphological analysis is dependent on **morphological awareness**, which is *the understanding that many words can be broken down into smaller meaningful units, or morphemes* (Ram et al., 2013). Children perform better at morphological analysis when they're given formal instruction that raises their level of morphological awareness. Many of the words encountered in school are composed of multiple morphemes. For example, *psychologist* can be broken down into *psycho* meaning "mind," *log* meaning "study," and *ist* meaning "person," in other words, "a person who studies the mind." Thus, morphological awareness and the ability to do morphological analysis are essential for proficient reading.

As children learn more words and develop reading proficiency, they need to deal more frequently with words that have multiple meanings (Corthals, 2010). Younger children, as well as older children who are poor readers, are prone to consider alternative meanings of homonyms that are inconsistent with the context, such as considering a *river bank* as a possible place to keep money. However, older children with strong reading skills are better able to inhibit inappropriate meanings by considering sentence context.

In addition to making inferences about the meanings of words from context, schoolchildren also need to learn how to make inferences about information that isn't explicitly stated in the text (Karasinski & Weismer, 2010). Much of the research on children's and adult's abilities to make bridging inferences (see Chapter 7) is based on Kintsch's (1988) construction-integration model. This is *a theory that explains how a reader's ability to make inferences is based on the linguistic input, the reader's real-world knowledge, and working memory constraints*. In this model, the reader first extracts meaning from the text in the form of propositions, or simple sentences. The reader then uses real-world knowledge to fill in logical gaps in the text. To do this, the reader needs to hold two propositions in working memory while searching long-term memory for the appropriate connecting information. Thus, working memory constraints limit the reader's ability to make inferences.

Table 11.2 Construction-Integration Model and Bridging Inferences	
Context	A princess was walking along a pond when she saw a frog. "Kiss me," croaked the frog, "and I'll turn into a handsome prince."
Proposition 1	The princess carefully considered the proposition. [Logical gap.]
Proposition 2	That night, she had frog legs for supper.
Logical inference	The princess decided not to kiss the frog after all. *Or maybe:* She kissed the frog, but it didn't turn into a handsome prince, so she ate it out of revenge.

Producing Discourse

Show and tell is a common classroom activity in the early school years, and it gives children practice in producing oral narratives. Over the next few years, the emphasis shifts more toward written narratives, in the form of essays and other writing assignments. But the ability to produce coherent oral narratives is a vital skill for success both in school and in professional life as an adult.

Researchers looking at the development of oral and written narrative skills in schoolchildren make a distinction between the narrative's microstructure and macrostructure (Heilman et al., 2010; Terry et al., 2013). Microstructure refers to *the linguistic form and content of a narrative at the sentence level*, and it's usually measured in terms of mean length of utterance and number of different words. On the other hand,

macrostructure refers to *the global hierarchical structure of a narrative as it flows logically from beginning to conclusion*, and this is usually analyzed in terms of story grammar. (You can refer back to Chapter 7 for a review of story grammar and the elements of narrative.) Cohesion is another aspect of macrostructure that develops during the school years, as children get better at using referring expressions and conjunctions more effectively.

In addition to well-developed microstructure and macrostructure, advanced narratives also include the use of **literate language**, which refers to *the particular syntactic structures and vocabulary used in academic situations* (Heilman et al., 2010). Literate language makes extensive use of abstract nouns, such as *anticipation* or *curiosity*. Another feature of literate language is the **metacognitive verb**, which is *a verb that describes a mental state* (Sun & Nippold, 2012). Metacognitive verbs like *think* and *believe* demand the use of complex syntactic structures, such as embedded sentences. For example, the sentence *The princess decided she would kiss the frog* has the metacognitive verb *decide* as its main verb and the embedded sentence *she would kiss the frog* as its object or complement. This kind of syntactic structure is far less common in the speech of preschoolers as well as in the spoken language of older children with language impairments. Proper use of metacognitive verbs requires a well-developed theory of mind, that is, the ability to infer the mental states of others.

In the early years of school, when children are still developing literacy skills, the emphasis is placed on comprehending and producing narratives, or stories. However, once children become fluent readers, the focus shifts to a new sort of text known as **expository discourse**, which is *a monologue that provides a factual description or an explanation of an event* (Westerveld & Moran, 2011). "What I Did on My Summer Vacation" is the stereotypical example of expository discourse, which can be produced either orally or in writing. Expository discourse is a form of language that is quite different in structure from the conversations and narratives that make up the bulk of social interactions. Over the school years, children become more adept at constructing expository discourse, which tends to become longer and more complex as children get older. Furthermore, after about the third grade, the bulk of schoolchildren's reading material is in the form of expository discourse.

Oral language skill on entering school has a major impact not only on the development of reading but also on the formation of math skills. Phonological awareness is an important component of the computation of math problems, since both the numerals and the operations need to be manipulated in phonological short-term memory (Ostad, 2011). At first, children say math problems out loud as they solve them—*seven plus eight is fifteen*. This is an example of what is known as **private speech**, which is *self-talk that is not addressed to other people*.

Preschoolers often use private speech as they play or engage in particular activities, and it's believed to be a form of thinking out loud and directing behavior. As we get older, we learn to turn private speech inward and silent so that it's nothing more than our voice in our head. Still, even as adults we resort to private speech spoken out loud when we are struggling to find the solution to a problem. Further evidence that oral language skills underlie the development of math performance comes from the observation that children with specific language disorder also tend to perform poorly at math, even though they show no other cognitive deficits (Nys, Content, & Leybaert, 2013).

In Sum

Children who do well in school already have strong oral language and preliteracy skills when they enter kindergarten, and these abilities underlie the successful development of reading. Since reading involves the conversion of written symbols into spoken-word mental representations, readers need to have sufficient capacity in short-term memory to hold on to these phonological word forms while they rapidly access their meanings from long-term memory. Schoolchildren learn tens of thousands of words over the course of primary and secondary education, with the majority acquired incidentally while reading. Readers use two strategies for learning the meanings of unfamiliar words. First, they can use contextual cues from the surrounding text, including both the meanings of neighboring words as well as the syntactic structure in which the new word is found, to infer meaning. Second, they can do a morphological analysis of the novel word, breaking it down into its component morphemes, or meaningful units. A reader's ability to make bridging inferences is explained by the construction-integration model in terms of the information present in the text, real-world knowledge, and working memory constraints. Children in school are also expected to produce both oral and written discourse. In the early years, the emphasis is on narratives, or storytelling; later there's a gradual shift toward expository discourse, in which the speaker or writer is expected to use the specialized vocabulary and syntactic structures of academic and professional settings.

Review Questions

1. Describe the kinds of language skills children need to already have when they enter school in order to become successful readers. Explain the relationship between oral language and literacy.

2. Describe vocabulary growth during the school years. What strategies do readers use to infer the meaning of unknown words?

3. Distinguish between the microstructure and the macrostructure of narrative. What is literate language, and how is it related to expository discourse?

4. What is private speech, and how is it related to the development of math skills?

Thought Questions

1. Although novice readers tend to show a trochaic (strong-weak) bias for unfamiliar words, van Rees et al. (2012) found that skilled

readers assign stress to new words based on their similarities to known words. For example, *bedoon* is usually stressed on the second syllable because words like *believe* and *cartoon* have iambic stress. Consider where you would place the stress on the following nonwords: *abade, mambey, copet, bevade*. What are some familiar English words that provide a model for assigning stress to these nonwords? (Hint: Consider real words that begin and end in the same way as these nonwords.)

2. The construction-integration model explains how we make bridging inferences when processing discourse. What are the three components of the model? Consider the following example: *Mark reached into the picnic basket. The beer was warm.* What bridging inference needs to be made to understand the relationship between these two sentences? How do the three components of the model interact in this case to generate this bridging inference? Under what circumstances might it be difficult for the reader or listener to make this inference?

Google It! Language and Math Skills

Although language and mathematics are treated as separate subjects in school, there's a growing consensus among researchers and educators that **language and math skills** are interrelated and support each other. You can find articles and videos on the Internet that explain this position.

SECTION 11.4: ADULTHOOD AND AGING

- People continue learning new words across the lifespan; as a result, older adults have larger vocabularies than younger adults. Older adults use this vocabulary advantage to offset cognitive declines that have a negative impact on language processing.

- Some hearing loss is inevitable in later adulthood; however, many older adults experience difficulties in auditory processing despite normal hearing. Ambient noise and multitalker situations make speech comprehension especially difficult for many older adults.

- Older adults experience cognitive reductions in attention, working memory, and processing speed; all of these losses have a negative impact on language processing. Nevertheless, aging adults find strategies to compensate for cognitive decline.

- Younger adults tend to use more complex syntax but simpler vocabulary, and they also speak at a faster rate; in contrast, older adults speak more slowly, and they use simpler syntax but more sophisticated vocabulary.

- The tip-of-the-tongue phenomenon increases with age, and hence older people often make use of circumlocutions, giving a description or definition of the word they're struggling to recall; this phenomenon may occur because the connections from word meaning to word form weaken with age.

- In spite of physical and cognitive declines, older adults tend to be happier than younger adults; however, social and intellectual engagement is key, and difficulties in language comprehension arising from auditory deficits can start a downward spiral of social isolation and mental deterioration.

If you're a typical college student, you're a young adult at the peak of your physical and cognitive abilities. But that still doesn't mean it's all downhill from here. As adults move through middle age and into their later years, they experience a gradual cognitive decline, as their working memory capacity decreases, their processing speed slows down, and their ability to control attention is reduced (Kemper et al., 2010). This cognitive decline impacts all aspects of life, including language processing. At the same time, adults accumulate a lifetime of experience as they age. Older adults not only have larger vocabularies than younger adults, they also are more aware of their limitations and make allowances for them. Despite the physical and cognitive declines that come with aging, older adults are, on average, happier than young adults, so maybe growing old isn't as bad as young people think it is.

You're Not Getting Older, You're Getting Better

Although our phonological and syntactic abilities are set by adolescence, we continue to learn new words throughout our lives. Preschoolers mainly learn words incidentally through interactions with caregivers, but during the school years reading becomes the primary vehicle for vocabulary acquisition. There's also a shift in school toward intentional word learning, as for example when students learn lists of terms and definitions or when they are taught strategies for morphological analysis. Although the rate of vocabulary development slows down in adulthood, people continue absorbing new words throughout their lives, both through reading and through exposure to new words in speech.

Different brain areas appear to be involved in vocabulary acquisition depending on whether the learning is intentional or incidental (Richardson et al., 2009). In teenagers, vocabulary size is correlated with the density of gray matter in the region of the left parietal lobe known as the posterior supramarginal gyrus. This area seems to be related to the explicit learning of new words and concepts. In older adults, however, vocabulary size is associated with gray matter increases in the left posterior temporal regions. It's believed that this area is involved in the learning of new words through contextual cues.

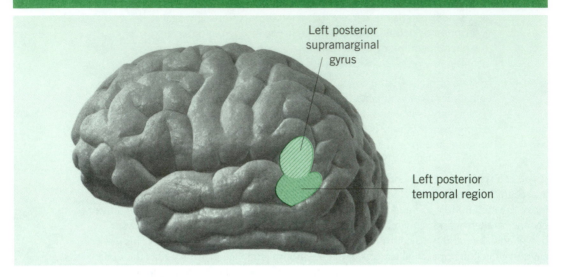

Left posterior supramarginal gyrus

Left posterior temporal region

Mostly Downhill, But With Some High Points

As they get older, most adults experience some loss of auditory processing abilities. This can happen both at the sensory level from damage to the cochlea and at the perceptual level due to changes in the brain (Tun et al., 2012). Loss of sensitivity to pure tones is normal in middle and later adulthood. In particular, a decline in sensitivity to the higher frequencies is common, and this can have a major impact on speech perception, since important information about consonants and vowels is carried in the higher frequencies. In fact, most older adults experience difficulty understanding speech in the presence of background noise.

Even when older adults have hearing within the normal range, they still often report that they have difficulty understanding speech in noise (Woods et al., 2012). This suggests an impairment in phonological processing, particularly in terms of processing speech sounds of short duration, such as stop consonants. In the lab, older adults with normal hearing have more difficulty identifying consonants in nonsense words compared with young adults. However, this problem with consonant identification goes away in clear speech, apparently because older adults can use context cues to make reasonable guesses about the consonants they missed.

Multitalker situations also pose challenges in speech perception for older adults (Passow et al., 2012). Imagine you're chatting with your friends in the school cafeteria during the crowded lunch hour. If you're in your late teens or early twenties, you may have no difficulty keeping your attention focused on the conversation at your table, in spite of all the other conversations going on around you. However, as adults pass through middle age, they have more difficulty inhibiting distractions, and so it takes them more effort to keep their attention directed on the conversation at hand. If they're also experiencing the beginnings of hearing loss, they may become overwhelmed by the ambient noise and unable to understand what's said to them.

Aging adults typically display cognitive reductions in attention and working memory as well as processing speed, which in turn have a negative effect on language processing (Tun et al., 2012). Speech perception and production place significant demands on working memory and attention in young adults too, but even more so in older adults who are experiencing reductions in these resources. Long-term memory is affected as well, and older adults tend to perform more poorly on tests of comprehension or recall, especially when the sentences or texts are complex (Kail, Lemaire, & Lecacheur, 2012). Older adults also have more difficulty using context cues in a sentence to predict what's coming next (Meyer & Federmeier, 2010).

Despite these reductions in cognitive functioning and the impact they have on language processing, older adults in good health display few obvious performance issues in everyday language use, and in some ways they even outperform young adults (Sauzéon et al., 2010). Since older adults have larger vocabularies and are more familiar with the kinds of contexts in which particular words are used, they can use semantic and pragmatic knowledge to compensate for processing impairments.

Multitasking

In spite of its apparent effortlessness, language processing requires a lot of cognitive resources. Think about a time when you're driving with a friend. On the open road, conversation is easy and free-flowing, but the idle chit-chat suddenly stops once you encounter heavy traffic or hazardous road conditions. Because older adults are aware, at some level, of their cognitive limitations, they're generally more careful about allocating mental resources when performing two tasks at once (Kemper et al., 2010). When the second task, such as driving, becomes demanding, older adults tend to slow down their speaking rate, trading speed for accuracy. Young adults tend to emphasize speed over accuracy, and as a result they're more likely to make errors when talking during a dual-task situation than are their elders.

Younger adults also tend to use more complex sentence structures in their speech as well as more conversational fillers such as "like" and "you know" than do older adults (Kemper et al., 2010). Despite the syntactic complexity of their sentences, though, young adults use simpler vocabulary, presumably because they know fewer words. In contrast, older adults tend to use simpler sentence structures but more rich and varied vocabulary, and they're also less likely to use conversational fillers. This conservative style of speaking is probably an accommodation for declines in processing speed and working memory.

On the other hand, young adults do make accommodations for those they perceive as having cognitive impairments by using a form of speech known as **elderspeak** (Kemper et al., 2010). This is *a manner of speaking that young people adopt when addressing older adults who appear to have difficulties with hearing or language perception.* This style is characterized by a slow rate of speaking and the use of short, simple sentences as well as by a considerable amount of repetition. Elderspeak provides one more example of how adult speakers modify their language to fit the needs and limitations of their interlocutor, as we've already seen the case of infant-directed speech and in interactions with non-native speakers.

Speech is laid atop respiration, and we try to line up our breaths with syntactic or prosodic boundaries when we speak. As adults age, their patterns of breath-pausing change (Huber et al., 2012). Younger adults take fewer breaths while speaking and locate them mostly at major linguistic boundaries. Older adults, however, breathe more often while speaking, pausing more frequently at minor syntactic boundaries. Nevertheless, they generally take breaths at locations that have negligible impact on naturalness and intelligibility.

More frequent pauses in older adults' speech may be due, at least in part, to a reduction in respiratory capacity (Huber et al., 2012). However, similar patterns of pausing are also observed during silent reading. Compared with younger adults, older adults tend to pause a longer time at minor syntactic boundaries, such as between subject and verb, and a shorter time at major syntactic boundaries, such as between sentences. Although it's possible that they're lining up their breathing with the syntactic structures of the text they're reading, a more plausible explanation is that working memory limitations force older adults to break sentences into smaller chunks.

The Aging Brain

A notable finding in the neuroscience of aging is that the brain tends to reorganize as we get older. Cognitive functions related to language are more clearly lateralized in young adults, but they tend to diffuse across hemispheres as we get older (Meyer & Federmeier, 2010). This suggests that aging brains need to draw on additional resources to perform the same functions that they managed with more limited processing areas when they were younger. In other words, the compensation strategies that we observe in the behavior of older adults is also reflected in the neural reorganization we can see in their brains (Shafto et al., 2012).

You should recall from Chapter 6 that the N400 is an ERP component that's a signal of semantic processing. N400s are evoked not only by sentence-level context but also by discourse-level information and even by real-world knowledge (Wlotko & Federmeier, 2012). In younger adults, an N400 clearly indicates a violation of an expectation in a text, thus showing that they're constantly thinking ahead and making guesses about what comes next. However, the N400 response is much weaker in older adults, suggesting that they don't use context to predict what's coming next the way younger adults do. As we've already seen, older adults rely heavily on context to overcome perceptual difficulties, and so perhaps they have fewer cognitive resources left over to make inferences about what follows.

It's on the Tip of My Tongue

Just because we know a word, that doesn't mean we always have access to it whenever we need it. All of us have suffered the **tip-of-the-tongue phenomenon**, which is *the experience of being temporarily unable to recall a familiar word* (Shafto, 2010). Oftentimes we can even name characteristics of the word, such as what sound it begins with or what other words it's related to, even though we can't access the word form itself. While even young people have this experience, naming difficulties increase with age. By the early fifties, the tip-of-the-tongue phenomenon becomes a fairly common occurrence with a steep increase in the incidence of naming difficulties during the seventies and later.

While difficulties in finding words may be an early symptom of a disease such as Alzheimer's, lexical retrieval failures are common even among healthy older adults (Conner et al., 2011). As a result, the speech patterns of older adults include more **circumlocution**, which is *the use of a roundabout description in place of a single word or phrase*. Older people are also more likely to use generalized terms in place of specific words, as for example when Grandma asks Grandpa to "get me the thingamajig from the whatchamacallit." (And Grandpa knows exactly what she means.) Circumlocutions and generalized terms are even more common in the speech of Alzheimer's patients (Gayraud, Lee, & Barkat-Defradas, 2011).

The tip-of-the-tongue phenomenon even extends to the recall of proper nouns. No doubt you've been in the situation where you've run into a person and couldn't remember his or her name, even though you knew you knew it. This kind of retrieval failure for personal and place names also increases with age (Martins, Mares, & Stilwell, 2012). Some older adults even report more difficulty recalling names than recalling words. Perhaps this is because there's no acceptable circumlocution for a person's name, at least when you're addressing that person.

Although the tip-of-the-tongue phenomenon, or TOT, is perceived as a temporary inability to retrieve a word, research shows that what's really happening is specifically a failure to retrieve the phonological word form (Farrell & Abrams, 2011). After all, TOT'ed speakers can tell you the meaning of the word, since that's exactly what they do when they resort to circumlocution. TOTs can be induced in the laboratory, and participants can often recall the word if they're provided with the first syllable, although usually not if they're only given the first sound or letter. These observations suggest that the source of the TOT lies in the connections between the word's meaning and its pronunciation.

The tip-of-the-tongue phenomenon is often explained in terms of the **transmission deficit hypothesis**. This is *the proposal that the connections between a word's semantic representation and its phonological representation weaken with age* (White et al., 2012). According to this model, word meanings are stable because they're highly interconnected. That is to say, you define a word in terms of other words, and there are multiple ways of explaining what a word means. However, each word meaning has a single specific word form, and so if the link from the word's meaning to its pronunciation is disrupted, there's no workaround.

The TOT phenomenon increases with age despite the fact that vocabulary continues to expand well into a person's fifties and even later (Kavé, Knafo, & Gilboa, 2010). However, processing efficiency peaks earlier, generally before age twenty, and then steadily declines after that. Thus, while older people can recognize more words than younger people, they also have more difficulty producing the words they do know.

Interestingly, the reverse of the TOT phenomenon rarely occurs. That is to say, given the phonological or written word form, people of any age almost never have any

Figure 11.9 Transmission Deficit Hypothesis

The word *computer* has many links to related concepts, but only a single link connects the word to each of the letters that make up the word form. The tip-of-the-tongue phenomenon occurs when links to the semantic system are sufficiently activated but the links to the orthographic system are not sufficiently activated.

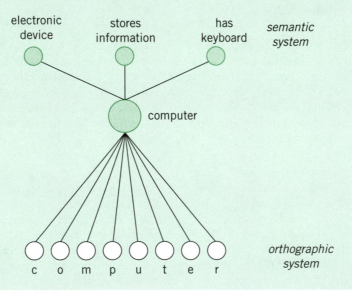

Source: Shafto (2010).

difficulty accessing its meaning (assuming they know the word). This observation reflects a more general pattern of language processing known as the **input/output asymmetry**, referring to *the observation that language perception processes are generally spared even when language production processes are impaired* (Shafto, 2010). This asymmetry is also reflected in the fact that we can recognize words we don't know how to use and that we can read words we can't spell.

Generally speaking, language comprehension abilities remain stable well into healthy old age, at least in situations without noise or distractions (Price & Sanford, 2011). Likewise, older adults are usually just as good at reading, if not better, than young adults, since they have a long lifetime of reading experience to draw on. Because reading is self-paced, older people aren't hampered by slower processing speeds or working memory constraints the way they are in speech perception. However, when the text structure is very complex, they can have more difficulty recalling details or making inferences than younger adults.

Happy Ever After

Despite declines in physical and mental prowess, old age is a happy time for many people. Researchers analyzing the content of Facebook messages found that older people use more positive expressions of emotion and make more references to the future than do younger people, who tend to express more negative emotions and make more references to themselves and to the past (Kern et al., 2013). *The observation that people tend to get happier as they get older* is known as the **aging positivity effect**.

This effect is also dependent on a number of behavioral and lifestyle factors (Tun et al., 2012). Older adults with a satisfying social support system and a mentally engaging environment show the effect, but those suffering from isolation exhibit rapid cognitive decline. Since people experiencing difficulties with language comprehension often withdraw from social circles, a vicious cycle of social isolation and cognition decline is all too often set in motion.

In Sum

Although your phonological and syntactic abilities are set by adolescence, you continue to learn new words throughout your life. As people grow older, they experience physical and cognitive declines that have a negative effect on language. While many older adults experience some degree of hearing loss, a more important obstacle to language comprehension is a decline in auditory processing in the brain as well as reductions in other cognitive functions such as working memory and attention. Despite these declines, older adults find ways to compensate, and as a result, they sometimes outperform younger adults on language tasks. They accomplish this mainly by employing the conservative strategy of speaking slower and using simpler syntactic structures. Younger adults, on the other hand, use a riskier strategy of faster speaking

Kern and colleagues analyzed a dataset of over 70,000 Facebook users to identify the most commonly used words in text messages, with senders categorized by age and gender. More word clouds and other graphs can be viewed on the World Well-Being Project website at www.wwbp.org/age-plot.html.

Source: Kern et al. (2014).

rate and more complex syntactic structure. While all adults experience the tip-of-the-tongue phenomenon, it becomes increasingly common as they get older. The problem seems to occur because the links from word meaning to word form weaken with age. Although many young adults dread the dismal future of old age, people in their later years are generally happier than those in their early adulthood. However, social and intellectual engagement is key, and social isolation can lead to a downward spiral of cognitive decline.

Review Questions

1. How does vocabulary learning differ between adolescence and adulthood? How are these differences reflected in the brain?

2. Although some hearing loss is normal as we age, why do many older adults with normal hearing still have trouble understanding speech in certain circumstances? Consider both cognitive and environmental factors.

3. How does breath-pausing in speech change with age? Do we also see a similar pattern of pausing while reading? What factors may be influencing this change?

4. What is the tip-of-the-tongue phenomenon? How do older adults compensate for TOT? How does the transmission deficit hypothesis explain the TOT phenomenon?

Thought Questions

1. Can you think of some other examples of the input/output asymmetry besides those given in the text? Do you think this asymmetry is limited to language, or might it extend to other areas of cognition. If so, can you give any examples?

2. The reverse of the TOT phenomenon rarely occurs, but it can. What would the experience be like? Have you ever had the experience?

3. Why do you think older adults are generally happier than younger adults, despite physical and cognitive declines?

Google It! Hearing and Happiness

Recently, the mosquito ringtone has become popular among teenagers because their parents and teachers can't hear it. YouTube has clips that play it. You can also search hearing test to find your hearing threshold. If you're interested in learning more about how the language people use changes as they get older, google World Well-Being Project, where researchers have analyzed thousands of social media texts.

CONCLUSION

As our bodies and minds change throughout the lifespan, so do our language abilities. Some aspects of language, such as phonology and syntax, peak before adolescence and remain fairly stable well into healthy old age. On the other hand, we continue to learn vocabulary our whole life long, although the pace of growth is certainly faster in childhood. Still, a lifetime of experience with language means that older adults not only know more words but also have a deeper understanding of their meanings and the contexts in which they're used.

Language development is also tied to physical development. As infants, we can't utter our first words until we have control over the muscles that articulate speech. In older adulthood, declines in respiratory capacity mean that we have to stop to breathe more frequently when we speak.

Changes in cognitive processes over the lifespan influence language development as well. Working memory capacity is quite limited in infancy, but this actually helps language learners focus on the relevant aspects of the linguistic input. During childhood and adolescence, working memory capacity increases, but it declines again in middle and later adulthood. As a result, older adults tend to speak in shorter sentences, and they may also have difficulty recalling information or making inferences when dealing with complex texts.

In American culture, youth is revered and old age is feared. Yet, in spite of physical and cognitive declines, older adults are generally happier than young adults. Perhaps this should give us all something to look forward to.

CROSS-CULTURAL PERSPECTIVE: The Noun Bias in Children's First Words

Developmental psychologists in the United States have long noted that most of the words in children's early vocabulary are nouns (Katerelos, Poulin-Dubois, & Oshima-Takane, 2011). In more recent years, cross-cultural studies have confirmed this early noun bias in other languages as well, including French, Italian, Spanish, and Hebrew. This suggests that the noun bias may be universal.

Perhaps there's something in the cognitive makeup of human toddlers that make them predisposed to learning nouns more than verbs. After all, nouns refer to objects that are concrete and easy to perceive, such as *cup* and *chair*. Even before they speak, toddlers have experience manipulating many of these objects. This familiarity then should make learning the names of the objects easier. Furthermore, many of the word-learning strategies that young children use, such as the whole object assumption (Chapter 5), work only with nouns.

Verbs, on the other hand, are more abstract in their meaning. Unlike nouns, which refer to objects, verbs signify relationships between nouns participating in events that unfold over time. This is true even for action verbs that the child can easily perform, such as *eat* or *run*. In other words, there can be no *eat* without someone to eat and something to be eaten. Likewise, *run* only has meaning in the context of a runner.

Perhaps, then, toddlers learn more nouns than verbs because they're easier to learn. Nouns are perceptually salient and oftentimes manipulable. Verbs, on the other hand, may be harder to learn because they're more abstract.

However, studies on vocabulary development in East Asian languages such as Japanese, Korean, and Mandarin have challenged this assumption that the noun bias is universal. Toddlers learning these languages show a weaker noun bias than do English-learning children (Rescorla et al., 2013). So perhaps the noun bias isn't universal after all.

It could be that the noun bias isn't due to cognitive factors but rather comes from the structure of the language being learned. The two most salient positions in a sentence are the beginning and the end. Since English generally follows a subject-verb-object word order, nouns show up at the beginning and the end of most sentences, with the verb buried in the middle. That is to say, nouns stand out in English, but verbs don't. French, Italian, Spanish, and Hebrew all have subject-verb-object word order as well, which may be why the noun bias is also found in those languages.

Korean and Japanese, however, follow subject-object-verb word order, and so both languages highlight verbs at the ends of sentences much more so than English does. Furthermore, both Korean and Japanese simply leave out noun phrases that are obvious from context, and this is true of Mandarin as well. In all three of these languages, it's not uncommon, especially in casual speech, for a sentence to consist solely of a verb phrase without an expressed subject or object. As a result, children learning these languages hear a lot more verbs, and verbs stand out more in sentences that also contain nouns.

Discourse factors may play a role as well (Rescorla et al., 2013). When Korean mothers talk with their children, they're more likely to discuss activities and actions; hence the focus is on verbs. American mothers, on the other hand, are more likely to point to and talk about objects in the environment; hence the focus is on nouns. Some evidence suggests that the Korean pattern of mother-child interaction is more typical of East Asian culture, whereas the American style is more typical of Western culture.

In the end, most of the words that young Korean children learn are still nouns. It's just that they also know more verbs than English-learning youngsters. So perhaps the noun bias is universal after all, but culture can influence how much of a bias there is.

KEY TERMS

Aging positivity effect

Alphabet knowledge

Basic level category

Business talk

Circumlocution

Construction-integration
model

Contextual abstraction

Decoding

Descriptive talk

Developmental cascade

Elderspeak

Expository discourse

Homonym advantage

Input/output asymmetry

Less-is-more hypothesis

Lexical configuration

Lexical engagement

Literate language

Macrostructure

Metacognitive verb

Microstructure

Morphological analysis

Morphological awareness

Morphosyntax

Oral language skills

Polyseme

Print knowledge

Private speech

Protoconversation

Salient

Slow mapping

Tip-of-the-tongue
phenomenon

Transmission deficit
hypothesis

Trochaic bias

Language, Culture, and Thought

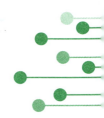

In his novel *Nineteen Eighty-Four*, George Orwell (1949) describes a totalitarian society where every aspect of people's lives is controlled by the government. To limit people's thought processes, the government invents a language called Newspeak, which is intended to replace English. Because Newspeak only has words for politically acceptable concepts, people who use the language will be unable to commit thought crimes against the state.

The motivation behind Newspeak is the idea that we can only think in terms that are provided to us by our language. At the time that Orwell wrote the novel, many psychologists equated thought with language, and so the notion that people were constrained in their thoughts by the language they spoke was widely accepted. Today, however, we understand that the relationship between language and thought is far more complex that was believed in Orwell's day.

In this chapter, we explore the ways in which language, culture, and thought interact. We'll see that the vocabulary and structure of our language guide our perception and attention, and they may make certain ways of thinking easier. At the same time, we'll find that languages are flexible, and they change to accommodate new ways of thinking. We'll also explore how culture, as a shared system of learned behaviors and thought processes, influences both the ways we speak and the ways we think.

SECTION 12.1: WORDS AND THOUGHT

- Linguistic relativity is the idea that the language we speak influences the way we perceive and think about the world around us; since each language carves up the world in a somewhat different manner, we should expect to see perceptual and cognitive differences between speakers of different languages.

- Innatism is the position that perceptual and cognitive processes are biologically based and therefore universal; thus, the language we speak should have no influence on how we perceive or think about the world.

- Languages vary in the number of basic color terms they have; thus, color perception provides a test case for linguistic relativity versus innatism; the data suggest an underlying core of color perception that is innate, but language can also have some influence on the perception of color.

- The visual system is maximally sensitive to four focal colors, red, green, yellow, and blue; in addition to black and white, these are the most common color categories across languages, and a language will not have other color terms such as brown or purple unless it also has terms for the first six.

- The perception of emotion in facial expressions is another example of a perceptual process that has an innate core but can be influenced by the emotion terms available in a given language.

- Language influences our perceptions by directing our attention toward certain distinctions and away from others; by giving labels to categories, members of those categories become easier to discriminate and also easier to remember.

We not only use language to communicate with others, we also use it to think to ourselves. We saw in Chapter 11 that toddlers use private speech to direct their actions. As we grow older, we turn that private speech inward, generating a more or less constant monologue in our heads as we go through the day. Faced with a problem to solve, we often find ourselves muttering or even speaking aloud as we think it through. Clearly, much of our conscious experience as humans is in a linguistic form.

In Chapter 9, we also found that there are no exact translation equivalents between languages. For example, English divides the set of all drinking vessels into two categories, *glass* and *cup*, depending on what substance they're made of. Russian also divides the set of all drinking vessels into two categories, *chashka* and *stakan*, depending on whether they have a handle or not. Thus, none of these words has a direct translation in the other language. This observation suggests the possibility that the language we speak could influence the way we think.

What Language Do You Think In?

In the mid-twentieth century, American linguist Benjamin Whorf (1956) seriously considered these two facts: (1) much of our conscious thinking is in the form of language; and (2) each language carves up the world in somewhat different ways.

Therefore, he reasoned, the language we speak must influence the way we think, including the way that we perceive the world.

The strong version of the Whorf hypothesis is known as **linguistic determinism**. This is *the proposal that people can only perceive and categorize the world according to the structures offered by their language* (Kousta, Vinson, & Vigliocco, 2008). Nowadays it may seem an exaggeration to claim that people can only think in terms of the language they speak. However, given the standard behaviorist view that thought was nothing more than subvocalized speech, it wouldn't have seemed like an unreasonable proposal at the time.

Few researchers take linguistic determinism seriously today. First of all, we now recognize that there are other modes of thought besides language, such as when an artist uses visual imagery to create a painting or a musician uses auditory imagery to compose a piece of music. Furthermore, we have plenty of evidence that people can perceive and categorize beyond the limits of their language. For instance, the Japanese language doesn't usually make a distinction between singular and plural, such that the word *hon* means either *book* or *books*. This doesn't mean that Japanese people can't conceive of the difference between one and more than one book. For that matter, some nouns in English aren't marked for plural either, as in *one fish, two fish*, but that doesn't mean we don't notice the difference in number.

A more reasonable interpretation of the Whorf hypothesis is **linguistic relativity**. This is *the proposal that the language people speak influences the way they perceive and think about the world* (Kersten et al., 2010). Thus, while Japanese nouns aren't overtly marked for singular or plural, speakers of the language *can* distinguish one book from more than one book simply by including a quantity word, just as we do in English with words like *fish*. Since Japanese speakers aren't required to make a singular-plural distinction the way English speakers are, linguistic relativity suggests that they pay less attention to the quantity of objects, and this subtle distinction between Japanese and English speakers has been verified in laboratory experiments (Domahs et al., 2012).

When it comes to the ways people use language to talk about the world around them, the idea of linguistic relativity seems to be obviously true (Bowers & Pleydell-Pearce, 2011). However, what's more controversial is the claim that even at the basic level perceptual processes are influenced by the structure of the language we speak. Some psychologists, especially those whose research focuses on the physiology of the nervous system, argue in favor of **innatism**, which is *the proposal that perceptual and cognitive processes are not influenced by language in any way* (Da Pos & Albertazzi, 2010).

The data so far are ambiguous. A number of cross-linguistic studies have yielded findings that seem to support the idea of linguistic relativity. However, many of these findings can also be interpreted to support the innatism position. Let's review some of these studies and see what conclusions we can draw from them.

The Amazing Technicolor World

When you look at a rainbow, you see colored bands of light. In grade school, you probably learned the mnemonic ROY G. BIV to remember the order of the colors—red, orange, yellow, green, blue, indigo, and violet. The first five and the last are no doubt familiar colors, but if you're like me, you've never, ever, named the color of any other object as "indigo."

If you took physics in high school, you may have learned that the visible light spectrum is continuous and doesn't naturally break up into distinct color bands (Delgado, 2004). Nevertheless, we see distinct regions of different colors, suggesting that our perception of color is categorical. (See Chapter 3 for a discussion of the categorical perception of phonemes, which also vary continuously.) This observation then raises the question: Are the distinct colors we see and can name with words like "red" and "blue" a product of innate perceptual processes or of learned linguistic categories?

In a survey of color terms in languages around the world, Berlin and Kay (1969) found that different languages have different numbers of basic color terms. In fact, some languages distinguish only two color categories, black and white, which lump together all the dark colors and all the light colors. We do this as well in English when we describe the red-yellow half of the spectrum as "warm colors" and the green-blue half of the spectrum as "cool colors."

At first glance, these findings suggest strong support for the linguistic relativity hypothesis, in that different languages categorize colors differently. However, Berlin and Kay (1969) also found consistent patterns of color categorization across languages. For example, a three-color system would always consist of black, white,

Figure 12.1 The Visible Light Spectrum

The visible light spectrum ranges roughly from 400 to 750 nanometers. We perceive the spectrum as bands of color traditionally named red, orange, yellow, green, blue, indigo, and violet. However, the spectrum is continuous, with no physical boundaries between the perceived color bands. Google "visible light spectrum" to see figures like this in color.

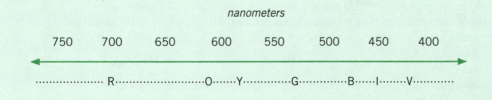

Table 12.1 Order of Color Terms

Although languages differ in the number of basic color terms they have, there are consistent patterns of color categorization across languages.

Number	Colors
2	Black *and* White
3	Red
4	Yellow *or* Green
5	Green *or* Yellow
6	Blue
7	Brown
>7	Pink, Purple, Orange, Grey *in no particular order.*

Source: Berlin and Kay (1969).

and red, while a six-color system would include these three as well as yellow, green, and blue.

In languages across the globe, color systems tend to be organized around six focal colors—white, black, red, green, yellow, and blue (Regier, Kay, & Cook, 2005). A **focal color** is *the best example of a color name and the center of a color category*. That is to say, in any language that has the Red color category, speakers will generally agree on the same shade of red as the best example of that color, typically somewhere around the color of fresh blood or of a bright red apple.

Strictly speaking, white and black aren't colors but opposite poles of a grayscale continuum representing the amount of light present (Da Pos & Albertazzi, 2010). The other four focal colors, red, green, yellow, and blue, are ubiquitous in modern society. These are the four colors that make up an Uno deck, and they also make up the logos for Microsoft and Google.

Although the colors of visible light vary along a continuum, our visual system is maximally sensitive to four specific regions, which we perceive as the four focal colors of red, green, yellow, and blue (Da Pos & Albertazzi, 2010). Furthermore, because of the way it processes light, the visual system wraps the visible spectrum into a circle defined by two pairs of opposing colors, red-green and yellow-blue. If you imagine the white-black scale extending above and below the color wheel, you can see how the visible colors arrange themselves with lighter shades tending toward white and the darker shades toward black.

Figure 12.2   Four Focal Colors

The four focal colors come in two opponent pairs of red-green and yellow-blue. We can think of these focal colors as occupying four quadrants of a circle. We can perceive adjacent colors as blending into each other. For example, a blend of yellow and red could be perceived as orange. However, we can't perceive blends of opponent colors. Google "color wheel" to see similar images in full color.

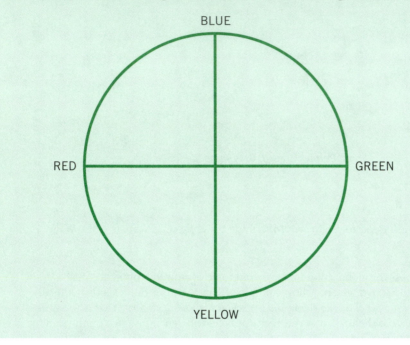

Fifty Shades of Grue

The color systems of the world vary somewhat in the way they divide up the color wheel, but color categories always consist of continuous regions, and boundaries are always some distance away from the focal points. It's not uncommon to have *a single basic color term in a language that includes both blue and green*, a color category researchers refer to as **grue** (Delgado, 2004). The Japanese word *ao* is a good example of "grue" because it can be used to refer to the color of grass or the color of the sky. And since the Japanese words for "leaf" and "tooth" are homophones, the word *aoba* can mean either "greenleaf" or "bluetooth," depending on context.

You may wonder how Japanese speakers can use the same word to refer to both green and blue. However, Russian speakers are equally surprised to learn that English uses the same color term, *blue*, to refer to what they regard as two separate color categories. Russian distinguishes between *goluboy*, or light blue, and *siniy*, or dark blue, and native speakers of the language are quite consistent about which shades of blue go in each category (Zhou et al., 2010). Greek and Turkish make a similar light blue–dark blue distinction.

Research into the categorical perception of color often involves asking speakers of different languages to sort color samples into groups (Wright, 2012). Not surprisingly, speakers of languages with only the single color term for grue tend to group green and blue color samples together, while speakers of languages with a blue-green distinction generally agree on which samples go in which category. When speakers of a grue language are given blue and green focal examples and asked to sort the rest of the samples as blue or green, they vary widely on how they divide up the two colors.

New color categories can be learned through extensive training. The Chinese language has separate color terms for green and blue, but researchers taught Chinese participants to distinguish two types of green and two types of blue by assigning different names to each of them (Zhou et al., 2010). Language clearly plays a role in learning and using novel color categories. When participants are given a concurrent verbal task such as repeating a list of digits, they can no longer separate color samples according to the new categories they've learned. In other words, when the participants can't access the novel color names, they have more difficulty sorting colors into the newly learned categories.

Speakers of a grue language can certainly perceive a difference between blue and green, just as you can perceive a difference between light blue and dark blue. However, language can interact with memory to influence the categorical perception of color (Wright, 2012). A **delayed match-to-sample task** is *an experimental procedure in which a participant first sees a target item and then after a delay is asked to choose which of two novel items is more like the target*. When asked to discriminate blue and green targets, speakers of blue-green languages can use the "blue" and "green" color labels as a memory aid, and so they perform better on this task than do speakers of grue languages.

In a nutshell, findings from color categorization studies suggest a middle road between relativism and innatism. The human visual system is maximally sensitive to the four focal colors of red, green, yellow, and blue, and even prelinguistic infants show categorical perception of these colors (Ozturk et al., 2013). Nevertheless, the language we speak does influence the way we think about color differences, as for example whether we consider blue and green to be separate colors or else different shades of grue.

Language and the Perception of Emotion

Cross-cultural research suggests that there are six basic facial expressions in humans, namely happiness, sadness, fear, surprise, anger, and disgust (Damjanovic et al., 2010).

Around the world, people are very accurate at matching pictures of facial expressions to these six labels of emotion (translated into their language, of course). At first glance, these results suggest an innate ability to categorically perceive these six emotions. However, critics argue that this apparent categorical perception of emotion is driven by the linguistic labels that have been provided.

When people are instead shown pictures of facial expressions and asked to name the emotion, researchers find considerable variation both within and across

Figure 12.3   Categorical Perception of Emotional Facial Expressions

The German language has separate words for "disgust" and "anger," whereas the Yucatec language uses the same term for both emotions. However, in a delayed match-to-sample task, Yucatec speakers performed similarly to German speakers. Both groups were more accurate when the distractor item came from the other category than when it came from the same category. This result suggests that separate linguistic labels are not necessary for distinguishing emotional facial expressions.

(a) Sample stimuli

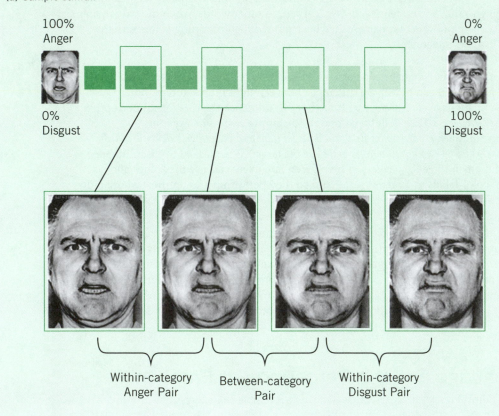

100%
Anger

0%
Disgust

0%
Anger

100%
Disgust

Within-category
Anger Pair

Between-category
Pair

Within-category
Disgust Pair

(b) Results

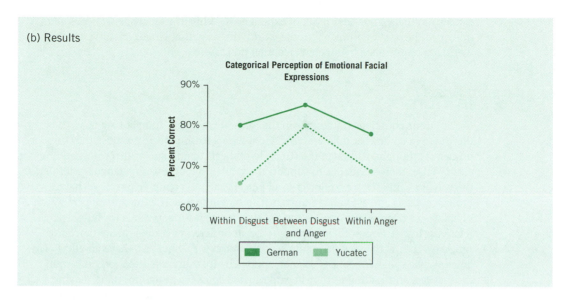

Categorical Perception of Emotional Facial Expressions

Source: Sauter, LeGuen, and Haun (2011).

cultures. There is even more disagreement across participants when they are simply asked to judge whether two faces express the same emotion or not (Gendron et al., 2012). These findings suggest that providing linguistic labels for emotions helps reduce the uncertainty that people otherwise experience when trying to recognize facial expressions, especially when there are no other context cues available.

Languages vary in the set of words they have to describe emotions, just as they do for colors (Sauter, et al., 2011). When German speakers were asked to name the emotion expressed in pictures of faces, they distinguished between those showing anger and those showing disgust. However, speakers of Yucatec Maya, an indigenous language of Mexico, use the same term to describe both emotions. Nevertheless, in a delayed match-to-sample task, the speakers of Yucatec Maya performed similarly to the speakers of German, indicating that linguistic labels aren't necessary to distinguish the two emotions.

In the case of emotion perception, as in color perception, the relationship between innate perceptual processes and linguistic influences is complex. In both cases, there appear to be core perceptual processes that are biologically based and therefore universal. However, there's still leeway within the parameters of these innate processes for language to have an effect. By providing category labels in the form of words, our language guides us to attend to certain differences and ignore others, and these labels can also influence our later recall of experiences. While the language we speak does influence the way we think about the world, the ways that languages carve up the world are constrained by innate perceptual processes.

In Sum

Much of our conscious thinking is in the form of language, and yet languages carve up the world in somewhat different ways. So it seems reasonable to suppose that language influences thought. Although the strong hypothesis that language determines thought is clearly false, there's evidence to support the weaker hypothesis that language influences the way we think. However, lower-level perceptual and cognitive processes have a biological basis and as such are universal among humans. The categorical perception of color and of emotional expression have served as testing grounds for linguistic relativity. In both cases, there appears to be an underlying core of innate perceptual processes, but within certain confines there's room for language to have an effect. The language we speak influences our perceptions by focusing our attention on certain distinctions and leading us to disregard other differences as unimportant. Having a label makes a category easier to learn, and it also helps in the discrimination and recall of category members.

Review Questions

1. Distinguish between linguistic determinism and linguistic relativity. What is innatism?

2. In what sense are the color bands of the rainbow an illusion?

3. What are focal colors, and why do they exist? How do the focal colors influence color naming patterns in languages around the world?

4. What is the evidence to support the position that color categories can be learned?

5. What do studies on the perception of emotion tell us about linguistic relativity and innatism?

Thought Questions

1. Consider the visible light spectrum as illustrated in Figure 12.1 and the arrangement of the four focal colors as illustrated in Figure 12.2. What do these diagrams tell us about the relationship between reality and perception?

2. The study of linguistic influences on color perception is complicated by the fact that there's no clear definition of a basic color term. In our culture, we say that indigo is one of the seven colors of the rainbow,

and yet indigo is rarely used as a color term in other contexts. While it's clear that black, white, and the four focal colors are basic in the sense that they have a biological basis, what about other color terms such a brown or purple? And what about more specific color terms like turquoise, teal, and aquamarine?

3. Even within a language, color terms aren't always consistent. The Japanese word *ao* clearly refers to both green and blue. Yet Japanese also has the word *midori*, which specifically means "green" and definitely not "blue." However, it has no word that specifically means just "blue" and not "green." What does this say about the relationship between language and reality?

Google It! What Colors Can You See?

Why is **indigo** considered one of the colors of the rainbow? Do an Internet search and see if you can find the answer. Many of the experiments on color perception reported in this section make use of the **Munsell color system**. You can see the array of colors for yourself, and you can read about how the colors are arranged. You can also check your color acuity by trying a **Munsell color test**, which you can find online.

SECTION 12.2: GRAMMAR AND THOUGHT

- English has a semantic gender system that classifies nouns as masculine, feminine, or neuter according to their natural type, but many European languages have a formal gender system that arbitrarily assigns a gender to each noun.

- Speakers of languages with formal gender systems show evidence of thinking about inanimate objects as having gender, and those thought patterns carry over to a second language like English that has no formal gender.

- Another way that languages categorize nouns is through the use of classifiers, which are used in conjunction with a noun to indicate its shape or function; native speakers are sensitive to the perceptual similarities among nouns that share the same classifier.

- The human perceptual system naturally distinguishes between objects with a stable shape and those without; many languages encode this distinction in their grammar, categorizing nouns as count or mass.

- Some languages focus on the manner of actions, while others focus on the path of actions; some encode information about the temporal flow of events, but others do not. Speakers' attention to events is guided by the requirements of their language.

- The thinking-for-speaking hypothesis suggests that speakers organize their cognitive processes as they speak to meet the requirements of their language.

In recent decades, there's been a movement toward using gender-neutral language in an effort to promote gender equality. Words like *chairman, mailman,* and *fireman,* which could refer to either a man or woman, have been changed to gender-neutral terms like *chair, letter carrier,* and *firefighter.* Likewise, male-female pairs like *waiter-waitress* and *steward-stewardess* have been replaced by single nongendered terms like *server* and *flight attendant.*

Replacing gender-specific terms with neutral equivalents isn't that difficult, since vocabulary changes somewhat from generation to generation anyway. However, when sex differences are encoded in the grammar, it's more difficult to find gender-neutral alternatives. Before the 1980s, masculine pronouns were considered acceptable in situations where they could refer to either males or females, as in the sentence: *Each student should raise his hand before he speaks.* Ladies, that includes you too.

Since then, writers and speakers of English have struggled with workarounds to gendered pronouns. Most of these are clunky, as in *he/she, s/he, he or she,* and so on. In writing, one workaround is to write in the plural, as in: *All students should raise their hand before they speak.* This works because the plural pronouns aren't marked for gender. But this strategy fails when the referent is clearly singular but we don't want to indicate the gender. In casual speech, most of us resort to the singular *they,* as in: *My friend left their bike at my house, but they're coming to get it later.* Your English teacher won't approve, but the rest of us know what you mean.

In short, the campaign advocating for the use of gender-neutral language is premised on the belief that language influences thought. In this case, however, the implication is that even the grammar of our language—and not just the words we use—can affect the way we think about the world.

Is That Apple Male or Female?

English has what's called a **semantic gender system**, by which we mean *a pattern of classifying nouns and pronouns according to their natural type* (Irmen & Roβberg, 2006). In a semantic gender system, males are classified as masculine, females as feminine, and nongendered things as neuter. However, not all languages work that way. Some languages, such as Chinese, or Hungarian, or Turkish, make no gender distinctions, simply using a single pronoun for *he, she,* or *it.* Other languages assign gender to nouns in a rather arbitrary fashion.

Many of the languages Europe, and well as a number of languages elsewhere in the world, employ what is called a **formal gender system** (Kousta et al., 2008). In these languages, we find *a pattern of classifying nouns and pronouns that arbitrarily assigns a gender to inanimate objects*. The Romance languages, such as French, Spanish, and Italian, distinguish all nouns as either masculine or feminine, including inanimate objects like books and tables and even abstract concepts like freedom and courage. German and Russian make a three-way distinction of masculine-feminine-neuter. Nouns referring to humans usually are marked with their natural gender, but not always, as in the case of the German word for "girl," *Mädchen*, which is neuter. Nor are inanimate objects or abstract concepts usually neuter. In German, the word for "table," *Tisch*, is masculine and the word for "freedom," *Freiheit*, is feminine.

Grammatical gender provides another testing ground for the linguistic relativity hypothesis. Specifically, researchers ask whether speakers of a language with a formal gender system actually think of objects in the real world as having the masculine or feminine gender assigned to the nouns that refer to them. It's important to note that the gender assignment of inanimate objects is arbitrary and varies from language to language (Cubelli et al., 2011). If grammatical gender influences thought, then a German speaker should treat an apple as a male, and a Spanish speaker should treat it as a female, because that's the way gender is assigned in those two languages.

In a series of studies, German-English and Spanish-English bilinguals were tested to see whether the formal gender systems of their first language influenced the way they thought about inanimate objects when speaking in their second language (Boroditsky, Schmidt, & Phillips, 2003). One study used a **paired-associate learning task.** This is *an experimental procedure in which participants are asked to memorize unrelated word pairs*. The study was conducted in English, and the word pairs associated inanimate objects like *apple* with personal names like *Patrick* or *Patricia*. The participants were better at remembering pairs in which the gender of the personal name matched the grammatical gender of the object name in their first language. In other words, German speakers were better at remembering *apple-Patrick*, and Spanish speakers were better at remembering *apple-Patricia*. This is still a rather superficial test of linguistic relativity.

Stronger evidence for linguistic relativity comes from a more subtle probe of German and Spanish speakers' cognitions about the gender of objects (Boroditsky et al., 2003). Working in English, these participants were shown pictures of objects and asked to write down the first three adjectives that came to mind. Afterward, an independent group of native English speakers rated each adjective on a scale ranging from masculine to feminine. It was found that participants tended use more masculine or more feminine adjectives depending on the gender of the object in their first language. For example, the word for *bridge* is feminine in German but masculine in Spanish. German speakers described bridges as *beautiful, elegant,* and *peaceful*, while Spanish speakers described them as *big, strong,* and *towering* (Boroditsky et al., 2003).

It's a Piece of Cake

Instead of sorting out nouns by gender, many languages sort out nouns by means of classifiers. A **classifier** is *a grammatical word used in conjunction with a noun to indicate its shape or function*. As a grammatical means of categorizing nouns, classifiers are somewhat like formal gender in that the assignment of a noun to a particular class is partially based on real-world attributes and partially arbitrary. However, unlike formal gender, which rarely exceeds two or three types, a language might use dozens of classifiers.

Classifiers are frequently found in languages that don't distinguish singular and plural, in which case they're used to join a number or quantity word with a noun. They're also used to a more limited extent in other languages as well, including English. Consider words for concrete nouns like *bread* and *cabbage*. Due to the vagaries of English grammar, we don't usually say *two breads* or *three cabbages*. Instead, we say *two loaves of bread* and *three heads of cabbage*. The words *loaf* and *head* are classifiers for *bread* and *cabbage* respectively. Just imagine being a speaker of Chinese, or a signer of American Sign Language, and having to learn which classifier to use with each noun in the language.

Typically, classifiers focus on the shape, size, or function of the noun. In Mandarin, *tiáo* is the classifier for long, slender objects like rivers, snakes, and legs, but it's also used metaphorically as the classifier for dogs, underwear, and news (as in, a *piece* of news). Mandarin speakers perceive same-classifier noun pairs as more similar than different-classifier noun pairs, suggesting that the language has some influence on the way the speakers think about the world (Saalbach & Imai, 2007). However, even a control group of German speakers rated the same-classifier pairs as more similar, although to a lesser degree than did the Mandarin speakers. This suggests that classifiers are based on some sort of innate perceptual similarity.

As a more subtle test of linguistic relativity, Mandarin and non-Mandarin speakers were asked to rate their preferences for objects in mock advertisements (Zhang & Schmitt, 1998). In Mandarin, the classifier *bǎ* is used for objects that are typically grasped by the hand, such as umbrellas. The researchers found that Mandarin speakers rated an advertisement for an umbrella higher when it was pictured with a hand grasping it than when no hand was shown. On the other hand, they had no preference for a rope when it was held in the hand. Although ropes are certainly graspable, they take the long, slender classifier *tiáo* instead of the graspable classifier *bǎ*. Non-Mandarin speakers were not influenced by the presence or absence of a hand with either object.

In an eye-tracking procedure, Mandarin speakers tended to divert their attention more to other objects in a visual array that shared a classifier with the target object (Huettig et al., 2010). However, this effect was only found when the participants were engaged in a language-oriented task and not when they were engaged in a task that didn't require overt language use. As a result, the researchers suggested that the question of linguistic relativity—how language influences thought—is too simplistic. Instead, they suggest the emphasis of research should be on how linguistic structure specifically influences thought during language-processing tasks.

Figure 12.4   Influence of Noun Classifiers on Product Preferences

In Chinese, umbrellas take the graspable classifier *bǎ*, whereas ropes take the long, slender classifier *tiáo*. Chinese speakers preferred the mock advertisement of an umbrella with a hand, but showed no preference for one of a rope with a hand. In Japanese, both umbrellas and ropes take the long, slender classifier *hon*, and Japanese speakers showed no preference for the presence of a hand in any of the mock advertisements.

(a) Chinese responses

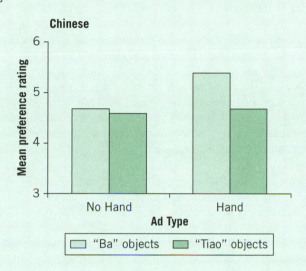

(b) Japanese responses

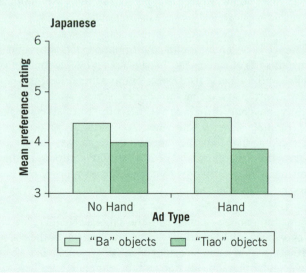

Source: Zhang and Schmitt (1998).

Too Much Stuff, Too Many Things

Some things tend to keep their shape over time. Not only do objects like cups, tables, and chairs have a permanent shape to them, we recognize these objects by their shape. Smash a chair to pieces, and it's no longer a chair. Other things tend to go all over the place, but we still recognize them as the same stuff. Liquids, like water, milk, or shampoo, are examples of things that don't hold their shape. Even some solid materials, like flour, sugar, or sand, tend to spread out as well. This perceptual distinction between rigidly shaped objects and shape-shifting substances often gets encoded in the grammars of languages.

English is an example of a language that makes a difference between mass nouns and count nouns. A **mass noun** is *a noun that represents a substance without a consistent shape and therefore cannot be counted*, while a **count noun** is *a noun that represents an object with a consistent shape and therefore can be counted*. Count nouns typically have separate singular and plural forms and can be used with numbers—*one cup, two cups*. Since mass nouns can't be counted, they don't have separate singular and plural forms. Most have only a singular form, no matter how much of the stuff there is—*water is everywhere*. Some mass nouns, though, are treated as plural—*people are everywhere*.

The shape-substance distinction may be an example of a universal perceptual process influencing the structure of language, since even prelinguistic infants demonstrate an understanding of the difference between shaped objects and shapeless substances (Domahs et al., 2012). However, languages differ somewhat in what they treat as countable or not. In English you cut your hair (uncountable), but in French or Italian you cut your hairs (countable). Even within a language, the same concept may have both mass and count forms. Compare the uncountable *My luggage is in the car* with the countable *My suitcases are in the car*. We also extend the mass-count distinction to the realm of abstract nouns, where we apply it in seemingly random fashion. For example, *sleep* is a mass noun while *dream* is a count noun.

The difference between mass and count nouns extends beyond semantics to syntax, triggering all sorts of agreement. For instance, this morning at breakfast I had too *much* coffee and too *many* pancakes. And in general I eat too *little* fruit and too *few* vegetables. Word pairs like *much/many* and *little/few* are known as quantifiers, and we quantify mass and count nouns differently. You may have also noticed in the last example the inconsistency with which we distinguish mass and count nouns, since *fruit* is treated as shapeless substance while *vegetables* is treated as shaped objects. As we learned in Chapter 6, the P600 is an ERP component signaling a syntax error, and a mismatch of quantifier with a mass or count noun will elicit a P600 (Chiarelli et al., 2011).

Mass nouns can only be counted with the aid of a classifier. *Two breads* is awkward, but *two loaves of bread* or *two pieces of bread* is not. In a sense, the classifier gives shape to the substance so that it can be counted. Some languages, like Chinese and Japanese, make no singular-plural distinction and therefore use classifiers to count all nouns.

At first, linguists thought that meant that speakers of those languages perceived all entities as substances and not objects. However, electrophysiological evidence indicates that people perceive the substance-shape distinction even though it's not encoded in their language (Domahs et al., 2012). Furthermore, learning a language that enforces the encoding of singular and plural forms on count nouns has an early influence on cognitive development, in that English- and Russian-learning toddlers learn the exact meaning of the numbers *one, two,* and *three* before Chinese or Japanese youngsters do.

Languages differ in the degree to which they discriminate entities on the basis of shape or substance, and this can influence the way their speakers view the world (Kersten et al., 2010). Nouns in the Mexican language Yucatec are more likely refer to the substance their referent is made of rather than to the shape it takes, whereas English emphasizes shape over substance. And in a categorization task, speakers of the Mexican language Yucatec tended to sort objects by substance, but speakers of English tended to sort by shape. This finding provides some support for linguistic relativity.

Jumping Jack Rabbit, or Down the Bunny Hole

Imagine a rabbit in a garden, munching on some leafy greens. It sees the gardener approaching, and so it hops away some distance and then goes into a hole in the ground. If you wanted to describe this complex event in a single sentence, you would have to focus attention on some elements of the event and disregard others. You could focus on the manner of the action, *hop*, or on the path of the action, *go into the hole*. Likewise, you could focus on the ongoing nature of the action, *was hopping*, or the end result, *hopped*. The language we speak tends to direct our attention towards certain elements of an event and away from others.

Most English speakers would describe the scenario above with a sentence like: *The rabbit hopped into the hole*. That is, they tend to focus on the manner of the action. But this isn't the case with Spanish speakers, who attend more to the path of the action: *The rabbit went into the hole*, or in Spanish: *El conejo entró al hueco*. In fact, the Spanish equivalent of *The rabbit hopped into the hole* is considered ungrammatical (Kersten et al., 2010). Other languages like English that focus on the manner of an action include German, Russian, and Chinese, while other languages like Spanish that focus on the path of an action include Hebrew, Turkish, and Japanese.

English and Spanish monolinguals as well as English-Spanish bilinguals were asked to categorize novel animated objects they watched moving on a computer screen (Kersten et al., 2010). In support of the linguistic relativity hypothesis, the English speakers sorted the objects by the manner in which they moved, while the Spanish speakers sorted them by the path along which they moved. The bilinguals performed like English monolinguals when the experiment was conducted in English and like Spanish monolinguals when it was conducted in Spanish. Apparently, when bilinguals switch languages, they also change the way they think.

In Chapter 10, we saw that English speakers use verb aspect to describe the temporal flow of the event, as for example in the sentence: *The bat phone rang while Batman was shaving.* The verb form *rang* indicates an event of relatively short duration, while *was shaving* marks an ongoing event. Although German is closely related to English, it lacks a verb aspect system, presenting all verbs as simple events: *The bat phone rang while Batman shaved.*

In an eye-tracking study, English and German speakers were shown pictures of events, such as a drawing of two people walking on a road that leads to a house in the distance (Bylund, Athanasopouolos, & Oostendorp, 2013). The English speakers were more likely to describe the ongoing event, as in *They were walking*, while the German speakers were more likely to describe the end result, as in *They walked to the house*. Furthermore, the English speakers fixated more on the walking couple and less on the house at the end of the road, but looking times were opposite for the German speakers. This suggests that the presence of a verb aspect system draws English speakers' attention to the action itself while the lack of one in German leads its speakers to look more toward the end result of the action.

The results outlined in this section suggest a more nuanced version of linguistic relativity known as **thinking-for-speaking**. This is *the claim that speakers organize their thought processes to meet the requirements of their language as they speak* (Bowers & Pleydell-Pearce, 2011). English speakers need to pay attention to whether each noun is singular or plural, but Chinese speakers don't. Spanish speakers need to consider whether their friend is male (*amigo*) or female (*amiga*), but English speakers don't. Chinese speakers focus on the manner in which an action is performed, while Japanese speakers focus on path that the action follows, because the structures of their respective languages requires them to. In other words, while the language we speak doesn't constrain the way we think, it does lead us into habitual ways of viewing the world around us.

In Sum

The English pronouns *he, she,* and *it* indicate the natural gender of their referents, but many European languages classify even inanimate objects as masculine or feminine. Experimental evidence suggests that speakers of languages with formal gender systems tend to think of objects as male or female, and this way of thinking can even carry over to a second language like English, which has no formal gender. Instead of categorizing nouns by gender, many languages pair each noun with a classifier that indicates its shape or function. These classifiers tend to suggest subtle perceptual similarities among nouns that share a common classifier. Many languages encode a difference between nouns that can be counted and those that cannot, reflecting a natural tendency of the human perceptual system to distinguish consistently shaped objects from shapeless substances. Languages differ in which elements of events they encode in their verbs. A language may emphasize either the manner of the action or its path, and it may emphasize the temporal flow of the event or else the resulting state of the event. The thinking-for-speaking hypothesis is a nuanced version of linguistic relativity proposing that speakers organize their thinking during speech to meet the requirements of their language.

Review Questions

1. What is the difference between a semantic and a formal gender system? Discuss the evidence suggesting that formal gender systems influence the way speakers think about the gender of inanimate objects.

2. How do classifier systems differ from gender systems? What is the relationship between the use of classifiers and the singular-plural distinction?

3. Distinguish between mass nouns and count nouns. What are some ways in which this distinction is encoded in the grammar of English?

4. Explain the thinking-for-speaking hypothesis. What is the evidence for it? How does it differ from the linguistic relativity hypothesis?

Thought Questions

1. Sometimes category names are mass nouns while the member names are count nouns. For example, *furniture* is a mass noun, but *sofa*, *chair*, and *table* are all count nouns. Can you think of other examples like this?

2. In English, mass nouns can be made countable by use of a classifier. We've already met two examples, *a loaf of bread* and *a head of cabbage*. Can you think of some other classifier-mass noun pairs? In what sense does the classifier constrain the shape or function of the noun so that it can be counted?

Google It! Mark Twain and "The Awful German Language"

The nineteenth-century American humorist Mark Twain spent some time in Germany and even learned to speak German. In his classic essay "The Awful German Language," Twain recounts his struggles with the language. The highlight of the essay is "The Tale of the Fishwife and Its Sad Fate," which Twain writes in a mock German style, with all of the pronouns reflecting the gender of their German referents. Although the tale is meant to be satirical, it does give you a taste of how a formal gender system works.

SECTION 12.3: FIGURATIVE LANGUAGE

- Figurative language refers to any expression with a literal meaning that is different from its intended meaning; metaphors and metonyms are common figures of speech that draw connections between concepts that are not obviously similar.

- Indirect access models propose that the literal meaning of a figurative expression is always accessed first before a nonliteral interpretation is considered, whereas direct access models propose that a nonliteral meaning can be accessed without considering the literal meaning if context strongly biases a figurative interpretation.

- Idioms are set expressions whose meanings cannot be understood based on the meanings of the individual words they are composed of. Early models of idiom processing treated them as "words with spaces"; the more recent configuration hypothesis proposes that idioms can be comprehended either literally or figuratively depending on context.

- Verbal irony expresses an intended meaning that is the opposite of its literal meaning; unlike deception, the speaker fully expects the listener to understand the intended meaning. Sarcasm is a special case of verbal irony that is intended to verbally injure another person.

- The graded salience hypothesis proposes that situational factors can bias the listener toward either a literal or ironic interpretation of an utterance; since recognizing irony involves making inferences about others' intentions, children are not especially good at detecting irony until adolescence.

- Whereas literal language processing involves activity in the left hemisphere, figurative language processing draws on activity from both hemispheres; the brain's default mode network, which becomes active when we turn our attention inward, also plays a role in verbal irony processing.

In Chapter 7, we visited a family at dinner time, when Dad asked if someone could pass him the salt. His teenage daughter replied, "Yes, I could," but then her younger brother handed his father the salt. According to speech act theory, we evaluate utterances not by their literal meaning but rather by what we think the speaker intended. Yet speech act theory is only the tip of the iceberg—metaphorically speaking—when it comes to using language in nonliteral ways.

It's Just a Figure of Speech

Figurative language is *any expression whose intended meaning is different from its literal meaning* (Palmer & Brooks, 2004). Indirect requests such as "Could you pass the salt?" constitute one common type of figurative language, and metaphorical expressions like "tip of the iceberg" constitute another. Additionally, we need to include idioms, irony, and sarcasm in the list (Laval & Bert-Erboul, 2005).

Figurative language is so pervasive in our daily lives that it mostly goes unnoticed, both by the listener and by the speaker (Bosco, Vallana, & Bucciarelli, 2012). We say things we don't mean and expect others to read our minds, which they do with a high degree of accuracy. As listeners, we pay scant attention to the literal meanings of utterances and instead rely on our theory of mind abilities (Chapter 7) to infer the speaker's intentions.

A common type of figurative language is **metaphor**. This is *figurative language that draws a comparison between two concepts that are not generally considered to be similar* (Palmer & Brooks, 2004). When the poet Robert Burns wrote, "My love is like a red, red rose," he wasn't suggesting that his sweetheart had red petals, a slender green stem and prickly thorns. Rather, he's asking us to infer his intended comparison between the beauty of a rose and the beauty of the woman he loves. (To the English majors: Burns's verse is strictly speaking a simile, which is a form of metaphor.)

Another kind of nonliteral language that's commonly used is **metonymy**. This is *figurative language that refers to an entity in terms of one of its salient characteristics* (Lowder & Gordon, 2013). In the following sentences, consider what the italicized portion is referring to:

1. *The ham sandwich* is sitting at table 5.

2. Sally petitioned *the college* for a fee waiver.

3. Sebastian read *Dickens* at Oxford.

If you need the answers, here they are: (1) the customer that ordered the ham sandwich; (2) the administration that runs the college; and (3) the books that Charles Dickens wrote.

Notice how metonymy allows for conciseness of expression. However, ease of understanding a metonym depends on how familiar it is. In an eye-tracking experiment, participants read the sentence *Many Americans protested during Vietnam* with ease, but they had considerably more difficulty with the parallel sentence *Many Americans protested during Finland* (Frisson & Pickering, 1999). This result suggests that familiar metonyms are understood automatically.

Many different theories of figurative language processing have been proposed, but these can generally be sorted into two types (Lowder & Gordon, 2013). One type of theory is the **indirect access model**, which is *the proposal that the literal meaning of a figurative expression is always accessed first before a nonliteral interpretation is considered.* Generally, these models propose that a figurative meaning is only computed if the literal meaning doesn't in any way match the surrounding context. The other type of theory is the **direct access model**, which is *the proposal that the nonliteral meaning of a figurative expression can be accessed without considering the literal meaning first.* Direct access models consider the role of context, common ground, and familiarity in the processing of figurative expressions. Thus, a metonym like *during Vietnam* can be read quickly because it's familiar and also because the context (*Many Americans protested . . .*) is consistent with the implied meaning of *during the Vietnam War.*

Who Spilled the Beans?

Some figurative expressions are so commonly used in the language that their literal meaning is highly unlikely in any situation. An example of this is the **idiom**, which is *a formulaic phrase whose meaning cannot be derived from the meanings of the words that make it up* (Conner et al., 2011). The meanings of some idioms, such as *spill the beans* or *let the cat out of the bag*, are fairly transparent in that the metaphorical relationship between the literal and figurative interpretations is straightforward, as when *revealing a secret* is compared with *releasing something from a container* (Nippold & Duthie, 2003). On the other hand, opaque idioms like *kick the bucket* and *paint the town red* may contain a historical reference that's usually unknown to the speakers of the language. All idioms are language specific and can't be directly translated into other languages (Palmer & Brooks, 2004).

Early research into the processing of idioms was based on the **words-with-spaces model**, which is *the view that idioms are set phrases that behave syntactically like single words* (Holsinger, 2013). However, there are problems with this approach. Although idioms, like words, have meaning, they also have syntactic structure. In particular, the verb that forms the heart of many English idioms must be modified according to the rules of morphosyntax (see Chapter 11). Furthermore, some idioms can undergo transformations such as the passive voice: *The beans would have been spilled if Jeremy hadn't told Margaret to hold her tongue in the nick of time.*

More recent models of idiom comprehension don't just treat idioms as megawords but rather take their internal structure into account (Holsinger, 2013). For instance, the **configuration hypothesis** makes *the proposal that the language processing system goes first with a literal interpretation of an idiom unless context biases it toward the idiomatic interpretation.* This is different from the indirect access model in that both literal and figurative meanings are considered. Thus, context calls for a literal interpretation in the sentence *Gabe kicked the bucket down the stairs*, but it calls for an idiomatic interpretation in the sentence *Grandpa was ninety-two when he kicked the bucket.*

Many expressions can have both literal and idiomatic meanings, depending on context (Sidtis, 2004). For example, the phrase *break the ice* needs to be interpreted literally in the sentence *We need an icepick to break the ice*, but it has to be interpreted figuratively in the sentence *We need a party game to break the ice*. Literal and figurative versions of an expression have different prosodic contours, and native speakers listening to a recording of a phrase like *break the ice* can tell which meaning was intended even without any context.

Children begin learning the meanings of idioms in early childhood, but the process continues well into adulthood (Nippold & Duthie, 2003). Developmental evidence suggests that children attempt to understand idioms by analyzing the words that compose them. Thus, a transparent idiom like *paddle your own canoe* can be readily learned as a metaphor for self-reliance. However, children may need to experience an opaque idiom like *bring down the house* in a number of different contexts before grasping its full meaning. As people learn idioms, they tend to associate mental models with them, and the richness of the imagery they report is a good indicator of how well they understand the meaning and usage of that idiom.

Isn't That Ironic?

The words we speak don't match the thoughts in our heads. Sometimes we intentionally deceive others for socially acceptable reasons, such as telling someone you really love a gift when in fact you don't like it. Other times we deceive others for our own selfish reasons, such as when we deny wrongdoing or try to take advantage of someone. In these cases, we hope our listener will take our words at face value and not see through to our hidden intentions. And then there are the times when we say something that's the opposite of what we intended, fully expecting our listener to see through our words and understand our true meaning.

When we produce *an utterance that conveys an understood meaning that is the opposite of its literal meaning*, we're using **verbal irony** (Scharrer & Christmann, 2011). Oftentimes verbal irony has a negative connotation, especially when it's used to express frustration or disappointment in yourself or others (Pexman, 2008). For instance, you might mutter "Well that's just wonderful" when you get a bad grade on an assignment, or you might say "That was smooth!" when a friend trips for no obvious reason. In these cases, the positive literal meaning is contradicted by the negative context. However, we can also use verbal irony to convey a positive intended meaning with words that have a negative literal meaning. This would be the case if your friend told you she just got an A on an exam and you replied, "That's too bad." Discourse analyses reveal that verbal irony is fairly common in casual conversation between friends, occurring on about 8% of turns.

Sarcasm is the special case of *verbal irony that is intended to criticize or ridicule another person* (Scharrer & Christmann, 2011). In other words, not all irony is sarcastic, but all sarcasm is ironic. Observational studies show that males make almost twice as many sarcastic remarks in ordinary discourse compared with females (Katz, Blasko, & Kazmerski, 2004). Listeners are also more likely to interpret a remark as sarcastic

Figure 12.5   Casual Conversation

Verbal irony and sarcasm are fairly common in the casual conversations of young people, occurring on about 8% of turns.

Source: ©iStockphoto.com/kali9.

if it is made by someone in an occupation such as comedian or factory worker that's stereotypically associated with sarcasm, compared with remarks from teachers and clergy, who aren't expected to use sarcasm.

Verbal irony fulfills a number of social functions (Recchia et al, 2010). As we learned in Chapter 7, people often communicate their intentions in indirect ways with the expectation that the listener will understand the underlying meaning. Polite requests like *Could you pass the salt?* and rhetorical questions like *How many times do I have to tell you to stop?* are examples of indirect speech acts. Verbal irony entails a kind of indirect speech act as well. Irony is often used to voice dissatisfaction, and depending on context it can either soften the complaint or emphasize the speaker's irritation (Angeleri & Airenti, 2014). Conversely, verbal irony can also be used to voice praise in a situation where the interlocutors may be uncomfortable expressing their true emotions too strongly.

Listeners are generally able to distinguish between ironic and non-ironic interpretations of utterances that are presented to them out of context (Scharrer & Christmann, 2011). This is true not only for English but also for a number of other languages that have been studied as well. It's generally believed that speakers use prosodic cues to signal an ironic interpretation. The data so far are inconsistent, with some but not all acoustic analyses showing ironic statements to have different prosodic contours from their literal counterparts. Thus, it's still not clear which acoustic cues listeners use to recognize irony.

Other factors besides acoustic cues may help listeners recognize that an utterance was intended to be ironic (Scharrer & Christmann, 2011). As we learned in Chapter 7, the common ground, or shared knowledge, between speaker and listener plays an important role in discourse processing. Common ground can provide the listener with cues that the utterance should be taken either literally or ironically. Verbal cues, such as exaggerated adjectives and adverbs, in addition to nonverbal cues, such as facial expressions, can also bias the listener toward one interpretation or the other. Perhaps most important of all, theory of mind plays an important role in irony comprehension (Gaudreau et al., 2013). Recall from Chapter 7 that the ability to make inferences about the mental states is essential for successful communication, and identifying a mismatch between speakers' intentions and their literal utterances is what irony comprehension is all about.

The direct access and indirect access models of figurative language comprehension apply to irony comprehension as well (Akimoto, et al., 2012). The direct access model predicts that irony detection will occur rapidly when the context is heavily biased toward that interpretation, and some experimental evidence supports this model. On the other hand, the indirect access model predicts that we always make a literal interpretation first and then reject it in favor of an ironic interpretation if the context warrants it. This means that it should take longer to process ironic utterances compared with their literal counterparts, and there's some experimental evidence supporting this model as well.

Situational factors may influence whether the direct access or indirect access model is more appropriate. The **graded salience hypothesis** is *the proposal that the literal meaning of an utterance is processed first but that an ironic meaning may be considered in parallel when the context biases such an interpretation* (Regel, Gunter, & Friederici, 2010). When you're hanging out with friends who frequently make ironic or sarcastic remarks, you're probably going to pick up on the irony a lot faster than if, for example, your professor makes an unexpected ironic remark in the middle of a serious lecture.

The ability to comprehend irony depends on the ability to make inferences about other people's mental states, and so children's irony comprehension develops along with their theory of mind abilities (Angeleri & Airenti, 2013). Before the age of five or six, children have great difficulty recognizing the ironic meanings of utterances, and even early teenagers can sometimes have difficulty distinguishing between irony and deception. However, by around the ages of eight to ten, children understand the humor and teasing functions of irony and can even use irony for these purposes in their own speech (Recchia et al, 2010).

Left Brain, Right Brain

Evidence from brain-imaging studies suggests that irony and other types of figurative language are processed differently from literal language (Rapp et al., 2013). Traditionally, it was believed that literal language was processed in the left hemisphere while figurative language was processed in the right hemisphere. However, we now know that the situation is more complex. While literal language is mainly processed in the left hemisphere, both hemispheres are actively involved in the processing of figurative language, including irony.

The brain's **default mode network** plays a role in figurative language processing. This is *the system of brain regions that are active when our attention turns inward* (Rapp et al., 2013). The default mode network is engaged when we daydream or retrieve memories. However, it's also active during theory of mind tasks, including the making of inferences about other people's intentions, which is essential to figurative language interpretation. As we learned in Chapter 3, the mirror neuron system enables us to take the perspective of another person, and so it's also important in making inferences about other people's intentions.

ERP research on irony processing has yielded mixed results. Some studies have found an N400 response to ironic statements (Katz et al., 2004). Recall from Chapter 6 that an N400 component signals the processing of a semantic inconsistency, presumably in this case a mismatch between the literal and inferred meanings. However, other researchers have found a P600 response instead of an N400 (Regel et al., 2010). Usually a P600 signals the detection of a syntactic inconsistency, but it can also reflect the integration of contextual information with the literal meaning of the utterance. Clearly, much more research is needed in the area of figurative language processing.

In Sum

Figurative language involves a mismatch between literal and intended meaning, and the speaker expects the listener to be able to recover the hidden meaning. Metaphors and metonyms are common figures of speech that make implicit comparisons between concepts that aren't obviously similar. Research on figurative language processing has so far led to conflicting results. Some data support indirect models, which propose that the literal meaning is always considered first before a nonliteral interpretation is attempted. Other data support direct access models, which propose that figurative meanings are accessed without first considering literal meanings. Idioms are set expressions whose meanings are not based on the literal meanings of the words that compose them. Traditional models of idiom processing treat them as "words with spaces," but the configuration hypothesis deals with evidence suggesting that idioms can be comprehended either literally or figuratively in accordance with contextual cues. In the case of verbal irony, the expressed meaning is the opposite of the intended meaning but without the intention to deceive. Sarcasm is a type of verbal irony that includes the intention to criticize or ridicule another person. The processing of literal language mainly involves only the left hemisphere, but the processing of figurative language relies on considerable activity in both hemispheres.

Review Questions

1. What is the difference between a metaphor and a metonym? Illustrate with examples.

2. Distinguish between indirect access and direct access models of figurative language processing. In what sense should proposals such

as the configuration hypothesis and the graded salience hypothesis be considered hybrid models?

3. What is the difference between verbal irony and deception? What about verbal irony and sarcasm?

4. The traditional view is that the left hemisphere processes literal language and the right hemisphere processes figurative language. What is the current thinking on this issue?

Thought Questions

1. It seems that direct communication would be more effective, so why do we even use figurative language? Consider various cognitive or social purposes that might be served by figurative language.

2. Sarcasm can be thought of as an indirect form of criticism. Why might sarcasm be even more hurtful than direct criticism?

Google It! The Brain's Default Mode Network

Figurative language processing activates the brain's **default mode network**. You can find videos on YouTube that will tell more about what the brain does when our thoughts turn inward.

SECTION 12.4: TABOO LANGUAGE

- Taboo words are considered inappropriate in many situations because they are so emotionally arousing; despite the widespread belief that swear words are harmful, all people know them and many use them in their daily lives.

- Children learn swear words early, not only repeating adult curse words without knowing what they mean but also using childish insults that they later outgrow; by adolescence they have mastered the adult taboo vocabulary.

- Learning the taboo words of a language is part of the child's enculturation process; second-language learners also have to master these terms, although they may not have the emotional impact of taboo words in their first language.

- A number of laboratory tasks demonstrate the emotional costs of processing taboo words; these typically measure reaction time, response accuracy, or skin conductance when participants see, hear, or are asked to produce taboo words.

- Compulsive swearing is a condition that occurs with a number of brain disorders; patients who experience severe language loss, as in the case of Alzheimer's disease or Broca's aphasia, often find their ability to swear unimpaired.

- Euphemisms provide us with ways of discussing unpleasant topics without experiencing uncomfortable levels of emotional arousal.

In the United States, we value our freedom of speech. Nevertheless, the Federal Communication Commission (FCC) has deemed seven words of the English language as so offensive that they're not allowed on the public airwaves, and violators face heavy fines (Kaye & Sapolsky, 2009). Yet we all know these "seven dirty words," and we've all used them at one time or another, some of us quite regularly. There's plenty of evidence that some words have strong emotional content, and they can profoundly affect us, both physiologically and psychologically (Söderholm et al., 2013). In this section, we'll explore the emotional impact that some words have on us as well as ways we try to get around the negative psychological effects that these taboo words can have.

Emotional Words

Emotions are physiological and psychological reactions to stimuli that motivate us to respond in particular ways. Many psychologists nowadays ascribe to the **dimensional model of emotion**, which is *the proposal that emotional content can be described in terms of arousal (high-low) and valence (positive-negative)* (Söderholm et al., 2013). **Arousal** is *the physiological component of emotion that represents the degree to which the body is ready for action.* Emotions like anger and fear are high in arousal, while sadness is low in arousal. **Valence** is *the psychological component that evaluates the emotional experience.* Receiving an A on a test generally leads to an emotional experience with positive valence, when getting an F usually leads to one with a negative valence.

Table 12.2 Dimensional Model of Emotion		
	Positive Valence	**Negative Valence**
High arousal	You got an A on the exam. It was tough, but you'd studied hard, and you weren't expecting an A. *You feel good (positive valence), and you're very excited (high arousal).*	You got an F on the exam. It was tough, and you'd studied hard, so you were expecting to pass. *You feel bad (negative valence), and you're very upset (high arousal).*
Low arousal	You got an A on the exam. It was easy, and you didn't even have to study for it. You were expecting an A. *You feel good (positive valence), but you're not excited (low arousal).*	You got an F on the exam. It wasn't tough, but you didn't study, so you were expecting to fail. *You feel bad (negative valence), but you're not very upset (low arousal).*

Words have both semantic and emotional content. *The literal meaning of a word* is its **denotation**, while *the emotion evoked by a word* is its **connotation**. Two words can have similar denotations but different connotations. For example, you can describe someone as *determined* or *stubborn*, depending on whether you view this behavior as positive or negative. Words likewise have the power to arouse us. Any term that conveys a threat, such as *war* or *attack*, is likely to elicit arousal.

There are some *words that are so emotionally arousing that they are considered inappropriate to use in many social situations*. These are known as **taboo words** (Jay, Caldwell-Harris, & King, 2008). The categories represented by taboo words vary somewhat from culture to culture, but in English-speaking countries they tend to make references to certain body parts and products, sexual acts, ethnic or gender slurs, and certain religious concepts (Jay et al., 2008). Many taboo words are curse words or swear words, but we can also include words like *death* that refer to concepts we prefer not to think about.

Societies restrict the use of taboo words because of the general belief that they will do harm if spoken or heard (Jay, 2009). This is the rationale behind the FCC's prohibition on the use of the "seven dirty words." Taboo words certainly do have emotional impact, and insults can be psychologically harmful. Still, their psychological effect can range from mildly to severely offensive, depending not only on the specific word but also on the circumstances in which it's uttered.

Despite the social injunctions against swear words, they're used frequently in conversations by people of all ages and all social groups. In fact, it's the emotional connotations of taboo words that make them so useful in conversation (Jay, 2009). No measured prose can convey the intensity of emotion that's packed into any of the "dirty words." The main reason why people swear is to express emotions of high arousal and negative valence, such as frustration or anger, and they can also be used in conjunction with other words of positive valence to heighten the level of arousal they elicit in the listener (Jay & Janschewitz, 2008).

Soap in Your Mouth

Despite the best efforts of the FCC and many parents to protect children from offensive language, kids nevertheless manage to learn taboo words, and they do so at an early age (Jay & Jay, 2013). Toddlers as young as one or two years-old will repeat offensive words without understanding what they mean, and over the next few years they develop a good understanding of what a taboo word is and the emotion it evokes. Although preschoolers don't use the offensive language of adults, they have their own words with high emotional impact. Three-year-olds hurl insults like *poopyface* at each other with malicious intent, and taunts like *You're such a baby!* are fighting words to a grade-schooler.

Children continue to swear despite their parents' best efforts to eradicate the habit, and their offensive vocabulary becomes more adult-like as they enter adolescence (Jay &

Janschewitz, 2008). Most likely, children learn the emotional connotations of taboo words from the aversive reactions of parents and elders. As a six-year-old, you may have repeated a word you heard your father utter when he was angry. You may not have even known what the word meant, although you did have a sense of its emotional force. However, getting your mouth washed out with soap didn't teach you not to say that word anymore. Rather, it taught you its full emotional impact.

Learning about taboo words is part of the socialization process of childhood (Jay, 2009). Native speakers of a language know all the taboo words and what they mean, even if they make their best efforts never to use them. Indeed, an important part of the enculturation process is learning under which situations and with which persons the use of swear words is appropriate. Adult second-language learners become acquainted with the taboo words of their new language, and they may even learn when and with whom to use them. However, taboo words generally elicit less emotional arousal in a person's nondominant language (Simcox et al., 2011).

Colorful Language

If I showed you red, green, yellow, and blue color swatches, you could name the colors with ease. Likewise, if I showed you a series of color terms, such *red, green, yellow, blue,* you could read these words quickly. Even if the words were in colored ink, such that *red* was in yellow ink and *green* was in blue ink, the task should still be easy. But what if I asked you to name the ink color instead of the word? That is, you see the word *red* written in yellow ink, and the proper response is "yellow," not "red." You can probably imagine that this task is considerably harder, because reading words is a highly practiced task, whereas naming ink colors is not.

The situation in which reaction time in a color-naming task is slowed due to cognitive interference is known as the **Stroop effect**, named after John Ridley Stroop, who first reported the effect (Stroop, 1935). We also get a Stroop effect when we use other words besides color terms, such as *leaf* or *chair*. However, when we use emotionally arousing words like *war* or *fear*, participants take even more time to name the ink color (Bertels et al., 2011). This result is known as the emotional Stroop effect, although strictly speaking it only occurs for emotional words that are both negative in valence and high in arousal (Eilola & Havelka, 2010).

Psychologists believe that the arousal caused by these words interferes with the process of recalling and naming the ink color. It should come as no surprise then that we also find a Stroop effect for taboo words (Eilola, Havelka, & Sharma, 2007). Even though we don't have to say the "naughty words" out loud, their mere presence interferes with our ability to name the ink colors.

You sweat when you're aroused, and this moisture on your skin conducts electricity. Thus, emotional arousal can be assessed through the **skin conductance response**, which is *a change in how easily a mild electric current can pass between two electrodes* *placed on the skin* (Eilola & Havelka, 2010). The skin conductance response occurs one or two seconds after the presentation of an arousing or painful stimulus and typically lasts for several seconds before returning to baseline. Taboo words typically elicit a skin conductance response, whereas words with negative valence but low arousal, such as *sorrow*, do not (Jay et al., 2008).

We all make errors when we speak, sometimes with embarrassing consequences. The **SLIP task** is *a technique for inducing speech errors in the laboratory* (Severens et al., 2011). SLIP stands for "Spoonerisms of a Laboratory Induced Predisposition," and it's also a nod to the notion of a Freudian slip. A **spoonerism** is *a speech error that involves switching the initial sounds of word pairs*. For instance, saying *belly jean* for *jelly bean* is a spoonerism.

In the SLIP task, we first have participants read lists of word pairs, each beginning with the same two consonants, such as *cat-tongue, car-trunk,* and *cow-trough,* followed by a word pair that the participant reads aloud (Severens et al., 2011). In this procedure, the word pair *tool-cart* often comes out as *cool-tart,* resulting in a spoonerism. Other participants are led to produce a spoonerism of the word pair *tool-kits,* and when this happens, there's a spike in the skin conductance response, indicating arousal in response to the embarrassing slip of the tongue.

As any two-year-old knows, swear words grab your attention, and we can demonstrate this in the laboratory. The **RSVP task** (Rapid Serial Visual Presentation) is *an experimental technique in which the participant is asked to watch for target words within a rapidly presented list* (Colbeck & Bowers, 2012). Imagine you're asked to press a button every time you see either of two words, for example *house* or *tray*. The stream consists of words presented one at a time:

CAR . . . TREE . . . CHAIR . . . HOUSE. . . . FOOT . . . TRAY . . . RUG . . .

The second target (in this case *tray*) is frequently missed if it's presented within 500 milliseconds of the first target (in this case *house*). *The case where attending to one stimulus leads to reduced detection of a second stimulus* is known as the **attentional blink**. Taboo words also cause an attentional blink if they are included in the presentation stream just before a target word. Thus, the participant is likely to miss the first target word (*house*) if it's immediately preceded by a taboo word, in this case where *chair* is located.

Dirty Mind

People swear for many different reasons, but some really can't help themselves. **Coprolalia** is *a condition characterized by compulsive swearing due to a brain disorder* (Jay & Janschewitz, 2008). As we learned in Chapter 1, damage to Broca's area in the left frontal lobe can severely impact a patient's ability to produce speech. Broca's aphasics may experience severe language loss, but their ability to swear is often unimpaired. Damage to the frontal lobes can also lead to an increase in swearing (Jay, 2009). This isn't surprising, given that one of the roles of the frontal lobes is to inhibit socially inappropriate behavior. Likewise, Alzheimer's patients often begin swearing as they go into cognitive decline, even when they rarely swore before the disease.

Another condition that sometimes leads to coprolalia is **Tourette's syndrome** (Sidtis, 2004). This is *a disorder of the brain that involves motor and vocal tics and sometimes compulsive swearing.* Not all Tourette's patients swear, but for those who do, their vocal and motor tics generally include the most highly offensive terms and gestures in their language and culture (Jay, 2009). An interesting aspect of Tourette's syndrome is its cultural component. For example, American Tourette's patients typically shout the "seven dirty words," whereas Japanese Tourette's patients are more likely to curse their ancestors, as this is considered the most offensive verbal behavior in Japanese culture. Thus, the specific tics that Tourette's patients exhibit depend on where they grew up.

Two areas of the brain that seem to be involved in the processing of taboo words are the amygdala and the hippocampus (Jay & Janschewitz, 2008). As we learned in Chapter 2, these are subcortical structures deep inside the temporal lobes. The amygdala plays a role in regulating emotion and memory, while the hippocampus is involved in memory and learning. The activation of these areas is believed to account for why taboo words are so memorable.

Neuroimaging studies have shown that arousing and non-arousing words are processed along different neural pathways. When participants are asked to memorize word lists, arousing taboo words activate pathways between the hippocampus and the amygdala, but non-arousing words activate pathways between the hippocampus and the frontal lobe instead (Kensinger & Corkin, 2004). When participants were asked to divide their attention between memorizing the word lists and doing another unrelated task, their later recall of the non-arousing words was impaired. However, their recall of the taboo words wasn't affected. These findings are in line with results from other studies showing that arousing stimuli produce strong memories without the effortful processing of non-arousing stimuli.

Politely Speaking

We've seen that taboo words have emotional connotations that override their semantic denotations. However, we also sometimes need to talk about the concepts that taboo words refer to, although in a way that won't get us emotionally upset. In such a case, we often make use of a **euphemism**, which is *a word that has the same meaning as a taboo word but without the emotional connotation* (Jay & Janschewitz, 2008).

We use euphemisms not only to replace swear words but also other words referring to concepts that make us feel uncomfortable. For example, we say *pass away* instead of *die* or *get sick* instead of *vomit*. We also use medical terms to refer to body parts or products that would otherwise be taboo to mention. By using a neutral term, we can discuss a sensitive topic without using the taboo word and, hopefully, without arousing negative emotion.

Sometimes we need to refer to a particular taboo word without mentioning it. One strategy for doing this in English is to refer to it by its initial letter, as in: *Mom's washing Jacob's mouth out with soap because he used the f-word*. To test the hypothesis that euphemisms of this sort are less arousing than their taboo counterparts, researchers had participants read words out loud as they measured skin conductance response (Bowers & Pleydell-Pearce, 2011). Some of the items were swear words and others were swear word euphemisms, such as *f-word*. In two other conditions, the participants read neutral words, such as *drum*, or else the euphemism for that neutral word, such as *d-word*. The increase in skin conductance was significantly greater for the swear words than for the euphemisms or the neutral words. The researchers concluded that euphemisms are an example of "linguistic relativity par excellence" (p. 4) in that they allow us to think about concepts that would otherwise be too uncomfortable to consider.

Figure 12.6 Skin Conductance Response for Swear Words and Euphemisms

The skin conductance response is greater for swear words than for euphemisms or neutral terms, indicating greater arousal for the taboo items.

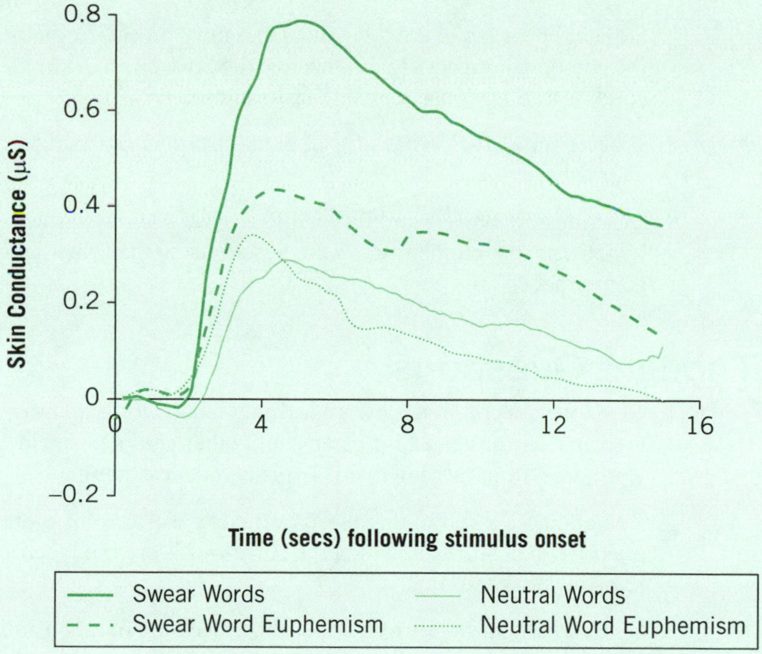

—— Swear Words	—— Neutral Words
– – · Swear Word Euphemism	········· Neutral Word Euphemism

Source: Bowers and Pleydell-Pearce (2011).

In Sum

Words have not only literal denotations but also emotional connotations. Taboo words are considered inappropriate to use in many social situations because of the negative emotions they arouse. People generally believe that swear words are not only offensive but also harmful, and they try to shield youngsters from hearing them. Nevertheless, learning the taboo words of a language and the restrictions on using them is a natural part of the enculturation process. All speakers of a language know which words are taboo, and many regularly use them. To a considerable degree, the emotional impact of taboo words depends on the situation and the participants in the discourse. Laboratory tasks demonstrate the emotional costs of processing taboo words by measuring reaction time, skin conductance, or response accuracy when participants see, hear, or speak taboo words. A number of brain disorders can lead to compulsive swearing, and it's not uncommon for a patient suffering from severe language loss to still be able to swear. We can avoid the emotional costs of taboo words by using euphemisms, which allow us to discuss topics that would otherwise be too uncomfortable to consider.

Review Questions

1. Describe the dimensional model of emotion, illustrating the concepts of valence and arousal with examples. Where in the model do taboo words fit?

2. Explain how each of the following laboratory procedures illustrate the emotional impact of taboo words: the Stroop task, skin conductance response, the SLIP task, and the RSVP task.

3. What is coprolalia? What sorts of brain disorders can lead to coprolalia?

4. Describe how Bowers and Pleydell-Pearce (2011) tested the hypothesis that euphemisms were less arousing than their taboo counterparts.

Thought Questions

1. Given that all children grow up learning taboo words anyway, is there really any need for parents and other adults to shield youngsters from hearing them? Explain your reasoning.

2. Do you find TV shows that bleep over curse words to be more or less offensive than shows in which the curse words are not bleeped out? Explain your reasoning.

3. Given what you've just read about the processing of taboo and nontaboo words, speculate on why patients with severe language loss may still be able to curse fluently.

Google It! The Seven Dirty Words

If you're not sure what the **seven dirty words** are, you can google them. Of course, you can also find the famous George Carlin routine about them. You can find videos on YouTube that demonstrate how **skin conductance response** is measured. Note that this measure is also known as **Galvanic skin response**. You can read more about the **Stroop task** and the **emotional Stroop task** online and see demonstrations of them. You can also find demonstrations of the **attentional blink**, which is the phenomenon of interest in the RSVP task. YouTube has a number of videos illustrating and explaining **Tourette's syndrome** as well.

CONCLUSION

In the fictional world of *Nineteen Eighty-Four*, a totalitarian government known as "Big Brother" attempts to control the thoughts of the people by limiting the language to politically correct expressions. It's unclear whether such a program of language control would ever succeed in preventing people from committing thought crimes.

Nevertheless, the society we live in does put pressure on us speak in politically correct or socially acceptable forms. If you want to be perceived as supportive of women's rights, you need to use gender-neutral language, no matter how unnatural or awkward it may feel to you. Indeed, if you're a strong advocate for gender equality, you probably find the "gender fair" forms to be more aesthetically pleasing than the older sexist terms.

Likewise, we all know that there are certain words we must not say in polite company, even though we may use them habitually with our friends. We may also be reluctant to use certain words because of the negative emotions they arouse. So instead we use euphemisms, which mean the same thing as the taboo words they replace but don't elicit the same level of emotional arousal.

Language, as a vehicle for thought, certainly influences the way we think. At the same time, modern society is rapidly changing, and our language needs to adapt by creating new words to represent concepts that didn't even exist a few years before. The impact that rapidly advancing technology has on the language we speak is the topic of the next chapter.

CROSS-CULTURAL PERSPECTIVE:
Gender-Fair Language

If you're a typical American college student, you grew up calling the person that brings your food in a restaurant a *server*, and the person that bring you a drink on an airplane a *flight attendant*. However, your parents—and certainly your grandparents—didn't use those terms when they were your age, and maybe they still don't today.

Before the 1980s, English-speaking Americans used gender-specific terms for many profession names. *Waiters* and *waitresses* worked in a restaurant, while *stewards* and *stewardesses* worked on an airplane. Other occupations had male-specific names, such as *mailman* and *fireman*, whether the person was a man or a woman.

Since the 1980s, however, there has been a movement in this country toward using gender-neutral language, such as *letter carrier* and *firefighter*, in an effort to promote gender equality. The rationale underlying the promotion of gender-neutral language is linguistic relativity, namely the idea that if our language doesn't discriminate between genders, our thoughts will be less likely to as well.

Other industrialized countries have also made efforts to achieve gender equality through gender-fair language, although the approach each society has taken depends in part on the structure of the language they use (Vervecken & Hannover, 2012). In Germany, the standard approach is to use "pair forms." Virtually all profession names have separate masculine and feminine forms. For example, *Astronaut* refers specifically to a male space traveler, and if the person is female, she must be referred to as *Astronautin*. A group of male space travelers are called *Astronauten*, and their female counterparts *Astronautinnen*.

Table 12.3   Masculine and Feminine Profession Names in German

In German, the names of professions must indicate gender as well as number, as in the example of *astronaut* below. Note that the default form is masculine singular; the suffix *-in* indicates feminine and the suffix *-en* indicates plural.

	Masculine	Feminine
Singular	Astronaut	Astronautin
Plural	Astronauten	Astronautinnen

How then do you refer to a mixed group of male and female space travelers in German? Until fairly recently, you simply used the masculine plural form to refer to a mixed group, even when the majority—or even all but one, were women. We used to have a similar practice in English with pronouns, using *he* to refer to either male or female, as in: *A student should raise his hand before he speaks.*

German speakers who wish to be gender-fair have opted for the use of pair forms instead of the generic masculine when referring to mixed-sex groups (Vervecken & Hannover, 2012). Thus, a group of male and female space travelers are now called

Astronauten und Astronautinnen, sometimes abbreviated as *Astronaut/innen* in writing. This practice is similar to the pair-form pronouns we now use in gender-neutral English, as in: *A student should raise his or her hand before he or she speaks.*

Norwegian, which is related to German, used to make a similar male/female distinction in occupation names by adding a feminine suffix when referring to women (Gabriel & Gygax, 2008). However, gender-equality-conscious Norwegian speakers have opted instead to banish the feminine suffix altogether, instead using the previously masculine form as gender-neutral. We have also taken this approach in English in the case of the word pair *actor-actress*. Many people nowadays habitually refer to female movie stars as *actors*. In these cases, there is the sense that the feminine ending *-ess* carries additional meanings (mostly related to appearance or a lack of seriousness) that the male forms don't.

The real question for us as psycholinguists is whether all this effort to promote gender-fair language has had any effect on how we think about gender roles. So far, there's some evidence that we're sensitive to gender stereotypes. People take more time to read a sentence when it contains a pronoun that doesn't match the gender stereotype of its referent, such as *she* for *carpenter* or *he* for *secretary* (Cacciari et al., 2011). In fact, a sentence such as *The electrician found herself humming as she worked* will often elicit a P600, which is an ERP component generally associated with the detection of a syntactic error.

As for using gender-neutral language, there's still a lot of variability among English speakers. When participants were asked to complete sentences such as: *When a teenager finishes high school . . .* , 65% used a masculine pronoun (*he/him/his*) in their sentence completion (Irmen & Roβberg, 2006). Only 5% used a feminine pronoun (*she/her*), while the remaining 35% made some attempt at gender neutrality, responding either with neutral expressions such as *he or she*, or else with the singular *they*.

In the end, it's still unclear whether gender-neutral language promotes gender equality in society. However, people who use gender-fair language are perceived by others as more competent and less sexist than those who do not (Vervecken & Hannover, 2012). Thus, people may use gender-neutral terms to signal their support for gender equality, even if their thinking on gender-role stereotypes remains unchanged.

KEY TERMS

Arousal	Classifier	Connotation
Attentional blink	Configuration hypothesis	Coprolalia

Count noun

Default mode network

Delayed match-to-sample task

Denotation

Dimensional model of emotion

Direct access model

Euphemism

Figurative language

Focal color

Formal gender system

Graded salience

hypothesis

Grue

Idiom

Indirect access model

Innatism

Linguistic determinism

Linguistic relativity

Mass noun

Metaphor

Metonymy

Paired-associate learning task

RSVP task

Sarcasm

Semantic gender system

Skin conductance response

SLIP task

Spoonerism

Stroop effect

Taboo words

Thinking-for-speaking

Tourette's syndrome

Valence

Verbal irony

Words-with-spaces model

Language and Technology

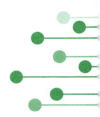

For most of our existence as humans, speech was the only mode of language available to us. We lived in small bands as hunter-gatherers, and speech gave us the ability to coordinate our endeavors in ways that our primate ancestors could not.

The invention of agriculture within the last 10,000 years sparked a technological revolution. Our numbers increased, and we started organizing ourselves in city-states. Kings needed to keep track of their tax revenues, and businessmen their transactions.

Writing evolved out of the tally sheets of early accountants. But more than just being a memory aid, writing became a new mode of communication. For the first time, humans could communicate across both distance and time. However, the writing mode also forced us to use language in a more careful manner to compensate for the lack of facial expressions and vocal inflections. Even today, new technology can influence the characteristics of the language we use.

The invention of writing enabled us to exchange messages with others at great distance, but those messages had to be physically carried from sender to receiver. That changed in the middle of the nineteenth century with the invention of the telegraph. Now written messages—transformed into a series of dots and dashes—could be sent rapidly along wires across great distances.

Sending telegrams was expensive, though, and a "telegraphic" manner of writing evolved that used only content words. This style was also adopted for newspaper headlines and postcards. A few decades later, the invention of the telephone enabled conversation at a distance for the first time. Still, a number of linguistic conventions evolved as we modified our natural form of communication to the new technology.

During the last few decades, many new modes of communication have emerged, from email to Skype, from SMS to Twitter. Each of these media has particular restrictions, and we quickly adapt our language use to fit them. In this chapter we explore how new technologies impact the way we use language.

SECTION 13.1: CELL PHONES

- Driving is significantly impaired by talking on a cell phone, and distracted driving leads to thousands of deaths and hundreds of thousands of injuries each year; talking on a cell phone impacts driving even more than being legally drunk.

- Hands-free cell phones are no improvement, since it is not the manipulation of the device that causes distracted driving; rather, it is the conversation itself, over a mobile device, that impairs driving. This is in contrast to listening to the radio, which does not negatively impact driving ability.

- When we multitask, we alternate our attention between two or more cognitive tasks; conversing on a cell phone draws heavily on attentional and cognitive resources, and drivers have difficulty diverting those resources back to the driving task when road conditions are hazardous.

- Conversation is an activity that engages joint attention. In the case of cell phone conversations, joint attention is drawn away from the driving environment; however, in the case of conversing with a front-seat passenger, joint attention is often directed toward road conditions. As a result, drivers have fewer accidents when driving with a passenger than when driving alone.

- Cell phone conversations lead to inattentional blindness, which is the failure to see or to remember objects or events directly in our visual field because our attention has been drawn elsewhere; both drivers and pedestrians are less likely to notice potential hazards when using a mobile device.

- Although cell phone calls in public are often perceived as obnoxious because they are loud, experimental studies indicate that only being able to hear half of the conversation is what actually makes them annoying.

Cell phones have truly turned the world into a global village. For the first time in the history of our species, a human being can initiate a conversation with another person without even knowing where on the planet he or she may be located. In fact, "Where are you?" has become a common way to start a cell phone conversation.

More than 80% of American adults own cell phones, and the percentage is similar throughout the developed and developing world (Beeson, Higginson, & Rising, 2013). Among young Americans in the eighteen- to twenty-nine-year-old range, ownership is virtually universal, at around 96% (Morrill, Jones, & Vaterlaus, 2013). For this population, cell phones aren't just a convenient tool for communication. They're an integral part of a young person's social identity, as brand name and model provide important information about the personality of the owner.

Many adolescents and young adults develop strong attachments to their cell phones (Weller et al., 2013). It's not unusual for young people to experience separation anxiety when they lose or misplace their mobile devices. In surveys, respondents in this age group often report that they feel naked without their cell phone and that they'd rather lose their wallet than their cell phone. The need to communicate is essential for well-being, and cell phones have become a major mode of communication for young adults.

Risky Business

As cell phone ownership has increased, so has the use of mobile devices while driving, with a resulting rise in the incidence of traffic accidents due to distracted driving (Ferdinand & Menachemi, 2014). A quarter of all accidents and fatalities on American roads are caused by drivers who are distracted by their mobile devices (Sanbonmatsu et al., 2013). This translates to 2,600 deaths and 330,000 injuries a year, all as a result of using a cell phone while driving (Wu & Weseley, 2013).

Talking on a cell phone clearly impairs driving performance. This is true for various age groups and as measured by a number of different methods (Drews, et al., 2008). Drivers using a cell phone have slower reaction times, fail to respond to objects and events in plain sight, are more likely to miss a turn, and check their mirrors less often compared with non–cell phone users (Rivardo, Pacella, & Klein, 2008). The amount of brain activity that drivers devote to the driving task is reduced by more than a third when talking on a cell phone (Sinsky & Beasley, 2013). Driving performance while talking on a cell phone is even worse than is driving while legally drunk (Hyman et al., 2010).

Despite the known risks of using a mobile device while driving, only 3% of respondents on surveys claim that they never use their phones while driving (Park et al., 2013). Furthermore, about half of survey respondents who view cell phone driving as an "extremely serious risk" also reported that they'd used their phones while driving within the last month. Such findings suggest that drivers seriously underestimate the very real dangers of talking on a cell phone.

While hands-free devices enable drivers to keep both hands on the steering wheel, they do little to mitigate the risks of talking on a cell phone when driving (Sawyer & Hancock, 2012). This finding indicates that it's not handling the device that leads to distracted driving. Rather, driving impairment is due to the cognitive demands of conversing over a cell phone. However, recent studies have found that people who use hand-held devices while driving also tend to engage in other risky behaviors like not wearing their seatbelt (Ferdinand & Menachemi, 2014). As a result, they're not only more likely to be involved in an accident, they're also more likely to be severely injured when they do have a crash.

The considerable impairment caused by cell phone use while driving is counterintuitive. After all, people have been driving cars for over a century, conversing with passengers without any apparent danger. In fact, having an adult passenger in the front seat lessens the risk of an accident (Ferdinand & Menachemi,

2014). This is especially true for novice and older drivers, who are at greater risk of accident in comparison with seasoned adult drivers. Furthermore, listening to the radio or other audio media had no effect on driving performance (Strayer & Drews, 2007).

There are several reasons why conversing with a passenger isn't distracting in the way that talking on a cell phone is. First, passengers often help drivers by pointing out traffic obstacles and landmarks. Second, adult passengers regulate the flow of conversation depending on traffic conditions. In other words, when drivers and passengers converse, they tend to engage in the joint activity of shared attention to road conditions and of navigating the car to their destination (Drews et al., 2008). Cell phone conversants, on the other hand, can't do this because they're unaware of road conditions (Hyman et al., 2010).

Many studies investigating the impact of cell phone use on driving are conducted in high-fidelity driving simulators. Not only are studies easier to control in simulators, they're also safer. In one study, drivers were asked to navigate a multilane freeway for a distance of about eight miles and then to exit the highway at a designated rest stop (Strayer & Drews, 2007). During the simulated trip, the driver conversed with a friend in the passenger seat or else via cell phone. Drivers conversing with a passenger successfully navigated to the destination 88% of the time, compared with only 50% for those conversing over a cell phone.

Figure 13.1 Navigation Task

In a driving simulator task, participants were instructed to navigate to a rest area about eight miles up the road. While 88% of drivers conversing with a passenger successfully navigated to the destination, only 50% of those talking on a cell phone successfully completed the task.

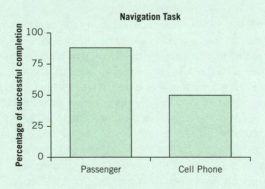

Source: Adapted from data in Strayer and Drews (2007).

Some researchers have questioned whether simulator studies accurately portray the performance decrements created by cell phone use (Hyman et al., 2010). The simulated environment may in fact make driving more difficult, as can the fact that both the car and the phone are unfamiliar to the driver. Furthermore, these studies don't take into account individual differences, in that some people may be more practiced at multitasking than others. Nevertheless, it's clear that cell phone use does have some impact on driving.

Blinded by the Phone

Attention is a bottleneck in cognitive processing, and strictly speaking it's impossible to do two things at once if both of those tasks require attentional resources. Thus, **multitasking** involves *the alternation of attention between two or more cognitive tasks that take in different inputs, engage in different processes, and produce different outputs* (Sanbonmatsu et al., 2013). Anyone can chew gum and walk, because chewing is a fully automated task and walking on even terrain requires only minimal attention. Much of the time, people can walk and talk at the same time as well. Maintaining a conversation is cognitively demanding, but there's still enough attentional reserve for walking, which is largely automatic under normal circumstances. However, people do tend to stop talking when they have to navigate difficult terrain.

Talking with a passenger while driving is similar. Drivers and passengers converse when road conditions are clear, but they stop chatting during congested or hazardous

Figure 13.2 Participant Talking on a Cell Phone While Driving in a Simulator

A participant conversing on a hands-free cell phone while driving in a high-fidelity driving simulator.

Source: Drews, Pasupathi, and Strayer (2008).

conditions. Talking on a cell phone is even more cognitively demanding than conversing in person. Not all frequencies of the voice are carried over the cell phone, and noise is often mixed in with the signal. This means that we have to work harder to understand the other person, and so more attention is shifted to the task. If you're doing nothing else, talking on a cell phone isn't that challenging. But if you engage in another cognitively demanding task such as driving, you may not have enough cognitive capacity to perform both tasks well. In that case, you need to focus on one of the tasks and ignore the other. For safety's sake you should ignore the cell phone conversation and focus on the driving, but in reality that's rarely what we do.

People vary in their ability to multitask, but more importantly, perceived ability to multitask is an especially poor indicator of actual ability (Sanbonmatsu et al., 2013). In general, people overestimate their ability to focus on two tasks at the same time, and those with the most inflated view of their capacity for multitasking tend also to be the ones who are the worst at it. As a result, those drivers who habitually talk on the cell phone while driving are also the ones that are least able to regulate their attention. Researchers have linked cell phone use while driving to personality traits like impulsivity and sensation seeking. Even more dangerous is the fact that these people are oblivious to their poor performance on the road (Hyman et al., 2010).

Perhaps it's because talking seems so automatic that we don't realize just how cognitively demanding it is. At any rate, talking on a cell phone often leads to **inattentional blindness**, which is *the failure to perceive or remember a stimulus directly in the visual field because another cognitively demanding task is being performed* (Hyman et al., 2010). Strayer and Drews (2007) used an **incidental-recognition-memory paradigm** to measure participant's recall of road signs they had passed while driving in a simulator. This is *a procedure in which participants are tested on their ability to remember items that they were not specifically instructed to pay attention to*.

Those participants who had driven while conversing on a hands-free cell phone only recalled half as many roadway signs as those who'd driven without talking on the cell phone. Furthermore, the traffic relevance of the roadway signs was no indicator of how likely the cell phone drivers were to remember them. That is, drivers distracted by their cell phone were just as likely to miss a hazard warning as they were an "adopt-a-highway" sign. These results show that drivers are not able to strategically allocate attention to road conditions when needed.

This inattentional blindness hypothesis is further supported by electrophysiological studies. The **P300** is *an ERP component that indicates how much attention is allocated to a task* (Strayer & Drews, 2007). Furthermore, the amplitude of the P300 is a good predictor of memory performance on a subsequent incidental-recognition-memory task. There was a 50% reduction in the amplitude of the P300 when drivers in a simulator talked on a cell phone. This finding suggests that even when they fixated on an object in the visual field, they failed to encode it as well as did drivers who weren't distracted by the cell phone. Simply put, they didn't see things that were right before their eyes because they were too busy talking.

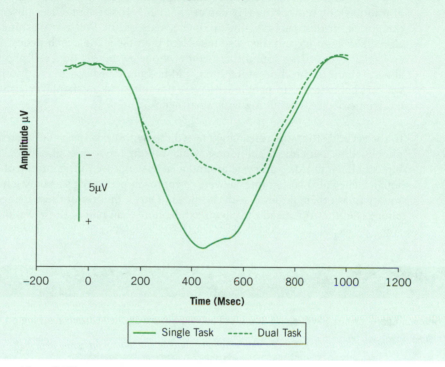

Figure 13.3   Cell Phone Driving and the P300

Average event-related potential (ERP) elicited by the participants' perception of a brake light on the car they were following. The amplitude of the P300 component, which reflects memory encoding, was reduced by half with the participant was talking on a cell phone.

Amplitude µV

5µV

Time (Msec)

Single Task   ----- Dual Task

Source: Strayer and Drews (2007).

Send in the Clowns

People generally understand the potentially deadly risks of not paying attention while driving even if they underestimate their ability to regulate their attention while multitasking. The risks involved in using a cell phone while walking are less obvious, but they can be just as deadly.

Observational studies have found that people who talk on a cell phone while walking engage in the same precautionary behaviors as other pedestrians (Lopresti-Goodman, Rivera, & Dressel, 2012). Cell phone walkers visually scan their pathway for obstacles, and they look left and right before stepping out into the street. Still, they get involved in more accidents with oncoming traffic and experience more near misses than do pedestrians not using mobile devices. They also cross traffic with less time to spare and miss more safe opportunities for crossing compared with those who aren't using a cell phone. In other words, pedestrians who use cell phones appear to be experiencing inattentional blindness, in that they go through the motions of safe walking behavior but fail to detect many of the dangers they're looking out for.

Even when someone is walking in a pedestrian-only area where there's no danger from vehicular traffic, talking on a cell phone leads to impaired performance. In a set of observational studies, Hyman and colleagues investigated the effect of multitasking on walking (Hyman et al., 2010). In the first study, observers categorized pedestrians crossing an open square on the Western Washington University campus, and they also measured the time it took each pedestrian to cross the square. They found that people who were talking on a cell phone walked slower, changed direction more often, and had more near misses with other walkers compared with people who were listening to a music player, using no electronic device, or walking with a partner.

In the second study, the researchers tested the hypothesis that talking on a cell phone led to inattentional blindness while walking (Hyman et al., 2010). They hired a clown to ride a unicycle around a large sculpture in the middle of the square. They also posted interviewers to approach pedestrians as they left the square to ask them if they'd seen the clown. Only a quarter of those using a cell phone said they'd noticed the clown, while more than half of those walking alone

Figure 13.4 Photo of the Unicycling Clown

Clown unicycling around the Sky-Viewing Sculpture on Red Square on the Western Washington University campus.

Source: Hyman et al. (2010, Fig. 2). © John Wiley & Sons, Ltd.

with no electronic device saw the clown. Interestingly, those listening to an MP3 player were just as likely to have seen the clown as those who weren't, which parallels the finding that listening to the radio doesn't impair driving while talking on a cell phone does. Nearly three-quarters of those walking in pairs saw the clown, which is similar to the finding that conversing with a front-seat passenger improves driving performance. This result also points to the role of joint attention in conversation. Just as a passenger may point out a safety hazard to the driver, pedestrians who notice a unicycling clown are likely to point it out to their partner.

Need to Listen

Most people consider cell phone conversations conducted in public places to be annoying (Monk, Fellas, & Ley, 2004). A common perception is that people talk louder on cell phones than they do in face-to-face interactions. While this may be true, controlled studies have found overheard cell phone conversations to be rated more annoying than overhead face-to-face interactions, even when the sound volume was the same in both cases.

This has led researchers to consider *the proposal that only being able to hear half of the conversation is what makes public cell phone calls so annoying.* Monk and colleagues

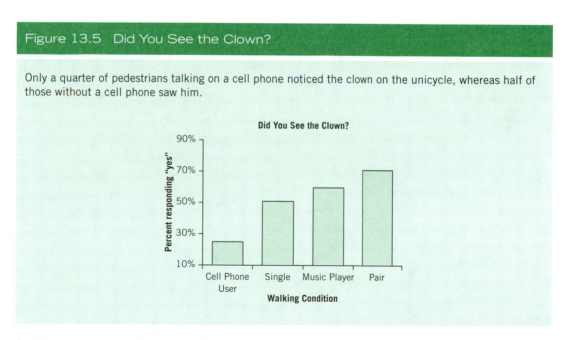

Figure 13.5   Did You See the Clown?

Only a quarter of pedestrians talking on a cell phone noticed the clown on the unicycle, whereas half of those without a cell phone saw him.

Source: Based on data from Hyman et al. (2010).

(2004) tested the **need-to-listen hypothesis** by staging conversations on trains in England. Two actors sat behind a passenger and performed a scripted conversation. In the first condition, both actors spoke in a clearly audible voice, while in the second condition only one of the actors spoke in an audible voice. In the third condition, one of the actors performed the scripted conversation via cell phone with an actor in another train car.

After the one-minute conversation was over, the actors left the train car. A researcher then approached the targeted passenger and interviewed him or her about the overheard conversation. On average, the respondents rated the conversation in which both partners could be overheard to be less annoying than either the cell phone or one-audible conversations, which were both rated as annoying to the same degree. Since all conversations were controlled for sound volume, this result indicates that what was annoying was the inability to hear half of the conversation.

In Sum

Taking on a cell phone impacts driving ability even more so than being legally drunk, and it leads to thousands of deaths and hundreds of thousands of injuries each year. Since holding the cell phone is not what impairs driving performance, hands-free devices yield no improvement in safety. When we multitask, we

Figure 13.6 The Conversation Was Annoying

Although all three conversation conditions were performed with the same sound volume, the condition in which both sides of the conversation were audible was rated less annoying than the two conditions in which only one side of the conversation was audible.

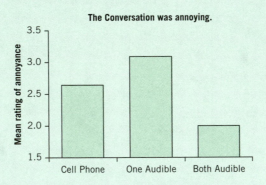

Source: Based on data from Monk, Fellas, and Ley (2004).

alternate our attention between two or more cognitive tasks. Talking on a cell phone makes considerable demands on cognitive and attentional resources, and we often fail to divert those resources back to the driving task when road conditions become hazardous. This isn't the case with listening to the radio, since we can easily disengage from it when traffic conditions require our full attention. Likewise, having an adult passenger in the front seat decreases the risk of an accident, since the topic of conversation often directs joint attention to the navigation task. Cell phone conversations while driving or walking are dangerous because of inattentional blindness. Because our attention is directed toward the conversation, we fail to process important objects or events in our visual field. Most people find public cell phone calls to be annoying. While loudness may account for some of the irritation, mostly these calls are obnoxious because we can only hear half of the conversation.

Review Questions

1. Explain why conversing with a passenger is safer than driving alone, and why conversing on a cell phone is more dangerous.

2. Multitasking involves engaging in two different tasks at the same time, but can you really pay attention to two different things simultaneously? Explain.

3. What is inattentional blindness? How is it measured using the incidental-recognition-memory paradigm?

4. Describe the method and results of the clown on a unicycle study (Hyman et al., 2010).

5. Describe method and results of the experiment that tested the need-to-listen hypothesis (Monk et al., 2004).

Thought Questions

1. Conduct a survey of your classmates or friends regarding attitudes toward cell phone use while driving. Ask your research participants to respond to the question: *How dangerous is it to use a cell phone? (1) Not very dangerous, (2) Somewhat dangerous, or (3) Very dangerous.* Then, follow up with the question: *How often do you use a cell phone while driving? (1) Rarely, (2) Sometimes, or (3) Frequently.* Do you detect any patterns in your data? What do they suggest?

2. Brainstorming with your classmates, generate ideas for convincing people not to use cell phones while driving. Based on your general knowledge of human behavior, which approaches do you think will be most effective?

Google It! Did You See the Clown?

There are plenty of quality videos on YouTube that demonstrate **inattentional blindness**. The **moonwalking bear** and the **gorilla on the court** are classic demonstrations. Check them out. You can also find a video demonstration of the **clown on a unicycle experiment**. For a humorous take on dealing with annoying people who talk on their cell phone in public, check out **cell phone crashing**.

SECTION 13.2: TEXTING

- Keyboards and keypads provide a means for entering text into a machine; the various keyboard and keypad layouts in use today are the result of both practical considerations and historical legacy. Human factors is an interdisciplinary field that studies how humans interact with machines.

- Statistical properties of language have been an important factor in the design of text-input systems for a century and a half. The QWERTY keyboard separates commonly co-occurring letters to prevent mechanical jamming, thus allowing for rapid typing; predictive text software enables one-thumb text input at an efficient speed.

- Texting on a cell phone is an inexpensive and private means of communication that meets the needs of adolescents and young adults, who use it to build and maintain their network of social relationships; about half of all text messages can be categorized as phatic, or social, communication.

- Social media are designed to help people build and maintain relationships; however, frequent use of social media can have a negative impact on subjective well-being. This is in contrast to face-to-face interactions, which generally increase subjective well-being.

- Texting while driving leads to a 400% increase in time spent looking away from the road and a twenty-three-fold increase in risk of accident; texting while walking is dangerous as well, and although texting pedestrians go through the motions of exercising caution, they're still more prone to accidents than nontexters.

- Despite fears that texting leads to declines in spelling and reading abilities, research shows the opposite to be true. The use of homophones and alternate spellings in text messages requires a high degree of phonological awareness; furthermore, habitual texters are sensitive to the situations in which it's appropriate to use textisms.

If you're like most college students, you probably send and receive around forty text messages every day (Morrill et al., 2013). Texting is much cheaper than talking on a cell phone, and oftentimes more convenient. (Just try talking on your cell phone instead of texting in class and see if your professor doesn't notice!) However, texting does have its drawbacks. Unlike making a phone call, which enables you to talk directly with someone a great distance away, texting requires you to enter written language into a machine for transmission. This is generally done by pressing keys to input letters, numbers, and other symbols.

Keyboards provide a separate key for each letter or number, although auxiliary keys like "Shift" and "Control" give the keys alternative functions. More than three dozen keys are needed to represent the letters, numbers and punctuation marks used in English, and so keyboards generally require the use of both hands. You're no doubt acquainted with the QWERTY keyboard used with computers, but some smartphones provide an alphabetically arranged keyboard.

Keypads, on the other hand, are designed for use by a single hand, or even a single finger, and they do this by placing multiple letters on the same key. You're certainly familiar with two different keypad systems, although you may never have noticed before that they're different. The calculator keypad arranges the numbers in descending order, while the telephone keypad arranges them in ascending order. (Go ahead and compare your cell phone keypad to a calculator keypad!)

The point of this discussion is that there's no natural or optimal way to enter text into a machine. Rather, the various keyboard and keypad arrangements we have today are due as much to historical accident as they are to practical considerations.

A Brief History of Texting

The history of texting goes back more than a century and a half with the invention of the typewriter. In the middle of the nineteenth century, various typing machines—each with a different keyboard layout—were developed. However, it wasn't until some decades later that the typewriter and its QWERTY keyboard were standardized (Bi et al., 2012).

According to urban legend, the QWERTY keyboard was designed to slow down the typist to avoid jamming levers, but in fact this is only half true. Letters that commonly co-occur were placed on opposite sides of the keyboard to keep levers from jamming, and as a result skilled typists could enter text much faster that they could on an alphabetic keyboard (Higginbotham et al., 2012).

Even though lever-jamming isn't a problem for computers, the QWERTY keyboard still has its advantages. Skilled typists can type faster when alternating hand and finger movements are required for entering letter sequences (Kozlik et al., 2013). They also report that these sequences are easier to type than sequences using the same hand or finger.

You may have learned touch typing in school, meaning that you can type without looking at the keyboard. If so, you've developed a set of complex and automatic motor skills that enable you to enter text quickly and with relatively few errors. Now that computers have pervaded virtually every aspect of modern life, keyboarding skills are essential.

Your parents and teachers may type faster and more accurately than you because they've had decades more experience on the keyboard. However, you're no doubt faster and more accurate than your elders when it comes to entering text on a keypad (Beeson et al., 2013). Because text messaging is still a new technology, the older generation has no practice advantage, and furthermore they're less likely to send text messages compared with adolescents and young adults. As a result, many young people can touch type on a keypad, oftentimes holding the cell phone in one hand and composing messages with their thumb.

As a memory aid, letters were originally associated with the numbers on the telephone dial, which predated the telephone keypad. The letters provide the opportunity to associate difficult to remember number sequences with easy to remember words, a practice that's still widely used in advertising today. The arrangement of letters on the keypad isn't optimized for inputting text, and cell phone manufacturers have developed a variety of keypad layouts that are more efficient. However, since so many people are already familiar with the existing systems, they're reluctant to spend the time and effort to learn more efficient methods for inputting text (Zhai & Kristensson, 2012). Thus, the traditional telephone keypad, like the QWERTY keyboard, is a historic relic that has become deeply ingrained in our society.

We can think of keypad design as "legacy" technology that isn't well fitted to modern needs. Originally, text was input to a cell phone via **multitap**, which is *a keypad entry method that cycles through the letter values of the key* (Sawyer & Hancock, 2012). Let's say you want to send the simple message *thanks*. In the multitap method, you need to press the 8 key one time for T, the 4 key two times for H, the 2 key one time for A, the 6 key two times for N, the 5 key two times for K, and the 7 key four times for S. That's twelve key presses for six letters.

Since then, newer technology has been developed to make text messaging more efficient. **Predictive text** is *software that uses the probabilities of language to make text entry on a keypad more efficient* (Sawyer & Hancock, 2012). Because no other common word can be spelled with the number sequence 842657, predictive text software will interpret it as *thanks*.

Many times a particular number sequence maps onto multiple potential words. In that case, predictive text software takes into account the preceding few words to make its best guess (Higginbotham et al., 2012). For example, the number sequence 7243 could make at least half a dozen different common English words, such as *page, rage, sage, paid, raid,* and *said.* However, if you've just typed *What she*, then by far the most likely next word is *said*. Predictive software allows people to enter text fluently and within the normal range of language processing speed.

The recent introduction of tablets has presented a new challenge to keyboard design (Trudeau et al., 2013). As mobile computing devices, tablets are generally held in both hands, and a virtual QWERTY keyboard on the touch screen is provided for text entry. However, because of the way the tablet is held, users generally type with their thumbs, as they do on a cell phone. This anatomical limitation has led to the design of the split keyboard when the tablet is held in landscape orientation.

Keyboard and keypad designs are the product of an area of applied research known as **human factors**. This is *an interdisciplinary field that studies the ways that people interact with the machines they use*. We've already seen that human factors generally involves a trade-off between ease of learning and efficiency of use. As a rule, consumers tend to prefer methods that are easy to learn, even if they're inefficient to use.

Texting Today

Some three-quarters of adult cell phone owners also use their mobile devices for sending and receiving text messages (Beeson et al., 2013). This figure no doubt reaches close to 100% for adolescent and young adult cell phone users. About half of all text messages can be categorized as **phatic communication**, that is, *language exchange for the sole purpose of building and maintaining social relationships* (Morrill et al., 2013). The bulk of face-to-face language interaction is also phatic in nature, but mobile technology has also opened the opportunity to maintain social relationships at a distance.

Texting is an inexpensive and private form of communication that is especially well suited to adolescents and young adults, who are actively building their network of social relationships (Conti-Ramsden, Durkin, & Simkin, 2010). However, it lacks the visual and auditory components of talk-in-interaction that convey emotion and underlying meaning (Tulane & Beckert, 2013). As a result, receivers are prone to misunderstanding intended messages, which they incorrectly perceive as offensive.

Although young adults use texting and instant messaging on social media to enhance relationships, research suggests that too much "face time" on Facebook can make you sad (Kross et al., 2013). In a longitudinal study, researchers tracked Facebook use and **subjective well-being** in young adults five times a day for fourteen days. When people engage in face-to-face social interaction, their *personal rating of happiness and life satisfaction* generally increases afterward. However, after interacting on Facebook, the participants' mood tended to become more negative, regardless of what their level of subject well-being was before the Facebook session.

Texting in the classroom has become a contentious issue in high schools and on college campuses. In one survey, both high school and college students believed they were adept at texting in class without their instructors knowing about it (Tulane & Beckert, 2013). Some respondents even reported that they'd observed their teachers texting during class! However, McDonald (2013) found a negative correlation between in-class texting and final grade in a freshman-level social science course. Although GPA, ACT score, and attendance were the three biggest predictors of final grade, in-class texting behavior also had a significant impact on class performance.

Although frequent texting may satisfy a psychological need for connecting with others, it may also have negative health consequences. Researchers monitored two key indicators of stress, heart rate and respiratory rate, of young people as they sent and received text messages. Both heart rate and breathing rate increased as the participants composed messages, and heart rate shot up every time a text message was received. This finding suggests that frequent texters may be subjecting themselves to unhealthy levels of stress.

Texting on the Go

In the last section, we saw how talking on a cell phone impairs driving to a greater degree than being drunk. It only follows then that texting and driving are a bad mix. Simply put, time spent looking at a cell phone screen is time spent not looking at the road. In simulator studies, drivers who texted increased the time they looked away from the road by 400% compared with nontexters (Park et al., 2013).

Texting while driving leads to a twenty-three-fold increase in risk of accident, and it's illegal in most states (Sinsky & Beasley, 2013). Still, more than a third of young Americans admit to sending and receiving text messages while they drive on a regular basis (Lopresti-Goodman et al., 2012). Here's a case where people's confidence in their abilities clearly doesn't match up with their actual performance.

Texting while walking is dangerous as well. In one survey, more than a third of respondents admitted to colliding with another person or an object while sending or receiving text messages (Schaburn et al., 2014). Observational studies have found that when people text while walking, they tend to reduce their pace and deviate more frequently from a straight path (Schaburn et al., 2014). Although texters may be slowing down in an attempt to compensate for the distraction of texting, they still put themselves in danger. In simulator studies, texting pedestrians both looked away from traffic more and experienced more hits by motor vehicles than nontexters.

People who text while walking often go through the motions of exercising caution, but in fact they experience more accidents than nontexting pedestrians. In one study, researchers observed how texting and nontexting walkers passed through doorframes of varying width (Lopresti-Goodman et al., 2012). Nontexters were very consistent in their judgments of whether they could walk straight through the doorframes or would have to turn their shoulders to fit through. Texters, on the other hand, rotated their shoulders to pass through doorways that they walked straight through when not texting. They also slowed down more than nontexters.

Figure 13.7   Passing Through Doorways While Texting

Nontexters did not significantly decrease their walking speed as they passed through an experimental doorway. However, the texters did slow down, even though they had plenty of room to pass. They were also more likely to bump into the door frame than were the nontexters.

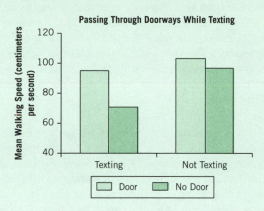

Source: Based on data from Lopresti-Goodman, Rivera, and Dressel (2012).

Texting impacts safety while walking in other ways, too. Because of the need to hold the mobile device steady in the field of vision, texting pedestrians assume a posture that's not optimal for walking (Schaburn et al., 2014). When we walk, we alternate the swing of our arms to help maintain balance, and we hold our head relatively stable as the rest of our body moves. However, texters hold their upper bodies more rigid than nontexters, which has a negative effect on balance. Texters walk slower in an apparent attempt to compensate for their poor posture, but they're still more prone to mishaps.

CUL8R

There's clearly a generation gap in texting culture. Older adults bemoan the death of the English language at the hands of young texters who have no respect for proper grammar or spelling. However, it's important to keep in mind that languages are living systems that are always in flux. A close inspection of the texting language that adolescents and young adults use shows that it is highly creative and works within established rules (Tulane & Beckert, 2013).

The widespread use of instant messaging technology in the twenty-first century has led to the rise of a new language form that very much parallels the development of creoles and signed language. We've seen in other chapters how children who don't share a common tongue will collaboratively build a language when they're brought together as a social group. The generation that grew up with instant messaging capability have likewise developed an economical and expressive language style based on written English that's well suited to the limitations of the text message format (Anjaneyulu, 2013).

Although text messages are composed in written language, they don't strictly adhere to the traditional conventions of formal writing (Conti-Ramsden et al., 2010). The rules of grammar and spelling are relaxed, and a certain degree of typing errors is tolerated. However, texters are expected to follow the rules of texting etiquette. For example, texters are allowed a certain amount of creative freedom with abbreviations, but these must be transparent to the receiver. *An innovative use of language in text messaging* is known as a **textism**.

Despite anecdotes of textisms creeping into standard English writing as well as concerns about a general decline in the quality of schoolwork, there's little hard evidence to support these claims (Plester, Wood, & Joshi, 2009). In fact, research shows that skill in the use of textisms in instant messaging is positively correlated reading and spelling abilities in the classroom. This is because the use of textisms, with their widespread use of homophones and alternate spellings, requires a high degree of phonological awareness, a necessary precursor to developing strong reading and spelling skills.

An important part of being a fluent speaker (and writer) of a language is knowing how to adjust the style and level of formality to fit the demands of the social context and the expectations of the audience. Using appropriate texting language is simply part of the skill set any communicator in the twenty-first century needs have.

In Sum

Since the invention of the typewriter in the mid-1800s, various schemes have been devised for entering text into machines. Many keyboard and keypad designs are informed by human factors research, which studies the ways that people interact with machines. Taking into consideration the statistical properties of language enables designers to build text-input systems that are efficient both for the machine and for the human operator. Texting on cell phones has become an important means of communication for young people, who use the technology for building and maintaining social relationships. While face-to-face interactions generally lead to an increase in subjective well-being, interactions via social media are more likely to lead to a decrease in happiness and life satisfaction. Texting while driving is exceedingly risky and frequently has lethal consequences; however, texting while walking is also fraught with danger. A new texting culture has arisen that makes creative use of written language. In spite of fears to the contrary, young people who use frequent textisms also have a strong command of spelling and grammar conventions in formal writing.

Review Questions

1. What is human factors research? Discuss some ways that human factors research has informed the design of keyboards and keypads for entering text into machines.

2. What is phatic communication, and what is its relationship to subjective well-being? How do face-to-face and social media interactions differ in terms of subjective well-being?

3. Discuss the dangers of texting while driving and while walking. Based on the results of the doorway experiment (Lopresti-Goodman et al., 2012), do you think it's possible for people to be careful enough to walk and text at the same time? Explain your reasoning.

Thought Questions

1. If you're a regular user of social media, you might have some intuitions about why social media use can lead to a decrease in subjective well-being. What do your intuitions tell you? Can you formulate these intuitions as hypotheses that you could test with experiments?

2. If you know someone who habitually texts while driving, what can you say or do to convince him or her of the dangers? Why do you think people engage in such risky behaviors as texting while driving or walking?

3. You hear an older person complain that text messaging is destroying the English language. How do you respond?

Google It! The Dvorak Keyboard

If you never learned how to touch type on the QWERTY keyboard, you may instead be interested in learning the **Dvorak keyboard**, which many claim allows for faster typing. You can find descriptions and tutorials online. Most computers have Dvorak as an optional keyboard setting.

SECTION 13.3: NATURAL LANGUAGE PROCESSING

- The term *natural language processing* refers to software that responds to, transforms, or produces speech or text; its three main tasks involve (1) converting speech to text, (2) transforming text, and (3) converting text to speech.

- Natural language processing programs use statistical learning mechanisms to extract patterns from a large corpus of text or speech, building up a grammar of the language in much the same way that human infants do.

- Automatic speech recognition refers to the process of converting spoken language input into a text format; common speech-to-text programs include dictation software and programs that output closed captioning for TV.

- A speech-generating device is a computer that converts text into spoken language output, in the form of either prerecorded messages or synthesized speech; assistive reading software is an example of text-to-speech software that is widely used.

- Natural language processing devices that integrate all three tasks (speech-to-text, text-to-text, and text-to-speech) allow for complex human-machine interactions; the personal assistant Siri on Apple's iPhone and Google Translate are examples of interactive natural language processors that are commercially available.

- Many natural language processing devices provide augmentative and alternative communication methods for users who have lost the ability to speak due to disease or injury; while synthetic voices sound unnatural, sometimes individuals can preserve samples of their speech through voice banking.

In the last two sections, we explored how technology has enabled us to communicate *through* machines. In other words, we use machines to convey human language to others who are distant from us in space or time. In this section, we'll consider ways that technology now lets us use human language to communicate directly *with* our machines. **Natural language processing** refers to *software that responds to, transforms, or produces speech or text* (Higginbotham et al., 2012). While talking computers and robots have long been a staple of science fiction, we've now reached an era when talking with our machines, from personal assistants on our smart phones to GPS devices in our cars, has become commonplace.

When HAL Met Siri . . .

HAL 9000 was a computer with natural language processing abilities in the fictional *2001: A Space Odyssey* film and novel series by Arthur C. Clarke. We've long passed the year 2001, when HAL was already operational, and no natural language processing device currently on the market even comes close to HAL's abilities; but in the last few years we've seen significant progress.

Early attempts at developing natural language processing software took the approach of directly encoding the rules of the language into the program. These early programs generally didn't perform very well, or else they only worked within a narrow scope of contexts. In part, the problem was that the structure of language is just too complex to write out as an explicit computer program. Furthermore, all language rules have exceptions, and these need to be encoded as well.

Modern approaches to natural language processing take a statistical approach (Higginbotham et al., 2012). Instead of writing explicit rules, programmers first create a **corpus**, which is *a large selection of text or speech that is used to train natural language processing software*. Oftentimes a training corpus will contain more than ten million words. The software works through the corpus, tracking co-occurrence frequencies and detecting patterns. In other words, natural language processors use statistical learning mechanisms to build up a grammar, just like human infants do. This statistical approach is what accounts for the great strides researchers have recently made in producing practical natural language processing devices for the market.

We can divide natural language processing into three broad tasks: (1) converting speech to text, (2) transforming text, and (3) converting text to speech. These three tasks are combined in various ways to provide useful devices that humans can interact with using natural human language.

Listen to Me

Automatic speech recognition refers to *the machine process of converting spoken language into text* (Zhang, Sun, & Luo, 2014). As symbol manipulators, computers are well suited to processing text, which is composed of a discrete set of alphanumeric characters. It's no surprise that text editors and word processors were among the first computer programs developed, available even in the days of huge mainframe computers before PCs were invented. Recognizing speech, on the other hand, is a far more challenging task for a computer.

Although we perceive the continuous speech stream as being composed of a series of separate phonemes, we learned in Chapter 3 that these speech sounds blend into and overlap one another, and they also take different forms depending on context. Human infants use categorical perception mechanisms to extract the phonemes from the speech stream. Automatic speech recognition software is trained by exposing it to vast amounts of speech along with its corresponding text transcription. As the computer chugs through the data, it learns to associate various speech patterns with particular phonemes (Higginbotham et al., 2012). Trained software can then take speech input and produce an output either in phonetic symbols or in standard written language format.

Speech-to-text programs have a number of useful applications. Depending on the make and model of your laptop or desktop computer, you may already have dictation software installed. If so, you should give it a try. You'll probably find that touch typing is still faster and more accurate. However, you can imagine how convenient this kind of software is for people who lack full use of their hands.

Another application of speech-to-text software is in the production of closed captioning for television programs (Razik et al., 2011). Closed captioning is commonly displayed on TV screens in noisy public locations, such as airports and fitness centers, where the spoken content can't be heard. It also enables deaf and hard-of-hearing people to understand the programs they're watching. In some cases, captioning can be a fully automated process, but usually it requires the assistance of a human moderator. This in part accounts for the time lag between when the lines are spoken and when the captions appear on screen. Despite human moderation, real-time closed captioning can sometimes be difficult to comprehend.

Early automatic speech recognition programs had to be trained on the voice of each speaker that used it (Young & Mihailidis, 2010). This usually involves having the user read a specific script into the computer, which allows it to learn the unique vocal characteristics of the speaker. Dictation software trained in this way can achieve a fairly high level of accuracy. However, other programs, such as customer service applications, need to be able to respond to a wide variety of voices. These programs work well so long as the speech input is limited. If you've ever checked a bank or credit card balance over the telephone, you've had the experience of interacting with automatic speech recognition software.

"Press 1 for . . ."

A **speech-generating device** is *a computer program that produces spoken language output* (Drager, Reichle, & Pinkoski, 2010). Some speech-generating devices play back prerecorded messages spoken by a real human. Those annoying "Press 1 for . . ." telephone menus are of this type. Other speech-generating devices output **synthesized speech**, which is *computer-generated sound output that mimics the fluctuations in fundamental frequencies and formants of human speech*. Synthesized speech allows for more flexibility in how the system responds, since it isn't limited to a set of prerecorded messages. On the other hand, synthesized speech lacks the acoustic detail of real human speech, especially the overtones that provide emotional information, and so it can be difficult to understand.

Synthesized speech is an important component in text-to-speech software. Many computers now have text-to-speech software installed, often with a selection of voices to choose from. If you haven't already, you should try out the text-to-speech program on your computer to hear what it sounds like. You'll probably find the voices monotonous and difficult to pay attention to if they're reading long passages. Nevertheless, synthesized speech is a great boon to those with visual impairments since it enables them interact with their computers, read email, and surf the Internet— activities we take for granted in the twenty-First century but until recently were limited to the visual modality.

People with reading disabilities also benefit from text-to-speech software. **Assistive reading software** is *a computer program that extracts text from a scanned document and then converts the text to synthesized speech*. Studies have found that assistive reading software can help children with learning difficulties improve their reading skill (Chiang & Liu, 2011). Having the computer read aloud as the child reads silently helps the learner develop decoding skills (Chapter 11). Furthermore, children with attention-deficit disorder who use assistive reading software pay more attention to what they read, are less distracted, and read faster with better comprehension. Rather than removing the incentive to read, assistive reading software helps struggling readers develop stronger literacy skills and encourages them to read more.

Q & A

A **question-answering system** is *a computer program that takes natural language inquiries as input, searches databases or the Internet for information, and then provides answers in the form of natural language* (Furbach, Glöckner, & Pelzer, 2010). When search engines were first developed, you could only search the Internet by using keywords. A simple question like *Who was the first president of the United States?* would stump the search engine, because it would not only search for *first president* and *United States* but also *who*, *was*, *the*, and *of*. Later search engines such as Ask Jeeves (now Ask.com) could handle questions in natural language, mainly by filtering out the function words and doing searches on the content words that remained. Recently marketed personal assistants like Apple's Siri on the iPhone are true question-answering systems in that they take natural spoken language as input and produce synthesized speech as output.

Machine translation is another example of a question-answering system (Green, 2011). These programs take text in one language and convert it into text in another language. As we learned in Chapter 9, you can't just translate word-for-word from one language to another. Each language has a unique vocabulary and set of syntactic structures. Again, taking a statistical learning approach is what has driven rapid improvements in machine translation over the last few years.

Let's suppose we want to build an English-Thai translator. First, we need to find a large number of parallel texts in English and Thai, that is, documents in one language that have already been translated (by humans) into the other language. As the computer works through these texts, consisting of many millions of words, it looks for phrase-by-phrase correspondences between the two languages. It then uses these correspondences to translate from one language to the other.

Notice that the machine translator knows nothing about the vocabulary or grammar of either language. Rather, it only knows typical phrase-by-phrase correspondences between languages. This means that a separate translator needs to be trained for each language pair, for example, English-Thai, English-Chinese, Thai-Chinese, and so on. Given that there are some 3,000 languages spoken in the world, we'd need to train some nine million different translation programs to have a true universal translator. While many of the common language pairs now have machine translators on the market, I wouldn't expect to see a Choctaw-Cherokee translator available anytime soon.

Commercially available machine translation software such as Google Translate does a fairly good job with conventional prose such as business letters and instruction manuals. However, translating technical or creative writing still requires a human translator, although machine translation can provide a first draft for the human translator to clean up.

The ultimate goal is to produce a voice-to-voice machine translation system, and rapid progress is being made in that direction (Hyman, 2014). The basic plan is straightforward. First, an automatic speech recognition system takes input in the form of the spoken source language and converts it to text. Next, a machine translation system converts the text in the source language into text in the target language. Finally, a speech synthesis system produces output in the form of the spoken target language. notice that the speech recognition and synthesis programs need to be able to take inputs and produce outputs in both languages. The main hurdle at this point is getting all of these systems to work together seamlessly and in real time.

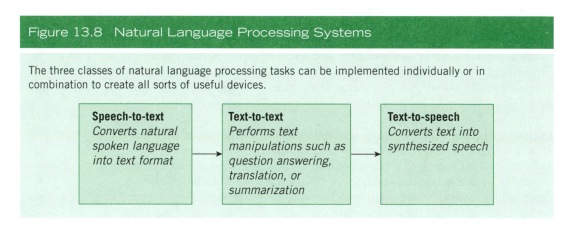

Figure 13.8   Natural Language Processing Systems

The three classes of natural language processing tasks can be implemented individually or in combination to create all sorts of useful devices.

Speech-to-text
Converts natural spoken language into text format

Text-to-text
Performs text manipulations such as question answering, translation, or summarization

Text-to-speech
Converts text into synthesized speech

Giving Voice to the Silenced

Language is what makes us human. Losing the ability to communicate with others due to brain disease or injury is perhaps the worst possible fate, as it condemns the person to an existence of social isolation. Over 100,000 Americans acquire aphasia each year, mainly due to stroke (Fried-Oken, Beukelman, & Hux, 2012). Although many regain their language faculties, many others don't recover and must rely on technological aids to interact with others. **Augmentative and alternative communication** is *an umbrella term for strategies and devices that help those with language impairments to engage in social interactions*. While the term includes low-tech methods such as note cards and gesturing, it has increasingly come to refer to high-tech devices that supplement or replace a person's ability to speak.

Tablets and smartphones provide convenient platforms for augmentative and alternative communication software. Aphasic patients with intact reading abilities can navigate through the various functions of their device by following written labels. However, aphasia oftentimes disrupts reading as well as speech. In this case, an effective approach is to provide **visual scene displays**, which are *contextually rich and personally relevant digital images that convey content on mobile devices* (Fried-Oken et al., 2012). These naturalistic scenes immediately capture visual attention and are easier to process than are line drawings or abstract symbols (Light & McNaughton, 2012). Each visual scene display has a number of prerecorded messages associated with it.

Stroke can also lead to loss of manual dexterity, in which case pressing buttons on a tablet is impractical. When some speaking ability still remains, as in the case of dysarthria (Chapter 4), using automatic speech recognition software may be a feasible approach (Mustafa et al., 2014). Typically, speech recognition programs don't perform well with dysarthric speech. However, when the software can be trained so that it adapts to the user's particular speech characteristics, satisfactory results can sometimes be obtained. In other cases, a multimodal approach works better (Higginbotham et al., 2012). For example, the user can type the initial letter before speaking the word. The keyboard input then helps the software identify the spoken word input.

Figure 13.9 Visual Scene Display

Visual scene displays on mobile devices enable individuals with aphasia to socially interact with other people.

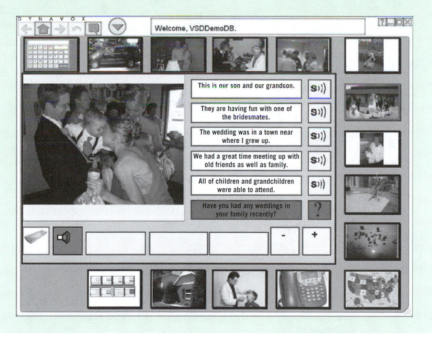

Source: Fried-Oken, Beukelman, & Hux (2012).

Speech-generating devices can be used to give a voice to those who've lost the ability to speak (Baxter et al., 2012). However, many aphasic patients are reluctant to use synthetic speech to communicate (Khan et al., 2011). Voice is an important component of one's personal identity, and if the user doesn't like the synthetic voice, he or she may feel embarrassed and thus have less motivation to engage in social interaction. In the case of sudden language loss, synthetic speech is the only option; but attempts are made to match the new voice to the original as much as possible.

Sometimes patients still have an intact voice, but they know that they'll lose it soon due to a degenerative disease or impending surgery. In such a case, patients can prepare by going through *the process of recording voice samples for later use in a speech-generating device*. This is known as **voice banking** (Khan et al., 2011). In most cases, the best the patient can hope for is to record a good number of useful sentences that can later be selected and played back as needed.

When sufficient recordings of a person's speech exist, it's possible to create a synthetic voice that sounds quite similar to the original. This was the case with movie critic Roger Ebert, who lost the ability to speak after cancer surgery on his jaw. Because he was a noted TV personality, there were hundreds of hours of recorded speech providing raw material for a speech synthesizer. You can learn more in his TED Talk, available at ted.com.

In Sum

Natural language processing involves any software that responds to, transforms, or produces speech or text. It involves three classes of processes: (1) converting speech to text, (2) transforming text, and (3) converting text to speech. Natural language software uses statistical learning mechanisms to extract patterns from a large corpus of speech or text in much the same way that human infants learn their language. Automatic speech recognition software converts spoken input into text format, and useful applications include programs for taking dictation and for closed captioning TV shows. A speech-generating device converts text into spoken language, either as prerecorded messages or else as synthesized speech. Assistive reading software makes use of synthesized speech. Question-answering systems and machine translation devices incorporate all three natural language processing tasks to create a rich experience of human-machine interaction. Natural language processing in the form of augmentative and alternative communication has given individuals with language loss the opportunity to interact socially in ways they could not have before.

Review Questions

1. What is natural language processing? What approach did researchers first take, and why did it fail? Which approach has proven more successful?

2. Describe the three broad categories of natural language processing. Give some examples of practical devices that employ each process. Also give some examples of devices that combine these tasks.

3. Describe some of the natural language processing devices that have been developed for augmentative and alternative communication in recent years.

Thought Questions

1. Cross-cultural researchers who want to administer the same survey in multiple languages often use a technique known as back-translation to ensure that no meaning has been lost or changed. Let's say we have an English-language survey that we want to administer in Chinese. First, we translate the survey into Chinese, and then we translate it back into English. After that, we compare the original English document against the back-translated document to see if there are any discrepancies. Use the back-translation method to test Google Translate. Try different types of documents to see if some topics or genres work better than others.

2. Current machine translation programs are developed for specific pairs of languages, for example English and Chinese. This means that millions of translation programs will need to be developed, one for each possible language pair. One way to reduce that number is to use a pivot language such as English. Then all we need to do is develop a machine translation program between English and each other language. Thus, to translate from Choctaw to Cherokee, we would first do Choctaw to English and then do English to Cherokee. Based on your experience with back-translation in the previous question, what problems would you expect to encounter? How can you expand on the back-translation method to test the practicality of using a pivot language?

Google It! Remaking a Voice

Search **Roger Ebert TED Talk** to learn more about his heroic struggle to remake his voice after losing his lower jaw to cancer. You'll get to compare his synthetic voice against his original, and you can judge for yourself how good it is.

SECTION 13.4: ARTIFICIAL INTELLIGENCE

- The AI debate centers around the question of whether we can build machines that are intelligent in the same way that humans are; the

Turing test proposes that a machine should be considered intelligent if its ability to hold a conversation is indistinguishable from that of a human being.

- ELIZA was an early program that appeared to have the potential to pass the Turing test; people interacting with the program often treated it as if it were human, in what is known as the ELIZA effect. Programs like ELIZA that can converse within restricted topics are called chatbots.

- The Loebner Prize is an annual award given to the program that comes closest to passing the Turing test; researchers debate which kinds of questions would best distinguish humans from computers, but these often lead judges to misidentify humans as computers, in what is known as the confederate effect.

- Good Old Fashioned Artificial Intelligence (GOFAI) takes the position that intelligence is nothing more than complex symbol manipulation. The Chinese Room argument is intended to show that the GOFAI approach is misguided; the symbol grounding problem asserts that symbols only take on meaning outside of the system in which they are manipulated.

- The embodied cognition approach maintains that machines can only become truly intelligent if they have bodies that can sense and interact with the environment; this has led to research in the development of embodied conversational agents. The view of language as social interaction is important to this approach.

- CAPTCHAs are an example of computers using the Turing test to distinguish humans from bots. Humans can rapidly decipher these distorted letter sequences, but computers cannot; however, humans' ability to do this is still poorly understood.

In the 2013 movie *Her*, a lonely man falls in love with his computer's operating system (Ellison, Jonze, & Landay, 2013). Samantha doesn't just respond to voice commands, she engages him in wide-ranging conversation and expresses her emotions. She also displays personality and conscious self-awareness. Except for the fact that she has no physical form, Samantha is in all other aspects indistinguishable from a human being.

Language has been at the center of discussion on artificial intelligence since the field began in the 1950s. Today we're surrounded by "smart" devices that navigate our cars, find information for us, help us schedule appointments, and even vacuum floors. From the start, however, the Holy Grail of artificial intelligence has been to build a machine that's linguistically and socially indistinguishable in its behavior from a human being (Wallis, 2011). In this section, we go beyond the field of natural language to consider the question: Can machines think?

Talk to Me

In the mid-twentieth century, philosophers were already debating whether machines might someday become as intelligent as humans (Hoffmann, 2010). On the one hand, proponents of artificial intelligence argued that any cognitive processes performed by a brain could, in principle, be performed on a computer of sufficient complexity. On the other hand, opponents of artificial intelligence insisted that brains don't process information that same way that computers do, and thus only brains can give rise to truly intelligent behavior. The crux of the issue centers on your definition of intelligence. *The question of whether we can build machines that are truly intelligent* is known as the **AI debate**, and philosophers still dispute this issue.

British mathematician Alan Turing cleverly sidestepped this philosophical quagmire by instead proposing an operational definition for artificial intelligence (Cullen, 2009). Recall from Chapter 2 that scientists often define abstract concepts in terms of concrete measurements. Turing urged computer scientists to do the same. Specifically, he made *the proposal that a machine should be considered intelligent if its ability to hold a conversation is indistinguishable from that of a human being*. This criterion is now known as the **Turing test**.

Turing justified his test by insisting that we should hold computers to the same standard as humans (Schweizer, 2012). After all, philosophers can't agree on a definition for human intelligence either. Nevertheless, we go through life informally evaluating the intelligence of the people we interact with. How do we do that? Think about it: We judge people as smart or stupid based on their behavior, especially the way they talk. Thus, Turing brought linguistic ability to the forefront of the AI debate.

In Turing's day, synthetic speech software hadn't been developed yet, and even today it fools no one for the real thing; so Turing (1950) restricted the format of the conversation to text messaging instead. Imagine you're chatting online with two friends. Now suppose I told you that one of those friends was actually a computer. Do you think you could tell which was the computer and which was the human? Remember, the machine is trying to convince you it's human, so if you directly ask if it's a computer, it will deny it!

The original version of the Turing test works exactly this way. A human Judge communicates with two different Entities. One Entity is a human and is trying to convince you that he or she is human. The other Entity is a computer, and it's also trying to convince you that it's human. After a certain time period has elapsed, we ask the Judge to determine which Entity was the computer. Of course, the Judge has a 50% chance of guessing correctly, but if we run the test on multiple Judges, we can see if group performance is at or above chance. If the group can't reliably distinguish the computer from the human, then the computer passes the Turing test (Pfeiffer et al., 2011).

In an alternative version of the Turing test, each Judge converses with only one Entity, which could be either a person or a machine (Shah & Warwick, 2010). Again, if the Judges perform at chance level, the computer passes the test.

Figure 13.10 The Turing Test °

In the paired version, the Judge converses with two Entities and then decides which is the computer. In the single version, the Judge converses with one Entity and then decides if it is a human or a computer.

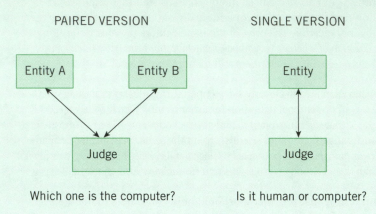

PAIRED VERSION

SINGLE VERSION

Entity A

Entity B

Entity

Judge

Judge

Which one is the computer?

Is it human or computer?

Passing the Test

Early advances in natural language processing lead to the development of computer programs that appeared capable of passing the Turing test. The most notable of these was ELIZA. Weizenbaum (1966) designed ELIZA to mimic a technique of Rogerian psychotherapy known as reflective listening. Instead of actively engaging in conversation, she waits for the client to write something, and then she responds to that.

ELIZA performs simple grammatical transformations such as changing *I* to *you*. So, if you write *I am feeling a little down today*, she will likely respond with something like *Tell me why you are feeling a little down today*. She also looks for certain keywords, such as terms for family members. So, if you write *My mother really frustrates me*, ELIZA is likely to respond with something like *Tell me about your mother*. She also deftly evades personal questions by insisting that she'd rather talk about you.

If you know in advance that you're texting with a computer, it's fairly easy to see through the simple tricks that Weizenbaum employed in designing ELIZA. However, if you enter into the conversation with the expectation that you're interacting with a human, ELIZA will give you no particular reason to suspect that she's nothing more than software. Certainly she'll make incongruent responses from time to time, but real people chatting on the Internet often spout nonsense as well. And if you're looking for someone to tell your problems to, ELIZA acts more sympathetic than most strangers.

The tendency to misidentify computer-generated text messages as coming from a human is known as the **ELIZA effect** (Shah & Warwick, 2010). The success of ELIZA led to the development of other similar programs. Today, *a computer program that can simulate an intelligent conversation within a restricted topic* is known as a **chatbot**, chatterbot, or conversational agent. In recent years, chatbots have been incorporated into all sorts of natural language programs, including programs that provide customer service online and that serve as virtual characters in video games. However, if you like to chat with strangers online, watch for malicious chatbots posing as real people that try to get you to reveal personal information such as credit card numbers or account passwords.

Eyes on the Prize

So far, no chatbot has been designed that convincingly mimics intelligent conversation over a wide range of topics, as most humans are capable of doing. Since 1991, however, computer scientists have been competing for the **Loebner Prize**, which is *an annual award presented to the computer program that comes closest to passing the Turing test* (Shah & Warwick, 2010).

This contest has spurred a debate about the best approach to take as the Judge in a Turing test. Some Judges take a "power" approach in which they assume the Entity is a computer until they are completely convinced that it's a human. In a study of the transcripts from the 2008 Loebner Prize competition, Shah and Warwick (2010) found that this approach wasn't the most effective. Rather, it tended to lead to what they called the **confederate effect**, which is *the tendency to misidentify human-generated text messages as coming from a computer*. (A confederate is an accomplice of the researcher in an experiment.) It seems that prior expectations strongly affect our perceptions in the Turing test, as they do in the real world.

Another approach is to ask questions that probe emotions or intuitions (French, 2012). For example, if you ask a group of native English speakers whether *Flugbots* is a good name for a new breakfast cereal, nearly all will say no because it just sounds ugly. This kind of question is designed to trip up a computer in a Turing test because it's not likely to have access to this sort of information. This type of question is an acknowledged weakness of the Turing test as a measure of artificial intelligence, since the machine fails not through lack of intelligence but rather lack of human experience (Cullen, 2009).

Back in the Chinese Room

In Chapter 5, we learned about the Chinese Room argument and the symbol grounding problem in the context of understanding how words get meaning. These issues were first presented as potential problems with the Turing test.

The original version of the Chinese Room argument, Searle (1980), asked us to imagine the following scenario. You're inside a room that has a narrow slit through which people outside the room pass slips of paper with Chinese writing on them. You don't know Chinese, but you have a book that allows you to match each input with the proper response. To people standing outside the room, you appear to know Chinese, but of course you don't. In other words, you passed the Chinese Turing test, even though all you did was manipulate symbols that were meaningless to you. ELIZA and similar programs are all Chinese rooms, according to Searle.

The Chinese Room argument wasn't just intended to challenge the validity of the Turing test. It also attacked *the assumption that many aspects of intelligence can be achieved through the complex manipulation of symbols*. This approach is commonly known as **Good Old Fashioned Artificial Intelligence**, or GOFAI for short (Rodríguez, Hermosillo, & Lara, 2012). According to Searle, the Chinese Room argument demonstrates that mere symbol manipulation can only lead to the appearance of intelligence but not to true understanding. GOFAI supporters conceded that Searle-in-the-room didn't understand Chinese, but some maintained that the room as a whole *did* understand Chinese, an argument that few philosophers or scientists accept nowadays (Ford, 2011).

The Chinese Room argument leads us to the symbol grounding problem, namely the question of how symbols get their meaning (Rodríguez et al., 2012). According to the GOFAI view, symbols acquire meaning through their relationships with other symbols. For example, every entry in a dictionary is defined in terms of other entries in the dictionary, so the whole enterprise seems to be circular, and yet somehow it works. However, English dictionaries are useful to us because we already know many of the words in them, and you certainly can't learn Chinese by memorizing a Chinese dictionary.

Figure 13.11   Setup for the Chinese Room Argument

The Chinese speaker outside the room thinks that the person inside the room must know Chinese. In fact, the person in the room knows no Chinese but only follows instructions in a manual.

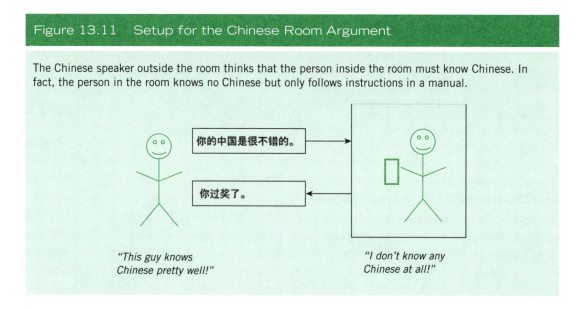

"This guy knows Chinese pretty well!"

"I don't know any Chinese at all!"

As White (2011a, 2011b) points out, symbol systems have both internal and external properties. Internally, symbols have relationships with other symbols inside the system. A dictionary is a symbol system with only internal properties. However, meaningful symbol systems also have external properties. That is, symbols refer to entities or events outside of the symbol system, and this is where their meaning comes from. A dictionary only makes sense if we've already established these external connections between words and their referents.

We still haven't solved the symbol grounding problem. But one approach that's gained currency in recent years is embodied cognition, which we learned about in Chapter 3. In this view, we derive meaning through our interaction with the world. For example, I know what the word *cold* means because I've experienced cold. Since a computer in a box has no experience of the world, it can't understand the symbols it manipulates.

Full Body Workout

The embodied cognition approach has led some researchers in recent years to propose that a truly intelligent machine must have a body with a full range of senses and with freedom to explore and act on its environment (Schweizer, 2012). In other words, it would need to be a robot, not disembodied software. This robot wouldn't be preprogrammed with knowledge of the world but rather it would be outfitted with the ability to learn through experience, just as a human child does. Even then, it's not clear that an intelligent robot's experiences of the world would be the same as those of a human.

Artificial intelligence researchers are also beginning to pay more attention to the fact that language is about much more than just exchanging information (Wallis, 2011). A recurrent theme in this textbook has been the observation that the purpose of most talk-in-interaction is to build and maintain social relationships. Furthermore, meaning in discourse is conveyed not just through words but also—and perhaps even more importantly—through vocal inflections and facial expressions.

Taking a sociocultural view of language use, some computer scientists have turned their attention to the concept of an **embodied conversational agent** (Wallis, 2011). This is *a spoken dialog system that also includes a virtual or physical body*. Many people find computer interactions more natural when they can look at a face that provides them with emotional cues.

Embodied conversational agents currently in use have a limited range of topics and are designed for very specific types of interactions, such as helping online customers place orders. They are also frequently perceived as being cold or condescending (Wallis, 2011). This is because their conversational abilities are still highly scripted. They also don't have the capacity to read their human interlocutor's facial expressions to sense when offense has been taken. Instead of assuaging their partner's hurt feelings, they continue with their scripts, only aggravating the irritation. Machines still have a lot to learn about what makes humans tick.

Turning the Tables on the Turing Test

Humans only account for a portion of online activity. The Internet is full of intelligent software casually known as bots that interact with other bots without any sort of supervision from humans. Bots run the stock market, buying and trading faster than any human can, making fortunes for their masters. They sign up for free email accounts from which to send spam. Countries and companies unleash bots on their enemies and competitors to spy on them. Organized crime rings release bots into social media to flood them with advertisements or to go on phishing expeditions for private information.

When websites need to distinguish between human and computer visitors, they turn to the Turing test. One common test for humanness is the CAPTCHA, which stands for Completely Automated Public Turing test to tell Computers and Humans Apart (Hannagan et al., 2012). Since computers use them to detect humans, CAPTCHAs are sometimes referred to as reverse Turing tests.

CAPTCHAs not only reveal the limitations of the current state of artificial intelligence, they also show us how little we still understand about human perception and cognition (Hannagan et al., 2012). It takes relatively little distortion of an alphanumeric sequence to stump a bot, while humans usually have little difficulty deciphering these twisted letters. Still, it's not clear how people accomplish this task.

Hannigan and colleagues used a priming task to test the hypothesis that our extensive experience with reading in difficult situations, such as reading terrible handwriting, enables us to quickly recognize distorted text (Hannagan et al., 2012). Recall from Chapter 2 that priming refers to enhanced recall due to previous exposure. CAPTCHA primes led to only small decreases in priming compared with printed primes, lending support for the hypothesis.

Clearly, computers still have a long way to go before they can match us in the everyday tasks we perform with seeming effortlessness. This observation brings us to the great paradox of artificial intelligence. Tasks that are difficult for humans, such as solving math problems or winning at chess, tend to be easy for computers. Meanwhile, the easy stuff we do without conscious thought still stumps even the most powerful computer.

In Sum

With the invention of the computer in the mid-twentieth century, philosophers and scientists began to take the idea of artificial intelligence seriously. The Turing

Figure 13.12 CAPTCHA Priming Task

Each trial began with a mask for 500 milliseconds, followed by either a CAPTCHA or printed prime for 50 milliseconds. Immediately following that, either a related or unrelated target appeared on screen and remained until the participant responded.

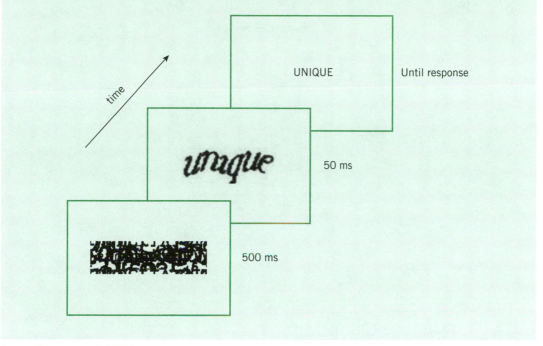

UNIQUE — Until response

50 ms

500 ms

time

Source: Hannagan et al. (2012).

test considers conversational ability to be the hallmark of human intelligence and the appropriate measure of machine intelligence. Many people willingly respond to ELIZA and other conversational agents as if they were human, and this observation is known as the ELIZA effect. On the other hand, judges in a Turing test often misidentify humans as computers, reflecting the way that expectations guide perception more generally. Good Old Fashioned Artificial Intelligence proposes that intelligence can be achieved through complex symbol manipulation, but the Chinese Room argument refutes that claim. The embodied cognition approach contends that machines can only become truly intelligent like humans if they have bodies that can sense and act on the environment. To protect against attacks by malicious software, many websites require their users to prove themselves as human, often by using a reverse Turing test such as CAPTCHA. Little is known about why humans are so good at deciphering distorted text while computers quickly fail at the task.

Figure 13.13 CAPTCHA and Printed Primes

Reaction times were faster in the Related than the Unrelated conditions for both CAPTCHA and Printed primes. A similar pattern of results was obtained for measures of error rate as well. Since the primes were only shown for 50 milliseconds each, these results support the hypothesis that CAPTCHAs are deciphered rapidly in the early stages of reading.

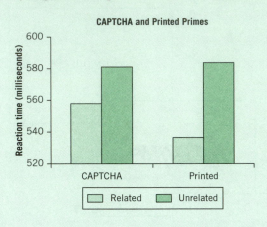

Source: Hannagan et al. (2012).

Review Questions

1. What is the AI debate? How does the Turing test propose to settle that debate?

2. What is a chatbot? What is the ELIZA effect, and what is it named after? Explain the Loebner Prize and the confederate effect.

3. Explain Good Old Fashioned Artificial Intelligence and its relevance to the Chinese Room argument and the symbol grounding problem.

4. Why are CAPTCHAs considered a "reverse" Turing test?

Thought Questions

1. If you were a Judge in a Turing test, what sorts of questions would you ask? You can even conduct a Turing test yourself by finding a version of ELIZA online. How well does she respond to your questions?

2. Have you ever suspected that someone on a social media site was a chatbot instead of a human? What made you suspicious? Try exploring your intuitions on this.

Google It! Chatbots

Many versions of ELIZA are available online. Engage in a conversation with her and try to find patterns that she uses to respond in a seemingly intelligent manner. You can also find plenty of videos on the Turing test and the Loebner Prize on YouTube. While you're on YouTube, look up some demos of a chatbot or an embodied conversational agent. Do any of them pass the Turing test?

CONCLUSION

"The report of my death was an exaggeration," wrote Mark Twain in response to the premature publication of his obituary. The same can be said of the English language, which is not only alive but thriving. Pedants and purists may complain that the younger generation is destroying the language with texting slang like ILBL8 and W84M, but nothing could be farther from the truth.

Languages are like living organisms. They're complex systems that are constantly adapting to a changing environment. Only dead languages never change. But then again, nobody speaks a dead language.

All living languages are in constant flux. You don't talk like your grandparents, and they don't talk like theirs. When Shakespeare wrote, "There is a tide in the affairs of men, which taken at the flood, leads on to fortune," he was being poetic but not pretentious. The Bard wrote in the colloquial English of his day, but the language has shape-shifted over the last four centuries.

You, the readers of this book, are the new stewards of the language, the ones who'll remake it to meet the needs of a future we can scarcely imagine. Be bold, be creative. Go ahead and bend the rules—they won't break! After all, the joy of language play is the thing that makes us uniquely human.

CROSS-CULTURAL PERSPECTIVE: Typing and Texting in Other Languages

The QWERTY keyboard was designed with the English language in mind. To prevent typewriter keys from jamming during rapid typing, its inventor placed common letter pairs on opposite sides of the keyboard. While QWERTY is a reasonably efficient layout for typing English, it's not necessarily well suited to other languages. Still, it's become the standard keyboard throughout most of the world.

Shortly after the typewriter was invented in the United States, it was introduced to Europe with only minor tweaks (Bi, Smith, & Zhai, 2012). German-speaking countries swapped the Y and Z keys to make a QWERTZ keyboard. Meanwhile, French-speaking countries made two swaps —A with Q and Z with W—to form the AZERTY keyboard. In both cases, additional keys were added for special letters used in those languages.

Typewriters work well with alphabetic scripts, but not with the logographic systems used in East Asia. There's no straightforward way to accommodate thousands of characters on a two-handed keyboard. As a result, the typewriter never caught on in Japan or China. However, the widespread availability of the personal computer in the 1980s changed all that.

During the twentieth century, both Japan and China had developed romanization schemes for writing their languages in the Roman alphabet, *romaji* and *pinyin,* respectively. There was no intention to replace native scripts, but these schemes do provide a consistent way of representing Japanese or Chinese names in European languages like English.

Figure 13.14   The QWERTZ Keyboard

The QWERTZ keyboard is used in German-speaking countries and other parts of central Europe.

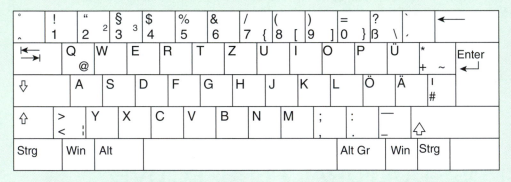

Source: Kozlik, Neumann, and Kunde (2013).

The Japanese learn *romaji* in school, and the Chinese learn *pinyin*; so the letters on the QWERTY keyboard are familiar. All that was needed was a program to convert *romaji* into Japanese script and *pinyin* into Chinese script. In short, the Japanese and Chinese leapfrogged over the typewriter era. In the span of about a decade, they transitioned from cultures where nearly all documents were written by hand to cultures where nearly all documents were composed by word processor.

Typing in Japanese or Chinese is a two-step process. First you type a word or phrase in Roman letters. Then you press a key—typically the spacebar—to tell the computer to convert the letter string into the native script. In the case of homophones, a list of possible equivalents appears, and you press a number to make your selection. Japanese and Chinese word processors also use predictive text software to make good guesses, and so you don't always have to type the entire word or phrase before the software can complete the transcription for you. Texting on a cell phone keypad works similarly. You type in *romaji* or *pinyin*, and software converts it into Japanese or Chinese.

In China, a texting slang has evolved that parallels the textisms of young Americans. Homophonic plays on words are common, swapping Chinese characters with similar pronunciations. As a result, older people often have difficulty understanding the texts of younger folk, just as is the case in the United States.

It's also not uncommon to see letters and numbers mixed in with Chinese-character text messages. For example, MM stands for *mèimei*, written 妹妹 and meaning "sister," while GG stands for *gēge*, written 哥哥 and meaning "brother." These are common terms of address among members of the young, tech-savvy generation in China.

Just as you might text 4U, G2G, or CUL8R, young Chinese texters also use letters and numbers for their sound value. For instance, the number sequence 520 sounds sort of like "I love you" in Chinese. But if you're not ready to commit, it's to time say 886—"goodbye!"

KEY TERMS

AI debate

Assistive reading software

Augmentative
and alternative
communication

Automatic speech
recognition

Chatbot

Confederate effect

Corpus

ELIZA effect

Embodied conversational
agent

Good Old Fashioned
Artificial Intelligence

Human factors

Inattentional blindness

Incidental-recognition-
memory paradigm

Loebner prize

Multitap

Multitasking

Natural language
processing

Need-to-listen hypothesis

P300

Phatic communication

Predictive text

Question-answering
system

Speech-generating device

Subjective well-being

Synthesized speech

Textism

Turing test

Visual scene displays

Voice banking

GLOSSARY

Accuracy: The percentage of correct responses over a set of trials. (2.3)

Acquired dyslexia: An impairment in reading ability due to brain damage in a person who had previously been a skilled reader. (8.2)

Active voice: A sentence structure in which the agent is mapped onto the subject position. (6.1)

Adaptive control hypothesis: A proposal suggesting that bilinguals' constant need to monitor and control their languages leads to benefits in nonverbal cognition. (9.3)

Affricate: A consonant that is produced by momentarily blocking the airflow and then releasing it through a tight constriction. (4.1)

Age of arrival: The time when the learner receives the first intensive exposure to the second language in the country where it is spoken. (9.4)

Agent: The entity that causes the event portrayed in a sentence to occur. (6.1)

Aging positivity effect: The observation that people tend to get happier as they get older. (11.4)

Agreement: A set of syntactic devices for linking related elements within and between sentences. (6.1)

AI debate: The question of whether we can build machines that are truly intelligent. (13.4)

Alarm call: A vocalization to warn other members of the group about an approaching predator. (1.1)

Alphabet: A writing system that represents each phoneme with a different symbol. (8.1)

Alphabet knowledge: An understanding of the name of each letter and the sounds associated with it. (11.2)

Alphabetic principle: The process by which readers associate written symbols with speech sounds. (8.3)

Alveolar: A consonant produced by pressing the blade of the tongue against the fleshy area behind the upper teeth. (4.1)

Alveolar ridge: The fleshy region of the mouth covering the bone where the upper teeth are anchored. (4.1)

American Sign Language: The sign language used by many deaf communities in the United States and Canada. (10.1)

Amplitude: The amount of change that a wave undergoes during one cycle. (3.1)

Amygdala: A subcortical structure of the temporal lobe that plays a role in regulating emotion and memory. (2.4)

Anaphor: A word or phrase that refers back to a previously mentioned entity in the discourse. (7.3)

Anaphora: The process of an anaphor referring back to an antecedent. (7.3)

Antecedent: The entity in a discourse that an anaphor refers back to. (7.3)

Anterior: Toward the front of the brain. (2.4)

Anterior cingulate cortex: A region deep inside the longitudinal fissure that is believed to be involved in error detection and monitoring conflict. (4.2)

Anterior insula: A region deep within the lateral sulcus that has been implicated in language processing. (4.2)

Anthropomorphism: The tendency to assign human-like qualities to animals, natural phenomena, and even abstract concepts. (1.4)

Aperiodic sound: A sound with no regularly repeating pattern. (3.1)

Aphasia: A language deficit due to brain damage. (1.4)

Approximant: A consonant that is produced by diverting the airflow without constricting it. (4.1)

Arbitrariness of the sign: The observation that the sound of a word gives virtually no information about its meaning. (5.1)

Arbitrary symbol: A symbol that bears no resemblance to what it refers to. (1.2).

Arcuate fasciculus: A band of neural fibers extending from the temporal lobe to the frontal lobe. (4.2)

Arousal: The physiological component of emotion that represents the degree to which the body is ready for action. (12.4)

Aspiration: The puff of air accompanying the release of some plosives. (3.2)

Assistive reading software: A computer program that extracts text from a scanned document and then converts the text to synthesized speech. (13.3)

Attentional blink: The case in which attending to one stimulus leads to reduced detection of a second stimulus. (12.4)

Auditory perturbation technique: A procedure in which participants repeat syllables into a microphone and listen through headphones as their voice is modified by a computer. (4.3)

Auditory processing deficit hypothesis: The proposal that dyslexia stems from an underlying difficulty in accurately detecting and remembering rapid sound changes. (8.3)

Augmentative and alternative communication: An umbrella term for strategies and devices that help those with language impairments to engage in social interactions. (13.3)

Automatic speech recognition: The machine process of converting spoken language into text. (13.3)

Backchannels: Signals like "mmhmm" and "uhhuh" from the listener that indicate engagement and encourage the speaker to continue. (7.1)

Balanced bilingual: A person who grows up speaking two languages and can communicate equally well in either language. (9.1)

Basal ganglia: A set of subcortical structures located where the brain stem joins the cerebrum that are responsible for procedural learning and the execution of routine actions. (2.4)

Base frequency effect: The observation that the frequency effect of the base form extends to its inflected forms. (5.3)

Basic level category: A class of objects or events that is cognitively salient and is neither too specific nor too general. (11.2)

Basilar membrane: A structure that extends inside the length of the cochlea and divides it in two. (3.1)

Beat: The average time it takes to produce a syllable, as set by the speaking rate of the last turn. (7.1)

Behaviorism: A school of psychology that emphasizes the role of learning in shaping behavior. (1.4)

Between-subjects design: An experiment design that assigns each participant to only one condition. (2.2)

Bilabial: A consonant sound that is produced by bringing the upper and lower lips together. (4.1)

Bilingual: Someone able to speak two or more languages. (9.1)

Bilingual accommodation: Sensitivity to the identity or ethnic background of the interlocutor in selecting a language to use. (9.1)

Bilingual disadvantage: The observation that bilinguals have smaller vocabularies in each of their languages and more difficulty retrieving words compared with monolinguals. (9.2)

Bimodal bilingual: Someone able to communicate in both spoken and signed language. (10.3)

Bottom-up process: A process that is driven solely by the input without consideration of context or expectations. (5.4)

Brainstem: The interior portion of the brain that is charged with regulating body functions and keeping the body alive. (2.3)

Bridging inference: The use of logic or real-world experience to fill in gaps in a discourse. (7.3)

Broca's aphasia: A type of aphasia characterized by disjointed or ungrammatical speech. (1.4)

Broca's area: An area of the brain that plays a role in speech production. (1.4)

Burst: A period of active text composition bounded by pauses at both ends. (8.4)

Business talk: Caregiver speech that consists mainly of instructions and prohibitions. (11.1)

Canonical babbling: Prelinguistic vocalization characterized by sequences of clearly formed consonant-vowel syllables. (4.4)

Canonical word order: The typical sequence of sentence elements. (6.1)

Categorical perception: The process of experiencing continuously changing stimuli as belonging to two or more discrete sets. (3.2)

Category anaphor: A noun phrase anaphor that names the category that the antecedent is a member of. (7.3)

Centrality of syntax: The view that the ability to organize words into phrases and sentences according to recursive rules is the distinguishing feature of language. (1.3)

Cerebellum: The walnut-sized structure behind the brainstem that is responsible for coordinating movement. (2.3)

Cerebral cortex: The outer covering of the cerebrum where most of the brain activity giving rise to conscious experience takes place. (2.4)

Cerebral plasticity: The brain's ability to modify its structure in response to new experiences. (9.4)

Chatbot: A computer program that can simulate an intelligent conversation within a restricted topic. (13.4)

Childhood apraxia of speech: A condition in which children experience severe difficulty in producing speech even though their cognitive, perceptual, and motor skills are otherwise in the normal range. (4.4)

Chinese Room argument: A demonstration of why meaning cannot arise solely from the relationships among symbols. (5.1)

Chunking: A process that groups meaningless items into larger meaningful units in order to increase working memory capacity. (1.2)

Circumlocution: The use of a roundabout description in place of a single word or phrase. (11.4)

Classifier: A grammatical word used in conjunction with a noun to indicate its shape or function. (12.2)

Clause: A simple sentence that is part of a larger complex sentence. (6.1)

Cleft sentence: A syntactic structure that attaches an introductory clause to the beginning of a sentence for the purpose of highlighting one of the participants in the event. (6.1)

Cloze probability: The likelihood that a person will complete a sentence with a particular word. (6.2)

Coarticulation: The process of overlapping phonemes in the speech stream. (3.2)

Cochlea: The organ of auditory sensation. (3.1)

Cochlear implant: An electronic device attached to an external microphone that directly stimulates the auditory nerve. (3.1)

Code blending: Discourse in which signed and spoken language are produced simultaneously. (10.3)

Codeswitching: A change from one language to another within a single interaction. (9.1)

Cognates: Words in two languages that have similar form and meaning. (9.2)

Cognitive reserve: The notion that engaging in stimulating mental or physical activity on a regular basis helps maintain cognitive functioning as we age and protects against dementia. (9.3)

Coherence: The use of schemas and logical relations to bind the sentences of a discourse together. (7.3)

Cohesion: The use of linguistic devices to tie together the sentences of a discourse. (7.3)

Cohort: The set of all words that begin with the same sequence of phonemes. (5.4)

Cohort model: A model of word recognition proposing that listeners initially consider all possible word matches to the incoming speech stream but identify the word as soon as a recognition point is reached. (5.4)

Collocation: A sequence of words that frequently go to together. (6.4)

Common ground: The pool of information that all participants of a conversation share. (7.1)

Communication: Any behavior on the part of one organism intended to influence the emotions, thoughts, or behaviors of another organism. (1.1)

Component: A specific ERP waveform that is tied to a particular cognitive process. (2.4)

Computational model: A computer program that simulates a cognitive process in a manner that is consistent with what is currently known about human cognition. (4.3)

Concept: A mental representation of some sort of statistical regularity in our experience. (5.1)

Conditioned head turn technique: An experimental method that trains infants to turn their heads in a particular direction when they detect a change in the auditory stimulus. (3.3)

Conduction aphasia: A language disorder characterized by preserved speech perception and production capabilities but with a marked difficulty in repeating spoken language. (4.2)

Confederate effect: The tendency to misidentify human-generated text messages as coming from a computer. (13.4)

Configuration hypothesis: The proposal that the language processing system goes first with a literal interpretation of an idiom unless context biases it toward the idiomatic interpretation. (12.3)

Connectionist network: A computer program that models statistical learning. (6.4)

Connotation: The emotion evoked by a word. (12.4)

Conspecific: A member of the same species. (1.1)

Constraint-based model: The proposal that syntactic analysis and semantic interpretation occur simultaneously and influence each other. (6.2)

Construct: A label given to a set of observations that seem to be related. (2.1)

Construction integration model: A theory that explains a reader's ability to make inferences based on the linguistic input, the reader's real-world knowledge, and working memory constraints. (11.3)

Content words: Words that carry the bulk of meaning in language. (1.4)

Contextual abstraction: The use of surrounding text to determine the meaning of a word. (11.3)

Continuity debate: The question of whether human language evolved gradually or rapidly. (1.3)

Continuity theories: Theories that propose a steady transition from animal communication systems to human language. (1.3)

Control condition: The group that is not given the experimental treatment but rather provides a baseline for comparison with the experimental condition. (2.2)

Conversational fillers: Words like "uh" and "um" that are semantically empty but are used to signal planning difficulties. (7.1)

Cooperative principle: The proposal that speakers should follow social norms to tailor their utterances to fit the current needs of the conversation. (7.3)

Coprolalia: A condition characterized by compulsive swearing due to a brain disorder. (12.4)

Corpus: A large selection of text or speech that is used to train natural language processing software. (13.3)

Corpus callosum: A band of fibers connecting the left and right hemispheres, allowing for communication between the two hemispheres of the brain. (2.4)

Correlation: A mathematical technique that searches for relationships among variables in a set of data. (2.1)

Cospeech gestures: Hand movements that speakers make while they talk. (7.4)

Count noun: A noun that represents an object with a consistent shape and therefore can be counted. (12.2)

Creole: A full-fledged language based on a pidgin. (1.3)

Critical period hypothesis: The idea that children have a biological predisposition to learn languages that they lose around puberty. (9.4)

Cross-language priming: The situation in which a word in one language aids the retrieval of a word with a related meaning in another language. (9.2)

Cross-situational word learning: The ability to learn to associate novel words with novel objects even in cases of referential ambiguity by tracking co-occurrence statistics. (5.2)

Cultural model: The position that deafness is within the normal range of human variation and provides an alternative experience that is visually oriented and centered on signed language. (10.4)

Culture: A system of learned behaviors and thought processes shared by a group. (10.4)

Dative construction: A syntactic structure that entails the meaning of doing something for the benefit of someone else. (6.1)

Deaf community sign language: A sign language that naturally emerges whenever a group of unrelated deaf individuals is brought together to form a community. (10.1)

Decoding: The process of converting printed symbols into a spoken word format. (11.3)

Decontextualization: The distancing of thought, language, and behavior from the current situation. (7.2)

Deduction: The logical process of going from general statements to specific examples. (2.1)

Deep orthography: The situation in which spelling and pronunciation are poorly matched. (8.1)

Default mode network: The system of brain regions that are active when our attention turns inward. (12.3)

Delayed auditory feedback technique: A procedure in which research participants speak while listening through headphones to their own voice, which is delayed a fraction of a second. (4.3)

Delayed match-to-sample task: An experimental procedure in which a participant first sees a target item and then after a delay is asked to choose which of two novel items is more like the target. (12.1)

Delayed recall task: A memory task in which participants hear or see a series of items and then recall those items after a delay. (2.3)

Denotation: The literal meaning of a word. (12.4)

Dependent variable: The measurement of the response each participant makes to the treatment in an experiment. (2.2)

Derivational suffix: A suffix that changes the meaning and grammatical category of a word. (5.3)

Descriptive talk: Caregiver speech that involves labeling objects of joint attention and commenting on them. (11.1)

Developmental cascade: The observation that early developmental processes in one area have an impact on later developmental processes in other areas. (11.1)

Developmental dyslexia: A reading disability in children that cannot be attributed to a lack of intelligence, motivation, or educational opportunity. (8.3)

Developmental language delay: A condition marked by slower than normal development of expressive language during the first few years of life even though hearing, motor, and cognitive functions are otherwise in the normal range. (7.4)

Diffusion tensor imaging: An fMRI technique that enables researchers to trace the pathways of white matter tracts. (8.3)

Digit span task: A procedure that assesses short-term memory capacity by having research participants repeat lists of digits. (2.1)

Dimensional model of emotion: The proposal that emotional content can be described in terms of arousal (high-low) and valence (positive-negative). (12.4)

Diphthong: A vowel combination that is perceived as a single phoneme. (4.1)

Direct access model: The proposal that the nonliteral meaning of a figurative expression can be accessed without considering the literal meaning first. (12.3)

Direct realism: The theory that we have direct awareness of the world because the sensory input is sufficiently rich for us to completely recover the object of perception. (3.4)

Direct route: The process of going straight from the written word to its meaning. (8.2)

Discontinuity theories: Theories that propose a sudden transition from animal communication systems to human language. (1.3)

Discourse: A language structure consisting of a sequence of sentences that are ordered according to rules. (1.2)

Displacement: The ability to refer to things and events beyond the here and now. (1.2)

Distributional learning: The tracking of the frequency and location of various sounds in the speech stream. (3.3)

Dominance hierarchy: A social system in which each member of a group knows who ranks above and who ranks below. (1.1)

Dominant language: The language of political and economic power within a bilingual society. (9.1)

Dorsal: Toward the back. (2.4)

Dorsal stream: A left-hemisphere processing pathway that links the incoming speech signal with speech motor programs. (4.3)

Dorsolateral prefrontal cortex: An area of the brain involved in executive control. (9.3)

Dual lexicon model: The proposal that there are two mental lexicons, one for the dorsal sound-to-action stream and another for the ventral sound-to-meaning stream. (5.3)

Dual route model: The proposal that readers can either first access a word's meaning and then its pronunciation or else first access a word's pronunciation and then its meaning. (8.2)

Duality of patterning: A structuring process that takes units at a lower level and combines them according to rules into new units at a higher level. (1.2)

Dysarthria: A motor speech disorder due to neural injury that is characterized by poor articulation of phonemes and prosody. (4.2)

Elderspeak: A manner of speaking that young people adopt when addressing older adults who appear to have difficulties with hearing or language perception. (11.4)

Electroencephalography: A technique that uses electrodes attached to various locations on the scalp to record voltage fluctuations originating in the brain. (2.4)

ELIZA effect: The tendency to misidentify computer-generated text messages as coming from a human. (13.4)

Ellipsis: The deletion of sentence elements that can be inferred from context. (7.4)

Embodied cognition: The point of view arguing that cognition is rooted in the body's interactions with the world around it. (3.4)

Embodied conversational agent: A spoken dialogue system that also includes a virtual or physical body. (13.4)

Embodied representation: A symbol that is understood in terms of the perceptual and motor experiences it evokes. (5.1)

Embodied semantics: The proposal that we understand the meaning of a word by simulating it in the sensorimotor cortex. (5.3)

Endogenous oscillators: Neural circuits that fire at regular intervals and thus serve as internal timekeepers for the brain. (7.1)

English language learners: Children entering school whose native language is not English. (9.4)

Entrainment: The synchronization of rhythmic behavior in social interactions. (7.1)

Episode: The fundamental building block of a story. (7.2)

Error rate: The percentage of incorrect responses over a set of trials. (2.3)

Ethologist: A scientist who studies animal behavior. (1.1)

Euphemism: A word that has the same meaning as a taboo word but without the emotional connotation. (12.4)

Event-related potential: A waveform extracted from the EEG that signifies a specific cognitive process. (2.4)

Executive control: The management of cognitive resources to perform tasks efficiently. (9.3)

Executive functions: Memory allocation, planning, inhibition, and other cognitive processes necessary for guiding intentional behavior. (7.2)

Exner's area: A brain region located in the left frontal premotor cortex just above Broca's area that stores the motor programs for handwriting gestures. (8.4)

Expansion stage: The period from four to six months of age when infants produce a variety of different sounds. (4.4)

Experiment: A tightly controlled situation that has been intentionally designed to test a hypothesis. (2.2)

Experimental condition: The group that is given a treatment to test the hypothesis. (2.2)

Experimental method: A means for systematically testing hypotheses in controlled situations. (2.1)

Expository discourse: A monologue that provides a factual description or an explanation of an event. (11.3)

Expressive aphasia: A condition in which brain damage leads to a loss of speech production without a loss of speech comprehension. (4.2)

Face: The personal need to be viewed as competent and to have one's actions unimpeded by others. (7.3)

Falsifiability criterion: The principle that a theory must make predictions that have the potential to be disconfirmed by data. (2.1)

Fast mapping: The ability to learn a new word after only one or a few exposures. (5.2)

Feedback control: The process that adjusts the forward trajectory based on real-time information about the likely success of the movement. (4.3)

Feedforward control: The process that provides the general motor plan for moving a body part toward a goal position. (4.3)

Feedforward model: A model in which each process is performed in a serial fashion. (5.4)

Field study: A study conducted under natural circumstances outside of the laboratory. (2.1)

Figurative language: Any expression whose intended meaning is different from its literal meaning. (12.3)

Fingerspelling: A method for representing the letters of the alphabet with hand gestures. (10.3)

First language attrition: The situation where a bilingual favors the second language to the extent that first language ability is lost. (9.4)

Fis phenomenon: A condition in which a child can clearly hear a distinction between two phonemes but uses only one of them when speaking. (4.4)

Fixation: Momentary gaze of the eyes on a single location while reading. (2.3)

Flanker task: An experimental procedure in which participants respond to the direction of the central arrow in an array, regardless of direction the other arrows are pointing. (9.3)

fMRI: A brain-imaging technique that makes use of differences in magnetic properties between oxygenated and deoxygenated hemoglobin to track blood flow. (2.4)

Focal color: The best example of a color name and the center of a color category. (12.1)

Formal gender system: A pattern of classifying nouns and pronouns that arbitrarily assigns a gender to inanimate objects. (12.2)

Formant: A band of high-amplitude sound above the fundamental frequency. (3.2)

Formant transition: A modification of a formant due to a preceding or following consonant. (3.2)

Forward model: A model that explains sensory suppression by proposing that each time the sensorimotor system generates a motor command it also generates a predicted sensory consequence for comparison against the actual sensory input. (4.3)

Fovea: The region of the retina directly behind the pupil where vision is most acute. (8.2)

FOXP2: A gene found widely among vertebrates that plays a role in brain development as well as serving other functions. (1.3)

Frames-then-content model: A theory that explains babbling in terms of repeated jaw movements. (4.4)

Free recall task: A memory task in which participants are allowed to repeat the items in any order. (2.3)

Frequency: The number of wavelengths that pass by a given point in a given amount of time. (3.1)

Frequency effect: The observation that low-frequency words are fixated longer than high-frequency words. (8.2)

Fricative: A consonant that is produced by constricting the airstream to create friction. (3.2)

Frontal lobe: The lobe at the front of the head that generates motor movement and is also responsible for planning and decision making. (2.4)

Function words: Words that express grammatical relationships but carry little meaning. (1.4)

Fundamental frequency: The lowest frequency produced by a vibrating object. (3.1)

Fuzzy-logical model of perception: A theory that proposes we arrive at perceptual decisions by matching the relative goodness of various sensory inputs against the values of particular prototypes stored in memory. (3.4)

Garden path model: A two-staged model of sentence processing in which syntactic analysis precedes semantic interpretation. (6.2)

Garden path sentence: A sentence that deviates significantly from expected structure, making it difficult to process. (6.2)

Gating task: A procedure in which participants are presented with increasingly longer increments of a word and asked to guess what they think the word will be. (5.4)

Gaze contingency paradigm: An experimental procedure in which a narrow window of text surrounding the fixation point is displayed on a computer screen. (8.2)

General auditory framework: The assumption that speech perception operates by means of the same mechanisms that have evolved in humans and other animals to perceive environmental sounds. (3.4)

Givenness: The degree to which an antecedent is likely to be within the memory and attention span of the listener. (7.3)

Glottal stop: A consonant produced by constricting the vocal folds. (4.1)

Good Old Fashioned Artificial Intelligence: The assumption that many aspects of intelligence can be achieved through the complex manipulation of symbols. (13.4)

Gooing stage: The period from two to four months of age when infants produce syllable-like sounds in the back of the vocal tract. (4.4)

Graded salience hypothesis: The proposal that the literal meaning of an utterance is processed first but that an ironic meaning may be considered in parallel when the context biases such an interpretation. (12.3)

Gray matter: Brain tissue that is mainly composed of neuron cell bodies and whose function is to process information. (8.3)

Gricean maxims: Aspects of a speaker's utterance that the listener attends to in deciding whether to accept the statement at face value. (7.3)

Grue: A single basic color term in a language that includes both blue and green. (12.1)

Gyrus: A protruding region of the cerebral cortex. (4.2)

Hair cells: Specialized cells of the basilar membrane that are sensitive to movements in the cochlear fluid. (3.1)

Handshape: The configuration of the fingers during the production of a sign. (10.2)

Hard palate: The bony region along the roof of the mouth. (4.1)

Hayes model: An influential theory of the writing process that has guided research since the 1980s. (8.4)

Heritage language: The language spoken in an immigrant's country of origin. (9.1)

Hertz: Cycles per second. (3.1)

Heuristic: A mental shortcut to problem solving that usually, but not always, gives the correct answer. (6.2)

Hierarchical structure in advance planning: A programming approach that makes a general plan at the highest level while restricting the scope of planning at lower levels. (6.3)

High attachment: The parsing strategy of attaching a prepositional phrase to the verb. (6.2)

High-amplitude sucking technique: An experimental procedure that measures the frequency of an infant's sucking on a non-nutritive nipple. (3.3)

Hippocampus: A subcortical structure of the temporal lobe that plays an important role in memory and learning. (2.4)

Holophrase: A single vocalization or gesture that refers to the entire situation and not to the specific objects and events in that situation. (1.1)

Homesign: A gestural communication system for interactions with a deaf family member. (10.1)

Homographs: Words that are spelled the same but pronounced differently. (8.1)

Homonym advantage: The observation that children learn a new word faster when it sounds like a familiar word. (11.2)

Homophones: Words with the same pronunciation but different meanings. (8.1)

Hopeful monster hypothesis: The idea that a single mutation could lead to a rapid transition from one form to another. (1.3)

Horizontal transmission: The learning of language and culture through interactions with peers. (10.4)

Human factors: An interdisciplinary field that studies the ways that people interact with the machines they use. (13.2)

Hypothesis: A prediction about future observations that is derived from a theory. (2.1)

Iambic: A weak-strong stress pattern. (5.2)

Iconic gesture: A movement of one or both upper limbs to imitate an action. (7.4)

Iconic symbol: A symbol that bears a clear resemblance to what it refers to. (1.2)

Iconicity: The degree to which a symbol resembles its referent. (10.2)

Idiom: A formulaic phrase whose meaning cannot be derived from the meanings of the words that make it up. (12.3)

Illocution: The speaker's intended meaning behind the utterance. (7.3)

Immediate recall task: A memory task in which participants hear or see a series of items and then repeat them without delay. (2.3)

Implicit learning: A form of learning that takes place outside of conscious awareness. (2.3)

Implicit prosody hypothesis: The proposal that skilled readers organize the material they read into prosodic phrases similar to the way they would when they speak. (8.2)

Inattentional blindness: The failure to perceive or remember a stimulus directly in the visual field because another cognitively demanding task is being performed. (13.1)

Incidental recognition memory paradigm: A procedure in which participants are tested on their ability to remember items that they were not specifically instructed to pay attention to. (13.1)

Incomplete first-language acquisition: The failure to attain full native-speaker proficiency of the first language. (9.1)

Incremental model: A model in which the processing at one step is still underway when the processing at the next step begins. (6.3)

Independent variable: The various types of treatment given to the different groups in an experiment. (2.2)

Indexical gesture: A movement of an upper limb to point out a referent in a conversation. (7.4)

Indirect access model: The proposal that the literal meaning of a figurative expression is always accessed first before a nonliteral interpretation is considered. (12.3)

Indirect route: The process of accessing the meaning of a written word by first reconstructing its pronunciation. (8.2)

Indirect speech act: An utterance whose literal and intended messages are not the same. (7.3)

Induction: The logical process of going from specific examples to general statements. (2.1)

Infant-directed speech: A manner of speaking to infants that attracts their attention and helps them learn language. (3.3)

Inferior: Toward the bottom of the brain. (2.4)

Inflectional suffix: A suffix that is added to words for the purposes of grammar. (5.3)

Innatism: The proposal that perceptual and cognitive processes are not influenced by language in any way. (12.1)

Input/output asymmetry: The observation that language perception processes are generally intact even when language production processes are impaired. (11.4)

Interactive model: A model in which higher and lower levels of processing influence each other. (5.4)

Interdental: A consonant that is produced by protruding the tongue between the upper and lower teeth. (4.1)

Interference hypothesis: The proposal that the bilingual disadvantage can be explained in terms of interference from translation equivalents in the unused language. (9.2)

Interference inhibition: The ability to ignore distracting or misleading information. (9.3)

Interlingual homographs: Words in two languages that have similar form but different meanings. (9.2)

Interlocutors: The participants in a conversation. (7.1)

Intonational phrase boundary: A prosodic cue consisting of a change in pitch, usually downward, and a lengthening of the final syllable that signals the end of a syntactic phrase. (6.4)

Irreversible sentence: A sentence that no longer makes real-world sense if the agent and patient swap subject and object positions. (6.1)

Isolated spelling disorder. A specific and significant impairment in spelling skills even though reading ability is in the normal range: (8.4)

Jaw perturbation technique: A procedure that involves attaching a robotic arm to the jaw of the research participant, who articulates syllables as the robot applies an upward or downward force. (4.3)

Joint attention: A situation in which all participants in an interaction have focused their attention on the same object or event. (5.2)

KE family: An extended family living in London that exhibits a language disorder appearing to have a genetic cause. (1.3)

Labiodental: A consonant that is produced by bringing the lower lip against the upper teeth. (4.1)

Lack of invariance: The observation that there is no reliable relationship between a phoneme and the acoustic signal. (3.4)

Language acquisition device: A specialized set of processing units in the brain that guides the rapid development of language in human infants. (3.4)

Language negotiation: A process in which bilingual interlocutors work together to decide which language to use. (9.1)

Late closure: A syntactic parsing strategy that continues to add new words to the current structure unless there is sufficient evidence that a new structure should begin. (6.2)

Late language emergence: A condition in which children are initially delayed in language development but eventually catch up with their peers. (6.4)

Latency: The difference in time between the presentation of a stimulus and the initiation of a response by the participant. (2.3)

Lateral sulcus: The deep fold in the cerebral cortex that separates the temporal lobe from the frontal and parietal lobes. (4.2)

Lateral: Toward the side (either left or right) of the brain. (2.4)

Lateralization: The fact that some cognitive functions are processed in only one of the two hemispheres of the brain. (2.4)

Layering: The expression of multiple morphemes within a single sign. (10.2)

Lemma: The most basic form of a word. (5.1)

Length of residence: The number of years the learner has lived in the country where the second language is spoken. (9.4)

Less-is-more hypothesis: The proposal that working memory constraints help infants focus on the relevant cues to segmenting the speech stream. (11.1)

Letter position dyslexia: A rare form of reading disorder in which readers mix up the order of letters in words. (8.3)

Lexeme: The set of all forms a word can take. (5.1)

Lexical access: The process of matching the acoustic signal of the speech stream to candidate phonological representations stored in the mental lexicon. (5.4)

Lexical bias: A tendency among children to rely on the literal meaning of an utterance even when prosody strongly suggests a nonliteral meaning. (7.4)

Lexical boost: An increase in syntactic priming when the verb is repeated between the prime and target sentences. (6.2)

Lexical bootstrapping: The ability use word meanings to make inferences about syntactic structure. (6.4)

Lexical concept: A concept that can be expressed by a word. (5.4)

Lexical configuration: The process of associating a sound sequence with a particular meaning. (11.2)

Lexical decision task: An experimental procedure in which the participant sees a string of letters and responses and, as quickly as possible, indicates whether it is a word or not. (2.3)

Lexical engagement: The process of associating a newly learned word with other items that are already stored in the mental lexicon. (11.2)

Lexical integration: The process of linking the selected word form to the overall semantics and syntax of the utterance. (5.4)

Lexical selection: (1) The process of choosing the best-fitting word match to the acoustic input. (2) The process that goes from a particular concept to an abstract word form, or lemma. (5.4)

Lexigrams: Visual symbols that stand for words. (1.4)

Lingua franca: A second language in common to all ethnic groups in a given region. (9.1)

Linguistic determinism: The proposal that people can only perceive and categorize the world according to the structures offered by their language. (12.1)

Linguistic relativity: The proposal that the language people speak influences the way they perceive and think about the world. (12.1)

Literate language: The particular syntactic structures and vocabulary used in academic situations. (11.3)

Locution: The literal meaning of the utterance. (7.3)

Loebner Prize: An annual award presented to the computer program that comes closest to passing the Turing test. (13.4)

Logogram: A written symbol that represents a word or morpheme. (8.1)

Longitudinal fissure: The deep groove separating the left and right hemispheres. (4.2)

Loudness: The psychological perception of sound wave amplitude. (3.1)

Low attachment: The parsing strategy of attaching a prepositional phrase to the object. (6.2)

Macrostructure: The global hierarchical structure of a narrative as it flows logically from beginning to conclusion. (11.3)

Magnetoencephalography: A technique for recording brain activity by measuring subtle changes in the magnetic field surrounding the head produced by the electrical currents arising from neural events in the brain. (4.3)

Manner of articulation: The degree to which airflow is obstructed in the production of consonants. (4.1)

Manual babbling: The repeated movements of the hands and arms in ways that mimic the components of signed language. (10.3)

Manual-visual mode: Transmission from hand to eye. (10.1)

Manualism: An approach to deaf education that emphasizes signed language. (10.3)

Mass noun: A noun that represents a substance that lacks a consistent shape and therefore cannot be counted. (12.2)

McGurk effect: An artificially induced illusion in which the auditory information for one speech sound is combined with the visual information for another speech sound to produce the perception of a third speech sound. (3.2)

Mean length of utterance: The standard measure of children's syntactic complexity. (6.4)

Medial: Toward the midline of the brain. (2.4)

Medical model: The view that deafness is a disability that needs to be remediated or eliminated whenever possible. (10.4)

Mental flexibility: The ability to rapidly switch from one cognitive task to another. (9.3)

Mental lexicon: The storage of information about words in long-term memory. (5.3)

Metacognitive verb: A verb that describes a mental state. (11.3)

Metalinguistic awareness: An understanding about how language works. (9.3)

Metaphor: Figurative language that draws a comparison between two concepts that are not generally considered to be similar. (12.3)

Metonymy: Figurative language that refers to an entity in terms of one of its salient characteristics. (12.3)

Metrical segmentation strategy: A rule of thumb that both infants and adults use in segmenting the speech stream by assuming that English words begin on a stressed syllable. (3.3)

Microstructure: The linguistic form and content of a narrative at the sentence level. (11.3)

Minimal attachment: A syntactic parsing strategy that assumes the simplest possible sentence structure. (6.2)

Mirror neurons: Neurons in the brains of primates that fire not only when the primate performs an action but also when it observes somebody else performing that action. (3.4)

Missing letter effect: The observation that skilled readers skip over predictable words and thus cannot track the letters in those words. (8.2)

Model: A simplified version of the phenomenon under investigation, typically in the form of a graph or set of mathematical equations. (2.1)

Module: A dedicated neural system that has evolved to perform a specific function. (3.4)

Monolingual: The ability to speak only one language. (9.1)

Morphemes: The basic units of meaning in a language. (1.2)

Morphological analysis: The tactic of breaking down a word into its component parts to determine its meaning. (11.3)

Morphological awareness: The understanding that many words can be broken down into smaller meaningful units, or morphemes. (11.3)

Morphology: The set of rules for combining morphemes together to form words. (1.2)

Morphosyntax: The ways that a word changes its form according to the role it plays in a sentence. (11.2)

Mother tongue hypothesis: A model of language evolution proposing that maternal vocalizations took on meaning over the course of many generations, developing into a way for family members to communicate. (1.3)

Motherese: The type of language caregivers use to interact with their infants. (Also known as caregiver speech or infant-directed speech.) (1.3)

Motor theory: A theory of speech perception that proposes people perceive speech by inferring the movements of the vocal tract that produced those sounds. (3.4)

Multimodal perception: The idea that the senses strongly interact with each other to produce our rich experience of the world. (3.2)

Multitap: A keypad entry method that cycles through the letter values of the key. (13.2)

Multitasking: The alternation of attention between two or more cognitive tasks that take

in different inputs, engage in different processes, and produce different outputs. (13.1)

Mutual exclusivity assumption: The assumption that no two words mean exactly the same thing. (5.2)

Mutual intelligibility: The degree to which speakers of two different languages or dialects can understand each other. (9.1)

N400: A negative-going ERP waveform that begins about 400 milliseconds after a semantically inconsistent stimulus is presented. (6.2)

Narrative: A form of discourse in which one participant dominates as the active speaker while the other participants assume passive roles as listeners. (7.2)

Nativism: The view that behavior is mainly shaped by natural selection and thus encoded in our genes. (3.4)

Natural language processing: Software that responds to, transforms, or produces speech or text. (13.3)

Naturalistic observation: The process of observing and describing a phenomenon. (2.1)

Need-to-listen hypothesis: The proposal that only being able to hear half of the conversation is what makes public cell phone calls so annoying. (13.1)

Neighborhood density: A measure of how many other words differ from a particular word by substitution of a single phoneme. (5.2)

Network model: A conceptualization of the mental lexicon as a network of words or concepts connected to each other by semantic links. (5.3)

Neuronal recycling hypothesis: The proposal that brain areas designed for one function can be reorganized to perform another, somewhat similar function. (8.1)

Nonmanual markers: Conventionalized expressions of the face and movements of the head that convey specific meanings in signed languages. (10.2)

Nonword: A pronounceable letter string that just happens to not be a word in English. (2.3)

Number of different words: A common measure of the child's productive vocabulary. (6.4)

Object-directed vocalization: Babbling uttered as an infant approaches and manipulates a novel object. (4.4)

Occipital lobe: The lobe at the back of the head that processes visual input from the eyes. (2.4)

One-language-at-home–one-language-outside approach: A strategy for raising bilingual children in which the heritage language is learned from family members and the societal language is learned at school. (9.4)

One-parent–one-language approach: A strategy for raising bilingual children that has one parent speaking the heritage language and the other parent speaking the societal language. (9.4)

Onomatopoeia: A word that represents a sound. (5.1)

Operant conditioning: A method for reinforcing desired behavior through the use of systematic rewards and punishments. (1.4)

Operational definition: A definition of a construct in terms of how the construct is measured. (2.1)

Oral language skills: The ability to produce accurate pronunciation, appropriate vocabulary, sophisticated syntax, and discourse structure. (11.3)

Oral-aural mode: Transmission from mouth to ear. (10.1)

Oralism: An approach to deaf education that emphasizes spoken language instruction. (10.3)

Orthography: The set of rules for writing the words of a language. (8.1)

Overgeneralization: The treatment of irregular words as if they were regularly inflected. (6.4)

Overlaps: Instances when multiple interlocutors speak at the same time. (7.1)

Overtones: Frequencies higher than the fundamental that are also produced by a vibrating object. (3.1)

P300: An ERP component that indicates how much attention is allocated to a task. (13.1)

P600: A positive-going ERP waveform that starts about 600 milliseconds after a syntactically inconsistent stimulus is presented. (6.2)

Paired-associate learning task: An experimental procedure in which participants are asked to memorize unrelated word pairs. (12.2)

Parafovea: The area surrounding the fovea, where vision is less acute. (8.2)

Parafovea-on-fovea effect: The case in which characteristics of the following word affect the fixation duration of the current word. (8.2)

Parallel model: A model in which the processing at one step occurs simultaneously with the same processing at other steps. (6.3)

Parietal lobe: The lobe at the top of the head that monitors body position and navigation through the environment. (2.4)

Passive voice: A sentence structure in which the patient is mapped onto the subject position. (6.1)

Patient: The entity that is acted upon in the event that is portrayed in a sentence. (6.1)

Perceptual narrowing: The process of transitioning from more universal or unconstrained perceptual abilities to those that are more narrow or constrained. (3.3)

Perceptual span: The range of letters that can be processed during one fixation. (8.2)

Periodic sound: A sound with a regularly repeating pattern. (3.1)

Perisylvian cortex: The region inside of and surrounding the lateral sulcus. (4.2)

Perlocution: The listener's perception of the speaker's intended meaning. (7.3)

Perturbation paradigm: An experimental procedure that disrupts normal infant-caregiver interaction to observe the infant's response. (7.4)

PET: A brain imaging technique that produces a three-dimensional moving picture of blood flow by tracking gamma rays emitted from a mildly radioactive substance injected into the bloodstream. (2.4)

Phatic communication: Language exchange for the sole purpose of building and maintaining social relationships. (13.2)

Phonation: The sound resulting from vibrations of the vocal folds as air is expelled from the lungs. (3.2)

Phonation stage: The period from birth to two months when infants produce vowel-like sounds by vibrating the vocal folds. (4.4)

Phonemes: Meaningless speech sounds that serve as the fundamental building blocks of language. (1.2)

Phonemic restoration: The process of filling in missing segments of the speech stream with contextually appropriate material. (3.2)

Phonics-based approach: A method of teaching reading that explicitly trains children to recognize consistent relationships between letters and sounds. (8.3)

Phonological awareness: An understanding that words can be broken down into smaller sound structures. (8.3)

Phonological dyslexia: A condition in which reading is relatively intact but the ability to sound out unfamiliar words is lost. (8.2)

Phonological encoding: The process that goes from abstract word form, or lemma, to its phonological representation. (5.4)

Phonological loop: A short-term memory buffer that can hold about two seconds of spoken language. (2.1)

Phonology: The set of rules for combining phonemes into larger units. (1.2)

Phonotactic probability: The likelihood that a particular sequence of phonemes will occur in a language. (5.2)

Phonotactic rules: Rules for combining phonemes into sequences to form words. (5.1)

Picture-word interference task: An experimental procedure in which the participant is asked to name a picture while ignoring a simultaneously presented distractor word. (5.3)

Pidgin: A simple language consisting of a few hundred words and a very basic grammar. (1.3)

Pitch: The psychological perception of sound wave frequency. (3.1)

Place of articulation: The location in the oral cavity where the airflow is obstructed to produce a consonant sound. (4.1)

Plosive: A consonant that is produced by momentarily blocking and then releasing the airstream. (3.2)

Polyseme: A word that has multiple related meanings, or senses. (11.2)

Postalveolar: A consonant produced by pressing the tip of the tongue against the region between the alveolar ridge and the hard palate. (4.1)

Posterior. Toward the back of the brain. (2:4)

Poverty-of-the-stimulus argument. The position that the linguistic input children receive is insufficient for them to learn the language. (6.4)

Pragmatic language impairment. A developmental disorder in which a child has structural language skills intact but still experiences difficulties with the social and contextual aspects of discourse, such as inferring nonliteral meanings of utterances. (7.4)

Pragmatics: The various ways in which context contributes to the meaning of a discourse. (7.1)

Predictability effect: The observation that less predictable words are fixated longer than more highly predictable words. (8.2)

Predictive inference: An expectation of what comes next in a discourse based on the sequence of events so far. (7.3)

Predictive text: Software that uses the probabilities of language to make text entry on a keypad more efficient. (13.2)

Prefrontal cortex: The most forward area of the frontal lobe, known to be responsible for executive functioning. (7.2)

Prelingually deaf: Having lost hearing before learning language. (10.3)

Primacy and recency effects: The observation that the first and last items in a list are more accurately recalled than those in the middle. (2.3)

Primary auditory cortex: The region of the superior temporal lobe that does the initial processing of the input from the cochlea. (3.1)

Primary motor cortex: The region of the brain that programs commands to move the body, including the articulators for speech. (4.2)

Primacy of speech: The observation that virtually all language use is in the spoken mode.

Priming: An implicit memory process in which the recall of a particular item is enhanced due to previous exposure of similar items: (2.3)

Principle of no gaps/no overlaps: The tendency to avoid leaving a noticeable silence between turns of conversation and to instead begin a new turn before the current turn is finished. (7.1)

Print knowledge: Familiarity with how to hold a book and turn pages as well as with how print is organized on a page. (11.3)

Private speech: Self-talk that is not addressed to other people. (11.3)

Privileged ground: Information that one interlocutor knows but the other one doesn't. (7.2)

Productive vocabulary: The set of words a person is able to produce in appropriate contexts. (5.2)

Prosodic bootstrapping: A hypothesis proposing that infants use intonation and stress patterns to infer phrase and word boundaries. (3.3) The use of prosodic patterns to identify syntactic structure. (6.4)

Prosody: Fluctuations of the fundamental frequency during an utterance. (3.2)

Protoconversation: Social exchange in which an infant and a caregiver convey emotions through facial expressions and mutual gaze while taking turns gesturing and vocalizing. (11.1)

Protolanguage: A hypothetical pidgin-like language spoken by ancestral humans. (1.3)

Psycholinguistics: The scientific study of the cognitive processes involved in comprehending and producing language. (2.3)

Question-answering system: A computer program that takes natural language inquiries as input, searches databases or the Internet for information, and then provides answers in the form of natural language. (13.3)

Rapid automatized naming: A diagnostic for dyslexia in which the child is asked to name written letters, numbers, or other familiar symbols as quickly as possible. (8.3)

Recall: The intentional retrieval of information from long-term memory. (5.4)

Receptive aphasia: A condition in which brain damage leads to a loss of speech comprehension and to fluent but meaningless speech production. (4.2)

Receptive bilingualism: The ability to understand a second language without being able to speak it. (9.1)

Receptive vocabulary: The set of words a person is able to recognize and understand the meaning of. (5.2)

Recognition: A search of long-term memory to find a stored match with the current stimulus. (5.4)

Recognition point: The point at which a string of phonemes provides enough evidence for identifying a word. (5.4)

Recursion: The process of extending a pattern by placing it inside itself. (1.3)

Reduced relative clause: A kind of embedded syntactic structure that allows for economy of expression but can be extremely difficult to process in some cases. (6.2)

Reference: The process of using a word or phrase to represent an entity. (7.2)

Referent: The entity that is represented by a particular word or phrase. (7.2)

Referential locus: A region of the signing space that serves as a referring expression during a discourse. (10.2)

Referential priming: An experimental procedure in which the participant is first shown only one of the items of a visual display before the full display is presented. (6.3)

Referential uncertainty: The observation that there is no direct link between the word and the object or event it refers to. (5.2)

Referring expression: A word or phrase that is used to represent a particular entity or event. (7.2)

Regression: A movement of the eyes back to a previously viewed location. (2.3)

Relative clause: A sentence that is placed inside of another sentence for the purpose of describing a noun. (6.1)

Relevance theory: The proposal that speakers strive for a balance between providing too much and too little information in choosing referring expressions. (7.2)

Reliability: The degree to which an instrument gives consistent measurements for the same thing. (2.1)

Repeated name penalty: A delay in processing when the same referring expression is used on multiple consecutive occasions in a narrative. (7.3)

Repetition suppression: A reduction in brain activity when a syntactically primed sentence is processed. (6.3)

Residual speech sound errors: Misarticulations that persist into the elementary school years. (4.4)

Reversible sentence: A sentence that still makes sense, but with a different meaning, if the agent and patient swap subject and object positions. (6.1)

Revised hierarchical model: A theory of bilingual language processing that assumes separate lexicons for each language connected by a common underlying conceptual level. (9.2)

Revision: A disruption of speech that changes the syntactic structure of the utterance. (6.4)

RSVP task: An experimental technique in which the participant is asked to watch for target words within a rapidly presented list. (12.4)

Saccade: A quick movement of the eyes while reading. (2.3)

Salient: Prominent and easy to notice. (11.1)

Sarcasm: Verbal irony that is intended to criticize or ridicule another person. (12.3)

Scalar implicature: A listener's inference that a speaker's use of a weaker term means that a stronger term is not true. (7.4)

Schema: A mental framework for organizing our understanding of how some aspect of the world works. (7.2)

Schwa: A neutral mid-central vowel occurring in many unstressed syllables in English. (4.1)

Scrambling: The syntactic process of putting the object before the subject. (6.3)

Selective attention: The ability to direct and focus attention on the current task. (9.3)

Semantic anomaly: A condition in which a grammatically correct sentence does not make sense because of a mismatch between the meaning of one or more words and the sentence as a whole. (2.4)

Semantic categorization task: An experimental procedure that asks participants to name members of a given category. (9.2)

Semantic facilitation effect: The observation that thematic relations lead to faster naming times. (5.3)

Semantic gender system: A pattern of classifying nouns and pronouns according to their natural type. (12.2)

Semantic interference effect: The observation that taxonomic relations lead to slower naming times. (5.3)

Semantic neighbors: Concepts with related meanings. (5.4)

Semantic primes: Innately meaningful concepts that are used to define all other concepts. (5.1)

Semantic priming effect: The observation that target words are recognized faster when they are preceded by related primes rather than unrelated primes. (5.3)

Semantic priming task: An experimental technique that presents a pair of words and measures the participant's reaction time. (5.3)

Sense model: A theory of bilingual language processing that takes into account the fact that most words have multiple meanings that do not fully overlap across languages. (9.2)

Sensitive period: The time early in life when language learning is more likely to be successful. (9.4)

Sentence superiority effect: The improved ability to identify a word within a sentence as opposed to by itself. (5.4)

Sentence-picture matching task: A procedure in which the respondent selects from a set of pictures the one that is described by the prompt sentence. (6.2)

Serial model: A model in which all of the processing at one step needs to be completed before moving on to the next step. (6.3)

Serial recall task: A memory task in which participants are required to repeat the items in the correct order. (2.3)

Shadowing task: A procedure in which the participant is asked to repeat a continuous flow of speech out loud and as quickly as possible. (5.4)

Shallow orthography: The situation in which spelling and pronunciation are closely matched. (8.1)

Sign language: A linguistic system that is perceived visually and produced through hand movements and facial expressions. (10.1)

Sign language advantage: The observation that infants can produce their first signed word earlier than they can produce their first spoken word. (10.3)

Signed English: An artificial sign language for use in the classroom that uses ASL signs in English word order. (10.1)

Signed language: The expression of language in the manual-visual mode. (10.1)

Signing space: The three-dimensional space within arms' reach in front of the signer. (10.2)

Simon task: An experimental procedure that requires participants to respond to the color of a stimulus regardless of its location. (9.3)

Sine wave: A wave that can be described by a trigonometric sine function. (3.1)

Singing Neanderthal hypothesis: Model of language evolution proposing that both music and language derive from the same source, the humming of pre-human social interactions. (1.3)

Situation model: A mental representation of the entities and events in a story and how they are related. (7.2)

Skin conductance response: A change in how easily a mild electric current can pass between two electrodes placed on the skin. (12.4)

SLIP task: A technique for inducing speech errors in the laboratory. (12.4)

Slow expressive development: A delay in babbling or talking in spite of developing receptive language and social interaction skills at a normal rate. (4.4)

Slow mapping: The extended process of consolidating the pronunciation and meaning of a word through multiple encounters. (11.2)

Social grooming: The practice of picking fleas and dirt from the fur of conspecifics. (1.1)

Social grooming hypothesis: A model of language evolution proposing that gossip for humans serves the same purpose of social network building as does grooming for chimpanzees. (1.3)

Societal language: The language spoken by the majority of people in a given society. (9.1)

Somatosensory cortex: The region of the brain that processes the body senses to keep track of what the various body parts are doing, including the articulators for speech. (4.2)

Sonorant: A speech sound that usually serves a consonant but sometimes as a vowel. (3.2)

Speciation: The processes involved in the evolution of new species. (1.3)

Specific language impairment: A language processing and production disorder that cannot be attributed to other causes such as brain damage or hearing loss. (1.3):

Spectrogram: A chart displaying the pattern of frequencies in the speech stream and how those patterns change over time. (3.2)

Speech act theory: The position that the value of an utterance lies not in the literal meaning of its words but rather in the intention of the speaker and the effect it has on the listener. (7.3)

Speech is special: The view that speech perception is a distinct cognitive module that operates independently of and differently from other perceptual systems. (3.4)

Speech learning model: The proposal that a foreign accent is the result of an imbalance between the amounts of time spent using the first and second languages. (9.4)

Speech-generating device: A computer program that produces spoken language output. (13.3)

Speechreading: The perception of spoken language by observing the movements of the face, lips, and tongue. (10.3)

Spillover effect: The case in which processing difficulties of the preceding word cause the fixation duration of the current word to be extended. (8.2)

Spoonerism: A speech error that involves switching the initial sounds of word pairs. (12.4)

Spreading activation model: A model of the mental lexicon that proposes that activation of one node spreads out to other nodes linked to it. (5.3)

Stall: A disruption of speech that does not change the syntactic structure of the utterance. (6.4)

Story grammar: The framework guiding the presentation of events and characters in a narrative. (7.2)

Stroop effect: The situation in which reaction time in a color-naming task is slowed due to cognitive interference. (12.4)

Subcortical structures: A set of distinct brain structures located below the cerebral cortex. (2.4)

Subjective well-being: Personal rating of happiness and life satisfaction. (13.2)

Sulcus: A region of the cerebral cortex that is folded inward. (4.2)

Superior: Toward the top of the brain. (2.4)

Supplementary motor area: A brain region that is believed to be responsible for programming intentional actions. (4.2)

Supramarginal gyrus: A region of the inferior parietal lobe that is adjacent to the lateral fissure. (5.3)

Surface dyslexia: A condition in which the ability to read regularly spelled words and pseudowords is intact while the ability to read irregularly spelled words is lost. (8.2)

Syllabary: A writing system that represents each syllable with a different symbol. (8.1)

Symbol grounding problem: The question of where the meaning of a symbol comes from. (5.1)

Syntactic bootstrapping: The use of syntactic information to infer the meaning of verbs. (5.2)

Syntactic priming: The tendency to repeat a previously heard sentence structure. (6.2)

Syntax: A set of rules for ordering words in a sentence. (1.2, 6.1)

Synthesized speech: Computer-generated sound output that mimics the fluctuations in fundamental frequencies and formants of human speech. (13.3)

Taboo words: Words that are so emotionally arousing that they are considered inappropriate to use in many social situations. (12.4)

Talk-in-interaction: The spontaneous speech people use as they engage in joint activities. (7.1)

Taxonomic assumption: The assumption that a newly learned word extends to other similar referents. (5.2)

Taxonomic relation: A relationship between two words that belong to the same semantic category. (5.3)

Temporal lobe: The lobe at the side of the head that processes auditory input from the ears and is also responsible for object recognition. (2.4)

Textism: An innovative use of language in text messaging. (13.2)

Thalamus: A midbrain structure traditionally thought of as a sensorimotor relay from various brain structures up to the cerebral cortex. (4.2)

Thematic relation: A relationship between two words based on frequency of co-occurrence. (5.3)

Thematic role assignment: The mapping of thematic roles onto syntactic positions such as subject and object. (6.1)

Thematic roles: The various types of participants involved in an event portrayed in a sentence. (6.1)

Theory: A conceptual framework that explains a set of observations in such a way that it also makes predictions about future observations. (2.1)

Theory of mind: The ability to make inferences about the mental states and intentions of others. (7.3)

Thinking-for-speaking: The claim that speakers organize their thought processes to meet the requirements of their language as they speak. (12.2)

Timbre: The psychological perception of sound wave complexity. (3.1)

Tip-of-the-tongue phenomenon: The experience of being temporarily unable to recall a familiar word. (11.4)

Tonotopic organization: The progressive arrangement of cells sensitive to different frequencies. (3.1)

Tourette's syndrome: A disorder of the brain that involves motor and vocal tics and sometimes compulsive swearing. (12.4)

Transition relevance place: A point in the conversation where the listener can expect the current speaker to end a turn. (7.1)

Transitional probability: The likelihood that a particular event will occur next given the current event. (3.3)

Transitional program: A form of bilingual education that is intended to assimilate heritage-language students into the mainstream language and culture. (9.4)

Translation equivalents: Words in two different languages that refer to the same concept. (9.2)

Transmission deficit hypothesis: The proposal that the connections between a word's semantic representation and its phonological representation weakens with age. (11.4)

Trial: A single application of the treatment in an experiment. (2.2)

Trochaic: A strong-weak stress pattern. (5.2)

Trochaic bias: The observation that young children produce the strong-weak stress pattern earlier and with more ease than the weak-strong stress pattern. (11.1)

Turing test: The proposal that a machine should be considered intelligent if its ability to hold a conversation is indistinguishable from that of a human being. (13.4)

Turn-constructional unit: A syntactic structure, ranging from a single word to a sentence, that can make up a turn in a conversation. (7.1)

Two-alternative forced-choice task: An experimental task requiring the participant to decide between two options. (2.3)

Two-way immersion program: A form of bilingual education that is intended to develop fully bilingual and biliterate students. (9.4)

Ultimate attainment: Second language acquisition that typically falls short of full mastery. (9.4)

Unbalanced bilingual: A person who has limited ability in a second language. (9.2)

Unheralded pronoun: A pronoun without an antecedent. (7.3)

Unimodal bilingual: Able to communicate in two spoken languages. (10.3)

Usage-based framework: The position that the child uses general cognitive mechanisms like pattern detection and categorization to gradually build an understanding of the grammar of the language. (6.4)

Valence: The psychological component that evaluates the emotional experience. (12.4)

Validity: The degree to which the measuring instrument actually measures what it is claimed to measure. (2.1)

Velar: Consonants produced by pressing the root of the tongue against the soft palate at the back of the mouth. (4.1)

Velum: The fleshy region behind the hard palate; the soft palate. (4.1)

Ventral: Toward the belly. (2.4)

Ventral stream: A bilateral processing pathway that interprets the meaning of the incoming speech signal. (4.3)

Verb agreement: The incorporation of referential loci in the signing of verbs. (10.2)

Verb aspect: The temporal flow of the event expressed by a verb. (10.2)

Verbal irony: An utterance that conveys an understood meaning that is the opposite of its literal meaning. (12.3)

Vertical transmission: The learning of language and culture through interactions with parents and elders. (10.4)

Village sign language: A sign language used by both deaf and hearing members of a community with a high incidence of deafness. (10.1)

Visual prosody: The facial expressions and body movements that convey an extra layer of meaning in a signed language. (10.2)

Visual scene displays: Contextually rich and personally relevant digital images that convey content on mobile devices. (13.3)

Visual word form area: A region between the occipital and temporal lobes where the symbols of the writing system are stored, regardless of the language or the type of script. (8.1)

Visual world paradigm: A task in which participants are asked to interact with objects or pictures in the visual environment according to spoken instructions. (5.4)

Vocabulary spurt: A time in which the child begins learning new words at a rapid pace, usually starting around eighteen months of age. (1.4)

Vocal folds: A pair of membranes stretched across the opening of the glottis that can be vibrated to produce sound. (4.1)

Vocal tract: The system of air passages, including the throat, mouth and nose, where speech is produced. (1.4)

Voice banking: The process of recording voice samples for later use in a speech-generating device. (13.3)

Voice onset time: The difference in time between the release of a plosive consonant and the beginning of vocal fold vibration. (3.2)

Weaker links hypothesis: The proposal that the bilingual disadvantage can be explained in terms of lower word frequencies. (9.2)

Wernicke's aphasia: A condition characterized by speech that is filled with vocabulary and

grammatical errors accompanied by difficulty in comprehending speech. (2.3)

Wernicke's area: A region in the left temporal lobe that is generally described as the language comprehension area of the brain. (2.4)

White matter tracts: Bundles of fibers that connect various regions of the brain and whose function is to transmit information. (8.3)

Whole object assumption: The assumption that a new word refers to the entire object and not just a part of it. (5.2)

Within-subjects design: An experiment design that assigns each participant to every condition. (2.2)

Word: A minimal unit of meaningful speech that can stand alone. (5.1)

Word association task: A procedure in which the participant is asked to produce a word in response to a prompt. (5.3)

Word frequency: A measure of how often a particular word in all its forms occurs in the language. (5.2)

Word production: The process of finding phonological word forms in the mental lexicon to express underlying semantic representations or thoughts. (5.4)

Word recognition: The process of extracting phonological word forms from the speech stream and linking them by way of the mental lexicon to their semantic representations. (5.4)

Words-with-spaces model: The view that idioms are set phrases that behave syntactically like single words. (12.3)

Working memory: A kind of short-term memory that holds whatever we are currently thinking about. (1.2)

Zero anaphora: The case in which no overt anaphor is used even though an anaphoric reference can easily be inferred. (7.3)

REFERENCES

Ackermann, H. (2008). Cerebellar contributions to speech production and speech perception: Psycholinguistic and neurobiological perspectives. *Trends in Neurosciences, 31,* 265–272.

Aguert, M., Laval, V., Le Bigot, L., & Bernicot, J. (2010). Understanding expressive speech acts: The role of prosody and situational context in French-speaking 5- to 9-year-olds. *Journal of Speech, Language, and Hearing Research, 53,* 1629–1641.

Akimoto, Y., Miyazawa, S., & Muramoto, T. (2012). Comprehension processes of verbal irony: The effects of salience, egocentric context, and allocentric theory of mind. *Metaphor and Symbol, 27,* 217–242.

Akre, K. L., & Ryan, M. J. (2010). Proximity-dependent response to variably complex mating signals in túngara frogs (Physalaemus pustulosus). *Ethology, 116,* 1138–1145.

Alain, C., Arnott, S. R., Hevenor, S., Graham, S., & Grady, C. L. (2001). "What" and "where" in the human auditory system. *Proceedings of the National Academy of Science USA, 98,* 12301–12306.

Allum, P. H., & Wheeldon, L. R. (2007). Planning scope in spoken sentence production: The role of grammatical units. *Journal of Experimental Psychology: Learning, Memory, and Cognition, 33,* 791–810.

Almor, A., & Eimas, P. D. (2008). Focus and noun phrase anaphors in spoken language comprehension. *Language and Cognitive Processes, 23,* 201–225.

Altmann, L. J. P., & Kemper, S. (2006). Effects of age, animacy and activation order on sentence production. *Language and Cognitive Processes, 21,* 322–354.

Altmann, L. J. P., Lombardino, L. J., & Puranik, C. (2008). Sentence production in students with dyslexia. *International Journal of Language and Communication Disorders, 43,* 55–76.

Alves, R. A., Castro, S. L., & Olive, T. (2008). Execution and pauses in writing narratives: Processing time, cognitive effort and typing skill. *International Journal of Psychology, 43,* 969–979.

Amengual, M. (2011). Interlingual influence in bilingual speech: Cognate status effect in a continuum of bilingualism. *Bilingualism: Language and Cognition, 15,* 517–530.

Anderson, C., & Carlson, K. (2010). Syntactic structure guides prosody in temporarily ambiguous sentences. *Language and Speech, 53,* 472–493.

Angeleri, R., & Airenti, G. (2014). The development of joke and irony understanding: A study with 3- to 6-year-old children. *Canadian Journal of Experimental Psychology/ Revue Canadienne de Psychologie Expérimentale, 68,* 133–146.

Angermeyer, P. S. (2010). Interpreter-mediated interaction as bilingual speech: Bridging macro- and micro-sociolinguistics in codeswitching research. *International Journal of Bilingualism, 14,* 466–489.

Anjaneyulu, T. (2013). A glossary: Usage of abbreviations of mobile phone SMS. *ETC: A Review of General Semantics, 70,* 141–171.

Arnold, J. E. (2008). Reference production: Production-internal and addressee-oriented processes. *Language and Cognitive Processes, 23,* 495–527.

Arnon, I., & Clark, E. V. (2011). Why brush your teeth is better than teeth: Children's word production is facilitated in familiar sentence-frames. *Language Learning and Development, 7,* 107–129.

Aronoff, M., Meir, I., & Sandler, W. (2005). The paradox of sign language morphology. *Language, 81,* 301–344.

Arts, A., Maes, A., Noordman, L., & Jansen, C. (2011). Overspecification facilitates object identification. *Journal of Pragmatics, 43,* 361–374.

Arunchalam, S., & Waxman, S. R. (2010). Meaning from syntax: Evidence from 2-year-olds. *Cognition, 114,* 442–446.

Ash, S., Xie, S. X., Gross, R. G., Dreyfuss, M., Boller, A., Camp, E., . . . Grossman, M. (2012). The organization and anatomy of narrative comprehension and expression in Lewy body spectrum disorders. *Neuropsychology, 26,* 368–384.

Austin, J. (1962). *How to do things with words.* London: Oxford University Press.

Baars, B. J., Motley, M. T., & MacKay, D. G. (1975). Output editing for lexical status in artificially elicited slips of the tongue. *Journal of Verbal Learning and Verbal Behavior, 14*(4), 382–391.

Bachorowski, J. (1999). Vocal expression and perception of emotion. *Current Directions in Psychological Science, 8,* 53–57.

Baddeley, A. D., Thomson, N., & Buchanan, M. (1975). Word length and the structure of short-term memory. *Journal of Verbal Learning and Verbal Behavior, 14*(6), 575–589.

Bahr, R. H., Silliman, E. R., Berninger, V. W., & Dow, M. (2012). Linguistic pattern analysis of misspellings of typically developing writers in grades 1–9. *Journal of Speech, Language, and Hearing Research, 55,* 1587–1599.

Baldwin, D., Andersson, A., Saffran, J., & Meyer, M. (2008). Segmenting dynamic human action via statistical structure. *Cognition, 106,* 1382–1407.

Ballard, K. J., Djaja, D., Arciuli, J., James, D. G. H., & van Doorn, J. (2012). Developmental trajectory of production of prosody: Lexical stress contrastivity in children ages 3 to 7 years and in adults. *Journal of Speech, Language, and Hearing Research, 55,* 1822–1835.

Banks, W. E., d'Errico, F., Peterson, A., Kageyama, M., Sima, A., & Sánchez-Goñi, M. (2008). Neanderthal extinction by competitive exclusion. *PLoS ONE, 3,* e3972.

Barbieri, C., Butthof, A., Koen B., & Pakendorf, B. (2013). Genetic perspectives on the origin of clicks in Bantu languages from southwestern Zambia. *European Journal of Human Genetics, 21,* 430–436.

Barfield, C. H., Tang-Martinez, Z., & Trainer, J. M. (1994). Domestic calves (Bos taurus) recognize their own mothers by auditory cues. *Ethology, 97,* 257–264.

Barreña, A., & Almgren, M. (2012). Object-verb and verb-object in Basque and Spanish monolinguals. *International Journal of Bilingualism, 17,* 337–356.

Bavelas, J. B., Coates, L., & Johnson, T. (2000). Listeners as co-narrators. *Journal of Personality and Social Psychology, 79,* 941–952.

Baxter, S., Enderby, P., Evans, P., & Judge, S. (2012). Barriers and facilitators to the use of high-technology augmentative and alternative communication devices: A systematic review and qualitative synthesis. *International Journal of Language and Communication Disorders, 47,* 115–129.

Beeson, P. M., Higginson, K., & Rising, K. (2013). Writing treatment for aphasia: A texting approach. *Journal of Speech, Language, and Hearing Research, 56,* 945–955.

Ben-Ari, M. (2005). *Just a theory: Exploring the nature of science.* Amherst, NY: Prometheus.

Ben-Dor, M., Gopher, A., Hershkovitz, I., & Barkai, R. (2011). Man the fat hunter: The demise of *Homo erectus* and the emergence of a new hominin lineage in the Middle Pleistocene (ca. 400 kyr) Levant. *PLoS ONE, 6,* e28689.

Beňuš, Š., Gravano, A., & Hirschberg, J. (2011). Pragmatic aspects of temporal accommodation in turn-taking. *Journal of Pragmatics, 43,* 3001–3027.

Berducci, D. (2010). From infants' reacting to understanding: Grounding mature communication and sociality through turn-taking and sequencing. *Psychology of Language and Communication, 14,* 3–28.

Berko, J., & Brown, R. (1960). Psycholinguistic research methods. In P. Mussen (Ed.), *Handbook of research methods in child development.* New York: John Wiley.

Berlin, B., & Kay, P. (1969). *Basic color terms: Their universality and evolution.* Berkeley: University of California Press.

Bertels, J., Kolinsky, R., Pietrons, E., & Morais, J. (2011). Long-lasting attentional influence of negative and taboo words in an auditory variant of the emotional Stroop task. *Emotion, 11,* 29–37.

Bi, X., Smith, B. A., & Zhai, S. (2012). Multilingual

touchscreen keyboard design and optimization. *Human-Computer Interaction, 27,* 352–382.

Bialystok, E. (2011). Reshaping the mind: The benefits of bilingualism. *Canadian Journal of Experimental Psychology, 65,* 229–235.

Bialystok, E., & Barac, R. (2012). Emerging bilingualism: Dissociating advantages for metalinguistic awareness and executive control. *Cognition, 122,* 67–73.

Bialystok, E., Craik, F. I. M., & Luk, G. (2012). Bilingualism: Consequences for mind and brain. *Trends in Cognitive Science, 16,* 240–250.

Bickerton, D. (1981). *Roots of language.* Ann Arbor, MI: Karoma.

Bickerton, D. (1990). *Language and species.* Chicago: University of Chicago Press.

Bickerton, D. (2009). *Adam's tongue.* New York: Hill and Wang.

Bidelman, G. M., Hutka, S., & Moreno, S. (2013). Tone language speakers and musicians share enhanced perceptual and cognitive abilities for musical pitch: Evidence for bidirectionality between the domains of language and music. *PLoS ONE, 8,* e60676.

Binder, J. R., Frost, J. A., Hammeke, T. A., & Cox, R. W. (1997). Human brain language areas identified by functional magnetic resonance imaging. *Journal of Neuroscience, 17*(1), 353–362.

Bion, R. A. H., Borovsky, A., & Fernald, A. (2012). Fast mapping, slow learning: Disambiguation of novel word-object mappings in relation to vocabulary learning at 18, 24, and 30 months. *Cognition, 126,* 39–53.

Bloom, L. (1993). *The transition from infancy to language: Acquiring the power of expression.* New York: Cambridge University Press.

Bobb, S. C., Wodniecka, Z., & Kroll, J. F. (2013). What bilinguals tell us about cognitive control: Overview to the special issue. *Journal of Cognitive Psychology, 25,* 493–496.

Bock, J. K. (1986). Syntactic persistence in language production. *Cognitive Psychology, 18,* 355–387.

Boë, L., Heim, J., Abry, C., & Badin, P. (2004). Neandertal vocal tract: Which potential for vowel acoustics? *Interaction Studies: Social Behaviour and Communication in Biological and Artificial Systems, 5,* 409–429.

Bohland, J. W., Bullock, D., & Guenther, F. H. (2010). Neural representations and mechanisms for the performance of simple speech sequences. *Journal of Cognitive Neuroscience, 22,* 1504–1529.

Bohrn, I. C., Altmann, U., & Jacobs, A. M. (2012). Looking at the brains behind figurative language: A quantitative meta-analysis of neuroimaging studies on metaphor, idiom, and irony processing. *Neuropsychologia, 50*(11), 2669–2683.

Bolhuis, J., Okanoya, K., & Scharff, C. (2010). Twitter evolution: Converging mechanisms in birdsong and human speech. *Nature Reviews: Neuroscience, 11,* 747–759.

Bolton, K. K. (2002). Chinese Englishes: From Canton jargon to global English. *World Englishes, 21,* 181–199.

Bonvillian, J. D., & Patterson, F. G. (1993). Early sign language acquisition in children and gorillas: Vocabulary content and sign iconicity. *First Language, 13,* 315–338.

Boring, E. G. (1923). Intelligence as the tests test it. *New Republic, 36,* 35–37.

Bornkessel-Schlesewsky, I., & Schlesewsky, M. (2013). Reconciling time, space and function: A new dorsal-ventral stream model of sentence comprehension. *Brain and Language, 125,* 60–76.

Boroditsky, L., Schmidt, L., & Phillips, W. (2003). Sex, syntax, and semantics. In D. Gentner & S. Goldin-Meadow (Eds.), *Language in mind: Advances in the study of language and cognition* (pp. 61–80). Cambridge, MA: MIT Press.

Bortfeld, H., Shaw, K., & Depowski, N. (2013). Disentangling the influence of salience and familiarity on infant word learning: Methodological advances. *Frontiers in Psychology, 4,* Art. 175.

Bosco, F. M., Vallana, M., & Bucciarelli, M. (2012). The inferential chain makes the difference between familiar and novel figurative expressions. *Journal of Cognitive Psychology, 24,* 525–540.

Boudreault, P., & Mayberry, R. I. (2006). Grammatical processing in American Sign Language: Age of first-language acquisition effects in relation to syntactic structure. *Language and Cognitive Processes, 21,* 608–635.

Bowers, J. S., & Pleydell-Pearce, C. W. (2011). Swearing, euphemisms, and linguistic relativity. *PLoS ONE, 6,* e22341.

Bradley, B. J. (2008). Reconstructing phylogenies and phenotypes: A molecular view of human evolution. *Journal of Anatomy, 212,* 337–353.

Braine, M. D. (1974). Length constraints, reduction rules, and holophrastic processes in children's word combinations. *Journal of Verbal Learning and Verbal Behavior, 13,* 448–456.

Branigan, H. P., Pickering, M. J., & McLean, J. F. (2005). Priming prepositional-phrase attachment during comprehension. *Journal of Experimental Psychology: Learning, Memory, and Cognition, 31,* 468–481.

Bransford, J. D., & Johnson, M. K. (1972). Contextual prerequisites for understanding: Some investigations of comprehension and recall. *Journal of Verbal Learning and Verbal Behavior, 11,* 717–726.

Breheny, R., Ferguson, H. J., & Katsos, N. (2013). Investigating the timecourse of accessing conversational implicatures during incremental sentence interpretation. *Language and Cognitive Processes, 28*(4), 443–467.

Brentari, D., González, C., Seidl, A., & Wilbur, R. (2010). Sensitivity to visual prosodic cues in signers and nonsigners. *Language and Speech, 54,* 49–72.

Brito, N., & Barr, R. (2012). Influence of bilingualism on memory generalization during infancy. *Developmental Science, 15,* 812–816.

Brown-Schmidt, S. (2012). Beyond common and privileged: Gradient representations of common ground in real-time language use. *Language and Cognitive Processes, 27,* 62–89.

Brown-Schmidt, S., Gunlogson, C., & Tanenhaus, M. K. (2008). Addressees distinguish shared from private information when interpreting questions during interactive conversation. *Cognition, 107,* 1122–1134.

Brunelli, S. A., Shair, H. N., & Hofer, M. A. (1994). Hypothermic vocalizations of rat pups (Rattus norvegicus) and direct maternal search behavior. *Journal of Comparative Psychology, 108,* 298–303.

Burchert, F., Hanne, S., & Vasishth, S. (2013). Sentence comprehension disorders in aphasia: The concept of chance performance revisited. *Aphasiology, 27*(1), 112–125.

Bürki, A., & Gaskell, M. G. (2012). Lexical representation of schwa words: Two mackerels, but only one salami. *Journal of Experimental Psychology: Learning, Memory, and Cognition, 38,* 617–631.

Bush, G., Luu, P., & Posner, M. I. (2000). Cognitive and emotional influences in anterior cingulate cortex. *Trends in Cognitive Science, 4,* 215–222.

Bush, G., Vogt, B. A., Holmes J, Dale, A. M., Greve, D., Jenike, M. A., & Rosen, B. R. (2002). Dorsal anterior cingulate cortex: A role in reward-based decision making. *Proceedings of the National Academy of Sciences USA, 99,* 523–528.

Byers-Heinlein, K. (2013). Parental language mixing: Its measurement and the relation of mixed input to young bilingual children's vocabulary size. *Bilingualism: Language and Cognition, 16,* 32–48.

Bylund, E., Athanasopoulos, P., & Oostendorp, M. (2013). Motion event cognition and grammatical aspect: Evidence from Afrikaans. *Linguistics, 51,* 929–955.

Byun, T. M. (2012). Bidirectional perception-production relations in phonological development: Evidence from positional neutralization. *Clinical Linguistics and Phonetics, 26,* 397–413.

Cabell, S. Q., Justice, L. M., Piasta, S. B., Curenton, S. M., Wiggins, A., Turnbull, K. P., & Petscher, Y. (2011). The impact of teacher responsivity education on preschoolers' language and literacy skills. *American Journal of Speech-Language Pathology, 20,* 315–330.

Cabo, D. P. Y., & Rothman, J. (2012). The (il)logical problem of heritage speaker bilingualism and incomplete acquisition. *Applied Linguistics, 33,* 450–455.

Cacciari, C., Corradini, P., Padovani, R., & Carreiras, M. (2011). Pronoun resolution in Italian: The role of grammatical gender and context. *Journal of Cognitive Psychology, 23,* 416–434.

Cai, S., Ghosh, S. S., Guenther, F. H., & Perkell, J. S. (2011). Focal manipulations of formant trajectories reveal a role of auditory feedback in the online control of both within-syllable and between-syllable speech training. *Journal of Neuroscience, 31,* 16483–16490.

Cairns, P., Shillcock, R., Chater, N., & Levy, J. (1997). Bootstrapping word boundaries: A bottom-up corpus-based approach to speech segmentation. *Cognitive Psychology, 33,* 111–153.

Cantone, K. F. (2013). Comments on the paper *Gender acquisition in bilingual children: French-German, Italian-German, Spanish-German and Italian-French. International Journal of Bilingualism, 17,* 573–576.

Cao, F., Vu, M., Chan, D. H. L., Lawrence, J. M., Harris, L. N., Xu, Y., & Perfetti, C. A. (2012). Writing affects the brain network of reading in Chinese: A functional magnetic resonance imaging study. *Human Brain Mapping, 34,* 1670–1684.

Cashon, C. H., & DeNicola, C. A. (2011). Is perceptual narrowing too narrow? *Journal of Cognition and Development, 12,* 159–162.

Centers for Disease Control. (n.d.) *Hearing loss fact sheet.* Available at http://www.cdc.gov/ncbddd/actearly/pdf/parents_pdfs/hearinglossfactsheet.pdf.

Champagne-Lavau, M., & Joanette, Y. (2009). Pragmatics, theory of mind and executive functions after a right-hemisphere lesion: Different patterns of deficits. *Journal of Neurolinguistics, 22,* 413–426.

Changizi, M. A., & Shimojo, S. (2005). Character complexity and redundancy in writing systems over human history. *Proceedings of the Royal Society, B, 272,* 267–275.

Chen, S., & Bond, M. (2010). Two languages, two personalities? Examining language effects on the expression of personality in a bilingual context. *Personality and Social Psychology Bulletin, 36,* 1514–1528.

Chiang, H.-Y., & Liu, C.-H. (2011). Evaluation of the benefits of assistive reading software: Perceptions of high school students with learning disabilities. *Assistive Technology, 23,* 199–204.

Chiarelli, V., El Yagoubi, R., Mondini, S., Bisiacchi, P., & Semenza, C. (2011). The syntactic and semantic processing of mass and count nouns: An ERP study. *PLoS ONE, 6,* e25885.

Chomsky, N. (1957). *Syntactic structures.* The Hague: Mouton.

Chomsky, N. (1959). A review of B. F. Skinner's *Verbal Behavior. Language, 35,* 26–58.

Chomsky, N. (1980). *Rules and representations.* New York: Columbia University Press.

Chomsky, N. (2011). Language and other cognitive systems. What is special about language? *Language Learning and Development, 7,* 263–278.

Christianson, K., Hollingsworth, A., Halliwell, J. F., & Ferreira, F. (2001). Thematic roles assigned along the garden path linger. *Cognitive Psychology, 42,* 368–407.

Christoffels, I. K., Kroll, J. K., & Bajo, M. T. (2013). Introduction to *Bilingualism and Cognitive Control. Frontiers in Psychology, 4,* 199.

Christophe, A., Millotte, S., Bernal, S., & Lidz, J. (2008). Bootstrapping lexical and syntactic acquisition. *Language and Speech, 51,* 61–75.

Cicone, M. (1979). The relation between gesture and language in aphasic communication. *Brain and Language, 8,* 324–349.

Clay, Z., Smith, C. L., & Blumstein, D. T. (2012). Food-associated vocalizations in mammals and birds: What do these calls really mean? *Animal Behaviour, 83,* 323–330.

Coco, M. I., & Keller, F. (2012). Scan patterns predict sentence production in the cross-model processing of visual scenes. *Cognitive Science, 36,* 1204–1223.

Colbeck, K. L., & Bowers, J. S. (2012). Blinded by taboo words in L1 but not L2. *Emotion, 12,* 217–222.

Collins, A. M., & Quillian, M. R. (1969). Retrieval time from semantic memory. *Journal of Verbal Learning and Verbal Behavior, 8,* 240–247.

Collins, A. M., & Loftus, E. F. (1975). A spreading-activation theory of semantic processing. *Psychological Review, 82,* 407–428.

Collins, K. (2009). "Dear Prezadent Obama." *Maui Magazine,* http://www.mauimagazine.net/Maui-Magazine/January-February-2009/Dear-Prezadent-Obama/

Colozzo, P., Gillam, R. B., Wood, M., Schnell, R. D., & Johnston, J. R. (2011). Content and form in the narratives of children with specific language impairment. *Journal of Speech, Language, and Hearing Research, 54,* 1609–1627.

Connelly, V., Dockrell, J. E., Walter, K., & Critten, S. (2012). Predicting the quality of composition and written language bursts from oral language, spelling, and handwriting skills in children with and without specific language impairment. *Written Communication, 29,* 278–302.

Conner, P. S., Hyun, J., Wells, B. O., Anema, I., Goral, M., Monéreau-Merry, M.-M., . . . Obler, L. K. (2011). Age-related differences in idiom production in adulthood. *Clinical Linguistics and Phonetics, 25,* 899–912.

Conti-Ramsden, G., Durkin, K., & Simkin, Z. (2010). Language and social factors in the use of cell phone technology by adolescents with and without specific language impairment. *Journal of Speech, Language, and Hearing Research, 53,* 196–208.

Cook, P. S. (2011). Featuring in American Sign Language storytelling. *Storytelling, Self, Society, 7,* 36–62.

Cooper, F. S., Liberman, A. M., & Borst, J. (1950). Synthetic speech: A study of the auditory perception of complex sounds. *Science, 112,* 426.

Cooper, R., Abraham, J., Berman, S., & Staska, M. (1997). The development of infants' preference for motherese. *Infant Behavior and Development, 20,* 477–488.

Cope, N., Eicher, J. D., Meng, H., Gibson, C. J., Hager, L., Lacadie, C., . . . Gruen, J. R. (2012). Variants in the *DXY2* locus are associated with altered brain activation in reading-related brain regions in subjects with reading disability. *NeuroImage, 63,* 148–156.

Corthals, P. (2010). Nine- to twelve-year olds' metalinguistic awareness of homonymy. *International Journal of Language and Communication Disorders, 45,* 121–128.

Craig, A. D. (2009). How do you feel—now? The anterior insula and human awareness. *Nature Reviews: Neuroscience 10,* 59–70.

Cromdal, J. (2013). Bilingual and second language interactions: Views from Scandinavia. *International Journal of Bilingualism, 17,* 121–131.

Cross, D. V., Lane, H. L., & Sheppard, W. C. (1965). Identification and discrimination functions for a visual continuum and their relation to the motor theory of speech perception.

Journal of Experimental Psychology, 70(1), 63–74.

Crystal, D. (2000). *Language death.* Cambridge: Cambridge University Press.

Crystal, D. (2003). *English as a global language.* Cambridge: Cambridge University Press.

Cubelli, R., Paolieri, D., Lotto, L., & Job, R. (2011). The effect of grammatical gender on object categorization. *Journal of Experimental Psychology, 37,* 449–460.

Cullen, J. (2009). Imitation versus communication: Testing for human-like intelligence. *Minds and Machines, 19,* 237–254.

Cutler, A., & Mehler, J. (1993). The periodicity bias. *Journal of Phonetics, 21,* 103–108.

Cutler, A., & Norris, D. (1988). The role of strong syllables in segmentation for lexical access. *Journal of Experimental Psychology: Human Perception and Performance, 14,* 113–121.

Cuza, A. (2012). Crosslinguistic influence at the syntax proper: Interrogative subject-verb inversion in heritage Spanish. *International Journal of Bilingualism, 17,* 71–96.

Da Hawai'i Pidgin Bible. (2000). http://pidginbible.org.

Da Pos, O., & Albertazzi, L. (2010). It is in the nature of colors. *Seeing and Perceiving, 23,* 39–73.

Dalal, R. H., & Loeb, D. F. (2005). Imitative production of regular past tense -ed by

English-speaking children with specific language impairment. *International Journal of Language and Communication Disorders, 40,* 67–82.

Damjanovic, L., Roberson, D., Athanasopoulos, P., Kasai, C., & Dyson, M. (2010). Searching for happiness across cultures. *Journal of Cognition and Culture, 10,* 85–107.

Darwin, C. (1859). *On the origin of species: Or the preservation of favoured races in the struggle for life.* London: John Murray.

Davies, B. L. (2007). Grice's cooperative principle: Meaning and rationality. *Journal of Pragmatics, 39,* 2308–2331.

Davila-Ross, M., Allcock, B., Thomas, C., & Bard, K. A. (2011). Aping expressions? Chimpanzees produce distinct laugh types when responding to laughter of others. *Emotion, 11,* 1013–1020.

Davis, B. L., & MacNeilage, P. F. (1994). Organization of babbling: A case study. *Language and Speech, 37,* 341–355.

Davis, M. (n.d.) MRC Cognition and Brain Sciences Unit. http://www.mrc-cbu.cam.ac.uk/people/matt.davis/cmabridge/

de Leeuw, E., Mennen, I., & Scobbie, J. M. (2011). Singing a different tune in your native language: First language attrition of prosody. *International Journal of Bilingualism, 16,* 101–116.

De Raeve, L., Baerts, J., Colleye, E., & Croux, E. (2012). Changing schools for the deaf: Updating the educational setting for our deaf children in the 21st century, a big challenge. *Deafness and Education International, 14,* 48–59.

de Zubicaray, G. I., Hansen, S., & McMahon, K. L. (2013). Differential processing of thematic and categorical conceptual relations in spoken word production. *Journal of Experimental Psychology: General, 142,* 131–142.

DeCasper, A. J., & Fifer, W. P. (1980). Of human bonding: Newborns prefer their mothers' voices. *Science, 208,* 1174–1176.

DeCasper, A. J., & Spence, M. J. (1986). Prenatal maternal speech influences newborns' perception of speech sounds. *Infant Behavior and Development, 9,* 133–150.

DeCasper, A. J., Lecanuet, J., Busnel, M., Granier-Deferre, C., & Maugeais, R. (1994). Fetal reactions to recurrent maternal speech. *Infant Behavior and Development, 17,* 159–164.

Dehaene, S. (2009). *Reading in the brain: The new science of how we read.* New York: Hudson.

Dehaene, S., & Cohen, L. (2011). The unique role of the visual word form area in reading. *Trends in Cognitive Sciences, 15,* 254–262

DeKeyser, R. M. (2013). Age effects in second language learning: Stepping stones toward better understanding. *Language Learning, 63,* Suppl. 1, 52–67.

Delgado, A. R. (2004). Order in Spanish colour words: Evidence against linguistic relativity. *British Journal of Psychology, 95,* 81–90.

Dell, G. S. (1986). A spreading-activation theory of retrieval in sentence production. *Psychological Review, 9,* 283–321.

Dell, G. S., Schwartz, M. F., Martin, N., Saffran, E. M., & Gagnon, D. A. (1997). Lexical access in aphasic and nonaphasic speakers. *Psychological Review, 104,* 801–838.

Deng, Y., Guo, R., Ding, G., & Peng, D. (2012). Top-down modulations from dorsal stream in lexical recognition: An effective connectivity fMRI study. *PLoS ONE, 7,* e33337.

DeThorne, L. S., Petrill, S. A., Schatschneider, C., & Cutting, L. (2010). Conversational language use as a predictor of early reading development: Language history as a moderating variable. *Journal of Speech, Language, and Hearing Research, 53,* 209–223.

Diehl, R. L., Lotto, A. J., & Holt, L. L. (2004). Speech perception. *Annual Review of Psychology, 55,* 149–179.

Digweed, S. M., & Rendall, D. (2009). Predator-associated vocalizations in North American red squirrels (Tamiasciurus hudsonicus): To whom are alarm calls addressed and how do they function? *Ethology, 115,* 1190–1199.

Digweed, S. M., & Rendall, D. (2010). Are the alarm calls of North American red squirrels (Tamiasciurus hudsonicus) functionally referential? *Behaviour, 147,* 1201–1218.

Dijkerman, H., & de Haan, E. F. (2007). Somatosensory processes subserving perception and action. *Behavioral and Brain Sciences, 30,* 189–201.

Dimigen, O., Kliegl, R., & Sommer, W. (2012). Trans-saccadic parafoveal preview benefits in fluent reading: A study with fixation-related brain potentials. *NeuroImage, 62,* 381–393.

Disotell, T. R. (2012). Archaic human genomics. *American Journal of Physical Anthropology, 149,* 24–39.

Ditman, T., Holcomb, P. J., & Kuperberg, G. R. (2007). The contributions of lexico-semantic discourse information to the resolution of ambiguous categorical anaphors. *Language and Cognitive Processes, 22,* 793–827.

Dixon, L. Q., Wu, S., & Daraghmeh, A. (2012). Profiles in bilingualism: Factors influencing kindergartners' language proficiency. *Early Childhood Education Journal, 40,* 25–34.

Dixon, L. Q., Zhao, J., Quiroz, B. G., & Shin, J.-Y. (2012). Home and community factors influencing bilingual children's ethnic language vocabulary development. *International Journal of Bilingualism, 16,* 541–565.

Domahs, F., Nagels, A., Domahs, U., Whitney, C., Wiese, R., & Kircher, T. (2012). Where the mass counts: Common cortical activation for different kinds of nonsingularity. *Journal of Cognitive Neuroscience, 24,* 915–932.

Domsch, C., Richels, C., Saldana, M., Coleman, C., Wimberly, C., & Maxwell, L. (2012). Narrative skill and syntactic complexity in school-age children with and without late language emergence. *International Journal of Language and Communication Disorders, 47,* 197–207.

Dooling, R. J., Best, C. T., & Brown, S. D. (1995). Discrimination of synthetic full-formant and sinewave /ra-la/ continua by budgerigars (*Melopsittacus undulatus*) and zebra finches (*Taeniopygia guttata*). *Journal of the Acoustical Society of America, 97,* 1893–1846.

Dopkins, S., & Nordlie, J. (2011). Exploring a decrease in recognition performance for non-antecedents following the processing of anaphors. *Discourse Processes, 48,* 432–451.

Dore, J. (1975). Holophrases, speech acts and language universals. *Journal of Child Language, 2,* 21–40.

Drager, K. D. R., Reichle, J., & Pinkoski, C. (2010). Synthesized speech output and children: A scoping review. *American Journal of Speech-Language Pathology, 19,* 259–273.

Drews, F. A., Pasupathi, M., & Strayer, D. L. (2008). Passenger and cell phone conversations in simulated driving. *Journal of Experimental Psychology: Applied, 14,* 392–400.

Du, Y., Zhang, Q., & Zhang, J. X. (2014). Does N200 reflect semantic processing? An ERP study on Chinese visual word recognition. *PLoS ONE, 9,* e90794.

Duff, M. C., & Schmidt, S. (2012). The hippocampus and the flexible use and processing of language. *Frontiers in Human Neuroscience, 6,* 69.

Dunbar, R. (1998). *Grooming, gossip and the evolution of language.* Cambridge, MA: Harvard University Press.

Eilola, T. M., & Havelka, J. (2010). Behavioral and physiological responses to the emotional and taboo Stroop tasks in native and non-native speakers of English. *International Journal of Bilingualism, 15,* 353–369.

Eilola, T. M., Havelka, J., & Sharma, D. (2007). Emotional activation in the first and second language. *Cognition and Emotion, 21,* 1064–1076.

Eimas, P. D. (1974). Auditory and linguistic processing of cues for place of articulation by infants. *Perception and Psychophysics, 16*(3), 513–521.

Eimas, P. D. (1975). Auditory and phonetic coding of the cues for speech: Discrimination of the (r-l) distinction by young infants. *Perception and Psychophysics, 18*(5), 341–347.

Eimas, P. D., Siqueland, E. R., Jusczyk, P., & Vigorito, J. (1971). Speech perception in infants. *Science, 171,* 303–306.

Ellison, M. (Producer), Jonze, S. (Producer, Director), & Landay, V. (Producer). (2013). *Her* [Motion picture]. United States: Warner Bros. Pictures.

Enard, W. (2011). FOXP2 and the role of cortico-basal ganglia circuits in speech and language evolution. *Current Opinion in Neurobiology, 21*(3), 415–424.

Engel de Abreu, P. M. J. (2011). Working memory in multilingual children: Is there a bilingual effect? *Memory, 19,* 529–537.

Engel de Abreu, P. M. J., Cruz-Santos, A., Tourinho, C. J., Martin, R., & Bialystok, E. (2012). Bilingualism enriches the poor: Enhanced cognitive control in low-income minority children. *Psychological Science, 23,* 1364–1371.

Eskritt, M., Whalen, J., & Lee, K. (2008). Preschoolers can recognize violations of the Gricean maxims. *British Journal of Developmental Psychology, 26,* 435–443.

Esseily, R., Jacquet, A.-Y., & Fagard, J. (2011). Handedness for grasping objects and pointing and the development of language in 14-month-old infants. *Laterality, 16,* 565–585.

Estes, K., & Bowen, S. (2013). Learning about sounds contributes to learning about words: Effects of prosody and phonotactics on infant word learning. *Journal of Experimental Child Psychology, 114,* 405–417.

Estigarriba, B. (2010). Facilitation by variation: Right-to-left learning of English yes/no questions. *Cognitive Science 34,* 68–93.

Ettlinger, M., Lanter, J., & Van Pay, C. K. (2013, June 17). Learning to remember by learning to speak. *Developmental Psychology.* Advance online publication. doi: 10.1037/a0033317

Fairbanks, G. (1955). Selective vocal effects of delayed auditory feedback. *Journal of Speech and Hearing Disorders, 20,* 333–345.

Falk, D. (2009). *Finding our tongues: Mothers, infants and the origin of language.* New York: Basic Books.

Fant, G. (1970). *Acoustic theory of speech production.* The Hague: Mouton.

Farrell, M. T., & Abrams, L. (2011). Tip-of-the-tongue states reveal age differences in the syllable frequency effect. *Journal of Experimental Psychology: Learning, Memory, and Cognition, 37,* 277–285.

Fasolo, M., Majorano, M., & D'Odorico, L. (2008). Babbling and first words in children with slow expressive development. *Clinical Linguistics and Phonetics, 22,* 83–94.

Fedurek, P., & Dunbar, R. M. (2009). What does mutual grooming tell us about why chimpanzees groom? *Ethology, 115,* 566–575.

Feeney, A., & Bonnefon, J.-P. (2012). Politeness and honesty contribute additively to the interpretations of scalar implicatures. *Journal of Language and Social Psychology, 32,* 181–190.

Feldman, H. M., Lee, E. S., Yeatman, J. D., & Yeom, K. W. (2011). Language and reading skills in school-aged children and adolescents born preterm are associated with white matter properties on diffusion tensor imaging. *Neuropsychologia, 50,* 3384–3362.

Fenlon, J., Denmark, T., Campbell, R., & Woll, B. (2007). Seeing sentence boundaries. *Sign Language and Linguistics, 10,* 177–200.

Ferdinand, A. O., & Menachemi, N. (2014). Associations between driving performance and engaging in secondary tasks: A systematic review. *American Journal of Public Health, 104,* e39–e48.

Ferguson, C. J., & Donnellan, M. B. (2014). Is the association between children's baby video viewing and poor language development robust? A reanalysis of Zimmerman, Christakis, and Meltzoff (2007). *Developmental Psychology, 50,* 129–137.

Fernald, A. (1985). Four-month-old infants prefer to listen to motherese. *Infant Behavior and Development, 8,* 181–195.

Fernald, A., & Kuhl, P. K. (1987). Acoustic determinants of infant preference for motherese speech. *Infant Behavior and Development, 10,* 279–293.

Fernald, A., & McRoberts, G. (1996). Prosodic bootstrapping: A critical analysis of the argument and the evidence. In J. L. Morgan & K. Demuth (Eds.), *Signal to syntax: Bootstrapping from speech to grammar in early acquisition* (pp. 365–388). London: Psychology Press.

Ferrier, S., Dunham, P., & Dunham, F. (2000). The confused robot: Two-year-olds' responses to breakdowns in conversation. *Social Development, 9,* 337–347.

Festman, J. (2013). The complexity-cost factor in bilingualism. *Behavioral and Brain Sciences, 36,* 355–356.

Fielding-Barnsley, R., & Hay, I. (2012). Comparative effectiveness of phonological awareness and oral language intervention for children with low emergent literacy skills. *Australian Journal of Language and Literacy, 35,* 271–286.

Finkbeiner, M., Forster, K., Nicol, J., & Nakamura, K. (2004). The role of polysemy in masked semantic and translation priming. *Journal of Memory And Language, 51,* 1–22.

Fischer, S. R. (2001). *A history of writing.* London: Reaktion Books.

Fitzgerald, C. E., Hadley, P. A., & Rispoli, M. (2013). Are some parents' interaction styles associated with richer grammatical input? *American Journal of Speech-Language Pathology, 22,* 476–488.

Fodor, J. A. (1983). *The modularity of the mind.* Cambridge, MA: MIT Press.

Foppolo, F., Guasti, M. T., & Chierchia, G. (2012). Scalar implicatures in child language: Give children a chance. *Language Learning and Development, 8,* 365–394.

Ford, J. (2011). Helen Keller was never in a Chinese room. *Minds and Machines, 21,* 57–72.

Frazier, L., & Rayner, K. (1982). Making and correcting errors during sentence comprehension: Eye movements in the analysis of structurally ambiguous sentences. *Cognitive Psychology, 14,* 178–210.

French, R. M. (2012). Moving beyond the Turing test. *Communications of the ACM, 55* (12), 74–77.

Frie, R. (2013). Culture and language: Bilingualism in the German-Jewish experience and across contexts. *Clinical Social Work Journal, 41,* 11–19.

Fried-Oken, M., Beukelman, D. R., & Hux, K. (2012). Current and future AAC research considerations for adults with acquired cognitive and communication impairments. *Assistive Technology, 24,* 56–66.

Friederici, A. D., Brauer, J., & Lohmann, G. (2011). Maturation of the language network: From inter- to intrahemispheric connectivities. *PLoS ONE, 6,* e20726.

Friederici, A. D., Oberecker, R., & Brauer, J. (2012). Neurophysiological preconditions of syntax acquisition. *Psychological Research, 76,* 204–211.

Frisson, S., & Pickering, M. J. (1999). The processing of metonymy: Evidence from eye movements. *Journal of Experimental Psychology: Learning, Memory, and Cognition, 25,* 1366–1383.

Fromkin, V. A. (1971). The non-anomalous nature of anomalous utterances. *Language, 27,* 27–52.

Furbach, U., Glöckner, I., & Pelzer, B. (2010). An application of automated reasoning in natural language question answering. *AI Communications, 23,* 241–265.

Gabriel, U., & Gygax, P. (2008). Can societal language amendments change gender representation? The case of Norway. *Scandinavian Journal of Psychology, 49,* 451–457.

Gaißert, N., Waterkamp, S., Fleming, R. W., Bülthoff, I., & Proulx, M. J. (2012). Haptic categorical perception of shape. *PLoS ONE, 7*(8), 1–7.

Galantucci, B., Fowler, C. A., & Turvey, M. T. (2006). The motor theory of speech perception reviewed. *Psychonomic Bulletin and Review 13,* 361–377.

Ganger, J., & Brent, M. R. (2004). Reexamining the vocabulary spurt. *Developmental Psychology, 40,* 621–632.

Garbin, G., Sanjuan, A., Forn, C., Bustamante, J. C., Rodriguez-Pujadas, A., Belloch, B., . . . Ávila, C. (2010). Bridging language and attention: Brain basis of the impact of bilingualism on cognitive control. *NeuroImage, 53,* 1272–1278.

García, E. E., & Náñez, J. E. (2010). *Bilingualism and cognition: Informing research, pedagogy, and policy.* Washington, DC: American Psychological Association.

Gardner, B. T., & Gardner, R. (1975). Evidence for sentence constituents in the early utterances of child and chimpanzee. *Journal of Experimental Psychology: General, 104,* 244–267.

Gardner, R. A., & Gardner, B. T. (1969). Teaching sign language to a chimpanzee. *Science, 165*, 664–672.

Gardner, R. A., & Gardner, B. T. (1984). A vocabulary test for chimpanzees. *Journal of Comparative Psychology, 98*, 381–404.

Gardner, R. A., & Gardner, B. T. (1998). *The structure of learning from sign stimuli to sign language*. Hillsdale, NJ: Lawrence Erlbaum Associates.

Gardner, R., Gardner, B. T., & Van Cantfort, T. E. (1989). *Teaching sign language to chimpanzees*. Albany:State University of New York Press.

Gaudreau, G., Monetta, L., Macoir, J., Laforce, R., Jr., Poulin, S., & Hudon, C. (2013). Verbal irony comprehension in older adults with amnestic mild cognitive impairment. *Neuropsychology, 27*, 702–712.

Gautreau, A., Hoen, M., & Meunier, F. (2013). Let's all speak together! Exploring the masking effects of various languages on spoken word identification in multi-linguistic babble. *PLoS ONE, 8*, e65668.

Gayraud, F., Lee, H.-R., & Barkat-Defradas, M. (2011). Syntactic and lexical context of pauses and hesitations in the discourse of Alzheimer patients and healthy elderly subjects. *Clinical Linguistics and Phonetics, 25*, 198–209.

Gebauer, D., Enzinger, C., Kronbichler, M., Schurz, M., Reishofer, G., Koschutnig, K., . . . Fink, A. (2012). Distinct patterns of brain function in children with isolated spelling impairment. *Neuropsychologia, 50*, 1353–1361.

Gebauer, D., Fink, A., Kargl, R., Reishofer, G., Koschutnig, K., Purgstaller, C., . . . Enzinger, C. (2012). Differences in brain function and changes with intervention in children with poor spelling and reading abilities. *PLoS ONE, 7, 5*, e38201.

Gell-Mann, M., & Ruhlen, M. (2011). The origin and evolution of word order. *Proceedings of the National Academy of Sciences USA, 108*, 17290–17295.

Gendron, M., Lindquist, K. A., Barsalou, L., & Barrett, L. F. (2012). Emotion words shape emotion percepts. *Emotion, 12*, 314–325.

Geng, J., Kirchgessner, M., & Schnur, T. (2013). The mechanism underlying lexical selection: Evidence from the picture–picture interference paradigm. *Quarterly Journal of Experimental Psychology, 66*, 261–276.

Geranmayeh, F., Brownsett, S., Leech, R., Beckmann, C., Woodhead, Z., & Wise, R. (2012). The contribution of the inferior parietal cortex to spoken language production. *Brain and Language, 121*(1), 47–57.

Ghosh, S. S., Tourville, J. A., & Guenther, F. H. (2008). A neuroimaging study of premotor lateralization and cerebellar involvement in the production of phonemes and syllables. *Journal of Speech, Language and Hearing Research, 51*, 1183–1202.

Gibbs, R. W., Jr., & Bryant, G. A. (2008). Striving for optimal relevance when answering questions. *Cognition, 106*, 345–369.

Gibson, E., Bergen, L., & Piantadosi, S. T. (2013). Rational integration of noisy evidence and prior semantic expectations in sentence interpretation. *Proceedings of the National Academy of Sciences USA, 20*, 8051–8056.

Gibson, J.J. (1979). *The ecological approach to visual perception*. Boston: Houghton Mifflin.

Gil-da-Costa, R., Martin, A., Lopes, M. A., Muñoz, M., Fritz, J. B., & Braun, A. R. (2006). Species-specific calls activate homologs of Broca's and Wernicke's areas in the macaque. *Nature Neuroscience, 9*, 1064–1070.

Gildersleeve-Neumann, C. E., Davis, B. L., & MacNeilage, P. F. (2013). Syllabic patterns in the early vocalizations of Quichua children. *Applied Psycholinguistics, 34*, 111–134.

Gillespie-Lynch, K., Greenfield, P. M., Lyn, H., & Savage-Rumbaugh, S. (2011). The role of dialogue in the ontogeny and phylogeny of early symbol combinations: A cross-species comparison of bonobo, chimpanzee, and human learners. *First Language, 31*, 442–460.

Givón, T. T., & Rumbaugh, S. (2009). Can apes learn grammar? A short detour into language evolution. In J. Guo, E. Lieven, N. Budwig, S. Ervin-Tripp, K.

Nakamura, & Ş. Özçalişkan (Eds.), *Crosslinguistic approaches to the psychology of language: Research in the tradition of Dan Isaac Slobin* (pp. 299–309). New York: Psychology Press.

Gleitman, L. (1990). Structural sources of verb learning. *Language Acquisition, 1,* 1–63.

Glenberg, A. M., & Kaschak, M. P. (2002). Grounding language in action. *Psychonomic Bulletin and Review, 9*(3), 558–565.

Glenberg, A. M., Robertson, D. A., Kaschak, M. P., & Malter, A. J. (2003). Embodied meaning and negative priming. *Behavioral and Brain Sciences, 26,* 644–647.

Gnanadesikan, A. E. (2009). *The writing revolution: Cuneiform to the Internet*. Malden, MA: Wiley-Blackwell.

Goddard, C. (2002). The search for the shared semantic core of all languages. In C. Goddard & A. Wierzbicka (Eds.), *Meaning and universal grammar: Theory and empirical findings (Vol. I)* (pp. 5–40). Amsterdam: John Benjamins.

Goetry, V., & Kolinsky, R. (2000). The role of rhythmic cues for speech segmentation in monolingual and bilingual listeners. *Psychologica Belgica, 40,* 115–152.

Goldfield, B. A., & Reznick, J. (1990). Early lexical acquisition: Rate, content, and the vocabulary spurt. *Journal of Child Language, 17,* 171–183.

Goldman, J. G., & Manis, F. R. (2013). Relationships among cortical thickness, reading skill, and print exposure in adults. *Scientific Study of Reading, 17,* 163–176.

Goldstein, M. H., & Schwade, J. A. (2008). Social feedback to infants' babbling facilitates rapid phonological learning. *Psychological Science, 19,* 515–523.

Goldstein, M. H., Schwade, J., Briesch, J., & Syal, S. (2010). Learning while babbling: Prelinguistic object-directed vocalizations indicate a readiness to learn. *Infancy, 15,* 362–391.

Golfinopoulos, E., Tourville, J. A., Bohland, J. W., Ghosh, S. S., Nieto-Castanon, A., & Guenther, F. H. (2011). fMRI investigation of unexpected somatosensory feedback perturbation during speech. *NeuroImage, 55,* 1324–1338.

Gollan, T. H., & Goldrick, M. (2012). Does bilingualism twist your tongue? *Cognition, 125,* 491–497.

Gollan, T. H., Salmon, D. P., Montoya, R. I., & Galasko, D. R. (2011). Degree of bilingualism predicts age of diagnosis of Alzheimer's disease in low-education but not in highly educated Hispanics. *Neuropsychologia, 49,* 3826–3830.

Gómez-Velázquez, F. R., González-Garrido, A. A., & Vega-Gutiérrez, O. L. (2013). Naming abilities and orthographic recognition during childhood: An event-related brain potential study. *International Journal of Psychology Studies, 5,* 55–68.

Gonnerman, L. M., Seidenberg, M. S., & Andersen, E. S. (2007). Graded semantic and phonological similarity effects in priming: Evidence for a distributed connectionist approach to morphology. *Journal of Experimental Psychology: General, 136,* 323–345.

Gonzalez-Gomez, N., & Nazzi, T. (2013). Effects of prior phonotactic knowledge on infant word segmentation: The case of nonadjacent dependencies. *Journal of Speech, Language, and Hearing Research, 56,* 840–849.

Goodman, N. D., & Stuhlmüller, A. (2013). Knowledge and implicature: Modeling language understanding as social cognition. *Topics in Cognitive Science, 5,* 173–184.

Gopnik, M. (1990). Feature-blind grammar and dysphasia. *Nature,344,* 715.

Gow, D. R. (2012). The cortical organization of lexical knowledge: A dual lexicon model of spoken language processing. *Brain and Language, 121,* 273–288.

Grande, M., Meffert, E., Shoenberger, E., Jung, S., Frauenrath, T., Huber, W., . . . Heim, S. (2012). From a concept to a word in a syntactically complete sentence: An fMRI study on spontaneous language production in an overt picture description task. *NeuroImage, 61,* 702–714.

Granier-Deferre, C., Bassereau, S., Ribeiro, A., Jacquet, A., & DeCasper, A. J. (2011). A melodic contour repeatedly experienced by human near-term fetuses elicits a profound cardiac reaction one month after birth. *PloS ONE, 6*(2), 1–10.

Graves, W. W., Grabowski, T. J., Mehta, S., & Gupta, P. (2008). The left posterior superior temporal gyrus participates specifically in accessing lexical phonology. *Journal of Cognitive Neuroscience, 20,* 1698–1710.

Gray, S., Brinkley, S., & Svetina, D. (2012). Word learning by preschoolers with SLI: Effect of phonotactic probability and object familiarity. *Journal of Speech, Language, and Hearing Research, 55,* 1289–1300.

Graziano, M.S.A. (2008). *The intelligent movement machine.* Oxford: Oxford University Press.

Graziano, M. S. A., and Aflalo, T. N. (2007). Mapping behavioral repertoire onto the cortex. *Neuron, 56,* 239–251.

Green, L. B., & Klecan-Aker, J. S. (2012). Teaching story-grammar components to increase oral narrative ability: A group intervention study. *Child Language Teaching and Therapy, 28,* 263–276.

Green, S. (2011). Life, translated. *Communications of the ACM, 54*(8), 19–21.

Greenberg, J. H. (1963). Some universals of grammar with particular reference to the order of meaningful elements. In J. H. Greenberg (Ed.), *Universals of language* (pp. 73–113). Cambridge, MA: MIT Press.

Greenfield, P. M. (1991). Language, tools and brain: The ontogeny and phylogeny of hierarchically organized

sequential behavior. *Behavioral and Brain Sciences, 14,* 531–595.

Greer, T. (2013). Scandinavian bilingual and L2 interaction: A view from afar. *International Journal of Bilingualism, 17,* 237–244.

Gregg, M. K., & Samuel, A. G. (2012). Feature assignment in perception of auditory figure. *Journal of Experimental Psychology: Human Perception and Performance, 38*(4), 998–1013.

Grice, H. P. (1975). Logic and conversation. In P. Cole & J. Morgan (Eds.), *Syntax and semantics: Vol. 3. Speech acts* (pp. 41–58). New York: Academic Press.

Grieser, D. L., & Kuhl, P. K. (1988). Maternal speech to infants in a tonal language: Support for universal prosodic features in motherese. *Developmental Psychology, 24,* 14–20.

Grimme, B., Fuchs, S., Perrier, P., & Schöner, G. (2011). Limb versus speech motor control: A conceptual review. *Motor Control, 15*(1), 5–33.

Guellai, B., & Streri, A. (2011). Cues for early social skills: Direct gaze modulates newborns' recognition of talking faces. *PLoS ONE, 6*(4), 1–6.

Guenther, F. H., & Vladusich, T. (2012). A neural theory of speech acquisition and production. *Journal of Neurolinguistics, 25,* 408–422.

Güldemann, T., & Stoneking, M. (2008). A historical appraisal of clicks: A linguistic and genetic

population perspective. *Annual Review of Anthropology, 37,* 93–109.

Gupta, P. (2005). Primacy and recency in nonword repetition. *Memory, 13,* 318–324.

Gupta, P., & Tinsdale, J. (2009). Word learning, phonological short-term memory, phonotactic probability and long-term memory: Towards an integrated framework. *Philosophical Transactions of the Royal Science B, 364,* 3755–3771.

Gupta, R., Duff, M. C., & Tranel, D. (2011). Bilateral amygdala damage impairs the acquisition and use of common ground in social interaction. *Neuropsychology, 25,* 137–146.

Gutierrez, A., Pilotti, M., Romero, E., Mahamane, S., & Broderick, T. (2012). Proactive interference between languages: Do task demands matter? *International Journal of Bilingualism, 17,* 505–524.

Hall, S. J., Vince, M. A., Walser, E. S., & Garson, P. J. (1988). Vocalisations of the Chillingham cattle. *Behaviour, 104,* 78–104.

Hamill, A. C., & Stein, C. H. (2011). Culture and empowerment in the deaf community: An analysis of Internet weblogs. *Journal of Community and Applied Social Psychology, 21,* 388–406.

Han, W.-J. (2012). Bilingualism and academic achievement. *Child Development, 83,* 300–321.

Han, W.-J., & Huang, C.-C. (2010). The forgotten treasure: Bilingualism and Asian children's emotional and behavioral health. *American Journal of Public Health, 100,* 831–838.

Hanna, J. E., & Tanenhaus, M. K. (2004). Pragmatic effects on reference resolution in the collaborative task: Evidence from eye movements. *Cognitive Science, 28,* 105–115.

Hannagan, T., Ktori, M., Chanceaux, M., & Grainger, J. (2012). Deciphering CAPTCHAs: What a Turing test reveals about human cognition. *PLoS ONE, 7,* e32121.

Harold, M., & Barlow, S. M. (2013). Effects of environmental stimulation on infant vocalizations and orofacial dynamics at the onset of canonical babbling. *Infant Behavior and Development, 36,* 84–93.

Harris, M., & Chasin, J. (2005). Visual attention in deaf and hearing infants: The role of auditory cues. *Journal of Child Psychology and Psychiatry, 46,* 1116–1123.

Hauser, M. D., Chomsky, N., & Fitch, W. (2002). The faculty of language: What is it, who has it, and how did it evolve? *Science, 298,* 1569–1579.

Hay, J. F., & Saffran, J. R. (2012). Rhythmic grouping biases constrain infant statistical learning. *Infancy, 17,* 610–641.

Hayashi, Y., & Murphy, V. A. (2013). On the nature of morphological awareness in Japanese-English bilingual children: A cross-linguistic perspective. *Bilingualism: Language and Cognition, 16,* 49–67.

Hayden, B. (2012). Neandertal social structure? *Oxford Journal of Archaeology, 31,* 1–26.

Hayes, C. (1951). *The ape in our house.* New York: Harper.

Hayes, J. R. (2012). Modeling and remodeling. *Written Communication, 29,* 369–388.

Hayes, K. J., & Hayes, C. (1952). Imitation in a home-raised chimpanzee. *Journal of Comparative and Physiological Psychology, 45,* 450–459.

Hayes, K. J., & Hayes, C. (1953). Picture perception in a home-raised chimpanzee. *Journal of Comparative and Physiological Psychology, 46,* 470–474.

Hayes, K. J., & Nissen, C. H. (1971). Higher mental functions of a home-raised chimpanzee. In A. M. Schrier & F. Stollnitz (Eds.), *Behaviour of non-human primates* (Vol. 4, pp. 50–115). New York: Academic Press.

Heilman, J., Miller, J. F., Nockerts, A., & Dunaway, C. (2010). Properties of the narrative scoring scheme using narrative retells in young school-age children. *American Journal of Speech-Language Pathology, 19,* 15–166.

Heinks-Maldonado, T. M. (2005). Fine-tuning of auditory cortex during speech production. *Psychophysiology, 42,* 180–190.

Henning, A., & Striano, T. (2011). Infant and maternal sensitivity to interpersonal timing. *Child Development, 82,* 916–931.

Herkenrath, A. (2011). Receptive multilingualism in an immigrant constellation: Examples from Turkish-German children's language. *International Journal of Bilingualism, 16,* 287–314.

Heselwood, B. (2007). Schwa and the phonotactics of RP English. *Transactions of the Philological Society, 105,* 148–187.

Hickok, G., & Poeppel, D. (2007). The cortical organization of speech processing. *Nature Reviews Neuroscience, 8,* 393–402.

Higginbotham, D. J., Lesher, G. W., Moulton, B. J., & Roark, B. (2012). The application of natural language processing to augmentative and alternative communication. *Assistive Technology, 24,* 14–24.

Highman, C., Leitao, S., Hennessey, N., & Piek, J. (2012). Prelinguistic communication development in children with childhood apraxia of speech: A retrospective analysis. *International Journal of Speech-Language Pathology, 14,* 35–47.

Higuchi, S., Chaminade, T., Imamizu, H., & Kawato, M. (2009). Shared neural correlates for language and tool use in Broca's area. *Neuroreport: For Rapid Communication of Neuroscience Research, 20,* 1376–1381.

Hirsh-Pasek, K., & Treiman, R. (1982). Doggerel: Motherese in a new context. *Journal of Child Language, 9,* 229–237.

Hockett, C. F. (1960). The origin of speech. *Scientific American, 203,* 89–97.

Hoffmann, A. (2010). Can machines think? An old question reformulated. *Minds and Machines, 20,* 203–212.

Holden, C. (1999). Neandertals left speechless? *Science, 283,* 1111.

Holden, C. (2006). Court revives Georgia sticker case. *Science, 312,* 1292.

Holm, J. A. (2000). *Introduction to pidgins and creoles.* Cambridge: Cambridge University Press.

Holsinger, E. (2013). Representing idioms: Syntactic and contextual effects on idiom processing. *Language and Speech, 56,* 373–394.

Holtgraves, T. (2008). Conversation, speech acts, and memory. *Memory and Cognition, 36,* 361–374.

Hoonhorst, I. I., Medina, V. V., Colin, C. C., Markessis, E. E., Radeau, M. M., Deltenre, P. P., & Serniclaes, W. W. (2011). Categorical perception of voicing, colors and facial expressions: A developmental study. *Speech Communication, 53,* 417–430.

Hopkins, W. D. (2010). The comparative neuropsychology of tool use in primates with specific reference to chimpanzees and capuchin monkeys. In M. L. Platt & A. A. Ghazanfar (Eds.), *Primate neuroethology* (pp. 587–614). New York: Oxford University Press

Hopp, H., & Schmid, M. S. (2013). Perceived foreign accent in first language attrition and second language acquisition: The impact of age of acquisition and bilingualism. *Applied Psycholinguistics, 34,* 361–394.

Horwitz, B., Amunts, K., Bhattacharyya, R., Patkin, D., Jeffries, K., Zilles, K., & Braun, A. R. (2003). Activation of Broca's area during the production of spoken and signed language: A combined cytoarchitectonic mapping and PET analysis. *Neuropsychologia, 41,* 1868.

Hosseini, S. M. H., Black, J. M., Soriano, T., Bugescu, N., Martinez, R., Raman, M. M., . . . Hoeft, F. (2013). Topological properties of large-scale structural brain networks in children with familial risk for reading difficulties. *NeuroImage, 71,* 260–274.

Houde, J. F., & Nagarajan, S. S. (2011). Speech production as state feedback control. *Frontiers in Human Neuroscience, 5.*

Hsu, H. (2014). Effects of bilingualism and trilingualism in L2 production: Evidence from errors and self-repairs in early balanced bilingual and trilingual adults. *Journal of Psycholinguistic Research, 43*(4), 357–379. doi:10.1007/s10936-013-9257-3.

Huber, J. E., Darling, M., Francis, E. J., & Zhang, D. (2012). Impact of typical aging and Parkinson's disease on the relationship among breath pausing, syntax, and punctuation. *American Journal of Speech-Language Pathology, 21,* 368–379.

Hublin, J. J. (2009). The origin of Neandertals. *Proceedings of the National Academy of Sciences USA, 106,* 16022–16027.

Huettig, F., Chen, J., Bowerman, M., & Majid, A. (2010). Do language-specific categories shape conceptual processing? Mandarin classifier distinctions influence eye gaze behavior, but only during linguistic processing. *Journal of Cognition and Culture, 10,* 39–58.

Hunt, L., Ahles, S. P., Gibson, L., Minai, U., & Fiorentino, R. (2013). Pragmatic inferences modulate N400 during sentence comprehension: Evidence from picture-sentence verification. *Neuroscience Letters, 534,* 246–251.

Hupp, J. M., & Jungers, M. K. (2013). Beyond words: Comprehension and production of pragmatic prosody in adults and children. *Journal of Experimental Child Psychology, 115,* 536–551.

Hyde, M., & Power, D. (2005). Some ethical dimensions of cochlear implantation for deaf children and their families. *Journal of Deaf Studies and Deaf Education, 11,* 102–111.

Hyman, I. E., Jr., Boss, M. S., Wise, B. M., McKenzie, K. E., & Caggiano, J. M. (2010). Did you see the unicycling clown? Inattentional blindness while walking and talking on a cell phone. *Applied Cognitive Psychology, 24,* 597–607.

Hyman, P. (2014). Speech-to-speech translations stutter, but researchers see mellifluous future. *Communications of the ACM, 57,* 4, 16–19.

Iacoboni, M., Woods, R. P., Brass, M., Bekkering, H., Mazziotta, J. C., & Rizzolatti, G. (1999). Cortical mechanisms of human imitation. *Science, 286,* 2526–2528.

Iordanescu, L., Grabowecky, M., & Suzuki, S. (2013). Action enhances auditory but not visual temporal sensitivity. *Psychonomic Bulletin and Review, 20*(1), 108–114.

Irmen, L., & Roßberg, N. (2006). How formal versus semantic gender influences the interpretation of person denotations. *Swiss Journal of Psychology, 65,* 157–165.

Ivanova, I., Pickering, M. J., Branigan, H. P., McLean, J. F., & Costa, A. (2011). The comprehension of anomalous sentences: Evidence from structural priming. *Cognition, 122,* 193–209.

Ivry, R. B., Spencer, R. M., Zelaznik, H. N., & Diedrichsen, J. (2002). The cerebellum and event timing. *Annals of the New York Academy of Sciences USA, 978,* 302–317.

Ivy, L. J., & Masterson, J. J. (2011). A comparison of oral and written English styles in African American students at different stages of writing development. *Language, Speech, and Hearing Services in Schools, 42,* 31–40.

Iyer, S., & Oller, D. (2008). Prelinguistic vocal development in infants with typical hearing and infants with severe-to-profound hearing loss. *Volta Review, 108,* 115–138.

Jaeger, T. F., Furth, K., & Hilliard, C. (2012). Phonological overlap affects lexical selection during sentence production. *Journal of Experimental Psychology: Learning, Memory, and Cognition, 38,* 1439–1449.

Jakobson, R. (1962). Why "mama" and "papa"? In R. Jakobson, *Selected writings: Vol. I. Phonological studies* (pp. 538–545). The Hague: Mouton.

Jakobson, R. (1968). *Child language, aphasia and phonological universals.* The Hague: Mouton.

James, L. E., & Burke, D. M. (2000). Phonological priming effects on word retrieval and tip-of-the-tongue experiences in young and older adults. *Journal of Experimental Psychology: Learning, Memory, and Cognition, 26,* 1378–1391.

James, W. (1981). *The principles of psychology*, Cambridge, MA: Harvard University Press. (Original work published 1890)

Jared, D., Poh, R. P. Y., & Paivio, A. (2013). L1 and L2 picture naming in Mandarin-English bilinguals: A test of bilingual dual coding theory. *Bilingualism: Language and Cognition, 16,* 383–396.

Jaszczolt, K. M. (2013). First-person reference in discourse: Aims and strategies. *Journal of Pragmatics, 48,* 57–70.

Jay, K. L., & Jay, T. B. (2013). A children's garden of curses: A gender, historical, and age-related evaluation of the taboo lexicon. *American Journal of Psychology, 126,* 459–475.

Jay, T. (2009). The utility and ubiquity of taboo words. *Perspectives on Psychological Science, 4,* 153–161.

Jay, T., Caldwell-Harris, C., & King, K. (2008). Recalling taboo and nontaboo words. *American Journal of Psychology, 121,* 88–103.

Jay, T., & Janschewitz, K. (2008). The pragmatics of swearing. *Journal of Politeness Research, 4,* 267–288.

Jobard, G., Vigneau, M., Simon, G., & Tzouriou-Mazoyer, N. (2011). The weight of skill: Interindividual variability of reading related brain activation patterns in fluent readers. *Journal of Neurolinguistics, 24,* 113–132.

Johnson, B. W., McArthur, G., Hautus, M., Reid, M., Brock, J., Castles, A., & Crain, S. (2013). Lateralized auditory brain function in children with normal reading ability and in children with dyslexia. *Neuropsychologia, 51,* 633–641.

Johnson, M. D., & Ojemann, G. A. (2000). The role of the human thalamus in language and memory: Evidence from electrophysiological studies. *Brain and Cognition, 42,* 218–230.

Jones, M. N., Johns, B. T., & Recchia, G. (2012). The role of semantic diversity in lexical organization. *Canadian Journal of Experimental Psychology, 66,* 115–124.

Jones, Ö., Seghier, M. L., Duncan, K., Leff, A. P., Green, D. W., & Price, C. J. (2013). Auditory-motor interactions for the production of native and non-native speech. *Journal of Neuroscience, 33,* 2376–2387.

Junge, C., Cutler, A., & Hagoort, P. (2012). Electrophysiological evidence of early word learning. *Neuropsychologia, 50,* 3702–3712.

Junge, C., Kooijman, V., Hagoort, P., & Cutler, A. (2012). Rapid recognition at 10 months as a predictor of language development. *Developmental Science, 15,* 463–473.

Kail, M., Lemaire, P., & Lecacheur, M. (2012). Online grammaticality judgments in French young and older adults. *Experimental Aging Research, 38,* 186–207.

Kamat, R., Ghate, M., Gollan, T. H., Meyer, R., Vaida, F., Heaton, R. K., . . . Marcotte, T. D. (2012). Effects of Marathi-Hindi bilingualism on neuropsychological performance. *Journal of the International Neuropsychological Society, 18,* 305–313.

Kaplan, P. S., Bachorowski, J., Smoski, M. J., & Hudenko, W. J. (2002). Infants of depressed mothers, although competent learners, fail to learn in response to their own mothers' infant-directed speech. *Psychological Science, 13,* 268–271.

Karasinski, C., & Weismer, S. E. (2010). Comprehension of inferences in discourse processing by adolescents with and without language impairment. *Journal of Speech, Language, and Hearing Research, 53,* 1268–1279.

Kassubek, J., Hickok, G., & Erhard, P. (2004). Involvement of classical anterior and posterior language areas in sign language production, as investigated by 4 T functional magnetic resonance imaging. *Neuroscience Letters, 364,* 168–172.

Katerelos, M., Poulin-Dubois, D., & Oshima-Takane, Y. (2011). A cross-linguistic study of word-mapping in 18- to 20-month-old infants. *Infancy, 16,* 508–534.

Katz, A. N., Blasko, D. G., & Kazmerski, V. A. (2004). Saying what you don't mean: Social influences on sarcastic language processing. *Current Directions in Psychological Science, 13,* 186–189.

Kauschanskaya, M., & Rechtzigel, K. (2012). Concreteness effects in bilingual and monolingual word learning. *Psychonomic Bulletin Review, 19,* 935–941.

Kavé, G., Knafo, A., & Gilboa, A. (2010). The rise and fall of word retrieval across the lifespan. *Psychology and Aging, 25,* 719–724.

Kay-Raining Bird, E., Lamond, E., & Holden, J. (2012). Survey of bilingualism in autism spectrum disorders. *International Journal of Language Communication Disorders, 47,* 52–64.

Kaye, B. K., & Sapolsky, B. S. (2009). Taboo or not taboo? That is the question: Offensive language on prime-time broadcast and cable programming. *Journal of Broadcasting and Electronic Media, 53,* 22–37.

Kellogg, W. N., & Kellogg, L.A. (1933). *The ape and the child: A study of environmental influence upon early behavior.* New York: Whittlesey House.

Kelly, S. D., Creigh, P., & Bartolotti, J. (2010). Integrating speech and iconic gestures in a Stroop-like task: Evidence for automatic processing. *Journal of Cognitive Neuroscience, 22,* 683–694.

Kemler Nelson, D. G., Hirsh-Pasek, K., Jusczyk, P. W., & Cassidy, K. W. (1989). How the prosodic cues in motherese might assist language learning. *Journal of Child Language, 16,* 55–68.

Kemper, S., Schmalzried, R., Hoffman, L., & Herman, R. (2010). Aging and the vulnerability of speech to dual task demands. *Psychology and Aging, 4,* 949–962.

Kensinger, E., & Corkin, S. (2004). Two routes to emotional memory: Distinct neural process for valence and arousal. *Proceedings of the National Academy of Sciences USA, 16,* 3310–3315.

Keren-Portnoy, T., & Keren, M. (2011). The dynamics of syntax acquisition: Facilitation between syntactic structures. *Journal of Child Language, 38,* 404–432.

Kern, M. L., Eichstaedt, J. C., Schwartz, H. A., Park, G., Ungar, L. H., Stillwell, D. J., . . . Seligman, M. E. P. (2013). From "Sooo Excited!!!" to "So Proud": Using language to study development. *Developmental Psychology, 50,* 178–188.

Kersten, A. W., Meissner, C. A., Lechuga, J., Schwartz, B. L.,

Albrechtsen, J. S., & Iglesias, A. (2010). English speakers attend more strongly than Spanish speakers to manner of motion when classifying novel objects and events. *Journal of Experimental Psychology: General, 139,* 638–653.

Ketelaars, M. P., Cuperus, J., Jansonius, K., & Verhoeven, L. (2010). Pragmatic language impairment and associated behavioural problems. *International Journal of Language Communication Disorders, 45,* 204–215.

Keyes, H. (2012). Categorical perception effects for facial identity in robustly represented familiar and self-faces: The role of configural and featural information. *Quarterly Journal of Experimental Psychology*, 65, 760–772.

Khan, Z. A., Green, P., Creer, S., & Cunningham, S. (2011). Reconstructing the voice of an individual following laryngectomy. *Augmentative and Alternative Communications, 27,* 61–66.

Khattab, G. (2013). Phonetic convergence and divergence strategies in English-Arabic bilingual children. *Linguistics, 51,* 439–472.

Kidd, E. (2011). Implicit statistical learning is directly associated with the acquisition of syntax. *Developmental Psychology, 48,* 171–184.

Kidd, E. (2012a). Implicit statistical learning is directly associated with the acquisition of syntax. *Developmental Psychology, 48,* 171–184.

Kidd, E. (2012b). Individual differences in syntactic priming in language acquisition. *Applied Psycholinguistics, 33,* 393–418.

Kim, S., Yoon, M., Kim, W., Lee, S., & Kang, E. (2012). Neural correlates of bridging inferences and coherence processing. *Journal of Psycholinguistic Research, 41*(4), 311–321.

Kintsch, W. (1988). The role of knowledge in discourse comprehension: A construction integration model. *Psychological Review, 95,* 163–182.

Kisilevsky, B. S., Hains, S. J., Brown, C. A., Lee, C. T., Cowperthwaite, B. B., Stutzman, S. S., & . . . Wang, Z. Z. (2009). Fetal sensitivity to properties of maternal speech and language. *Infant Behavior and Development*, 32, 59–71.

Kitzinger, C., Shaw, R., & Toerien, M. (2012). Referring to persons without using a full-form reference: Locally initial indexicals in action. *Research on Language and Social Interaction, 45,* 116–136.

Kitzmann, C. D., & Caine, N. G. (2009). Marmoset (Callithrix geoffroyi) food-associated calls are functionally referential. *Ethology*, 115, 439–448.

Klein, H. B., Moses, N., & Jean-Baptiste, R. (2010). Influence of context on the production of complex sentences by typically developing children. *Language, Speech, and Hearing Services in Schools, 41,* 289–302.

Kliegl, R., Dambacher, M., Dimigen, O., Jacobs, A. M., & Sommer, W. (2012). Eye movements and brain potentials during reading. *Psychological Research, 76,* 145–158.

Klima, E. S., & Bellugi, U. (1979). *The signs of language.* Cambridge, MA: Harvard University Press.

Kluender, K. R., Diehl, R. L., & Killeen, P. R. (1987). Japanese quail can learn phonetic categories. *Science, 237,* 1195–1197.

Kluender, K. R., Lotto, A. J., Holt, L. L., & Bloedel, S. L. (1998). Role of experience for language-specific functional mappings of vowel sounds. *Journal of the Acoustical Society of America*, *104*, 3568–3582.

Komatsu, M. (2007). Acoustic constituents of prosodic typology. *Dissertation Abstracts International Section A, 68.*

Konopka, G., Bomar, J. M., Winden, K., Coppola, G., Jonsson, Z. O., Gao, F., & . . . Geschwind, D. H. (2009). Human-specific transcriptional regulation of CNS development genes by FOXP2. *Nature, 462,* 213–217.

Koopmans-van Beinum, F. J., Clement, C. J., & van den Dikkenberg-Pot, I. (2001). Babbling and the lack of auditory speech perception: A matter of coordination? *Developmental Science, 4,* 61.

Korinth, S. P., Sommer, W., & Breznitz, Z. (2013). Does silent reading speed in normal adult readers depend on early visual processes? Evidence from event-related brain potential. *Brain and Language, 120,* 15–26.

Korkman, M., Stenroos, M., Mickos, A., Westman, M.,

Ekholm, P., & Byring, R. (2012). Does simultaneous bilingualism aggravate children's specific language problems. *Acta Paediatrica, 101,* 946–952.

Kouremenos, D., Fotinea, S.-E., Efthimiou, E., & Ntalianis, K. (2010). A prototype Greek text to Greek Sign Language conversion system. *Behavior and Information Technology, 29,* 467–481.

Kousta, S.-T., Vinson, D. P., & Vigliocco, G. (2008). Investigating linguistic relativity through bilingualism: The case of grammatical gender. *Journal of Experimental Psychology: Learning, Memory, and Cognition, 34,* 843–858.

Koutsoftas, A. D., & Gray, S. (2012). Comparison of narrative and expository writing in students with and without language-learning disabilities. *Language, Speech, and Hearing Services in Schools, 43,* 395–409.

Kozlik, J., Neumann, R., & Kunde, W. (2013). ABC versus QWERTZ: Interference from mismatching sequences of letters in the alphabet and on the keyboard. *Journal of Experimental Psychology: Human Perception and Performance, 39,* 1085–1099.

Krause, J., Lalueza-Fox, C., Orlando, L., Enard, W., Green, R. E., Burbano, H. A., & . . . Pääbo, S. (2007). The derived FOXP2 variant of modern humans was shared with Neandertals. *Current Biology, 17,* 1908–1912.

Krentz, U. C., & Corina, D. P. (2008). Preference for language in early infancy: The human language bias is not speech specific. *Developmental Science, 11,* 1–9.

Kroll, J. F., & Stewart, E. (1994). Category interference in translation and picture naming: Evidence for asymmetric connections between bilingual memory representations. *Journal of Memory and Language, 33,* 149–174.

Kross, E., Verduyn, P., Demiralp, E., Park, J., Lee, D. S., Lin, N., . . . Ybarra, O. (2013). Facebook use predicts declines in subjective well-being in young adults. *PLoS ONE, 8,* e69841.

Kruchinina, O. V., Galperina, E. I., Kats, E. E., & Shepoval'nikov, A. N. (2012). Factors affecting the variability of the central mechanisms for maintaining bilingualism. *Human Physiology, 38,* 571–585.

Krueger, C., Holditch-Davis, D., Quint, S., & DeCasper, A. (2004). Recurring auditory experience in the 28- to 34-week-old fetus. *Infant Behavior and Development, 27*(4), 537–543.

Kuhl, P. K. (2010). Brain mechanisms in early language acquisition. *Neuron, 67,* 713–727.

Kuhl, P. K., & Miller, J. D. (1975). Speech perception by the chinchilla: Voiced-voiceless distinction in alveolar plosive consonants. *Science, 190,* 69–72.

Kuhl, P. K., & Miller, J. D. (1978). Speech perception by the chinchilla: Identification functions for synthetic VOT stimuli. *Journal of the Acoustical Society of America, 63,* 905–917.

Kuhl, P. K., & Padden, D. M. (1982). Enhanced discriminability at the phonetic boundaries for the voicing feature in macaques. *Perception and Psychophysics, 32,* 542–550.

Kuhl, P. K., Stevens, E., Hayashi, A., Deguchi, T., Kiritani, S., & Iverson, P. (2006). Infants show a facilitation effect for native language phonetic perception between 6 and 12 months. *Developmental Science, 9,* F13–F21.

Kuhl, P. K., Williams, K. A., Lacerda, F., Stevens, K. N., & Lindblom, B. (1992). Linguistic experience alters phonetic perception in infants by 6 months of age. *Science, 255,* 606–608.

Kuperberg, G. R. (2007). Neural mechanisms of language comprehension: Challenges to syntax. *Brain Research, 1146,* 23–49.

Kurata, K. (2005). Activity properties and location of neurons in the motor thalamus that project to the cortical motor areas in monkeys. *Journal of Neurophysiology, 94,* 550–566.

Kutas, M., & Hillyard, S. A. (1980). Reading senseless sentences: Brain potentials reflect semantic incongruity. *Science, 207,* 203–208.

Ladefoged, P. (2001). *Vowels and consonants: An introduction to the sounds of language.* Malden, MA: Blackwell.

Ladefoged, P. (2006). *A course in phonetics* (5th ed.). Boston: Thomson Wadsworth.

Ladefoged, P., & Disner, S. F. (2012). *Vowels and consonants.* Malden, MA: Wiley-Blackwell.

Ladefoged, P., & Maddieson, I. (1996). *The sounds of the world's languages.* Malden, MA: Wiley-Blackwell.

Lakoff, G., & Johnson M. (2003). *Metaphors we live by.* Chicago: University of Chicago Press.

Lamb, T. D., Collin, S. P., & Pugh, E. R. (2007). Evolution of the vertebrate eye: Opsins, photoreceptors, retina and eye cup. *Nature Reviews Neuroscience, 8,* 960–975.

Land, M. F., & Nilsson, D.-E. (2002). *Animal eyes.* Oxford: Oxford University Press.

Lany, J., & Saffran, J. R. (2011). Interactions between statistical and semantic information in infant language development. *Developmental Science, 14,* 1207–1219.

Lauchlan, F., Parisi, M., & Fadda, R. (2012). Bilingualism in Sardinia and Scotland: Exploring the cognitive benefits of speaking a "minority" language. *International Journal of Bilingualism, 17,* 43–56.

Laval, V., & Bert-Erboul, A. (2005). French-speaking children's understanding of sarcasm: The role of intonation and context. *Journal of Speech, Language, and Hearing Research, 48,* 610–620.

Lê, K., Coelho, C., Mozeiko, J., & Grafman, J. (2011). Measuring goodness of story narratives. *Journal of Speech, Language, and Hearing Science, 54,* 118–126.

Le Bihan, D., & Jezzard, P. (1995). Functional magnetic resonance imaging of the brain. *Annals of Internal Medicine, 122*(4), 296–303.

Lea, A. J., Barrera, J. P., Tom, L. M., & Blumstein, D. T. (2008). Heterospecific eavesdropping in a nonsocial species. *Behavioral Ecology, 19,* 1041–1046.

Lebel, C., Shaywitz, B., Holahan, J., Shaywitz, S., Marchione, K., & Beaulieu, C. (2013). Diffusion tensor imaging correlates of reading ability in dysfluent and non-impaired readers. *Brain and Language, 125,* 215–222.

Lecanuet, J. P., Graniere-Deferre, C. C., Jacquet, A. Y., & DeCasper, A. J. (2000). Fetal discrimination of low-pitched musical notes. *Developmental Psychobiology, 36*(1), 29–39.

Lecanuet, J., Granier-Deferre, C., Jacquet, A., & Busnel, M. (1992). Decelerative cardiac responsiveness to acoustical stimulation in the near term fetus. *Quarterly Journal of Experimental Psychology B: Comparative and Physiological Psychology, 44B,* 279–303.

Lee-Goldman, R. (2011). *No* as a discourse marker. *Journal of Pragmatics, 43,* 2627–2649.

Lee, H., & Kim, K. H. (2011). Can speaking more languages enhance your creativity? Relationship between bilingualism and creative potential among Korean American students with multicultural link. *Personality and Individual Differences, 50,* 1186–1190.

Lee, J., & Thompson, C. K. (2011). Real-time production of arguments and adjuncts in normal and agrammatic speakers. *Language and Cognitive Processes, 26,* 985–1021.

Lehti-Eklund, H. (2012). Code-switching to first language in repair: A resource for students' problem solving in a foreign language classroom. *International Journal of Bilingualism, 17,* 132–152.

Leijten, M., & van Waes, L. (2013). Keystroke logging in writing research: Using Inputlog to analyze and visualize writing processes. *Written Communication, 30,* 358–392.

Leikin, M. (2012). The effect of bilingualism on creativity: Developmental and educational perspectives. *International Journal of Bilingualism, 17,* 431–447.

Lempert, H. (1989). Animacy constraints on preschool children's acquisition of syntax. *Child Development, 60,* 237–245.

Levelt, W. J. M. (1989). *Speaking: From intention to articulation.* Cambridge, MA: MIT Press.

Levelt, W. J. M., Roelofs, A., & Meyer, A. S. (1999). A theory of lexical access in speech production. *Behavioral and Brain Sciences, 22,* 1–38.

Levelt, W. J. M., & Wheeldon, L. (1994). Do speakers have a mental syllabary? *Cognition, 50,* 239–269.

Levy, J., Pernet, C., Treserras, S., Boulaouar, K., Aubry, F.,

Démonet, J.-F., & Celsis, P. (2009). Testing for the dual-route cascade reading model in the brain: An fMRI effective connectivity account of an efficient reading style. *PLoS ONE, 4*, e6675.

Lewis, B. A., Avrich, A. A., Freebairn, L. A., Hansen, A. J., Sucheston, L. E., Kuo, I., . . . Stein, C. M. (2011). Literacy outcomes of children with early childhood speech sound disorders: Impact of endophenotypes. *Journal of Speech, Language, and Hearing Research, 54*, 1628–1643.

Lewkowicz, D. J., & Ghazanfar, A. A. (2009). The emergence of multisensory systems through perceptual narrowing. *Trends in Cognitive Sciences, 13*, 470–478.

Lewkowicz, D. J., & Hansen-Tift, A. M. (2012). Infants deploy selective attention to the mouth of a talking face when learning speech. *Proceedings of the National Academy of Sciences USA, 109*, 1431–1436.

Li, P., Zhao, X., & MacWhinney, B. (2007). Dynamic self-organization and early lexical development in children. *Cognitive Science, 31*, 581–612.

Li, X., Bicknell, K., Liu, P., Wei, W., & Rayner, K. (2014). Reading is fundamentally similar across disparate writing systems: A systematic characterization of how words and characters influence eye movements in Chinese reading. *Journal of Experimental Psychology: General, 143*, 895–913.

Liberman, A. (1996). *Speech: A special code*. Cambridge, MA: MIT Press.

Liberman, A. M. (1957). Some results of research on speech perception. *Journal of the Acoustical Society of America, 29*, 117–123.

Liberman, A. M. (1982). On finding that speech is special. *American Psychologist, 37*(2), 148–167.

Liberman, A. M., Cooper, F. S., Shankweiler, D. P., & Studdert-Kennedy, M. (1967). Perception of speech code. *Psychological Review, 74*, 431–461.

Liberman, A. M., Harris, K. S., Kinney, J., & Lane, H. H. (1961). The discrimination of relative onset-time of the components of certain speech and nonspeech patterns. *Journal of Experimental Psychology, 61*(5), 379–388.

Lieberman, P. (2012). Vocal tract anatomy and the neural bases of talking. *Journal of Phonetics, 40*, 608–622.

Lieberman, P., Crelin, E. S., & Klatt, D. H. (1972). Phonetic ability and related anatomy of the newborn and adult human, Neanderthal man, and the chimpanzee. *American Anthropologist, 74*, 287–307.

Lieberman, P., & McCarthy, R. (2007). Tracking the evolution of language and speech. *Expedition, 49*, 15–20.

Light, J., & McNaughton, D. (2012). Supporting the communication, language, and literacy development of children with complex communication needs: State of the science and future research priorities. *Assistive Technology, 24*, 34–44.

Lindgren, K. A. (2012). Contact zones and border crossings: Writing deaf lives. *Biography, 35*, 342–359.

Lisker, L., & Abramson, A. S. (1964). A cross-language study of voicing in initial stops: Acoustical measurements. *Word, 20*, 384–422.

Liu, H., Kuhl, P. K., & Tsao, F. (2003). An association between mothers' speech clarity and infants' speech discrimination skills. *Developmental Science, 6*, 1–10.

Liu, P., Li, W., Lin, N., & Li, X. (2013). Do Chinese readers follow the national standard rules for word segmentation during reading? *PLoS ONE, 8*, e55440.

Locke, J. L. (2006). Parental selection of vocal behavior: Crying, cooing, babbling, and the evolution of language. *Human Nature, 17*, 155–168.

Loncke, M., Desmet, T., Vandierendonck, A., & Hartsuiker, R. J. (2011). Executive control is shared between sentence processing and digit maintenance: Evidence from a strictly timed dual-task paradigm. *Journal of Cognitive Psychology, 23*, 886–911.

Lopresti-Goodman, S. M., Rivera, A., & Dressel, C. (2012). Practicing safe text: The impact of texting on walking behavior. *Applied Cognitive Psychology, 26*, 644–648.

Lorch, M. (2011). Re-examining Paul Broca's initial presentation of M. Leborgne: Understanding the impetus for brain and language research. *Cortex, 47,* 1228–1235.

Lotto, A. J., Kluender, K. R., & Holt, L. L. (1997). Perceptual compensation for coarticulation by Japanese quail (*Coturnix coturnix japonica*). *Journal of the Acoustical Society of America, 102,* 1134–1140.

Lowder, M. W., & Gordon, P. C. (2013). It's hard to offend the college: Effects of sentence structure on figurative-language processing. *Journal of Experimental Psychology: Learning, Memory, and Cognition, 39,* 993–1011.

Lucas, G., & Spielberg, S. (1981). *Raiders of the lost ark* [Motion picture]. UK: Elstree Studios.

Luck, S. J. (2005). *An introduction to the event-related potential technique.* London: MIT Press.

Luk, G., Bialystok, E., Craik, F. I., & Grady, C. L. (2011). Lifelong bilingualism maintains white matter integrity in older adults. *Journal of Neuroscience, 16,* 16808–16813.

Luk, G., De Sa, E., & Bialystok, E. (2011). Is there a relation between onset age of bilingualism and enhancement of cognitive control? *Bilingualism: Language and Cognition, 14,* 588–595.

Luo, L., Craik, F. I. M., Moreno, S., & Bialystok, E. (2013). Bilingualism interacts with domain in a working memory task: Evidence from aging. *Psychology and Aging 28*(1)*,* 28–34.

Luo, X., Cheung, H., Bel, D., Li, L., Chen, L., & Mo, L. (2013). The roles of semantic sense and form-meaning connection in translation priming. *Psychological Record, 63,* 193–208.

Luo, Y., Yan, M., & Zhou, X. (2013). Prosodic boundaries delay the processing of upcoming lexical information during silent sentence reading. *Journal of Experimental Psychology: Learning, Memory, and Cognition, 39,* 915–930.

Lyn, H., Greenfield, P. M., Savage-Rumbaugh, S., Gillespie-Lynch, K., & Hopkins, W. D. (2011). Nonhuman primates do declare! A comparison of declarative symbol and gesture use in two children, two bonobos, and a chimpanzee. *Language and Communication, 31,* 63–74.

Määttä, S., Laakso, M.-L., Tolvanen, A., Ahonen, T., & Aro, T. (2012). Developmental trajectories of early communication skills. *Journal of Speech, Language, and Hearing Research, 55,* 1086–1096.

MacKenzie, C. (2011). Dysarthria in stroke: A narrative review of its description and the outcome of intervention. *International Journal of Speech-Language Pathology, 13,* 125–136.

Maddieson, I. (1984). *Patterns of sounds.* New York: Cambridge University Press.

Magrath, R. D., Pitcher, B. J., & Gardner, J. L. (2009). An avian eavesdropping network: Alarm signal reliability and heterospecific response. *Behavioral Ecology, 20,* 745–752.

Majorano, M., & D'Odorico, L. (2011). The transition into ambient language: A longitudinal study of babbling and first word production of Italian children. *First Language, 31,* 47–66.

Mampe, B., Friederici, A. D., Christophe, A., & Wermke, K. (2009). Newborns' cry melody is shaped by their native language. *Current Biology, 19,* 1994–1997.

Mann, V. A., & Liberman, A. M. (1983). Some differences between phonetic and auditory modes of perception. *Cognition, 14,* 211–235.

Männel, C., & Friederici, A. D. (2009). Pauses and intonational phrasing: ERP Studies in 5-month-old German infants and adults. *Journal of Cognitive Neuroscience, 21,* 1988–2006.

Männel, C., & Friederici, A. D. (2011). Intonational phrase structure processing at different stages of syntax acquisition: ERP studies in 2-, 3-, and 6-year-old children. *Developmental Science, 14,* 786–798.

Marcus, G. F., Vijayan, S. S., Bandi Rao, S. S., & Vishton, P. M. (1999). Rule learning by seven-month-old infants. *Science, 283,* 77.

Marian, V., Spivey, M., & Hirsch, J. (2003). Shared and separate systems in bilingual language processing: Converging evidence from eyetracking and brain imaging. *Brain and Language, 86,* 70–82.

Marslen-Wilson, W. D. (1987). Functional parallelism in spoken word recognition. *Cognition, 25,* 71–102.

Martin, C. D., Costa, A., Dering, B., Hoshino, N., Wu, Y. J., & Thierry, G. (2012). Effects of speed of word processing on semantic access: The case of bilingualism. *Brain and Language, 120,* 61–65.

Martin, R. C., Crowther, J. E., Knight, M., Tamborello, F. P., II, & Yang, C. (2010). Planning in sentence production: Evidence for the phrase as a default planning scope. *Cognition, 116,* 117–192.

Martins, I. P., Mares, I., & Stilwell, P. A. (2012). How subjective are subjective language complaints? *European Journal of Neurology, 19,* 666–671.

Massaro, D. W. (1989). Testing between the TRACE model and the fuzzy logical model of speech perception. *Cognitive Psychology, 21,* 398–421.

Massaro, D. W., & Chen, T. H. (2008). The motor theory of speech perception revisited. *Psychonomic Bulletin and Review, 15*(2), 453–457.

Mastropieri, D., & Turkewitz, G. (1999). Prenatal experience and neonatal responsiveness to vocal expressions of emotion. *Developmental Psychobiology, 35,* 204–214.

Mauldin, L. (2012). Parents of deaf children with cochlear implants: A study of technology and community. *Sociology of Health and Illness, 34,* 529–543.

Mayor, J., & Plunkett, K. (2010). A neurocomputational account of taxonomic responding and fast mapping in early word learning. *Psychological Review, 117,* 1–31.

McArthur, G., Atkinson, C., & Ellis, D. (2009). Atypical brain responses to sounds in children with specific language and reading impairments. *Developmental Science, 12,* 768–783.

McCarthy, G., Blamire, A. M., Rothman, D. L., Gruetter, R., & Shulman, R. G. (1993). Echo-planar magnetic resonance imaging studies of frontal cortex activation during word generation in humans. *Proceedings of the National Academy of Sciences USA, 90,* 4952–4956.

McCrae, R. R., & Costa, P. T. (1990). *Personality in adulthood.* New York: Guilford Press.

McDonald, S. E. (2013). The effects and predictor value of in-class texting behavior on final course grades. *College Student Journal, 47,* 34–40.

McEachern, D., & Haynes, W. O. (2004). Gesture: Speech combinations as a transition to multiword utterances. *American Journal of Speech-Language Pathology, 13,* 227–235.

McGregor, K. K., Berns, A. J., Owen, A. J., Michels, S. A., Duff, D., Bahsen, A. J., & Lloyd, M. (2012). Associations between syntax and the lexicon among children with and without ASD and language impairment. *Journal of Autism and Developmental Disorders, 42,* 35–47.

McGurk, H., & MacDonald, J. (1976). Hearing lips and seeing voices. *Nature, 264,* 746–748.

McKee, M., Schlehofer, D., & Thew, D. (2013). Ethical issues in conducting research with deaf populations. *American Journal of Public Health, 103,* 2174–2178.

McKoon, G., & Ratcliff, R. (2003). Meaning through syntax: Language comprehension and the reduced relative clause construction. *Psychological Review, 110,* 490–525.

McMurray, B., Horst, J. S., & Samuelson, L. K. (2012). Word learning emerges from the interaction of online referent selection and slow associative learning. *Psychological Review, 119,* 831–877.

McWhorter, J. H. (1999). *Language change and language contact in pidgins and creoles.* Amsterdam: John Benjamins Publishing.

Mealings, K. T., Cox, F., & Demuth, K. (2013). Acoustic investigations into the later acquisition of syllabic -*es* plurals. *Journal of Speech, Language, and Hearing Research, 56,* 1260–1271.

Mehler, J., Jusczyk, P., Lambertz, G., & Halsted, N. (1988). A precursor of language acquisition in young infants. *Cognition, 29,* 143–178.

Mehu, M., & Dunbar, R. M. (2008). Naturalistic observations of smiling and laughter in human group interactions. *Behaviour, 145,* 1747–1780.

Meir, I., Sandler, W., Padden, C., & Aronoff, M. (2010). Emerging sign languages. In M. Marschark & P. E. Spencer (Eds.), *Oxford handbook of deaf studies, language, and education, Vol. 2*. Oxford: Oxford University Press.

Meisel, J. M. (2012). Remarks on the acquisition of Basque-Spanish bilingualism. *International Journal of Bilingualism, 17*, 392–399.

Mendelsohn, A. L., Brockmeyer, C. A., Dreyer, B. P., Fierman, A. H., Berkule-Silberman, S. B., & Tomopoulos, S. (2010). Do verbal interactions with infants during electronic media exposure mitigate adverse impacts on their language development as toddlers? *Infant and Child Development, 19*, 577–593.

Messenger, K., Branigan, H. P., & McLean, J. (2012). Is children's acquisition of the passive a staged process? Evidence from six- and nine-year-olds' production of passives. *Journal of Child Language, 39*, 991–1016.

Meyer, A. M., & Federmeier, K. D. (2010). Event-related potentials reveal the effects of aging on meaning selection and revision. *Psychophysiology, 47*, 673–686.

Meyer, D. E., & Schvaneveldt, R. W. (1971). Facilitation in recognizing pairs of words: Evidence of a dependence between retrieval operations. *Journal of Experimental Psychology, 90*, 227–234.

Miller, B., & O'Donnell, C. (2013). Opening a window into reading development: Eye movements' role within a broader literacy research framework.

School Psychology Review, 42, 123–139.

Miller, G. A. (1956). The magical number seven, plus or minus two: Some limits on our capacity for processing information. *Psychological Review, 63*(2), 81–97.

Miller, M. S. (2010). Epistemology and people who are deaf: Deaf worldviews, views of the deaf world, or my parents are hearing. *American Annals of the Deaf, 154*, 479–485.

Mithen, S. J. (2005) *The singing Neanderthals: The origins of music, language, mind and body*. Cambridge, MA: Harvard University Press.

Monaghan, P., Christiansen, M. H., & Fitneva, S. A. (2011). The arbitrariness of the sign: Learning advantages from the structure of the vocabulary. *Journal of Experimental Psychology: General, 140*, 325–347.

Monaghan, P., Mattock, K., & Walker, P. (2012). The role of sound symbolism in language learning. *Journal of Experimental Psychology: Learning, Memory, and Cognition, 38*, 1152–1164.

Monk, A., Fellas, E., & Ley, E. (2004). Hearing only one side of normal and mobile phone conversations. *Behavior and Information Technology, 23*, 301–305.

Moon, C., Lagercrantz, H., & Kuhl, P. (2013). Language experienced in utero affects vowel perception after birth: A two-country study. *Acta Paediatrica, 102*(2), 156–160.

Mora, J. C., & Nadeu, M. (2012). L2 effects on the perception and production of a native vowel contrast in early bilinguals. *International Journal of Bilingualism, 16*, 484–500.

Morford, J. P., Grieve-Smith, A. B., MacFarlane, J., Staley, J., & Waters, G. (2008). Effects of language experience on the perception of American Sign Language. *Cognition, 109*, 41–53.

Morgan, J. L. (1996). A rhythmic bias in preverbal speech segmentation. *Journal of Memory And Language, 35*, 666–688.

Morken, F., & Helland, T. (2013). Writing in dyslexia: Product and process. *Dyslexia, 19*, 131–148.

Morrill, T. B., Jones, R. M., & Vaterlaus, J. M. (2013). Motivations for text messaging: Gender and age differences among young adults. *North American Journal of Psychology, 15*, 1–16.

Morris, S. (2010). Clinical application of the mean babbling level and syllable structure level. *Language, Speech and Hearing Services in Schools, 41*, 223–230.

Moseley, R., Pulvermüller, F., Mohr, B., Lombardo, M., Baron-Cohen, S., & Shtyrov, Y. (2014). Brain routes for reading in adults with and without autism: EMEG evidence . . . combined electroencephalography and magnetoencephalography. *Journal of Autism and Developmental Disorders, 44*, 137–153.

Motley, M. T., & Baars, B. J. (1979). Effects of cognitive set upon laboratory induced verbal

(Freudian) slips. *Journal of Speech and Hearing Research, 22*(3), 421–432.

Mozeiko, J., Le, K., Coelho, C., Krueger, F., & Grafman, J. (2011). The relationship of story grammar and executive function following TBI. *Aphasiology, 25,* 826–835.

Mustafa, M. B., Salim, S. S., Mohamed, N., Al-Qatab, B., & Siong, C. E. (2014). Severity-based adaptation with limited data for ASR to aid dysarthric speakers. *PLoS ONE, 9, e86285.*

Myachykov, A., Garrod, S., & Scheepers, C. (2012) Determinants of structural choice in visually situated sentence production. *Acta Psychologica, 141,* 304–315.

Myachykov, A., Thompson, D., Scheepers, C., & Garrod, S. (2011). Visual attention and structural choice in sentence production across languages. *Language and Linguistics Compass 52,* 95–107.

Nakamura, K., Kuo, W.-J., Pegado, F., Cohen, L., Tzeng, O. J. L., & Dehaene, S. (2012). Universal brain systems for recognizing word shapes and handwriting gestures during reading. *Proceedings of the National Academy of Sciences USA, 109,* 20762–20767.

Nathani, S., Oller, D., & Neal, A. (2007). On the robustness of vocal development: An examination of infants with moderate-to-severe hearing loss and additional risk factors. *Journal of Speech, Language and Hearing Research, 50,* 1425–1444.

Nazzi, T. & Bertoncini, J. J. (2003). Before and after the vocabulary spurt: Two modes of word acquisition? *Developmental Science, 6,* 136–142.

Nazzi, T., Bertoncini, J., & Mehler, J. (1998). Language discrimination by newborns: Toward an understanding of the role of rhythm. *Journal of Experimental Psychology: Human Perception and Performance, 24,* 756–766.

Nelson, L. H., White, K. R., & Grewe, J. (2012). Evidence for website claims about the benefits of teaching sign language to infants and toddlers with normal hearing. *Infant and Child Development, 21,* 474–502.

Newman, A. J., Kenny, S., Saint-Aubin, J., & Klein, R. M. (2013). Can skilled readers perform a second task in parallel? A functional connectivity MRI study. *Brain and Language, 124,* 84–95.

Newport, E. L. (1990). Maturational constraints on language learning. *Cognitive Science, 14,* 11–28.

Nicolay, A.-C., & Poncelet, M. (2013). Cognitive advantage in children enrolled in a second-language immersion elementary school program for three years. *Bilingualism: Language and Cognition, 16,* 597–607.

Nippold, M. A., & Duthie, J. K. (2003). Mental imagery and idiom comprehension: A comparison of school-age children and adults. *Journal of Speech, Language, and Hearing Research, 46,* 788–799.

Norrick, N. R. (2011). Conversational recipe telling. *Journal of Pragmatics, 43,* 2740–2761.

Norris, D., McQueen, J. M., & Cutler, A. (1995). Competition and segmentation in spoken-word recognition. *Journal of Experimental Psychology: Learning, Memory, and Cognition, 21,* 1209–1228.

Nys, J., Content, A., & Leybaert, J. (2013). Impact of language abilities on exact and approximate number skills development: Evidence from children with specific language impairment. *Journal of Speech, Language, and Hearing Research, 56,* 956–970.

O'Brien, B. A., Wolf, M., Miller, L. T., Lovett, M. W., & Morris, R. (2011). Orthographic processing efficiency in developmental dyslexia: An investigation of age and treatment factors at the sublexical level. *Annals of Dyslexia, 61,* 111–135.

Oden, G. C., & Massaro, D. W. (1978). Integration of featural information in speech perception. *Psychological Review, 85,* 172–191.

Olive, T., & Passerault, J.-M. (2012). The visuospatial dimension of writing. *Written Communication, 29,* 326–344.

Oller, D. K., Buder, E. H., Ramsdell, H. L., Warlaumont, A. S., Chorna, L., & Bakeman, R. (2013). Functional flexibility of infant vocalization and the emergence of language. *Proceedings of the National Academy of Sciences USA, 110,* 6318–6323.

Oller, D. K., & Eilers, R. E. (1988). The role of audition in infant babbling. *Child Development, 59*, 441–449.

Oller, D., Eilers, R. E., & Basinger, D. (2001). Intuitive identification of infant vocal sounds by parents. *Developmental Science, 4*, 49.

Oloff, F. (2013). Embodied withdrawal after overlap resolution. *Journal of Pragmatics, 46*, 139–156.

Orwell, G. (1949). *Nineteen eighty-four*. London: Secker & Warburg.

Ostad, S. A. (2011). Private speech use in arithmetical calculation: Contributory role of phonological awareness of children with and without mathematical difficulties. *Journal of Learning Disabilities, 46*, 291–303.

Osterhout, H., & Holcomb, P. (1992). Event related brain potentials elicited by syntactic anomaly. *Language and Cognitive Processes, 8*, 785–802.

Owen, A. J. (2010). Factors affecting accuracy of past tense production in children with specific language impairment and their typically developing peers: The influence of verb transitivity, clause location, and sentence type. *Journal of Speech, Language, and Hearing Research, 53*, 993–1014.

Ozturk, O., Shayan, S., Liszkowski, U., & Majid, A. (2013). Language is not necessary for color categories. *Developmental Science, 16*, 111–115.

Özyürek, A., Kita, S., Allen, S., Brown, A., Furman, R., & Ishizuka, T. (2008). Development of cross-linguistic variation in speech and gesture: Motion events in English and Turkish. *Developmental Psychology, 44*, 1040–1054.

Palagi, E., & Mancini, G. (2011). Playing with the face: Playful facial "chattering" and signal modulation in a monkey species (Theropithecus gelada). *Journal of Comparative Psychology, 125*, 11–21.

Palmer, B. C., & Brooks, M. A. (2004). Reading until the cows come home: Figurative language and reading comprehension. *Journal of Adolescent and Adult Literacy, 47*, 370–379.

Papoušek, M., Papoušek, H., & Symmes, D. (1991). The meanings of melodies in motherese in tone and stress languages. *Infant Behavior and Development, 14*, 415–440.

Park, A., Salsbury, J., Corbett, K., & Aiello, J. (2013). The effects of text messaging during dual-task driving simulation on cardiovascular and respiratory responses and reaction time. *Ohio Journal of Science, 111*, 42–44.

Passow, S., Westerhausen, R., Wartenburger, I., Hugdahl, K., Heekeren, H. R., Lindenberger, U., & Li, S.-C. (2012). Human aging compromises attentional control of auditory perception. *Psychology of Aging, 27*, 99–105.

Paterson, K. B., McGowan, V. A., & Jordan, T. R. (2013). Filtered text reveals adult age differences in reading: Evidence from eye movements. *Psychology and Aging, 28*, 352–364.

Patson, N. D., Darowski, E. S., Moon, N., & Ferreira, F. (2009). Lingering misinterpretations in garden-path sentences: Evidence from a paraphrasing task. *Journal of Experimental Psychology: Learning, Memory, and Cognition, 35*, 280–285.

Patterson, F. G. (1978). The gesture of a gorilla: Language acquisition in another pongid. *Brain and Language, 5*, 72–97.

Pennisi, E. (2004). The first language? *Science, 303*, 1319–1320.

Pepperberg, I. (2002). Cognitive and communicative abilities of grey parrots. *Current Directions in Psychological Science, 11*, 83–87.

Perea, M., Abu Mallouh, R., & Carreiras, M. (2013). Early access to abstract representations in developing readers: Evidence from masked priming. *Developmental Science, 16*, 564–573.

Pérez-Leroux, A. T., Castilla-Earls, A. P., & Brunner, J. (2012). general and specific effects of lexicon in grammar: Determiner and object pronoun omissions in child Spanish. *Journal of Speech, Language, and Hearing Research, 55*, 313–327.

Perfetti, C. A., & Tan, L.-H. (2013). Write to read: The brain's universal reading and writing network. *Trends in Cognitive Sciences, 17*, 56–57.

Perlmutter, D. M. (n.d.) *What is sign language?* Washington, DC: Linguistic Society of

America. Available at http://www.linguisticsociety.org/files/Sign_Language.pdf.

Perrone-Bertolotti, M., Kujala, J., Vidal, J. R., Hamame, C. M., Ossandon, T., Bertrand, O., . . . Lachaux, J.-P. (2012). How silent is silent reading? Intracerebral evidence for top-down activation of temporal voice areas during reading. *Journal of Neuroscience, 32,* 17554–17562.

Petersen, S. E., Fox, P. T., Posner, M. I., & Mintun, M. M. (1988). Positron emission tomographic studies of the cortical anatomy of single-word processing. *Nature, 331*(6157), 585–589.

Pexman, P. M. (2008). It's fascinating research: The cognition of verbal irony. *Current Directions in Psychological Science, 17,* 286–290.

Pfeiffer, U. J., Timmermans, B., Bente, G., Vogeley, K., & Schilbach, L. (2011). A non-verbal Turing test: Differentiating mind from machine in gaze-based social interaction. *PLoS ONE, 6,* e327591.

Pfister, J. (2010). Is there a need for a maxim of politeness? *Journal of Pragmatics, 42,* 1266–1282.

Pickering, M. J., McLean, J. F., & Branigan, H. P. (2013). Persistent structural priming and frequency effects during comprehension. *Journal of Experimental Psychology: Learning, Memory, and Cognition, 39,* 890–897.

Pinker, S. (1999). *Words and rules: The ingredients of language.* New York: Science Masters.

Pinker, S., & Bloom, P. (1990). Natural language and natural selection. *Behavior and Brain Sciences, 13,* 707–784.

Plester, B., Wood, C., & Joshi, P. (2009). Exploring the relationship between children's knowledge of text message abbreviations and school literacy outcomes. *British Journal of Developmental Psychology, 27,* 145–161.

Poeppel, D., & Monahan, P. J. (2008). Speech perception: Cognitive foundations and cortical implementation. *Current Directions in Psychological Science, 17,* 80–85.

Politzer-Ahles, S., Fiorentino, R., Jiang, X., & Zhou, X. (2013). Distinct neural correlates for pragmatic and semantic meaning processing: An event-related potential investigation of scalar implicature processing using picture-sentence verification. *Brain Research, 1490,* 134–152.

Pons, F. (2006). The effects of distributional learning on rats' sensitivity to phonetic information. *Journal of Experimental Psychology: Animal Behavior Processes, 32,* 97–101.

Pons, F., Lewkowicz, D. J., Soto-Faraco, S., & Sebastián-Gallés, N. (2009). Narrowing of intersensory speech perception in infancy. *PNAS Proceedings of the National Academy of Sciences USA, 106,* 10598–10602.

Popper, K. (1959). *The logic of scientific discovery.* New York: Harper & Row.

Poulin-Dubois, D., Bialystok, E., Blaye, A., Polonia, A., & Yott, J. (2012). Lexical access and vocabulary development in very young bilinguals. *International Journal of Bilingualism, 17,* 57–70.

Premack, D., & Premack, A. J. (1984). *The mind of an ape.* New York: W. W. Norton.

Preston, J. L., Felsenfeld, S., Frost, S. J., Mencl, W., Fulbright, R. K., Grigorenko, E. L., & . . . Joanisse, M. (2012). Functional brain activation differences in school-age children with speech sound errors: Speech and print processing. *Journal of Speech, Language and Hearing Research, 55,* 1068–1082.

Price, C. J. (2012). A review and synthesis of the first 20 years of PET and fMRI studies of heard speech, spoken language and reading. *NeuroImage, 62*(2), 816–847.

Price, C. J., & Devlin, J. T. (2003). The myth of the visual word form area. *NeuroImage, 19,* 473–481.

Price, J. M., & Sanford, A. J. (2011). Reading in healthy ageing: The influence of information structuring in sentences. *Psychology and Aging, 27,* 529–540.

Provine, R. R. (2004). Laughing, tickling, and the evolution of speech and self. *Current Directions in Psychological Science, 13,* 215–218.

Pugh, K. R., Landi, N., Preston, J. L., Mencl, W. E., Austin, A. C., Sibley, D., . . . Frost, S. J. (2013). The relationship between phonological and auditory processing and brain organization in beginning readers. *Brain and Language, 125,* 173–183.

Pyers, J. E., & Emmorey, K. (2008). The face of bimodal bilingualism: Grammatical markers in American Sign Language are produced when bilinguals speak to English monolinguals. *Psychological Science, 19,* 531–536.

Quine, W. V. O. (1960). *Word and object.* Cambridge, MA: MIT Press.

Quinlan, T., Loncke, M., Leijten, M., & van Waes, L. (2012). Coordinating the cognitive processes of writing: The role of the monitor. *Written Communication, 29,* 345–368.

Quinto-Pozos, D., Forber-Pratt, A. J., & Singleton, J. L. (2011). Do developmental communication disorders exist in the signed modality? Perspectives from professionals. *Language, Speech and Hearing Services in Schools, 42,* 423–433.

Rabagliati, H., Pylkkänen, L., & Marcus, G. F. (2013). Top-down influence in young children's linguistic ambiguity resolution. *Developmental Psychology, 49,* 1076–1089.

Ram, G., Marinellie, S. A., Benigno, J., & McCarthy, J. (2013). Morphological analysis in context versus isolation: Use of a dynamic assessment task with school-age children. *Language, Speech, and Hearing Services in Schools, 44,* 32–47.

Ramírez-Esparza, N., Gosling, S. D., Benet-Martínez, V., Potter, J. P., & Pennebaker, J. W. (2006). Do bilinguals have two personalities? A special case of cultural frame switching. *Journal of Research in Personality, 40,* 99–120.

Ramsdell, H. L., Oller, D., Buder, E. H., Ethington, C. A., Chorna, L., Oetting, J., & Rvachew, S. (2012). Identification of prelinguistic phonological categories. *Journal of Speech, Language and Hearing Research, 55,* 1626–1639.

Rapp, A. M., Langohr, K., Mutschler, D. E., Klingberg, S., Wild, B., & Erb, M. (2013). Isn't it ironic? Neural correlates of irony comprehension in schizophrenia. *PLoS ONE, 8,* e74224.

Rapp, D. N., & van den Broek, P. (2005). Dynamic text comprehension. *Current Directions in Psychological Science, 14,* 276–279.

Raschle, N. M., Chang, M., & Gaab, N. (2011). Structural brain alterations with dyslexia predate reading onset. *NeuroImage, 57,* 742–749.

Raschle, N. M., Zuk, J., & Gaab, N. (2012). Functional characteristics of developmental dyslexia in left-hemispheric posterior brain regions predate reading onset. *Proceedings of the National Academy of Sciences USA, 109*(6), 2156–2161.

Rauch, D. P., Naumann, J., & Jude, N. (2011). Metalinguistic awareness mediates effects of full biliteracy on third-language reading in Turkish-German bilinguals. *International Journal of Bilingualism, 16,* 402–418.

Rayner, K. (1978). Eye movements in reading and information processing. *Psychological Bulletin, 85,* 618–660.

Rayner, K. (1998). Eye movements in reading and information processing: 20 years of research. *Psychological Bulletin, 124*(3), 372–422.

Rayner, K., White, S. J., Johnson, R. L., & Liversedge, S. P. (2006). Raeding wrods with jumbled lettres: There is a cost. *Psychological Science, 17,* 192–193.

Razik, J., Mella, O., Fohr, D., & Haton, J.-P. (2011). Frame-synchronous and local confidence measures for automatic speech recognition. *International Journal of Pattern Recognition and Artificial Intelligence, 25,* 157–182.

Reber, A.S. (1967). Implicit learning of artificial grammars. *Verbal Learning and Verbal Behavior, 5,* 855–863.

Recchia, H. E., Howe, N., Ross, H. S., & Alexander, S. (2010). Children's understanding and production of verbal irony in family conversations. *British Journal of Developmental Psychology, 28,* 255–274.

Regel, S., Gunter, T. C., & Friederici, A. D. (2010). Isn't it ironic? An electrophysiological exploration of figurative language processing. *Journal of Cognitive Neuroscience, 23,* 277–293.

Regier, T., Kay, P., & Cook, R. S. (2005). Focal colors are universal after all. *Proceedings of the National Academy of Sciences USA, 102,* 8386–8391.

Reissland, N., & Stephenson, T. (1999). Turn-taking in early vocal interaction: A comparison of premature and term infants' vocal interaction with their mothers. *Child: Care, Health, and Development, 25,* 447–456.

Rescorla, L., Lee, Y. M. C., Oh, K. J., & Kim, Y. A. (2013). Lexical development in Korean: Vocabulary size, lexical composition, and late talking. *Journal of Speech, Language, and Hearing Research, 56,* 735–747.

Ressel, V., Pallier, C., Ventura-Campos, N., Díaz, B., Roessler, A. Ávila, & Sebastián-Gallés, N. (2012). An effect of bilingualism on the auditory cortex. *Journal of Neuroscience, 47,* 16597–16601.

Revill, K. P., & Spieler, D. H. (2012). The effect of lexical frequency on spoken word recognition in young and older listeners. *Psychology and Aging, 27,* 80–87.

Richardson, F. M., Thomas, M. S. C., Filippi, R., Harth, H., & Price, C. J. (2009). Contrasting effects of vocabulary knowledge on temporal and parietal brain structure across lifespan. *Journal of Cognitive Neuroscience, 22,* 943–954.

Richardson, J. D., Fillmore, P., Rorden, C., LaPointe, L. L., & Fridriksson, J. (2012). Re-establishing Broca's initial findings. *Brain and Language, 123,* 125–130.

Riecker, A., Brendel, B., Ziegler, W., Erb, M., & Ackermann, H. (2008). The influence of syllable onset complexity and syllable frequency on speech motor control. *Brain and Language, 107,* 102–113.

Rispoli, M., Hadley, P., & Holt, J. (2008). Stalls and revisions: A developmental perspective on sentence production. *Journal of Speech, Language, and Hearing Research, 51,* 953–966.

Rivardo, M. G., Pacella, M. L., & Klein, B. A. (2008). Simulated driving performance is worse with a passenger than a simulated cellular telephone converser. *North American Journal of Psychology, 10,* 265–276.

Rizzolatti, G., & Arbib, M. A. (1998). Language within our grasp. *Trends in Neurosciences, 21,* 188–194.

Rizzolatti, G., Camarda, R., Fogassi, L., Gentilucci, M., Luppino, G., & Matelli, M. (1988). Functional organization of inferior area 6 in the macaque monkey: II. Area F5 and the control of distal movements. *Experimental Brain Research, 71,* 491–507.

Rizzolatti, G., & Craighero, L. (2004). The mirror-neuron system. *Annual Review of Neuroscience, 27,* 169–192.

Rizzolatti, G., Fogassi, L., & Gallese, V. (1997). Parietal cortex from sight to action. *Current Opinion in Neurobiology, 7,* 562–567.

Rochat, P., Querido, J. G., & Striano, T. (1999). Emerging sensitivity to the timing and structure of protoconversation in early infancy. *Developmental Psychology, 35,* 950–957.

Rochon, E., Saffran, E. M., Berndt, R., & Schwartz, M. F. (2000). Quantitative analysis of aphasic sentence production: Further development and new data. *Brain and Language, 72,* 193–218.

Rodd, J. M., Berriman, R., Landau, M., Lee, T., Ho, C., Gaskell, M., & Davis, M. H. (2012). Learning new meanings for old words: Effects of semantic relatedness. *Memory and Cognition, 40,* 1095–1108.

Rodríguez, D., Hermosillo, J., & Lara, B. (2012). Meaning in artificial agents: The symbol grounding problem revisited. *Minds and Machines, 22,* 25–34.

Rogalsky, C., & Hickok, G. (2011). The role of Broca's area in sentence comprehension. *Journal of Cognitive Neuroscience, 23,* 1664–1680.

Roll, M., Lindgren, M., Alter, K., & Horne, M. (2012). Time-driven effects on parsing during reading. *Brain and Language, 121,* 267–272.

Rommers, J., Meyer, A. S., Praamstra, P., & Huettig, F. (2013). The contents of predictions in sentence comprehension: Activation of the shape of objects before they are referred to. *Neuropsychologia, 51,* 437–447.

Rontu, H. (2007). Codeswitching in triadic conversational situations in early bilingualism. *International Journal of Bilingualism, 11,* 337–358.

Ross, B. (2009). Challenges facing theories of music and language co-evolution. *Journal of the Musical Arts in Africa, 6,* 61–76.

Rothenberg, M. (2009). Voice onset time versus articulatory modeling for stop consonants. *Logopedics Phoniatrics Vocology, 34*, 171–180.

Rothman, J. (2009). Understanding the nature and outcomes of early bilingualism: Romance languages as heritage languages. *International Journal of Bilingualism, 13,* 155–163.

Rumbaugh, D. M. (Ed.). (1977). *Language learning by a chimpanzee. THE LANA Project.* New York: Academic Press.

Rumelhart, D., & McClelland, J. (Eds.). (1986). *Parallel distributed processing* (Vol. 1). Cambridge, MA: MIT Press.

Saalbach, H., & Imai, M. (2007). Scope of linguistic influence: Does a classifier system alter object concepts? *Journal of Experimental Psychology: General, 136*, 485–501.

Sacco, D. F., Wirth, J. H., Hugenberg, K., Chen, Z., & Williams, K. D. (2011). The world in black and white: Ostracism enhances the categorical perception of social information. *Journal of Experimental Social Psychology, 47*, 836–842.

Sacks, H. (1992). *Lectures on conversation, Vol. 1–2.* Oxford: Blackwell.

Sacks, H., Schegloff, E. A., & Jefferson, G. (1974). A simplest systematics for the organization of turn-taking for conversation. *Language, 50*(4), 696–735.

Saffran, J. R., Aslin, R. N., & Newport, E. L. (1996). Statistical learning by 8-month-old infants. *Science, 274*, 1926–1928.

Saffran, J. R., Johnson, E. K., Aslin, R. N., & Newport, E. L. (1999). Statistical learning of tone sequences by human infants and adults. *Cognition, 70*, 27–52.

Saffran, J. R., Pollak, S. D., Seibel, R. L., & Shkolnik, A. (2007). Dog is a dog is a dog: Infant rule learning is not specific to language. *Cognition, 105*(3), 669–680.

Saffran, J. R., & Thiessen, E. D. (2007). Domain-general learning capacities. In E. Hoff & M. Shatz (Eds.), *Blackwell handbook of language development* (pp. 68–86). Malden, MA: Blackwell Publishing.

Sahni, S. D., Seidenberg, M. S., & Saffran, J. R. (2010). Connecting cues: Overlapping regularities support cue discovery in infancy. *Child Development, 81*, 727–736.

Sahraoui, H., & Nespoulous, J. (2012). Across-task variability in agrammatic performance. *Aphasiology, 26*, 785–810.

Saito, K., & Brajot, F.-X. (2013). Scrutinizing the role of length of residence and age of acquisition in the interlanguage pronunciation development of English /r/ by late Japanese bilinguals. *Bilingualism: Language and Cognition 16*, 847–863.

Sakoda, K., & Siegel, J. (2003). *Pidgin grammar: An introduction to the creole language of Hawai'i.* Honolulu, HI: Bess Press.

Salvatierra, J. L., & Rosselli, M. (2010). The effect of bilingualism and age on inhibitory control. *International Journal of Bilingualism, 15*, 26–37.

Samuelson, L. K., Smith, L. B., Perry, L. K., & Spencer, J. P. (2011). Grounding word learning in space. *PLoS ONE, 6,* e28095.

Sanbonmatsu, D. M., Strayer, D. L., Medeiros-Ward, N., & Watson, J. M. (2013). Who multi-tasks and why? Multi-tasking ability, perceived multi-tasking ability, impulsivity, and sensation seeking. *PLoS ONE, 8,* e54402.

Sandler, W. (2003). Sign language phonology. In W. Frawley (Ed.), *The Oxford international encyclopedia of linguistics.* Oxford: Oxford University Press.

Sass, K., Heim, S., Sachs, O., Theede, K., Muehlhaus, J., Krach, S., & Kircher, T. (2010). Why the leash constrains the dog: The impact of semantic associations on sentence production. *Actae Neurobiologiae Experimentalis, 70*, 435–453.

Sauter, D. A., LeGuen, O., & Haun, D. B. M. (2011). Categorical perception of emotional facial expressions does not require lexical categories. *Emotion, 11*, 1479–1483.

Sauzéon, H., Rabouet, C., Rodrigues, J., Langevin, S., Schelstraete, M. A., Feyereisen, P., . . . N'Kaoua, B. (2010). Verbal knowledge as a compensation determinant of adult age differences in verbal fluency tasks over time. *Journal of Adult Development, 18*, 144–154.

Savage-Rumbaugh, S., & Lewin, R. (1994). *Kanzi: The ape at the brink of the human mind.* Hoboken, NJ: Wiley.

Savage-Rumbaugh, S., Shanker, S. G., & Taylor, T. J. (1998). *Apes, language, and the human mind.* New York: Oxford University Press.

Sawyer, B. D., & Hancock, P. A. (2012). Assisted entry mitigates text messaging-based driving detriment. *Work, 41,* 4279–4282.

Schaburn, S. M., van den Hoorn, W., Moorcroft, A., Greenland, C., & Hodges, P. W. (2014). Texting and walking: Strategies for postural control and implications for safety. *PLoS ONE, 9,* e84312.

Scharrer, L., & Christmann, U. (2011). Voice modulations in German ironic speech. *Language and Speech, 54,* 435–465.

Schlaggar, B. L., & Church, J. A. (2009). Functional neuroimaging insights into the development of skilled reading. *Current Directions in Psychological Science, 18,* 21–26.

Schneidman, L. A., & Goldin-Meadow, S. (2012). Language input and acquisition in a Mayan village: How important is directed speech? *Developmental Science, 15,* 659–673.

Schuele, M. C., & Dykes, J. C. (2005). Complex syntax acquisition: A longitudinal case study of a child with specific language impairment. *Clinical Linguistics and Phonetics, 19,* 295–318.

Schüppert, A., & Gooskens, C. (2011). The role of extra-linguistic factors in receptive bilingualism: Evidence from Danish and Swedish pre-schoolers. *International Journal of Bilingualism, 16,* 332–347.

Schweizer, P. (2012). The externalist foundations of a truly total Turing test. *Minds and Machines, 22,* 191–212.

Schweizer, T. A., Ware, J., Fischer, C. E., Craik, F. I. M., & Bialystok, E. (2012). Bilingualism as a contributor to cognitive reserve: Evidence from brain atrophy in Alzheimer's disease. *Cortex, 48,* 991–996.

Scott, K. (2005). Auditory processing: Speech, space, and auditory objects. *Current Opinion in Neurobiology, 15,* 197–201.

Scott, K. A., Pollock, K., Roberts, J. A., & Krakow, R. (2013). Phonological processing skills of children adopted internationally. *American Journal of Speech-Language Pathology, 22,* 673–683.

Searle, J. (1980). Minds, brains, and programs. *Behavior and Brain Sciences, 3,* 417–424.

Searle, J. R. (1969). *Speech acts: An essay in the philosophy of language.* Cambridge: Cambridge University Press.

Segaert, K., Kempen, G., Petersson, K. M., & Hagoort, P. (2013). Syntactic priming and the lexical boost effect during sentence production and sentence comprehension: An fMRI study. *Brain and Language, 124,* 174–183.

Segal, O., & Kishon-Rabin, L. (2012). Evidence for language-specific influence on the preference of stress patterns in infants learning an iambic language (Hebrew). *Journal of Speech, Language, and Hearing Research, 55,* 1329–1341.

Seidenberg, M. S. (2005). Connectionist models of word reading. *Current Directions in Psychological Science, 14,* 238–242.

Senghas, A., & Coppola, M. (2001). Children creating language: How Nicaraguan Sign Language acquired a spatial grammar. *Psychological Science, 12,* 323–328.

Senghas, R. J., & Monaghan, L. (2002). Signs of their times: Deaf communities and the culture of language. *Annual Review of Anthropology, 31,* 69–97.

Serratrice, L. (2013). Acquisition of features in the nominal domain in bilingual acquisition. *International Journal of Bilingualism, 17,* 657–664.

Severens, E., Janssens, I., Kühn, S., Brass, M., & Hartsuiker, R. J. (2011). When the brain tames the tongue: Covert editing of inappropriate language. *Psychophysiology, 48,* 1252–1257.

Seyfarth, R. M., Cheney, D. L., & Marler, P. (1980a). Monkey responses to three different alarm calls: Evidence of predator classification and semantic communication. *Science, 210,* 801–803.

Seyfarth, R. M., Cheney, D. L., & Marler, P. (1980b). Vervet monkey alarm calls: Semantic communication in a free-ranging primate. *Animal Behaviour, 28,* 1070–1094.

Shafto, M. (2010). Orthographic error monitoring in old age: Lexical and sublexical availability during perception and production. *Psychology and Aging, 25,* 991–1001.

Shafto, M., Randall, B., Stamatakis, E. A., Wright, P., & Tyler, L. K. (2012). Age-related neural reorganization during spoken word recognition: The interaction of form and meaning. *Journal of Cognitive Neuroscience, 24,* 1434–1446.

Shah, H., & Warwick, K. (2010). Hidden interlocutor misidentification in practical Turing tests. *Minds and Machines, 20,* 441–454.

Shankweiler, D., Mencl, W. E., Braze, D., Tabor, W., Pugh, K. R., & Fulbright, R. K. (2008). Reading differences and brain: Cortical integration of speech and print in sentence processing varies with reader skill. *Developmental Neuropsychology, 33,* 745–775.

Shaywitz, S. E., Mody, M., & Shaywitz, B. A. (2006). Neural mechanisms in dyslexia. *Current Directions in Psychological Science, 15,* 278–281.

Sheng, L., & McGregor, K. K. (2010). Lexical-semantic organization in children with specific language impairment. *Journal of Speech, Language, and Hearing Research, 53,* 146–159.

Sheng, L., McGregor, K. K., & Marian, V. (2006). Lexical-semantic organization in bilingual children: Evidence from a repeated word association task. *Journal of Speech, Language, and Hearing Research, 49,* 572–587.

Shin, H., & Alba, R. (2009). The economic value of bilingualism for Asians and Hispanics. *Sociological Forum, 24,* 254–275.

Shu, W., et al. (2005). Altered ultrasonic vocalization in mice with a disruption in the *Foxp2* gene. *Proceedings of the National Academy of Sciences USA, 102,* 9643–9648.

Shum, M., Shiller, D. M., Baum, S. R., & Gracco, V. L. (2011). Sensorimotor integration for speech motor learning involves the inferior parietal cortex. *European Journal of Neuroscience, 34,* 1817–1822.

Shuster, L. L., & Lemieux, S. K. (2005). An fMRI investigation of covertly and overtly produced mono- and multisyllabic words. *Brain and Language, 93,* 20–31.

Sidtis, D. V. L. (2004). When novel sentences spoken or heard for the first time in the history of the universe are not enough: Toward a dual-process model of language. *International Journal of Language Communication Disorders, 39,* 1–44.

Simcox, T., Pilotti, M., Mahamane, S., & Romero, E. (2011). Does the language in which aversive stimuli are presented affect their processing? *International Journal of Bilingualism, 16,* 419–427.

Simonyan, K., & Horwitz, B. (2011). Laryngeal motor cortex and control of speech in humans. *Neuroscientist, 17,* 197–208.

Singh, L., Reznick, J. S., & Liang, X. (2012). Infant word segmentation and childhood vocabulary development: A longitudinal analysis. *Developmental Science, 15,* 482–495.

Singleton, N. C. (2012). Can semantic enrichment lead to naming in a word extension task? *American Journal of Speech-Language Pathology, 21,* 279–292.

Sinsky, C. A., & Beasley, J. W. (2013). Texting while doctoring: A patient safety hazard. *Annals of Internal Medicine, 159,* 782–784.

Skinner, B. F. (1957). *Verbal behavior.* New York: Appleton-Century-Crofts.

Slevc, L. R., & Ferreira, V. S. (2013). To err is human; to structurally prime from errors is also human. *Journal of Experimental Psychology: Learning, Memory, and Cognition, 39,* 985–992.

Smith, F. H., Janković, I., & Karavanić, I. (2005). The assimilation model, modern human origins in Europe, and the extinction of Neandertals. *Quaternary International, 137,* 7–19.

Smith, K., Smith, A. D. M., & Blythe, R. A. (2011). Cross-situational learning: An experimental study of word-learning mechanisms. *Cognitive Science, 35,* 480–498.

Smith, L. B. (2013). It's all connected: Pathways in visual object recognition and early noun learning. *American Psychologist,* November, 618–629.

Smith, M., & Wheeldon, L. (2004). Horizontal

information flow in spoken sentence production. *Journal of Experimental Psychology: Learning, Memory, and Cognition, 30,* 675–686.

Snow, C. E. (1977). The development of conversation between mothers and babies. *Journal of Child Language, 4,* 1–22.

So, W. C., & Lim, J. Y. (2012). Point to a referent, and say, "what is this?" Gesture as a potential cue to identify referents in a discourse. *Applied Psycholinguistics, 33,* 329–342.

Söderholm, C., Häyry, E., Laine, M., & Karrasch, M. (2013). Valence and arousal ratings for 420 Finnish nouns by age and gender. *PLoS ONE, 8,* e72859.

Soderstrom, M., Seidl, A., Nelson, D., & Jusczyk, P. (2003). The prosodic bootstrapping of phrases: Evidence from prelinguistic infants. *Journal of Memory and Language, 49,* 249–267.

Song, L., Tamis-LeMonda, C. S., Yoshikawa, H., Kahana-Kalman, R., & Wu, I. (2012). Language experiences and vocabulary development in Dominican and Mexican infants across the first 2 years. *Developmental Psychology, 48,* 1106–1123.

Spanoudis, G., Natsopoulos, D., & Panayiotou, G. (2007). Mental verbs and pragmatic language difficulties. *International Journal of Language Communication Disorders, 42,* 487–504.

Spence, M. J., & DeCasper, A. J. (1987). Prenatal experience with low-frequency maternal-voice sounds influence neonatal perception of maternal voice samples. *Infant Behavior and Development, 10,* 133–142.

Spitzer, S. M., Liss, J. M., & Mattys, S. L. (2007). Acoustic cues to lexical segmentation: A study of resynthesized speech. *Journal of the Acoustical Society of America, 122,* 3678–3687.

Spivey, M. J., Tanenhaus, M. K., Eberhard, K. M., & Sedivy, J. C. (2002). Eye movements and spoken language comprehension: Effects of visual context on syntactic ambiguity resolution. *Cognitive Psychology, 45*(4), 447–481.

Stadler, S. A. (2011). Coding speech acts for their degree of explicitness. *Journal of Pragmatics, 43,* 36–50.

Stanger-Hall, K. F., Lloyd, J. E., & Hillis, D. M. (2007). Phylogeny of North American fireflies (Coleoptera: Lampyridae): Implications for the evolution of light signals. *Molecular Phylogenetics and Evolution, 45,* 33–49.

Stanovich, K. E. (2007). *How to think straight about psychology* (8th ed.). Boston. Pearson.

Starr, S. (1975). The relationship of single words to two-word sentences. *Child Development, 46,* 701–708.

Stern, J. M. (1997). Offspring-induced nurturance: Animal–human parallels. *Developmental Psychobiology, 31,* 19–37.

Stivers, T., Enfield, N. J., Brown, P., Englert, C., Hayashi, M., Heinemann, T., . . . Levinson, S. C. (2009). Universals and cultural variation in turn-taking in conversation. *Proceedings of the National Academy of Sciences USA, 106,* 10587–10592.

Stokes, S. F., Bleses, D., Basbøll, H., & Lambertsen, C. (2012). Statistical learning in emerging lexicons: The case of Danish. *Journal of Speech, Language, and Hearing Research, 55,* 1265–1273.

Stokoe, W. C. (1960). *Sign language structure.* Silver Spring, MD: Linstok Press.

Stoodley, C. J., & Stein, J. F. (2013). Cerebellar function in developmental dyslexia. *Cerebellum, 12,* 267–276.

Storkel, H. L., Maekawa, J., & Aschenbrenner, A. J. (2013). The effect of homonymy on learning correctly articulated versus misarticulated words. *Journal of Speech, Language, and Hearing Research, 56,* 694–707.

Strayer, D. L., & Drews, F. A. (2007). Cell-phone-induced driver distraction. *Current Directions in Psychological Science, 16,* 128–131.

Streeter, L. A. (1976). Language perception of 2-mo-old infants shows effects of both innate mechanisms and experience. *Nature, 259,* 39–41.

Stroop, J. R. (1935). Studies of interference in serial verbal reactions. *Journal of Experimental Psychology, 18,* 643–662.

Suh, M.-W., Lee, H.-J., Kim, J. S., Chung, C. K., & Oh, S. H. (2009). Speech experience shapes the speechreading network and subsequent deafness facilitates it. *Brain, 132,* 2761–2771.

Sun, L., & Nippold, M. A. (2012). Narrative writing in children and adolescents: Examining the literate lexicon. *Language, Speech, and Hearing Services in Schools, 44,* 291–305.

Sundara, M., Demuth, K., & Kuhl, P. K. (2011). Sentence-position effects on children's perception and production of English third person singular -s. *Journal of Speech, Language, and Hearing Research, 54,* 55–71.

Sutton-Spence, R. (2010). The role of sign language narratives in developing identity for deaf children. *Journal of Folklore Research, 47,* 265–305.

Sutton-Spence, R., & Napoli, D. J. (2012). Deaf jokes and sign language humor. *Humor, 25,* 311–337.

Svennevig, J. (2010). Pre-empting reference problems in conversation. *Language in Society, 39,* 173–202.

Swinney, D. A., Onifer, W., Prather, P., & Hirshkowitz, M. (1979). Semantic facilitation across sensory modalities in the processing of individual words and sentences. *Memory and Cognition, 7*(3), 159–165.

Szagun, G., Stumper, B., Oetting, J., & Tobey, E. (2012). Age or experience? The influence of age at implantation and social and linguistic environment on language development in children with cochlear implants. *Journal of Speech,*

Language and Hearing Research, 55, 1640–1654.

Szewczyk, J. M., & Schriefers, H. (2013). Prediction in language comprehension beyond specific words: An ERP study on sentence comprehension in Polish. *Journal of Memory and Language, 68,* 297–314.

Takaso, H., Eisner, F., Wise, R. S., & Scott, S. K. (2010). The effect of delayed auditory feedback on activity in the temporal lobe while speaking: A positron emission tomography study. *Journal of Speech, Language and Hearing Research, 53,* 226–236.

Tanaka, M. N., Branigan, H. P., McLean, J. F., & Pickering, M. J. (2011). Conceptual influences on word order and voice in sentence production: Evidence from Japanese. *Journal of Memory and Language, 65,* 318–330.

Tanenhaus, M. K., & Spivey-Knowlton, M. J. (1995). Integration of visual and linguistic information in spoken language comprehension. *Science, 268*(5217), 1632.

Tanenhaus, M. K., Spivey-Knowlton, M. J., Eberhard, K. M., & Sedivy, J. C. (1995). Integration of visual and linguistic information in spoken language comprehension. *Science, 268,* 1632–1634.

Tanenhaus, M. K., & Trueswell, J. C. (1995). Sentence comprehension. In J. L. Miller & P. D. Eimas (Eds.), *Handbook of perception and cognition: Vol. 11. Speech, language, and communication* (pp. 217–262). Orlando, FL: Academic Press.

Taylor, S. F., Martis, B., Fitzgerald, K. D., Welsh, R. C., Abelson, J. L., Liberzon, I., . . . Gehring, W. J. (2006). Medial frontal cortex activity and loss-related responses to errors. *Journal of Neuroscience, 26,* 4063–4070.

ten Bosch, L., Oostdijk, N., & Boves, L. (2005). On temporal aspects of turn taking in conversational dialogues. *Speech Communication, 47,* 80–86.

ter Maat, M., Truong, K. P., & Heylen, D. (2011). How agents' turn-taking strategies influence impressions and response behaviors. *Presence, 20,* 412–430.

Terrace, H. S., Petitto, L. A., Sanders, R. J., & Bever, T. G. (1979). Can an ape create a sentence? *Science, 206,* 891–902.

Terry, N. P., Mills, M. T., Bingham, G. E., Mansour, S., & Marencin, N. (2013). Oral narrative performance of African American prekindergartners who speak nonmainstream American English. *Language, Speech, and Hearing Services in Schools, 44,* 291–305.

Theakston, A., Lieven, E., Pine, J., & Rowland, C. (2004). Semantic generality, input frequency and the acquisition of syntax. *Journal of Child Language, 31,* 61–99.

Theißen, G. (2006). The proper place of hopeful monsters in evolutionary biology. *Theory in Biosciences, 124,* 349–369.

Thiessen, E. D., Kronstein, A. T., & Hufnagle, D. G. (2012). The extraction and integration framework: A two-process account of statistical learning. *Psychological Bulletin,* December 10.

Thiessen, E. D., & Saffran, J. R. (2003). When cues collide: Use of stress and statistical cues to word boundaries by 7- to 9-month-old infants. *Developmental Psychology*, 39, 706–716.

Thothathiri, M., Kimberg, D. Y., & Schwartz, M. F. (2011). The neural basis of reversible sentence comprehension: Evidence from voxel-based lesion symptom mapping in aphasia. *Journal of Cognitive Neuroscience,* 24, 212–222.

Tian, Z., Moon, C., Lagercrantz, H., & Kuhl, P. (2011). Prenatal motherese? Newborn speech perception may be enhanced by having a young sibling. *Psi Chi Journal of Undergraduate Research*, 16, 90–94.

Tooley, K. M., Traxler, M. J., & Swaab, T. Y. (2009). Electrophysiological and behavioral evidence of syntactic priming in sentence comprehension. *Journal of Experimental Psychology: Learning, Memory, and Cognition*, 35(1), 19–45.

Tourville, J. A., & Guenther, F. H. (2011). The DIVA model: A neural theory of speech acquisition and production. *Language and Cognitive Processes*, 26, 952–981.

Trachsel, M. (2010). Human uniqueness in the age of ape language research. *Society and Animals: Journal of Human-Animal Studies*, 18, 397–412.

Trudeau, M. B., Catalano, P. J., Jindrich, D. L., & Dennerlein, J. T. (2013). Tablet keyboard configuration affects performance, discomfort and task difficulty for thumb typing in a two-handed grip. *PLoS ONE, 8,* e67525.

Trueswell, J. C., Medina, T. N., Hafri, A., & Gleitman, L. R. (2012). Propose but verify: Fast mapping meets cross-situational word learning. *Cognitive Psychology, 66,* 126–156.

Tulane, S., & Beckert, T. E. (2013). Perceptions of texting: A comparison of female high school and college students. *North American Journal of Psychology, 15,* 395–404.

Tun, P. A., Williams, V. A., Small, B. J., & Hafter, E. R. (2012). The effects of aging on auditory processing and cognition. *American Journal of Audiology, 21,* 344–350.

Turing, A. M. (1950). Computing, machinery, and intelligence. *Mind, 59,* 433–460.

Ungerleider, L. G., & Mishkin, M. (1982). Two cortical visual systems. In D. J. Ingle, M. A. Goodale, & R. J. W. Mansfield (Eds.), *Analysis of visual behavior*. Cambridge, MA: MIT Press.

Vaala, S. E., Linebarger, D. L., Fenstermacher, S. K., Tedone, A., Brey, E., Barr, R., . . . Calvert, S. L. (2010). Content analysis of language-promoting teaching strategies used in infant-directed media. *Infant and Child Development, 19,* 628–648.

Valencia-Laver, D. L., & Light, L. L. (2000). The occurrence of causal bridging and predictive inferences in young and older adults. *Discourse Processes, 30,* 27–56.

Valicenti-McDermott, M., Tarshis, N., Schouls, M., Galdston, M., Hottinger, K., Seijo, R., . . . Shinnar, S. (2013). Language differences between monolingual English and bilingual English-Spanish young children with autism spectrum disorders. *Journal of Child Neurology*, 28, 945–948.

Valle, A., Binder, K. S., Walsh, C. B., Nemier, C., & Bangs, K. E. (2013). Eye movements, prosody, and word frequency among average- and high-skilled second-grade readers. *School Psychology Review, 42,* 171–190.

van Balkom, H., Verhoeven, L., & van Weerdenburg, M. (2010). Conversational behaviour of children with developmental language delay and their caretakers. *International Journal of Language and Communication Disorders, 45,* 295–319.

van Petten, C., Federmeier, K. D., & Holcomb, P. J. (2010). For distinguished contributions to psychophysiology: Marta Kutas. *Psychophysiology, 47,* 403–409.

van Rees, L. J., Ballard, K. J., McCabe, P., Macdonald-D'Silva, A. G., & Arciuli, J. (2012). Training production of lexical stress in typically developing children using orthographically biased stimuli and principles of motor learning. *American Journal* of Speech-Language Pathology, 21, 197–206.

van Staden, A. (2013). An evaluation of an intervention using sign language and multi-sensory coding to support word learning and reading comprehension of deaf signing children. Child Language Teaching and Therapy, 29, 305–318.

Vanhove, J. (2013). The critical period hypothesis in second language acquisition: A statistical critique and a reanalysis. PLoS ONE, 8, e69172.

Vannest, J., Newport, E. L., Newman, A. J., & Bavelier, D. (2011). Interplay between morphology and frequency in lexical access: The case of the base frequency effect. Brain Research, 1373, 144–159.

Velan, H., Deutsch, A., & Frost, R. (2013). The flexibility of letter-position flexibility: Evidence from eye movements in reading Hebrew. Journal of Experimental Psychology: Human Perception and Performance, 39, 1143–1152.

Veltkamp, G. M., Recio, G., Jacobs, A. M., & Conrad, M. (2012). Is personality modulated by language? International Journal of Bilingualism, 17, 496–504.

Vervecken, D., & Hannover, B. (2012). Ambassadors of gender equality? How use of pair forms versus masculines as generics impacts perception of the speaker. European Journal of Social Psychology, 42, 754–762.

Vettin, J., & Todt, D. (2005). Human laughter, social play, and play vocalizations of non-human primates: An evolutionary approach. Behaviour, 142, 217–240.

Vogel, A. C., Church, J. A., Power, J. D., Miezin, F. M., Petersen, S. E., & Schlaggar, B. L. (2013). Functional network architecture of reading-related regions across development. Brain and Language, 125, 231–243.

von Frisch, K. (1967). The dance language and orientation of bees. Cambridge, MA: The Belknap Press of Harvard University Press.

von Hapsburg, D., & Davis, B. (2006). Auditory sensitivity and the prelinguistic vocalizations of early-amplified infants. Journal of Speech, Language and Hearing Research, 49, 809–822.

von Hapsburg, D., Davis, B., & MacNeilage, P. (2008). Frame dominance in infants with hearing loss. Journal of Speech, Language and Hearing Research, 51, 306–320.

Vouloumanos, A., & Werker, J. F. (2009). Infants' learning of novel words in a stochastic environment. Developmental Psychology,45, 1611–1617.

Wagner, V., Jescheniak, J. D., & Scriefers, H. (2010). On the flexibility of grammatical advance planning during sentence production: Effects of cognitive load on multiple lexical access. Journal of Experimental Psychology: Learning, Memory, and Cognition, 36, 423–440.

Wagovich, S. A., Pak, Y., & Miller, M. D. (2012). Orthographic word knowledge growth in school-age children. American Journal of Speech-Language Pathology, 21, 140–153.

Walle, E. A., & Campos, J. J. (2014). Infant language development is related to the acquisition of walking. Developmental Psychology, 50, 336–348.

Wallis, P. (2011). From data to design. Applied Artificial Intelligence, 25, 530–548.

Wandell, B. A., & Yeatman, J. D. (2013). Biological development of reading circuits. Current Opinion in Neurobiology, 23, 261–268.

Wang, X. (2013). Language dominance in translation priming: Evidence from balanced and unbalanced Chinese-English bilinguals. Quarterly Journal of Experimental Psychology, 66, 727–743.

Wang, X., Georgiou, G. K., Das, J. P., & Li, Q. (2012). Cognitive processing skills and developmental dyslexia in Chinese. Journal of Learning Disabilities, 45, 526–537.

Wankoff, L. S. (2011). Warning signs in the development of speech, language, and communication: When to refer to a speech-language pathologist. Journal of Child and Adolescent Psychiatric Nursing, 24, 175–184.

Warren, R. M. (1970). Perceptual restoration of missing speech sounds. Science, 167, 392–393.

Warren, R. M., & Warren, R. P. (1970). Auditory illusions and confusions. *Scientific American*, *223*, 30–36.

Watts, J. M., & Stookey, J. M. (2000). Vocal behaviour in cattle: The animal's commentary on its biological processes and welfare. *Applied Animal Behaviour Science*, *67*, 15–33.

Weber, A., & Crocker, M. W. (2012). On the nature of semantic constraints on lexical access. *Journal of Psycholinguistic Research, 41*, 195–214.

Weizenbaum, J. (1966). ELIZA: A computer program for the study of natural language communication between man and machine. *Communications of the ACM, 9*, 36–45.

Welcome, S. E., & Joanisse, M. F. (2012). Individual differences in skilled adult readers reveal dissociable patterns of neural activity with component processes of reading. *Brain and Language, 120*, 360–371.

Weller, J. A., Shackleford, C., Dieckmann, N., & Slovic, P. (2013). Possession attachment predicts cell phone use while driving. *Health Psychology, 32*, 379–387.

Weltman, K., & Lavidor, M. (2013). Modulating lexical and semantic processing by transcranial direct current stimulation. *Experimental Brain Research, 226*, 121–135.

Werker, J. F., Gilbert, J. V., & Humphrey, K. (1981). Developmental aspects of cross-language speech perception. *Child Development, 52*, 349–355.

Werker, J. F., & Tees, R. C. (1983). Developmental changes across childhood in the perception of non-native speech sounds. *Canadian Journal of Psychology/Revue Canadienne de Psychologie, 37*, 278–286.

Werker, J. F., & Tees, R. C. (2002). Cross-language speech perception: Evidence for perceptual reorganization during the first year of life. *Infant Behavior and Development, 25*, 121.

Werker, J. F., Yeung, H., & Yoshida, K. A. (2012). How do infants become experts at native-speech perception? *Current Directions in Psychological Science, 21*, 221–226.

Westerveld, M. F., & Moran, C. A. (2011). Expository language skills of young school-age children. *Language, Speech, and Hearing Services in Schools, 42*, 182–193.

Whalen, D. H., Giulivi, S., Nam, H., Levitt, A. G., Hallé, P., & Goldstein, L. M. (2012). Biomechanically preferred consonant-vowel combinations fail to appear in adult spoken corpora. *Language and Speech, 55*, 503–515.

White, G. (2011a). Bootstrapping normativity. *Philosophy of Technology, 24*, 35–53.

White, G. (2011b). Descartes among the robots: Computer science and the inner/outer distinction. *Minds and Machines, 21*, 179–202.

White, K. K., Palm, G. M., Abrams, L., & Protasi, M. A. (2012). Age-related influences on lexical selection and orthographic encoding during homophone spelling. *Psychology and Aging, 27*, 67–79.

Whorf, B. (1956). *Language, thought, and reality: Selected writings of Benjamin Lee Whorf* (J. B. Carroll, Ed.). Cambridge, MA: MIT Press.

Wilbur, R. B. (2009). Effects of varying rate of signing on ASL manual signs and nonmanual markers. *Language and Speech, 52*, 245–285.

Wilcox, S. (2004). Cognitive iconicity: Conceptual spaces, meaning, and gesture in signed languages. *Cognitive Linguistics, 15*, 119–147.

Wilkinson, R., Beeke, S., & Maxim, J. (2010). Formulating actions and events with limited linguistic resources: Enactment and iconicity in agrammatic aphasic talk. *Research on Language and Social Interaction, 43*, 57–84.

Wilson, M. (2002). Six views of embodied cognition. *Psychonomic Bulletin and Review, 9*, 625–636.

Wilson, M., & Wilson, T. P. (2005). An oscillator model of the timing of turn-taking. *Psychonomic Bulletin and Review, 12*, 957–968.

Wlotko, E. W., & Federmeier, K. D. (2012). Age-related changes in the impact of contextual strength on multiple aspects of sentence comprehension. *Psychophysiology, 49*, 770–785.

Wodniecka, Z., Craik, F. I. M., Luo, L., & Bialystok, E. (2010). Does bilingualism help memory? Competing effects of verbal ability and executive control. *International Journal of Bilingual Education and Bilingualism, 13,* 575–595.

Wolpoff, M. H., Mannheim, B., Mann, A., Hawks, J., Caspari, R., Rosenberg, K. R., . . . Clark, G. (2004). Why not the Neandertals? *World Archaeology, 36,* 527–546.

Wood, C. C. (1976). Discriminability, response bias, and phoneme categories in discriminative voice onset time. *Journal of the Acoustic Society of America, 60,* 1381–1389.

Woods, D. L., Doss, Z., Herron, T. J., & Yund, E. W. (2012). Age-related changes in consonant and sentence processing. *Journal of Rehabilitation Research and Development, 49,* 1277–1292.

Wright, O. (2012). Categorical influences on chromatic search asymmetries. *Visual Cognition, 20,* 947–987.

Wu, A., & Weseley, A. J. (2013). The effects of statistical format and population specificity on adolescent perceptions of cell phone use while driving. *Current Psychology, 32,* 32–43.

Wynn, T., & Coolidge, F. L. (2012). *How to think like a Neandertal.* New York: Oxford University Press.

Xu, F., Spelke, E. S., & Goddard, S. (2005). Number sense in human infants. *Developmental Science, 8,* 88–101.

Yang, J., & Yang, Y. (2008). Horizontal flow of semantic and phonological information in Chinese spoken sentence production. *Language and Speech, 51,* 267–284.

Yap, M. J., Balota, D. A., & Tan, S. E. (2013). Additive and interactive effects in semantic priming: Isolating lexical and decision processes in the lexical decision task. *Journal of Experimental Psychology: Learning, Memory, and Cognition, 39,* 140–158.

Yeung, H., Chen, K., & Werker, J. F. (2013). When does native language input affect phonetic perception? The precocious case of lexical tone. *Journal of Memory and Language, 68,* 123–139.

Yoon, S. O., Koh, S., & Brown-Schmidt, S. (2012). Influence of perspective and goals on reference production. *Psychonomics Bulletin and Review, 19,* 699–707.

Yoshida, K. A., Pons, F., Maye, J., & Werker, J. F. (2010). Distributional phonetic learning at 10 months of age. *Infancy, 15,* 420–433.

Young, V., & Mihailidis, A. (2010). Difficulties in automatic speech recognition of dysarthric speakers and implications for speech-based applications used by the elderly: A literature review. *Assistive Technology, 22,* 99–112.

Yu, B. (2013). Issues in bilingualism and heritage language maintenance: Perspectives of minority-language mothers of children with autism spectrum disorders. *American Journal of Speech-Language Pathology, 22,* 10–24.

Yu, C., & Smith, L. B. (2012a). Embodied attention and word learning by toddlers. *Cognition, 125,* 244–262.

Yu, C., & Smith, L. B. (2012b). Modeling cross-situational word-referent learning: Prior questions. *Psychological Review, 119,* 21–39.

Yuan, D., Guo, R., Ding, G., & Peng, D. (2012). Top-down modulations from dorsal stream in lexical recognition: An effective connectivity fMRI study. *PLoS ONE, 7,* e33337.

Yuan, J. (2011). Perception of intonation in Mandarin Chinese. *Journal of the Acoustic Society of America, 130,* 4063–4069.

Yuan, S., & Fisher, C. (2009). "Really? She blicked the baby?" Two-year-olds learn combinatorial facts about verbs by listening. *Psychological Science, 20,* 619–626.

Zanobini, M., Viterbori, P., & Saraceno, F. (2012). Phonology and language development in Italian children: An analysis of production and accuracy. *Journal of Speech, Language, and Hearing Research, 55,* 16–31.

Zhai, S., & Kristensson, P. O. (2012). The word-gesture keyboard: Reimagining keyboard interaction. *Communications of the ACM, 55,* 91–101.

Zhang, J., Randall, B., Stamatakis, E. A., Marslen-Wilson, W. D., & Tyler, L. K. (2011). The interaction of lexical semantics and cohort competition in spoken word recognition: An fMRI study. *Journal of Cognitive Neuroscience, 23,* 3778–3790.

Zhang, M., Li, J., Chen, C., Mei, L., Xue, G., Lu, Z., . . . Dong, Q. (2013). The contribution of the left mid-fusiform cortical thickness to Chinese and English reading in a large Chinese sample. *NeuroImage, 65,* 250–256.

Zhang, S., & Schmitt, B. (1998). Language-dependent classification: The mental representation of classifiers in cognition, memory, and evaluations. *Journal of Experimental Psychology: Applied, 4,* 375–385.

Zhang, X., Sun, J., & Luo, Z. (2014). One-against-all weighted dynamic time warping for language-independent and speaker-dependent speech recognition in adverse conditions. *PLoS ONE, 9,* e85458.

Zhang, Y., Whitfield-Gabrieli, S., Christodoulou, J. A., & Gabrieli, J. D. E. (2013). Atypical balance between occipital and fronto-parietal activation for visual shape extraction in dyslexia. *PLoS ONE, 8*(6), e67331.

Zhou, K., Mo, L., Kay, P., Kwok, V. P. Y., Ip, T. N. M., & Tan, L. H. (2010). Newly trained lexical categories produce lateralized categorical perception of color. *Proceedings of the National Academy of Sciences USA, 107,* 9974–9978.

Zhou, P., Crain, S., & Zhan, L. (2012). Sometimes children are as good as adults: The pragmatic use of prosody in children's on-line sentence processing. *Journal of Memory and Language, 67,* 149–164.

Zuberbühler, K. (2005). The phylogenetic roots of language: Evidence from primate communication and cognition. *Current Directions in Psychological Science 14,* 126–130.

Zuberbühler, K., Cheney, D. L., & Seyfarth, R. M. (1999). Conceptual semantics in a nonhuman primate. *Journal of Comparative Psychology, 113,* 33–42.

Zurif, E., Swinney, D. Prather, P., & Solomon, J. (1993). An on-line analysis of syntactic processing in Broca's and Wernicke's aphasia. *Brain and Language, 45*(3), 448–464.

INDEX

Broca's aphasia, 40, 64–65, 74, 125, 136, 228–230, 241, 483–484
Broca's area, 40–41, 74, 135, 136, 138, 140, 149, 228–230
Brown, R., 158
Bryant, G. A., 268
Burns, Robert, 473
Bursts of active text composition, 328
Business talk, 420

Canonical babbling, 153–155
Canonical word order, 211–214, 246, 251–253
Cantonese. *See also* Chinese language
CAPTCHA, 524, 525*f*
Caregiver imitation of infant speech, 152, 153, 282
Caregiver speech, 29, 106. *See also* Infant-caregiver interactions
Carlin, George, 487
Catalan, 349
Categorical perception, 98–99, 109
Category anaphor, 273
Cell phone conversations, overheard, 499–500
Cell phone texting, 502–509. *See also* Texting
Cell phone use and safety issues, 492–499
    conversing with passengers while driving, 494, 495–496
    drunk driving versus, 262–263
    hands-free devices, 493
    Internet or YouTube activities, 502
    multitasking cognitive demands, 496
    pedestrian using cell phones, 497–498
    texting while driving, 502, 506
    texting while walking, 506–507
Cerebellum, 140–141, 296, 321
Cerebral cortex, 73, 137–139, 320
Cerebral plasticity, 366
Chatbot, 521, 527
Cheney, D. L., 5–6, 7*f*
CHILDES, 185
Childhood apraxia of speech, 152, 158, 160
Child language development
    adult-child interactions, 420
    common speech disruptions, 243–244
    developmental stages in syntactic processing, 243
    expectations for kindergarten, 433
    fast mapping and word learning, 177, 425–426
    gestures, 284
    Gricean maxims, 287

    inflections, 244–245
    late talkers, 283
    learning swear words, 481–482
    math skills and, 438–439
    noun bias, 450–451
    oral language and literacy, 433–435
    phonology, 424–425
    preschool child lexicon, 425–427
    preschool years, 423–432
    private self-talk, 454
    producing discourse, 437–438
    school-age years, 432–440
    vocabulary growth, 176, 425–427, 435–437. *See also* Word learning
    See also Infant language development; Language learning and development; Sign language acquisition; Syntax acquisition and development; Word learning
Chimpanzee laughter, 11–12, 21
Chimpanzees and bonobos, use of human languages, 1–2, 36–39. *See also* Primate use of human languages
Chinchillas, 115, 116*f*
Chinese language
    babbling development and, 156
    classifiers, 466, 467*f*
    color categorization, 459
    dialects, 338
    "ee" sound, 132
    English translation equivalents, 350
    focus on manner of action, 469, 470
    gender system, 464
    infant tonal discrimination, 109–110
    Internet or YouTube activities, 432
    keyboard layout, 529
    learning to read, 315, 318–319
    learning to write, 324
    lexical decision task studies, 82–83
    logographic system, 297–298, 301, 318
    mutually unintelligible dialects and tonal systems, 110
    noun bias and, 451
    pronunciation, 298, 301, 318
    romanization scheme (*pinyin*), 528–529
    second-person pronoun, 292
    singular/plural distinction, 468
    texting slang, 529
    use of tone, 122–123
    word boundaries and, 206

⑤SAGE research**methods**

The essential online tool for researchers from the world's leading methods publisher

Find exactly what you are looking for, from basic explanations to advanced discussion

More content and new features added this year!

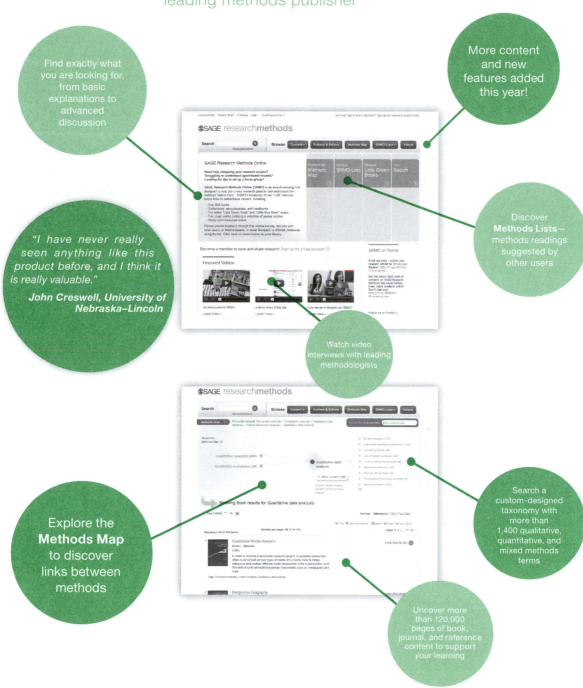

"I have never really seen anything like this product before, and I think it is really valuable."

John Creswell, University of Nebraska–Lincoln

Discover **Methods Lists**— methods readings suggested by other users

Watch video interviews with leading methodologists

Explore the **Methods Map** to discover links between methods

Search a custom-designed taxonomy with more than 1,400 qualitative, quantitative, and mixed methods terms

Uncover more than 120,000 pages of book, journal, and reference content to support your learning

Find out more at
www.sageresearchmethods.com